MASSACHUSETTS
RULES OF COURT

FEDERAL

2005

Mat#40271575

PREFACE

This edition of the *Massachusetts Rules of Court, Federal, 2005*, replaces the 2004 edition. This volume provides in convenient form court rules governing federal practice in Massachusetts and is current with amendments received through January 1, 2005.

THE PUBLISHER

February 2005

*

RELATED PRODUCTS FROM WEST

RELATED PRODUCTS

Federal Civil Practice
Savery, Corso and Harrington

Juvenile Law
Ireland

Landlord and Tenant Law with Forms, Third Edition
Daher and Chopp

Legal Forms, Fourth Edition
Hovey and Koenig

Mediation and Arbitration
Finn

Methods of Practice with Forms, Fourth Edition
Talty, Talty and Braunstein

Motor Vehicle Law and Practice and Related Topics with Forms, Third Edition
Kenney and Farris

Municipal Law and Practice, Fourth Edition
Randall and Franklin

Probate Law and Practice with Forms, Second Edition
Dunphy

Prima Facie Case—Proof and Defense, Fourth Edition
Bishop

Procedural Forms Annotated, Fifth Edition
Rodman, Perlin and Blum

Real Estate Law with Forms, Fourth Edition
Eno and Hovey

Rules Practice
Smith, Zobel, Murphy

Summary of Basic Law, Third Edition
Alperin, Shubow and Chase

Taxation, Fourth Edition
Bailey and Van Dorn

Tort Law, Second Edition
Nolan and Sartorio

Trial Practice
Flanagan

Uniform Commercial Code Manual, Third Edition
Lemelman

Uniform Commercial Code Forms Annotated, Second Edition
Lemelman

Workers' Compensation, Third Edition
Nason, Koziol and Wall

RELATED PRODUCTS

Newhall's Settlement of Estates and Fiduciary Law in Massachusetts, Fifth Edition
Belknap

The Law of Chapter 93A
Gilleran

Massachusetts Litigation Forms and Analysis
Doniger and Truesdell

Trial Handbook for Massachusetts Lawyers, Third Edition
Swartz

Massachusetts Conveyancers' Handbook with Forms, Third Edition
Mendler

**Kindregan & Inker's Massachusetts Domestic Relations
Rules and Statutes Annotated**

Massachusetts General Laws Annotated

**Massachusetts Rules of Court
State and Federal**

**West's Massachusetts Civil Actions
and Procedure**

West's Massachusetts Criminal Justice

**West's Massachusetts Motor Vehicle
and Traffic Laws and Regulations**

West's Massachusetts Probate Law and Rules

Massachusetts Decisions

Massachusetts Digest

MASSTAX Guide

West's Massachusetts Law Finder

Westlaw

WESTCheck® and WESTMATE®

West CD–ROM Libraries™

Massachusetts Practice CD–ROM

RELATED PRODUCTS

To order any of these Massachusetts practice tools, please
call your West Representative or 1–800–328–9352.

NEED RESEARCH HELP?

You can get quality research results with free help—call the West Reference Attorneys when
you have questions concerning Westlaw or West Publications at 1–800–733–2889.

INTERNET ACCESS

Contact the West Editorial Department directly with your questions and suggestions by
e-mail at west.editor@thomson.com. Visit West's home page at west.thomson.com.

WESTLAW ELECTRONIC RESEARCH GUIDE

Westlaw—Expanding the Reach of Your Library

Westlaw is West's online legal research service. With Westlaw, you experience the same quality and integrity that you have come to expect from West books, plus quick, easy access to West's vast collection of statutes, case law materials, public records, and other legal resources, in addition to current news articles and business information. For the most current and comprehensive legal research, combine the strengths of West books and Westlaw.

When you research with westlaw.com you get the convenience of the Internet combined with comprehensive and accurate Westlaw content, including exclusive editorial enhancements, plus features found only in westlaw.com such as ResultsPlus™ or StatutesPlus.™

Accessing Databases Using the Westlaw Directory

The Westlaw Directory lists all databases on Westlaw and contains links to detailed information relating to the content of each database. Click Directory on the westlaw.com toolbar. There are several ways to access a database even when you don't know the database identifier. Browse a directory view. Scan the directory. Type all or part of a database name in the Search these Databases box. The Find a Database Wizard can help you select relevant databases for your search. You can access up to ten databases at one time for user-defined multibase searching.

Retrieving a Specific Document

To retrieve a specific document by citation or title on westlaw.com click **Find** on the toolbar to display the Find a Document page. If you are unsure of the correct citation format, type the publication abbreviation, e.g., **xx st** (where xx is a state's two-letter postal abbreviation), in the Enter Citation box and click **Go** to display a fill-in-the-blank template. To retrieve a specific case when you know one or more parties' names, click **Find by Title**.

KeyCite®

KeyCite, West's citation research service on Westlaw, makes it easy to trace the history of your case, statute, administrative decision or regulation to determine if there are recent updates, and to find other documents that cite your document. KeyCite will also find pending legislation relating to federal or state statutes. Access the powerful features of KeyCite from the westlaw.com toolbar, the **Links** tab, or KeyCite flags in a document display. KeyCite's red and yellow warning flags tell you at a glance whether your document has negative history. Depth-of-treatment stars help you focus on the most important citing references. KeyCite Alert allows you to monitor the status of your case, statute or rule, and automatically sends you updates at the frequency you specify.

ResultsPlus™

ResultsPlus is a Westlaw technology that automatically suggests additional information related to your search. The suggested materials are accessible by a set of links that appear to the right of your westlaw.com search results:

- Go directly to relevant ALR® articles and Am Jur® annotations.
- Find on-point resources by key number.
- See information from related treatises and law reviews.

StatutesPlus™

When you access a statutes database in westlaw.com you are brought to a powerful Search Center which collects, on one toolbar, the tools that are most useful for fast, efficient retrieval of statutes documents:

- Have a few key terms? Click **Index**.
- Know the common name? Click **Popular Name Table**.
- Familiar with the subject matter? Click **Table of Contents**.
- Have a citation or section number? Click **Find by Citation**.
- Or, simply search with **Natural Language** or **Terms and Connectors.**

When you access a statutes section, click on the **Links** tab for all relevant links for the current document that will also include a KeyCite section with a description of the KeyCite status flag. Depending on your document, links may also include administrative, bill text, and other sources that were previously only available by accessing and searching other databases.

Additional Information

Westlaw is available on the Web at www.westlaw.com.

For search assistance, call the West Reference Attorneys at:
1–800–REF–ATTY (1–800–733–2889).

For technical assistance, call West Customer Technical Support at:
1–800–WESTLAW (1–800–937–8529).

TABLE OF CONTENTS

*

FEDERAL RULES OF CIVIL PROCEDURE

Effective September 16, 1938

Including Amendments Effective December 1, 2003

Research Note

Rule requirements, case law applications, commentary, and references to treatises and law reviews are available in Wright, Miller, et al., Federal Practice and Procedure, *Volumes 4 to 19; and in Baicker–McKee, Janssen & Corr,* Federal Civil Rules Handbook.

Use WESTLAW ® *to find cases citing a rule. In addition, use* WESTLAW *to search for specific terms or to update a rule; see the US–RULES, US–ORDERS and US–PL Scope Screens for further information.*

Amendments to Federal Rules of Civil Procedure are published, as received, in Supreme Court Reporter, Federal Reporter 3d, Federal Supplement 2d, Federal Rules Decisions *and* Bankruptcy Reporter *advance sheets.*

Table of Rules

FEDERAL RULES OF CIVIL PROCEDURE

* Suggested title added by Publisher.

I. SCOPE OF RULES—ONE FORM OF ACTION

RULE 1. SCOPE AND PURPOSE OF RULES

These rules govern the procedure in the United States district courts in all suits of a civil nature whether cognizable as cases at law or in equity or in admiralty, with the exceptions stated in Rule 81. They shall be construed and administered to secure the just, speedy, and inexpensive determination of every action.

[Amended December 29, 1948, effective October 20, 1949; February 28, 1966, effective July 1, 1966; April 22, 1993, effective December 1, 1993.]

RULE 2. ONE FORM OF ACTION

There shall be one form of action to be known as "civil action."

II. COMMENCEMENT OF ACTION; SERVICE OF PROCESS, PLEADINGS, MOTIONS, AND ORDERS

RULE 3. COMMENCEMENT OF ACTION

A civil action is commenced by filing a complaint with the court.

RULE 4. SUMMONS

(a) Form. The summons shall be signed by the clerk, bear the seal of the court, identify the court and the parties, be directed to the defendant, and state the name and address of the plaintiff's attorney or, if unrepresented, of the plaintiff. It shall also state the time within which the defendant must appear and defend, and notify the defendant that failure to do so will result in a judgment by default against the defendant for the relief demanded in the complaint. The court may allow a summons to be amended.

(b) Issuance. Upon or after filing the complaint, the plaintiff may present a summons to the clerk for signature and seal. If the summons is in proper form, the clerk shall sign, seal, and issue it to the plaintiff for service on the defendant. A summons, or a copy of the summons if addressed to multiple defendants, shall be issued for each defendant to be served.

(c) Service With Complaint; by Whom Made.

(1) A summons shall be served together with a copy of the complaint. The plaintiff is responsible for service of a summons and complaint within the time allowed under subdivision (m) and shall furnish the person effecting service with the necessary copies of the summons and complaint.

(2) Service may be effected by any person who is not a party and who is at least 18 years of age. At the request of the plaintiff, however, the court may direct that service be effected by a United States marshal, deputy United States marshal, or other person or officer specially appointed by the court for that purpose. Such an appointment must be made when the plaintiff is authorized to proceed in forma pauperis pursuant to 28 U.S.C. § 1915 or is authorized to proceed as a seaman under 28 U.S.C. § 1916.

(d) Waiver of Service; Duty to Save Costs of Service; Request to Waive.

(1) A defendant who waives service of a summons does not thereby waive any objection to the venue or to the jurisdiction of the court over the person of the defendant.

(2) An individual, corporation, or association that is subject to service under subdivision (e), (f), or (h) and that receives notice of an action in the manner provided in this paragraph has a duty to avoid unnecessary costs of serving the summons. To avoid costs, the plaintiff may notify such a defendant of the commencement of the action and request that the defendant waive service of a summons. The notice and request

(A) shall be in writing and shall be addressed directly to the defendant, if an individual, or else to an officer or managing or general agent (or other agent authorized by appointment or law to receive service of process) of a defendant subject to service under subdivision (h);

(B) shall be dispatched through first-class mail or other reliable means;

(C) shall be accompanied by a copy of the complaint and shall identify the court in which it has been filed;

(D) shall inform the defendant, by means of a text prescribed in an official form promulgated pursuant to Rule 84, of the consequences of compliance and of a failure to comply with the request;

(E) shall set forth the date on which the request is sent;

(F) shall allow the defendant a reasonable time to return the waiver, which shall be at least 30 days from the date on which the request is sent, or 60 days from that date if the defendant is addressed outside any judicial district of the United States; and

(G) shall provide the defendant with an extra copy of the notice and request, as well as a prepaid means of compliance in writing.

If a defendant located within the United States fails to comply with a request for waiver made by a plaintiff located within the United States, the court shall impose the costs subsequently incurred in effecting service on the defendant unless good cause for the failure be shown.

(3) A defendant that, before being served with process, timely returns a waiver so requested is not required to serve an answer to the complaint until 60 days after the date on which the request for waiver of service was sent, or 90 days after that date if the defendant was addressed outside any judicial district of the United States.

(4) When the plaintiff files a waiver of service with the court, the action shall proceed, except as provided in paragraph (3), as if a summons and complaint had been served at the time of filing the waiver, and no proof of service shall be required.

(5) The costs to be imposed on a defendant under paragraph (2) for failure to comply with a request to waive service of a summons shall include the costs subsequently incurred in effecting service under subdivision (e), (f), or (h), together with the costs, including a reasonable attorney's fee, of any motion required to collect the costs of service.

(e) Service Upon Individuals Within a Judicial District of the United States. Unless otherwise provided by federal law, service upon an individual from whom a waiver has not been obtained and filed, other than an infant or an incompetent person, may be effected in any judicial district of the United States:

(1) pursuant to the law of the state in which the district court is located, or in which service is effected, for the service of a summons upon the defendant in an action brought in the courts of general jurisdiction of the State; or

(2) by delivering a copy of the summons and of the complaint to the individual personally or by leaving copies thereof at the individual's dwelling house or usual place of abode with some person of suitable age and discretion then residing therein or by delivering a copy of the summons and of the complaint to an agent authorized by appointment or by law to receive service of process.

(f) Service Upon Individuals in a Foreign Country. Unless otherwise provided by federal law, service upon an individual from whom a waiver has not been obtained and filed, other than an infant or an incompetent person, may be effected in a place not within any judicial district of the United States:

(1) by any internationally agreed means reasonably calculated to give notice, such as those means authorized by the Hague Convention on the Service Abroad of Judicial and Extrajudicial Documents; or

(2) if there is no internationally agreed means of service or the applicable international agreement allows other means of service, provided that service is reasonably calculated to give notice:

(A) in the manner prescribed by the law of the foreign country for service in that country in an action in any of its courts of general jurisdiction; or

(B) as directed by the foreign authority in response to a letter rogatory or letter of request; or

(C) unless prohibited by the law of the foreign country, by

(i) delivery to the individual personally of a copy of the summons and the complaint; or

(ii) any form of mail requiring a signed receipt, to be addressed and dispatched by the clerk of the court to the party to be served; or

(3) by other means not prohibited by international agreement as may be directed by the court.

(g) Service Upon Infants and Incompetent Persons. Service upon an infant or an incompetent person in a judicial district of the United States shall be effected in the manner prescribed by the law of the state in which the service is made for the service of summons or other like process upon any such defendant in an action brought in the courts of general jurisdiction of that state. Service upon an infant or an incompetent person in a place not within any judicial district of the United States shall be effected in the manner prescribed by paragraph (2)(A) or (2)(B) of subdivision (f) or by such means as the court may direct.

(h) Service Upon Corporations and Associations. Unless otherwise provided by federal law, service upon a domestic or foreign corporation or upon a partnership or other unincorporated association that is subject to suit under a common name, and from which a waiver of service has not been obtained and filed, shall be effected:

(1) in a judicial district of the United States in the manner prescribed for individuals by subdivision (e)(1), or by delivering a copy of the summons and of the complaint to an officer, a managing or general agent, or to any other agent authorized by appointment or by law to receive service of process and, if the agent is one authorized by statute to receive service and the statute so requires, by also mailing a copy to the defendant, or

(2) in a place not within any judicial district of the United States in any manner prescribed for individuals by subdivision (f) except personal delivery as provided in paragraph (2)(C)(i) thereof.

(i) Serving the United States, Its Agencies, Corporations, Officers, or Employees.

(1) Service upon the United States shall be effected

(A) by delivering a copy of the summons and of the complaint to the United States attorney for the district in which the action is brought or to an assistant United States attorney or clerical employee designated by the United States attorney in a writing filed with the clerk of the court or by sending a copy of the summons and of the complaint by registered or certified mail addressed to the civil process clerk at the office of the United States attorney and

(B) by also sending a copy of the summons and of the complaint by registered or certified mail to the Attorney General of the United States at Washington, District of Columbia, and

(C) in any action attacking the validity of an order of an officer or agency of the United States not made a party, by also sending a copy of the summons and of the complaint by registered or certified mail to the officer or agency.

(2)(A) Service on an agency or corporation of the United States, or an officer or employee of the United States sued only in an official capacity, is effected by serving the United States in the manner prescribed by Rule 4(i)(1) and by also sending a copy of the summons and complaint by registered or certified mail to the officer, employee, agency, or corporation.

(B) Service on an officer or employee of the United States sued in an individual capacity for acts or omission occurring in connection with the performance of duties on behalf of the United States—whether or not the officer or employee is sued also in an official capacity—is effected by serving the United States in the manner prescribed by Rule 4(i)(1) and by serving the officer or employee in the manner prescribed by Rule 4(e), (f), or (g).

(3) The court shall allow a reasonable time to serve process under Rule 4(i) for the purpose of curing the failure to serve:

(A) all persons required to be served in an action governed by Rule 4(i)(2)(A), if the plaintiff has served either the United States attorney or the Attorney General of the United States. or

(B) the United States in an action governed by Rule 4(i)(2)(B), if the plaintiff has served an officer or employee of the United State sued in an individual capacity.

(j) Service Upon Foreign, State, or Local Governments.

(1) Service upon a foreign state or a political subdivision, agency, or instrumentality thereof shall be effected pursuant to 28 U.S.C. § 1608.

(2) Service upon a state, municipal corporation, or other governmental organization subject to suit shall be effected by delivering a copy of the summons and of the complaint to its chief executive officer or by serving the summons and complaint in the manner prescribed by the law of that state for the service of summons or other like process upon any such defendant.

(k) Territorial Limits of Effective Service.

(1) Service of a summons or filing a waiver of service is effective to establish jurisdiction over the person of a defendant

(A) who could be subjected to the jurisdiction of a court of general jurisdiction in the state in which the district court is located, or

(B) who is a party joined under Rule 14 or Rule 19 and is served at a place within a judicial district of the United States and not more than 100 miles from the place from which the summons issues, or

(C) who is subject to the federal interpleader jurisdiction under 28 U.S.C. § 1335, or

(D) when authorized by a statute of the United States.

(2) If the exercise of jurisdiction is consistent with the Constitution and laws of the United States, serving a summons or filing a waiver of service is also effective, with respect to claims arising under federal law, to establish personal jurisdiction over the person of any defendant who is not subject to the jurisdiction of the courts of general jurisdiction of any state.

(l) **Proof of Service.** If service is not waived, the person effecting service shall make proof thereof to the court. If service is made by a person other than a United States marshal or deputy United States marshal, the person shall make affidavit thereof. Proof of service in a place not within any judicial district of the United States shall, if effected under paragraph (1) of subdivision (f), be made pursuant to the applicable treaty or convention, and shall, if effected under paragraph (2) or (3) thereof, include a receipt signed by the addressee or other evidence of delivery to the addressee satisfactory to the court. Failure to make proof of service does not affect the validity of the service. The court may allow proof of service to be amended.

(m) Time Limit for Service. If service of the summons and complaint is not made upon a defendant within 120 days after the filing of the complaint, the court, upon motion or on its own initiative after notice to the plaintiff, shall dismiss the action without prejudice as to that defendant or direct that service be effected within a specified time; provided that if the plaintiff shows good cause for the failure, the court shall extend the time for service for an appropriate period. This subdivision does not apply to service in a foreign country pursuant to subdivision (f) or (j)(1).

(n) Seizure of Property; Service of Summons Not Feasible.

(1) If a statute of the United States so provides, the court may assert jurisdiction over property. Notice to claimants of the property shall then be sent in the manner provided by the statute or by service of a summons under this rule.

(2) Upon a showing that personal jurisdiction over a defendant cannot, in the district where the action is brought, be obtained with reasonable efforts by service of summons in any manner authorized by this rule, the court may assert jurisdiction over any of the defendant's assets found within the district by seizing the assets under the circumstances and in the manner provided by the law of the state in which the district court is located.

[Amended January 21, 1963, effective July 1, 1963; February 28, 1966, effective July 1, 1966; April 29, 1980, effective August 1, 1980; amended by Pub.L. 97-462, § 2, January 12, 1983, 96 Stat. 2527, effective 45 days after January 12, 1983; amended March 2, 1987, effective August 1, 1987; April 22, 1993, effective December 1, 1993; April 17, 2000, effective December 1, 2000.]

RULE 4.1 SERVICE OF OTHER PROCESS

(a) Generally. Process other than a summons as provided in Rule 4 or subpoena as provided in Rule 45 shall be served by a United States marshal, a deputy United States marshal, or a person specially appointed for that purpose, who shall make proof of service as provided in Rule 4(*l*). The process may be served anywhere within the territorial limits of the state in which the district court is located, and, when authorized by a statute of the United States, beyond the territorial limits of that state.

(b) Enforcement of Orders: Commitment for Civil Contempt. An order of civil commitment of a person held to be in contempt of a decree or injunction issued to enforce the laws of the United States may be served and enforced in any district. Other orders in civil contempt proceedings shall be served in the state in which the court issuing the order to be enforced is located or elsewhere within the United States if not more than 100 miles from the place at which the order to be enforced was issued.

[Adopted April 22, 1993, effective December 1, 1993.]

RULE 5. SERVICE AND FILING PLEADINGS AND OTHER PAPERS

(a) Service: When Required. Except as otherwise provided in these rules, every order required by its terms to be served, every pleading subsequent to the original complaint unless the court otherwise orders because of numerous defendants, every paper relating to discovery required to be served upon a party unless the court otherwise orders, every written motion other than one which may be heard ex parte, and every written notice, appearance, demand, offer of judgment, designation of record on appeal, and similar paper shall be served upon each of the parties. No service need be made on parties in default for failure to appear except that pleadings asserting new or additional claims for relief against them shall be served upon them in the manner provided for service of summons in Rule 4.

In an action begun by seizure of property, in which no person need be or is named as defendant, any service required to be made prior to the filing of an answer, claim, or appearance shall be made upon the person having custody or possession of the property at the time of its seizure.

(b) Making Service.

(1) Service under Rules 5(a) and 77(d) on a party represented by an attorney is made on the attorney unless the court orders service on the party.

(2) Service under Rule 5(a) is made by:

    (A) Delivering a copy to the person served by:

        (i) handing it to the person;

        (ii) leaving it at the person's office with a clerk or other person in charge, or if no one is in charge leaving it in a conspicuous place in the office; or

        (iii) if the person has no office or the office is closed, leaving it at the person's dwelling house or usual place of abode with someone of suitable age and discretion residing there.

    (B) Mailing a copy to the last known address of the person served. Service by mail is complete on mailing.

    (C) If the person served has no known address, leaving a copy with the clerk of the court.

    (D) Delivering a copy by any other means, including electronic means, consented to in writing by the person served. Service by electronic means is complete on transmission; service by other consented means is complete when the person making service delivers the copy to the agency designated to make delivery. If authorized by local rule, a party may make service under this subparagraph (D) through the court's transmission facilities.

(3) Service by electronic means under Rule 5(b)(2)(D) is not effective if the party making service learns that the attempted service did not reach the person to be served.

(c) Same: Numerous Defendants. In any action in which there are unusually large numbers of defendants, the court, upon motion or of its own initiative, may order that service of the pleadings of the defendants and replies thereto need not be made as between the defendants and that any cross-claim, counterclaim, or matter constituting an avoidance or affirmative defense contained therein shall be deemed to be denied or avoided by all other parties and that the filing of any such pleading and service thereof upon the plaintiff constitutes due notice of it to the parties. A copy of every such order shall be served upon the parties in such manner and form as the court directs.

(d) Filing; Certificate of Service. All papers after the complaint required to be served upon a party, together with a certificate of service, must be filed with the court within a reasonable time after service, but disclosures under Rule 26(a)(1) or (2) and the following discovery requests and responses must not be filed until they are used in the proceeding or the court orders filing: (i) depositions, (ii) interrogatories, (iii) requests for documents or to permit entry upon land, and (iv) requests for admission.

(e) Filing With the Court Defined. The filing of papers with the court as required by these rules shall be made by filing them with the clerk of court, except that the judge may permit the papers to be filed with the judge, in which event the judge shall note thereon the filing date and forthwith transmit them to the office of the clerk. A court may by local rule permit papers to be filed, signed, or verified by electronic means that are consistent with technical standards, if any, that the Judicial Conference of the United States establishes. A paper filed by electronic means in compliance with a local rule constitutes a written paper for the purpose of applying these rules. The clerk shall not refuse to accept for filing any paper presented for that purpose solely because it is not presented in proper form as required by these rules or any local rules or practices.

[Amended January 21, 1963, effective July 1, 1963; March 30, 1970, effective July 1, 1970; April 29, 1980, effective August 1, 1980; March 2, 1987, effective August 1, 1987; April 30, 1991, effective December 1, 1991; April 22, 1993, effective December 1, 1993; April 23, 1996, effective December 1, 1996; April 17, 2000, effective December 1, 2000; April 23, 2001, effective December 1, 2001.]

RULE 6.   TIME

(a) Computation. In computing any period of time prescribed or allowed by these rules, by the local rules of any district court, by order of court, or by any applicable statute, the day of the act, event, or default from which the designated period of time begins to run shall not be included. The last day of the period so computed shall be included, unless it is a Saturday, a Sunday, or a legal holiday, or, when the act to be done is the filing of a paper in court, a day on which weather or other conditions have made the office of the clerk of the district court inaccessible, in which event the period runs until the end of the next day which is not one of the aforementioned days. When the period of time prescribed or allowed is less than 11 days, intermediate Saturdays, Sundays, and legal holidays shall be excluded in the computation. As used in this rule and in Rule 77(c), "legal holiday" includes New Year's Day, Birthday of Martin Luther King, Jr., Washington's Birthday, Memorial Day, Independence Day, Labor Day, Columbus Day, Veterans Day, Thanksgiving Day, Christmas Day, and any other day appointed as a holiday by the President or the Congress of the United States, or by the state in which the district court is held.

(b) Enlargement. When by these rules or by a notice given thereunder or by order of court an act is required or allowed to be done at or within a specified time, the court for cause shown may at any time in its discretion (1) with or without motion or notice order the period enlarged if request therefor is made before the expiration of the period originally prescribed or as extended by a previous order, or (2) upon motion made after the expiration of the specified period permit the act to be done where the failure to act was the result of excusable neglect; but it may not extend the time for taking any action under Rules 50(b) and (c)(2), 52(b), 59(b), (d) and (e) and 60(b), except to the extent and under the conditions stated in them.

(c) Unaffected by Expiration of Term [Rescinded].

(d) For Motions—Affidavits. A written motion, other than one which may be heard ex parte, and notice of the hearing thereof shall be served not later than 5 days before the time specified for the hearing, unless a different period is fixed by these rules or by order of the court. Such an order may for cause shown be made on ex parte application. When a motion is supported by affidavit, the affidavit shall be served with the motion; and, except as otherwise provided in Rule 59(c), opposing affidavits may be served not later than 1 day before the hearing, unless the court permits them to be served at some other time.

(e) Additional Time After Service Under Rule 5(b)(2)(B), (C), or (D). Whenever a party has the right or is required to do some act or take some proceedings within a prescribed period after the service of a notice or other paper upon the party and the notice or paper is served upon the party under Rule 5(b)(2)(B), (C), or (D), 3 days shall be added to the prescribed period.

[Amended December 27, 1946, effective March 19, 1948; January 21, 1963, effective July 1, 1963; February 28, 1966, effective July 1, 1966; December 4, 1967, effective July 1, 1968; March 1, 1971, effective July 1, 1971; April 28, 1983, effective August 1, 1983; April 29, 1985, effective August 1, 1985; March 2, 1987, effective August 1, 1987; April 29, 1999, effective December 1, 1999; April 23, 2001, effective December 1, 2001.]

III. PLEADINGS AND MOTIONS

RULE 7. PLEADINGS ALLOWED; FORM OF MOTIONS

(a) Pleadings. There shall be a complaint and an answer; a reply to a counterclaim denominated as such; an answer to a cross-claim, if the answer contains a cross-claim; a third-party complaint, if a person who was not an original party is summoned under the provisions of Rule 14; and a third-party answer, if a third-party complaint is served. No other pleading shall be allowed, except that the court may order a reply to an answer or a third-party answer.

(b) Motions and Other Papers.

(1) An application to the court for an order shall be by motion which, unless made during a hearing or trial, shall be made in writing, shall state with particularity the grounds therefor, and shall set forth the relief or order sought. The requirement of writing is fulfilled if the motion is stated in a written notice of the hearing of the motion.

(2) The rules applicable to captions and other matters of form of pleadings apply to all motions and other papers provided for by these rules.

(3) All motions shall be signed in accordance with Rule 11.

(c) Demurrers, Pleas, etc., Abolished. Demurrers, pleas, and exceptions for insufficiency of a pleading shall not be used.

[Amended December 27, 1946, effective March 19, 1948; January 21, 1963, effective July 1, 1963; April 28, 1983, effective August 1, 1983.]

RULE 7.1 DISCLOSURE STATEMENT

(a) Who Must File: Nongovernmental Corporate Party. A nongovernmental corporate party to an action or proceeding in a district court must file two copies of a statement that identifies any parent corporation and any publicly held corporation that owns 10% or more of its stock or states that there is no such corporation.

(b) Time for Filing; Supplemental Filing. A party must:

(1) file the Rule 7.1(a) statement with its first appearance, pleading, petition, motion, response, or other request addressed to the court, and

(2) promptly file a supplemental statement upon any change in the information that the statement requires.

[Adopted April 29, 2002, effective December 1, 2002.]

RULE 8. GENERAL RULES OF PLEADING

(a) Claims for Relief. A pleading which sets forth a claim for relief, whether an original claim, counterclaim, cross-claim, or third-party claim, shall contain (1) a short and plain statement of the grounds upon which the court's jurisdiction depends, unless the court already has jurisdiction and the claim needs no new grounds of jurisdiction to support it, (2) a short and plain statement of the claim showing that the pleader is entitled to relief, and (3) a demand for judgment for the relief the pleader seeks. Relief in the alternative or of several different types may be demanded.

(b) Defenses; Form of Denials. A party shall state in short and plain terms the party's defenses to each claim asserted and shall admit or deny the averments upon which the adverse party relies. If a party is without knowledge or information sufficient to form a belief as to the truth of an averment, the party shall so state and this has the effect of a denial. Denials shall fairly meet the substance of the averments denied. When a pleader intends in good faith to deny only a part or a qualification of an averment, the pleader shall specify so much of it as is true and material and shall deny only the remainder. Unless the pleader intends in good faith to controvert all the averments of the preceding pleading, the pleader may make denials as specific denials of designated averments or paragraphs or may generally deny all the averments except such designated averments or paragraphs as the pleader expressly admits; but, when the pleader does so intend to controvert all its averments, including averments of the grounds upon which the court's jurisdiction depends, the pleader may do so by general denial subject to the obligations set forth in Rule 11.

(c) Affirmative Defenses. In pleading to a preceding pleading, a party shall set forth affirmatively accord and satisfaction, arbitration and award, assumption of risk, contributory negligence, discharge in bankruptcy, duress, estoppel, failure of consideration, fraud, illegality, injury by fellow servant, laches, license, payment, release, res judicata, statute of frauds, statute of limitations, waiver, and any other matter constituting an avoidance or affirmative defense. When a party has mistakenly designated a defense as a counterclaim or a counterclaim as a defense, the court on terms, if justice so requires, shall treat the pleading as if there had been a proper designation.

(d) Effect of Failure to Deny. Averments in a pleading to which a responsive pleading is required, other than those as to the amount of damage, are admitted when not denied in the responsive pleading.

Averments in a pleading to which no responsive pleading is required or permitted shall be taken as denied or avoided.

(e) Pleading to Be Concise and Direct; Consistency.

(1) Each averment of a pleading shall be simple, concise, and direct. No technical forms of pleading or motions are required.

(2) A party may set forth two or more statements of a claim or defense alternately or hypothetically, either in one count or defense or in separate counts or defenses. When two or more statements are made in the alternative and one of them if made independently would be sufficient, the pleading is not made insufficient by the insufficiency of one or more of the alternative statements. A party may also state as many separate claims or defenses as the party has regardless of consistency and whether based on legal, equitable, or maritime grounds. All statements shall be made subject to the obligations set forth in Rule 11.

(f) Construction of Pleadings. All pleadings shall be so construed as to do substantial justice.

[Amended February 28, 1966, effective July 1, 1966; March 2, 1987, effective August 1, 1987.]

RULE 9.   PLEADING SPECIAL MATTERS

(a) Capacity. It is not necessary to aver the capacity of a party to sue or be sued or the authority of a party to sue or be sued in a representative capacity or the legal existence of an organized association of persons that is made a party, except to the extent required to show the jurisdiction of the court. When a party desires to raise an issue as to the legal existence of any party or the capacity of any party to sue or be sued or the authority of a party to sue or be sued in a representative capacity, the party desiring to raise the issue shall do so by specific negative averment, which shall include such supporting particulars as are peculiarly within the pleader's knowledge.

(b) Fraud, Mistake, Condition of the Mind. In all averments of fraud or mistake, the circumstances constituting fraud or mistake shall be stated with particularity. Malice, intent, knowledge, and other condition of mind of a person may be averred generally.

(c) Conditions Precedent. In pleading the performance or occurrence of conditions precedent, it is sufficient to aver generally that all conditions precedent have been performed or have occurred. A denial of performance or occurrence shall be made specifically and with particularity.

(d) Official Document or Act. In pleading an official document or official act it is sufficient to aver that the document was issued or the act done in compliance with law.

(e) Judgment. In pleading a judgment or decision of a domestic or foreign court, judicial or quasi-judicial tribunal, or of a board or officer, it is sufficient to aver the judgment or decision without setting forth matter showing jurisdiction to render it.

(f) Time and Place. For the purpose of testing the sufficiency of a pleading, averments of time and place are material and shall be considered like all other averments of material matter.

(g) Special Damage. When items of special damage are claimed, they shall be specifically stated.

(h) Admiralty and Maritime Claims. A pleading or count setting forth a claim for relief within the admiralty and maritime jurisdiction that is also within the jurisdiction of the district court on some other ground may contain a statement identifying the claim as an admiralty or maritime claim for the purposes of Rules 14(c), 38(e), 82, and the Supplemental Rules for Certain Admiralty and Maritime Claims. If the claim is cognizable only in admiralty, it is an admiralty or maritime claim for those purposes whether so identified or not. The amendment of a pleading to add or withdraw an identifying statement is governed by the principles of Rule 15. A case that includes an admiralty or maritime claim within this subdivision is an admiralty case within 28 U.S.C. § 1292(a)(3).

[Amended February 28, 1966, effective July 1, 1966; December 4, 1967, effective July 1, 1968; March 30, 1970, effective July 1, 1970; March 2, 1987, effective August 1, 1987; April 11, 1997, effective December 1, 1997.]

RULE 10.   FORM OF PLEADINGS

(a) Caption; Names of Parties. Every pleading shall contain a caption setting forth the name of the court, the title of the action, the file number, and a designation as in Rule 7(a). In the complaint the title of the action shall include the names of all the parties, but in other pleadings it is sufficient to state the name of the first party on each side with an appropriate indication of other parties.

(b) Paragraphs; Separate Statements. All averments of claim or defense shall be made in numbered paragraphs, the contents of each of which shall be limited as far as practicable to a statement of a single set of circumstances; and a paragraph may be referred to by number in all succeeding pleadings. Each claim founded upon a separate transaction or occurrence and each defense other than denials shall be stated in a separate count or defense whenever a separation facilitates the clear presentation of the matters set forth.

(c) Adoption by Reference; Exhibits. Statements in a pleading may be adopted by reference in a different part of the same pleading or in another pleading or in any motion. A copy of any written instrument which is an exhibit to a pleading is a part thereof for all purposes.

RULE 11. SIGNING OF PLEADINGS, MOTIONS, AND OTHER PAPERS; REPRESENTATIONS TO COURT; SANCTIONS

(a) Signature. Every pleading, written motion, and other paper shall be signed by at least one attorney of record in the attorney's individual name, or, if the party is not represented by an attorney, shall be signed by the party. Each paper shall state the signer's address and telephone number, if any. Except when otherwise specifically provided by rule or statute, pleadings need not be verified or accompanied by affidavit. An unsigned paper shall be stricken unless omission of the signature is corrected promptly after being called to the attention of the attorney or party.

(b) Representations to Court. By presenting to the court (whether by signing, filing, submitting, or later advocating) a pleading, written motion, or other paper, an attorney or unrepresented party is certifying that to the best of the person's knowledge, information, and belief, formed after an inquiry reasonable under the circumstances,—

(1) it is not being presented for any improper purpose, such as to harass or to cause unnecessary delay or needless increase in the cost of litigation;

(2) the claims, defenses, and other legal contentions therein are warranted by existing law or by a nonfrivolous argument for the extension, modification, or reversal of existing law or the establishment of new law;

(3) the allegations and other factual contentions have evidentiary support or, if specifically so identified, are likely to have evidentiary support after a reasonable opportunity for further investigation or discovery; and

(4) the denials of factual contentions are warranted on the evidence or, if specifically so identified, are reasonably based on a lack of information or belief.

(c) Sanctions. If, after notice and a reasonable opportunity to respond, the court determines that subdivision (b) has been violated, the court may, subject to the conditions stated below, impose an appropriate sanction upon the attorneys, law firms, or parties that have violated subdivision (b) or are responsible for the violation.

(1) *How Initiated.*

(A) By Motion. A motion for sanctions under this rule shall be made separately from other motions or requests and shall describe the specific conduct alleged to violate subdivision (b). It shall be served as provided in Rule 5, but shall not be filed with or presented to the court unless, within 21 days after service of the motion (or such other period as the court may prescribe), the challenged paper, claim, defense, contention, allegation, or denial is not withdrawn or appropriately corrected. If

warranted, the court may award to the party prevailing on the motion the reasonable expenses and attorney's fees incurred in presenting or opposing the motion. Absent exceptional circumstances, a law firm shall be held jointly responsible for violations committed by its partners, associates, and employees.

(B) On Court's Initiative. On its own initiative, the court may enter an order describing the specific conduct that appears to violate subdivision (b) and directing an attorney, law firm, or party to show cause why it has not violated subdivision (b) with respect thereto.

(2) *Nature of Sanction; Limitations.* A sanction imposed for violation of this rule shall be limited to what is sufficient to deter repetition of such conduct or comparable conduct by others similarly situated. Subject to the limitations in subparagraphs (A) and (B), the sanction may consist of, or include, directives of a nonmonetary nature, an order to pay a penalty into court, or, if imposed on motion and warranted for effective deterrence, an order directing payment to the movant of some or all of the reasonable attorneys' fees and other expenses incurred as a direct result of the violation.

(A) Monetary sanctions may not be awarded against a represented party for a violation of subdivision (b)(2).

(B) Monetary sanctions may not be awarded on the court's initiative unless the court issues its order to show cause before a voluntary dismissal or settlement of the claims made by or against the party which is, or whose attorneys are, to be sanctioned.

(3) *Order.* When imposing sanctions, the court shall describe the conduct determined to constitute a violation of this rule and explain the basis for the sanction imposed.

(d) Inapplicability to Discovery. Subdivisions (a) through (c) of this rule do not apply to disclosures and discovery requests, responses, objections, and motions that are subject to the provisions of Rules 26 through 37.

[Amended April 28, 1983, effective August 1, 1983; March 2, 1987, effective August 1, 1987; April 22, 1993, effective December 1, 1993.]

RULE 12. DEFENSES AND OBJECTIONS—WHEN AND HOW PRESENTED—BY PLEADING OR MOTION—MOTION FOR JUDGMENT ON THE PLEADINGS

(a) When Presented.

(1) Unless a different time is prescribed in a statute of the United States, a defendant shall serve an answer

(A) within 20 days after being served with the summons and complaint, or

(B) if service of the summons has been timely waived on request under Rule 4(d), within 60 days after the date when the request for waiver was sent, or within 90 days after that date if the defendant was addressed outside any judicial district of the United States.

(2) A party served with a pleading stating a cross-claim against that party shall serve an answer thereto within 20 days after being served. The plaintiff shall serve a reply to a counterclaim in the answer within 20 days after service of the answer, or, if a reply is ordered by the court, within 20 days after service of the order, unless the order otherwise directs.

(3)(A) The United States, an agency of the United States, or an officer or employee of the United States sued in an official capacity, shall serve an answer to the complaint or cross-claim—or a reply to a counterclaim—within 60 days after the United States attorney is served with the pleading asserting the claim.

(B) An officer or employee of the United States sued in an individual capacity for acts or omissions occurring in connection with the performance of duties on behalf of the United States shall serve an answer to the complaint or cross-claim—or a reply to a counterclaim—within 60 days after service on the officer or employee, or service on the United States attorney, whichever is later.

(4) Unless a different time is fixed by court order, the service of a motion permitted under this rule alters these periods of time as follows:

(A) if the court denies the motion or postpones its disposition until the trial on the merits, the responsive pleading shall be served within 10 days after notice of the court's action; or

(B) if the court grants a motion for a more definite statement, the responsive pleading shall be served within 10 days after the service of the more definite statement.

(b) How Presented. Every defense, in law or fact, to a claim for relief in any pleading, whether a claim, counterclaim, cross-claim, or third-party claim, shall be asserted in the responsive pleading thereto if one is required, except that the following defenses may at the option of the pleader be made by motion: (1) lack of jurisdiction over the subject matter, (2) lack of jurisdiction over the person, (3) improper venue, (4) insufficiency of process, (5) insufficiency of service of process, (6) failure to state a claim upon which relief can be granted, (7) failure to join a party under Rule 19. A motion making any of these defenses shall be made before pleading if a further pleading is permitted. No defense or objection is waived by being joined with one or more other defenses or objections in a responsive pleading or motion. If a pleading sets forth a claim for relief to which the adverse party is

not required to serve a responsive pleading, the adverse party may assert at the trial any defense in law or fact to that claim for relief. If, on a motion asserting the defense numbered (6) to dismiss for failure of the pleading to state a claim upon which relief can be granted, matters outside the pleading are presented to and not excluded by the court, the motion shall be treated as one for summary judgment and disposed of as provided in Rule 56, and all parties shall be given reasonable opportunity to present all material made pertinent to such a motion by Rule 56.

(c) Motion for Judgment on the Pleadings. After the pleadings are closed but within such time as not to delay the trial, any party may move for judgment on the pleadings. If, on a motion for judgment on the pleadings, matters outside the pleadings are presented to and not excluded by the court, the motion shall be treated as one for summary judgment and disposed of as provided in Rule 56, and all parties shall be given reasonable opportunity to present all material made pertinent to such a motion by Rule 56.

(d) Preliminary Hearings. The defenses specifically enumerated (1)–(7) in subdivision (b) of this rule, whether made in a pleading or by motion, and the motion for judgment mentioned in subdivision (c) of this rule shall be heard and determined before trial on application of any party, unless the court orders that the hearing and determination thereof be deferred until the trial.

(e) Motion for More Definite Statement. If a pleading to which a responsive pleading is permitted is so vague or ambiguous that a party cannot reasonably be required to frame a responsive pleading, the party may move for a more definite statement before interposing a responsive pleading. The motion shall point out the defects complained of and the details desired. If the motion is granted and the order of the court is not obeyed within 10 days after notice of the order or within such other time as the court may fix, the court may strike the pleading to which the motion was directed or make such order as it deems just.

(f) Motion to Strike. Upon motion made by a party before responding to a pleading or, if no responsive pleading is permitted by these rules, upon motion made by a party within 20 days after the service of the pleading upon the party or upon the court's own initiative at any time, the court may order stricken from any pleading any insufficient defense or any redundant, immaterial, impertinent, or scandalous matter.

(g) Consolidation of Defenses in Motion. A party who makes a motion under this rule may join with it any other motions herein provided for and then available to the party. If a party makes a motion under this rule but omits therefrom any defense or objection then available to the party which this rule permits to be raised by motion, the party shall not thereafter make a motion based on the defense or objection so omitted, except a motion as provided in subdivision (h)(2) hereof on any of the grounds there stated.

(h) Waiver or Preservation of Certain Defenses.

(1) A defense of lack of jurisdiction over the person, improper venue, insufficiency of process, or insufficiency of service of process is waived (A) if omitted from a motion in the circumstances described in subdivision (g), or (B) if it is neither made by motion under this rule nor included in a responsive pleading or an amendment thereof permitted by Rule 15(a) to be made as a matter of course.

(2) A defense of failure to state a claim upon which relief can be granted, a defense of failure to join a party indispensable under Rule 19, and an objection of failure to state a legal defense to a claim may be made in any pleading permitted or ordered under Rule 7(a), or by motion for judgment on the pleadings, or at the trial on the merits.

(3) Whenever it appears by suggestion of the parties or otherwise that the court lacks jurisdiction of the subject matter, the court shall dismiss the action.

[Amended December 27, 1946, effective March 19, 1948; January 21, 1963, effective July 1, 1963; February 28, 1966, effective July 1, 1966; March 2, 1987, effective August 1, 1987; April 22, 1993, effective December 1, 1993; April 17, 2000, effective December 1, 2000.]

RULE 13.   COUNTERCLAIM AND CROSS–CLAIM

(a) Compulsory Counterclaims. A pleading shall state as a counterclaim any claim which at the time of serving the pleading the pleader has against any opposing party, if it arises out of the transaction or occurrence that is the subject matter of the opposing party's claim and does not require for its adjudication the presence of third parties of whom the court cannot acquire jurisdiction. But the pleader need not state the claim if (1) at the time the action was commenced the claim was the subject of another pending action, or (2) the opposing party brought suit upon the claim by attachment or other process by which the court did not acquire jurisdiction to render a personal judgment on that claim, and the pleader is not stating any counterclaim under this Rule 13.

(b) Permissive Counterclaims. A pleading may state as a counterclaim any claim against an opposing party not arising out of the transaction or occurrence that is the subject matter of the opposing party's claim.

(c) Counterclaim Exceeding Opposing Claim. A counterclaim may or may not diminish or defeat the recovery sought by the opposing party. It may claim relief exceeding in amount or different in kind from that sought in the pleading of the opposing party.

(d) Counterclaim Against the United States. These rules shall not be construed to enlarge beyond the limits now fixed by law the right to assert counterclaims or to claim credits against the United States or an officer or agency thereof.

(e) Counterclaim Maturing or Acquired After Pleading. A claim which either matured or was acquired by the pleader after serving a pleading may, with the permission of the court, be presented as a counterclaim by supplemental pleading.

(f) Omitted Counterclaim. When a pleader fails to set up a counterclaim through oversight, inadvertence, or excusable neglect, or when justice requires, the pleader may by leave of court set up the counterclaim by amendment.

(g) Cross-Claim Against Co-party. A pleading may state as a cross-claim any claim by one party against a co-party arising out of the transaction or occurrence that is the subject matter either of the original action or of a counterclaim therein or relating to any property that is the subject matter of the original action. Such cross-claim may include a claim that the party against whom it is asserted is or may be liable to the cross-claimant for all or part of a claim asserted in the action against the cross-claimant.

(h) Joinder of Additional Parties. Persons other than those made parties to the original action may be made parties to a counterclaim or cross-claim in accordance with the provisions of Rules 19 and 20.

(i) Separate Trials; Separate Judgments. If the court orders separate trials as provided in Rule 42(b), judgment on a counterclaim or cross-claim may be rendered in accordance with the terms of Rule 54(b) when the court has jurisdiction so to do, even if the claims of the opposing party have been dismissed or otherwise disposed of.

[Amended December 27, 1946, effective March 19, 1948; January 21, 1963, effective July 1, 1963; February 28, 1966, effective July 1, 1966; March 2, 1987, effective August 1, 1987.]

RULE 14.   THIRD–PARTY PRACTICE

(a) When Defendant May Bring in Third Party. At any time after commencement of the action a defending party, as a third-party plaintiff, may cause a summons and complaint to be served upon a person not a party to the action who is or may be liable to the third-party plaintiff for all or part of the plaintiff's claim against the third-party plaintiff. The third-party plaintiff need not obtain leave to make the service if the third-party plaintiff files the third-party complaint not later than 10 days after serving the original answer. Otherwise the third-party plaintiff must obtain leave on motion upon notice to all parties to the action. The person served with the summons and third-party complaint, hereinafter called the third-party defendant, shall make any defenses to the third-party plaintiff's claim as provided in Rule 12 and any counterclaims against the third-party plaintiff and cross-claims against other third-party defendants as provided in Rule 13. The third-party defendant may assert against the plaintiff any defenses which the third-party plaintiff has to the plaintiff's claim. The third-party defendant may also assert any claim against the plaintiff arising out of the transaction or occurrence that is the subject matter of the plaintiff's claim against the third-party plaintiff. The plaintiff may assert any claim against the third-party defendant arising out of the transaction or occurrence that is the subject matter of the plaintiff's claim against the third-party plaintiff, and the third-party defendant thereupon shall assert any defenses as provided in Rule 12 and any counterclaims and cross-claims as provided in Rule 13. Any party may move to strike the third-party claim, or for its severance or separate trial. A third-party defendant may proceed under this rule against any person not a party to the action who is or may be liable to the third-party defendant for all or part of the claim made in the action against the third-party defendant. The third-party complaint, if within the admiralty and maritime jurisdiction, may be in rem against a vessel, cargo, or other property subject to admiralty or maritime process in rem, in which case references in this rule to the summons include the warrant of arrest, and references to the third-party plaintiff or defendant include, where appropriate, a person who asserts a right under Supplemental Rule C(6)(b)(i) in the property arrested.

(b) When Plaintiff May Bring in Third Party. When a counterclaim is asserted against a plaintiff, the plaintiff may cause a third party to be brought in under circumstances which under this rule would entitle a defendant to do so.

(c) Admiralty and Maritime Claims. When a plaintiff asserts an admiralty or maritime claim within the meaning of Rule 9(h), the defendant or person who asserts a right under Supplemental Rule C(6)(b)(i), as a third-party plaintiff, may bring in a third-party defendant who may be wholly or partly liable, either to the plaintiff or to the third-party plaintiff, by way of remedy over, contribution, or otherwise on account of the same transaction, occurrence, or series of transactions or occurrences. In such a case the third-party plaintiff may also demand judgment against the third-party defendant in favor of the plaintiff, in which event the third-party defendant shall make any defenses to the claim of the plaintiff as well as to that of the third-party plaintiff in the manner provided in Rule 12 and the action shall proceed as if the plaintiff had commenced it against the third-party defendant as well as the third-party plaintiff.

[Amended December 27, 1946, effective March 19, 1948; January 21, 1963, effective July 1, 1963; February 28, 1966, effective July 1, 1966; March 2, 1987, effective August 1, 1987; April 17, 2000, effective December 1, 2000.]

RULE 15. AMENDED AND SUPPLEMENTAL PLEADINGS

(a) Amendments. A party may amend the party's pleading once as a matter of course at any time before a responsive pleading is served or, if the pleading is one to which no responsive pleading is permitted and the action has not been placed upon the trial calendar, the party may so amend it at any time within 20 days after it is served. Otherwise a party may amend the party's pleading only by leave of court or by written consent of the adverse party; and leave shall be freely given when justice so requires. A party shall plead in response to an amended pleading within the time remaining for response to the original pleading or within 10 days after service of the amended pleading, whichever period may be the longer, unless the court otherwise orders.

(b) Amendments to Conform to the Evidence. When issues not raised by the pleadings are tried by express or implied consent of the parties, they shall be treated in all respects as if they had been raised in the pleadings. Such amendment of the pleadings as may be necessary to cause them to conform to the evidence and to raise these issues may be made upon motion of any party at any time, even after judgment; but failure so to amend does not affect the result of the trial of these issues. If evidence is objected to at the trial on the ground that it is not within the issues made by the pleadings, the court may allow the pleadings to be amended and shall do so freely when the presentation of the merits of the action will be subserved thereby and the objecting party fails to satisfy the court that the admission of such evidence would prejudice the party in maintaining the party's action or defense upon the merits. The court may grant a continuance to enable the objecting party to meet such evidence.

(c) Relation Back of Amendments. An amendment of a pleading relates back to the date of the original pleading when

(1) relation back is permitted by the law that provides the statute of limitations applicable to the action, or

(2) the claim or defense asserted in the amended pleading arose out of the conduct, transaction, or occurrence set forth or attempted to be set forth in the original pleading, or

(3) the amendment changes the party or the naming of the party against whom a claim is asserted if the foregoing provision (2) is satisfied and, within the period provided by Rule 4(m) for service of the summons and complaint, the party to be brought in by amendment (A) has received such notice of the institution of the action that the party will not be prejudiced in maintaining a defense on the merits, and (B) knew or should have known that, but for a mistake concern-

ing the identity of the proper party, the action would have been brought against the party.

The delivery or mailing of process to the United States Attorney, or United States Attorney's designee, or the Attorney General of the United States, or an agency or officer who would have been a proper defendant if named, satisfies the requirement of subparagraphs (A) and (B) of this paragraph (3) with respect to the United States or any agency or officer thereof to be brought into the action as a defendant.

(d) Supplemental Pleadings. Upon motion of a party the court may, upon reasonable notice and upon such terms as are just, permit the party to serve a supplemental pleading setting forth transactions or occurrences or events which have happened since the date of the pleading sought to be supplemented. Permission may be granted even though the original pleading is defective in its statement of a claim for relief or defense. If the court deems it advisable that the adverse party plead to the supplemental pleading, it shall so order, specifying the time therefor.

[Amended January 21, 1963, effective July 1, 1963; February 28, 1966, effective July 1, 1966; March 2, 1987, effective August 1, 1987; April 30, 1991, effective December 1, 1991; amended by Pub.L. 102–198, § 11, December 9, 1991, 105 Stat. 1626; amended April 22, 1993, effective December 1, 1993.]

RULE 16. PRETRIAL CONFERENCES; SCHEDULING; MANAGEMENT

(a) Pretrial Conferences; Objectives. In any action, the court may in its discretion direct the attorneys for the parties and any unrepresented parties to appear before it for a conference or conferences before trial for such purposes as

(1) expediting the disposition of the action;

(2) establishing early and continuing control so that the case will not be protracted because of lack of management;

(3) discouraging wasteful pretrial activities;

(4) improving the quality of the trial through more thorough preparation; and

(5) facilitating the settlement of the case.

(b) Scheduling and Planning. Except in categories of actions exempted by district court rule as inappropriate, the district judge, or a magistrate judge when authorized by district court rule, shall, after receiving the report from the parties under Rule 26(f) or after consulting with the attorneys for the parties and any unrepresented parties by a scheduling conference, telephone, mail, or other suitable means, enter a scheduling order that limits the time

(1) to join other parties and to amend the pleadings;

(2) to file motions; and

(3) to complete discovery.

The scheduling order may also include

(4) modifications of the times for disclosures under Rules 26(a) and 26(e)(1) and of the extent of discovery to be permitted;

(5) the date or dates for conferences before trial, a final pretrial conference, and trial; and

(6) any other matters appropriate in the circumstances of the case.

The order shall issue as soon as practicable but in any event within 90 days after the appearance of a defendant and within 120 days after the complaint has been served on a defendant. A schedule shall not be modified except upon a showing of good cause and by leave of the district judge or, when authorized by local rule, by a magistrate judge.

(c) Subjects for Consideration at Pretrial Conferences. At any conference under this rule consideration may be given, and the court may take appropriate action, with respect to

(1) the formulation and simplification of the issues, including the elimination of frivolous claims or defenses;

(2) the necessity or desirability of amendments to the pleadings;

(3) the possibility of obtaining admissions of fact and of documents which will avoid unnecessary proof, stipulations regarding the authenticity of documents, and advance rulings from the court on the admissibility of evidence;

(4) the avoidance of unnecessary proof and of cumulative evidence, and limitations or restrictions on the use of testimony under Rule 702 of the Federal Rules of Evidence;

(5) the appropriateness and timing of summary adjudication under Rule 56;

(6) the control and scheduling of discovery, including orders affecting disclosures and discovery pursuant to Rule 26 and Rules 29 through 37;

(7) the identification of witnesses and documents, the need and schedule for filing and exchanging pretrial briefs, and the date or dates for further conferences and for trial;

(8) the advisability of referring matters to a magistrate judge or master;

(9) settlement and the use of special procedures to assist in resolving the dispute when authorized by statute or local rule;

(10) the form and substance of the pretrial order;

(11) the disposition of pending motions;

(12) the need for adopting special procedures for managing potentially difficult or protracted actions

that may involve complex issues, multiple parties, difficult legal questions, or unusual proof problems;

(13) an order for a separate trial pursuant to Rule 42(b) with respect to a claim, counterclaim, cross-claim, or third-party claim, or with respect to any particular issue in the case;

(14) an order directing a party or parties to present evidence early in the trial with respect to a manageable issue that could, on the evidence, be the basis for a judgment as a matter of law under Rule 50(a) or a judgment on partial findings under Rule 52(c);

(15) an order establishing a reasonable limit on the time allowed for presenting evidence; and

(16) such other matters as may facilitate the just, speedy, and inexpensive disposition of the action.

At least one of the attorneys for each party participating in any conference before trial shall have authority to enter into stipulations and to make admissions regarding all matters that the participants may reasonably anticipate may be discussed. If appropriate, the court may require that a party or its representative be present or reasonably available by telephone in order to consider possible settlement of the dispute.

(d) Final Pretrial Conference. Any final pretrial conference shall be held as close to the time of trial as reasonable under the circumstances. The participants at any such conference shall formulate a plan for trial, including a program for facilitating the admission of evidence. The conference shall be attended by at least one of the attorneys who will conduct the trial

for each of the parties and by any unrepresented parties.

(e) Pretrial Orders. After any conference held pursuant to this rule, an order shall be entered reciting the action taken. This order shall control the subsequent course of the action unless modified by a subsequent order. The order following a final pretrial conference shall be modified only to prevent manifest injustice.

(f) Sanctions. If a party or party's attorney fails to obey a scheduling or pretrial order, or if no appearance is made on behalf of a party at a scheduling or pretrial conference, or if a party or party's attorney is substantially unprepared to participate in the conference, or if a party or party's attorney fails to participate in good faith, the judge, upon motion or the judge's own initiative, may make such orders with regard thereto as are just, and among others any of the orders provided in Rule 37(b)(2)(B), (C), (D). In lieu of or in addition to any other sanction, the judge shall require the party or the attorney representing the party or both to pay the reasonable expenses incurred because of any noncompliance with this rule, including attorney's fees, unless the judge finds that the noncompliance was substantially justified or that other circumstances make an award of expenses unjust.

[Amended April 28, 1983, effective August 1, 1983; March 2, 1987, effective August 1, 1987; April 22, 1993, effective December 1, 1993.]

IV. PARTIES

RULE 17. PARTIES PLAINTIFF AND DEFENDANT; CAPACITY

(a) Real Party in Interest. Every action shall be prosecuted in the name of the real party in interest. An executor, administrator, guardian, bailee, trustee of an express trust, a party with whom or in whose name a contract has been made for the benefit of another, or a party authorized by statute may sue in that person's own name without joining the party for whose benefit the action is brought; and when a statute of the United States so provides, an action for the use or benefit of another shall be brought in the name of the United States. No action shall be dismissed on the ground that it is not prosecuted in the name of the real party in interest until a reasonable time has been allowed after objection for ratification of commencement of the action by, or joinder or substitution of, the real party in interest; and such ratification, joinder, or substitution shall have the same effect as if the action had been commenced in the name of the real party in interest.

(b) Capacity to Sue or Be Sued. The capacity of an individual, other than one acting in a representa-

tive capacity, to sue or be sued shall be determined by the law of the individual's domicile. The capacity of a corporation to sue or be sued shall be determined by the law under which it was organized. In all other cases capacity to sue or be sued shall be determined by the law of the state in which the district court is held, except (1) that a partnership or other unincorporated association, which has no such capacity by the law of such state, may sue or be sued in its common name for the purpose of enforcing for or against it a substantive right existing under the Constitution or laws of the United States, and (2) that the capacity of a receiver appointed by a court of the United States to sue or be sued in a court of the United States is governed by Title 28, U.S.C., Sections 754 and 959(a).

(c) Infants or Incompetent Persons. Whenever an infant or incompetent person has a representative, such as a general guardian, committee, conservator, or other like fiduciary, the representative may sue or defend on behalf of the infant or incompetent person. An infant or incompetent person who does not have a duly appointed representative may sue by a next friend or by a guardian ad litem. The court shall appoint a guardian ad litem for an infant or incompetent person not otherwise represented in an action or shall make such other order as it deems proper for the protection of the infant or incompetent person.

[Amended December 27, 1946, effective March 19, 1948; December 29, 1948, effective October 20, 1949; February 28, 1966, effective July 1, 1966; March 2, 1987, effective August 1, 1987; April 25, 1988, effective August 1, 1988; amended by Pub.L. 100–690, Title VII, § 7049, November 18, 1988, 102 Stat. 4401 (although amendment by Pub.L. 100–690 could not be executed due to prior amendment by Court order which made the same change effective August 1, 1988).]

RULE 18. JOINDER OF CLAIMS AND REMEDIES

(a) **Joinder of Claims.** A party asserting a claim to relief as an original claim, counterclaim, cross-claim, or third-party claim, may join, either as independent or as alternate claims, as many claims, legal, equitable, or maritime, as the party has against an opposing party.

(b) **Joinder of Remedies; Fraudulent Conveyances.** Whenever a claim is one heretofore cognizable only after another claim has been prosecuted to a conclusion, the two claims may be joined in a single action; but the court shall grant relief in that action only in accordance with the relative substantive rights of the parties. In particular, a plaintiff may state a claim for money and a claim to have set aside a conveyance fraudulent as to that plaintiff, without first having obtained a judgment establishing the claim for money.

[Amended February 28, 1966, effective July 1, 1966; March 2, 1987, effective August 1, 1987.]

RULE 19. JOINDER OF PERSONS NEEDED FOR JUST ADJUDICATION

(a) **Persons to Be Joined if Feasible.** A person who is subject to service of process and whose joinder will not deprive the court of jurisdiction over the subject matter of the action shall be joined as a party in the action if (1) in the person's absence complete relief cannot be accorded among those already parties, or (2) the person claims an interest relating to the subject of the action and is so situated that the disposition of the action in the person's absence may (i) as a practical matter impair or impede the person's ability to protect that interest or (ii) leave any of the persons already parties subject to a substantial risk of incurring double, multiple, or otherwise inconsistent obligations by reason of the claimed interest. If the person has not been so joined, the court shall order that the person be made a party. If the person should join as a plaintiff but refuses to do so, the person may be made a defendant, or, in a proper case, an involuntary plaintiff. If the joined party objects to venue and joinder of that party would render the

venue of the action improper, that party shall be dismissed from the action.

(b) **Determination by Court Whenever Joinder Not Feasible.** If a person as described in subdivision (a)(1)–(2) hereof cannot be made a party, the court shall determine whether in equity and good conscience the action should proceed among the parties before it, or should be dismissed, the absent person being thus regarded as indispensable. The factors to be considered by the court include: first, to what extent a judgment rendered in the person's absence might be prejudicial to the person or those already parties; second, the extent to which, by protective provisions in the judgment, by the shaping of relief, or other measures, the prejudice can be lessened or avoided; third, whether a judgment rendered in the person's absence will be adequate; fourth, whether the plaintiff will have an adequate remedy if the action is dismissed for nonjoinder.

(c) **Pleading Reasons for Nonjoinder.** A pleading asserting a claim for relief shall state the names, if known to the pleader, of any persons as described in subdivision (a)(1)–(2) hereof who are not joined, and the reasons why they are not joined.

(d) **Exception of Class Actions.** This rule is subject to the provisions of Rule 23.

[Amended February 28, 1966, effective July 1, 1966; March 2, 1987, effective August 1, 1987.]

RULE 20. PERMISSIVE JOINDER OF PARTIES

(a) **Permissive Joinder.** All persons may join in one action as plaintiffs if they assert any right to relief jointly, severally, or in the alternative in respect of or arising out of the same transaction, occurrence, or series of transactions or occurrences and if any question of law or fact common to all these persons will arise in the action. All persons (and any vessel, cargo or other property subject to admiralty process in rem) may be joined in one action as defendants if there is asserted against them jointly, severally, or in the alternative, any right to relief in respect of or arising out of the same transaction, occurrence, or series of transactions or occurrences and if any question of law or fact common to all defendants will arise in the action. A plaintiff or defendant need not be interested in obtaining or defending against all the relief demanded. Judgment may be given for one or more of the plaintiffs according to their respective rights to relief, and against one or more defendants according to their respective liabilities.

(b) **Separate Trials.** The court may make such orders as will prevent a party from being embarrassed, delayed, or put to expense by the inclusion of a party against whom the party asserts no claim and who asserts no claim against the party, and may order separate trials or make other orders to prevent delay or prejudice.

[Amended February 28, 1966, effective July 1, 1966; March 2, 1987, effective August 1, 1987.]

RULE 21. MISJOINDER AND NON-JOINDER OF PARTIES

Misjoinder of parties is not ground for dismissal of an action. Parties may be dropped or added by order of the court on motion of any party or of its own initiative at any stage of the action and on such terms as are just. Any claim against a party may be severed and proceeded with separately.

RULE 22. INTERPLEADER

(1) Persons having claims against the plaintiff may be joined as defendants and required to interplead when their claims are such that the plaintiff is or may be exposed to double or multiple liability. It is not ground for objection to the joinder that the claims of the several claimants or the titles on which their claims depend do not have a common origin or are not identical but are adverse to and independent of one another, or that the plaintiff avers that the plaintiff is not liable in whole or in part to any or all of the claimants. A defendant exposed to similar liability may obtain such interpleader by way of cross-claim or counterclaim. The provisions of this rule supplement and do not in any way limit the joinder of parties permitted in Rule 20.

(2) The remedy herein provided is in addition to and in no way supersedes or limits the remedy provided by Title 28, U.S.C., §§ 1335, 1397, and 2361. Actions under those provisions shall be conducted in accordance with these rules.

[Amended December 29, 1948, effective October 20, 1949; March 2, 1987, effective August 1, 1987.]

RULE 23. CLASS ACTIONS

(a) **Prerequisites to a Class Action.** One or more members of a class may sue or be sued as representative parties on behalf of all only if (1) the class is so numerous that joinder of all members is impracticable, (2) there are questions of law or fact common to the class, (3) the claims or defenses of the representative parties are typical of the claims or defenses of the class, and (4) the representative parties will fairly and adequately protect the interests of the class.

(b) **Class Actions Maintainable.** An action may be maintained as a class action if the prerequisites of subdivision (a) are satisfied, and in addition:

(1) the prosecution of separate actions by or against individual members of the class would create a risk of

(A) inconsistent or varying adjudications with respect to individual members of the class which

would establish incompatible standards of conduct for the party opposing the class, or

(B) adjudications with respect to individual members of the class which would as a practical matter be dispositive of the interests of the other members not parties to the adjudications or substantially impair or impede their ability to protect their interests; or

(2) the party opposing the class has acted or refused to act on grounds generally applicable to the class, thereby making appropriate final injunctive relief or corresponding declaratory relief with respect to the class as a whole; or

(3) the court finds that the questions of law or fact common to the members of the class predominate over any questions affecting only individual members, and that a class action is superior to other available methods for the fair and efficient adjudication of the controversy. The matters pertinent to the findings include: (A) the interest of members of the class in individually controlling the prosecution or defense of separate actions; (B) the extent and nature of any litigation concerning the controversy already commenced by or against members of the class; (C) the desirability or undesirability of concentrating the litigation of the claims in the particular forum; (D) the difficulties likely to be encountered in the management of a class action.

(c) **Determining by Order Whether to Certify a Class Action; Appointing Class Counsel; Notice and Membership in Class; Judgment; Multiple Classes and Subclasses.**

(1) (A) When a person sues or is sued as a representative of a class, the court must—at an early practicable time—determine by order whether to certify the action as a class action.

(B) An order certifying a class action must define the class and the class claims, issues, or defenses, and must appoint class counsel under Rule 23(g).

(C) An order under Rule 23(c)(1) may be altered or amended before final judgment.

(2) (A) For any class certified under Rule 23(b)(1) or (2), the court may direct appropriate notice to the class.

(B) For any class certified under Rule 23(b)(3), the court must direct to class members the best notice practicable under the circumstances, including individual notice to all members who can be identified through reasonable effort. The notice must concisely and clearly state in plain, easily understood language:

● the nature of the action,

● the definition of the class certified,

● the class claims, issues, or defenses,

● that a class member may enter an appearance through counsel if the member so desires,

• that the court will exclude from the class any member who requests exclusion, stating when and how members may elect to be excluded, and

• the binding effect of a class judgment on class members under Rule 23(c)(3).

(3) The judgment in an action maintained as a class action under subdivision (b)(1) or (b)(2), whether or not favorable to the class, shall include and describe those whom the court finds to be members of the class. The judgment in an action maintained as a class action under subdivision (b)(3), whether or not favorable to the class, shall include and specify or describe those to whom the notice provided in subdivision (c)(2) was directed, and who have not requested exclusion, and whom the court finds to be members of the class.

(4) When appropriate (A) an action may be brought or maintained as a class action with respect to particular issues, or (B) a class may be divided into subclasses and each subclass treated as a class, and the provisions of this rule shall then be construed and applied accordingly.

(d) Orders in Conduct of Actions. In the conduct of actions to which this rule applies, the court may make appropriate orders: (1) determining the course of proceedings or prescribing measures to prevent undue repetition or complication in the presentation of evidence or argument; (2) requiring, for the protection of the members of the class or otherwise for the fair conduct of the action, that notice be given in such manner as the court may direct to some or all of the members of any step in the action, or of the proposed extent of the judgment, or of the opportunity of members to signify whether they consider the representation fair and adequate, to intervene and present claims or defenses, or otherwise to come into the action; (3) imposing conditions on the representative parties or on intervenors; (4) requiring that the pleadings be amended to eliminate therefrom allegations as to representation of absent persons, and that the action proceed accordingly; (5) dealing with similar procedural matters. The orders may be combined with an order under Rule 16, and may be altered or amended as may be desirable from time to time.

(e) Settlement, Voluntary Dismissal, or Compromise.

(1) (A) The court must approve any settlement, voluntary dismissal, or compromise of the claims, issues, or defenses of a certified class.

(B) The court must direct notice in a reasonable manner to all class members who would be bound by a proposed settlement, voluntary dismissal, or compromise.

(C) The court may approve a settlement, voluntary dismissal, or compromise that would bind class members only after a hearing and on finding that the settlement, voluntary dismissal, or compromise is fair, reasonable, and adequate.

(2) The parties seeking approval of a settlement, voluntary dismissal, or compromise under Rule 23(e)(1) must file a statement identifying any agreement made in connection with the proposed settlement, voluntary dismissal, or compromise.

(3) In an action previously certified as a class action under Rule 23(b)(3), the court may refuse to approve a settlement unless it affords a new opportunity to request exclusion to individual class members who had an earlier opportunity to request exclusion but did not do so.

(4) (A) Any class member may object to a proposed settlement, voluntary dismissal, or compromise that requires court approval under Rule 23(e)(1)(A).

(B) An objection made under Rule 23(e)(4)(A) may be withdrawn only with the court's approval.

(f) Appeals. A court of appeals may in its discretion permit an appeal from an order of a district court granting or denying class action certification under this rule if application is made to it within ten days after entry of the order. An appeal does not stay proceedings in the district court unless the district judge or the court of appeals so orders.

(g) Class Counsel.

(1) *Appointing Class Counsel.*

(A) Unless a statute provides otherwise, a court that certifies a class must appoint class counsel.

(B) An attorney appointed to serve as class counsel must fairly and adequately represent the interests of the class.

(C) In appointing class counsel, the court

(i) must consider:

• the work counsel has done in identifying or investigating potential claims in the action,

• counsel's experience in handling class actions, other complex litigation, and claims of the type asserted in the action,

• counsel's knowledge of the applicable law, and

• the resources counsel will commit to representing the class;

(ii) may consider any other matter pertinent to counsel's ability to fairly and adequately represent the interests of the class;

(iii) may direct potential class counsel to provide information on any subject pertinent to the appointment and to propose terms for attorney fees and nontaxable costs; and

(iv) may make further orders in connection with the appointment.

(2) *Appointment Procedure.*

(A) The court may designate interim counsel to act on behalf of the putative class before determining whether to certify the action as a class action.

(B) When there is one applicant for appointment as class counsel, the court may appoint that applicant only if the applicant is adequate under Rule 23(g)(1)(B) and (C). If more than one adequate applicant seeks appointment as class counsel, the court must appoint the applicant best able to represent the interests of the class.

(C) The order appointing class counsel may include provisions about the award of attorney fees or nontaxable costs under Rule 23(h).

(h) Attorney Fees Award. In an action certified as a class action, the court may award reasonable attorney fees and nontaxable costs authorized by law or by agreement of the parties as follows:

(1) *Motion for Award of Attorney Fees.* A claim for an award of attorney fees and nontaxable costs must be made by motion under Rule 54(d)(2), subject to the provisions of this subdivision, at a time set by the court. Notice of the motion must be served on all parties and, for motions by class counsel, directed to class members in a reasonable manner.

(2) *Objections to Motion.* A class member, or a party from whom payment is sought, may object to the motion.

(3) *Hearing and Findings.* The court may hold a hearing and must find the facts and state its conclusions of law on the motion under Rule 52(a).

(4) *Reference to Special Master or Magistrate Judge.* The court may refer issues related to the amount of the award to a special master or to a magistrate judge as provided in Rule 54(d)(2)(D).

[Amended February 28, 1966, effective July 1, 1966; March 2, 1987, effective August 1, 1987; April 24, 1998, effective December 1, 1998; March 27, 2003, effective December 1, 2003.]

RULE 23.1 DERIVATIVE ACTIONS BY SHAREHOLDERS

In a derivative action brought by one or more shareholders or members to enforce a right of a corporation or of an unincorporated association, the corporation or association having failed to enforce a right which may properly be asserted by it, the complaint shall be verified and shall allege (1) that the plaintiff was a shareholder or member at the time of the transaction of which the plaintiff complains or that the plaintiff's share or membership thereafter devolved on the plaintiff by operation of law, and (2) that the action is not a collusive one to confer jurisdiction on a court of the United States which it would not otherwise have. The complaint shall also allege with particularity the efforts, if any, made by the plaintiff

to obtain the action the plaintiff desires from the directors or comparable authority and, if necessary, from the shareholders or members, and the reasons for the plaintiff's failure to obtain the action or for not making the effort. The derivative action may not be maintained if it appears that the plaintiff does not fairly and adequately represent the interests of the shareholders or members similarly situated in enforcing the right of the corporation or association. The action shall not be dismissed or compromised without the approval of the court, and notice of the proposed dismissal or compromise shall be given to shareholders or members in such manner as the court directs.

[Adopted February 28, 1966, effective July 1, 1966; amended March 2, 1987, effective August 1, 1987.]

RULE 23.2 ACTIONS RELATING TO UNINCORPORATED ASSOCIATIONS

An action brought by or against the members of an unincorporated association as a class by naming certain members as representative parties may be maintained only if it appears that the representative parties will fairly and adequately protect the interests of the association and its members. In the conduct of the action the court may make appropriate orders corresponding with those described in Rule 23(d), and the procedure for dismissal or compromise of the action shall correspond with that provided in Rule 23(e).

[Adopted February 28, 1966, effective July 1, 1966.]

RULE 24. INTERVENTION

(a) Intervention of Right. Upon timely application anyone shall be permitted to intervene in an action: (1) when a statute of the United States confers an unconditional right to intervene; or (2) when the applicant claims an interest relating to the property or transaction which is the subject of the action and the applicant is so situated that the disposition of the action may as a practical matter impair or impede the applicant's ability to protect that interest, unless the applicant's interest is adequately represented by existing parties.

(b) Permissive Intervention. Upon timely application anyone may be permitted to intervene in an action: (1) when a statute of the United States confers a conditional right to intervene; or (2) when an applicant's claim or defense and the main action have a question of law or fact in common. When a party to an action relies for ground of claim or defense upon any statute or executive order administered by a federal or state governmental officer or agency or upon any regulation, order, requirement, or agreement issued or made pursuant to the statute or executive order, the officer or agency upon timely application may be permitted to intervene in the action. In exercising its discretion the court shall consider whether the intervention will unduly delay or prejudice the adjudication of the rights of the original parties.

(c) Procedure. A person desiring to intervene shall serve a motion to intervene upon the parties as provided in Rule 5. The motion shall state the grounds therefor and shall be accompanied by a pleading setting forth the claim or defense for which intervention is sought. The same procedure shall be followed when a statute of the United States gives a right to intervene. When the constitutionality of an act of Congress affecting the public interest is drawn in question in any action in which the United States or an officer, agency, or employee thereof is not a party, the court shall notify the Attorney General of the United States as provided in Title 28, U.S.C. § 2403. When the constitutionality of any statute of a State affecting the public interest is drawn in question in any action in which that State or any agency, officer, or employee thereof is not a party, the court shall notify the attorney general of the State as provided in Title 28, U.S.C. § 2403. A party challenging the constitutionality of legislation should call the attention of the court to its consequential duty, but failure to do so is not a waiver of any constitutional right otherwise timely asserted.

[Amended December 27, 1946, effective March 19, 1948; December 29, 1948, effective October 20, 1949; January 21, 1963, effective July 1, 1963; February 28, 1966, effective July 1, 1966; March 2, 1987, effective August 1, 1987; April 30, 1991, effective December 1, 1991.]

RULE 25. SUBSTITUTION OF PARTIES

(a) Death.

(1) If a party dies and the claim is not thereby extinguished, the court may order substitution of the proper parties. The motion for substitution may be made by any party or by the successors or representatives of the deceased party and, together with the notice of hearing, shall be served on the parties as provided in Rule 5 and upon persons not parties in the manner provided in Rule 4 for the service of a summons, and may be served in any judicial district. Unless the motion for substitution is made not later than 90 days after the death is suggested upon the record by service of a statement of the fact of the death as provided herein for the service of the motion, the action shall be dismissed as to the deceased party.

(2) In the event of the death of one or more of the plaintiffs or of one or more of the defendants in an action in which the right sought to be enforced survives only to the surviving plaintiffs or only against the surviving defendants, the action does not abate. The death shall be suggested upon the record and the action shall proceed in favor of or against the surviving parties.

(b) Incompetency. If a party becomes incompetent, the court upon motion served as provided in subdivision (a) of this rule may allow the action to be continued by or against the party's representative.

(c) Transfer of Interest. In case of any transfer of interest, the action may be continued by or against the original party, unless the court upon motion directs the person to whom the interest is transferred to be substituted in the action or joined with the original party. Service of the motion shall be made as provided in subdivision (a) of this rule.

(d) Public Officers; Death or Separation From Office.

(1) When a public officer is a party to an action in an official capacity and during its pendency dies, resigns, or otherwise ceases to hold office, the action does not abate and the officer's successor is automatically substituted as a party. Proceedings following the substitution shall be in the name of the substituted party, but any misnomer not affecting the substantial rights of the parties shall be disregarded. An order of substitution may be entered at any time, but the omission to enter such an order shall not affect the substitution.

(2) A public officer who sues or is sued in an official capacity may be described as a party by the officer's official title rather than by name; but the court may require the officer's name to be added.

[Amended December 29, 1948, effective October 20, 1949; April 17, 1961, effective July 19, 1961; January 21, 1963, effective July 1, 1963; March 2, 1987, effective August 1, 1987.]

V. DEPOSITIONS AND DISCOVERY

RULE 26. GENERAL PROVISIONS GOVERNING DISCOVERY; DUTY OF DISCLOSURE

(a) Required Disclosures; Methods to Discover Additional Matter.

(1) *Initial Disclosures.* Except in categories of proceedings specified in Rule 26(a)(1)(E), or to the extent otherwise stipulated or directed by order, a party must, without awaiting a discovery request, provide to other parties:

(A) the name and, if known, the address and telephone number of each individual likely to have discoverable information that the disclosing party may use to support its claims or defenses, unless solely for impeachment, identifying the subjects of the information;

(B) a copy of, or a description by category and location of, all documents, data compilations, and tangible things that are in the possession, custody, or control of the party and that the disclosing party may use to support its claims or defenses, unless solely for impeachment;

(C) a computation of any category of damages claimed by the disclosing party, making available for inspection and copying as under Rule 34 the documents or other evidentiary material, not privileged or protected from disclosure, on which such computation is based, including materials bearing on the nature and extent of injuries suffered; and

(D) for inspection and copying as under Rule 34 any insurance agreement under which any person carrying on an insurance business may be liable to satisfy part or all of a judgment which may be entered in the action or to indemnify or reimburse for payments made to satisfy the judgment.

(E) The following categories of proceedings are exempt from initial disclosure under Rule 26(a)(1):

(i) an action for review on an administrative record;

(ii) a petition for habeas corpus or other proceeding to challenge a criminal conviction or sentence;

(iii) an action brought without counsel by a person in custody of the United States, a state, or a state subdivision;

(iv) an action to enforce or quash an administrative summons or subpoena;

(v) an action by the United States to recover benefit payments;

(vi) an action by the United States to collect on a student loan guaranteed by the united States;

(vii) a proceeding ancillary to proceedings in other courts; and

(viii) an action to enforce an arbitration award.

These disclosures must be made at or within 14 days after the Rule 26(f) conference unless a different time is set by stipulation or court order, or unless a party objects during the conference that initial disclosures are not appropriate in the circumstances of the action and states the objection in the Rule 26(f) discovery plan. In ruling on the objection, the court must determine what disclosures—if any—are to be made, and set the time for disclosure. Any party first served or otherwise joined after the Rule 26(f) conference must make these disclosures within 30 days after being served or joined unless a different time is set by stipulation or court order. A party must make its initial disclosures based on the information then reasonably available to it and is not excused from making its disclosures because it has not fully completed its investigation of the case or because it challenges the

sufficiency of another party's disclosures or because another party has not made its disclosures.

(2) *Disclosure of Expert Testimony.*

(A) In addition to the disclosures required by paragraph (1), a party shall disclose to other parties the identity of any person who may be used at trial to present evidence under Rules 702, 703, or 705 of the Federal Rules of Evidence.

(B) Except as otherwise stipulated or directed by the court, this disclosure shall, with respect to a witness who is retained or specially employed to provide expert testimony in the case or whose duties as an employee of the party regularly involve giving expert testimony, be accompanied by a written report prepared and signed by the witness. The report shall contain a complete statement of all opinions to be expressed and the basis and reasons therefor; the data or other information considered by the witness in forming the opinions; any exhibits to be used as a summary of or support for the opinions; the qualifications of the witness, including a list of all publications authored by the witness within the preceding ten years; the compensation to be paid for the study and testimony; and a listing of any other cases in which the witness has testified as an expert at trial or by deposition within the preceding four years.

(C) These disclosures shall be made at the times and in the sequence directed by the court. In the absence of other directions from the court or stipulation by the parties, the disclosures shall be made at least 90 days before the trial date or the date the case is to be ready for trial or, if the evidence is intended solely to contradict or rebut evidence on the same subject matter identified by another party under paragraph (2)(B), within 30 days after the disclosure made by the other party. The parties shall supplement these disclosures when required under subdivision (e)(1).

(3) *Pretrial Disclosures.* In addition to the disclosures required by Rule 26(a)(1) and (2), a party must provide to other parties and promptly file with the court the following information regarding the evidence that it may present at trial other than solely for impeachment:

(A) the name and, if not previously provided, the address and telephone number of each witness, separately identifying those whom the party expects to present and those whom the party may call if the need arises;

(B) the designation of those witnesses whose testimony is expected to be presented by means of a deposition and, if not taken stenographically, a transcript of the pertinent portions of the deposition testimony; and

(C) an appropriate identification of each document or other exhibit, including summaries of other evidence, separately identifying those which the party expects to offer and those which the party may offer if the need arises.

Unless otherwise directed by the court, these disclosures must be made at least 30 days before trial. Within 14 days thereafter, unless a different time is specified by the court, a party may serve and promptly file a list disclosing (i) any objections to the use under Rule 32(a) of a deposition designated by another party under Rule 26(a)(3)(B) and (ii) any objection, together with the grounds therefor, that may be made to the admissibility of materials identified under Rule 26(a)(3)(C). Objections not so disclosed, other than objections under Rules 402 and 403 of the Federal Rules of Evidence, are waived unless excused by the court for good cause.

(4) *Form of Disclosures.* Unless the court orders otherwise, all disclosures under Rules 26(a)(1) through (3) must be made in writing, signed, and served.

(5) *Methods to Discover Additional Matter.* Parties may obtain discovery by one or more of the following methods: depositions upon oral examination or written questions; written interrogatories; production of documents or things or permission to enter upon land or other property under Rule 34 or 45(a)(1)(C), for inspection and other purposes; physical and mental examinations; and requests for admission.

(b) Discovery Scope and Limits. Unless otherwise limited by order of the court in accordance with these rules, the scope of discovery is as follows:

(1) *In General.* Parties may obtain discovery regarding any matter, not privileged, that is relevant to the claim or defense of any party, including the existence, description, nature, custody, condition, and location of any books, documents, or other tangible things and the identity and location of persons having knowledge of any discoverable matter. For good cause, the court may order discovery of any matter relevant to the subject matter involved in the action. Relevant information need not be admissible at the trial if the discovery appears reasonably calculated to lead to the discovery of admissible evidence. All discovery is subject to the limitations imposed by Rule 26(b)(2)(i), (ii), and (iii).

(2) *Limitations.* By order, the court may alter the limits in these rules on the number of depositions and interrogatories or the length of depositions under Rule 30. By order or local rule, the court may also limit the number of requests under Rule 36. The frequency or extent of use of the discovery methods otherwise permitted under these rules and by any local rule shall be limited by the court if it determines that: (i) the discovery sought is unreasonably cumulative or duplicative, or is obtainable from some other source that is more convenient, less burdensome, or less expensive; (ii) the party seeking discovery has had ample opportunity by discovery in the action to

obtain the information sought; or (iii) the burden or expense of the proposed discovery outweighs its likely benefit, taking into account the needs of the case, the amount in controversy, the parties' resources, the importance of the issues at stake in the litigation, and the importance of the proposed discovery in resolving the issues. The court may act upon its own initiative after reasonable notice or pursuant to a motion under Rule 26(c).

(3) *Trial Preparation: Materials.* Subject to the provisions of subdivision (b)(4) of this rule, a party may obtain discovery of documents and tangible things otherwise discoverable under subdivision (b)(1) of this rule and prepared in anticipation of litigation or for trial by or for another party or by or for that other party's representative (including the other party's attorney, consultant, surety, indemnitor, insurer, or agent) only upon a showing that the party seeking discovery has substantial need of the materials in the preparation of the party's case and that the party is unable without undue hardship to obtain the substantial equivalent of the materials by other means. In ordering discovery of such materials when the required showing has been made, the court shall protect against disclosure of the mental impressions, conclusions, opinions, or legal theories of an attorney or other representative of a party concerning the litigation.

A party may obtain without the required showing a statement concerning the action or its subject matter previously made by that party. Upon request, a person not a party may obtain without the required showing a statement concerning the action or its subject matter previously made by that person. If the request is refused, the person may move for a court order. The provisions of Rule 37(a)(4) apply to the award of expenses incurred in relation to the motion. For purposes of this paragraph, a statement previously made is (A) a written statement signed or otherwise adopted or approved by the person making it, or (B) a stenographic, mechanical, electrical, or other recording, or a transcription thereof, which is a substantially verbatim recital of an oral statement by the person making it and contemporaneously recorded.

(4) *Trial Preparation: Experts.*

(A) A party may depose any person who has been identified as an expert whose opinions may be presented at trial. If a report from the expert is required under subdivision (a)(2)(B), the deposition shall not be conducted until after the report is provided.

(B) A party may, through interrogatories or by deposition, discover facts known or opinions held by an expert who has been retained or specially employed by another party in anticipation of litigation or preparation for trial and who is not expected to be called as a witness at trial only as provided in

Rule 35(b) or upon a showing of exceptional circumstances under which it is impracticable for the party seeking discovery to obtain facts or opinions on the same subject by other means.

(C) Unless manifest injustice would result, (i) the court shall require that the party seeking discovery pay the expert a reasonable fee for time spent in responding to discovery under this subdivision; and (ii) with respect to discovery obtained under subdivision (b)(4)(B) of this rule the court shall require the party seeking discovery to pay the other party a fair portion of the fees and expenses reasonably incurred by the latter party in obtaining facts and opinions from the expert.

(5) *Claims of Privilege or Protection of Trial Preparation Materials.* When a party withholds information otherwise discoverable under these rules by claiming that it is privileged or subject to protection as trial preparation material, the party shall make the claim expressly and shall describe the nature of the documents, communications, or things not produced or disclosed in a manner that, without revealing information itself privileged or protected, will enable other parties to assess the applicability of the privilege or protection.

(c) Protective Orders. Upon motion by a party or by the person from whom discovery is sought, accompanied by a certification that the movant has in good faith conferred or attempted to confer with other affected parties in an effort to resolve the dispute without court action, and for good cause shown, the court in which the action is pending or alternatively, on matters relating to a deposition, the court in the district where the deposition is to be taken may make any order which justice requires to protect a party or person from annoyance, embarrassment, oppression, or undue burden or expense, including one or more of the following:

(1) that the disclosure or discovery not be had;

(2) that the disclosure or discovery may be had only on specified terms and conditions, including a designation of the time or place;

(3) that the discovery may be had only by a method of discovery other than that selected by the party seeking discovery;

(4) that certain matters not be inquired into, or that the scope of the disclosure or discovery be limited to certain matters;

(5) that discovery be conducted with no one present except persons designated by the court;

(6) that a deposition, after being sealed, be opened only by order of the court;

(7) that a trade secret or other confidential research, development, or commercial information not be revealed or be revealed only in a designated way; and

(8) that the parties simultaneously file specified documents or information enclosed in sealed envelopes to be opened as directed by the court.

If the motion for a protective order is denied in whole or in part, the court may, on such terms and conditions as are just, order that any party or other person provide or permit discovery. The provisions of Rule 37(a)(4) apply to the award of expenses incurred in relation to the motion.

(d) Timing and Sequence of Discovery. Except in categories of proceedings exempted from initial disclosure under Rule 26(a)(1)(E), or when authorized under these rules or by order or agreement of the parties, a party may not seek discovery from any source before the parties have conferred as required by Rule 26(f). Unless the court upon motion, for the convenience of parties and witnesses and in the interests of justice, orders otherwise, methods of discovery may be used in any sequence, and the fact that a party is conducting discovery, whether by deposition or otherwise, does not operate to delay any other party's discovery.

(e) Supplementation of Disclosures and Responses. A party who has made a disclosure under subdivision (a) or responded to a request for discovery with a disclosure or response is under a duty to supplement or correct the disclosure or response to include information thereafter acquired if ordered by the court or in the following circumstances:

(1) A party is under a duty to supplement at appropriate intervals its disclosures under subdivision (a) if the party learns that in some material respect the information disclosed is incomplete or incorrect and if the additional or corrective information has not otherwise been made known to the other parties during the discovery process or in writing. With respect to testimony of an expert from whom a report is required under subdivision (a)(2)(B) the duty extends both to information contained in the report and to information provided through a deposition of the expert, and any additions or other changes to this information shall be disclosed by the time the party's disclosures under Rule 26(a)(3) are due.

(2) A party is under a duty seasonably to amend a prior response to an interrogatory, request for production, or request for admission if the party learns that the response is in some material respect incomplete or incorrect and if the additional or corrective information has not otherwise been made known to the other parties during the discovery process or in writing.

(f) Conference of Parties; Planning for Discovery. Except in categories of proceedings exempted from initial disclosure under Rule 26(a)(1)(E) or when otherwise ordered, the parties must, as soon as practicable and in any event at least 21 days before a scheduling conference is held or a scheduling order is due under Rule 16(b), confer to consider the nature and basis of their claims and defenses and the possibilities for a prompt settlement or resolution of the case, to make or arrange for the disclosures required by Rule 26(a)(1), and to develop a proposed discovery plan that indicates the parties' views and proposals concerning:

(1) what changes should be made in the timing, form, or requirement for disclosures under Rule 26(a), including a statement as to when disclosures under Rule 26(a)(1) were made or will be made;

(2) the subjects on which discovery may be needed, when discovery should be completed, and whether discovery should be conducted in phases or be limited to or focused upon particular issues;

(3) what changes should be made in the limitations on discovery imposed under these rules or by local rule, and what other limitations should be imposed; and

(4) any other orders that should be entered by the court under Rule 26(c) or under Rule 16(b) and (c).

The attorneys of record and all unrepresented parties that have appeared in the case are jointly responsible for arranging the conference, for attempting in good faith to agree on the proposed discovery plan, and for submitting to the court within 14 days after the conference a written report outlining the plan. A court may order that the parties or attorneys attend the conference in person. If necessary to comply with its expedited schedule for Rule 16(b) conferences, a court may by local rule (i) require that the conference between the parties occur fewer than 21 days before the scheduling conference is held or a scheduling order is due under Rule 16(b), and (ii) require that the written report outlining the discovery plan be filed fewer than 14 days after the conference between the parties, or excuse the parties from submitting a written report and permit them to report orally on their discovery plan at the Rule 16(b) conference.

(g) Signing of Disclosures, Discovery Requests, Responses, and Objections.

(1) Every disclosure made pursuant to subdivision (a)(1) or subdivision (a)(3) shall be signed by at least one attorney of record in the attorney's individual name, whose address shall be stated. An unrepresented party shall sign the disclosure and state the party's address. The signature of the attorney or party constitutes a certification that to the best of the signer's knowledge, information, and belief, formed after a reasonable inquiry, the disclosure is complete and correct as of the time it is made.

(2) Every discovery request, response, or objection made by a party represented by an attorney shall be signed by at least one attorney of record in the attorney's individual name, whose address shall be stated. An unrepresented party shall sign the request, response, or objection and state the party's

address. The signature of the attorney or party constitutes a certification that to the best of the signer's knowledge, information, and belief, formed after a reasonable inquiry, the request, response, or objection is:

(A) consistent with these rules and warranted by existing law or a good faith argument for the extension, modification, or reversal of existing law;

(B) not interposed for any improper purpose, such as to harass or to cause unnecessary delay or needless increase in the cost of litigation; and

(C) not unreasonable or unduly burdensome or expensive, given the needs of the case, the discovery already had in the case, the amount in controversy, and the importance of the issues at stake in the litigation.

If a request, response, or objection is not signed, it shall be stricken unless it is signed promptly after the omission is called to the attention of the party making the request, response, or objection, and a party shall not be obligated to take any action with respect to it until it is signed.

(3) If without substantial justification a certification is made in violation of the rule, the court, upon motion or upon its own initiative, shall impose upon the person who made the certification, the party on whose behalf the disclosure, request, response, or objection is made, or both, an appropriate sanction, which may include an order to pay the amount of the reasonable expenses incurred because of the violation, including a reasonable attorney's fee.

[Amended December 27, 1946, effective March 19, 1948; January 21, 1963, effective July 1, 1963; February 28, 1966, effective July 1, 1966; March 30, 1970, effective July 1, 1970; April 29, 1980, effective August 1, 1980; April 28, 1983, effective August 1, 1983; March 2, 1987, effective August 1, 1987; April 22, 1993, effective December 1, 1993; April 17, 2000, effective December 1, 2000.]

RULE 27. DEPOSITIONS BEFORE ACTION OR PENDING APPEAL

(a) Before Action.

(1) *Petition.* A person who desires to perpetuate testimony regarding any matter that may be cognizable in any court of the United States may file a verified petition in the United States district court in the district of the residence of any expected adverse party. The petition shall be entitled in the name of the petitioner and shall show: 1, that the petitioner expects to be a party to an action cognizable in a court of the United States but is presently unable to bring it or cause it to be brought, 2, the subject matter of the expected action and the petitioner's interest therein, 3, the facts which the petitioner desires to establish by the proposed testimony and the reasons for desiring to perpetuate it, 4, the names or a description of the

persons the petitioner expects will be adverse parties and their addresses so far as known, and 5, the names and addresses of the persons to be examined and the substance of the testimony which the petitioner expects to elicit from each, and shall ask for an order authorizing the petitioner to take the depositions of the persons to be examined named in the petition, for the purpose of perpetuating their testimony.

(2) *Notice and Service.* The petitioner shall thereafter serve a notice upon each person named in the petition as an expected adverse party, together with a copy of the petition, stating that the petitioner will apply to the court, at a time and place named therein, for the order described in the petition. At least 20 days before the date of hearing the notice shall be served either within or without the district or state in the manner provided in Rule 4(d) for service of summons; but if such service cannot with due diligence be made upon any expected adverse party named in the petition, the court may make such order as is just for service by publication or otherwise, and shall appoint, for persons not served in the manner provided in Rule 4(d), an attorney who shall represent them, and, in case they are not otherwise represented, shall cross-examine the deponent. If any expected adverse party is a minor or incompetent the provisions of Rule 17(c) apply.

(3) *Order and Examination.* If the court is satisfied that the perpetuation of the testimony may prevent a failure or delay of justice, it shall make an order designating or describing the persons whose depositions may be taken and specifying the subject matter of the examination and whether the depositions shall be taken upon oral examination or written interrogatories. The depositions may then be taken in accordance with these rules; and the court may make orders of the character provided for by Rules 34 and 35. For the purpose of applying these rules to depositions for perpetuating testimony, each reference therein to the court in which the action is pending shall be deemed to refer to the court in which the petition for such deposition was filed.

(4) *Use of Deposition.* If a deposition to perpetuate testimony is taken under these rules or if, although not so taken, it would be admissible in evidence in the courts of the state in which it is taken, it may be used in any action involving the same subject matter subsequently brought in a United States district court, in accordance with the provisions of Rule 32(a).

(b) **Pending Appeal.** If an appeal has been taken from a judgment of a district court or before the taking of an appeal if the time therefor has not expired, the district court in which the judgment was rendered may allow the taking of the depositions of witnesses to perpetuate their testimony for use in the event of further proceedings in the district court. In such case the party who desires to perpetuate the testimony may make a motion in the district court for

leave to take the depositions, upon the same notice and service thereof as if the action was pending in the district court. The motion shall show (1) the names and addresses of persons to be examined and the substance of the testimony which the party expects to elicit from each; (2) the reasons for perpetuating their testimony. If the court finds that the perpetuation of the testimony is proper to avoid a failure or delay of justice, it may make an order allowing the depositions to be taken and may make orders of the character provided for by Rules 34 and 35, and thereupon the depositions may be taken and used in the same manner and under the same conditions as are prescribed in these rules for depositions taken in actions pending in the district court.

(c) **Perpetuation by Action.** This rule does not limit the power of a court to entertain an action to perpetuate testimony.

[Amended December 27, 1946, effective March 19, 1948; December 29, 1948, effective October 20, 1949; March 1, 1971, effective July 1, 1971; March 2, 1987, effective August 1, 1987.]

RULE 28. PERSONS BEFORE WHOM DEPOSITIONS MAY BE TAKEN

(a) **Within the United States.** Within the United States or within a territory or insular possession subject to the jurisdiction of the United States, depositions shall be taken before an officer authorized to administer oaths by the laws of the United States or of the place where the examination is held, or before a person appointed by the court in which the action is pending. A person so appointed has power to administer oaths and take testimony. The term officer as used in Rules 30, 31 and 32 includes a person appointed by the court or designated by the parties under Rule 29.

(b) **In Foreign Countries.** Depositions may be taken in a foreign country (1) pursuant to any applicable treaty or convention, or (2) pursuant to a letter of request (whether or not captioned a letter rogatory), or (3) on notice before a person authorized to administer oaths in the place where the examination is held, either by the law thereof or by the law of the United States, or (4) before a person commissioned by the court, and a person so commissioned shall have the power by virtue of the commission to administer any necessary oath and take testimony. A commission or a letter of request shall be issued on application and notice and on terms that are just and appropriate. It is not requisite to the issuance of a commission or a letter of request that the taking of the deposition in any other manner is impracticable or inconvenient; and both a commission and a letter of request may be issued in proper cases. A notice or commission may designate the person before whom the deposition is to be taken either by name or descriptive title. A letter of request may be addressed "To the Appropriate Authority in [here name the country]." When a letter of request or any other device is used pursuant to any applicable treaty or convention, it shall be captioned in the form prescribed by that treaty or convention. Evidence obtained in response to a letter of request need not be excluded merely because it is not a verbatim transcript, because the testimony was not taken under oath, or because of any similar departure from the requirements for depositions taken within the United States under these rules.

(c) Disqualification for Interest. No deposition shall be taken before a person who is a relative or employee or attorney or counsel of any of the parties, or is a relative or employee of such attorney or counsel, or is financially interested in the action.

[Amended December 27, 1946, effective March 19, 1948; January 21, 1963, effective July 1, 1963; April 29, 1980, effective August 1, 1980; March 2, 1987, effective August 1, 1987; April 22, 1993, effective December 1, 1993.]

RULE 29.   STIPULATIONS REGARDING DISCOVERY PROCEDURE

Unless otherwise directed by the court, the parties may by written stipulation (1) provide that depositions may be taken before any person, at any time or place, upon any notice, and in any manner and when so taken may be used like other depositions, and (2) modify other procedures governing or limitations placed upon discovery, except that stipulations extending the time provided in Rules 33, 34, and 36 for responses to discovery may, if they would interfere with any time set for completion of discovery, for hearing of a motion, or for trial, be made only with the approval of the court.

[Amended March 30, 1970, effective July 1, 1970; April 22, 1993, effective December 1, 1993.]

RULE 30.   DEPOSITIONS UPON ORAL EXAMINATION

(a) When Depositions May Be Taken; When Leave Required.

(1) A party may take the testimony of any person, including a party, by deposition upon oral examination without leave of court except as provided in paragraph (2). The attendance of witnesses may be compelled by subpoena as provided in Rule 45.

(2) A party must obtain leave of court, which shall be granted to the extent consistent with the principles stated in Rule 26(b)(2), if the person to be examined is confined in prison or if, without the written stipulation of the parties,

(A) a proposed deposition would result in more than ten depositions being taken under this rule or Rule 31 by the plaintiffs, or by the defendants, or by third-party defendants;

(B) the person to be examined already has been deposed in the case; or

(C) a party seeks to take a deposition before the time specified in Rule 26(d) unless the notice contains a certification, with supporting facts, that the person to be examined is expected to leave the United States and be unavailable for examination in this country unless deposed before that time.

(b) Notice of Examination: General Requirements; Method of Recording; Production of Documents and Things; Deposition of Organization; Deposition by Telephone.

(1) A party desiring to take the deposition of any person upon oral examination shall give reasonable notice in writing to every other party to the action. The notice shall state the time and place for taking the deposition and the name and address of each person to be examined, if known, and, if the name is not known, a general description sufficient to identify the person or the particular class or group to which the person belongs. If a subpoena duces tecum is to be served on the person to be examined, the designation of the materials to be produced as set forth in the subpoena shall be attached to, or included in, the notice.

(2) The party taking the deposition shall state in the notice the method by which the testimony shall be recorded. Unless the court orders otherwise, it may be recorded by sound, sound-and-visual, or stenographic means, and the party taking the deposition shall bear the cost of the recording. Any party may arrange for a transcription to be made from the recording of a deposition taken by nonstenographic means.

(3) With prior notice to the deponent and other parties, any party may designate another method to record the deponent's testimony in addition to the method specified by the person taking the deposition. The additional record or transcript shall be made at that party's expense unless the court otherwise orders.

(4) Unless otherwise agreed by the parties, a deposition shall be conducted before an officer appointed or designated under Rule 28 and shall begin with a statement on the record by the officer that includes (A) the officer's name and business address; (B) the date, time, and place of the deposition; (C) the name of the deponent; (D) the administration of the oath or affirmation to the deponent; and (E) an identification of all persons present. If the deposition is recorded other than stenographically, the officer shall repeat items (A) through (C) at the beginning of each unit of recorded tape or other recording medium. The appearance or demeanor of deponents or attorneys shall not be distorted through camera or sound-recording techniques. At the end of the deposition, the officer shall state on the record that the deposition is com-

plete and shall set forth any stipulations made by counsel concerning the custody of the transcript or recording and the exhibits, or concerning other pertinent matters.

(5) The notice to a party deponent may be accompanied by a request made in compliance with Rule 34 for the production of documents and tangible things at the taking of the deposition. The procedure of Rule 34 shall apply to the request.

(6) A party may in the party's notice and in a subpoena name as the deponent a public or private corporation or a partnership or association or governmental agency and describe with reasonable particularity the matters on which examination is requested. In that event, the organization so named shall designate one or more officers, directors, or managing agents, or other persons who consent to testify on its behalf, and may set forth, for each person designated, the matters on which the person will testify. A subpoena shall advise a non-party organization of its duty to make such a designation. The persons so designated shall testify as to matters known or reasonably available to the organization. This subdivision (b)(6) does not preclude taking a deposition by any other procedure authorized in these rules.

(7) The parties may stipulate in writing or the court may upon motion order that a deposition be taken by telephone or other remote electronic means. For the purposes of this rule and Rules 28(a), 37(a)(1), and 37(b)(1), a deposition taken by such means is taken in the district and at the place where the deponent is to answer questions.

(c) Examination and Cross–Examination; Record of Examination; Oath; Objections. Examination and cross-examination of witnesses may proceed as permitted at the trial under the provisions of the Federal Rules of Evidence except Rules 103 and 615. The officer before whom the deposition is to be taken shall put the witness on oath or affirmation and shall personally, or by someone acting under the officer's direction and in the officer's presence, record the testimony of the witness. The testimony shall be taken stenographically or recorded by any other method authorized by subdivision (b)(2) of this rule. All objections made at the time of the examination to the qualifications of the officer taking the deposition, to the manner of taking it, to the evidence presented, to the conduct of any party, or to any other aspect of the proceedings shall be noted by the officer upon the record of the deposition; but the examination shall proceed, with the testimony being taken subject to the objections. In lieu of participating in the oral examination, parties may serve written questions in a sealed envelope on the party taking the deposition and the party taking the deposition shall transmit them to the officer, who shall propound them to the witness and record the answers verbatim.

(d) Schedule and Duration; Motion to Terminate or Limit Examination.

(1) Any objection during a deposition must be stated concisely and in a non-argumentative and non-suggestive manner. A person may instruct a deponent not to answer only when necessary to preserve a privilege, to enforce a limitation directed by the court, or to present a motion under Rule 30(d)(4).

(2) Unless otherwise authorized by the court or stipulated by the parties, a deposition is limited to one day of seven hours. The court must allow additional time consistent with Rule 26(b)(2) if needed for a fair examination of the deponent or if the deponent or another person, or other circumstance, impedes or delays the examination.

(3) If the court finds that any impediment, delay, or other conduct has frustrated the fair examination of the deponent, it may impose upon the persons responsible an appropriate sanction, including the reasonable costs and attorney's fees incurred by any parties as a result thereof.

(4) At any time during a deposition, on motion of a party or of the deponent and upon a showing that the examination is being conducted in bad faith or in such manner as unreasonably to annoy, embarrass, or oppress the deponent or party, the court in which the action is pending or the court in the district where the deposition is being taken may order the officer conducting the examination to cease forthwith from taking the deposition, or may limit the scope and manner of the taking of the deposition as provided in Rule 26(c). If the order made terminates the examination, it may be resumed thereafter only upon the order of the court in which the action is pending. Upon demand of the objecting party or deponent, the taking of the deposition must be suspended for the time necessary to make a motion for an order. The provisions of Rule 37(a)(4) apply to the award of expenses incurred in relation to the motion.

(e) Review by Witness; Changes; Signing. If requested by the deponent or a party before completion of the deposition, the deponent shall have 30 days after being notified by the officer that the transcript or recording is available in which to review the transcript or recording and, if there are changes in form or substance, to sign a statement reciting such changes and the reasons given by the deponent for making them. The officer shall indicate in the certificate prescribed by subdivision (f)(1) whether any review was requested and, if so, shall append any changes made by the deponent during the period allowed.

(f) Certification and Delivery by Officer; Exhibits; Copies.

(1) The officer must certify that the witness was duly sworn by the officer and that the deposition is a true record of the testimony given by the witness.

This certificate must be in writing and accompany the record of the deposition. Unless otherwise ordered by the court, the officer must securely seal the deposition in an envelope or package indorsed with the title of the action and marked "Deposition of [here insert name of witness]" and must promptly send it to the attorney who arranged for the transcript or recording, who must store it under conditions that will protect it against loss, destruction, tampering, or deterioration. Documents and things produced for inspection during the examination of the witness must, upon the request of a party, be marked for identification and annexed to the deposition and may be inspected and copied by any party, except that if the person producing the materials desires to retain them the person may (A) offer copies to be marked for identification and annexed to the deposition and to serve thereafter as originals if the person affords to all parties fair opportunity to verify the copies by comparison with the originals, or (B) offer the originals to be marked for identification, after giving to each party an opportunity to inspect and copy them, in which event the materials may then be used in the same manner as if annexed to the deposition. Any party may move for an order that the original be annexed to and returned with the deposition to the court, pending final disposition of the case.

(2) Unless otherwise ordered by the court or agreed by the parties, the officer shall retain stenographic notes of any deposition taken stenographically or a copy of the recording of any deposition taken by another method. Upon payment of reasonable charges therefor, the officer shall furnish a copy of the transcript or other recording of the deposition to any party or to the deponent.

(3) The party taking the deposition shall give prompt notice of its filing to all other parties.

(g) Failure to Attend or to Serve Subpoena; Expenses.

(1) If the party giving the notice of the taking of a deposition fails to attend and proceed therewith and another party attends in person or by attorney pursuant to the notice, the court may order the party giving the notice to pay to such other party the reasonable expenses incurred by that party and that party's attorney in attending, including reasonable attorney's fees.

(2) If the party giving the notice of the taking of a deposition of a witness fails to serve a subpoena upon the witness and the witness because of such failure does not attend, and if another party attends in person or by attorney because that party expects the deposition of that witness to be taken, the court may order the party giving the notice to pay to such other party the reasonable expenses incurred by that party

and that party's attorney in attending, including reasonable attorney's fees.

[Amended January 21, 1963, effective July 1, 1963; March 30, 1970, effective July 1, 1970; March 1, 1971, effective July 1, 1971; November 20, 1972, effective July 1, 1975; April 29, 1980, effective August 1, 1980; March 2, 1987, effective August 1, 1987; April 22, 1993, effective December 1, 1993; April 17, 2000, effective December 1, 2000.]

RULE 31. DEPOSITIONS UPON WRITTEN QUESTIONS

(a) Serving Questions; Notice.

(1) A party may take the testimony of any person, including a party, by deposition upon written questions without leave of court except as provided in paragraph (2). The attendance of witnesses may be compelled by the use of subpoena as provided in Rule 45.

(2) A party must obtain leave of court, which shall be granted to the extent consistent with the principles stated in Rule 26(b)(2), if the person to be examined is confined in prison or if, without the written stipulation of the parties,

(A) a proposed deposition would result in more than ten depositions being taken under this rule or Rule 30 by the plaintiffs, or by the defendants, or by third-party defendants;

(B) the person to be examined has already been deposed in the case; or

(C) a party seeks to take a deposition before the time specified in Rule 26(d).

(3) A party desiring to take a deposition upon written questions shall serve them upon every other party with a notice stating (1) the name and address of the person who is to answer them, if known, and if the name is not known, a general description sufficient to identify the person or the particular class or group to which the person belongs, and (2) the name or descriptive title and address of the officer before whom the deposition is to be taken. A deposition upon written questions may be taken of a public or private corporation or a partnership or association or governmental agency in accordance with the provisions of Rule 30(b)(6).

(4) Within 14 days after the notice and written questions are served, a party may serve cross questions upon all other parties. Within 7 days after being served with cross questions, a party may serve redirect questions upon all other parties. Within 7 days after being served with redirect questions, a party may serve recross questions upon all other parties. The court may for cause shown enlarge or shorten the time.

(b) Officer to Take Responses and Prepare Record. A copy of the notice and copies of all questions served shall be delivered by the party taking the deposition to the officer designated in the notice, who shall proceed promptly, in the manner provided by Rule 30(c), (e), and (f), to take the testimony of the witness in response to the questions and to prepare, certify, and file or mail the deposition, attaching thereto the copy of the notice and the questions received by the officer.

(c) Notice of Filing. When the deposition is filed the party taking it shall promptly give notice thereof to all other parties.

[Amended March 30, 1970, effective July 1, 1970; March 2, 1987, effective August 1, 1987; April 22, 1993, effective December 1, 1993.]

RULE 32. USE OF DEPOSITIONS IN COURT PROCEEDINGS

(a) Use of Depositions. At the trial or upon the hearing of a motion or an interlocutory proceeding, any part or all of a deposition, so far as admissible under the rules of evidence applied as though the witness were then present and testifying, may be used against any party who was present or represented at the taking of the deposition or who had reasonable notice thereof, in accordance with any of the following provisions:

(1) Any deposition may be used by any party for the purpose of contradicting or impeaching the testimony of deponent as a witness, or for any other purpose permitted by the Federal Rules of Evidence.

(2) The deposition of a party or of anyone who at the time of taking the deposition was an officer, director, or managing agent, or a person designated under Rule 30(b)(6) or 31(a) to testify on behalf of a public or private corporation, partnership or association or governmental agency which is a party may be used by an adverse party for any purpose.

(3) The deposition of a witness, whether or not a party, may be used by any party for any purpose if the court finds:

(A) that the witness is dead; or

(B) that the witness is at a greater distance than 100 miles from the place of trial or hearing, or is out of the United States, unless it appears that the absence of the witness was procured by the party offering the deposition; or

(C) that the witness is unable to attend or testify because of age, illness, infirmity, or imprisonment; or

(D) that the party offering the deposition has been unable to procure the attendance of the witness by subpoena; or

(E) upon application and notice, that such exceptional circumstances exist as to make it desirable, in the interest of justice and with due regard to the importance of presenting the testimony of witnesses

orally in open court, to allow the deposition to be used.

A deposition taken without leave of court pursuant to a notice under Rule 30(a)(2)(C) shall not be used against a party who demonstrates that, when served with the notice, it was unable through the exercise of diligence to obtain counsel to represent it at the taking of the deposition; nor shall a deposition be used against a party who, having received less than 11 days notice of a deposition, has promptly upon receiving such notice filed a motion for a protective order under Rule 26(c)(2) requesting that the deposition not be held or be held at a different time or place and such motion is pending at the time the deposition is held.

(4) If only part of a deposition is offered in evidence by a party, an adverse party may require the offeror to introduce any other part which ought in fairness to be considered with the part introduced, and any party may introduce any other parts.

Substitution of parties pursuant to Rule 25 does not affect the right to use depositions previously taken; and, when an action has been brought in any court of the United States or of any State and another action involving the same subject matter is afterward brought between the same parties or their representatives or successors in interest, all depositions lawfully taken and duly filed in the former action may be used in the latter as if originally taken therefor. A deposition previously taken may also be used as permitted by the Federal Rules of Evidence.

(b) Objections to Admissibility. Subject to the provisions of Rule 28(b) and subdivision (d)(3) of this rule, objection may be made at the trial or hearing to receiving in evidence any deposition or part thereof for any reason which would require the exclusion of the evidence if the witness were then present and testifying.

(c) Form of Presentation. Except as otherwise directed by the court, a party offering deposition testimony pursuant to this rule may offer it in stenographic or nonstenographic form, but, if in nonstenographic form, the party shall also provide the court with a transcript of the portions so offered. On request of any party in a case tried before a jury, deposition testimony offered other than for impeachment purposes shall be presented in nonstenographic form, if available, unless the court for good cause orders otherwise.

(d) Effect of Errors and Irregularities in Depositions.

(1) *As to Notice.* All errors and irregularities in the notice for taking a deposition are waived unless written objection is promptly served upon the party giving the notice.

(2) *As to Disqualification of Officer.* Objection to taking a deposition because of disqualification of the

officer before whom it is to be taken is waived unless made before the taking of the deposition begins or as soon thereafter as the disqualification becomes known or could be discovered with reasonable diligence.

(3) *As to Taking of Deposition.*

(A) Objections to the competency of a witness or to the competency, relevancy, or materiality of testimony are not waived by failure to make them before or during the taking of the deposition, unless the ground of the objection is one which might have been obviated or removed if presented at that time.

(B) Errors and irregularities occurring at the oral examination in the manner of taking the deposition, in the form of the questions or answers, in the oath or affirmation, or in the conduct of parties, and errors of any kind which might be obviated, removed, or cured if promptly presented, are waived unless seasonable objection thereto is made at the taking of the deposition.

(C) Objections to the form of written questions submitted under Rule 31 are waived unless served in writing upon the party propounding them within the time allowed for serving the succeeding cross or other questions and within 5 days after service of the last questions authorized.

(4) *As to Completion and Return of Deposition.* Errors and irregularities in the manner in which the testimony is transcribed or the deposition is prepared, signed, certified, sealed, indorsed, transmitted, filed, or otherwise dealt with by the officer under Rules 30 and 31 are waived unless a motion to suppress the deposition or some part thereof is made with reasonable promptness after such defect is, or with due diligence might have been, ascertained.

[Amended March 30, 1970, effective July 1, 1970; November 20, 1972, effective July 1, 1975; April 29, 1980, effective August 1, 1980; March 2, 1987, effective August 1, 1987; April 22, 1993, effective December 1, 1993.]

RULE 33. INTERROGATORIES TO PARTIES

(a) Availability. Without leave of court or written stipulation, any party may serve upon any other party written interrogatories, not exceeding 25 in number including all discrete subparts, to be answered by the party served or, if the party served is a public or private corporation or a partnership or association or governmental agency, by any officer or agent, who shall furnish such information as is available to the party. Leave to serve additional interrogatories shall be granted to the extent consistent with the principles of Rule 26(b)(2). Without leave of court or written stipulation, interrogatories may not be served before the time specified in Rule 26(d).

(b) Answers and Objections.

(1) Each interrogatory shall be answered separately and fully in writing under oath, unless it is objected to, in which event the objecting party shall state the reasons for objection and shall answer to the extent the interrogatory is not objectionable.

(2) The answers are to be signed by the person making them, and the objections signed by the attorney making them.

(3) The party upon whom the interrogatories have been served shall serve a copy of the answers, and objections if any, within 30 days after the service of the interrogatories. A shorter or longer time may be directed by the court or, in the absence of such an order, agreed to in writing by the parties subject to Rule 29.

(4) All grounds for an objection to an interrogatory shall be stated with specificity. Any ground not stated in a timely objection is waived unless the party's failure to object is excused by the court for good cause shown.

(5) The party submitting the interrogatories may move for an order under Rule 37(a) with respect to any objection to or other failure to answer an interrogatory.

(c) Scope; Use at Trial. Interrogatories may relate to any matters which can be inquired into under Rule 26(b)(1), and the answers may be used to the extent permitted by the rules of evidence.

An interrogatory otherwise proper is not necessarily objectionable merely because an answer to the interrogatory involves an opinion or contention that relates to fact or the application of law to fact, but the court may order that such an interrogatory need not be answered until after designated discovery has been completed or until a pre-trial conference or other later time.

(d) Option to Produce Business Records. Where the answer to an interrogatory may be derived or ascertained from the business records of the party upon whom the interrogatory has been served or from an examination, audit or inspection of such business records, including a compilation, abstract or summary thereof, and the burden of deriving or ascertaining the answer is substantially the same for the party serving the interrogatory as for the party served, it is a sufficient answer to such interrogatory to specify the records from which the answer may be derived or ascertained and to afford to the party serving the interrogatory reasonable opportunity to examine, audit or inspect such records and to make copies, compilations, abstracts or summaries. A specification shall be in sufficient detail to permit the interrogating party to locate and to identify, as readily as can the party served, the records from which the answer may be ascertained.

[Amended December 27, 1946, effective March 19, 1948; March 30, 1970, effective July 1, 1970; April 29, 1980, effective August 1, 1980; April 22, 1993, effective December 1, 1993.]

RULE 34. PRODUCTION OF DOCUMENTS AND THINGS AND ENTRY UPON LAND FOR INSPECTION AND OTHER PURPOSES

(a) **Scope.** Any party may serve on any other party a request (1) to produce and permit the party making the request, or someone acting on the requestor's behalf, to inspect and copy, any designated documents (including writings, drawings, graphs, charts, photographs, phonorecords, and other data compilations from which information can be obtained, translated, if necessary, by the respondent through detection devices into reasonably usable form), or to inspect and copy, test, or sample any tangible things which constitute or contain matters within the scope of Rule 26(b) and which are in the possession, custody or control of the party upon whom the request is served; or (2) to permit entry upon designated land or other property in the possession or control of the party upon whom the request is served for the purpose of inspection and measuring, surveying, photographing, testing, or sampling the property or any designated object or operation thereon, within the scope of Rule 26(b).

(b) **Procedure.** The request shall set forth, either by individual item or by category, the items to be inspected, and describe each with reasonable particularity. The request shall specify a reasonable time, place, and manner of making the inspection and performing the related acts. Without leave of court or written stipulation, a request may not be served before the time specified in Rule 26(d).

The party upon whom the request is served shall serve a written response within 30 days after the service of the request. A shorter or longer time may be directed by the court or, in the absence of such an order, agreed to in writing by the parties, subject to Rule 29. The response shall state, with respect to each item or category, that inspection and related activities will be permitted as requested, unless the request is objected to, in which event the reasons for the objection shall be stated. If objection is made to part of an item or category, the part shall be specified and inspection permitted of the remaining parts. The party submitting the request may move for an order under Rule 37(a) with respect to any objection to or other failure to respond to the request or any part thereof, or any failure to permit inspection as requested.

A party who produces documents for inspection shall produce them as they are kept in the usual course of business or shall organize and label them to correspond with the categories in the request.

(c) **Persons Not Parties.** A person not a party to the action may be compelled to produce documents and things or to submit to an inspection as provided in Rule 45.

[Amended December 27, 1946, effective March 19, 1948; March 30, 1970, effective July 1, 1970; April 29, 1980, effective August 1, 1980; March 2, 1987, effective August 1, 1987; April 30, 1991, effective December 1, 1991; April 22, 1993, effective December 1, 1993.]

RULE 35. PHYSICAL AND MENTAL EXAMINATIONS OF PERSONS

(a) **Order for Examination.** When the mental or physical condition (including the blood group) of a party or of a person in the custody or under the legal control of a party, is in controversy, the court in which the action is pending may order the party to submit to a physical or mental examination by a suitably licensed or certified examiner or to produce for examination the person in the party's custody or legal control. The order may be made only on motion for good cause shown and upon notice to the person to be examined and to all parties and shall specify the time, place, manner, conditions, and scope of the examination and the person or persons by whom it is to be made.

(b) **Report of Examiner.**

(1) If requested by the party against whom an order is made under Rule 35(a) or the person examined, the party causing the examination to be made shall deliver to the requesting party a copy of the detailed written report of the examiner setting out the examiner's findings, including results of all tests made, diagnoses and conclusions, together with like reports of all earlier examinations of the same condition. After delivery the party causing the examination shall be entitled upon request to receive from the party against whom the order is made a like report of any examination, previously or thereafter made, of the same condition, unless, in the case of a report of examination of a person not a party, the party shows that the party is unable to obtain it. The court on motion may make an order against a party requiring delivery of a report on such terms as are just, and if an examiner fails or refuses to make a report the court may exclude the examiner's testimony if offered at trial.

(2) By requesting and obtaining a report of the examination so ordered or by taking the deposition of the examiner, the party examined waives any privilege the party may have in that action or any other involving the same controversy, regarding the testimony of every other person who has examined or may thereafter examine the party in respect of the same mental or physical condition.

(3) This subdivision applies to examinations made by agreement of the parties, unless the agreement expressly provides otherwise. This subdivision does not preclude discovery of a report of an examiner or

the taking of a deposition of the examiner in accordance with the provisions of any other rule.

[Amended March 30, 1970, effective July 1, 1970; March 2, 1987, effective August 1, 1987; amended by Pub.L. 100–690, Title VII, § 7047(b), November 18, 1988, 102 Stat. 4401; amended April 30, 1991, effective December 1, 1991.]

RULE 36. REQUESTS FOR ADMISSION

(a) **Request for Admission.** A party may serve upon any other party a written request for the admission, for purposes of the pending action only, of the truth of any matters within the scope of Rule 26(b)(1) set forth in the request that relate to statements or opinions of fact or of the application of law to fact, including the genuineness of any documents described in the request. Copies of documents shall be served with the request unless they have been or are otherwise furnished or made available for inspection and copying. Without leave of court or written stipulation, requests for admission may not be served before the time specified in Rule 26(d).

Each matter of which an admission is requested shall be separately set forth. The matter is admitted unless, within 30 days after service of the request, or within such shorter or longer time as the court may allow or as the parties may agree to in writing, subject to Rule 29, the party to whom the request is directed serves upon the party requesting the admission a written answer or objection addressed to the matter, signed by the party or by the party's attorney. If objection is made, the reasons therefor shall be stated. The answer shall specifically deny the matter or set forth in detail the reasons why the answering party cannot truthfully admit or deny the matter. A denial shall fairly meet the substance of the requested admission, and when good faith requires that a party qualify an answer or deny only a part of the matter of which an admission is requested, the party shall specify so much of it as is true and qualify or deny the remainder. An answering party may not give lack of information or knowledge as a reason for failure to admit or deny unless the party states that the party has made reasonable inquiry and that the information known or readily obtainable by the party is insufficient to enable the party to admit or deny. A party who considers that a matter of which an admission has been requested presents a genuine issue for trial may not, on that ground alone, object to the request; the party may, subject to the provisions of Rule 37(c), deny the matter or set forth reasons why the party cannot admit or deny it.

The party who has requested the admissions may move to determine the sufficiency of the answers or objections. Unless the court determines that an objection is justified, it shall order that an answer be served. If the court determines that an answer does not comply with the requirements of this rule, it may order either that the matter is admitted or that an amended answer be served. The court may, in lieu of

these orders, determine that final disposition of the request be made at a pre-trial conference or at a designated time prior to trial. The provisions of Rule 37(a)(4) apply to the award of expenses incurred in relation to the motion.

(b) **Effect of Admission.** Any matter admitted under this rule is conclusively established unless the court on motion permits withdrawal or amendment of the admission. Subject to the provision of Rule 16 governing amendment of a pre-trial order, the court may permit withdrawal or amendment when the presentation of the merits of the action will be subserved thereby and the party who obtained the admission fails to satisfy the court that withdrawal or amendment will prejudice that party in maintaining the action or defense on the merits. Any admission made by a party under this rule is for the purpose of the pending action only and is not an admission for any other purpose nor may it be used against the party in any other proceeding.

[Amended December 27, 1946, effective March 19, 1948; March 30, 1970, effective July 1, 1970; March 2, 1987, effective August 1, 1987; April 22, 1993, effective December 1, 1993.]

RULE 37. FAILURE TO MAKE DISCLOSURE OR COOPERATE IN DISCOVERY; SANCTIONS

(a) **Motion for Order Compelling Disclosure or Discovery.** A party, upon reasonable notice to other parties and all persons affected thereby, may apply for an order compelling disclosure or discovery as follows:

(1) *Appropriate Court.* An application for an order to a party shall be made to the court in which the action is pending. An application for an order to a person who is not a party shall be made to the court in the district where the discovery is being, or is to be, taken.

(2) *Motion.*

(A) If a party fails to make a disclosure required by Rule 26(a), any other party may move to compel disclosure and for appropriate sanctions. The motion must include a certification that the movant has in good faith conferred or attempted to confer with the party not making the disclosure in an effort to secure the disclosure without court action.

(B) If a deponent fails to answer a question propounded or submitted under Rules 30 or 31, or a corporation or other entity fails to make a designation under Rule 30(b)(6) or 31(a), or a party fails to answer an interrogatory submitted under Rule 33, or if a party, in response to a request for inspection submitted under Rule 34, fails to respond that inspection will be permitted as requested or fails to permit inspection as requested, the discovering party may move for an order compelling an answer, or a designation, or an order compelling inspection in accordance with the request. The motion must include a certification that the movant has in good faith conferred or attempted to confer with the person or party failing to make the discovery in an effort to secure the information or material without court action. When taking a deposition on oral examination, the proponent of the question may complete or adjourn the examination before applying for an order.

(3) *Evasive or Incomplete Disclosure, Answer, or Response.* For purposes of this subdivision an evasive or incomplete disclosure, answer, or response is to be treated as a failure to disclose, answer, or respond.

(4) *Expenses and Sanctions.*

(A) If the motion is granted or if the disclosure or requested discovery is provided after the motion was filed, the court shall, after affording an opportunity to be heard, require the party or deponent whose conduct necessitated the motion or the party or attorney advising such conduct or both of them to pay to the moving party the reasonable expenses incurred in making the motion, including attorney's fees, unless the court finds that the motion was filed without the movant's first making a good faith effort to obtain the disclosure or discovery without court action, or that the opposing party's nondisclosure, response, or objection was substantially justified, or that other circumstances make an award of expenses unjust.

(B) If the motion is denied, the court may enter any protective order authorized under Rule 26(c) and shall, after affording an opportunity to be heard, require the moving party or the attorney filing the motion or both of them to pay to the party or deponent who opposed the motion the reasonable expenses incurred in opposing the motion, including attorney's fees, unless the court finds that the making of the motion was substantially justified or that other circumstances make an award of expenses unjust.

(C) If the motion is granted in part and denied in part, the court may enter any protective order authorized under Rule 26(c) and may, after affording an opportunity to be heard, apportion the reasonable expenses incurred in relation to the motion among the parties and persons in a just manner.

(b) Failure to Comply With Order.

(1) *Sanctions by Court in District Where Deposition Is Taken.* If a deponent fails to be sworn or to answer a question after being directed to do so by the court in the district in which the deposition is being taken, the failure may be considered a contempt of that court.

(2) *Sanctions by Court in Which Action Is Pending.* If a party or an officer, director, or managing agent of a party or a person designated under Rule 30(b)(6) or 31(a) to testify on behalf of a party fails to obey an order to provide or permit discovery, including an order made under subdivision (a) of this rule or Rule 35, or if a party fails to obey an order entered under Rule 26(f), the court in which the action is pending may make such orders in regard to the failure as are just, and among others the following:

(A) An order that the matters regarding which the order was made or any other designated facts shall be taken to be established for the purposes of the action in accordance with the claim of the party obtaining the order;

(B) An order refusing to allow the disobedient party to support or oppose designated claims or defenses, or prohibiting that party from introducing designated matters in evidence;

(C) An order striking out pleadings or parts thereof, or staying further proceedings until the order is obeyed, or dismissing the action or proceeding or any part thereof, or rendering a judgment by default against the disobedient party;

(D) In lieu of any of the foregoing orders or in addition thereto, an order treating as a contempt of court the failure to obey any orders except an order to submit to a physical or mental examination;

(E) Where a party has failed to comply with an order under Rule 35(a) requiring that party to produce another for examination, such orders as are listed in paragraphs (A), (B), and (C) of this subdivision, unless the party failing to comply shows that that party is unable to produce such person for examination.

In lieu of any of the foregoing orders or in addition thereto, the court shall require the party failing to obey the order or the attorney advising that party or both to pay the reasonable expenses, including attorney's fees, caused by the failure, unless the court finds that the failure was substantially justified or that other circumstances make an award of expenses unjust.

(c) Failure to Disclose; False or Misleading Disclosure; Refusal to Admit.

(1) A party that without substantial justification fails to disclose information required by Rule 26(a) or 26(e)(1) or to amend a prior response to discovery as required by Rule 26(e)(2), is not, unless such failure is harmless, permitted to use as evidence at a trial, at a hearing, or on a motion any witness or information not so disclosed. In addition to or in lieu of this sanction, the court, on motion and after affording an opportunity to be heard, may impose other appropriate sanctions. In addition to requiring payment of reasonable expenses, including attorney's fees, caused by the failure, these sanctions may include any of the actions authorized under Rule 37(b)(2)(A), (B), and (C) and

may include informing the jury of the failure to make the disclosure.

(2) If a party fails to admit the genuineness of any document or the truth of any matter as requested under Rule 36, and if the party requesting the admissions thereafter proves the genuineness of the document or the truth of the matter, the requesting party may apply to the court for an order requiring the other party to pay the reasonable expenses incurred in making that proof, including reasonable attorney's fees. The court shall make the order unless it finds that (A) the request was held objectionable pursuant to Rule 36(a), or (B) the admission sought was of no substantial importance, or (C) the party failing to admit had reasonable ground to believe that the party might prevail on the matter, or (D) there was other good reason for the failure to admit.

(d) Failure of Party to Attend at Own Deposition or Serve Answers to Interrogatories or Respond to Request for Inspection. If a party or an officer, director, or managing agent of a party or a person designated under Rule 30(b)(6) or 31(a) to testify on behalf of a party fails (1) to appear before the officer who is to take the deposition, after being served with a proper notice, or (2) to serve answers or objections to interrogatories submitted under Rule 33, after proper service of the interrogatories, or (3) to serve a written response to a request for inspection submitted under Rule 34, after proper service of the request, the court in which the action is pending on motion may make such orders in regard to the failure as are just, and among others it may take any action authorized under subparagraphs (A), (B), and (C) of subdivision (b)(2) of this rule. Any motion specifying a failure under clause (2) or (3) of this subdivision shall include a certification that the movant has in good faith conferred or attempted to confer with the party failing to answer or respond in an effort to obtain such answer or response without court action. In lieu of any order or in addition thereto, the court shall require the party failing to act or the attorney advising that party or both to pay the reasonable expenses, including attorney's fees, caused by the failure unless the court finds that the failure was substantially justified or that other circumstances make an award of expenses unjust.

The failure to act described in this subdivision may not be excused on the ground that the discovery sought is objectionable unless the party failing to act has a pending motion for a protective order as provided by Rule 26(c).

(e) Subpoena of Person in Foreign Country [Abrogated].

(f) Expenses Against United States [Repealed].

(g) Failure to Participate in the Framing of a Discovery Plan. If a party or a party's attorney fails to participate in good faith in the development and submission of a proposed discovery plan as required by Rule 26(f), the court may, after opportunity for hearing, require such party or attorney to pay to any other party the reasonable expenses, including attorney's fees, caused by the failure.

[Amended December 29, 1948, effective October 20, 1949; March 30, 1970, effective July 1, 1970; April 29, 1980, effective August 1, 1980; amended by Pub.L. 96–481, Title II, § 205(a), October 21, 1980, 94 Stat. 2330, effective October 1, 1981; amended March 2, 1987, effective August 1, 1987; April 22, 1993, effective December 1, 1993; April 17, 2000, effective December 1, 2000.]

VI. TRIALS

RULE 38. JURY TRIAL OF RIGHT

(a) Right Preserved. The right of trial by jury as declared by the Seventh Amendment to the Constitution or as given by a statute of the United States shall be preserved to the parties inviolate.

(b) Demand. Any party may demand a trial by jury of any issue triable of right by a jury by (1) serving upon the other parties a demand therefor in writing at any time after the commencement of the action and not later than 10 days after the service of the last pleading directed to such issue, and (2) filing the demand as required by Rule 5(d). Such demand may be indorsed upon a pleading of the party.

(c) Same: Specification of Issues. In the demand a party may specify the issues which the party wishes so tried; otherwise the party shall be deemed to have demanded trial by jury for all the issues so triable. If the party has demanded trial by jury for only some of the issues, any other party within 10 days after service of the demand or such lesser time as the court may order, may serve a demand for trial by jury of any other or all of the issues of fact in the action.

(d) Waiver. The failure of a party to serve and file a demand as required by this rule constitutes a waiver by the party of trial by jury. A demand for trial by jury made as herein provided may not be withdrawn without the consent of the parties.

(e) Admiralty and Maritime Claims. These rules shall not be construed to create a right to trial by jury of the issues in an admiralty or maritime claim within the meaning of Rule 9(h).

[Amended February 28, 1966, effective July 1, 1966; March 2, 1987, effective August 1, 1987; April 22, 1993, effective December 1, 1993.]

RULE 39. TRIAL BY JURY OR BY THE COURT

(a) By Jury. When trial by jury has been demanded as provided in Rule 38, the action shall be designated upon the docket as a jury action. The trial of all issues so demanded shall be by jury, unless (1) the parties or their attorneys of record, by written stipulation filed with the court or by an oral stipulation made in open court and entered in the record, consent to trial by the court sitting without a jury or (2) the court upon motion or of its own initiative finds that a right of trial by jury of some or of all those issues does not exist under the Constitution or statutes of the United States.

(b) By the Court. Issues not demanded for trial by jury as provided in Rule 38 shall be tried by the court; but, notwithstanding the failure of a party to demand a jury in an action in which such a demand might have been made of right, the court in its discretion upon motion may order a trial by a jury of any or all issues.

(c) Advisory Jury and Trial by Consent. In all actions not triable of right by a jury the court upon motion or of its own initiative may try any issue with an advisory jury or, except in actions against the United States when a statute of the United States provides for trial without a jury, the court, with the consent of both parties, may order a trial with a jury whose verdict has the same effect as if trial by jury had been a matter of right.

RULE 40. ASSIGNMENT OF CASES FOR TRIAL

The district courts shall provide by rule for the placing of actions upon the trial calendar (1) without request of the parties or (2) upon request of a party and notice to the other parties or (3) in such other manner as the courts deem expedient. Precedence shall be given to actions entitled thereto by any statute of the United States.

RULE 41. DISMISSAL OF ACTIONS

(a) Voluntary Dismissal: Effect Thereof.

(1) *By Plaintiff; By Stipulation.* Subject to the provisions of Rule 23(e), of Rule 66, and of any statute of the United States, an action may be dismissed by the plaintiff without order of court (i) by filing a notice of dismissal at any time before service by the adverse party of an answer or of a motion for summary judgment, whichever first occurs, or (ii) by filing a stipulation of dismissal signed by all parties who have appeared in the action. Unless otherwise stated in the notice of dismissal or stipulation, the dismissal is without prejudice, except that a notice of dismissal operates as an adjudication upon the merits when filed by a plaintiff who has once dismissed in any court of the United States or of any state an action based on or including the same claim.

(2) *By Order of Court.* Except as provided in paragraph (1) of this subdivision of this rule, an action shall not be dismissed at the plaintiff's instance save upon order of the court and upon such terms and conditions as the court deems proper. If a counterclaim has been pleaded by a defendant prior to the service upon the defendant of the plaintiff's motion to dismiss, the action shall not be dismissed against the defendant's objection unless the counterclaim can remain pending for independent adjudication by the court. Unless otherwise specified in the order, a dismissal under this paragraph is without prejudice.

(b) Involuntary Dismissal: Effect Thereof. For failure of the plaintiff to prosecute or to comply with these rules or any order of court, a defendant may move for dismissal of an action or of any claim against the defendant. Unless the court in its order for dismissal otherwise specifies, a dismissal under this subdivision and any dismissal not provided for in this rule, other than a dismissal for lack of jurisdiction, for improper venue, or for failure to join a party under Rule 19, operates as an adjudication upon the merits.

(c) Dismissal of Counterclaim, Cross–Claim, or Third–Party Claim. The provisions of this rule apply to the dismissal of any counterclaim, cross-claim, or third-party claim. A voluntary dismissal by the claimant alone pursuant to paragraph (1) of subdivision (a) of this rule shall be made before a responsive pleading is served or, if there is none, before the introduction of evidence at the trial or hearing.

(d) Costs of Previously–Dismissed Action. If a plaintiff who has once dismissed an action in any court commences an action based upon or including the same claim against the same defendant, the court may make such order for the payment of costs of the action previously dismissed as it may deem proper and may stay the proceedings in the action until the plaintiff has complied with the order.

[Amended December 27, 1946, effective March 19, 1948; January 21, 1963, effective July 1, 1963; February 28, 1966, effective July 1, 1966; December 4, 1967, effective July 1, 1968; March 2, 1987, effective August 1, 1987; April 30, 1991, effective December 1, 1991.]

RULE 42. CONSOLIDATION; SEPARATE TRIALS

(a) Consolidation. When actions involving a common question of law or fact are pending before the court, it may order a joint hearing or trial of any or all the matters in issue in the actions; it may order all the actions consolidated; and it may make such orders concerning proceedings therein as may tend to avoid unnecessary costs or delay.

(b) Separate Trials. The court, in furtherance of convenience or to avoid prejudice, or when separate trials will be conducive to expedition and economy, may order a separate trial of any claim, cross-claim, counterclaim, or third-party claim, or of any separate issue or of any number of claims, cross-claims, counterclaims, third-party claims, or issues, always preserving inviolate the right of trial by jury as declared by the Seventh Amendment to the Constitution or as given by a statute of the United States.

[Amended February 28, 1966, effective July 1, 1966.]

RULE 43. TAKING OF TESTIMONY

(a) Form. In every trial, the testimony of witnesses shall be taken in open court, unless a federal law, these rules, the Federal Rules of Evidence, or other rules adopted by the Supreme Court provide otherwise. The court may, for good cause shown in compelling circumstances and upon appropriate safeguards, permit presentation of testimony in open court by contemporaneous transmission from a different location.

(b) Scope of Examination and Cross–Examination [Abrogated].

(c) Record of Excluded Evidence [Abrogated].

(d) Affirmation in Lieu of Oath. Whenever under these rules an oath is required to be taken, a solemn affirmation may be accepted in lieu thereof.

(e) Evidence on Motions. When a motion is based on facts not appearing of record the court may hear the matter on affidavits presented by the respective parties, but the court may direct that the matter be heard wholly or partly on oral testimony or deposition.

(f) Interpreters. The court may appoint an interpreter of its own selection and may fix the interpreter's reasonable compensation. The compensation shall be paid out of funds provided by law or by one or more of the parties as the court may direct, and may be taxed ultimately as costs, in the discretion of the court.

[Amended February 28, 1966, effective July 1, 1966; November 20, 1972, and December 18, 1972, effective July 1, 1975; March 2, 1987, effective August 1, 1987; April 23, 1996, effective December 1, 1996.]

RULE 44. PROOF OF OFFICIAL RECORD

(a) Authentication.

(1) *Domestic.* An official record kept within the United States, or any state, district, or commonwealth, or within a territory subject to the administrative or judicial jurisdiction of the United States, or an entry therein, when admissible for any purpose, may be evidenced by an official publication thereof or by a copy attested by the officer having the legal custody of the record, or by the officer's deputy, and accompanied by a certificate that such officer has the custody.

The certificate may be made by a judge of a court of record of the district or political subdivision in which the record is kept, authenticated by the seal of the court, or may be made by any public officer having a seal of office and having official duties in the district or political subdivision in which the record is kept, authenticated by the seal of the officer's office.

(2) *Foreign.* A foreign official record, or an entry therein, when admissible for any purpose, may be evidenced by an official publication thereof; or a copy thereof, attested by a person authorized to make the attestation, and accompanied by a final certification as to the genuineness of the signature and official position (i) of the attesting person, or (ii) of any foreign official whose certificate of genuineness of signature and official position relates to the attestation or is in a chain of certificates of genuineness of signature and official position relating to the attestation. A final certification may be made by a secretary of embassy or legation, consul general, vice consul, or consular agent of the United States, or a diplomatic or consular official of the foreign country assigned or accredited to the United States. If reasonable opportunity has been given to all parties to investigate the authenticity and accuracy of the documents, the court may, for good cause shown, (i) admit an attested copy without final certification or (ii) permit the foreign official record to be evidenced by an attested summary with or without a final certification. The final certification is unnecessary if the record and the attestation are certified as provided in a treaty or convention to which the United States and the foreign country in which the official record is located are parties.

(b) Lack of Record. A written statement that after diligent search no record or entry of a specified tenor is found to exist in the records designated by the statement, authenticated as provided in subdivision (a)(1) of this rule in the case of a domestic record, or complying with the requirements of subdivision (a)(2) of this rule for a summary in the case of a foreign record, is admissible as evidence that the records contain no such record or entry.

(c) Other Proof. This rule does not prevent the proof of official records or of entry or lack of entry therein by any other method authorized by law.

[Amended February 28, 1966, effective July 1, 1966; March 2, 1987, effective August 1, 1987; April 30, 1991, effective December 1, 1991.]

RULE 44.1 DETERMINATION OF FOREIGN LAW

A party who intends to raise an issue concerning the law of a foreign country shall give notice by pleadings or other reasonable written notice. The court, in determining foreign law, may consider any relevant material or source, including testimony, whether or not submitted by a party or admissible under the Federal Rules of Evidence. The court's determination shall be treated as a ruling on a question of law.

[Adopted February 28, 1966, effective July 1, 1966; amended November 20, 1972, effective July 1, 1975; March 2, 1987, effective August 1, 1987.]

RULE 45. SUBPOENA

(a) Form; Issuance.

(1) Every subpoena shall

(A) state the name of the court from which it is issued; and

(B) state the title of the action, the name of the court in which it is pending, and its civil action number; and

(C) command each person to whom it is directed to attend and give testimony or to produce and permit inspection and copying of designated books, documents or tangible things in the possession, custody or control of that person, or to permit inspection of premises, at a time and place therein specified; and

(D) set forth the text of subdivisions (c) and (d) of this rule.

A command to produce evidence or to permit inspection may be joined with a command to appear at trial or hearing or at deposition, or may be issued separately.

(2) A subpoena commanding attendance at a trial or hearing shall issue from the court for the district in which the hearing or trial is to be held. A subpoena for attendance at a deposition shall issue from the court for the district designated by the notice of deposition as the district in which the deposition is to be taken. If separate from a subpoena commanding the attendance of a person, a subpoena for production or inspection shall issue from the court for the district in which the production or inspection is to be made.

(3) The clerk shall issue a subpoena, signed but otherwise in blank, to a party requesting it, who shall complete it before service. An attorney as officer of the court may also issue and sign a subpoena on behalf of

(A) a court in which the attorney is authorized to practice; or

(B) a court for a district in which a deposition or production is compelled by the subpoena, if the deposition or production pertains to an action pending in a court in which the attorney is authorized to practice.

(b) Service.

(1) A subpoena may be served by any person who is not a party and is not less than 18 years of age. Service of a subpoena upon a person named therein shall be made by delivering a copy thereof to such person and, if the person's attendance is commanded, by tendering to that person the fees for one day's attendance and the mileage allowed by law. When the subpoena is issued on behalf of the United States or an officer or agency thereof, fees and mileage need not be tendered. Prior notice of any commanded production of documents and things or inspection of premises before trial shall be served on each party in the manner prescribed by Rule 5(b).

(2) Subject to the provisions of clause (ii) of subparagraph (c)(3)(A) of this rule, a subpoena may be served at any place within the district of the court by which it is issued, or at any place without the district that is within 100 miles of the place of the deposition, hearing, trial, production, or inspection specified in the subpoena or at any place within the state where a state statute or rule of court permits service of a subpoena issued by a state court of general jurisdiction sitting in the place of the deposition, hearing, trial, production, or inspection specified in the subpoena. When a statute of the United States provides therefor, the court upon proper application and cause shown may authorize the service of a subpoena at any other place. A subpoena directed to a witness in a foreign country who is a national or resident of the United States shall issue under the circumstances and in the manner and be served as provided in Title 28, U.S.C. § 1783.

(3) Proof of service when necessary shall be made by filing with the clerk of the court by which the subpoena is issued a statement of the date and manner of service and of the names of the persons served, certified by the person who made the service.

(c) Protection of Persons Subject to Subpoenas.

(1) A party or an attorney responsible for the issuance and service of a subpoena shall take reasonable steps to avoid imposing undue burden or expense on a person subject to that subpoena. The court on behalf of which the subpoena was issued shall enforce this duty and impose upon the party or attorney in breach of this duty an appropriate sanction, which may include, but is not limited to, lost earnings and a reasonable attorney's fee.

(2)(A) A person commanded to produce and permit inspection and copying of designated books, papers, documents or tangible things, or inspection of premises need not appear in person at the place of production or inspection unless commanded to appear for deposition, hearing or trial.

(B) Subject to paragraph (d)(2) of this rule, a person commanded to produce and permit inspection and copying may, within 14 days after service of the subpoena or before the time specified for compliance if such time is less than 14 days after service, serve upon the party or attorney designated in the subpoena written objection to inspection or copying of any or all of the designated materials or of the premises. If objection is made, the party serving the subpoena shall not be entitled to inspect and copy the materials or inspect the premises except pursuant to an order of the court by which the subpoena was issued. If objection has been made, the party serving the subpoena may, upon notice to the person commanded to produce, move at any time for an order to compel the production. Such an order to compel production shall protect any person who is not a party or an officer of a party from significant expense resulting from the inspection and copying commanded.

(3)(A) On timely motion, the court by which a subpoena was issued shall quash or modify the subpoena if it

(i) fails to allow reasonable time for compliance;

(ii) requires a person who is not a party or an officer of a party to travel to a place more than 100 miles from the place where that person resides, is employed or regularly transacts business in person, except that, subject to the provisions of clause (c)(3)(B)(iii) of this rule, such a person may in order to attend trial be commanded to travel from any such place within the state in which the trial is held, or

(iii) requires disclosure of privileged or other protected matter and no exception or waiver applies, or

(iv) subjects a person to undue burden.

(B) If a subpoena

(i) requires disclosure of a trade secret or other confidential research, development, or commercial information, or

(ii) requires disclosure of an unretained expert's opinion or information not describing specific events or occurrences in dispute and resulting from the expert's study made not at the request of any party, or

(iii) requires a person who is not a party or an officer of a party to incur substantial expense to travel more than 100 miles to attend trial, the court may, to protect a person subject to or affected by the subpoena, quash or modify the subpoena or, if the party in whose behalf the subpoena is issued shows a substantial need for the testimony or material that cannot be otherwise met without undue hardship and assures that the person to whom the subpoena is addressed will be reasonably compensated, the court may order appearance or production only upon specified conditions.

(d) Duties in Responding to Subpoena.

(1) A person responding to a subpoena to produce documents shall produce them as they are kept in the usual course of business or shall organize and label them to correspond with the categories in the demand.

(2) When information subject to a subpoena is withheld on a claim that it is privileged or subject to protection as trial preparation materials, the claim shall be made expressly and shall be supported by a description of the nature of the documents, communications, or things not produced that is sufficient to enable the demanding party to contest the claim.

(e) Contempt. Failure by any person without adequate excuse to obey a subpoena served upon that person may be deemed a contempt of the court from which the subpoena issued. An adequate cause for failure to obey exists when a subpoena purports to require a non-party to attend or produce at a place not within the limits provided by clause (ii) of subparagraph (c)(3)(A).

[Amended December 27, 1946, effective March 19, 1948; December 29, 1948, effective October 20, 1949; March 30, 1970, effective July 1, 1970; April 29, 1980, effective August 1, 1980; April 29, 1985, effective August 1, 1985; March 2, 1987, effective August 1, 1987; April 30, 1991, effective December 1, 1991.]

RULE 46. EXCEPTIONS UNNECESSARY

Formal exceptions to rulings or orders of the court are unnecessary; but for all purposes for which an exception has heretofore been necessary it is sufficient that a party, at the time the ruling or order of the court is made or sought, makes known to the court the action which the party desires the court to take or the party's objection to the action of the court and the grounds therefor; and, if a party has no opportunity to object to a ruling or order at the time it is made, the absence of an objection does not thereafter prejudice the party.

[Amended March 2, 1987, effective August 1, 1987.]

RULE 47. SELECTION OF JURORS

(a) Examination of Jurors. The court may permit the parties or their attorneys to conduct the examination of prospective jurors or may itself conduct the examination. In the latter event, the court shall permit the parties or their attorneys to supplement the examination by such further inquiry as it deems proper or shall itself submit to the prospective jurors such additional questions of the parties or their attorneys as it deems proper.

(b) Peremptory Challenges. The court shall allow the number of peremptory challenges provided by 28 U.S.C. § 1870.

(c) Excuse. The court may for good cause excuse a juror from service during trial or deliberation.

[Amended February 28, 1966, effective July 1, 1966; April 30, 1991, effective December 1, 1991.]

RULE 48. NUMBER OF JURORS— PARTICIPATION IN VERDICT

The court shall seat a jury of not fewer than six and not more than twelve members and all jurors shall participate in the verdict unless excused from service by the court pursuant to Rule 47(c). Unless the parties otherwise stipulate, (1) the verdict shall be unanimous and (2) no verdict shall be taken from a jury reduced in size to fewer than six members.

[Amended April 30, 1991, effective December 1, 1991.]

RULE 49. SPECIAL VERDICTS AND INTERROGATORIES

(a) Special Verdicts. The court may require a jury to return only a special verdict in the form of a special written finding upon each issue of fact. In that event the court may submit to the jury written questions susceptible of categorical or other brief answer or may submit written forms of the several special findings which might properly be made under the pleadings and evidence; or it may use such other method of submitting the issues and requiring the written findings thereon as it deems most appropriate. The court shall give to the jury such explanation and instruction concerning the matter thus submitted as may be necessary to enable the jury to make its findings upon each issue. If in so doing the court omits any issue of fact raised by the pleadings or by the evidence, each party waives the right to a trial by jury of the issue so omitted unless before the jury retires the party demands its submission to the jury. As to an issue omitted without such demand the court may make a finding; or, if it fails to do so, it shall be deemed to have made a finding in accord with the judgment on the special verdict.

(b) General Verdict Accompanied by Answer to Interrogatories. The court may submit to the jury, together with appropriate forms for a general verdict, written interrogatories upon one or more issues of fact the decision of which is necessary to a verdict. The court shall give such explanation or instruction as may be necessary to enable the jury both to make answers to the interrogatories and to render a general verdict, and the court shall direct the jury both to make written answers and to render a general verdict. When the general verdict and the answers are harmonious, the appropriate judgment upon the verdict and answers shall be entered pursuant to Rule 58. When the answers are consistent with each other but one or more is inconsistent with the general verdict, judgment may be entered pursuant to Rule 58 in accordance with the answers, notwithstanding the general verdict, or the court may return the jury for further consideration of its answers and verdict or may order a new trial. When the answers are inconsistent with each other and one or more is likewise inconsistent with the general verdict, judgment shall not be entered, but the court shall return the jury for further

consideration of its answers and verdict or shall order a new trial.

[Amended January 21, 1963, effective July 1, 1963; March 2, 1987, effective August 1, 1987.]

RULE 50. JUDGMENT AS A MATTER OF LAW IN JURY TRIALS; ALTERNATIVE MOTION FOR NEW TRIAL; CONDITIONAL RULINGS

(a) Judgment as a Matter of Law.

(1) If during a trial by jury a party has been fully heard on an issue and there is no legally sufficient evidentiary basis for a reasonable jury to find for that party on that issue, the court may determine the issue against that party and may grant a motion for judgment as a matter of law against that party with respect to a claim or defense that cannot under the controlling law be maintained or defeated without a favorable finding on that issue.

(2) Motions for judgment as a matter of law may be made at any time before submission of the case to the jury. Such a motion shall specify the judgment sought and the law and the facts on which the moving party is entitled to the judgment.

(b) Renewing Motion for Judgment After Trial; Alternative Motion for New Trial. If, for any reason, the court does not grant a motion for judgment as a matter of law made at the close of all the evidence, the court is considered to have submitted the action to the jury subject to the court's later deciding the legal questions raised by the motion. The movant may renew its request for judgment as a matter of law by filing a motion no later than 10 days after entry of judgment—and may alternatively request a new trial or join a motion for a new trial under Rule 59. In ruling on a renewed motion, the court may:

(1) if a verdict was returned:

(A) allow the judgment to stand,

(B) order a new trial, or

(C) direct entry of judgment as a matter of law; or

(2) if no verdict was returned:

(A) order a new trial, or

(B) direct entry of judgment as a matter of law.

(c) Granting Renewed Motion for Judgment as a Matter of Law; Conditional Rulings; New Trial Motion.

(1) If the renewed motion for judgment as a matter of law is granted, the court shall also rule on the motion for a new trial, if any, by determining whether it should be granted if the judgment is thereafter vacated or reversed, and shall specify the grounds for granting or denying the motion for the new trial. If

the motion for a new trial is thus conditionally granted, the order thereon does not affect the finality of the judgment. In case the motion for a new trial has been conditionally granted and the judgment is reversed on appeal, the new trial shall proceed unless the appellate court has otherwise ordered. In case the motion for a new trial has been conditionally denied, the appellee on appeal may assert error in that denial; and if the judgment is reversed on appeal, subsequent proceedings shall be in accordance with the order of the appellate court.

(2) Any motion for a new trial under Rule 59 by a party against whom judgment as a matter of law is rendered shall be filed no later than 10 days after entry of the judgment.

(d) Same: Denial of Motion for Judgment as a Matter of Law. If the motion for judgment as a matter of law is denied, the party who prevailed on that motion may, as appellee, assert grounds entitling the party to a new trial in the event the appellate court concludes that the trial court erred in denying the motion for judgment. If the appellate court reverses the judgment, nothing in this rule precludes it from determining that the appellee is entitled to a new trial, or from directing the trial court to determine whether a new trial shall be granted.

[Amended January 21, 1963, effective July 1, 1963; March 2, 1987, effective August 1, 1987; April 30, 1991, effective December 1, 1991; April 22, 1993, effective December 1, 1993; April 27, 1995, effective December 1, 1995.]

RULE 51. INSTRUCTIONS TO JURY; OBJECTIONS; PRESERVING A CLAIM OF ERROR

(a) Requests.

(1) A party may, at the close of the evidence or at an earlier reasonable time that the court directs, file and furnish to every other party written requests that the court instruct the jury on the law as set forth in the requests.

(2) After the close of the evidence, a party may:

(A) file requests for instructions on issues that could not reasonably have been anticipated at an earlier time for requests set under Rule 51(a)(1), and

(B) with the court's permission file untimely requests for instructions on any issue.

(b) Instructions. The court:

(1) must inform the parties of its proposed instructions and proposed action on the requests before instructing the jury and before final jury arguments;

(2) must give the parties an opportunity to object on the record and out of the jury's hearing to the proposed instructions and actions on requests before the instructions and arguments are delivered; and

(3) may instruct the jury at any time after trial begins and before the jury is discharged.

(c) Objections.

(1) A party who objects to an instruction or the failure to give an instruction must do so on the record, stating distinctly the matter objected to and the grounds of the objection.

(2) An objection is timely if:

(A) a party that has been informed of an instruction or action on a request before the jury is instructed and before final jury arguments, as provided by Rule 51(b)(1), objects at the opportunity for objection required by Rule 51(b)(2); or

(B) a party that has not been informed of an instruction or action on a request before the time for objection provided under Rule 51(b)(2) objects promptly after learning that the instruction or request will be, or has been, given or refused.

(d) Assigning Error; Plain Error.

(1) A party may assign as error:

(A) an error in an instruction actually given if that party made a proper objection under Rule 51(c), or

(B) a failure to give an instruction if that party made a proper request under Rule 51(a), and— unless the court made a definitive ruling on the record rejecting the request—also made a proper objection under Rule 51(c).

(2) A court may consider a plain error in the instructions affecting substantial rights that has not been preserved as required by Rule 51(d)(1)(A) or (B).

[Amended March 2, 1987, effective August 1, 1987; March 27, 2003, effective December 1, 2003.]

RULE 52. FINDINGS BY THE COURT; JUDGMENT ON PARTIAL FINDINGS

(a) Effect. In all actions tried upon the facts without a jury or with an advisory jury, the court shall find the facts specially and state separately its conclusions of law thereon, and judgment shall be entered pursuant to Rule 58; and in granting or refusing interlocutory injunctions the court shall similarly set forth the findings of fact and conclusions of law which constitute the grounds of its action. Requests for findings are not necessary for purposes of review. Findings of fact, whether based on oral or documentary evidence, shall not be set aside unless clearly erroneous, and due regard shall be given to the opportunity of the trial court to judge of the credibility of the witnesses. The findings of a master, to the extent that the court adopts them, shall be considered as the findings of the court. It will be sufficient if the findings of fact and conclusions of law are stated orally and recorded in open court following the close of the evidence or appear in an opinion or memorandum of decision filed by the court. Findings of fact and conclusions of law are unnecessary on decisions of motions under Rule 12 or 56 or any other motion except as provided in subdivision (c) of this rule.

(b) Amendment. On a party's motion filed no later than 10 days after entry of judgment, the court may amend its findings—or make additional findings—and may amend the judgment accordingly. The motion may accompany a motion for a new trial under Rule 59. When findings of fact are made in actions tried without a jury, the sufficiency of the evidence supporting the findings may be later questioned whether or not in the district court the party raising the question objected to the findings, moved to amend them, or moved for partial findings.

(c) Judgment on Partial Findings. If during a trial without a jury a party has been fully heard on an issue and the court finds against the party on that issue, the court may enter judgment as a matter of law against that party with respect to a claim or defense that cannot under the controlling law be maintained or defeated without a favorable finding on that issue, or the court may decline to render any judgment until the close of all the evidence. Such a judgment shall be supported by findings of fact and conclusions of law as required by subdivision (a) of this rule.

[Amended December 27, 1946, effective March 19, 1948; January 21, 1963, effective July 1, 1963; April 28, 1983, effective August 1, 1983; April 29, 1985, effective August 1, 1985; April 30, 1991, effective December 1, 1991; April 22, 1993, effective December 1, 1993; April 27, 1995, effective December 1, 1995.]

RULE 53. MASTERS

(a) Appointment.

(1) Unless a statute provides otherwise, a court may appoint a master only to:

(A) perform duties consented to by the parties;

(B) hold trial proceedings and make or recommend findings of fact on issues to be decided by the court without a jury if appointment is warranted by

(i) some exceptional condition, or

(ii) the need to perform an accounting or resolve a difficult computation of damages; or

(C) address pretrial and post-trial matters that cannot be addressed effectively and timely by an available district judge or magistrate judge of the district.

(2) A master must not have a relationship to the parties, counsel, action, or court that would require disqualification of a judge under 28 U.S.C. § 455 unless the parties consent with the court's approval to appointment of a particular person after disclosure of any potential grounds for disqualification.

(3) In appointing a master, the court must consider the fairness of imposing the likely expenses on the parties and must protect against unreasonable expense or delay.

(b) Order Appointing Master.

(1) *Notice.* The court must give the parties notice and an opportunity to be heard before appointing a master. A party may suggest candidates for appointment.

(2) *Contents.* The order appointing a master must direct the master to proceed with all reasonable diligence and must state:

(A) the master's duties, including any investigation or enforcement duties, and any limits on the master's authority under Rule 53(c);

(B) the circumstances—if any—in which the master may communicate ex parte with the court or a party;

(C) the nature of the materials to be preserved and filed as the record of the master's activities;

(D) the time limits, method of filing the record, other procedures, and standards for reviewing the master's orders, findings, and recommendations; and

(E) the basis, terms, and procedure for fixing the master's compensation under Rule 53(h).

(3) *Entry of Order.* The court may enter the order appointing a master only after the master has filed an affidavit disclosing whether there is any ground for disqualification under 28 U.S.C. § 455 and, if a ground for disqualification is disclosed, after the parties have consented with the court's approval to waive the disqualification.

(4) *Amendment.* The order appointing a master may be amended at any time after notice to the parties, and an opportunity to be heard.

(c) Master's Authority. Unless the appointing order expressly directs otherwise, a master has authority to regulate all proceedings and take all appropriate measures to perform fairly and efficiently the assigned duties. The master may by order impose upon a party any noncontempt sanction provided by Rule 37 or 45, and may recommend a contempt sanction against a party and sanctions against a nonparty.

(d) Evidentiary Hearings. Unless the appointing order expressly directs otherwise, a master conducting an evidentiary hearing may exercise the power of the appointing court to compel, take, and record evidence.

(e) Master's Orders. A master who makes an order must file the order and promptly serve a copy on each party. The clerk must enter the order on the docket.

(f) Master's Reports. A master must report to the court as required by the order of appointment. The master must file the report and promptly serve a copy of the report on each party unless the court directs otherwise.

(g) Action on Master's Order, Report, or Recommendations.

(1) *Action.* In acting on a master's order, report, or recommendations, the court must afford an opportunity to be heard and may receive evidence, and may: adopt or affirm; modify; wholly or partly reject or reverse; or resubmit to the master with instructions.

(2) *Time To Object or Move.* A party may file objections to—or a motion to adopt or modify—the master's order, report, or recommendations no later than 20 days from the time the master's order, report, or recommendations are served, unless the court sets a different time.

(3) *Fact Findings.* The court must decide de novo all objections to findings of fact made or recommended by a master unless the parties stipulate with the court's consent that:

(A) the master's findings will be reviewed for clear error, or

(B) the findings of a master appointed under Rule 53(a)(1)(A) or (C) will be final.

(4) *Legal Conclusions.* The court must decide de novo all objections to conclusions of law made or recommended by a master.

(5) *Procedural Matters.* Unless the order of appointment establishes a different standard of review, the court may set aside a master's ruling on a procedural matter only for an abuse of discretion.

(h) Compensation.

(1) *Fixing Compensation.* The court must fix the master's compensation before or after judgment on the basis and terms stated in the order of appointment, but the court may set a new basis and terms after notice and an opportunity to be heard.

(2) *Payment.* The compensation fixed under Rule 53(h)(1) must be paid either:

(A) by a party or parties; or

(B) from a fund or subject matter of the action within the court's control.

(3) *Allocation.* The court must allocate payment of the master's compensation among the parties after considering the nature and amount of the controversy, the means of the parties, and the extent to which any party is more responsible than other parties for the reference to a master. An interim allocation may be amended to reflect a decision on the merits.

(i) Appointment of Magistrate Judge. A magistrate judge is subject to this rule only when the order referring a matter to the magistrate judge expressly provides that the reference is made under this rule.

[Amended February 28, 1966, effective July 1, 1966; April 28, 1983, effective August 1, 1983; March 2, 1987, effective August 1, 1987; April 30, 1991, effective December 1, 1991; April 22, 1993, effective December 1, 1993; March 27, 2003, effective December 1, 2003.]

VII. JUDGMENT

RULE 54. JUDGMENTS; COSTS

(a) Definition; Form. "Judgment" as used in these rules includes a decree and any order from which an appeal lies. A judgment shall not contain a recital of pleadings, the report of a master, or the record of prior proceedings.

(b) Judgment Upon Multiple Claims or Involving Multiple Parties. When more than one claim for relief is presented in an action, whether as a claim, counterclaim, cross-claim, or third-party claim, or when multiple parties are involved, the court may direct the entry of a final judgment as to one or more but fewer than all of the claims or parties only upon an express determination that there is no just reason for delay and upon an express direction for the entry of judgment. In the absence of such determination and direction, any order or other form of decision, however designated, which adjudicates fewer than all the claims or the rights and liabilities of fewer than all the parties shall not terminate the action as to any of the claims or parties, and the order or other form of decision is subject to revision at any time before the entry of judgment adjudicating all the claims and the rights and liabilities of all the parties.

(c) Demand for Judgment. A judgment by default shall not be different in kind from or exceed in amount that prayed for in the demand for judgment. Except as to a party against whom a judgment is entered by default, every final judgment shall grant the relief to which the party in whose favor it is rendered is entitled, even if the party has not demanded such relief in the party's pleadings.

(d) Costs; Attorneys' Fees.

(1) *Costs Other Than Attorneys' Fees.* Except when express provision therefor is made either in a statute of the United States or in these rules, costs other than attorneys' fees shall be allowed as of course to the prevailing party unless the court otherwise directs; but costs against the United States, its officers, and agencies shall be imposed only to the extent permitted by law. Such costs may be taxed by the clerk on one day's notice. On motion served within 5 days thereafter, the action of the clerk may be reviewed by the court.

(2) *Attorneys' Fees.*

(A) Claims for attorneys' fees and related nontaxable expenses shall be made by motion unless the substantive law governing the action provides for the recovery of such fees as an element of damages to be proved at trial.

(B) Unless otherwise provided by statute or order of the court, the motion must be filed no later than 14 days after entry of judgment; must specify the judgment and the statute, rule, or other grounds entitling the moving party to the award; and must state the amount or provide a fair estimate of the amount sought. If directed by the court, the motion shall also disclose the terms of any agreement with respect to fees to be paid for the services for which claim is made.

(C) On request of a party or class member, the court shall afford an opportunity for adversary submissions with respect to the motion in accordance with Rule 43(e) or Rule 78. The court may determine issues of liability for fees before receiving submissions bearing on issues of evaluation of services for which liability is imposed by the court. The court shall find the facts and state its conclusions of law as provided in Rule 52(a).

(D) By local rule the court may establish special procedures by which issues relating to such fees may be resolved without extensive evidentiary hearings. In addition, the court may refer issues relating to the value of services to a special master under Rule 53 without regard to the provisions of Rule 53(a)(1) and may refer a motion for attorneys' fees to a magistrate judge under Rule 72(b) as if it were a dispositive pretrial matter.

(E) The provisions of subparagraphs (A) through (D) do not apply to claims for fees and expenses as sanctions for violations of these rules or under 28 U.S.C. § 1927.

[Amended December 27, 1946, effective March 19, 1948; April 17, 1961, effective July 19, 1961; March 2, 1987, effective August 1, 1987; April 22, 1993, effective December 1, 1993; April 29, 2002, effective December 1, 2002; March 27, 2003, effective December 1, 2003.]

RULE 55.　DEFAULT

(a) **Entry.** When a party against whom a judgment for affirmative relief is sought has failed to plead or otherwise defend as provided by these rules and that fact is made to appear by affidavit or otherwise, the clerk shall enter the party's default.

(b) **Judgment.** Judgment by default may be entered as follows:

(1) *By the Clerk.* When the plaintiff's claim against a defendant is for a sum certain or for a sum which can by computation be made certain, the clerk upon request of the plaintiff and upon affidavit of the amount due shall enter judgment for that amount and costs against the defendant, if the defendant has been defaulted for failure to appear and is not an infant or incompetent person.

(2) *By the Court.* In all other cases the party entitled to a judgment by default shall apply to the court therefor; but no judgment by default shall be entered against an infant or incompetent person unless represented in the action by a general guardian, committee, conservator, or other such representative who has appeared therein. If the party against whom judgment by default is sought has appeared in the action, the party (or, if appearing by representative, the party's representative) shall be served with written notice of the application for judgment at least 3 days prior to the hearing on such application. If, in order to enable the court to enter judgment or to carry it into effect, it is necessary to take an account or to determine the amount of damages or to establish the truth of any averment by evidence or to make an investigation of any other matter, the court may conduct such hearings or order such references as it deems necessary and proper and shall accord a right of trial by jury to the parties when and as required by any statute of the United States.

(c) **Setting Aside Default.** For good cause shown the court may set aside an entry of default and, if a judgment by default has been entered, may likewise set it aside in accordance with Rule 60(b).

(d) **Plaintiffs, Counterclaimants, Cross-Claimants.** The provisions of this rule apply whether the party entitled to the judgment by default is a plaintiff, a third-party plaintiff, or a party who has pleaded a cross-claim or counterclaim. In all cases a judgment by default is subject to the limitations of Rule 54(c).

(e) **Judgment Against the United States.** No judgment by default shall be entered against the United States or an officer or agency thereof unless the claimant establishes a claim or right to relief by evidence satisfactory to the court.

[Amended March 2, 1987, effective August 1, 1987.]

RULE 56.　SUMMARY JUDGMENT

(a) **For Claimant.** A party seeking to recover upon a claim, counterclaim, or cross-claim or to obtain a declaratory judgment may, at any time after the expiration of 20 days from the commencement of the action or after service of a motion for summary judgment by the adverse party, move with or without supporting affidavits for a summary judgment in the party's favor upon all or any part thereof.

(b) **For Defending Party.** A party against whom a claim, counterclaim, or cross-claim is asserted or a declaratory judgment is sought may, at any time, move with or without supporting affidavits for a summary judgment in the party's favor as to all or any part thereof.

(c) **Motion and Proceedings Thereon.** The motion shall be served at least 10 days before the time fixed for the hearing. The adverse party prior to the day of hearing may serve opposing affidavits. The judgment sought shall be rendered forthwith if the pleadings, depositions, answers to interrogatories, and admissions on file, together with the affidavits, if any, show that there is no genuine issue as to any material fact and that the moving party is entitled to a judgment as a matter of law. A summary judgment, interlocutory in character, may be rendered on the issue of liability alone although there is a genuine issue as to the amount of damages.

(d) Case Not Fully Adjudicated on Motion. If on motion under this rule judgment is not rendered upon the whole case or for all the relief asked and a trial is necessary, the court at the hearing of the motion, by examining the pleadings and the evidence before it and by interrogating counsel, shall if practicable ascertain what material facts exist without substantial controversy and what material facts are actually and in good faith controverted. It shall thereupon make an order specifying the facts that appear without substantial controversy, including the extent to which the amount of damages or other relief is not in controversy, and directing such further proceedings in the action as are just. Upon the trial of the action the facts so specified shall be deemed established, and the trial shall be conducted accordingly.

(e) Form of Affidavits; Further Testimony; Defense Required. Supporting and opposing affidavits shall be made on personal knowledge, shall set forth such facts as would be admissible in evidence, and shall show affirmatively that the affiant is competent to testify to the matters stated therein. Sworn or certified copies of all papers or parts thereof referred to in an affidavit shall be attached thereto or served therewith. The court may permit affidavits to be supplemented or opposed by depositions, answers to interrogatories, or further affidavits. When a motion for summary judgment is made and supported as provided in this rule, an adverse party may not rest upon the mere allegations or denials of the adverse party's pleading, but the adverse party's response, by affidavits or as otherwise provided in this rule, must set forth specific facts showing that there is a genuine issue for trial. If the adverse party does not so respond, summary judgment, if appropriate, shall be entered against the adverse party.

(f) When Affidavits Are Unavailable. Should it appear from the affidavits of a party opposing the motion that the party cannot for reasons stated present by affidavit facts essential to justify the party's opposition, the court may refuse the application for judgment or may order a continuance to permit affidavits to be obtained or depositions to be taken or discovery to be had or may make such other order as is just.

(g) Affidavits Made in Bad Faith. Should it appear to the satisfaction of the court at any time that any of the affidavits presented pursuant to this rule are presented in bad faith or solely for the purpose of delay, the court shall forthwith order the party employing them to pay to the other party the amount of the reasonable expenses which the filing of the affidavits caused the other party to incur, including reasonable attorney's fees, and any offending party or attorney may be adjudged guilty of contempt.

[Amended December 27, 1946, effective March 19, 1948; January 21, 1963, effective July 1, 1963; March 2, 1987, effective August 1, 1987.]

RULE 57.   DECLARATORY JUDGMENTS

The procedure for obtaining a declaratory judgment pursuant to Title 28, U.S.C., § 2201, shall be in accordance with these rules, and the right to trial by jury may be demanded under the circumstances and in the manner provided in Rules 38 and 39. The existence of another adequate remedy does not preclude a judgment for declaratory relief in cases where it is appropriate. The court may order a speedy hearing of an action for a declaratory judgment and may advance it on the calendar.

[Amended December 29, 1948, effective October 20, 1949.]

RULE 58.   ENTRY OF JUDGMENT

(a) Separate Document.

(1) Every judgment and amended judgment must be set forth on a separate document, but a separate document is not required for an order disposing of a motion:

    (A) for judgment under Rule 50(b);

    (B) to amend or make additional findings of fact under Rule 52(b);

    (C) for attorney fees under Rule 54;

    (D) for a new trial, or to alter or amend the judgment, under Rule 59; or

    (E) for relief under Rule 60.

(2) Subject to Rule 54(b):

    (A) unless the court orders otherwise, the clerk must, without awaiting the court's direction, promptly prepare, sign, and enter the judgment when:

        (i) the jury returns a general verdict,

        (ii) the court awards only costs or a sum certain, or

        (iii) the court denies all relief;

    (B) the court must promptly approve the form of the judgment, which the clerk must promptly enter, when:

        (i) the jury returns a special verdict or a general verdict accompanied by interrogatories, or

        (ii) the court grants other relief not described in Rule 58(a)(2).

(b) Time of Entry. Judgment is entered for purposes of these rules:

(1) if Rule 58(a)(1) does not require a separate document, when it is entered in the civil docket under Rule 79(a), and

(2) if Rule 58(a)(1) requires a separate document, when it is entered in the civil docket under Rule 79(a) and when the earlier of these events occurs:

(A) when it is set forth on a separate document, or

(B) when 150 days have run from entry in the civil docket under Rule 79(a).

(c) Cost or Fee Awards.

(1) Entry of judgment may not be delayed, nor the time for appeal extended, in order to tax costs or award fees, except as provided in Rule 58(c)(2).

(2) When a timely motion for attorney fees is made under Rule 54(d)(2), the court may act before a notice of appeal has been filed and has become effective to order that the motion have the same effect under Federal Rule of Appellate Procedure 4(a)(4) as a timely motion under Rule 59.

(d) Request for Entry. A party may request that judgment be set forth on a separate document as required by Rule 58(a)(1).

[Amended December 27, 1946, effective March 19, 1948; January 21, 1963, effective July 1, 1963; April 22, 1993, effective December 1, 1993; April 29, 2002, effective December 1, 2002.]

RULE 59. NEW TRIALS; AMENDMENT OF JUDGMENTS

(a) Grounds. A new trial may be granted to all or any of the parties and on all or part of the issues (1) in an action in which there has been a trial by jury, for any of the reasons for which new trials have heretofore been granted in actions at law in the courts of the United States; and (2) in an action tried without a jury, for any of the reasons for which rehearings have heretofore been granted in suits in equity in the courts of the United States. On a motion for a new trial in an action tried without a jury, the court may open the judgment if one has been entered, take additional testimony, amend findings of fact and conclusions of law or make new findings and conclusions, and direct the entry of a new judgment.

(b) Time for Motion. Any motion for a new trial shall be filed no later than 10 days after entry of the judgment.

(c) Time for Serving Affidavits. When a motion for new trial is based on affidavits, they shall be filed with the motion. The opposing party has 10 days after service to file opposing affidavits, but that period may be extended for up to 20 days, either by the court for good cause or by the parties' written stipulation. The court may permit reply affidavits.

(d) On Court's Initiative; Notice; Specifying Grounds. No later than 10 days after entry of judgment the court, on its own, may order a new trial for any reason that would justify granting one on a party's motion. After giving the parties notice and an opportunity to be heard, the court may grant a timely motion for a new trial for a reason not stated in the motion. When granting a new trial on its own initiative or for a reason not stated in a motion, the court shall specify the grounds in its order.

(e) Motion to Alter or Amend Judgment. Any motion to alter or amend a judgment shall be filed no later than 10 days after entry of the judgment.

[Amended December 27, 1946, effective March 19, 1948; February 28, 1966, effective July 1, 1966; April 27, 1995, effective December 1, 1995.]

RULE 60. RELIEF FROM JUDGMENT OR ORDER

(a) Clerical Mistakes. Clerical mistakes in judgments, orders or other parts of the record and errors therein arising from oversight or omission may be corrected by the court at any time of its own initiative or on the motion of any party and after such notice, if any, as the court orders. During the pendency of an appeal, such mistakes may be so corrected before the appeal is docketed in the appellate court, and thereafter while the appeal is pending may be so corrected with leave of the appellate court.

(b) Mistakes; Inadvertence; Excusable Neglect; Newly Discovered Evidence; Fraud, etc. On motion and upon such terms as are just, the court may relieve a party or a party's legal representative from a final judgment, order, or proceeding for the following reasons: (1) mistake, inadvertence, surprise, or excusable neglect; (2) newly discovered evidence which by due diligence could not have been discovered in time to move for a new trial under Rule 59(b); (3) fraud (whether heretofore denominated intrinsic or extrinsic), misrepresentation, or other misconduct of an adverse party; (4) the judgment is void; (5) the judgment has been satisfied, released, or discharged, or a prior judgment upon which it is based has been reversed or otherwise vacated, or it is no longer equitable that the judgment should have prospective application; or (6) any other reason justifying relief from the operation of the judgment. The motion shall be made within a reasonable time, and for reasons (1), (2), and (3) not more than one year after the judgment, order, or proceeding was entered or taken. A motion under this subdivision (b) does not affect the finality of a judgment or suspend its operation. This rule does not limit the power of a court to entertain an independent action to relieve a party from a judgment, order, or proceeding, or to grant relief to a defendant not actually personally notified as provided in Title 28, U.S.C., § 1655, or to set aside a judgment for fraud upon the court. Writs of coram nobis, coram vobis, audita querela, and bills of review and bills in the nature of a bill of review, are abolished, and the procedure for obtaining any relief from a judgment shall be by motion as prescribed in these rules or by an independent action.

[Amended December 27, 1946, effective March 19, 1948; December 29, 1948, effective October 20, 1949; March 2, 1987, effective August 1, 1987.]

RULE 61. HARMLESS ERROR

No error in either the admission or the exclusion of evidence and no error or defect in any ruling or order or in anything done or omitted by the court or by any of the parties is ground for granting a new trial or for setting aside a verdict or for vacating, modifying, or otherwise disturbing a judgment or order, unless refusal to take such action appears to the court inconsistent with substantial justice. The court at every stage of the proceeding must disregard any error or defect in the proceeding which does not affect the substantial rights of the parties.

RULE 62. STAY OF PROCEEDINGS TO ENFORCE A JUDGMENT

(a) Automatic Stay; Exceptions—Injunctions, Receiverships, and Patent Accountings. Except as stated herein, no execution shall issue upon a judgment nor shall proceedings be taken for its enforcement until the expiration of 10 days after its entry. Unless otherwise ordered by the court, an interlocutory or final judgment in an action for an injunction or in a receivership action, or a judgment or order directing an accounting in an action for infringement of letters patent, shall not be stayed during the period after its entry and until an appeal is taken or during the pendency of an appeal. The provisions of subdivision (c) of this rule govern the suspending, modifying, restoring, or granting of an injunction during the pendency of an appeal.

(b) Stay on Motion for New Trial or for Judgment. In its discretion and on such conditions for the security of the adverse party as are proper, the court may stay the execution of or any proceedings to enforce a judgment pending the disposition of a motion for a new trial or to alter or amend a judgment made pursuant to Rule 59, or of a motion for relief from a judgment or order made pursuant to Rule 60, or of a motion for judgment in accordance with a motion for a directed verdict made pursuant to Rule 50, or of a motion for amendment to the findings or for additional findings made pursuant to Rule 52(b).

(c) Injunction Pending Appeal. When an appeal is taken from an interlocutory or final judgment granting, dissolving, or denying an injunction, the court in its discretion may suspend, modify, restore, or grant an injunction during the pendency of the appeal upon such terms as to bond or otherwise as it considers proper for the security of the rights of the adverse party. If the judgment appealed from is rendered by a district court of three judges specially constituted pursuant to a statute of the United States, no such order shall be made except (1) by such court sitting in open court or (2) by the assent of all the judges of such court evidenced by their signatures to the order.

(d) Stay Upon Appeal. When an appeal is taken the appellant by giving a supersedeas bond may obtain a stay subject to the exceptions contained in subdivision (a) of this rule. The bond may be given at or after the time of filing the notice of appeal or of procuring the order allowing the appeal, as the case may be. The stay is effective when the supersedeas bond is approved by the court.

(e) Stay in Favor of the United States or Agency Thereof. When an appeal is taken by the United States or an officer or agency thereof or by direction of any department of the Government of the United States and the operation or enforcement of the judgment is stayed, no bond, obligation, or other security shall be required from the appellant.

(f) Stay According to State Law. In any state in which a judgment is a lien upon the property of the judgment debtor and in which the judgment debtor is entitled to a stay of execution, a judgment debtor is entitled, in the district court held therein, to such stay as would be accorded the judgment debtor had the action been maintained in the courts of that state.

(g) Power of Appellate Court Not Limited. The provisions in this rule do not limit any power of an appellate court or of a judge or justice thereof to stay proceedings during the pendency of an appeal or to suspend, modify, restore, or grant an injunction during the pendency of an appeal or to make any order appropriate to preserve the status quo or the effectiveness of the judgment subsequently to be entered.

(h) Stay of Judgment as to Multiple Claims or Multiple Parties. When a court has ordered a final judgment under the conditions stated in Rule 54(b), the court may stay enforcement of that judgment until the entering of a subsequent judgment or judgments and may prescribe such conditions as are necessary to secure the benefit thereof to the party in whose favor the judgment is entered.

[Amended December 27, 1946, effective March 19, 1948; December 29, 1948, effective October 20, 1949; April 17, 1961, effective July 19, 1961; March 2, 1987, effective August 1, 1987.]

RULE 63. INABILITY OF A JUDGE TO PROCEED

If a trial or hearing has been commenced and the judge is unable to proceed, any other judge may proceed with it upon certifying familiarity with the record and determining that the proceedings in the case may be completed without prejudice to the parties. In a hearing or trial without a jury, the successor judge shall at the request of a party recall any witness whose testimony is material and disputed and who is available to testify again without undue burden. The successor judge may also recall any other witness.

[Amended March 2, 1987, effective August 1, 1987; April 30, 1991, effective December 1, 1991.]

VIII. PROVISIONAL AND FINAL REMEDIES

[Chapter heading amended April 30, 1991, effective December 1, 1991.]

RULE 64. SEIZURE OF PERSON OR PROPERTY

At the commencement of and during the course of an action, all remedies providing for seizure of person or property for the purpose of securing satisfaction of the judgment ultimately to be entered in the action are available under the circumstances and in the manner provided by the law of the state in which the district court is held, existing at the time the remedy is sought, subject to the following qualifications: (1) any existing statute of the United States governs to the extent to which it is applicable; (2) the action in which any of the foregoing remedies is used shall be commenced and prosecuted or, if removed from a state court, shall be prosecuted after removal, pursuant to these rules. The remedies thus available include arrest, attachment, garnishment, replevin, sequestration, and other corresponding or equivalent remedies, however designated and regardless of whether by state procedure the remedy is ancillary to an action or must be obtained by an independent action.

RULE 65. INJUNCTIONS

(a) Preliminary Injunction.

(1) *Notice.* No preliminary injunction shall be issued without notice to the adverse party.

(2) *Consolidation of Hearing With Trial on Merits.* Before or after the commencement of the hearing of an application for a preliminary injunction, the court may order the trial of the action on the merits to be advanced and consolidated with the hearing of the application. Even when this consolidation is not ordered, any evidence received upon an application for a preliminary injunction which would be admissible upon the trial on the merits becomes part of the record on the trial and need not be repeated upon the trial. This subdivision (a)(2) shall be so construed and applied as to save to the parties any rights they may have to trial by jury.

(b) Temporary Restraining Order; Notice; Hearing; Duration. A temporary restraining order may be granted without written or oral notice to the adverse party or that party's attorney only if (1) it clearly appears from specific facts shown by affidavit or by the verified complaint that immediate and irreparable injury, loss, or damage will result to the applicant before the adverse party or that party's attorney can be heard in opposition, and (2) the applicant's attorney certifies to the court in writing the efforts, if any, which have been made to give the notice and the reasons supporting the claim that notice should not be required. Every temporary restraining order granted without notice shall be indorsed with the date and hour of issuance; shall be filed forthwith in the clerk's office and entered of record; shall define the injury and state why it is irreparable and why the order was granted without notice; and shall expire by its terms within such time after entry, not to exceed 10 days, as the court fixes, unless within the time so fixed the order, for good cause shown, is extended for a like period or unless the party against whom the order is directed consents that it may be extended for a longer period. The reasons for the extension shall be entered of record. In case a temporary restraining order is granted without notice, the motion for a preliminary injunction shall be set down for hearing at the earliest possible time and takes precedence of all matters except older matters of the same character; and when the motion comes on for hearing the party who obtained the temporary restraining order shall proceed with the application for a preliminary injunction and, if the party does not do so, the court shall dissolve the temporary restraining order. On 2 days' notice to the party who obtained the temporary restraining order without notice or on such shorter notice to that party as the court may prescribe, the adverse party may appear and move its dissolution or modification and in that event the court shall proceed to hear and determine such motion as expeditiously as the ends of justice require.

(c) Security. No restraining order or preliminary injunction shall issue except upon the giving of security by the applicant, in such sum as the court deems proper, for the payment of such costs and damages as may be incurred or suffered by any party who is found to have been wrongfully enjoined or restrained. No such security shall be required of the United States or of an officer or agency thereof.

The provisions of Rule 65.1 apply to a surety upon a bond or undertaking under this rule.

(d) Form and Scope of Injunction or Restraining Order. Every order granting an injunction and every restraining order shall set forth the reasons for its issuance; shall be specific in terms; shall describe in reasonable detail, and not by reference to the complaint or other document, the act or acts sought to be restrained; and is binding only upon the parties to the action, their officers, agents, servants, employees, and attorneys, and upon those persons in active concert or participation with them who receive actual notice of the order by personal service or otherwise.

(e) Employer and Employee; Interpleader; Constitutional Cases. These rules do not modify any statute of the United States relating to temporary restraining orders and preliminary injunctions in actions affecting employer and employee; or the provisions of Title 28, U.S.C., § 2361, relating to preliminary injunctions in actions of interpleader or in the nature of interpleader; or Title 28, U.S.C., § 2284, relating to actions required by Act of Congress to be heard and determined by a district court of three judges.

(f) Copyright Impoundment. This rule applies to copyright impoundment proceedings.

[Amended December 27, 1946, effective March 19, 1948; December 29, 1948, effective October 20, 1949; February 28, 1966, effective July 1, 1966; March 2, 1987, effective August 1, 1987; April 23, 2001, effective December 1, 2001.]

RULE 65.1 SECURITY: PROCEEDINGS AGAINST SURETIES

Whenever these rules, including the Supplemental Rules for Certain Admiralty and Maritime Claims, require or permit the giving of security by a party, and security is given in the form of a bond or stipulation or other undertaking with one or more sureties, each surety submits to the jurisdiction of the court and irrevocably appoints the clerk of the court as the surety's agent upon whom any papers affecting the surety's liability on the bond or undertaking may be served. The surety's liability may be enforced on motion without the necessity of an independent action. The motion and such notice of the motion as the court prescribes may be served on the clerk of the court, who shall forthwith mail copies to the sureties if their addresses are known.

[Adopted February 28, 1966, effective July 1, 1966; amended March 2, 1987, effective August 1, 1987.]

RULE 66. RECEIVERS APPOINTED BY FEDERAL COURTS

An action wherein a receiver has been appointed shall not be dismissed except by order of the court. The practice in the administration of estates by receivers or by other similar officers appointed by the court shall be in accordance with the practice heretofore followed in the courts of the United States or as provided in rules promulgated by the district courts. In all other respects the action in which the appoint-ment of a receiver is sought or which is brought by or against a receiver is governed by these rules.

[Amended December 27, 1946, effective March 19, 1948; December 29, 1948, effective October 20, 1949.]

RULE 67. DEPOSIT IN COURT

In an action in which any part of the relief sought is a judgment for a sum of money or the disposition of a sum of money or the disposition of any other thing capable of delivery, a party, upon notice to every other party, and by leave of court, may deposit with the court all or any part of such sum or thing, whether or not that party claims all or any part of the sum or thing. The party making the deposit shall serve the order permitting deposit on the clerk of the court. Money paid into court under this rule shall be deposited and withdrawn in accordance with the provisions of Title 28, U.S.C., §§ 2041, and 2042; the Act of June 26, 1934, c. 756, § 23, as amended (48 Stat. 1236, 58 Stat. 845), U.S.C., Title 31, § 725v;* or any like statute. The fund shall be deposited in an interest-bearing account or invested in an interest-bearing instrument approved by the court.

* Law Revision Counsel Note: Repealed and reenacted as 28 U.S.C. §§ 572a and 2043 by Pub.L. 97–258, §§ 2(g)(3)(B), (4)(E), 5(b), September 13, 1982, 96 Stat. 1061, 1068.

[Amended December 29, 1948, effective October 20, 1949; April 28, 1983, effective August 1, 1983.]

RULE 68. OFFER OF JUDGMENT

At any time more than 10 days before the trial begins, a party defending against a claim may serve upon the adverse party an offer to allow judgment to be taken against the defending party for the money or property or to the effect specified in the offer, with costs then accrued. If within 10 days after the service of the offer the adverse party serves written notice that the offer is accepted, either party may then file the offer and notice of acceptance together with proof of service thereof and thereupon the clerk shall enter judgment. An offer not accepted shall be deemed withdrawn and evidence thereof is not admissible except in a proceeding to determine costs. If the judgment finally obtained by the offeree is not more favorable than the offer, the offeree must pay the costs incurred after the making of the offer. The fact that an offer is made but not accepted does not preclude a subsequent offer. When the liability of one party to another has been determined by verdict or order or judgment, but the amount or extent of the liability remains to be determined by further proceedings, the party adjudged liable may make an offer of judgment, which shall have the same effect as an offer made before trial if it is served within a reasonable time not less than 10 days prior to the commencement of hearings to determine the amount or extent of liability.

[Amended December 27, 1946, effective March 19, 1948; February 28, 1966, effective July 1, 1966; March 2, 1987, effective August 1, 1987.]

RULE 69. EXECUTION

(a) In General. Process to enforce a judgment for the payment of money shall be a writ of execution, unless the court directs otherwise. The procedure on execution, in proceedings supplementary to and in aid of a judgment, and in proceedings on and in aid of execution shall be in accordance with the practice and procedure of the state in which the district court is held, existing at the time the remedy is sought, except that any statute of the United States governs to the extent that it is applicable. In aid of the judgment or execution, the judgment creditor or a successor in interest when that interest appears of record, may obtain discovery from any person, including the judgment debtor, in the manner provided in these rules or in the manner provided by the practice of the state in which the district court is held.

(b) Against Certain Public Officers. When a judgment has been entered against a collector or other officer of revenue under the circumstances stated in Title 28, U.S.C., § 2006, or against an officer of Congress in an action mentioned in the Act of March 3, 1875, ch. 130, § 8 (18 Stat. 401), U.S.C., Title 2, § 118, and when the court has given the certificate of probable cause for the officer's act as provided in those statutes, execution shall not issue against the officer or the officer's property but the final judgment shall be satisfied as provided in such statutes.

[Amended December 29, 1948, effective October 20, 1949; March 30, 1970, effective July 1, 1970; March 2, 1987 effective August 1, 1987.]

RULE 70. JUDGMENT FOR SPECIFIC ACTS; VESTING TITLE

If a judgment directs a party to execute a conveyance of land or to deliver deeds or other documents or to perform any other specific act and the party fails to comply within the time specified, the court may direct the act to be done at the cost of the disobedient party by some other person appointed by the court and the act when so done has like effect as if done by the party. On application of the party entitled to performance, the clerk shall issue a writ of attachment or sequestration against the property of the disobedient party to compel obedience to the judgment. The court may also in proper cases adjudge the party in contempt. If real or personal property is within the district, the court in lieu of directing a conveyance thereof may enter a judgment divesting the title of any party and vesting it in others and such judgment has the effect of a conveyance executed in due form of law. When any order or judgment is for the delivery of possession, the party in whose favor it is entered is entitled to a writ of execution or assistance upon application to the clerk.

RULE 71. PROCESS IN BEHALF OF AND AGAINST PERSONS NOT PARTIES

When an order is made in favor of a person who is not a party to the action, that person may enforce obedience to the order by the same process as if a party; and, when obedience to an order may be lawfully enforced against a person who is not a party, that person is liable to the same process for enforcing obedience to the order as if a party.

[Amended March 2, 1987, effective August 1, 1987.]

IX. SPECIAL PROCEEDINGS

[Former Chapter IX heading and former Rules 72–76 abrogated December 4, 1967, effective July 1, 1968; new Chapter IX heading adopted and inserted between Rules 71 and 71A April 30, 1991, effective December 1, 1991.]

RULE 71A. CONDEMNATION OF PROPERTY

(a) Applicability of Other Rules. The Rules of Civil Procedure for the United States District Courts govern the procedure for the condemnation of real and personal property under the power of eminent domain, except as otherwise provided in this rule.

(b) Joinder of Properties. The plaintiff may join in the same action one or more separate pieces of property, whether in the same or different ownership and whether or not sought for the same use.

(c) Complaint.

(1) *Caption.* The complaint shall contain a caption as provided in Rule 10(a), except that the plaintiff shall name as defendants the property, designated generally by kind, quantity, and location, and at least one of the owners of some part of or interest in the property.

(2) *Contents.* The complaint shall contain a short and plain statement of the authority for the taking, the use for which the property is to be taken, a description of the property sufficient for its identification, the interests to be acquired, and as to each separate piece of property a designation of the defendants who have been joined as owners thereof or of some interest therein. Upon the commencement of the action, the plaintiff need join as defendants only the persons having or claiming an interest in the

property whose names are then known, but prior to any hearing involving the compensation to be paid for a piece of property, the plaintiff shall add as defendants all persons having or claiming an interest in that property whose names can be ascertained by a reasonably diligent search of the records, considering the character and value of the property involved and the interests to be acquired, and also those whose names have otherwise been learned. All others may be made defendants under the designation "Unknown Owners." Process shall be served as provided in subdivision (d) of this rule upon all defendants, whether named as defendants at the time of the commencement of the action or subsequently added, and a defendant may answer as provided in subdivision (e) of this rule. The court meanwhile may order such distribution of a deposit as the facts warrant.

(3) *Filing.* In addition to filing the complaint with the court, the plaintiff shall furnish to the clerk at least one copy thereof for the use of the defendants and additional copies at the request of the clerk or of a defendant.

(d) Process.

(1) *Notice; Delivery.* Upon the filing of the complaint the plaintiff shall forthwith deliver to the clerk joint or several notices directed to the defendants named or designated in the complaint. Additional notices directed to defendants subsequently added shall be so delivered. The delivery of the notice and its service have the same effect as the delivery and service of the summons under Rule 4.

(2) *Same; Form.* Each notice shall state the court, the title of the action, the name of the defendant to whom it is directed, that the action is to condemn property, a description of the defendant's property sufficient for its identification, the interest to be taken, the authority for the taking, the uses for which the property is to be taken, that the defendant may serve upon the plaintiff's attorney an answer within 20 days after service of the notice, and that the failure so to serve an answer constitutes a consent to the taking and to the authority of the court to proceed to hear the action and to fix the compensation. The notice shall conclude with the name of the plaintiff's attorney and an address within the district in which action is brought where the attorney may be served. The notice need contain a description of no other property than that to be taken from the defendants to whom it is directed.

(3) *Service of Notice.*

(A) Personal Service. Personal service of the notice (but without copies of the complaint) shall be made in accordance with Rule 4 upon a defendant whose residence is known and who resides within the United States or a territory subject to the administrative or judicial jurisdiction of the United States.

(B) Service by Publication. Upon the filing of a certificate of the plaintiff's attorney stating that the attorney believes a defendant cannot be personally served, because after diligent inquiry within the state in which the complaint is filed the defendant's place of residence cannot be ascertained by the plaintiff or, if ascertained, that it is beyond the territorial limits of personal service as provided in this rule, service of the notice shall be made on this defendant by publication in a newspaper published in the county where the property is located, or if there is no such newspaper, then in a newspaper having a general circulation where the property is located, once a week for not less than three successive weeks. Prior to the last publication, a copy of the notice shall also be mailed to a defendant who cannot be personally served as provided in this rule but whose place of residence is then known. Unknown owners may be served by publication in like manner by a notice addressed to "Unknown Owners."

Service by publication is complete upon the date of the last publication. Proof of publication and mailing shall be made by certificate of the plaintiff's attorney, to which shall be attached a printed copy of the published notice with the name and dates of the newspaper marked thereon.

(4) *Return; Amendment.* Proof of service of the notice shall be made and amendment of the notice or proof of its service allowed in the manner provided for the return and amendment of the summons under Rule 4.

(e) Appearance or Answer. If a defendant has no objection or defense to the taking of the defendant's property, the defendant may serve a notice of appearance designating the property in which the defendant claims to be interested. Thereafter, the defendant shall receive notice of all proceedings affecting it. If a defendant has any objection or defense to the taking of the property, the defendant shall serve an answer within 20 days after the service of notice upon the defendant. The answer shall identify the property in which the defendant claims to have an interest, state the nature and extent of the interest claimed, and state all the defendant's objections and defenses to the taking of the property. A defendant waives all defenses and objections not so presented, but at the trial of the issue of just compensation, whether or not the defendant has previously appeared or answered, the defendant may present evidence as to the amount of the compensation to be paid for the property, and the defendant may share in the distribution of the award. No other pleading or motion asserting any additional defense or objection shall be allowed.

(f) Amendment of Pleadings. Without leave of court, the plaintiff may amend the complaint at any time before the trial of the issue of compensation and as many times as desired, but no amendment shall be made which will result in a dismissal forbidden by subdivision (i) of this rule. The plaintiff need not serve a copy of an amendment, but shall serve notice of the filing, as provided in Rule 5(b), upon any party affected thereby who has appeared and, in the manner provided in subdivision (d) of this rule, upon any party affected thereby who has not appeared. The plaintiff shall furnish to the clerk of the court for the use of the defendants at least one copy of each amendment and shall furnish additional copies on the request of the clerk or of a defendant. Within the time allowed by subdivision (e) of this rule a defendant may serve an answer to the amended pleading, in the form and manner and with the same effect as there provided.

(g) Substitution of Parties. If a defendant dies or becomes incompetent or transfers an interest after the defendant's joinder, the court may order substitution of the proper party upon motion and notice of hearing. If the motion and notice of hearing are to be served upon a person not already a party, service shall be made as provided in subdivision (d)(3) of this rule.

(h) Trial. If the action involves the exercise of the power of eminent domain under the law of the United States, any tribunal specially constituted by an Act of Congress governing the case for the trial of the issue of just compensation shall be the tribunal for the determination of that issue; but if there is no such specially constituted tribunal any party may have a trial by jury of the issue of just compensation by filing a demand therefor within the time allowed for answer or within such further time as the court may fix, unless the court in its discretion orders that, because of the character, location, or quantity of the property to be condemned, or for other reasons in the interest of justice, the issue of compensation shall be determined by a commission of three persons appointed by it.

In the event that a commission is appointed the court may direct that not more than two additional persons serve as alternate commissioners to hear the case and replace commissioners who, prior to the time when a decision is filed, are found by the court to be unable or disqualified to perform their duties. An alternate who does not replace a regular commissioner shall be discharged after the commission renders its final decision. Before appointing the members of the commission and alternates the court shall advise the parties of the identity and qualifications of each prospective commissioner and alternate and may permit the parties to examine each such designee. The parties shall not be permitted or required by the court to suggest nominees. Each party shall have the right to object for valid cause to the appointment of any person as a commissioner or alternate. If a commission is appointed it shall have the authority of a master provided in Rule 53(c) and proceedings before it shall be governed by the provisions of Rule 53(d). Its action and report shall be determined by a majority and its findings and report shall have the effect, and be dealt with by the court in accordance with the

practice, prescribed in Rule 53(e), (f), and (g). Trial of all issues shall otherwise be by the court.

(i) Dismissal of Action.

(1) *As of Right.* If no hearing has begun to determine the compensation to be paid for a piece of property and the plaintiff has not acquired the title or a lesser interest in or taken possession, the plaintiff may dismiss the action as to that property, without an order of the court, by filing a notice of dismissal setting forth a brief description of the property as to which the action is dismissed.

(2) *By Stipulation.* Before the entry of any judgment vesting the plaintiff with title or a lesser interest in or possession of property, the action may be dismissed in whole or in part, without an order of the court, as to any property by filing a stipulation of dismissal by the plaintiff and the defendant affected thereby; and, if the parties so stipulate, the court may vacate any judgment that has been entered.

(3) *By Order of the Court.* At any time before compensation for a piece of property has been determined and paid and after motion and hearing, the court may dismiss the action as to that property, except that it shall not dismiss the action as to any part of the property of which the plaintiff has taken possession or in which the plaintiff has taken title or a lesser interest, but shall award just compensation for the possession, title or lesser interest so taken. The court at any time may drop a defendant unnecessarily or improperly joined.

(4) *Effect.* Except as otherwise provided in the notice, or stipulation of dismissal, or order of the court, any dismissal is without prejudice.

(j) Deposit and Its Distribution. The plaintiff shall deposit with the court any money required by law as a condition to the exercise of the power of eminent domain; and, although not so required, may make a deposit when permitted by statute. In such cases the court and attorneys shall expedite the proceedings for the distribution of the money so deposited and for the ascertainment and payment of just compensation. If the compensation finally awarded to any defendant exceeds the amount which has been paid to that defendant on distribution of the deposit, the court shall enter judgment against the plaintiff and in favor of that defendant for the deficiency. If the compensation finally awarded to any defendant is less than the amount which has been paid to that defendant, the court shall enter judgment against that defendant and in favor of the plaintiff for the overpayment.

(k) Condemnation Under a State's Power of Eminent Domain. The practice as herein prescribed governs in actions involving the exercise of the power of eminent domain under the law of a state, provided that if the state law makes provision for trial of any issue by jury, or for trial of the issue of compensation by jury or commission or both, that provision shall be followed.

(l) Costs. Costs are not subject to Rule 54(d).

[Adopted April 30, 1951, effective August 1, 1951; amended January 21, 1963, effective July 1, 1963; April 29, 1985, effective August 1, 1985; March 2, 1987, effective August 1, 1987; April 25, 1988, effective August 1, 1988; amended by Pub.L. 100–690, Title VII, § 7050, November 18, 1988, 102 Stat. 4401 (although amendment by Pub.L. 100–690 could not be executed due to prior amendment by Court order which made the same change effective August 1, 1988); amended April 22, 1993, effective December 1, 1993; March 27, 2003, effective December 1, 2003.]

RULE 72. MAGISTRATE JUDGES; PRETRIAL ORDERS

(a) Nondispositive Matters. A magistrate judge to whom a pretrial matter not dispositive of a claim or defense of a party is referred to hear and determine shall promptly conduct such proceedings as are required and when appropriate enter into the record a written order setting forth the disposition of the matter. Within 10 days after being served with a copy of the magistrate judge's order, a party may serve and file objections to the order; a party may not thereafter assign as error a defect in the magistrate judge's order to which objection was not timely made. The district judge to whom the case is assigned shall consider such objections and shall modify or set aside any portion of the magistrate judge's order found to be clearly erroneous or contrary to law.

(b) Dispositive Motions and Prisoner Petitions. A magistrate judge assigned without consent of the parties to hear a pretrial matter dispositive of a claim or defense of a party or a prisoner petition challenging the conditions of confinement shall promptly conduct such proceedings as are required. A record shall be made of all evidentiary proceedings before the magistrate judge, and a record may be made of such other proceedings as the magistrate judge deems necessary. The magistrate judge shall enter into the record a recommendation for disposition of the matter, including proposed findings of fact when appropriate. The clerk shall forthwith mail copies to all parties.

A party objecting to the recommended disposition of the matter shall promptly arrange for the transcription of the record, or portions of it as all parties may agree upon or the magistrate judge deems sufficient, unless the district judge otherwise directs. Within 10 days after being served with a copy of the recommended disposition, a party may serve and file specific, written objections to the proposed findings and recommendations. A party may respond to another party's objections within 10 days after being served with a copy thereof. The district judge to whom the case is assigned shall make a de novo determination upon the record, or after additional evidence, of any portion of the magistrate judge's disposition to which specific written objection has been made in accordance

with this rule. The district judge may accept, reject, or modify the recommended decision, receive further evidence, or recommit the matter to the magistrate judge with instructions.

[Former Rule 72 abrogated December 4, 1967, effective July 1, 1968; new Rule 72 adopted April 28, 1983, effective August 1, 1983; amended April 30, 1991, effective December 1, 1991; April 22, 1993, effective December 1, 1993.]

RULE 73. MAGISTRATE JUDGES; TRIAL BY CONSENT AND APPEAL OPTIONS

(a) Powers; Procedure. When specially designated to exercise such jurisdiction by local rule or order of the district court and when all parties consent thereto, a magistrate judge may exercise the authority provided by Title 28, U.S.C. § 636(c) and may conduct any or all proceedings, including a jury or nonjury trial, in a civil case. A record of the proceedings shall be made in accordance with the requirements of Title 28, U.S.C. § 636(c)(5).

(b) Consent. When a magistrate judge has been designated to exercise civil trial jurisdiction, the clerk shall give written notice to the parties of their opportunity to consent to the exercise by a magistrate judge of civil jurisdiction over the case, as authorized by Title 28, U.S.C. § 636(c). If, within the period specified by local rule, the parties agree to a magistrate judge's exercise of such authority, they shall execute and file a joint form of consent or separate forms of consent setting forth such election.

A district judge, magistrate judge, or other court official may again advise the parties of the availability of the magistrate judge, but, in so doing, shall also advise the parties that they are free to withhold consent without adverse substantive consequences. A district judge or magistrate judge shall not be informed of a party's response to the clerk's notification, unless all parties have consented to the referral of the matter to a magistrate judge.

The district judge, for good cause shown on the judge's own initiative, or under extraordinary circumstances shown by a party, may vacate a reference of a civil matter to a magistrate judge under this subdivision.

(c) Appeal. In accordance with Title 28, U.S.C. § 636(c)(3), appeal from a judgment entered upon direction of a magistrate judge in proceedings under this rule will lie to the court of appeals as it would from a judgment of the district court.

(d) Optional Appeal Route [Abrogated].

[Former Rule 73 abrogated December 4, 1967, effective July 1, 1968; new Rule 73 adopted April 28, 1983, effective August

1, 1983; amended March 2, 1987, effective August 1, 1987; April 22, 1993, effective December 1, 1993; April 11, 1997, effective December 1, 1997.]

RULE 74. METHOD OF APPEAL FROM MAGISTRATE JUDGE TO DISTRICT JUDGE UNDER TITLE 28, U.S.C. § 636(c)(4) AND RULE 73(d) [ABROGATED]

[Former Rule 74 abrogated December 4, 1967, effective July 1, 1968; new Rule 74 adopted April 28, 1983, effective August 1, 1983; amended April 22, 1993, effective December 1, 1993; abrogated April 11, 1997, effective December 1, 1997.]

RULE 75. PROCEEDINGS ON APPEAL FROM MAGISTRATE JUDGE TO DISTRICT JUDGE UNDER RULE 73(d) [ABROGATED]

[Former Rule 75 abrogated December 4, 1967, effective July 1, 1968; new Rule 75 adopted April 28, 1983, effective August 1, 1983; amended March 2, 1987, effective August 1, 1987; April 22, 1993, effective December 1, 1993; abrogated April 11, 1997, effective December 1, 1997.]

RULE 76. JUDGMENT OF THE DISTRICT JUDGE ON THE APPEAL UNDER RULE 73(d) AND COSTS [ABROGATED]

[Former Rule 76 abrogated December 4, 1967, effective July 1, 1968; new Rule 76 adopted April 28, 1983, effective August 1, 1983; amended April 22, 1993, effective December 1, 1993; abrogated April 11, 1997, effective December 1, 1997.]

X. DISTRICT COURTS AND CLERKS

RULE 77. DISTRICT COURTS AND CLERKS

(a) District Courts Always Open. The district courts shall be deemed always open for the purpose of filing any pleading or other proper paper, of issuing and returning mesne and final process, and of making and directing all interlocutory motions, orders, and rules.

(b) Trials and Hearings; Orders in Chambers. All trials upon the merits shall be conducted in open court and so far as convenient in a regular court room. All other acts or proceedings may be done or conducted by a judge in chambers, without the attendance of the clerk or other court officials and at any place either within or without the district; but no hearing, other than one ex parte, shall be conducted outside the district without the consent of all parties affected thereby.

(c) Clerk's Office and Orders by Clerk. The clerk's office with the clerk or a deputy in attendance shall be open during business hours on all days except Saturdays, Sundays, and legal holidays, but a district court may provide by local rule or order that its clerk's office shall be open for specified hours on Saturdays or particular legal holidays other than New Year's Day, Birthday of Martin Luther King, Jr., Washington's Birthday, Memorial Day, Independence Day, Labor Day, Columbus Day, Veterans Day, Thanksgiving Day, and Christmas Day. All motions and applications in the clerk's office for issuing mesne process, for issuing final process to enforce and execute judgments, for entering defaults or judgments by default, and for other proceedings which do not require allowance or order of the court are grantable of course by the clerk; but the clerk's action may be suspended or altered or rescinded by the court upon cause shown.

(d) Notice of Orders or Judgments. Immediately upon the entry of an order or judgment the clerk shall serve a notice of the entry in the manner provided for in Rule 5(b) upon each party who is not in default for failure to appear, and shall make a note in the docket of the service. Any party may in addition serve a notice of such entry in the manner provided in Rule 5(b) for the service of papers. Lack of notice of the entry by the clerk does not affect the time to appeal or relieve or authorize the court to relieve a party for failure to appeal within the time allowed, except as permitted in Rule 4(a) of the Federal Rules of Appellate Procedure.

[Amended December 27, 1946, effective March 19, 1948; January 21, 1963, effective July 1, 1963; December 4, 1967, effective July 1, 1968; March 1, 1971, effective July 1, 1971; March 2, 1987, effective August 1, 1987; April 30, 1991, effective December 1, 1991; April 23, 2001, effective December 1, 2001.]

RULE 78. MOTION DAY

Unless local conditions make it impracticable, each district court shall establish regular times and places, at intervals sufficiently frequent for the prompt dispatch of business, at which motions requiring notice and hearing may be heard and disposed of; but the judge at any time or place and on such notice, if any, as the judge considers reasonable may make orders for the advancement, conduct, and hearing of actions.

To expedite its business, the court may make provision by rule or order for the submission and determination of motions without oral hearing upon brief written statements of reasons in support and opposition.

[Amended March 2, 1987, effective August 1, 1987.]

RULE 79. BOOKS AND RECORDS KEPT BY THE CLERK AND ENTRIES THEREIN

(a) **Civil Docket.** The clerk shall keep a book known as "civil docket" of such form and style as may be prescribed by the Director of the Administrative Office of the United States Courts with the approval of the Judicial Conference of the United States, and shall enter therein each civil action to which these rules are made applicable. Actions shall be assigned consecutive file numbers. The file number of each action shall be noted on the folio of the docket whereon the first entry of the action is made. All papers filed with the clerk, all process issued and returns made thereon, all appearances, orders, verdicts, and judgments shall be entered chronologically in the civil docket on the folio assigned to the action and shall be marked with its file number. These entries shall be brief but shall show the nature of each paper filed or writ issued and the substance of each order or judgment of the court and of the returns showing execution of process. The entry of an order or judgment shall show the date the entry is made. When in an action trial by jury has been properly demanded or ordered the clerk shall enter the word "jury" on the folio assigned to that action.

(b) **Civil Judgments and Orders.** The clerk shall keep, in such form and manner as the Director of the Administrative Office of the United States Courts with the approval of the Judicial Conference of the United States may prescribe, a correct copy of every final judgment or appealable order, or order affecting title to or lien upon real or personal property, and any other order which the court may direct to be kept.

(c) **Indices; Calendars.** Suitable indices of the civil docket and of every civil judgment and order referred to in subdivision (b) of this rule shall be kept by the clerk under the direction of the court. There shall be prepared under the direction of the court calendars of all actions ready for trial, which shall distinguish "jury actions" from "court actions."

(d) **Other Books and Records of the Clerk.** The clerk shall also keep such other books and records as may be required from time to time by the Director of the Administrative Office of the United States Courts with the approval of the Judicial Conference of the United States.

[Amended December 27, 1946, effective March 19, 1948; December 29, 1948, effective October 20, 1949; January 21, 1963, effective July 1, 1963.]

RULE 80. STENOGRAPHER; STENOGRAPHIC REPORT OR TRANSCRIPT AS EVIDENCE

(a) **Stenographer [Abrogated].**

(b) **Official Stenographer [Abrogated].**

(c) **Stenographic Report or Transcript as Evidence.** Whenever the testimony of a witness at a trial or hearing which was stenographically reported is admissible in evidence at a later trial, it may be proved by the transcript thereof duly certified by the person who reported the testimony.

[Amended December 27, 1946, effective March 19, 1948.]

XI. GENERAL PROVISIONS

RULE 81. APPLICABILITY IN GENERAL

(a) **Proceedings to Which the Rules Apply.**

(1) These rules do not apply to prize proceedings in admiralty governed by Title 10, U.S.C., §§ 7651–7681. They do apply to proceedings in bankruptcy to the extent provided by the Federal Rules of Bankruptcy Procedure.

(2) These rules are applicable to proceedings for admission to citizenship, habeas corpus, and quo warranto, to the extent that the practice in such proceedings is not set forth in statutes of the United States, the Rules Governing Section 2254 Cases, or the Rules Governing Section 2255 Proceedings, and has heretofore conformed to the practice in civil actions.

(3) In proceedings under Title 9, U.S.C., relating to arbitration, or under the Act of May 20, 1926, ch. 347, § 9 (44 Stat. 585), U.S.C., Title 45, § 159, relating to boards of arbitration of railway labor disputes, these rules apply only to the extent that matters of procedure are not provided for in those statutes. These rules apply to proceedings to compel the giving of testimony or production of documents in accordance with a subpoena issued by an officer or agency of the United States under any statute of the United States except as otherwise provided by statute or by rules of the district court or by order of the court in the proceedings.

(4) These rules do not alter the method prescribed by the Act of February 18, 1922, c. 57, § 2 (42 Stat. 388), U.S.C., Title 7, § 292; or by the Act of June 10, 1930, c. 436, § 7 (46 Stat. 534), as amended, U.S.C., Title 7, § 499g(c), for instituting proceedings in the United States district courts to review orders of the Secretary of Agriculture; or prescribed by the Act of June 25, 1934, c. 742, § 2 (48 Stat. 1214), U.S.C., Title 15, § 522, for instituting proceedings to review orders of the Secretary of the Interior; or prescribed by the Act of February 22, 1935, c. 18, § 5 (49 Stat. 31), U.S.C., Title 15, § 715d(c), as extended, for instituting proceedings to review orders of petroleum control boards; but the conduct of such proceedings in the district courts shall be made to conform to these rules so far as applicable.

(5) These rules do not alter the practice in the United States district courts prescribed in the Act of July 5, 1935, c. 372, §§ 9 and 10 (49 Stat. 453), as amended, U.S.C., Title 29, §§ 159 and 160, for beginning and conducting proceedings to enforce orders of the National Labor Relations Board; and in respects not covered by those statutes, the practice in the district courts shall conform to these rules so far as applicable.

(6) These rules apply to proceedings for enforcement or review of compensation orders under the Longshoremen's and Harbor Workers' Compensation Act, Act of March 4, 1927, c. 509, §§ 18, 21 (44 Stat. 1434, 1436), as amended, U.S.C., Title 33, §§ 918, 921, except to the extent that matters of procedure are provided for in that Act. The provisions for service by publication and for answer in proceedings to cancel certificates of citizenship under the Act of June 27, 1952, c. 477, Title III, c. 2, § 340 (66 Stat. 260), U.S.C., Title 8, § 1451, remain in effect.

(7) [Abrogated].

(b) Scire Facias and Mandamus. The writs of scire facias and mandamus are abolished. Relief heretofore available by mandamus or scire facias may be obtained by appropriate action or by appropriate motion under the practice prescribed in these rules.

(c) Removed Actions. These rules apply to civil actions removed to the United States district courts from the state courts and govern procedure after removal. Repleading is not necessary unless the court so orders. In a removed action in which the defendant has not answered, the defendant shall answer or present the other defenses or objections available under these rules within 20 days after the receipt through service or otherwise of a copy of the initial pleading setting forth the claim for relief upon which the action or proceeding is based, or within 20 days after the service of summons upon such initial pleading, then filed, or within 5 days after the filing of the petition for removal, whichever period is longest. If at the time of removal all necessary pleadings have been served, a party entitled to trial by jury under Rule 38 shall be accorded it, if the party's demand therefor is served within 10 days after the petition for removal is filed if the party is the petitioner, or if not the petitioner within 10 days after service on the party of the notice of filing the petition. A party who, prior to removal, has made an express demand for trial by jury in accordance with state law, need not make a demand after removal. If state law applicable in the court from which the case is removed does not require the parties to make express demands in order to claim trial by jury, they need not make demands after removal unless the court directs that they do so within a specified time if they desire to claim trial by jury. The court may make this direction on its own motion and shall do so as a matter of course at the request of any party. The failure of a party to make demand as

directed constitutes a waiver by that party of trial by jury.

(d) District of Columbia; Courts and Judges [Abrogated].

(e) Law Applicable. Whenever in these rules the law of the state in which the district court is held is made applicable, the law applied in the District of Columbia governs proceedings in the United States District Court for the District of Columbia. When the word "state" is used, it includes, if appropriate, the District of Columbia. When the term "statute of the United States" is used, it includes, so far as concerns proceedings in the United States District Court for the District of Columbia, any Act of Congress locally applicable to and in force in the District of Columbia. When the law of a state is referred to, the word "law" includes the statutes of that state and the state judicial decisions construing them.

(f) References to Officer of the United States. Under any rule in which reference is made to an officer or agency of the United States, the term "officer" includes a district director of internal revenue, a former district director or collector of internal revenue, or the personal representative of a deceased district director or collector of internal revenue.

[Amended December 28, 1939, effective April 3, 1941; December 27, 1946, effective March 19, 1948; December 29, 1948, effective October 20, 1949; April 30, 1951, effective August 1, 1951; January 21, 1963, effective July 1, 1963; February 28, 1966, effective July 1, 1966; December 4, 1967, effective July 1, 1968; March 1, 1971, effective July 1, 1971; March 2, 1987, effective August 1, 1987; April 23, 2001, effective December 1, 2001; April 29, 2002, effective December 1, 2002.]

RULE 82. JURISDICTION AND VENUE UNAFFECTED

These rules shall not be construed to extend or limit the jurisdiction of the United States district courts or the venue of actions therein. An admiralty or maritime claim within the meaning of Rule 9(h) shall not be treated as a civil action for the purposes of Title 28, U.S.C., §§ 1391–1392.

[Amended December 29, 1948, effective October 20, 1949; February 28, 1966, effective July 1, 1966; April 23, 2001, effective December 1, 2001.]

RULE 83. RULES BY DISTRICT COURTS; JUDGE'S DIRECTIVES

(a) Local Rules.

(1) Each district court, acting by a majority of its district judges, may, after giving appropriate public notice and an opportunity for comment, make and amend rules governing its practice. A local rule shall be consistent with—but not duplicative of—Acts of Congress and rules adopted under 28 U.S.C. §§ 2072 and 2075, and shall conform to any uniform numbering

system prescribed by the Judicial Conference of the United States. A local rule takes effect on the date specified by the district court and remains in effect unless amended by the court or abrogated by the judicial council of the circuit. Copies of rules and amendments shall, upon their promulgation, be furnished to the judicial council and the Administrative Office of the United States Courts and be made available to the public.

(2) A local rule imposing a requirement of form shall not be enforced in a manner that causes a party to lose rights because of a nonwillful failure to comply with the requirement.

(b) Procedures When There Is No Controlling Law. A judge may regulate practice in any manner consistent with federal law, rules adopted under 28 U.S.C. §§ 2072 and 2075, and local rules of the district. No sanction or other disadvantage may be imposed for noncompliance with any requirement not in federal law, federal rules, or the local district rules unless the alleged violator has been furnished in the particular case with actual notice of the requirement.

[Amended April 29, 1985, effective August 1, 1985; April 27, 1995, effective December 1, 1995.]

RULE 84. FORMS

The forms contained in the Appendix of Forms are sufficient under the rules and are intended to indicate the simplicity and brevity of statement which the rules contemplate.

[Amended December 27, 1946, effective March 19, 1948.]

RULE 85. TITLE

These rules may be known and cited as the Federal Rules of Civil Procedure.

RULE 86. EFFECTIVE DATE

(a) Effective Date of Original Rules.* These rules will take effect on the day which is 3 months subsequent to the adjournment of the second regular session of the 75th Congress, but if that day is prior to September 1, 1938, then these rules will take effect on September 1, 1938. They govern all proceedings in actions brought after they take effect and also all further proceedings in actions then pending, except to the extent that in the opinion of the court their application in a particular action pending when the

rules take effect would not be feasible or would work injustice, in which event the former procedure applies.

(b) Effective Date of Amendments. The amendments adopted by the Supreme Court on December 27, 1946, and transmitted to the Attorney General on January 2, 1947, shall take effect on the day which is three months subsequent to the adjournment of the first regular session of the 80th Congress, but, if that day is prior to September 1, 1947, then these amendments shall take effect on September 1, 1947. They govern all proceedings in actions brought after they take effect and also all further proceedings in actions then pending, except to the extent that in the opinion of the court their application in a particular action pending when the amendments take effect would not be feasible or would work injustice, in which event the former procedure applies.

(c) Effective Date of Amendments. The amendments adopted by the Supreme Court on December 29, 1948, and transmitted to the Attorney General on December 31, 1948, shall take effect on the day following the adjournment of the first regular session of the 81st Congress.

(d) Effective Date of Amendments. The amendments adopted by the Supreme Court on April 17, 1961, and transmitted to the Congress on April 18, 1961, shall take effect on July 19, 1961. They govern all proceedings in actions brought after they take effect and also all further proceedings in actions then pending, except to the extent that in the opinion of the court their application in a particular action pending when the amendments take effect would not be feasible or would work injustice, in which event the former procedure applies.

(e) Effective Date of Amendments. The amendments adopted by the Supreme Court on January 21, 1963, and transmitted to the Congress on January 21, 1963, shall take effect on July 1, 1963. They govern all proceedings in actions brought after they take effect and also all further proceedings in actions then pending, except to the extent that in the opinion of the court their application in a particular action pending when the amendments take effect would not be feasible or would work injustice, in which event the former procedure applies.

[Amended December 27, 1946, effective March 19, 1948; December 29, 1948, effective October 20, 1949; April 17, 1961, effective July 19, 1961; January 21, 1963, and March 18, 1963, effective July 1, 1963.]

* Suggested title added by Publisher.

APPENDIX OF FORMS

(See Rule 84)

INTRODUCTORY STATEMENT

1. The following forms are intended for illustration only. They are limited in number. No attempt is made to furnish a manual of forms. Each form assumes the action to be brought in the Southern District of New York. If the district in which an action is brought has divisions, the division should be indicated in the caption.

2. Except where otherwise indicated each pleading, motion, and other paper should have a caption similar to that of the summons, with the designation of the particular paper substituted for the word "Summons". In the caption of the summons and in the caption of the complaint all parties must be named but in other pleadings and papers, it is sufficient to state the name of the first party on either side, with an appropriate indication of other parties. See Rules 4(b), 7(b)(2), and 10(a).

3. In Form 3 and the forms following, the words, "Allegation of jurisdiction," are used to indicate the appropriate allegation in Form 2.

4. Each pleading, motion, and other paper is to be signed in his individual name by at least one attorney of record (Rule 11). The attorney's name is to be followed by his address as indicated in Form 3. In forms following Form 3 the signature and address are not indicated.

5. If a party is not represented by an attorney, the signature and address of the party are required in place of those of the attorney.

FORM 1. SUMMONS

United States District Court for the Southern District of New York

Civil Action, File Number ——————

A. B., Plaintiff	)
v.	) *Summons*
C. D., Defendant	)

To the above-named Defendant:

You are hereby summoned and required to serve upon ——————, plaintiff's attorney, whose address is ——————, an answer to the complaint which is herewith served upon you, within 20 [1] days after service of this summons upon you, exclusive of the day of service. If you fail to do so, judgment by default will be taken against you for the relief demanded in the complaint.

———————————————————

Clerk of Court.

[Seal of the U.S. District Court]

Dated ——————

(This summons is issued pursuant to Rule 4 of the Federal Rules of Civil Procedure.)

1. If the United States or an officer or agency thereof is a defendant, the time to be inserted as to it is 60 days.

[Amended December 29, 1948, effective October 20, 1949.]

FORM 1A. NOTICE OF LAWSUIT AND REQUEST FOR WAIVER OF SERVICE OF SUMMONS

TO: _____ (A) _____

[as _____ (B) _____ of _____ (C) _____]

A lawsuit has been commenced against you (or the entity on whose behalf you are addressed). A copy of the complaint is attached to this notice. It has been filed in the United States District Court for the ___(D)___ and has been assigned docket number ___(E)___ .

This is not a formal summons or notification from the court, but rather my request that you sign and return the enclosed waiver of service in order to save the cost of serving you with a judicial summons and an additional copy of the complaint. The cost of service will be avoided if I receive a signed copy of the waiver within ___(F)___ days after the date designated below as the date on which this Notice and Request is sent. I enclose a stamped and addressed envelope (or other means of cost-free return) for your use. An extra copy of the waiver is also attached for your records.

If you comply with this request and return the signed waiver, it will be filed with the court and no summons will be served on you. The action will then proceed as if you had been served on the date the waiver is filed, except that you will not be obligated to answer the complaint before 60 days from the date designated below as the date on which this notice is sent (or before 90 days from that date if your address is not in any judicial district of the United States).

If you do not return the signed waiver within the time indicated, I will take appropriate steps to effect formal service in a manner authorized by the Federal Rules of Civil Procedure and will then, to the extent authorized by those Rules, ask the court to require you (or the party on whose behalf you are addressed) to pay the full costs of such service. In that connection, please read the statement concerning the duty of parties to waive the service of the summons, which is set forth on the reverse side (or at the foot) of the waiver form.

I affirm that this request is being sent to you on behalf of the plaintiff, this ___ day of _____, ___.

                                        _____
                                        Signature of Plaintiff's Attorney or
                                        Unrepresented Plaintiff

Notes:

A—Name of individual defendant (or name of officer or agent of corporate defendant)

B—Title, or other relationship of individual to corporate defendant

C—Name of corporate defendant, if any

D—District

E—Docket number of action

F—Addressee must be given at least 30 days (60 days if located in foreign country) in which to return waiver

[Adopted April 22, 1993, effective December 1, 1993.]

FORM 1B. WAIVER OF SERVICE OF SUMMONS

TO: __(name of plaintiff's attorney or unrepresented plaintiff)__

I acknowledge receipt of your request that I waive service of a summons in the action of __(caption of action)__ , which is case number __(docket number)__ in the United States District Court for the __(district)__ . I have also received a copy of the complaint in the action, two copies of this instrument, and a means by which I can return the signed waiver to you without cost to me.

I agree to save the cost of service of a summons and an additional copy of the complaint in this lawsuit by not requiring that I (or the entity on whose behalf I am acting) be served with judicial process in the manner provided by Rule 4.

I (or the entity on whose behalf I am acting) will retain all defenses or objections to the lawsuit or to the jurisdiction or venue of the court except for objections based on a defect in the summons or in the service of the summons.

I understand that a judgment may be entered against me (or the party on whose behalf I am acting) if an answer or motion under Rule 12 is not served upon you within 60 days after ___(date request was sent)___, or within 90 days after that date if the request was sent outside the United States.

_____   _____
Date   Signature
                                     Printed/typed name: _____
                                       [as _____]
                                       [of _____]

To be printed on reverse side of the waiver form or set forth
at the foot of the form:
Duty to Avoid Unnecessary Costs of Service of Summons

Rule 4 of the Federal Rules of Civil Procedure requires certain parties to cooperate in saving unnecessary costs of service of the summons and complaint. A defendant located in the United States who, after being notified of an action and asked by a plaintiff located in the United States to waive service of a summons, fails to do so will be required to bear the cost of such service unless good cause be shown for its failure to sign and return the waiver.

It is not good cause for a failure to waive service that a party believes that the complaint is unfounded, or that the action has been brought in an improper place or in a court that lacks jurisdiction over the subject matter of the action or over its person or property. A party who waives service of the summons retains all defenses and objections (except any relating to the summons or to the service of the summons), and may later object to the jurisdiction of the court or to the place where the action has been brought.

A defendant who waives service must within the time specified on the waiver form serve on the plaintiff's attorney (or unrepresented plaintiff) a response to the complaint and must also file a signed copy of the response with the court. If the answer or motion is not served within this time, a default judgment may be taken against that defendant. By waiving service, a defendant is allowed more time to answer than if the summons had been actually served when the request for waiver of service was received.

[Adopted April 22, 1993, effective December 1, 1993.]

FORM 2.   ALLEGATION OF JURISDICTION

(a) Jurisdiction Founded on Diversity of Citizenship and Amount.

Plaintiff is a [citizen of the State of Connecticut] [1] [corporation incorporated under the laws of the State of Connecticut having its principal place of business in the State of Connecticut] and defendant is a corporation incorporated under the laws of the State of New York having its principal place of business in a State other than the State of Connecticut. The matter in controversy exceeds, exclusive of interest and costs, the sum specified by 28 U.S.C. § 1332.

(b) Jurisdiction Founded on the Existence of a Federal Question.

The action arises under [the Constitution of the United States, Article ____, Section ____]; [the ____ Amendment to the Constitution of the United States, Section ____]; [the Act of ____, ____ Stat. ____; U.S.C., Title ____, § ____]; [the Treaty of the United States (here describe the treaty)] [2] as hereinafter more fully appears.

(c) Jurisdiction Founded on the Existence of a Question Arising Under Particular Statutes.

The action arises under the Act of _____, _____ Stat. _____; U.S.C., Title _____, § _____, as hereinafter more fully appears.

(d) Jurisdiction Founded on the Admiralty or Maritime Character of the Claim.

This is a case of admiralty and maritime jurisdiction, as hereinafter more fully appears. [If the pleader wishes to invoke the distinctively maritime procedures referred to in Rule 9(h), add the following or its substantial equivalent: This is an admiralty or maritime claim within the meaning of Rule 9(h).]

1. Form for natural person.

2. Use the appropriate phrase or phrases. The general allegation of the existence of a Federal question is ineffective unless the matters constituting the claim for relief as set forth in the complaint raise a Federal question.

[Amended April 17, 1961, effective July 19, 1961; February 28, 1966, effective July 1, 1966; April 22, 1993, effective December 1, 1993; April 29, 1999, effective December 1, 1999.]

Notes of Advisory Committee

1. Diversity of Citizenship. If the plaintiff is an assignee, he should allege such other facts of citizenship as will show that he is entitled to prosecute his action under U.S.C.A., Title 28, § 1332, formerly § 41(1).

2. Jurisdiction Founded on Some Fact Other Than Diversity of Citizenship. The allegation as to the matter in controversy may be omitted in any case where by law no jurisdictional amount is required. See for example, U.S.C.A., Title 28, former § 41(2)–(28).

3. Pleading Venue. Since improper venue is an affirmative dilatory defense, it is not necessary for plaintiff to include allegations showing the venue to be proper.

4. It is sufficient to allege that a corporation is incorporated in a particular state, there being, for jurisdictional purposes, a conclusive presumption that all of its members or stockholders are citizens of that State, Marshal v. Baltimore and Ohio R.R. Co., 1853, 16 How. 314; Henderson, Position of Foreign Corporations in American Constitutional Law (1918) 54–64.

FORM 3.   COMPLAINT ON A PROMISSORY NOTE

1.   Allegation of jurisdiction.

2.   Defendant on or about June 1, 1935, executed and delivered to plaintiff a promissory note [in the following words and figures: (here set out the note verbatim)]; [a copy of which is hereto annexed as Exhibit A]; [whereby defendant promised to pay to plaintiff or order on June 1, 1936 the sum of _____ dollars with interest thereon at the rate of six percent. per annum].

3.   Defendant owes to plaintiff the amount of said note and interest.

Wherefore plaintiff demands judgment against defendant for the sum of _____ dollars, interest, and costs.

Signed: _____

Attorney for Plaintiff.

Address: _____

[Amended January 21, 1963, effective July 1, 1963.]

Notes of Advisory Committee

1.   The pleader may use the material in one of the three sets of brackets. His choice will depend upon whether he desires to plead the document verbatim, or by exhibit, or according to its legal effect.

2.   Under the rules free joinder of claims is permitted. See Rules 8(e) and 18. Consequently the claims set forth in each and all of the following forms may be joined with this complaint or with each other. Ordinarily each claim should be stated in a separate division of the complaint, and the divisions should be designated as counts successively numbered. In particular the rules permit alternative and inconsistent pleading. See Form 10.

FORM 4.   COMPLAINT ON AN ACCOUNT

1.   Allegation of jurisdiction.

2.   Defendant owes plaintiff _____ dollars according to the account hereto annexed as Exhibit A.

Wherefore (etc. as in Form 3).

[Amended January 21, 1963, effective July 1, 1963.]

FORM 5.   COMPLAINT FOR GOODS SOLD AND DELIVERED

1.   Allegation of jurisdiction.

2.   Defendant owes plaintiff _____ dollars for goods sold and delivered by plaintiff to defendant between June 1, 1936 and December 1, 1936.

Wherefore (etc. as in Form 3).

[Amended January 21, 1963, effective July 1, 1963.]

Notes of Advisory Committee

This form may be used where the action is for an agreed price or for the reasonable value of the goods.

FORM 6.   COMPLAINT FOR MONEY LENT

1.   Allegation of jurisdiction.

2.   Defendant owes plaintiff _____ dollars for money lent by plaintiff to defendant on June 1, 1936.

Wherefore (etc. as in Form 3).

[Amended January 21, 1963, effective July 1, 1963.]

FORM 7.   COMPLAINT FOR MONEY PAID BY MISTAKE

1.   Allegation of jurisdiction.

2.   Defendant owes plaintiff _____ dollars for money paid by plaintiff to defendant by mistake on June 1, 1936, under the following circumstances: [here state the circumstances with particularity—see Rule 9(b)].

Wherefore (etc. as in Form 3).

[Amended January 21, 1963, effective July 1, 1963.]

FORM 8.   COMPLAINT FOR MONEY HAD AND RECEIVED

1.   Allegation of jurisdiction.

2.   Defendant owes plaintiff _____ dollars for money had and received from one G. H. on June 1, 1936, to be paid by defendant to plaintiff.

Wherefore (etc. as in Form 3).

[Amended January 21, 1963, effective July 1, 1963.]

FORM 9. COMPLAINT FOR NEGLIGENCE

1. Allegation of jurisdiction.

2. On June 1, 1936, in a public highway called Boylston Street in Boston, Massachusetts, defendant negligently drove a motor vehicle against plaintiff who was then crossing said highway.

3. As a result plaintiff was thrown down and had his leg broken and was otherwise injured, was prevented from transacting his business, suffered great pain of body and mind, and incurred expenses for medical attention and hospitalization in the sum of one thousand dollars.

Wherefore plaintiff demands judgment against defendant in the sum of _____ dollars and costs.

[Amended January 21, 1963, effective July 1, 1963.]

Notes of Advisory Committee

Since contributory negligence is an affirmative defense, the complaint need contain no allegation of due care of plaintiff.

FORM 10. COMPLAINT FOR NEGLIGENCE WHERE PLAINTIFF IS UNABLE TO DETERMINE DEFINITELY WHETHER THE PERSON RESPONSIBLE IS C. D. OR E. F. OR WHETHER BOTH ARE RESPONSIBLE AND WHERE HIS EVIDENCE MAY JUSTIFY A FINDING OF WILFULNESS OR OF RECKLESSNESS OR OF NEGLIGENCE

A. B., Plaintiff   )
         v.   ) *Complaint*
C. D. and E. F., Defendants   )

1. Allegation of jurisdiction.

2. On June 1, 1936, in a public highway called Boylston Street in Boston, Massachusetts, defendant C. D. or defendant E. F., or both defendants C. D. and E. F. wilfully or recklessly or negligently drove or caused to be driven a motor vehicle against plaintiff who was then crossing said highway.

3. As a result plaintiff was thrown down and had his leg broken and was otherwise injured, was prevented from transacting his business, suffered great pain of body and mind, and incurred expenses for medical attention and hospitalization in the sum of one thousand dollars.

Wherefore plaintiff demands judgment against C. D. or against E. F. or against both in the sum of _____ dollars and costs.

[Amended January 21, 1963, effective July 1, 1963.]

FORM 11. COMPLAINT FOR CONVERSION

1. Allegation of jurisdiction.

2. On or about December 1, 1936, defendant converted to his own use ten bonds of the _____ Company (here insert brief identification as by number and issue) of the value of _____ dollars, the property of plaintiff.

Wherefore plaintiff demands judgment against defendant in the sum of _____ dollars, interest, and costs.

[Amended January 21, 1963, effective July 1, 1963.]

FORM 12. COMPLAINT FOR SPECIFIC PERFORMANCE OF CONTRACT TO CONVEY LAND

1. Allegation of jurisdiction.

2. On or about December 1, 1936, plaintiff and defendant entered into an agreement in writing a copy of which is hereto annexed as Exhibit A.

3. In accord with the provisions of said agreement plaintiff tendered to defendant the purchase price and requested a conveyance of the land, but defendant refused to accept the tender and refused to make the conveyance.

4. Plaintiff now offers to pay the purchase price.

Wherefore plaintiff demands (1) that defendant be required specifically to perform said agreement, (2) damages in the sum of one thousand dollars, and (3) that if specific performance is not granted plaintiff have judgment against defendant in the sum of _____ dollars.

[Amended January 21, 1963, effective July 1, 1963.]

Notes of Advisory Committee

Here, as in Form 3, plaintiff may set forth the contract verbatim in the complaint or plead it, as indicated, by exhibit, or plead it according to its legal effect. Furthermore, plaintiff may seek legal or equitable relief or both even though this was impossible under the system in operation before these rules.

FORM 13. COMPLAINT ON CLAIM FOR DEBT AND TO SET ASIDE FRAUDULENT CONVEYANCE UNDER RULE 18(b)

A. B., Plaintiff   )
          v.   ) *Complaint*
C. D. and E. F., Defendants   )

1. Allegation of jurisdiction.

2. Defendant C. D. on or about _____ executed and delivered to plaintiff a promissory note [in the following words and figures: (here set out the note verbatim)]; [a copy of which is hereto annexed as Exhibit A]; [whereby defendant C. D. promised to pay to plaintiff or order on _____ the sum of five thousand dollars with interest thereon at the rate of _____ percent. per annum].

3. Defendant C. D. owes to plaintiff the amount of said note and interest.

4. Defendant C. D. on or about _____ conveyed all his property, real and personal [or specify and describe] to defendant E. F. for the purpose of defrauding plaintiff and hindering and delaying the collection of the indebtedness evidenced by the note above referred to.

Wherefore plaintiff demands:

(1) That plaintiff have judgment against defendant C. D. for _____ dollars and interest; (2) that the aforesaid conveyance to defendant E. F. be declared void and the judgment herein be declared a lien on said property; (3) that plaintiff have judgment against the defendants for costs.

[Amended January 21, 1963, effective July 1, 1963.]

FORM 14. COMPLAINT FOR NEGLIGENCE UNDER FEDERAL EMPLOYERS' LIABILITY ACT

1. Allegation of jurisdiction.

2. During all the times herein mentioned defendant owned and operated in interstate commerce a railroad which passed through a tunnel located at _____ and known as Tunnel No. _____.

3. On or about June 1, 1936, defendant was repairing and enlarging the tunnel in order to protect interstate trains and passengers and freight from injury and in order to make the tunnel more conveniently usable for interstate commerce.

4. In the course of thus repairing and enlarging the tunnel on said day defendant employed plaintiff as one of its workmen, and negligently put plaintiff to work in a portion of the tunnel which defendant had left unprotected and unsupported.

5. By reason of defendant's negligence in thus putting plaintiff to work in that portion of the tunnel, plaintiff was, while so working pursuant to defendant's orders, struck and crushed by a rock, which fell from the unsupported portion of the tunnel, and was (here describe plaintiff's injuries).

6. Prior to these injuries, plaintiff was a strong, able-bodied man, capable of earning and actually earning _____ dollars per day. By these injuries he has been made incapable of any gainful activity, has suffered great physical and mental pain, and has incurred expense in the amount of _____ dollars for medicine, medical attendance, and hospitalization.

Wherefore plaintiff demands judgment against defendant in the sum of _____ dollars and costs.

FORM 15. COMPLAINT FOR DAMAGES UNDER MERCHANT MARINE ACT

1. Allegation of jurisdiction. [If the pleader wishes to invoke the distinctively maritime procedures referred to in Rule 9(h), add the following or its substantial equivalent: This is an admiralty or maritime claim within the meaning of Rule 9(h).]

2. During all the times herein mentioned defendant was the owner of the steamship _____ and used it in the transportation of freight for hire by water in interstate and foreign commerce.

3. During the first part of (month and year) at _____ plaintiff entered the employ of defendant as an able seaman on said steamship under seamen's articles of customary form for a voyage from _____ ports to the Orient and return at a wage of _____ dollars per month and found, which is equal to a wage of _____ dollars per month as a shore worker.

4. On June 1, 1936, said steamship was about _____ days out of the port of _____ and was being navigated by the master and crew on the return voyage to _____ ports. (Here describe weather conditions and the condition of the ship and state as in an ordinary complaint for personal injuries the negligent conduct of defendant.)

5. By reason of defendant's negligence in thus (brief statement of defendant's negligent conduct) and the unseaworthiness of said steamship, plaintiff was (here describe plaintiff's injuries).

6. Prior to these injuries, plaintiff was a strong, able-bodied man, capable of earning and actually earning _____ dollars per day. By these injuries he has been made incapable of any gainful activity; has suffered great physical and mental pain, and has incurred expense in the amount of _____ dollars for medicine, medical attendance, and hospitalization.

Wherefore plaintiff demands judgment against defendant in the sum of _____ dollars and costs.

[Amended February 28, 1966, effective July 1, 1966.]

FORM 16. COMPLAINT FOR INFRINGEMENT OF PATENT

1. Allegation of jurisdiction.

2. On May 16, 1934, United States Letters Patent No. _____ were duly and legally issued to plaintiff for an invention in an electric motor; and since that date plaintiff has been and still is the owner of those Letters Patent.

3. Defendant has for a long time past been and still is infringing those Letters Patent by making, selling, and using electric motors embodying the patented invention, and will continue to do so unless enjoined by this court.

4. Plaintiff has placed the required statutory notice on all electric motors manufactured and sold by him under said Letters Patent, and has given written notice to defendant of his said infringement.

Wherefore plaintiff demands a preliminary and final injunction against continued infringement, an accounting for damages, and an assessment of interest and costs against defendant.

[Amended January 21, 1963, effective July 1, 1963.]

FORM 17. COMPLAINT FOR INFRINGEMENT OF COPYRIGHT AND UNFAIR COMPETITION

1. Allegation of jurisdiction.

2. Prior to March, 1936, plaintiff, who then was and ever since has been a citizen of the United States, created and wrote an original book, entitled _____.

3. This book contains a large amount of material wholly original with plaintiff and is copyrightable subject matter under the laws of the United States.

4. Between March 2, 1936, and March 10, 1936, plaintiff complied in all respects with the Act of (give citation) and all other laws governing copyright, and secured the exclusive rights and privileges in and to the copyright of said book, and received from the Register of Copyrights a certificate of registration, dated and identified as follows: "March 10, 1936, Class _____, No. _____."

5. Since March 10, 1936, said book has been published by plaintiff and all copies of it made by plaintiff or under his authority or license have been printed, bound, and published in strict conformity with the provisions of the Act of _____ and all other laws governing copyright.

6. Since March 10, 1936, plaintiff has been and still is the sole proprietor of all rights, title, and interest in and to the copyright in said book.

7. After March 10, 1936, defendant infringed said copyright by publishing and placing upon the market a book entitled _____, which was copied largely from plaintiff's copyrighted book, entitled _____.

8. A copy of plaintiff's copyrighted book is hereto attached as "Exhibit 1"; and a copy of defendant's infringing book is hereto attached as "Exhibit 2."

9. Plaintiff has notified defendant that defendant has infringed the copyright of plaintiff, and defendant has continued to infringe the copyright.

10. After March 10, 1936, and continuously since about _____, defendant has been publishing, selling and otherwise marketing the book entitled _____, and has thereby been engaging in unfair trade practices and unfair competition against plaintiff to plaintiff's irreparable damage.

Wherefore plaintiff demands:

(1) That defendant, his agents, and servants be enjoined during the pendency of this action and permanently from infringing said copyright of said plaintiff in any manner, and from publishing, selling, marketing or otherwise disposing of any copies of the book entitled _____.

(2) That defendant be required to pay to plaintiff such damages as plaintiff has sustained in consequence of defendant's infringement of said copyright and said unfair trade practices and unfair competition and to account for

(a) all gains, profits and advantages derived by defendant by said trade practices and unfair competition and

(b) all gains, profits, and advantages derived by defendant by his infringement of plaintiff's copyright or such damages as to the court shall appear proper within the provisions of the copyright statutes, but not less than two hundred and fifty dollars.

(3) That defendant be required to deliver up to be impounded during the pendency of this action all copies of said book entitled _____ in his possession or under his control and to deliver up for destruction all infringing copies and all plates, molds, and other matter for making such infringing copies.

(4) That defendant pay to plaintiff the costs of this action and reasonable attorney's fees to be allowed to the plaintiff by the court.

(5) That plaintiff have such other and further relief as is just.

[Amended December 27, 1946, effective March 19, 1948.]

FORM 18. COMPLAINT FOR INTERPLEADER AND DECLARATORY RELIEF

1. Allegation of jurisdiction.

2. On or about June 1, 1935, plaintiff issued to G. H. a policy of life insurance whereby plaintiff promised to pay to K. L. as beneficiary the sum of _____ dollars upon the death of G. H. The policy required the payment by G. H. of a stipulated premium on June 1, 1936, and annually thereafter as a condition precedent to its continuance in force.

3. No part of the premium due June 1, 1936, was ever paid and the policy ceased to have any force or effect on July 1, 1936.

4. Thereafter, on September 1, 1936, G. H. and K. L. died as the result of a collision between a locomotive and the automobile in which G. H. and K. L. were riding.

5. Defendant C. D. is the duly appointed and acting executor of the will of G. H.; defendant E. F. is the duly appointed and acting executor of the will of K. L.; defendant X. Y. claims to have been duly designated as beneficiary of said policy in place of K. L.

6. Each of defendants, C. D., E. F., and X. Y. is claiming that the above-mentioned policy was in full force and effect at the time of the death of G. H.; each of them is claiming to be the only person entitled to receive payment of the amount of the policy and has made demand for payment thereof.

7. By reason of these conflicting claims of the defendants, plaintiff is in great doubt as to which defendant is entitled to be paid the amount of the policy, if it was in force at the death of G. H.

Wherefore plaintiff demands that the court adjudge:

(1) That none of the defendants is entitled to recover from plaintiff the amount of said policy or any part thereof.

(2) That each of the defendants be restrained from instituting any action against plaintiff for the recovery of the amount of said policy or any part thereof.

(3) That, if the court shall determine that said policy was in force at the death of G. H., the defendants be required to interplead and settle between themselves their rights to the money due under said policy, and that plaintiff be discharged from all liability in the premises except to the person whom the court shall adjudge entitled to the amount of said policy.

(4) That plaintiff recover its costs.

[Amended January 21, 1963, effective July 1, 1963.]

FORM 18–A. NOTICE AND ACKNOWLEDGMENT FOR SERVICE BY MAIL [ABROGATED]

[Abrogated April 22, 1993, effective December 1, 1993.]

FORM 19. MOTION TO DISMISS, PRESENTING DEFENSES OF FAILURE TO STATE A CLAIM, OF LACK OF SERVICE OF PROCESS, OF IMPROPER VENUE, AND OF LACK OF JURISDICTION UNDER RULE 12(b)

The defendant moves the court as follows:

1. To dismiss the action because the complaint fails to state a claim against defendant upon which relief can be granted.

2. To dismiss the action or in lieu thereof to quash the return of service of summons on the grounds (a) that the defendant is a corporation organized under the laws of Delaware and was not and is not subject to service of process within the Southern District of New York, and (b) that the defendant has not been properly served with process in this action, all of which more clearly appears in the affidavits of M. N. and X. Y. hereto annexed as Exhibit A and Exhibit B respectively.

3. To dismiss the action on the ground that it is in the wrong district because (a) the jurisdiction of this court is invoked solely on the ground that the action arises under the Constitution and laws of the United States and (b) the defendant is a corporation incorporated under the laws of the State of Delaware and is not licensed to do or doing business in the Southern District of New York, all of which more clearly appears in the affidavits of K. L. and V. W. hereto annexed as Exhibits C and D respectively.

4. To dismiss the action on the ground that the court lacks jurisdiction because the amount actually in controversy is less than ten thousand dollars exclusive of interest and costs.*

Signed: _____

Attorney for Defendant.

Address: _____

Notice of Motion

To: _____
        Attorney for Plaintiff.

_____

Please take notice, that the undersigned will bring the above motion on for hearing before this Court at Room _____, United States Court House, Foley Square, City of New York, on the _____ day of _____, 20__, at 10 o'clock in the forenoon of that day or as soon thereafter as counsel can be heard.

Signed: _____

Attorney for Defendant.

Address: _____

[Amended December 29, 1948, effective October 20, 1949; April 17, 1961, effective July 19, 1961; March 27, 2003, effective December 1, 2003.]

Notes of Advisory Committee

1. The above motion and notice of motion may be combined and denominated Notice of Motion. See Rule 7(b).

2. As to paragraph 3, see U.S.C., Title 28, § 1391 (Venue generally), subsections (b) and (c).

3. As to paragraph 4, see U.S.C., Title 28, § 1331 (Federal question; amount in controversy; costs), as amended by P.L. 85–554, 72 Stat. 415, July 25, 1958, requiring that the amount in controversy, exclusive of interest and costs, be in excess of $10,000.*

* Pub. Note: The $10,000 minimum amount in controversy requirement of the federal question jurisdiction statute was repealed in 1980. 28 U.S.C.A. § 1331, as amended by Pub.L. 96–486, § 2(a), December 1, 1980, 94 Stat. 2369. Also note that the amount in controversy required in diversity of citizenship suits under 28 U.S.C.A. § 1332(a) was increased to $75,000 by Pub.L. 104–317, Title II, § 205(a), October 19, 1996, 110 Stat. 385.

FORM 20. ANSWER PRESENTING DEFENSES UNDER RULE 12(b)

First Defense

The complaint fails to state a claim against defendant upon which relief can be granted.

Second Defense

If defendant is indebted to plaintiffs for the goods mentioned in the complaint, he is indebted to them jointly with G. H. G. H. is alive; is a citizen of the State of New York and a resident of this district, is subject to the jurisdiction of this court, as to both service of process and venue; can be made a party without depriving this court of jurisdiction of the present parties, and has not been made a party.

Third Defense

Defendant admits the allegation contained in paragraphs 1 and 4 of the complaint; alleges that he is without knowledge or information sufficient to form a belief as to the truth of the allegations contained in paragraph 2 of the complaint; and denies each and every other allegation contained in the complaint.

Fourth Defense

The right of action set forth in the complaint did not accrue within six years next before the commencement of this action.

Counterclaim

(Here set forth any claim as a counterclaim in the manner in which a claim is pleaded in a complaint. No statement of the grounds on which the court's jurisdiction depends need be made unless the counterclaim requires independent grounds of jurisdiction.)

Cross-Claim Against Defendant M. N.

(Here set forth the claim constituting a cross-claim against defendant M. N. in the manner in which a claim is pleaded in a complaint. The statement of grounds upon which the court's jurisdiction depends need not be made unless the cross-claim requires independent grounds of jurisdiction.)

Notes of Advisory Committee

The above form contains examples of certain defenses provided for in Rule 12(b). The first defense challenges the legal sufficiency of the complaint. It is a substitute for a general demurrer or a motion to dismiss.

The second defense embodies the old plea in abatement; the decision thereon, however, may well provide under Rules 19 and 21 for the citing in of the party rather than an abatement of the action.

The third defense is an answer on the merits.

The fourth defense is one of the affirmative defenses provided for in Rule 8(c).

The answer also includes a counterclaim and a cross-claim.

[The Notes incorporate revisions made by the Advisory Committee at the same time amendments to certain other rules were made by Order dated December 27, 1946, effective March 19, 1948.]

FORM 21. ANSWER TO COMPLAINT SET FORTH IN FORM 8, WITH COUNTERCLAIM FOR INTERPLEADER

Defense

Defendant admits the allegations stated in paragraph 1 of the complaint; and denies the allegations stated in paragraph 2 to the extent set forth in the counterclaim herein.

Counterclaim for Interpleader

1. Defendant received the sum of _____ dollars as a deposit from E. F.

2. Plaintiff has demanded the payment of such deposit to him by virtue of an assignment of it which he claims to have received from E. F.

3. E. F. has notified the defendant that he claims such deposit, that the purported assignment is not valid, and that he holds the defendant responsible for the deposit.

Wherefore defendant demands:

(1) That the court order E. F. to be made a party defendant to respond to the complaint and to this counterclaim.[1]

(2) That the court order the plaintiff and E. F. to interplead their respective claims.

(3) That the court adjudge whether the plaintiff or E. F. is entitled to the sum of money.

(4) That the court discharge defendant from all liability in the premises except to the person it shall adjudge entitled to the sum of money.

(5) That the court award to the defendant its costs and attorney's fees.

1. Rule 13(h) provides for the court ordering parties to a counterclaim, but who are not parties to the original action, to be brought in as defendants.

[Amended January 21, 1963, effective July 1, 1963.]

FORM 22. MOTION TO BRING IN THIRD–PARTY DEFENDANT [SUPERSEDED]

[Superseded by Forms 22–A and 22–B January 21, 1963, effective July 1, 1963.]

FORM 22–A. SUMMONS AND COMPLAINT AGAINST THIRD–PARTY DEFENDANT

United States District Court for the Southern District of New York

Civil Action, File Number _____

A. B., Plaintiff   )

v.   )

C. D., Defendant and)

Third-Party Plaintiff) Summons

v.   )

E. F., Third-Party)

Defendant   )

To the above-named Third-Party Defendant:

You are hereby summoned and required to serve upon _____, plaintiff's attorney whose address is _____, and upon _____, who is attorney for C. D., defendant and third-party plaintiff, and whose address is _____, an answer to the third-party complaint which is herewith served upon you within 20 days after the service of this summons upon you exclusive of the day of service. If you fail to do so, judgment by default will be taken against you for the relief demanded in the third-party complaint. There is also served upon you herewith a copy of the complaint of the plaintiff which you may but are not required to answer.

Clerk of Court.

[Seal of District Court]

Dated _____

United States District Court for the Southern District of New York

Civil Action, File Number _____

A. B., Plaintiff   )

v.   )

C. D., Defendant and)

Third-Party Plaintiff) Third-Party Complaint

v.   )

E. F., Third-Party)

Defendant   )

1. Plaintiff A. B. has filed against defendant C. D. a complaint, a copy of which is hereto attached as "Exhibit A."

2. (Here state the grounds upon which C. D. is entitled to recover from E. F., all or part of what A. B. may recover from C. D. The statement should be framed as in an original complaint.)

Wherefore C. D. demands judgment against third-party defendant E. F. for all sums [1] that may be adjudged against defendant C. D. in favor of plaintiff A. B.

Signed: _____

Attorney for C. D.,

Third-Party Plaintiff.

Address: _____

1. Make appropriate change where C. D. is entitled to only partial recovery-over against E. F.

[Adopted January 21, 1963, effective July 1, 1963.]

FORM 22-B.   MOTION TO BRING IN THIRD–PARTY DEFENDANT

Defendant moves for leave, as third-party plaintiff, to cause to be served upon E. F. a summons and third-party complaint, copies of which are hereto attached as Exhibit X.

Signed: _____

Attorney for Defendant

C. D.

Address: _____

Notice of Motion

(Contents the same as in Form 19. The notice should be addressed to all parties to the action.)

Exhibit X

(Contents the same as in Form 22–A.)

[Adopted January 21, 1963, effective July 1, 1963.]

FORM 23.   MOTION TO INTERVENE AS
A DEFENDANT UNDER RULE 24

(Based upon the complaint, Form 16)

United States District Court for the Southern District of New York
Civil Action, File Number _____

A. B., Plaintiff	)	
v.	)	*Motion to intervene as*
C. D., Defendant	)	*a defendant*
E. F., Applicant for	)	
Intervention	)	

E. F. moves for leave to intervene as a defendant in this action, in order to assert the defenses set forth in his proposed answer, of which a copy is hereto attached, on the ground that he is the manufacturer and vendor to the defendant, as well as to others, of the articles alleged in the complaint to be an infringement of plaintiff's patent, and as such has a defense to plaintiff's claim presenting both questions of law and of fact which are common to the main action.[1]

Signed: _____ ,

Attorney for E. F.,

Applicant for

Intervention.

Address: _____

Notice of Motion
(Contents the same as in Form 19)

United States District Court for the Southern District of New York
Civil Action, File Number ———

<table>
<tr><td>A. B., Plaintiff</td><td>)</td><td rowspan="4">Intervener's Answer</td></tr>
<tr><td>v.</td><td>)</td></tr>
<tr><td>C. D., Defendant</td><td>)</td></tr>
<tr><td>E. F., Intervener</td><td>)</td></tr>
</table>

First Defense

Intervener admits the allegations stated in paragraphs 1 and 4 of the complaint; denies the allegations in paragraph 3, and denies the allegations in paragraph 2 in so far as they assert the legality of the issuance of the Letters Patent to plaintiff.

Second Defense

Plaintiff is not the first inventor of the articles covered by the Letters Patent specified in his complaint, since articles substantially identical in character were previously patented in Letters Patent granted to intervener on January 5, 1920.

Signed: ——————————————,

Attorney for E. F.,

Intervener.

Address: ————————————

   1. For other grounds of intervention, either of right or in the discretion of the court, see Rule 24(a) and (b).

[Amended December 29, 1948, effective October 20, 1949.]

FORM 24. REQUEST FOR PRODUCTION OF DOCUMENTS, ETC., UNDER RULE 34

Plaintiff A. B. requests defendant C. D. to respond within ——— days to the following requests:

(1) That defendant produce and permit plaintiff to inspect and to copy each of the following documents:

(Here list the documents either individually or by category and describe each of them.)

(Here state the time, place, and manner of making the inspection and performance of any related acts.)

(2) That defendant produce and permit plaintiff to inspect and to copy, test, or sample each of the following objects:

(Here list the objects either individually or by category and describe each of them.)

(Here state the time, place, and manner of making the inspection and performance of any related acts.)

(3) That defendant permit plaintiff to enter (here describe property to be entered) and to inspect and to photograph, test or sample (here describe the portion of the real property and the objects to be inspected).

(Here state the time, place, and manner of making the inspection and performance of any related acts.)

Signed: _____,

Attorney for Plaintiff.

Address: _____

[Amended March 30, 1970, effective July 1, 1970.]

FORM 25. REQUEST FOR ADMISSION UNDER RULE 36

Plaintiff A. B. requests defendant C. D. within _____ days after service of this request to make the following admissions for the purpose of this action only and subject to all pertinent objections to admissibility which may be interposed at the trial:

1. That each of the following documents, exhibited with this request, is genuine.

(Here list the documents and describe each document.)

2. That each of the following statements is true.

(Here list the statements.)

Signed: _____,

Attorney for Plaintiff.

Address: _____

[Amended December 27, 1946, effective March 19, 1948.]

FORM 26. ALLEGATION OF REASON FOR OMITTING PARTY

When it is necessary, under Rule 19(c), for the pleader to set forth in his pleading the names of persons who ought to be made parties, but who are not so made, there should be an allegation such as the one set out below:

John Doe named in this complaint is not made a party to this action [because he is not subject to the jurisdiction of this court]; [because he cannot be made a party to this action without depriving this court of jurisdiction].

FORM 27. NOTICE OF APPEAL TO COURT OF APPEALS UNDER [FORMER] RULE 73(b) [ABROGATED]

[Abrogated December 4, 1967, effective July 1, 1968.]

Notes of Advisory Committee

The form of notice of appeal is transferred to the Federal Rules of Appellate Procedure as Form 1.

FORM 28. NOTICE: CONDEMNATION

United States District Court for the Southern District of New York

CIVIL ACTION, FILE NUMBER _____

UNITED STATES OF AMERICA,   )
            PLAINTIFF   )
               v.   )
1,000 ACRES OF LAND IN [here insert)
    a general location as "City of) *Notice*
    _____" or "County of _____"],)
    JOHN DOE ET AL., AND UNKNOWN   )
        OWNERS, DEFENDANTS   )

To (here insert the names of the defendants to whom the notice is directed):

You are hereby notified that a complaint in condemnation has heretofore been filed in the office of the clerk of the United States District Court for the Southern District of New York, in the United States Court House in New York City, New York, for the taking (here state the interest to be acquired, as "an estate in fee simple") for use (here state briefly the use, "as a site for a post-office building") of the following described property in which you have or claim an interest.

(Here insert brief description of the property in which the defendants, to whom the notice is directed, have or claim an interest.)

The authority for the taking is (here state briefly, as "the Act of _____, _____ Stat. _____, U.S.C., Title _____, § _____".) [1]

You are further notified that if you desire to present any objection or defense to the taking of your property you are required to serve your answer on the plaintiff's attorney at the address herein designated within twenty days after _____. [2]

Your answer shall identify the property in which you claim to have an interest, state the nature and extent of the interest you claim, and state all of your objections and defenses to the taking of your property. All defenses and objections not so presented are waived. And in case of your failure so to answer the complaint, judgment of condemnation of that part of the above-described property in which you have or claim an interest will be rendered.

But without answering, you may serve on the plaintiff's attorney a notice of appearance designating the property in which you claim to be interested. Thereafter you will receive notice of all proceedings affecting it. At the trial of the issue of just compensation, whether or not you have previously appeared or answered, you may present evidence as to the amount of the compensation to be paid for your property, and you may share in the distribution of the award.

_____

                                   United States Attorney.

                    Address _____

(Here state an address within the district where the United States Attorney may be served as "United States Court House, New York, N. Y.")

Dated _____

1. And where appropriate add a citation to any applicable Executive Order.

2. Here insert the words "personal service of this notice upon you," if personal service is to be made pursuant to subdivision (d)(3)(i) of this rule [Rule 71A]; or, insert the date of the last publication of notice, if service by publication is to be made pursuant to subdivision (d)(3)(ii) of this rule. [*Pub. Note: Subdivisions (d)(3)(i) and (d)(3)(ii) were renumbered as (d)(3)(A) and (d)(3)(B), effective December 1, 1993.*]

[Adopted April 30, 1951, effective August 1, 1951.]

FORM 29. COMPLAINT: CONDEMNATION

United States District Court for the Southern District of New York

CIVIL ACTION, FILE NUMBER _____

UNITED STATES OF AMERICA,
    PLAINTIFF
        v.
1,000 ACRES OF LAND IN [here insert
    a general location as "City of
_____" or "County of _____"],
    JOHN DOE ET AL., AND UNKNOWN
        OWNERS, DEFENDANTS
	)
	)
	)
	)
	)
	)
	)
	)
	)
	)
		Complaint

1. This is an action of a civil nature brought by the United States of America for the taking of property under the power of eminent domain and for the ascertainment and award of just compensation to the owners and parties in interest.[1]

2. The authority for the taking is (here state briefly, as "the Act of _____, _____ Stat. _____, U.S.C., Title _____, § _____").[2]

3. The use for which the property is to be taken is (here state briefly the use, "as a site for a post-office building").

4. The interest to be acquired in the property is (here state the interest as "an estate in fee simple").

5. The property so to be taken is (here set forth a description of the property sufficient for its identification) or (described in Exhibit A hereto attached and made a part hereof).

6. The persons known to the plaintiff to have or claim an interest in the property [3] are:

    (Here set forth the names of such persons and the interests claimed.) [4]

7. In addition to the persons named, there are or may be others who have or may claim some interest in the property to be taken, whose names are unknown to the plaintiff and on diligent inquiry have not been ascertained. They are made parties to the action under the designation "Unknown Owners."

Wherefore the plaintiff demands judgment that the property be condemned and that just compensation for the taking be ascertained and awarded and for such other relief as may be lawful and proper.

_____

United States Attorney.

Address _____

    (Here state an address within the district where the United States Attorney may be served, as "United States Court House, New York, N. Y.")

    1. If the plaintiff is not the United States, but is, for example, a corporation invoking the power of eminent domain delegated to it by the state, then this paragraph 1 of the complaint should be appropriately modified and should be preceded by a paragraph appropriately alleging federal jurisdiction for the action, such as diversity. See Form 2.

    2. And where appropriate add a citation to any applicable Executive Order.

    3. At the commencement of the action the plaintiff need name as defendants only the persons having or claiming an interest in the property whose names are then known, but prior to any hearing involving the compensation to be paid for a particular piece of property the plaintiff must add as defendants all persons having or claiming an interest in that property whose names can be ascertained by an appropriate search of the records and also those whose names have otherwise been learned. See Rule 71A(c)(2).

    4. The plaintiff should designate, as to each separate piece of property, the defendants who have been joined as owners thereof or of some interest therein. See Rule 71A(c)(2).

[Adopted April 30, 1951, effective August 1, 1951.]

FORM 30. SUGGESTION OF DEATH UPON
THE RECORD UNDER RULE 25(a)(1)

A. B. [describe as a party, or as executor, administrator, or other representative or successor of C. D., the deceased party] suggests upon the record, pursuant to Rule 25(a)(1), the death of C. D. [describe as party] during the pendency of this action.

[Adopted January 21, 1963, effective July 1, 1963.]

FORM 31. JUDGMENT ON JURY VERDICT

United States District Court for the Southern District of New York

Civil Action, File Number _____

A. B., Plaintiff	)	
v.	)	*Judgment*
C. D., Defendant	)	

This action came on for trial before the Court and a jury, Honorable John Marshall, District Judge, presiding, and the issues having been duly tried and the jury having duly rendered its verdict,

It is Ordered and Adjudged

[that the plaintiff A. B. recover of the defendant C. D. the sum of _____, with interest thereon at the rate of _____ per cent as provided by law, and his costs of action.]

[that the plaintiff take nothing, that the action be dismissed on the merits, and that the defendant C. D. recover of the plaintiff A. B. his costs of action.]

Dated at New York, New York, this _____ day of _____, 20___.

_____

Clerk of Court.

[Adopted January 21, 1963, effective July 1 1963; March 27, 2003, effective December 1, 2003.]

Notes of Advisory Committee

1. This Form is illustrative of the judgment to be entered upon the general verdict of a jury. It deals with the cases where there is a general jury verdict awarding the plaintiff money damages or finding for the defendant, but is adaptable to other situations of jury verdicts.

2. The clerk, unless the court otherwise orders, is required forthwith to prepare, sign, and enter the judgment upon a general jury verdict without awaiting any direction by the court. The form of the judgment upon a special verdict or a general verdict accompanied by answers to interrogatories shall be promptly approved by the court, and the clerk shall thereupon enter it. See Rule 58, as amended.

3. The Rules contemplate a simple judgment promptly entered. See Rule 54(a). Every judgment shall be set forth on a separate document. See Rule 58, as amended.

4. Attorneys are not to submit forms of judgment unless directed in exceptional cases to do so by the court. See Rule 58, as amended.

FORM 32. JUDGMENT ON DECISION BY THE COURT

United States District Court for the Southern District of New York

Civil Action, File Number _____

A. B., Plaintiff) v.) *Judgment* C. D., Defendant)	

This action came on for [trial] [hearing] before the Court, Honorable John Marshall, District Judge, presiding, and the issues having been duly [tried] [heard] and a decision having been duly rendered,

It is Ordered and Adjudged

[that the plaintiff A. B. recover of the defendant C. D. the sum of _____, with interest thereon at the rate of _____ per cent as provided by law, and his costs of action.]

[that the plaintiff take nothing, that the action be dismissed on the merits, and that the defendant C. D. recover of the plaintiff A. B. his costs of action.]

Dated at New York, New York, this _____ day of _____, 20__.

_____

Clerk of Court.

[Adopted January 21, 1963, effective July 1, 1963;; March 27, 2003, effective December 1, 2003.]

Notes of Advisory Committee

1. This Form is illustrative of the judgment to be entered upon a decision of the court. It deals with the cases of decisions by the court awarding a party only money damages or costs, but is adaptable to other decisions by the court.

2. The clerk, unless the court otherwise orders, is required forthwith, without awaiting any direction by the court, to prepare, sign, and enter the judgment upon a decision by the court that a party shall recover only a sum certain or costs or that all relief shall be denied. The form of the judgment upon a decision by the court granting other relief shall be promptly approved by the court, and the clerk shall thereupon enter it. See Rule 58, as amended.

3. See also paragraphs 3–4 of the Explanatory Note to Form 31.

FORM 33. NOTICE OF AVAILABILITY OF MAGISTRATE JUDGE TO EXERCISE JURISDICTION

In accordance with the provisions of Title 28, U.S.C. § 636(c), you are hereby notified that a United States magistrate judge of this district court is available to exercise the court's jurisdiction and to conduct any or all proceedings in this case including a jury or nonjury trial, and entry of a final judgment. Exercise of this jurisdiction by a magistrate judge is, however, permitted only if all parties voluntarily consent.

You may, without adverse substantive consequences, withhold your consent, but this will prevent the court's jurisdiction from being exercised by a magistrate judge. If any party withholds consent, the identity of the parties consenting or withholding consent will not be communicated to any magistrate judge or to the district judge to whom the case has been assigned.

An appeal from a judgment entered by a magistrate judge may be taken directly to the United States court of appeals for this judicial circuit in the same manner as an appeal from any other judgment of a district court.

Copies of the Form for the "Consent to Jurisdiction by a United States Magistrate Judge" are available from the clerk of the court.

[Adopted April 28, 1983, effective August 1, 1983; amended April 22, 1993, effective December 1, 1993; April 11, 1997, effective December 1, 1997.]

FORM 34. CONSENT TO EXERCISE OF JURISDICTION
BY A UNITED STATES MAGISTRATE JUDGE

UNITED STATES DISTRICT COURT
_____ DISTRICT OF _____

	)	
Plaintiff,	)	
	)	
vs.	)	Docket No. _____
	)	
Defendant.	)	

CONSENT TO JURISDICTION BY A UNITED STATES MAGISTRATE JUDGE

In accordance with the provisions of Title 28, U.S.C. § 636(c), the undersigned party or parties to the above-captioned civil matter hereby voluntarily consent to have a United States magistrate judge conduct any and all further proceedings in the case, including trial, and order the entry of a final judgment.

_____   _____
            Date   Signature

Note: Return this form to the Clerk of the Court if you consent to jurisdiction by a magistrate judge. Do not send a copy of this form to any district judge or magistrate judge.

[Adopted April 28, 1983, effective August 1, 1983; amended April 22, 1993, effective December 1, 1993; April 11, 1997, effective December 1, 1997.]

FORM 34A. ORDER OF REFERENCE

UNITED STATES DISTRICT COURT
_____ DISTRICT OF _____

	)	
Plaintiff,	)	
	)	
vs.	)	Docket No. _____
	)	
Defendant.	)	

ORDER OF REFERENCE

IT IS HEREBY ORDERED that the above-captioned matter be referred to United States Magistrate Judge _____ for all further proceedings and entry of judgment in accordance with Title 28, U.S.C. § 636(c) and the consent of the parties.

_____
U. S. District Judge

[Adopted April 22, 1993, effective December 1, 1993.]

FORM 35.   REPORT OF PARTIES' PLANNING MEETING

[Caption and Names of Parties]

1. Pursuant to Fed.R.Civ.P. 26(f), a meeting was held on __(date)__ at __(place)__ and was attended by:

> __(name)__ for plaintiff(s)
> __(name)__ for defendant(s) __(party name)__
> __(name)__ for defendant(s) __(party name)__

2. **Pre-discovery Disclosures.** The parties [have exchanged] [will exchange by __(date)__] the information required by [Fed.R.Civ.P. 26(a)(1)] [local rule __].

3. **Discovery Plan.** The parties jointly propose to the court the following discovery plan: [Use separate paragraphs or subparagraphs as necessary if parties disagree.]

Discovery will be needed on the following subjects: __(brief description of subjects on which discovery will be needed)__
All discovery commenced in time to be completed by __(date)__ . [Discovery on __(issue for early discovery)__ to be completed by __(date)__ .]
Maximum of __ interrogatories by each party to any other party. [Responses due __ days after service.]
Maximum of __ requests for admission by each party to any other party. [Responses due __ days after service.]
Maximum of __ depositions by plaintiff(s) and __ by defendant(s).
Each deposition [other than of _____] limited to maximum of __ hours unless extended by agreement of parties.
Reports from retained experts under Rule 26(a)(2) due:
> from plaintiff(s) by __(date)__
> from defendant(s) by __(date)__
Supplementations under Rule 26(e) due __(time(s) or interval(s))__ .

4. **Other Items.** [Use separate paragraphs or subparagraphs as necessary if parties disagree.]

The parties [request] [do not request] a conference with the court before entry of the scheduling order.
The parties request a pretrial conference in __(month and year)__ .
Plaintiff(s) should be allowed until __(date)__ to join additional parties and until __(date)__ to amend the pleadings.
Defendant(s) should be allowed until __(date)__ to join additional parties and until __(date)__ to amend the pleadings.
All potentially dispositive motions should be filed by __(date)__ .
Settlement [is likely] [is unlikely] [cannot be evaluated prior to __(date)__] [*may be enhanced by use of the following alternative dispute resolution procedure: [_____].
Final lists of witnesses and exhibits under Rule 26(a)(3) should be due
> from plaintiff(s) by __(date)__
> from defendant(s) by __(date)__
Parties should have __ days after service of final lists of witnesses and exhibits to list objections under Rule 26(a)(3).
The case should be ready for trial by __(date)__ [and at this time is expected to take approximately __(length of time)__].
[Other matters.]

Date: _____

[Adopted April 22, 1993, effective December 1, 1993.]

* Pub. Note: So in original, without closed bracket.

SUPPLEMENTAL RULES FOR CERTAIN ADMIRALTY AND MARITIME CLAIMS

Effective July 1, 1966

Including Amendments Effective December 1, 2002

RULE A. SCOPE OF RULES

These Supplemental Rules apply to the procedure in admiralty and maritime claims within the meaning of Rule 9(h) with respect to the following remedies:

(1) Maritime attachment and garnishment;

(2) Actions in rem;

(3) Possessory, petitory, and partition actions;

(4) Actions for exoneration from or limitation of liability.

These rules also apply to the procedure in statutory condemnation proceedings analogous to maritime actions in rem, whether within the admiralty and maritime jurisdiction or not. Except as otherwise provided, references in these Supplemental Rules to actions in rem include such analogous statutory condemnation proceedings.

The general Rules of Civil Procedure for the United States District Courts are also applicable to the foregoing proceedings except to the extent that they are inconsistent with these Supplemental Rules.

RULE B. IN PERSONAM ACTIONS; ATTACHMENT AND GARNISHMENT

(1) When Available; Complaint, Affidavit, Judicial Authorization, and Process. In an in personam action:

(a) If a defendant is not found within the district, a verified complaint may contain a prayer for process to attach the defendant's tangible or intangible personal property—up to the amount sued for—in the hands of garnishees named in the process.

(b) The plaintiff or the plaintiff's attorney must sign and file with the complaint an affidavit stating that, to the affiant's knowledge, or on information and belief, the defendant cannot be found within the district. The court must review the complaint and affidavit and, if the conditions of this Rule B appear to exist, enter an order so stating and authorizing process of attachment and garnishment. The clerk may issue supplemental process enforcing the court's order upon application without further court order.

(c) If the plaintiff or the plaintiff's attorney certifies that exigent circumstances make court review impracticable, the clerk must issue the summons and process of attachment and garnishment. The plaintiff has the burden in any post-attachment hearing under Rule E(4)(f) to show that exigent circumstances existed.

(d)(i) If the property is a vessel or tangible property on board a vessel, the summons, process, and any supplemental process must be delivered to the marshal for service.

(ii) If the property is other tangible or intangible property, the summons, process, and any supplemental process must be delivered to a person or organization authorized to serve it, who may be (A) a marshal; (B) someone under contract with the United States; (C) someone specially appointed by the court for that purpose; or, (D) in an action brought by the United States, any officer or employee of the United States.

(e) The plaintiff may invoke state-law remedies under Rule 64 for seizure of person or property for the purpose of securing satisfaction of the judgment.

(2) Notice to Defendant. No default judgment may be entered except upon proof—which may be by affidavit—that:

(a) the complaint, summons, and process of attachment or garnishment have been served on the defendant in a manner authorized by Rule 4;

(b) the plaintiff or the garnishee has mailed to the defendant the complaint, summons, and process of attachment or garnishment, using any form of mail requiring a return receipt; or

(c) the plaintiff or the garnishee has tried diligently to give notice of the action to the defendant but could not do so.

(3) Answer.

(a) *By Garnishee.* The garnishee shall serve an answer, together with answers to any interrogatories served with the complaint, within 20 days after service of process upon the garnishee. Interrogatories to the garnishee may be served with the complaint without leave of court. If the garnishee refuses or neglects to answer on oath as to the debts, credits, or effects of the defendant in the garnishee's hands, or any interrogatories concerning such debts, credits, and effects that may be propounded by the plaintiff, the court may award compulsory process against the garnishee. If the garnishee admits any debts, credits, or effects, they shall be held in the garnishee's hands or paid into the registry of the court, and shall be held in either case subject to the further order of the court.

(b) *By Defendant.* The defendant shall serve an answer within 30 days after process has been executed, whether by attachment of property or service on the garnishee.

[Amended April 29, 1985, effective August 1, 1985; March 2, 1987, effective August 1, 1987; April 17, 2000, effective December 1, 2000.]

RULE C. IN REM ACTIONS: SPECIAL PROVISIONS

(1) When Available. An action in rem may be brought:

(a) To enforce any maritime lien;

(b) Whenever a statute of the United States provides for a maritime action in rem or a proceeding analogous thereto.

Except as otherwise provided by law a party who may proceed in rem may also, or in the alternative, proceed in personam against any person who may be liable.

Statutory provisions exempting vessels or other property owned or possessed by or operated by or for the United States from arrest or seizure are not affected by this rule. When a statute so provides, an action against the United States or an instrumentality thereof may proceed on in rem principles.

(2) Complaint. In an action in rem the complaint must:

(a) be verified;

(b) describe with reasonable particularity the property that is the subject of the action;

(c) in an admiralty and maritime proceeding, state that the property is within the district or will be within the district while the action is pending;

(d) in a forfeiture proceeding for violation of a federal statute, state:

(i) the place of seizure and whether it was on land or on navigable waters;

(ii) whether the property is within the district, and if the property is not within the district the statutory basis for the court's exercise of jurisdiction over the property; and

(iii) all allegations required by the statute under which the action is brought.

(3) Judicial Authorization and Process.

(a) *Arrest Warrant.*

(i) When the United States files a complaint demanding a forfeiture for violation of a federal stat-

ute, the clerk must promptly issue a summons and a warrant for the arrest of the vessel or other property without requiring a certification of exigent circumstances, but if the property is real property the United States must proceed under applicable statutory procedures.

(ii)(A) In other actions, the court must review the complaint and any supporting papers. If the conditions for an in rem action appear to exist, the court must issue an order directing the clerk to issue a warrant for the arrest of the vessel or other property that is the subject of the action.

(B) If the plaintiff or the plaintiff's attorney certifies that exigent circumstances make court review impracticable, the clerk must promptly issue a summons and a warrant for the arrest of the vessel or other property that is the subject of the action. The plaintiff has the burden in any post-arrest hearing under Rule E(4)(f) to show that exigent circumstances existed.

(b) *Service.*

(i) If the property that is the subject of the action is a vessel or tangible property on board a vessel, the warrant and any supplemental process must be delivered to the marshal for service.

(ii) If the property that is the subject of the action is other property, tangible or intangible, the warrant and any supplemental process must be delivered to a person or organization authorized to enforce it, who may be: (A) a marshal; (B) someone under contract with the United States; (C) someone specially appointed by the court for that purpose; or, (D) in an action brought by the United States, any officer or employee of the United States.

(c) *Deposit in Court.* If the property that is the subject of the action consists in whole or in part of freight, the proceeds of property sold, or other intangible property, the clerk must issue—in addition to the warrant—a summons directing any person controlling the property to show cause why it should not be deposited in court to abide the judgment.

(d) *Supplemental Process.* The clerk may upon application issue supplemental process to enforce the court's order without further court order.

(4) Notice. No notice other than execution of process is required when the property that is the subject of the action has been released under Rule E(5). If the property is not released within 10 days after execution, the plaintiff must promptly—or within the time that the court allows—give public notice of the action and arrest in a newspaper designated by court order and having general circulation in the district, but publication may be terminated if the property is released before publication is completed. The notice must specify the time under Rule C(6) to file a statement of interest in or right against the seized property and to answer. This rule does not affect the notice requirements in an action to foreclose a preferred ship mortgage under 46 U.S.C. §§ 31301 et seq., as amended.

(5) Ancillary Process. In any action in rem in which process has been served as provided by this rule, if any part of the property that is the subject of the action has not been brought within the control of the court because it has been removed or sold, or because it is intangible property in the hands of a person who has not been served with process, the court may, on motion, order any person having possession or control of such property or its proceeds to show cause why it should not be delivered into the custody of the marshal or other person or organization having a warrant for the arrest of the property, or paid into court to abide the judgment; and, after hearing, the court may enter such judgment as law and justice may require.

(6) Responsive Pleading; Interrogatories.

(a) *Civil Forfeiture.* In an in rem forfeiture action for violation of a federal statute:

(i) a person who asserts an interest in or right against the property that is the subject of the action must file a verified statement identifying the interest or right:

(A) within 30 days after the earlier of (1) the date of service of the Government's complaint or (2) completed publication of notice under Rule C(4), or

(B) within the time that the court allows.

(ii) an agent, bailee, or attorney must state the authority to file a statement of interest in or right against the property on behalf of another; and

(iii) a person who files a statement of interest in or right against the property must serve and file an answer within 20 days after filing the statement.

(b) *Maritime Arrests and Other Proceedings.* In an in rem action not governed by Rule C(6)(a):

(i) A person who asserts a right of possession or any ownership interest in the property that is the subject of the action must file a verified statement of right or interest:

(A) within 10 days after the earlier of (1) the execution of process, or (2) completed publication of notice under Rule C(4), or

(B) within the time that the court allows;

(ii) the statement of right or interest must describe the interest in the property that supports the person's demand for its restitution or right to defend the action;

(iii) an agent, bailee, or attorney must state the authority to file a statement of right or interest on behalf of another; and

(iv) a person who asserts a right of possession or any ownership interest must serve an answer within 20 days after filing the statement of interest or right.

(c) *Interrogatories.* Interrogatories may be served with the complaint in an in rem action without leave of court. Answers to the interrogatories must be served with the answer to the complaint.

[Amended April 29, 1985, effective August 1, 1985; March 2, 1987, effective August 1, 1987; April 30, 1991, effective December 1, 1991; April 17, 2000, effective December 1, 2000; April 29, 2002, effective December 1, 2002.]

RULE D. POSSESSORY, PETITORY, AND PARTITION ACTIONS

In all actions for possession, partition, and to try title maintainable according to the course of the admiralty practice with respect to a vessel, in all actions so maintainable with respect to the possession of cargo or other maritime property, and in all actions by one or more part owners against the others to obtain security for the return of the vessel from any voyage undertaken without their consent, or by one or more part owners against the others to obtain possession of the vessel for any voyage on giving security for its safe return, the process shall be by a warrant of arrest of the vessel, cargo, or other property, and by notice in the manner provided by Rule B(2) to the adverse party or parties.

RULE E. ACTIONS IN REM AND QUASI IN REM: GENERAL PROVISIONS

(1) Applicability. Except as otherwise provided, this rule applies to actions in personam with process of maritime attachment and garnishment, actions in rem, and petitory, possessory, and partition actions, supplementing Rules B, C, and D.

(2) Complaint; Security.

(a) *Complaint.* In actions to which this rule is applicable the complaint shall state the circumstances from which the claim arises with such particularity that the defendant or claimant will be able, without moving for a more definite statement, to commence an investigation of the facts and to frame a responsive pleading.

(b) *Security for Costs.* Subject to the provisions of Rule 54(d) and of relevant statutes, the court may, on the filing of the complaint or on the appearance of any defendant, claimant, or any other party, or at any later time, require the plaintiff, defendant, claimant, or other party to give security, or additional security, in such sum as the court shall direct to pay all costs and expenses that shall be awarded against the party by any interlocutory order or by the final judgment, or on appeal by any appellate court.

(3) Process.

(a) In admiralty and maritime proceedings process in rem or of maritime attachment and garnishment may be served only within the district.

(b) In forfeiture cases process in rem may be served within the district or outside the district when authorized by statute.

(c) Issuance and Delivery. Issuance and delivery of process in rem, or of maritime attachment and garnishment, shall be held in abeyance if the plaintiff so requests.

(4) Execution of Process; Marshal's Return; Custody of Property; Procedures for Release.

(a) *In General.* Upon issuance and delivery of the process, or, in the case of summons with process of attachment and garnishment, when it appears that the defendant cannot be found within the district, the marshal or other person or organization having a warrant shall forthwith execute the process in accordance with this subdivision (4), making due and prompt return.

(b) *Tangible Property.* If tangible property is to be attached or arrested, the marshal or other person or organization having the warrant shall take it into the marshal's possession for safe custody. If the character or situation of the property is such that the taking of actual possession is impracticable, the marshal or other person executing the process shall affix a copy thereof to the property in a conspicuous place and leave a copy of the complaint and process with the person having possession or the person's agent. In furtherance of the marshal's custody of any vessel the marshal is authorized to make a written request to the collector of customs not to grant clearance to such vessel until notified by the marshal or deputy marshal or by the clerk that the vessel has been released in accordance with these rules.

(c) *Intangible Property.* If intangible property is to be attached or arrested the marshal or other person or organization having the warrant shall execute the process by leaving with the garnishee or other obligor a copy of the complaint and process requiring the garnishee or other obligor to answer as provided in Rules B(3)(a) and C(6); or the marshal may accept for payment into the registry of the court the amount owed to the extent of the amount claimed by the plaintiff with interest and costs, in which event the garnishee or other obligor shall not be required to answer unless alias process shall be served.

(d) *Directions With Respect to Property in Custody.* The marshal or other person or organization having the warrant may at any time apply to the court for directions with respect to property that has been attached or arrested, and shall give notice of such application to any or all of the parties as the court may direct.

(e) *Expenses of Seizing and Keeping Property; Deposit.* These rules do not alter the provisions of Title 28, U.S.C., § 1921, as amended, relative to the expenses of seizing and keeping property attached or arrested and to the requirement of deposits to cover such expenses.

(f) *Procedure for Release From Arrest or Attachment.* Whenever property is arrested or attached, any person claiming an interest in it shall be entitled to a prompt hearing at which the plaintiff shall be required to show why the arrest or attachment should not be vacated or other relief granted consistent with these rules. This subdivision shall have no application to suits for seamen's wages when process is issued upon a certification of sufficient cause filed pursuant to Title 46, U.S.C. §§ 603 and 604* or to actions by the United States for forfeitures for violation of any statute of the United States.

(5) Release of Property.

(a) *Special Bond.* Except in cases of seizures for forfeiture under any law of the United States, whenever process of maritime attachment and garnishment or process in rem is issued the execution of such process shall be stayed, or the property released, on the giving of security, to be approved by the court or clerk, or by stipulation of the parties, conditioned to answer the judgment of the court or of any appellate court. The parties may stipulate the amount and nature of such security. In the event of the inability or refusal of the parties so to stipulate the court shall fix the principal sum of the bond or stipulation at an amount sufficient to cover the amount of the plaintiff's claim fairly stated with accrued interest and costs; but the principal sum shall in no event exceed (i) twice the amount of the plaintiff's claim or (ii) the value of the property on due appraisement, whichever is smaller. The bond or stipulation shall be conditioned for the payment of the principal sum and interest thereon at 6 per cent per annum.

(b) *General Bond.* The owner of any vessel may file a general bond or stipulation, with sufficient surety, to be approved by the court, conditioned to answer the judgment of such court in all or any actions that may be brought thereafter in such court in which the vessel is attached or arrested. Thereupon the execution of all such process against such vessel shall be stayed so long as the amount secured by such bond or stipulation is at least double the aggregate amount claimed by plaintiffs in all actions begun and pending in which such vessel has been attached or arrested. Judgments and remedies may be had on such bond or stipulation as if a special bond or stipulation had been filed in each of such actions. The district court may make necessary orders to carry this rule into effect, particularly as to the giving of proper notice of any action against or attachment of a vessel for which a general bond has been filed. Such bond or stipulation shall be indorsed by the clerk with a minute of the actions wherein process is so stayed. Further security may be required by the court at any time.

If a special bond or stipulation is given in a particular case, the liability on the general bond or stipulation shall cease as to that case.

(c) *Release by Consent or Stipulation; Order of Court or Clerk; Costs.* Any vessel, cargo, or other property in the custody of the marshal or other person or organization having the warrant may be released forthwith upon the marshal's acceptance and approval of a stipulation, bond, or other security, signed by the party on whose behalf the property is detained or the party's attorney and expressly authorizing such release, if all costs and charges of the court and its officers shall have first been paid. Otherwise no property in the custody of the marshal, other person or organization having the warrant, or other officer of the court shall be released without an order of the court; but such order may be entered as of course by the clerk, upon the giving of approved security as provided by law and these rules, or upon the dismissal or discontinuance of the action; but the marshal or other person or organization having the warrant shall not deliver any property so released until the costs and charges of the officers of the court shall first have been paid.

(d) *Possessory, Petitory, and Partition Actions.* The foregoing provisions of this subdivision (5) do not apply to petitory, possessory, and partition actions. In such cases the property arrested shall be released only by order of the court, on such terms and conditions and on the giving of such security as the court may require.

(6) Reduction or Impairment of Security. Whenever security is taken the court may, on motion and hearing, for good cause shown, reduce the amount of security given; and if the surety shall be or become insufficient, new or additional sureties may be required on motion and hearing.

(7) Security on Counterclaim.

(a) When a person who has given security for damages in the original action asserts a counterclaim that arises from the transaction or occurrence that is the subject of the original action, a plaintiff for whose benefit the security has been given must give security for damages demanded in the counterclaim unless the court, for cause shown, directs otherwise. Proceedings on the original claim must be stayed until this security is given, unless the court directs otherwise.

(b) The plaintiff is required to give security under Rule E(7)(a) when the United States or its corporate instrumentality counterclaims and would have been required to give security to respond in damages if a private party but is relieved by law from giving security.

(8) Restricted Appearance. An appearance to defend against an admiralty and maritime claim with respect to which there has issued process in rem, or process of attachment and garnishment, may be expressly restricted to the defense of such claim, and in that event is not an appearance for the purposes of any other claim with respect to which such process is not available or has not been served.

(9) Disposition of Property; Sales.

(a) *Actions for Forfeitures.* In any action in rem to enforce a forfeiture for violation of a statute of the United States the property shall be disposed of as provided by statute.

(b) *Interlocutory Sales; Delivery.*

(i) On application of a party, the marshal, or other person having custody of the property, the court may order all or part of the property sold—with the sales proceeds, or as much of them as will satisfy the judgment, paid into court to await further orders of the court—if:

(A) the attached or arrested property is perishable, or liable to deterioration, decay, or injury by being detained in custody pending the action;

(B) the expense of keeping the property is excessive or disproportionate; or

(C) there is an unreasonable delay in securing release of the property.

(ii) In the circumstances described in Rule E(9)(b)(i), the court, on motion by a defendant or a person filing a statement of interest or right under Rule C(6), may order that the property, rather than being sold, be delivered to the movant upon giving security under these rules.

(c) *Sales, Proceeds.* All sales of property shall be made by the marshal or a deputy marshal, or by other person or organization having the warrant, or by any other person assigned by the court where the marshal or other person or organization having the warrant is a party in interest; and the proceeds of sale shall be forthwith paid into the registry of the court to be disposed of according to law.

(10) Preservation of Property. When the owner or another person remains in possession of property attached or arrested under the provisions of Rule E(4)(b) that permit execution of process without taking actual possession, the court, on a party's motion or on its own, may enter any order necessary to preserve the property and to prevent its removal.

* Law Revision Counsel Note: Repealed by Pub.L. 98–89, § 4(b), August 26, 1983, 97 Stat. 600, section 1 of which enacted Title 46, Shipping.

[Amended April 29, 1985, effective August 1, 1985; March 2, 1987, effective August 1, 1987; April 30, 1991, effective December 1, 1991; April 17, 2000, effective December 1, 2000.]

RULE F. LIMITATION OF LIABILITY

(1) Time for Filing Complaint; Security. Not later than six months after receipt of a claim in writing, any vessel owner may file a complaint in the appropriate district court, as provided in subdivision (9) of this rule, for limitation of liability pursuant to statute. The owner (a) shall deposit with the court, for the benefit of claimants, a sum equal to the amount or value of the owner's interest in the vessel and pending freight, or approved security therefor, and in addition such sums, or approved security therefor, as the court may from time to time fix as necessary to carry out the provisions of the statutes as amended; or (b) at the owner's option shall transfer to a trustee to be appointed by the court, for the benefit of claimants, the owner's interest in the vessel and pending freight, together with such sums, or approved security therefor, as the court may from time to time fix as necessary to carry out the provisions of the statutes as amended. The plaintiff shall also give security for costs and, if the plaintiff elects to give security, for interest at the rate of 6 percent per annum from the date of the security.

(2) Complaint. The complaint shall set forth the facts on the basis of which the right to limit liability is asserted and all facts necessary to enable the court to determine the amount to which the owner's liability shall be limited. The complaint may demand exoneration from as well as limitation of liability. It shall state the voyage if any, on which the demands sought to be limited arose, with the date and place of its termination; the amount of all demands including all unsatisfied liens or claims of lien, in contract or in tort or otherwise, arising on that voyage, so far as known to the plaintiff, and what actions and proceedings, if any, are pending thereon; whether the vessel was damaged, lost, or abandoned, and, if so, when and where; the value of the vessel at the close of the voyage or, in case of wreck, the value of her wreckage, strippings, or proceeds, if any, and where and in whose possession they are; and the amount of any pending freight recovered or recoverable. If the plaintiff elects to transfer the plaintiff's interest in the vessel to a trustee, the complaint must further show any prior paramount liens thereon, and what voyages or trips, if any, she has made since the voyage or trip on which the claims sought to be limited arose, and any existing liens arising upon any such subsequent voyage or trip, with the amounts and causes thereof, and the names and addresses of the lienors, so far as known; and whether the vessel sustained any injury upon or by reason of such subsequent voyage or trip.

(3) Claims Against Owner; Injunction. Upon compliance by the owner with the requirements of subdivision (1) of this rule all claims and proceedings against the owner or the owner's property with respect to the matter in question shall cease. On application of the plaintiff the court shall enjoin the further prosecution of any action or proceeding against the plaintiff or the plaintiff's property with respect to any claim subject to limitation in the action.

(4) Notice to Claimants. Upon the owner's compliance with subdivision (1) of this rule the court shall issue a notice to all persons asserting claims with respect to which the complaint seeks limitation, admonishing them to file their respective claims with the clerk of the court and to serve on the attorneys for the plaintiff a copy thereof on or before a date to be named in the notice. The date so fixed shall not be less than 30 days after issuance of the notice. For cause shown, the court may enlarge the time within which claims may be filed. The notice shall be published in such newspaper or newspapers as the court may direct once a week for four successive weeks prior to the date fixed for the filing of claims. The plaintiff not later than the day of second publication shall also mail a copy of the notice to every person known to have made any claim against the vessel or the plaintiff arising out of the voyage or trip on which the claims sought to be limited arose. In cases involving death a copy of such notice shall be mailed to the decedent at the decedent's last known address, and also to any person who shall be known to have made any claim on account of such death.

(5) Claims and Answer. Claims shall be filed and served on or before the date specified in the notice provided for in subdivision (4) of this rule. Each claim shall specify the facts upon which the claimant relies in support of the claim, the items thereof, and the dates on which the same accrued. If a claimant desires to contest either the right to exoneration from or the right to limitation of liability the claimant shall file and serve an answer to the complaint unless the claim has included an answer.

(6) Information to Be Given Claimants. Within 30 days after the date specified in the notice for filing claims, or within such time as the court thereafter may allow, the plaintiff shall mail to the attorney for each claimant (or if the claimant has no attorney to the claimant) a list setting forth (a) the name of each claimant, (b) the name and address of the claimant's attorney (if the claimant is known to have one), (c) the nature of the claim, i.e., whether property loss, property damage, death, personal injury etc., and (d) the amount thereof.

(7) Insufficiency of Fund or Security. Any claimant may by motion demand that the funds deposited in court or the security given by the plaintiff be increased on the ground that they are less than the value of the plaintiff's interest in the vessel and pending freight. Thereupon the court shall cause due appraisement to be made of the value of the plaintiff's interest in the vessel and pending freight; and if the court finds that the deposit or security is either insufficient or excessive it shall order its increase or reduction. In like manner any claimant may demand that the deposit or security be increased on the ground that it is insufficient to carry out the provisions of the statutes relating to claims in respect of loss of life or bodily injury; and, after notice and hearing, the court may similarly order that the deposit or security be increased or reduced.

(8) Objections to Claims: Distribution of Fund. Any interested party may question or controvert any claim without filing an objection thereto. Upon determination of liability the fund deposited or secured, or the proceeds of the vessel and pending freight, shall be divided pro rata, subject to all relevant provisions of law, among the several claimants in proportion to the amounts of their respective claims, duly proved, saving, however, to all parties any priority to which they may be legally entitled.

(9) Venue; Transfer. The complaint shall be filed in any district in which the vessel has been attached or arrested to answer for any claim with respect to which the plaintiff seeks to limit liability; or, if the vessel has not been attached or arrested, then in any district in which the owner has been sued with respect to any such claim. When the vessel has not been attached or arrested to answer the matters aforesaid, and suit has not been commenced against the owner, the proceedings may be had in the district in which the vessel may be, but if the vessel is not within any district and no suit has been commenced in any district, then the complaint may be filed in any district. For the convenience of parties and witnesses, in the interest of justice, the court may transfer the action to any district; if venue is wrongly laid the court shall dismiss or, if it be in the interest of justice, transfer the action to any district in which it could have been brought. If the vessel shall have been sold, the proceeds shall represent the vessel for the purposes of these rules.

[Amended March 2, 1987, effective August 1, 1987.]

INDEX TO
FEDERAL RULES OF CIVIL PROCEDURE

AGENTS AND AGENCY—Cont'd
Managing Agent, generally, this index
Service,
    Process, admiralty and maritime claims, actions in rem and quasi in rem, **FRCVP E**

AGREEMENTS, PARTIES
Physical and mental examinations, **FRCVP 35**

ALTERATION
Class actions, orders, **FRCVP 23**
Judgments and decrees,
    Stay of proceedings pending motion, **FRCVP 62**
    Time for service of motion, **FRCVP 59**
Order, class action maintainable, determination, **FRCVP 23**

AMENDMENT
Admission, **FRCVP 36**
Class actions, orders, **FRCVP 23**
Conclusions of law on motion for new trial, **FRCVP 59**
Effective date of amendments to rules, **FRCVP 86**
Findings of court, **FRCVP 52**
    Extension of time, **FRCVP 6**
    Motion for new trial, **FRCVP 59**
    Stay of proceedings to enforce judgment, pending disposition of motion to amend, **FRCVP 62**
Judgments and decrees,
    Stay of proceedings pending motion, **FRCVP 62**
    Time for service of motion, **FRCVP 59**
Order, class action maintainable, determination, **FRCVP 23**
Pleadings, this index
Proof of service, **FRCVP 4(l)**
Rules by district courts, **FRCVP 83**
Summons, **FRCVP 4(a)**

AMOUNT
Jurisdiction, form of allegation, **FRCVP Form 2**
Liability, determination, further proceedings, offer of judgment, **FRCVP 68**

ANCILLARY PROCESS
Admiralty and maritime claims, actions in rem, **FRCVP C**

ANSWERS
Pleadings, this index

APPEAL AND REVIEW
Admiralty and maritime claims,
    Actions in rem and quasi in rem, security, **FRCVP E**
Application of rules, **FRCVP 81**
Class action certification, **FRCVP 23**
Correction of clerical errors, judgments, orders and record, pendency of appeal, **FRCVP 60**
Court of appeals, notice, form, **FRCVP Form 27**
Depositions pending appeal, **FRCVP 27**
District of Columbia courts, application of rules to appeals, **FRCVP 81**
Extension of time, taking appeal to court of appeals, **FRCVP 6**
Findings by court, requests for purpose of review, **FRCVP 52**
Habeas corpus cases, certification of probable cause, **FRCVP 81**
Injunctions, this index
Judgments and decrees, copy, clerk to keep correct copy of final judgment, **FRCVP 79**
Jury instructions, **FRCVP 23**
Longshoremen and Harbor Workers Compensation Act, application of rules, **FRCVP 81**
Magistrate judges,
    Judgment entered upon direction, **FRCVP 73**

APPEAL AND REVIEW—Cont'd
Notice of appeal, form on appeal, **FRCVP Form 27**
Record on appeal, service, **FRCVP 5**
Relief from failure to appeal within time, lack of notice of entry of judgment, **FRCVP 77**
Status quo, order preserving pending appeal, **FRCVP 62**
Stay pending appeal, **FRCVP 62**
Supersedeas bond, **FRCVP 62**
Taxation of costs by clerk, **FRCVP 54**
Time,
    Appeal to court of appeals, **FRCVP 6**
    Extension of time for taking, **FRCVP 6**
    Lack of notice of entry of judgment, **FRCVP 77**
    Supersedeas bond, giving, **FRCVP 62**
    Taxation of costs by clerk, **FRCVP 54**

APPEARANCE
Admiralty and maritime claims, actions in rem and quasi in rem, restricted, **FRCVP E**
Civil docket entry, **FRCVP 79**
Condemnation proceedings, **FRCVP 71A**
Service, **FRCVP 5(a)**

APPLICATION OF RULES
    Generally, **FRCVP 1, 81**
Personal property, rules governing procedure for condemnation, **FRCVP 71A**

APPLICATIONS
Intervention, **FRCVP 24**
Preliminary injunction, consolidation, hearing with trial on merits, **FRCVP 65**

APPOINTMENT
Class counsel, **FRCVP 23**
Interpreters, **FRCVP 43**
Masters, **FRCVP 53**
Process servers, **FRCVP 4(c)**

ARBITRATION AND AWARD
Affirmative defenses, **FRCVP 8**
Applicability of rules, **FRCVP 81**

ARREST
Admiralty and maritime claims, actions in rem, notice, **FRCVP C**
Satisfaction of judgment ultimately to be entered, **FRCVP 64**
Third party complaint, admiralty and maritime claims, **FRCVP 14**
United States vessels, exemptions, supplemental rules inapplicable, **FRCVP C**
Warrant for arrest,
    Admiralty and maritime claims,
        Actions in rem, **FRCVP C**
        Possessory or petitory actions, **FRCVP D**

ASSIGNMENT OF ERRORS
Jury instructions, **FRCVP 51**

ASSISTANCE
Writ, possession, delivery, **FRCVP 70**

ASSOCIATIONS AND SOCIETIES
Capacity to sue or be sued, **FRCVP 17**
Depositions,
    Oral examination,
        Failure of officer or director to attend at own deposition, sanctions, **FRCVP 37(d)**
        Failure to comply with order compelling designation, sanctions, **FRCVP 37(b)**
        Motion for order compelling designation, **FRCVP 37(a)**

STATUTORY CONDEMNATION PROCEEDINGS
Admiralty claims, applicability of supplemental rules, **FRCVP A**

STAY
Supersedeas or Stay, generally, this action

STENOGRAPHERS
Report or transcript as evidence, **FRCVP 80**

STIPULATIONS
Admiralty and maritime claims, actions in rem and quasi in rem, release, property, **FRCVP E**
Depositions,
  Taking, **FRCVP 29**
  Upon oral examination, recordation, **FRCVP 30**
Discovery procedure, **FRCVP 29**
Dismissal, **FRCVP 41**
  Action for condemnation of property, **FRCVP 71A**
Jury verdict, unanimity and size of jury, **FRCVP 48**
New trial, stipulations extending time for filing, **FRCVP 59**
Proceedings against sureties, **FRCVP 65.1**
Trial by court, **FRCVP 39**

STRIKING OF PLEADING
  Generally, **FRCVP 12**
Discovery, sanction for failure to comply with order compelling, **FRCVP 37(b)**
Motions, more definite statement, **FRCVP 12**
Third party claim, **FRCVP 14**

SUBCLASSES
Treatment, class actions, **FRCVP 23**

SUBJECT MATTER
Lack of jurisdiction, defense, **FRCVP 12**

SUBPOENAS
  Generally, **FRCVP 45**
Depositions, this index
Discovery, person in foreign country, **FRCVP 37(e)**
Masters, procuring attendance of witnesses, **FRCVP 53**
Production of documents, application of rules, **FRCVP 81**

SUBPOENA DUCES TECUM
Designation of materials in notice, taking deposition upon oral examination, **FRCVP 30**

SUBSTANTIAL RIGHTS
Disregard of error not affecting, **FRCVP 61**

SUBSTITUTION
Parties, this index

SUCCESSORS OF DECEASED PARTY
Motion for substitution, **FRCVP 25**

SUMMARIES
Business records, interrogatories, **FRCVP 33**
Foreign official records, evidence, **FRCVP 44**

SUMMARY JUDGMENT
  Generally, **FRCVP 56**
Motions, **FRCVP 12, 56**
  Findings of fact and conclusions of law, **FRCVP 52**
Pretrial conference, appropriateness and timing, **FRCVP 16**
Time, dismissal of action, **FRCVP 41**

SUMMONS
  Generally, **FRCVP 4**
Admiralty and maritime claims, actions in rem, **FRCVP C**

SUMMONS—Cont'd
Admiralty and maritime claims—Cont'd
  Attachment and garnishment, **FRCVP B**
Form, **FRCVP 4; FRCVP Form 1**
Service, **FRCVP 4**
  Application of rule to service of pleading, **FRCVP 5(a)**
  Copy of complaint to accompany, **FRCVP 4(b)**
  Third party practice, **FRCVP 14**
  Time, limit for service, **FRCVP 4(m)**
  Waiver, **FRCVP Form 1B**
    Request, **FRCVP Form 1A**
Third party defendant, **FRCVP Form 22-A**

SUNDAY
Clerks of court, business hours, **FRCVP 77**
Computation of time, **FRCVP 6**

SUPERSEDEAS OR STAY
  Generally, **FRCVP 62**
Admiralty and maritime claims, actions in rem and quasi in rem, **FRCVP E**
  Process, **FRCVP E**
Class action certification, stay pending appeal, **FRCVP 23**
Discovery, sanction for failure to comply with order compelling, **FRCVP 37(b)**
Payment of costs of previously dismissed action, **FRCVP 41**

SUPPLEMENTAL PLEADING
Generally, **FRCVP 15**

SUPPLEMENTAL PROCESS
Actions in rem, **FRCVP C**

SUPPLEMENTAL RULES
Admiralty and Maritime Claims, generally, this index

SUPPLEMENTARY PROCEEDINGS
Execution, **FRCVP 69**

SUPPLEMENTATION OF RESPONSES
Discovery, **FRCVP 26**

SURETIES AND SURETYSHIP
Admiralty and maritime claims, actions in rem and quasi in rem, security, reduction, **FRCVP E**
Proceedings against, **FRCVP 65.1**

SURPRISE
Relief from judgment on ground, **FRCVP 60**

SURVEYS OF PROPERTY OR OBJECTS
Entry Upon Land, generally, this index

TANGIBLE PROPERTY, CUSTODY
Admiralty and maritime claims, actions in rem and quasi in rem, **FRCVP E**

TELECOMMUNICATIONS
Depositions upon oral examination, **FRCVP 30**

TEMPORARY RESTRAINING ORDERS
Generally, **FRCVP 65**

TERMINATION OF ACTION
Claim or party disposed of by judgment, **FRCVP 54**

TERRITORIAL LIMITS
Service, process, admiralty and maritime claims, actions in rem and quasi in rem, **FRCVP E**

TERRITORIES
Official record, authentication, **FRCVP 44**

FEDERAL RULES OF EVIDENCE

Effective July 1, 1975

Including Amendments Effective December 1, 2003

Research Note

Rule requirements, case law applications, commentary, and references to treatises and law reviews are available in Wright and Miller, Federal Practice and Procedure, *Volume 21 et seq.; in Graham,* Handbook of Federal Evidence, 4th; *and in Goode & Wellborn,* Courtroom Handbook on Federal Evidence.

Use WESTLAW ® *to find cases citing a rule. In addition, use* WESTLAW *to search for specific terms or to update a rule; see the US–RULES, US–ORDERS and US–PL Scope Screens for further information.*

Amendments to the Federal Rules of Evidence are published, as received, in the Supreme Court Reporter, Federal Reporter 3d, Federal Supplement 2d, Federal Rules Decisions *and* Bankruptcy Reporter *advance sheets.*

Table of Rules

ARTICLE I.   GENERAL PROVISIONS

RULE 101.   SCOPE

These rules govern proceedings in the courts of the United States and before the United States bankruptcy judges and United States magistrate judges, to the extent and with the exceptions stated in rule 1101.

[Amended March 2, 1987, effective October 1, 1987; April 25, 1988, effective November 1, 1988; April 22, 1993, effective December 1, 1993.]

RULE 102.   PURPOSE AND CONSTRUCTION

These rules shall be construed to secure fairness in administration, elimination of unjustifiable expense and delay, and promotion of growth and development of the law of evidence to the end that the truth may be ascertained and proceedings justly determined.

RULE 103.   RULINGS ON EVIDENCE

(a) **Effect of Erroneous Ruling.** Error may not be predicated upon a ruling which admits or excludes evidence unless a substantial right of the party is affected, and

(1) *Objection.* In case the ruling is one admitting evidence, a timely objection or motion to strike appears of record, stating the specific ground of objection, if the specific ground was not apparent from the context; or

(2) *Offer of Proof.* In case the ruling is one excluding evidence, the substance of the evidence was made known to the court by offer or was apparent from the context within which questions were asked.

Once the court makes a definitive ruling on the record admitting or excluding evidence, either at or before trial, a party need not renew an objection or offer of proof to preserve a claim of error for appeal.

(b) **Record of Offer and Ruling.** The court may add any other or further statement which shows the character of the evidence, the form in which it was offered, the objection made, and the ruling thereon. It may direct the making of an offer in question and answer form.

(c) **Hearing of Jury.** In jury cases, proceedings shall be conducted, to the extent practicable, so as to prevent inadmissible evidence from being suggested to the jury by any means, such as making statements or offers of proof or asking questions in the hearing of the jury.

(d) **Plain Error.** Nothing in this rule precludes taking notice of plain errors affecting substantial rights although they were not brought to the attention of the court.

[Amended April 17, 2000, effective December 1, 2000.]

RULE 104.   PRELIMINARY QUESTIONS

(a) **Questions of Admissibility Generally.** Preliminary questions concerning the qualification of a person to be a witness, the existence of a privilege, or the admissibility of evidence shall be determined by the court, subject to the provisions of subdivision (b). In making its determination it is not bound by the rules of evidence except those with respect to privileges.

(b) **Relevancy Conditioned on Fact.** When the relevancy of evidence depends upon the fulfillment of a condition of fact, the court shall admit it upon, or subject to, the introduction of evidence sufficient to support a finding of the fulfillment of the condition.

(c) **Hearing of Jury.** Hearings on the admissibility of confessions shall in all cases be conducted out of the hearing of the jury. Hearings on other preliminary matters shall be so conducted when the interests of justice require, or when an accused is a witness and so requests.

(d) Testimony by Accused. The accused does not, by testifying upon a preliminary matter, become subject to cross-examination as to other issues in the case.

(e) Weight and Credibility. This rule does not limit the right of a party to introduce before the jury evidence relevant to weight or credibility.

[Amended March 2, 1987, effective October 1, 1987.]

RULE 105. LIMITED ADMISSIBILITY

When evidence which is admissible as to one party or for one purpose but not admissible as to another party or for another purpose is admitted, the court, upon request, shall restrict the evidence to its proper scope and instruct the jury accordingly.

RULE 106. REMAINDER OF OR RELATED WRITINGS OR RECORDED STATEMENTS

When a writing or recorded statement or part thereof is introduced by a party, an adverse party may require the introduction at that time of any other part or any other writing or recorded statement which ought in fairness to be considered contemporaneously with it.

[Amended March 2, 1987, effective October 1, 1987.]

ARTICLE II. JUDICIAL NOTICE

RULE 201. JUDICIAL NOTICE OF ADJUDICATIVE FACTS

(a) Scope of Rule. This rule governs only judicial notice of adjudicative facts.

(b) Kinds of Facts. A judicially noticed fact must be one not subject to reasonable dispute in that it is either (1) generally known within the territorial jurisdiction of the trial court or (2) capable of accurate and ready determination by resort to sources whose accuracy cannot reasonably be questioned.

(c) When Discretionary. A court may take judicial notice, whether requested or not.

(d) When Mandatory. A court shall take judicial notice if requested by a party and supplied with the necessary information.

(e) Opportunity to Be Heard. A party is entitled upon timely request to an opportunity to be heard as to the propriety of taking judicial notice and the tenor of the matter noticed. In the absence of prior notification, the request may be made after judicial notice has been taken.

(f) Time of Taking Notice. Judicial notice may be taken at any stage of the proceeding.

(g) Instructing Jury. In a civil action or proceeding, the court shall instruct the jury to accept as conclusive any fact judicially noticed. In a criminal case, the court shall instruct the jury that it may, but is not required to, accept as conclusive any fact judicially noticed.

ARTICLE III. PRESUMPTIONS IN CIVIL ACTIONS AND PROCEEDINGS

RULE 301. PRESUMPTIONS IN GENERAL IN CIVIL ACTIONS AND PROCEEDINGS

In all civil actions and proceedings not otherwise provided for by Act of Congress or by these rules, a presumption imposes on the party against whom it is directed the burden of going forward with evidence to rebut or meet the presumption, but does not shift to such party the burden of proof in the sense of the risk of nonpersuasion, which remains throughout the trial upon the party on whom it was originally cast.

RULE 302. APPLICABILITY OF STATE LAW IN CIVIL ACTIONS AND PROCEEDINGS

In civil actions and proceedings, the effect of a presumption respecting a fact which is an element of a claim or defense as to which State law supplies the rule of decision is determined in accordance with State law.

ARTICLE IV. RELEVANCY AND ITS LIMITS

RULE 401. DEFINITION OF "RELEVANT EVIDENCE"

"Relevant evidence" means evidence having any tendency to make the existence of any fact that is of consequence to the determination of the action more probable or less probable than it would be without the evidence.

RULE 402. RELEVANT EVIDENCE GENERALLY ADMISSIBLE; IRRELEVANT EVIDENCE INADMISSIBLE

All relevant evidence is admissible, except as otherwise provided by the Constitution of the United States, by Act of Congress, by these rules, or by other rules prescribed by the Supreme Court pursuant to statutory authority. Evidence which is not relevant is not admissible.

RULE 403. EXCLUSION OF RELEVANT EVIDENCE ON GROUNDS OF PREJUDICE, CONFUSION, OR WASTE OF TIME

Although relevant, evidence may be excluded if its probative value is substantially outweighed by the danger of unfair prejudice, confusion of the issues, or misleading the jury, or by considerations of undue delay, waste of time, or needless presentation of cumulative evidence.

RULE 404. CHARACTER EVIDENCE NOT ADMISSIBLE TO PROVE CONDUCT; EXCEPTIONS; OTHER CRIMES

(a) **Character Evidence Generally.** Evidence of a person's character or a trait of character is not admissible for the purpose of proving action in conformity therewith on a particular occasion, except:

(1) *Character of Accused.* Evidence of a pertinent trait of character offered by an accused, or by the prosecution to rebut the same, or if evidence of a trait of character of the alleged victim of the crime is offered by an accused and admitted under Rule 404(a)(2), evidence of the same trait of character of the accused offered by the prosecution;

(2) *Character of Alleged Victim.* Evidence of a pertinent trait of character of the alleged victim of the crime offered by an accused, or by the prosecution to rebut the same, or evidence of a character trait of peacefulness of the alleged victim offered by the prosecution in a homicide case to rebut evidence that the alleged victim was the first aggressor;

(3) *Character of Witness.* Evidence of the character of a witness, as provided in rules 607, 608, and 609.

(b) **Other Crimes, Wrongs, or Acts.** Evidence of other crimes, wrongs, or acts is not admissible to prove the character of a person in order to show action in conformity therewith. It may, however, be admissible for other purposes, such as proof of motive, opportunity, intent, preparation, plan, knowledge, identity, or absence of mistake or accident, provided that upon request by the accused, the prosecution in a criminal case shall provide reasonable notice in advance of trial, or during trial if the court excuses pretrial notice on good cause shown, of the general nature of any such evidence it intends to introduce at trial.

[Amended March 2, 1987, effective October 1, 1987; April 30, 1991, effective December 1, 1991; April 17, 2000, effective December 1, 2000.]

RULE 405. METHODS OF PROVING CHARACTER

(a) **Reputation or Opinion.** In all cases in which evidence of character or a trait of character of a person is admissible, proof may be made by testimony as to reputation or by testimony in the form of an opinion. On cross-examination, inquiry is allowable into relevant specific instances of conduct.

(b) **Specific Instances of Conduct.** In cases in which character or a trait of character of a person is an essential element of a charge, claim, or defense, proof may also be made of specific instances of that person's conduct.

[Amended March 2, 1987, effective October 1, 1987.]

RULE 406. HABIT; ROUTINE PRACTICE

Evidence of the habit of a person or of the routine practice of an organization, whether corroborated or not and regardless of the presence of eyewitnesses, is relevant to prove that the conduct of the person or organization on a particular occasion was in conformity with the habit or routine practice.

RULE 407. SUBSEQUENT REMEDIAL MEASURES

When, after an injury or harm allegedly caused by an event, measures are taken that, if taken previously, would have made the injury or harm less likely to occur, evidence of the subsequent measures is not admissible to prove negligence, culpable conduct, a defect in a product, a defect in a product's design, or a need for a warning or instruction. This rule does not require the exclusion of evidence of subsequent measures when offered for another purpose, such as proving ownership, control, or feasibility of precautionary measures, if controverted, or impeachment.

[Amended April 11, 1997, effective December 1, 1997.]

RULE 408. COMPROMISE AND OFFERS TO COMPROMISE

Evidence of (1) furnishing or offering or promising to furnish, or (2) accepting or offering or promising to accept, a valuable consideration in compromising or attempting to compromise a claim which was disputed as to either validity or amount, is not admissible to prove liability for or invalidity of the claim or its amount. Evidence of conduct or statements made in compromise negotiations is likewise not admissible. This rule does not require the exclusion of any evidence otherwise discoverable merely because it is presented in the course of compromise negotiations. This rule also does not require exclusion when the evidence is offered for another purpose, such as proving bias or prejudice of a witness, negativing a contention of undue delay, or proving an effort to obstruct a criminal investigation or prosecution.

RULE 409. PAYMENT OF MEDICAL AND SIMILAR EXPENSES

Evidence of furnishing or offering or promising to pay medical, hospital, or similar expenses occasioned by an injury is not admissible to prove liability for the injury.

RULE 410. INADMISSIBILITY OF PLEAS, PLEA DISCUSSIONS, AND RELATED STATEMENTS

Except as otherwise provided in this rule, evidence of the following is not, in any civil or criminal proceeding, admissible against the defendant who made the plea or was a participant in the plea discussions:

(1) a plea of guilty which was later withdrawn;

(2) a plea of nolo contendere;

(3) any statement made in the course of any proceedings under Rule 11 of the Federal Rules of Criminal Procedure or comparable state procedure regarding either of the foregoing pleas; or

(4) any statement made in the course of plea discussions with an attorney for the prosecuting authority which do not result in a plea of guilty or which result in a plea of guilty later withdrawn.

However, such a statement is admissible (i) in any proceeding wherein another statement made in the course of the same plea or plea discussions has been introduced and the statement ought in fairness be considered contemporaneously with it, or (ii) in a criminal proceeding for perjury or false statement if the statement was made by the defendant under oath, on the record and in the presence of counsel.

[Amended by Pub.L. 94–149, § 1(9), December 12, 1975, 89 Stat. 805; amended April 30, 1979, effective December 1, 1980 (effective date pursuant to Pub.L. 96–42, July 31, 1979, 93 Stat. 326).]

RULE 411. LIABILITY INSURANCE

Evidence that a person was or was not insured against liability is not admissible upon the issue whether the person acted negligently or otherwise wrongfully. This rule does not require the exclusion of evidence of insurance against liability when offered for another purpose, such as proof of agency, ownership, or control, or bias or prejudice of a witness.

[Amended March 2, 1987, effective October 1, 1987.]

RULE 412. SEX OFFENSE CASES; RELEVANCE OF ALLEGED VICTIM'S PAST SEXUAL BEHAVIOR OR ALLEGED SEXUAL PREDISPOSITION

(a) **Evidence Generally Inadmissible.** The following evidence is not admissible in any civil or criminal proceeding involving alleged sexual misconduct except as provided in subdivisions (b) and (c):

(1) Evidence offered to prove that any alleged victim engaged in other sexual behavior.

(2) Evidence offered to prove any alleged victim's sexual predisposition.

(b) **Exceptions.**

(1) In a criminal case, the following evidence is admissible, if otherwise admissible under these rules:

(A) evidence of specific instances of sexual behavior by the alleged victim offered to prove that a person other than the accused was the source of semen, injury or other physical evidence;

(B) evidence of specific instances of sexual behavior by the alleged victim with respect to the person accused of the sexual misconduct offered by the accused to prove consent or by the prosecution; and

(C) evidence the exclusion of which would violate the constitutional rights of the defendant.

(2) In a civil case, evidence offered to prove the sexual behavior or sexual predisposition of any alleged victim is admissible if it is otherwise admissible under these rules and its probative value substantially outweighs the danger of harm to any victim and of unfair prejudice to any party. Evidence of an alleged victim's reputation is admissible only if it has been placed in controversy by the alleged victim.

(c) **Procedure to Determine Admissibility.**

(1) A party intending to offer evidence under subdivision (b) must—

(A) file a written motion at least 14 days before trial specifically describing the evidence and stating the purpose for which it is offered unless the court, for good cause, requires a different time for filing or permits filing during trial; and

(B) serve the motion on all parties and notify the alleged victim or, when appropriate, the alleged victim's guardian or representative.

(2) Before admitting evidence under this rule the court must conduct a hearing in camera and afford the victim and parties a right to attend and be heard. The motion, related papers, and the record of the hearing must be sealed and remain under seal unless the court orders otherwise.

[Adopted by Pub.L. 95–540, § 2(a), October 28, 1978, 92 Stat. 2046, applicable to trials that begin more than 30 days after October 28, 1978; amended by Pub.L. 100–690, Title VII, § 7046(a), November 18, 1988, 102 Stat. 4400; amended April 29, 1994, effective December 1, 1994; amended by Pub.L. 103–322, Title IV, § 40141(b), September 13, 1994, 108 Stat. 1919, effective December 1, 1994.]

RULE 413. EVIDENCE OF SIMILAR CRIMES IN SEXUAL ASSAULT CASES

(a) In a criminal case in which the defendant is accused of an offense of sexual assault, evidence of the defendant's commission of another offense or offenses of sexual assault is admissible, and may be considered for its bearing on any matter to which it is relevant.

(b) In a case in which the Government intends to offer evidence under this rule, the attorney for the Government shall disclose the evidence to the defendant, including statements of witnesses or a summary of the substance of any testimony that is expected to be offered, at least fifteen days before the scheduled date of trial or at such later time as the court may allow for good cause.

(c) This rule shall not be construed to limit the admission or consideration of evidence under any other rule.

(d) For purposes of this rule and Rule 415, "offense of sexual assault" means a crime under Federal law or the law of a State (as defined in section 513 of title 18, United States Code) that involved—

(1) any conduct proscribed by chapter 109A of title 18, United States Code;

(2) contact, without consent, between any part of the defendant's body or an object and the genitals or anus of another person;

(3) contact, without consent, between the genitals or anus of the defendant and any part of another person's body;

(4) deriving sexual pleasure or gratification from the infliction of death, bodily injury, or physical pain on another person; or

(5) an attempt or conspiracy to engage in conduct described in paragraphs (1)–(4).

[Adopted by Pub.L. 103–322, Title XXXII, § 320935(a), September 13, 1994, 108 Stat. 2135, applicable to proceedings commenced on or after July 9, 1995, including all trials commenced on or after July 9, 1995 (Pub.L. 103–322, Title XXXII, § 320935(e), September 13, 1994, 108 Stat. 2137, as amended by Pub.L. 104–208, Div. A, Title I, § 101(a) [Title I, § 120], September 30, 1996, 110 Stat. 3009–25).]

RULE 414. EVIDENCE OF SIMILAR CRIMES IN CHILD MOLESTATION CASES

(a) In a criminal case in which the defendant is accused of an offense of child molestation, evidence of the defendant's commission of another offense or offenses of child molestation is admissible, and may be considered for its bearing on any matter to which it is relevant.

(b) In a case in which the Government intends to offer evidence under this rule, the attorney for the Government shall disclose the evidence to the defendant, including statements of witnesses or a summary of the substance of any testimony that is expected to be offered, at least fifteen days before the scheduled date of trial or at such later time as the court may allow for good cause.

(c) This rule shall not be construed to limit the admission or consideration of evidence under any other rule.

(d) For purposes of this rule and Rule 415, "child" means a person below the age of fourteen, and "offense of child molestation" means a crime under Federal law or the law of a State (as defined in section 513 of title 18, United States Code) that involved—

(1) any conduct proscribed by chapter 109A of title 18, United States Code, that was committed in relation to a child;

(2) any conduct proscribed by chapter 110 of title 18, United States Code;

(3) contact between any part of the defendant's body or an object and the genitals or anus of a child;

(4) contact between the genitals or anus of the defendant and any part of the body of a child;

(5) deriving sexual pleasure or gratification from the infliction of death, bodily injury, or physical pain on a child; or

(6) an attempt or conspiracy to engage in conduct described in paragraphs (1)–(5).

[Adopted by Pub.L. 103–322, Title XXXII, § 320935(a), September 13, 1994, 108 Stat. 2135, applicable to proceedings commenced on or after July 9, 1995, including all trials commenced on or after July 9, 1995 (Pub.L. 103–322, Title XXXII, § 320935(e), September 13, 1994, 108 Stat. 2137, as amended by Pub.L. 104–208, Div. A, Title I, § 101(a) [Title I, § 120], September 30, 1996, 110 Stat. 3009–25).]

RULE 415. EVIDENCE OF SIMILAR ACTS IN CIVIL CASES CONCERNING SEXUAL ASSAULT OR CHILD MOLESTATION

(a) In a civil case in which a claim for damages or other relief is predicated on a party's alleged commission of conduct constituting an offense of sexual assault or child molestation, evidence of that party's commission of another offense or offenses of sexual assault or child molestation is admissible and may be considered as provided in Rule 413 and Rule 414 of these rules.

(b) A party who intends to offer evidence under this Rule shall disclose the evidence to the party against whom it will be offered, including statements of witnesses or a summary of the substance of any testimony that is expected to be offered, at least fifteen days before the scheduled date of trial or at such later time as the court may allow for good cause.

(c) This rule shall not be construed to limit the admission or consideration of evidence under any other rule.

[Adopted by Pub.L. 103–322, Title XXXII, § 320935(a), September 13, 1994, 108 Stat. 2135, applicable to proceedings commenced on or after July 9, 1995, including all trials commenced on or after July 9, 1995 (Pub.L. 103–322, Title XXXII, § 320935(e), September 13, 1994, 108 Stat. 2137, as amended by Pub.L. 104–208, Div. A, Title I, § 101(a) [Title I, § 120], September 30, 1996, 110 Stat. 3009–25).]

ARTICLE V. PRIVILEGES

RULE 501. GENERAL RULE

Except as otherwise required by the Constitution of the United States or provided by Act of Congress or in rules prescribed by the Supreme Court pursuant to statutory authority, the privilege of a witness, person, government, State, or political subdivision thereof shall be governed by the principles of the common law as they may be interpreted by the courts of the United States in the light of reason and experience. However, in civil actions and proceedings, with respect to an element of a claim or defense as to which State law supplies the rule of decision, the privilege of a witness, person, government, State, or political subdivision thereof shall be determined in accordance with State law.

ARTICLE VI. WITNESSES

RULE 601. GENERAL RULE OF COMPETENCY

Every person is competent to be a witness except as otherwise provided in these rules. However, in civil actions and proceedings, with respect to an element of a claim or defense as to which State law supplies the rule of decision, the competency of a witness shall be determined in accordance with State law.

RULE 602. LACK OF PERSONAL KNOWLEDGE

A witness may not testify to a matter unless evidence is introduced sufficient to support a finding that the witness has personal knowledge of the matter. Evidence to prove personal knowledge may, but need not, consist of the witness' own testimony. This rule is subject to the provisions of rule 703, relating to opinion testimony by expert witnesses.

[Amended March 2, 1987, effective October 1, 1987; April 25, 1988, effective November 1, 1988.]

RULE 603. OATH OR AFFIRMATION

Before testifying, every witness shall be required to declare that the witness will testify truthfully, by oath or affirmation administered in a form calculated to awaken the witness' conscience and impress the witness' mind with the duty to do so.

[Amended March 2, 1987, effective October 1, 1987.]

RULE 604. INTERPRETERS

An interpreter is subject to the provisions of these rules relating to qualification as an expert and the administration of an oath or affirmation to make a true translation.

[Amended March 2, 1987, effective October 1, 1987.]

RULE 605. COMPETENCY OF JUDGE AS WITNESS

The judge presiding at the trial may not testify in that trial as a witness. No objection need be made in order to preserve the point.

RULE 606. COMPETENCY OF JUROR AS WITNESS

(a) At the Trial. A member of the jury may not testify as a witness before that jury in the trial of the case in which the juror is sitting. If the juror is called so to testify, the opposing party shall be afforded an opportunity to object out of the presence of the jury.

(b) Inquiry Into Validity of Verdict or Indictment. Upon an inquiry into the validity of a verdict or indictment, a juror may not testify as to any matter or statement occurring during the course of the jury's deliberations or to the effect of anything upon that or any other juror's mind or emotions as influencing the juror to assent to or dissent from the verdict or indictment or concerning the juror's mental processes in connection therewith, except that a juror may testify on the question whether extraneous prejudicial information was improperly brought to the jury's attention or whether any outside influence was improperly brought to bear upon any juror. Nor may a juror's affidavit or evidence of any statement by the juror concerning a matter about which the juror would be precluded from testifying be received for these purposes.

[Amended by Pub.L. 94–149, § 1(10), December 12, 1975, 89 Stat. 805; amended March 2, 1987, effective October 1, 1987.]

RULE 607. WHO MAY IMPEACH

The credibility of a witness may be attacked by any party, including the party calling the witness.

[Amended March 2, 1987, effective October 1, 1987.]

RULE 608. EVIDENCE OF CHARACTER AND CONDUCT OF WITNESS

(a) Opinion and Reputation Evidence of Character. The credibility of a witness may be attacked or supported by evidence in the form of opinion or reputation, but subject to these limitations: (1) the evidence may refer only to character for truthfulness or untruthfulness, and (2) evidence of truthful character is admissible only after the character of the witness for truthfulness has been attacked by opinion or reputation evidence or otherwise.

(b) Specific Instances of Conduct. Specific instances of the conduct of a witness, for the purpose of attacking or supporting the witness' character for truthfulness, other than conviction of crime as provided in rule 609, may not be proved by extrinsic evidence. They may, however, in the discretion of the court, if probative of truthfulness or untruthfulness, be inquired into on cross-examination of the witness (1) concerning the witness' character for truthfulness or untruthfulness, or (2) concerning the character for truthfulness or untruthfulness of another witness as to which character the witness being cross-examined has testified.

The giving of testimony, whether by an accused or by any other witness, does not operate as a waiver of the accused's or the witness' privilege against self-incrimination when examined with respect to matters that relate only to character for truthfulness.

[Amended March 2, 1987, effective October 1, 1987; April 25, 1988, effective November 1, 1988; March 27, 2003, effective December 1, 2003.]

RULE 609. IMPEACHMENT BY EVIDENCE OF CONVICTION OF CRIME

(a) General Rule. For the purpose of attacking the credibility of a witness,

(1) evidence that a witness other than an accused has been convicted of a crime shall be admitted, subject to Rule 403, if the crime was punishable by death or imprisonment in excess of one year under the law under which the witness was convicted, and evidence that an accused has been convicted of such a crime shall be admitted if the court determines that the probative value of admitting this evidence outweighs its prejudicial effect to the accused; and

(2) evidence that any witness has been convicted of a crime shall be admitted if it involved dishonesty or false statement, regardless of the punishment.

(b) Time Limit. Evidence of a conviction under this rule is not admissible if a period of more than ten years has elapsed since the date of the conviction or of the release of the witness from the confinement imposed for that conviction, whichever is the later date, unless the court determines, in the interests of justice, that the probative value of the conviction supported by specific facts and circumstances substantially outweighs its prejudicial effect. However, evidence of a conviction more than 10 years old as calculated herein, is not admissible unless the proponent gives to the adverse party sufficient advance written notice of intent to use such evidence to provide the adverse party with a fair opportunity to contest the use of such evidence.

(c) Effect of Pardon, Annulment, or Certificate of Rehabilitation. Evidence of a conviction is not admissible under this rule if (1) the conviction has been the subject of a pardon, annulment, certificate of rehabilitation, or other equivalent procedure based on a finding of the rehabilitation of the person convicted, and that person has not been convicted of a subsequent crime which was punishable by death or imprisonment in excess of one year, or (2) the conviction has been the subject of a pardon, annulment, or other equivalent procedure based on a finding of innocence.

(d) Juvenile Adjudications. Evidence of juvenile adjudications is generally not admissible under this rule. The court may, however, in a criminal case allow evidence of a juvenile adjudication of a witness other than the accused if conviction of the offense would be admissible to attack the credibility of an adult and the court is satisfied that admission in evidence is necessary for a fair determination of the issue of guilt or innocence.

(e) Pendency of Appeal. The pendency of an appeal therefrom does not render evidence of a conviction inadmissible. Evidence of the pendency of an appeal is admissible.

[Amended March 2, 1987, effective October 1, 1987; January 26, 1990, effective December 1, 1990.]

RULE 610. RELIGIOUS BELIEFS OR OPINIONS

Evidence of the beliefs or opinions of a witness on matters of religion is not admissible for the purpose of showing that by reason of their nature the witness' credibility is impaired or enhanced.

[Amended March 2, 1987, effective October 1, 1987.]

RULE 611. MODE AND ORDER OF INTERROGATION AND PRESENTATION

(a) Control by Court. The court shall exercise reasonable control over the mode and order of interrogating witnesses and presenting evidence so as to (1) make the interrogation and presentation effective for the ascertainment of the truth, (2) avoid needless consumption of time, and (3) protect witnesses from harassment or undue embarrassment.

(b) Scope of Cross-Examination. Cross-examination should be limited to the subject matter of the direct examination and matters affecting the credibility of the witness. The court may, in the exercise of discretion, permit inquiry into additional matters as if on direct examination.

(c) Leading Questions. Leading questions should not be used on the direct examination of a witness except as may be necessary to develop the witness' testimony. Ordinarily leading questions should be permitted on cross-examination. When a party calls a hostile witness, an adverse party, or a witness identified with an adverse party, interrogation may be by leading questions.

[Amended March 2, 1987, effective October 1, 1987.]

RULE 612. WRITING USED TO REFRESH MEMORY

Except as otherwise provided in criminal proceedings by section 3500 of title 18, United States Code, if a witness uses a writing to refresh memory for the purpose of testifying, either—

(1) while testifying, or

(2) before testifying, if the court in its discretion determines it is necessary in the interests of justice,

an adverse party is entitled to have the writing produced at the hearing, to inspect it, to cross-examine the witness thereon, and to introduce in evidence those portions which relate to the testimony of the witness. If it is claimed that the writing contains matters not related to the subject matter of the testimony the court shall examine the writing in camera, excise any portions not so related, and order delivery of the remainder to the party entitled thereto. Any portion withheld over objections shall be preserved and made available to the appellate court in the event of an appeal. If a writing is not produced or delivered pursuant to order under this rule, the court shall make any order justice requires, except that in criminal cases when the prosecution elects not to comply, the order shall be one striking the testimony or, if the court in its discretion determines that the interests of justice so require, declaring a mistrial.

[Amended March 2, 1987, effective October 1, 1987.]

RULE 613. PRIOR STATEMENTS OF WITNESSES

(a) Examining Witness Concerning Prior Statement. In examining a witness concerning a prior statement made by the witness, whether written or not, the statement need not be shown nor its contents disclosed to the witness at that time, but on request the same shall be shown or disclosed to opposing counsel.

(b) Extrinsic Evidence of Prior Inconsistent Statement of Witness. Extrinsic evidence of a prior inconsistent statement by a witness is not admissible unless the witness is afforded an opportunity to explain or deny the same and the opposite party is afforded an opportunity to interrogate the witness thereon, or the interests of justice otherwise require. This provision does not apply to admissions of a party-opponent as defined in rule 801(d)(2).

[Amended March 2, 1987, effective October 1, 1987; April 25, 1988, effective November 1, 1988.]

RULE 614. CALLING AND INTERROGATION OF WITNESSES BY COURT

(a) Calling by Court. The court may, on its own motion or at the suggestion of a party, call witnesses, and all parties are entitled to cross-examine witnesses thus called.

(b) Interrogation by Court. The court may interrogate witnesses, whether called by itself or by a party.

(c) Objections. Objections to the calling of witnesses by the court or to interrogation by it may be made at the time or at the next available opportunity when the jury is not present.

RULE 615. EXCLUSION OF WITNESSES

At the request of a party the court shall order witnesses excluded so that they cannot hear the testimony of other witnesses, and it may make the order of its own motion. This rule does not authorize exclusion of (1) a party who is a natural person, or (2) an officer or employee of a party which is not a natural person designated as its representative by its attorney, or (3) a person whose presence is shown by a party to be essential to the presentation of the party's cause, or (4) a person authorized by statute to be present.

[Amended March 2, 1987, effective October 1, 1987; April 25, 1988, effective November 1, 1988; amended by Pub.L. 100–690, Title VII, § 7075(a), November 18, 1988, 102 Stat. 4405 (although amendment by Pub.L. 100–690 could not be executed due to prior amendment by Court order which made the same change effective November 1, 1988); amended April 24, 1998, effective December 1, 1998.]

ARTICLE VII. OPINIONS AND EXPERT TESTIMONY

RULE 701. OPINION TESTIMONY BY LAY WITNESSES

If the witness is not testifying as an expert, the witness' testimony in the form of opinions or inferences is limited to those opinions or inferences which are (a) rationally based on the perception of the witness, (b) helpful to a clear understanding of the witness' testimony or the determination of a fact in issue, and (c) not based on scientific, technical, or other specialized knowledge within the scope of Rule 702.

[Amended March 2, 1987, effective October 1, 1987; April 17, 2000, effective December 1, 2000.]

RULE 702. TESTIMONY BY EXPERTS

If scientific, technical, or other specialized knowledge will assist the trier of fact to understand the evidence or to determine a fact in issue, a witness qualified as an expert by knowledge, skill, experience, training, or education, may testify thereto in the form of an opinion or otherwise, if (1) the testimony is based upon sufficient facts or data, (2) the testimony is the product of reliable principles and methods, and (3) the witness has applied the principles and methods reliably to the facts of the case.

[Amended April 17, 2000, effective December 1, 2000.]

RULE 703. BASES OF OPINION TESTIMONY BY EXPERTS

The facts or data in the particular case upon which an expert bases an opinion or inference may be those perceived by or made known to the expert at or before the hearing. If of a type reasonably relied upon by experts in the particular field in forming opinions or inferences upon the subject, the facts or data need not be admissible in evidence in order for the opinion or inference to be admitted. Facts or data that are otherwise inadmissible shall not be disclosed to the jury by the proponent of the opinion or inference unless the court determines that their probative value in assisting the jury to evaluate the expert's opinion substantially outweighs their prejudicial effect.

[Amended March 2, 1987, effective October 1, 1987; April 17, 2000, effective December 1, 2000.]

RULE 704. OPINION ON ULTIMATE ISSUE

(a) Except as provided in subdivision (b), testimony in the form of an opinion or inference otherwise admissible is not objectionable because it embraces an ultimate issue to be decided by the trier of fact.

(b) No expert witness testifying with respect to the mental state or condition of a defendant in a criminal case may state an opinion or inference as to whether the defendant did or did not have the mental state or condition constituting an element of the crime charged or of a defense thereto. Such ultimate issues are matters for the trier of fact alone.

[Amended by Pub.L. 98–473, Title II, § 406, October 12, 1984, 98 Stat. 2067.]

RULE 705. DISCLOSURE OF FACTS OR DATA UNDERLYING EXPERT OPINION

The expert may testify in terms of opinion or inference and give reasons therefor without first testifying to the underlying facts or data, unless the court requires otherwise. The expert may in any event be required to disclose the underlying facts or data on cross-examination.

[Amended March 2, 1987, effective October 1, 1987; April 22, 1993, effective December 1, 1993.]

RULE 706. COURT APPOINTED EXPERTS

(a) Appointment. The court may on its own motion or on the motion of any party enter an order to show cause why expert witnesses should not be appointed, and may request the parties to submit nominations. The court may appoint any expert witnesses agreed upon by the parties, and may appoint expert witnesses of its own selection. An expert witness shall not be appointed by the court unless the witness consents to act. A witness so appointed shall be informed of the witness' duties by the court in writing, a copy of which shall be filed with the clerk, or at a conference in which the parties shall have opportunity to participate. A witness so appointed shall advise the parties of the witness' findings, if any; the witness' deposition may be taken by any party; and the witness may be called to testify by the court or any party. The witness shall be subject to cross-examination by each party, including a party calling the witness.

(b) Compensation. Expert witnesses so appointed are entitled to reasonable compensation in whatever sum the court may allow. The compensation thus fixed is payable from funds which may be provided by law in criminal cases and civil actions and proceedings involving just compensation under the fifth amend-

ment. In other civil actions and proceedings the compensation shall be paid by the parties in such proportion and at such time as the court directs, and thereafter charged in like manner as other costs.

(c) Disclosure of Appointment. In the exercise of its discretion, the court may authorize disclosure to the jury of the fact that the court appointed the expert witness.

(d) Parties' Experts of Own Selection. Nothing in this rule limits the parties in calling expert witnesses of their own selection.

[Amended March 2, 1987, effective October 1, 1987.]

ARTICLE VIII. HEARSAY

RULE 801. DEFINITIONS

The following definitions apply under this article:

(a) Statement. A "statement" is (1) an oral or written assertion or (2) nonverbal conduct of a person, if it is intended by the person as an assertion.

(b) Declarant. A "declarant" is a person who makes a statement.

(c) Hearsay. "Hearsay" is a statement, other than one made by the declarant while testifying at the trial or hearing, offered in evidence to prove the truth of the matter asserted.

(d) Statements Which Are Not Hearsay. A statement is not hearsay if—

(1) *Prior Statement by Witness.* The declarant testifies at the trial or hearing and is subject to cross-examination concerning the statement, and the statement is (A) inconsistent with the declarant's testimony, and was given under oath subject to the penalty of perjury at a trial, hearing, or other proceeding, or in a deposition, or (B) consistent with the declarant's testimony and is offered to rebut an express or implied charge against the declarant of recent fabrication or improper influence or motive, or (C) one of identification of a person made after perceiving the person; or

(2) *Admission by Party-Opponent.* The statement is offered against a party and is (A) the party's own statement, in either an individual or a representative capacity or (B) a statement of which the party has manifested an adoption or belief in its truth, or (C) a statement by a person authorized by the party to make a statement concerning the subject, or (D) a statement by the party's agent or servant concerning a matter within the scope of the agency or employment, made during the existence of the relationship, or (E) a statement by a coconspirator of a party during the course and in furtherance of the conspiracy. The contents of the statement shall be considered but are not alone sufficient to establish the declarant's authority under subdivision (C), the agency or employ-

ment relationship and scope thereof under subdivision (D), or the existence of the conspiracy and the participation therein of the declarant and the party against whom the statement is offered under subdivision (E).

[Amended by Pub.L. 94–113, § 1, October 16, 1975, 89 Stat. 576; amended March 2, 1987, effective October 1, 1987; April 11, 1997, effective December 1, 1997.]

RULE 802. HEARSAY RULE

Hearsay is not admissible except as provided by these rules or by other rules prescribed by the Supreme Court pursuant to statutory authority or by Act of Congress.

RULE 803. HEARSAY EXCEPTIONS; AVAILABILITY OF DECLARANT IMMATERIAL

The following are not excluded by the hearsay rule, even though the declarant is available as a witness:

(1) Present Sense Impression. A statement describing or explaining an event or condition made while the declarant was perceiving the event or condition, or immediately thereafter.

(2) Excited Utterance. A statement relating to a startling event or condition made while the declarant was under the stress of excitement caused by the event or condition.

(3) Then Existing Mental, Emotional, or Physical Condition. A statement of the declarant's then existing state of mind, emotion, sensation, or physical condition (such as intent, plan, motive, design, mental feeling, pain, and bodily health), but not including a statement of memory or belief to prove the fact remembered or believed unless it relates to the execution, revocation, identification, or terms of declarant's will.

(4) Statements for Purposes of Medical Diagnosis or Treatment. Statements made for purposes of medical diagnosis or treatment and describing medical history, or past or present symptoms, pain, or sensations, or the inception or general character of the cause or external source thereof insofar as reasonably pertinent to diagnosis or treatment.

(5) Recorded Recollection. A memorandum or record concerning a matter about which a witness once had knowledge but now has insufficient recollection to enable the witness to testify fully and accurately, shown to have been made or adopted by the witness when the matter was fresh in the witness' memory and to reflect that knowledge correctly. If admitted, the memorandum or record may be read into evidence but may not itself be received as an exhibit unless offered by an adverse party.

(6) Records of Regularly Conducted Activity. A memorandum, report, record, or data compilation, in any form, of acts, events, conditions, opinions, or diagnoses, made at or near the time by, or from information transmitted by, a person with knowledge, if kept in the course of a regularly conducted business activity, and if it was the regular practice of that business activity to make the memorandum, report, record, or data compilation, all as shown by the testimony of the custodian or other qualified witness, or by certification that complies with Rule 902(11), Rule 902(12), or a statute permitting certification, unless the source of information or the method or circumstances of preparation indicate lack of trustworthiness. The term "business" as used in this paragraph includes business, institution, association, profession, occupation, and calling of every kind, whether or not conducted for profit.

(7) Absence of Entry in Records Kept in Accordance With the Provisions of Paragraph (6). Evidence that a matter is not included in the memoranda reports, records, or data compilations, in any form, kept in accordance with the provisions of paragraph (6), to prove the nonoccurrence or nonexistence of the matter, if the matter was of a kind of which a memorandum, report, record, or data compilation was regularly made and preserved, unless the sources of information or other circumstances indicate lack of trustworthiness.

(8) Public Records and Reports. Records, reports, statements, or data compilations, in any form, of public offices or agencies, setting forth (A) the activities of the office or agency, or (B) matters observed pursuant to duty imposed by law as to which matters there was a duty to report, excluding, however, in criminal cases matters observed by police officers and other law enforcement personnel, or (C) in civil actions and proceedings and against the Government in criminal cases, factual findings resulting from an investigation made pursuant to authority granted by law, unless the sources of information or other circumstances indicate lack of trustworthiness.

(9) Records of Vital Statistics. Records or data compilations, in any form, of births, fetal deaths, deaths, or marriages, if the report thereof was made to a public office pursuant to requirements of law.

(10) Absence of Public Record or Entry. To prove the absence of a record, report, statement, or data compilation, in any form, or the nonoccurrence or nonexistence of a matter of which a record, report, statement, or data compilation, in any form, was regularly made and preserved by a public office or agency, evidence in the form of a certification in accordance with rule 902, or testimony, that diligent search failed to disclose the record, report, statement, or data compilation, or entry.

(11) Records of Religious Organizations. Statements of births, marriages, divorces, deaths, legitimacy, ancestry, relationship by blood or marriage, or other similar facts of personal or family history, contained in a regularly kept record of a religious organization.

(12) Marriage, Baptismal, and Similar Certificates. Statements of fact contained in a certificate that the maker performed a marriage or other ceremony or administered a sacrament, made by a clergyman, public official, or other person authorized by the rules or practices of a religious organization or by law to perform the act certified, and purporting to have been issued at the time of the act or within a reasonable time thereafter.

(13) Family Records. Statements of fact concerning personal or family history contained in family Bibles, genealogies, charts, engravings on rings, inscriptions on family portraits, engravings on urns, crypts, or tombstones, or the like.

(14) Records of Documents Affecting an Interest in Property. The record of a document purporting to establish or affect an interest in property, as proof of the content of the original recorded document and its execution and delivery by each person by whom it purports to have been executed, if the record is a record of a public office and an applicable statute authorizes the recording of documents of that kind in that office.

(15) Statements in Documents Affecting an Interest in Property. A statement contained in a document purporting to establish or affect an interest in property if the matter stated was relevant to the purpose of the document, unless dealings with the property since the document was made have been inconsistent with the truth of the statement or the purport of the document.

(16) Statements in Ancient Documents. Statements in a document in existence twenty years or more the authenticity of which is established.

(17) Market Reports, Commercial Publications. Market quotations, tabulations, lists, directories, or other published compilations, generally used and relied upon by the public or by persons in particular occupations.

(18) Learned Treatises. To the extent called to the attention of an expert witness upon cross-examination or relied upon by the expert witness in direct examination, statements contained in published treatises, periodicals, or pamphlets on a subject of history, medicine, or other science or art, established as a reliable authority by the testimony or admission of the witness or by other expert testimony or by judicial notice. If admitted, the statements may be read into evidence but may not be received as exhibits.

(19) Reputation Concerning Personal or Family History. Reputation among members of a person's family by blood, adoption, or marriage, or among a person's associates, or in the community, concerning a person's birth, adoption, marriage, divorce, death, legitimacy, relationship by blood, adoption, or marriage, ancestry, or other similar fact of personal or family history.

(20) Reputation Concerning Boundaries or General History. Reputation in a community, arising before the controversy, as to boundaries of or customs affecting lands in the community, and reputation as to events of general history important to the community or State or nation in which located.

(21) Reputation as to Character. Reputation of a person's character among associates or in the community.

(22) Judgment of Previous Conviction. Evidence of a final judgment, entered after a trial or upon a plea of guilty (but not upon a plea of nolo contendere), adjudging a person guilty of a crime punishable by death or imprisonment in excess of one year, to prove any fact essential to sustain the judgment, but not including, when offered by the Government in a criminal prosecution for purposes other than impeachment, judgments against persons other than the accused. The pendency of an appeal may be shown but does not affect admissibility.

(23) Judgment as to Personal, Family, or General History, or Boundaries. Judgments as proof of matters of personal, family or general history, or boundaries, essential to the judgment, if the same would be provable by evidence of reputation.

(24) [Transferred to Rule 807.]

[Amended by Pub.L. 94–149, § 1(11), December 12, 1975, 89 Stat. 805; amended March 2, 1987, effective October 1, 1987; April 11, 1997, effective December 1, 1997; April 17, 2000, effective December 1, 2000.]

RULE 804. HEARSAY EXCEPTIONS; DECLARANT UNAVAILABLE

(a) Definition of Unavailability. "Unavailability as a witness" includes situations in which the declarant—

(1) is exempted by ruling of the court on the ground of privilege from testifying concerning the subject matter of the declarant's statement; or

(2) persists in refusing to testify concerning the subject matter of the declarant's statement despite an order of the court to do so; or

(3) testifies to a lack of memory of the subject matter of the declarant's statement; or

(4) is unable to be present or to testify at the hearing because of death or then existing physical or mental illness or infirmity; or

(5) is absent from the hearing and the proponent of a statement has been unable to procure the declarant's attendance (or in the case of a hearsay exception under subdivision (b)(2), (3), or (4), the declarant's attendance or testimony) by process or other reasonable means.

A declarant is not unavailable as a witness if exemption, refusal, claim of lack of memory, inability, or absence is due to the procurement or wrongdoing of the proponent of a statement for the purpose of preventing the witness from attending or testifying.

(b) Hearsay Exceptions. The following are not excluded by the hearsay rule if the declarant is unavailable as a witness:

(1) *Former Testimony.* Testimony given as a witness at another hearing of the same or a different proceeding, or in a deposition taken in compliance with law in the course of the same or another proceeding, if the party against whom the testimony is now offered, or, in a civil action or proceeding, a predecessor in interest, had an opportunity and similar motive to develop the testimony by direct, cross, or redirect examination.

(2) *Statement Under Belief of Impending Death.* In a prosecution for homicide or in a civil action or proceeding, a statement made by a declarant while believing that the declarant's death was imminent, concerning the cause or circumstances of what the declarant believed to be impending death.

(3) *Statement Against Interest.* A statement which was at the time of its making so far contrary to the declarant's pecuniary or proprietary interest, or so far tended to subject the declarant to civil or criminal liability, or to render invalid a claim by the declarant against another, that a reasonable person in the declarant's position would not have made the statement unless believing it to be true. A statement tending to expose the declarant to criminal liability and offered to exculpate the accused is not admissible unless corroborating circumstances clearly indicate the trustworthiness of the statement.

(4) *Statement of Personal or Family History.*

(A) A statement concerning the declarant's own birth, adoption, marriage, divorce, legitimacy, relationship by blood, adoption, or marriage, ancestry, or other similar fact of personal or family history, even though declarant had no means of acquiring personal knowledge of the matter stated; or

(B) a statement concerning the foregoing matters, and death also, of another person, if the declarant was related to the other by blood, adoption, or marriage or was so intimately associated with the other's family as to be likely to have accurate information concerning the matter declared.

(5) *[Transferred to Rule 807.]*

(6) *Forfeiture by Wrongdoing.* A statement offered against a party that has engaged or acquiesced in wrongdoing that was intended to, and did, procure the unavailability of the declarant as a witness.

[Amended by Pub.L. 94–149, § 1(12) and (13), December 12, 1975, 89 Stat. 806; amended March 2, 1987, effective October 1, 1987; amended by Pub.L. 100–690, Title VII, § 7075(b), November 18, 1988, 102 Stat. 4405; amended April 11, 1997, effective December 1, 1997.]

RULE 805. HEARSAY WITHIN HEARSAY

Hearsay included within hearsay is not excluded under the hearsay rule if each part of the combined statements conforms with an exception to the hearsay rule provided in these rules.

RULE 806. ATTACKING AND SUPPORTING CREDIBILITY OF DECLARANT

When a hearsay statement, or a statement defined in Rule 801(d)(2)(C), (D), or (E), has been admitted in evidence, the credibility of the declarant may be at-

tacked, and if attacked may be supported, by any evidence which would be admissible for those purposes if declarant had testified as a witness. Evidence of a statement or conduct by the declarant at any time, inconsistent with the declarant's hearsay statement, is not subject to any requirement that the declarant may have been afforded an opportunity to deny or explain. If the party against whom a hearsay statement has been admitted calls the declarant as a witness, the party is entitled to examine the declarant on the statement as if under cross-examination.

[Amended March 2, 1987, effective October 1, 1987; April 11, 1997, effective December 1, 1997.]

RULE 807. RESIDUAL EXCEPTION

A statement not specifically covered by Rule 803 or 804 but having equivalent circumstantial guarantees of trustworthiness, is not excluded by the hearsay rule, if the court determines that (A) the statement is offered as evidence of a material fact; (B) the statement is more probative on the point for which it is offered than any other evidence which the proponent can procure through reasonable efforts; and (C) the general purposes of these rules and the interests of justice will best be served by admission of the statement into evidence. However, a statement may not be admitted under this exception unless the proponent of it makes known to the adverse party sufficiently in advance of the trial or hearing to provide the adverse party with a fair opportunity to prepare to meet it, the proponent's intention to offer the statement and the particulars of it, including the name and address of the declarant.

[Adopted April 11, 1997, effective December 1, 1997.]

ARTICLE IX. AUTHENTICATION AND IDENTIFICATION

RULE 901. REQUIREMENT OF AUTHENTICATION OR IDENTIFICATION

(a) General Provision. The requirement of authentication or identification as a condition precedent to admissibility is satisfied by evidence sufficient to support a finding that the matter in question is what its proponent claims.

(b) Illustrations. By way of illustration only, and not by way of limitation, the following are examples of authentication or identification conforming with the requirements of this rule:

(1) *Testimony of Witness With Knowledge.* Testimony that a matter is what it is claimed to be.

(2) *Nonexpert Opinion on Handwriting.* Nonexpert opinion as to the genuineness of handwriting, based upon familiarity not acquired for purposes of the litigation.

(3) *Comparison by Trier or Expert Witness.* Comparison by the trier of fact or by expert witnesses with specimens which have been authenticated.

(4) *Distinctive Characteristics and the Like.* Appearance, contents, substance, internal patterns, or other distinctive characteristics, taken in conjunction with circumstances.

(5) *Voice Identification.* Identification of a voice, whether heard firsthand or through mechanical or electronic transmission or recording, by opinion based upon hearing the voice at any time under circumstances connecting it with the alleged speaker.

(6) *Telephone Conversations.* Telephone conversations, by evidence that a call was made to the number assigned at the time by the telephone company to a particular person or business, if (A) in the case of a person, circumstances, including self-identification, show the person answering to be the one called, or (B)

in the case of a business, the call was made to a place of business and the conversation related to business reasonably transacted over the telephone.

(7) *Public Records or Reports.* Evidence that a writing authorized by law to be recorded or filed and in fact recorded or filed in a public office, or a purported public record, report, statement, or data compilation, in any form, is from the public office where items of this nature are kept.

(8) *Ancient Documents or Data Compilation.* Evidence that a document or data compilation, in any form, (A) is in such condition as to create no suspicion concerning its authenticity, (B) was in a place where it, if authentic, would likely be, and (C) has been in existence 20 years or more at the time it is offered.

(9) *Process or System.* Evidence describing a process or system used to produce a result and showing that the process or system produces an accurate result.

(10) *Methods Provided by Statute or Rule.* Any method of authentication or identification provided by Act of Congress or by other rules prescribed by the Supreme Court pursuant to statutory authority.

RULE 902. SELF–AUTHENTICATION

Extrinsic evidence of authenticity as a condition precedent to admissibility is not required with respect to the following:

(1) **Domestic Public Documents Under Seal.** A document bearing a seal purporting to be that of the United States, or of any State, district, Commonwealth, territory, or insular possession thereof, or the Panama Canal Zone, or the Trust Territory of the Pacific Islands, or of a political subdivision, department, officer, or agency thereof, and a signature purporting to be an attestation or execution.

(2) **Domestic Public Documents Not Under Seal.** A document purporting to bear the signature in the official capacity of an officer or employee of any entity included in paragraph (1) hereof, having no seal, if a public officer having a seal and having official duties in the district or political subdivision of the officer or employee certifies under seal that the signer has the official capacity and that the signature is genuine.

(3) **Foreign Public Documents.** A document purporting to be executed or attested in an official capacity by a person authorized by the laws of a foreign country to make the execution or attestation, and accompanied by a final certification as to the genuineness of the signature and official position (A) of the executing or attesting person, or (B) of any foreign official whose certificate of genuineness of signature and official position relates to the execution or attestation or is in a chain of certificates of genuineness of signature and official position relating to the execution or attestation. A final certification may be made by a secretary of an embassy or legation, consul general,

consul, vice consul, or consular agent of the United States, or a diplomatic or consular official of the foreign country assigned or accredited to the United States. If reasonable opportunity has been given to all parties to investigate the authenticity and accuracy of official documents, the court may, for good cause shown, order that they be treated as presumptively authentic without final certification or permit them to be evidenced by an attested summary with or without final certification.

(4) **Certified Copies of Public Records.** A copy of an official record or report or entry therein, or of a document authorized by law to be recorded or filed and actually recorded or filed in a public office, including data compilations in any form, certified as correct by the custodian or other person authorized to make the certification, by certificate complying with paragraph (1), (2), or (3) of this rule or complying with any Act of Congress or rule prescribed by the Supreme Court pursuant to statutory authority.

(5) **Official Publications.** Books, pamphlets, or other publications purporting to be issued by public authority.

(6) **Newspapers and Periodicals.** Printed materials purporting to be newspapers or periodicals.

(7) **Trade Inscriptions and the Like.** Inscriptions, signs, tags, or labels purporting to have been affixed in the course of business and indicating ownership, control, or origin.

(8) **Acknowledged Documents.** Documents accompanied by a certificate of acknowledgment executed in the manner provided by law by a notary public or other officer authorized by law to take acknowledgments.

(9) **Commercial Paper and Related Documents.** Commercial paper, signatures thereon, and documents relating thereto to the extent provided by general commercial law.

(10) **Presumptions Under Acts of Congress.** Any signature, document, or other matter declared by Act of Congress to be presumptively or prima facie genuine or authentic.

(11) **Certified Domestic Records of Regularly Conducted Activity.** The original or a duplicate of a domestic record of regularly conducted activity that would be admissible under Rule 803(6) if accompanied by a written declaration of its custodian or other qualified person, in a manner complying with any Act of Congress or rule prescribed by the Supreme Court pursuant to statutory authority, certifying that the record—

(A) was made at or near the time of the occurrence of the matters set forth by, or from information transmitted by, a person with knowledge of those matters;

(B) was kept in the course of the regularly conducted activity; and

(C) was made by the regularly conducted activity as a regular practice.

A party intending to offer a record into evidence under this paragraph must provide written notice of that intention to all adverse parties, and must make the record and declaration available for inspection sufficiently in advance of their offer into evidence to provide an adverse party with a fair opportunity to challenge them.

(12) Certified Foreign Records of Regularly Conducted Activity. In a civil case, the original or a duplicate of a foreign record of regularly conducted activity that would be admissible under Rule 803(6) if accompanied by a written declaration by its custodian or other qualified person certifying that the record—

(A) was made at or near the time of the occurrence of the matters set forth by, or from information transmitted by, a person with knowledge of those matters;

(B) was kept in the course of the regularly conducted activity; and

(C) was made by the regularly conducted activity as a regular practice.

The declaration must be signed in a manner that, if falsely made, would subject the maker to criminal penalty under the laws of the country where the declaration is signed. A party intending to offer a record into evidence under this paragraph must provide written notice of that intention to all adverse parties, and must make the record and declaration available for inspection sufficiently in advance of their offer into evidence to provide an adverse party with a fair opportunity to challenge them.

[Amended March 2, 1987, effective October 1, 1987; April 25, 1988, effective November 1, 1988; April 17, 2000, effective December 1, 2000.]

RULE 903. SUBSCRIBING WITNESS' TESTIMONY UNNECESSARY

The testimony of a subscribing witness is not necessary to authenticate a writing unless required by the laws of the jurisdiction whose laws govern the validity of the writing.

ARTICLE X. CONTENTS OF WRITINGS, RECORDINGS, AND PHOTOGRAPHS

RULE 1001. DEFINITIONS

For purposes of this article the following definitions are applicable:

(1) Writings and Recordings. "Writings" and "recordings" consist of letters, words, or numbers, or their equivalent, set down by handwriting, typewriting, printing, photostating, photographing, magnetic impulse, mechanical or electronic recording, or other form of data compilation.

(2) Photographs. "Photographs" include still photographs, X-ray films, video tapes, and motion pictures.

(3) Original. An "original" of a writing or recording is the writing or recording itself or any counterpart intended to have the same effect by a person executing or issuing it. An "original" of a photograph includes the negative or any print therefrom. If data are stored in a computer or similar device, any printout or other output readable by sight, shown to reflect the data accurately, is an "original".

(4) Duplicate. A "duplicate" is a counterpart produced by the same impression as the original, or from the same matrix, or by means of photography, including enlargements and miniatures, or by mechanical or electronic re-recording, or by chemical reproduction, or by other equivalent techniques which accurately reproduces the original.

RULE 1002. REQUIREMENT OF ORIGINAL

To prove the content of a writing, recording, or photograph, the original writing, recording, or photograph is required, except as otherwise provided in these rules or by Act of Congress.

RULE 1003. ADMISSIBILITY OF DUPLICATES

A duplicate is admissible to the same extent as an original unless (1) a genuine question is raised as to the authenticity of the original or (2) in the circumstances it would be unfair to admit the duplicate in lieu of the original.

RULE 1004. ADMISSIBILITY OF OTHER EVIDENCE OF CONTENTS

The original is not required, and other evidence of the contents of a writing, recording, or photograph is admissible if—

(1) Originals Lost or Destroyed. All originals are lost or have been destroyed, unless the proponent lost or destroyed them in bad faith; or

(2) Original Not Obtainable. No original can be obtained by any available judicial process or procedure; or

(3) **Original in Possession of Opponent.** At a time when an original was under the control of the party against whom offered, that party was put on notice, by the pleadings or otherwise, that the contents would be a subject of proof at the hearing, and that party does not produce the original at the hearing; or

(4) **Collateral Matters.** The writing, recording, or photograph is not closely related to a controlling issue.

[Amended March 2, 1987, effective October 1, 1987.]

RULE 1005. PUBLIC RECORDS

The contents of an official record, or of a document authorized to be recorded or filed and actually recorded or filed, including data compilations in any form, if otherwise admissible, may be proved by copy, certified as correct in accordance with rule 902 or testified to be correct by a witness who has compared it with the original. If a copy which complies with the foregoing cannot be obtained by the exercise of reasonable diligence, then other evidence of the contents may be given.

RULE 1006. SUMMARIES

The contents of voluminous writings, recordings, or photographs which cannot conveniently be examined in court may be presented in the form of a chart, summary, or calculation. The originals, or duplicates, shall be made available for examination or copying, or both, by other parties at reasonable time and place. The court may order that they be produced in court.

RULE 1007. TESTIMONY OR WRITTEN ADMISSION OF PARTY

Contents of writings, recordings, or photographs may be proved by the testimony or deposition of the party against whom offered or by that party's written admission, without accounting for the nonproduction of the original.

[Amended March 2, 1987, effective October 1, 1987.]

RULE 1008. FUNCTIONS OF COURT AND JURY

When the admissibility of other evidence of contents of writings, recordings, or photographs under these rules depends upon the fulfillment of a condition of fact, the question whether the condition has been fulfilled is ordinarily for the court to determine in accordance with the provisions of rule 104. However, when an issue is raised (a) whether the asserted writing ever existed, or (b) whether another writing, recording, or photograph produced at the trial is the original, or (c) whether other evidence of contents correctly reflects the contents, the issue is for the trier of fact to determine as in the case of other issues of fact.

ARTICLE XI. MISCELLANEOUS RULES

RULE 1101. APPLICABILITY OF RULES

(a) **Courts and Judges.** These rules apply to the United States district courts, the District Court of Guam, the District Court of the Virgin Islands, the District Court for the Northern Mariana Islands, the United States courts of appeals, the United States Claims Court, and to United States bankruptcy judges and United States magistrate judges, in the actions, cases, and proceedings and to the extent hereinafter set forth. The terms "judge" and "court" in these rules include United States bankruptcy judges and United States magistrate judges.

(b) **Proceedings Generally.** These rules apply generally to civil actions and proceedings, including admiralty and maritime cases, to criminal cases and proceedings, to contempt proceedings except those in which the court may act summarily, and to proceedings and cases under title 11, United States Code.

(c) **Rule of Privilege.** The rule with respect to privileges applies at all stages of all actions, cases, and proceedings.

(d) **Rules Inapplicable.** The rules (other than with respect to privileges) do not apply in the following situations:

(1) *Preliminary Questions of Fact.* The determination of questions of fact preliminary to admissibility of evidence when the issue is to be determined by the court under rule 104.

(2) *Grand Jury.* Proceedings before grand juries.

(3) *Miscellaneous Proceedings.* Proceedings for extradition or rendition; preliminary examinations in criminal cases; sentencing, or granting or revoking probation; issuance of warrants for arrest, criminal summonses, and search warrants; and proceedings with respect to release on bail or otherwise.

(e) **Rules Applicable in Part.** In the following proceedings these rules apply to the extent that matters of evidence are not provided for in the statutes which govern procedure therein or in other rules prescribed by the Supreme Court pursuant to statutory authority: the trial of misdemeanors and other petty offenses before United States magistrate judges; review of agency actions when the facts are subject to trial de novo under section 706(2)(F) of title 5, United States Code; review of orders of the Secretary of Agriculture under section 2 of the Act entitled "An Act to authorize association of producers of agricultural products" approved February 18, 1922 (7 U.S.C. 292), and under sections 6 and 7(c) of the Perishable Agricultural Commodities Act, 1930 (7 U.S.C. 499f, 499g(c)); naturalization and revocation of naturalization under sections 310–318 of the Immigration and Nationality Act (8 U.S.C. 1421–1429); prize proceedings in admiralty under sections 7651–7681 of title 10, United States Code; review of orders of the Secretary of the Interior under section 2 of the Act entitled "An Act authorizing associations of producers of aquatic products" approved June 25, 1934 (15 U.S.C. 522); review of orders of petroleum control boards under section 5 of the Act entitled "An Act to regulate interstate and foreign commerce in petroleum and its products by prohibiting the shipment in such commerce of petroleum and its products produced in violation of State law, and for other purposes", approved February 22, 1935 (15 U.S.C. 715d); actions for fines, penalties, or forfeitures under part V of title IV of the Tariff Act of 1930 (19 U.S.C. 1581–1624), or under the Anti-Smuggling Act (19 U.S.C. 1701–1711); criminal libel for condemnation, exclusion of imports, or other proceedings under the Federal Food, Drug, and Cosmetic Act (21 U.S.C. 301–392); disputes between seamen under sections 4079, 4080, and 4081 of the Revised Statutes (22 U.S.C. 256–258); habeas corpus under sections 2241–2254 of title 28, United States Code; motions to vacate, set aside or correct sentence under section 2255 of title 28, United States Code; actions for penalties for refusal to transport destitute seamen under section 4578 of the Revised Statutes (46 U.S.C. 679);* actions against the United States under the Act entitled "An Act authorizing suits against the United States in admiralty for damage caused by and salvage service rendered to public vessels belonging to the United States, and for other purposes", approved March 3, 1925 (46 U.S.C. 781–790), as implemented by section 7730 of title 10, United States Code.

* Law Revision Counsel Note: Repealed and reenacted as 46 U.S.C. 11104(b)-(d) by Pub.L. 98–89, §§ 1, 2(a), 4(b), August 26, 1983, 97 Stat. 500.

[Amended by Pub.L. 94–149, § 1(14), December 12, 1975, 89 Stat. 806; Pub.L. 95–598, Title II, § 251, November 6, 1978, 92 Stat. 2673, effective October 1, 1979; Pub.L. 97–164, Title I, § 142, April 2, 1982, 96 Stat. 45, effective October 1, 1982; amended March 2, 1987, effective October 1, 1987; April 25, 1988, effective November 1, 1988; amended by Pub.L. 100–690, Title VII, § 7075(c)(1), November 18, 1988, 102 Stat. 4405 (although amendment by Pub.L. 100-690 could not be executed due to prior amendment by Court order which made the same change effective November 1, 1988); amended April 22, 1993, effective December 1, 1993.]

RULE 1102. AMENDMENTS

Amendments to the Federal Rules of Evidence may be made as provided in section 2072 of title 28 of the United States Code.

[Amended April 30, 1991, effective December 1, 1991.]

RULE 1103. TITLE

These rules may be known and cited as the Federal Rules of Evidence.

INDEX TO
FEDERAL RULES OF EVIDENCE

UNITED STATES COURT OF APPEALS FOR THE FIRST CIRCUIT

Summary of Contents

FEDERAL RULES OF APPELLATE PROCEDURE WITH LOCAL RULES OF THE FIRST CIRCUIT.

APPENDIX OF FORMS.

APPENDICES.

INTERNAL OPERATING PROCEDURES OF THE FIRST CIRCUIT.

INDEX.

FEDERAL RULES OF APPELLATE PROCEDURE WITH LOCAL RULES OF THE FIRST CIRCUIT

**Federal Rules of Appellate Procedure
Adopted Effective July 1, 1968**

**First Circuit Rules Adopted Effective
September 1, 1986**

Including Federal Rules of Appellate Procedure Amendments Effective December 1, 2003, and First Circuit Amendments Received Through January 1, 2005

Research Note

Rule requirements, case law applications, commentary, and references to treatises, form books and law reviews are available in Knibb, Federal Court of Appeals Manual; *and in Wright, Miller et al.,* Federal Practice and Procedure, *Volume 16.*

Use WESTLAW ® *to find cases citing a rule.* WESTLAW *may also be used to search for specific terms or to update a rule; see the US–RULES, US–ORDERS and US–PL Scope Screens for further information.*

Amendments to the Federal Rules of Appellate Procedure are published, as received, in the Supreme Court Reporter, Federal Reporter 3d, Federal Supplement 2d, Federal Rules Decisions *and* Bankruptcy Reporter *advance sheets. Amendments to the First Circuit Local Rules and Internal Operating Procedures are published, as received, in the* Federal Reporter 3d *and* Massachusetts Decisions *advance sheets.*

TITLE I. APPLICABILITY OF RULES

FRAP 1. SCOPE OF RULES; TITLE

(a) **Scope of Rules.**

(1) These rules govern procedure in the United States courts of appeals.

(2) When these rules provide for filing a motion or other document in the district court, the procedure must comply with the practice of the district court.

(b) [Abrogated].

(c) **Title.** These rules are to be known as the Federal Rules of Appellate Procedure.

[Amended April 30, 1979, effective August 1, 1979; April 25, 1989, effective December 1, 1989; former Rule 48 renumbered as Rule 1(c) April 29, 1994, effective December 1, 1994; April 24, 1998, effective December 1, 1998; April 29, 2002, effective December 1, 2002.]

FRAP 2. SUSPENSION OF RULES

On its own or a party's motion, a court of appeals may—to expedite its decision or for other good cause—suspend any provision of these rules in a particular case and order proceedings as it directs, except as otherwise provided in Rule 26(b).

[Amended April 24, 1998, effective December 1, 1998.]

TITLE II. APPEALS FROM A JUDGMENT OR ORDER OF A DISTRICT COURT

FRAP 3. APPEAL AS OF RIGHT— HOW TAKEN

(a) **Filing the Notice of Appeal.**

(1) An appeal permitted by law as of right from a district court to a court of appeals may be taken only by filing a notice of appeal with the district clerk within the time allowed by Rule 4. At the time of filing, the appellant must furnish the clerk with enough copies of the notice to enable the clerk to comply with Rule 3(d).

(2) An appellant's failure to take any step other than the timely filing of a notice of appeal does not affect the validity of the appeal, but is ground only for

the court of appeals to act as it considers appropriate, including dismissing the appeal.

(3) An appeal from a judgment by a magistrate judge in a civil case is taken in the same way as an appeal from any other district court judgment.

(4) An appeal by permission under 28 U.S.C. § 1292(b) or an appeal in a bankruptcy case may be taken only in the manner prescribed by Rules 5 and 6, respectively.

(b) **Joint or Consolidated Appeals.**

(1) When two or more parties are entitled to appeal from a district-court judgment or order, and their interests make joinder practicable, they may file a

joint notice of appeal. They may then proceed on appeal as a single appellant.

(2) When the parties have filed separate timely notices of appeal, the appeals may be joined or consolidated by the court of appeals.

(c) **Contents of the Notice of Appeal.**

(1) The notice of appeal must:

(A) specify the party or parties taking the appeal by naming each one in the caption or body of the notice, but an attorney representing more than one party may describe those parties with such terms as "all plaintiffs," "the defendants," "the plaintiffs A, B, et al.," or "all defendants except X";

(B) designate the judgment, order, or part thereof being appealed; and

(C) name the court to which the appeal is taken.

(2) A pro se notice of appeal is considered filed on behalf of the signer and the signer's spouse and minor children (if they are parties), unless the notice clearly indicates otherwise.

(3) In a class action, whether or not the class has been certified, the notice of appeal is sufficient if it names one person qualified to bring the appeal as representative of the class.

(4) An appeal must not be dismissed for informality of form or title of the notice of appeal, or for failure to name a party whose intent to appeal is otherwise clear from the notice.

(5) Form 1 in the Appendix of Forms is a suggested form of a notice of appeal.

(d) **Serving the Notice of Appeal.**

(1) The district clerk must serve notice of the filing of a notice of appeal by mailing a copy to each party's counsel of record—excluding the appellant's—or, if a party is proceeding pro se, to the party's last known address. When a defendant in a criminal case appeals, the clerk must also serve a copy of the notice of appeal on the defendant, either by personal service or by mail addressed to the defendant. The clerk must promptly send a copy of the notice of appeal and of the docket entries—and any later docket entries—to the clerk of the court of appeals named in the notice. The district clerk must note, on each copy, the date when the notice of appeal was filed.

(2) If an inmate confined in an institution files a notice of appeal in the manner provided by Rule 4(c), the district clerk must also note the date when the clerk docketed the notice.

(3) The district clerk's failure to serve notice does not affect the validity of the appeal. The clerk must note on the docket the names of the parties to whom the clerk mails copies, with the date of mailing. Service is sufficient despite the death of a party or the party's counsel.

(e) **Payment of Fees.** Upon filing a notice of appeal, the appellant must pay the district clerk all required fees. The district clerk receives the appellate docket fee on behalf of the court of appeals.

[Amended April 30, 1979, effective August 1, 1979; March 10, 1986, effective July 1, 1986; April 25, 1989, effective December 1, 1989; April 22, 1993, effective December 1, 1993; April 29, 1994, effective December 1, 1994; April 24, 1998, effective December 1, 1998.]

LOCAL RULE 3. DOCKETING STATEMENT REQUIRED; DISMISSALS FOR WANT OF DILIGENT PROSECUTION

(a) *Docketing Statement Required.* To provide the clerk of the Court of Appeals at the commencement of an appeal with the information needed for effective case management, within 14 days of filing the notice of appeal, the person or persons taking the appeal must submit a separate statement listing all parties to the appeal, the last known counsel, and last known addresses for counsel and unrepresented parties. Errors or omissions in this separate statement alone shall not otherwise affect the appeal if the notice of appeal itself complies with this rule.

(1) *Form.* Counsel filing an appeal must complete and file a docketing statement, using the form provided by the clerk of the appeals court.

(2) Service. A copy of the docketing statement and any attachments must be served on the opposing party or parties at the time the docketing statement is filed.

(3) Duty of Opposing Party. If an opposing party concludes that the docketing statement is in any way inaccurate, incomplete, or misleading, the clerk's office must be informed in writing of any errors and any proposed additions or corrections within seven days of service of the docketing statement, with copies to all other parties.

(b) If appellant does not pay the docket fee within 7 days of the filing of the notice of appeal, or does not file the docketing statement or any other paper within the time set by the court, the appeal may be dismissed for want of diligent prosecution.

Adopted effective Sept. 1, 1986. Amended September, 1999.

FRAP 3.1 APPEAL FROM A JUDGMENT OF A MAGISTRATE JUDGE IN A CIVIL CASE [ABROGATED]

[Adopted March 10, 1986, effective July 1, 1986; amended April 22, 1993, effective December 1, 1993; abrogated effective December 1, 1998.]

FRAP 4. APPEAL AS OF RIGHT— WHEN TAKEN

(a) **Appeal in a Civil Case.**

(1) *Time for Filing a Notice of Appeal.*

(A) In a civil case, except as provided in Rules 4(a)(1)(B), 4(a)(4), and 4(c), the notice of appeal required by Rule 3 must be filed with the district clerk within 30 days after the judgment or order appealed from is entered.

(B) When the United States or its officer or agency is a party, the notice of appeal may be filed by any party within 60 days after the judgment or order appealed from is entered.

(C) An appeal from an order granting or denying an application for a writ of error coram nobis is an appeal in a civil case for purposes of Rule 4(a).

(2) *Filing Before Entry of Judgment.* A notice of appeal filed after the court announces a decision or order—but before the entry of the judgment or order—is treated as filed on the date of and after the entry.

(3) *Multiple Appeals.* If one party timely files a notice of appeal, any other party may file a notice of appeal within 14 days after the date when the first notice was filed, or within the time otherwise prescribed by this Rule 4(a), whichever period ends later.

(4) *Effect of a Motion on a Notice of Appeal.*

(A) If a party timely files in the district court any of the following motions under the Federal Rules of Civil Procedure, the time to file an appeal runs for all parties from the entry of the order disposing of the last such remaining motion:

(i) for judgment under Rule 50(b);

(ii) to amend or make additional factual findings under Rule 52(b), whether or not granting the motion would alter the judgment;

(iii) for attorney's fees under Rule 54 if the district court extends the time to appeal under Rule 58;

(iv) to alter or amend the judgment under Rule 59;

(v) for a new trial under Rule 59; or

(vi) for relief under Rule 60 if the motion is filed no later than 10 days after the judgment is entered.

(B)(i) If a party files a notice of appeal after the court announces or enters a judgment—but before it disposes of any motion listed in Rule 4(a)(4)(A)—the notice becomes effective to appeal a judgment or order, in whole or in part, when the order disposing of the last such remaining motion is entered.

(ii) A party intending to challenge an order disposing of any motion listed in Rule 4(a)(4)(A), or a judgment altered or amended upon such a motion, must file a notice of appeal, or an amended notice of appeal—in compliance with Rule 3(c)—within the time prescribed by this Rule measured from the entry of the order disposing of the last such remaining motion.

(iii) No additional fee is required to file an amended notice.

(5) *Motion for Extension of Time.*

(A) The district court may extend the time to file a notice of appeal if:

(i) a party so moves no later than 30 days after the time prescribed by this Rule 4(a) expires; and

(ii) regardless of whether its motion is filed before or during the 30 days after the time prescribed by this Rule 4(a) expires, that party shows excusable neglect or good cause.

(B) A motion filed before the expiration of the time prescribed in Rule 4(a)(1) or (3) may be ex parte unless the court requires otherwise. If the motion is filed after the expiration of the prescribed time, notice must be given to the other parties in accordance with local rules.

(C) No extension under this Rule 4(a)(5) may exceed 30 days after the prescribed time or 10 days after the date when the order granting the motion is entered, whichever is later.

(6) *Reopening the Time to File an Appeal.* The district court may reopen the time to file an appeal for a period of 14 days after the date when its order to reopen is entered, but only if all the following conditions are satisfied:

(A) the motion is filed within 180 days after the judgment or order is entered or within 7 days after the moving party receives notice of the entry, whichever is earlier;

(B) the court finds that the moving party was entitled to notice of the entry of the judgment or order sought to be appealed but did not receive the notice from the district court or any party within 21 days after entry; and

(C) the court finds that no party would be prejudiced.

(7) *Entry Defined.*

(A) A judgment or order is entered for purposes of this Rule 4(a):

(i) if Federal Rule of Civil Procedure 58(a)(1) does not require a separate document, when the judgment or order is entered in the civil docket under Federal Rule of Civil Procedure 79(a); or

(ii) if Federal Rule of Civil Procedure 58(a)(1) requires a separate document, when the judgment or order is entered in the civil docket under Federal Rule of Civil Procedure 79(a) and when the earlier of these events occurs:

• the judgment or order is set forth on a separate document, or

• 150 days have run from entry of the judgment or order in the civil docket under Federal Rule of Civil Procedure 79(a).

(B) A failure to set forth a judgment or order on a separate document when required by Federal Rule of Civil Procedure 58(a)(1) does not affect the validity of an appeal from that judgment or order.

(b) Appeal in a Criminal Case.

(1) *Time for Filing a Notice of Appeal.*

(A) In a criminal case, a defendant's notice of appeal must be filed in the district court within 10 days after the later of:

(i) the entry of either the judgment or the order being appealed; or

(ii) the filing of the government's notice of appeal.

(B) When the government is entitled to appeal, its notice of appeal must be filed in the district court within 30 days after the later of:

(i) the entry of the judgment or order being appealed; or

(ii) the filing of a notice of appeal by any defendant.

(2) *Filing Before Entry of Judgment.* A notice of appeal filed after the court announces a decision, sentence, or order—but before the entry of the judgment or order—is treated as filed on the date of and after the entry.

(3) *Effect of a Motion on a Notice of Appeal.*

(A) If a defendant timely makes any of the following motions under the Federal Rules of Criminal Procedure, the notice of appeal from a judgment of conviction must be filed within 10 days after the entry of the order disposing of the last such remaining motion, or within 10 days after the entry of the judgment of conviction, whichever period ends later. This provision applies to a timely motion:

(i) for judgment of acquittal under Rule 29;

(ii) for a new trial under Rule 33, but if based on newly discovered evidence, only if the motion is made no later than 10 days after the entry of the judgment; or

(iii) for arrest of judgment under Rule 34.

(B) A notice of appeal filed after the court announces a decision, sentence, or order—but before it disposes of any of the motions referred to in Rule 4(b)(3)(A)—becomes effective upon the later of the following:

(i) the entry of the order disposing of the last such remaining motion; or

(ii) the entry of the judgment of conviction.

(C) A valid notice of appeal is effective—without amendment—to appeal from an order disposing of any of the motions referred to in Rule 4(b)(3)(A).

(4) *Motion for Extension of Time.* Upon a finding of excusable neglect or good cause, the district court may—before or after the time has expired, with or without motion and notice—extend the time to file a notice of appeal for a period not to exceed 30 days from the expiration of the time otherwise prescribed by this Rule 4(b).

(5) *Jurisdiction.* The filing of a notice of appeal under this Rule 4(b) does not divest a district court of jurisdiction to correct a sentence under Federal Rule of Criminal Procedure 35(a), nor does the filing of a motion under 35(a) affect the validity of a notice of appeal filed before entry of the order disposing of the motion. The filing of a motion under Federal Rule of Criminal Procedure 35(a) does not suspend the time for filing a notice of appeal from a judgment of conviction.

(6) *Entry Defined.* A judgment or order is entered for purposes of this Rule 4(b) when it is entered on the criminal docket.

(c) Appeal by an Inmate Confined in an Institution.

(1) If an inmate confined in an institution files a notice of appeal in either a civil or a criminal case, the notice is timely if it is deposited in the institution's internal mail system on or before the last day for filing. If an institution has a system designed for legal mail, the inmate must use that system to receive the benefit of this rule. Timely filing may be shown by a declaration in compliance with 28 U.S.C. § 1746 or by a notarized statement, either of which must set forth the date of deposit and state that first-class postage has been prepaid.

(2) If an inmate files the first notice of appeal in a civil case under this Rule 4(c), the 14–day period provided in Rule 4(a)(3) for another party to file a notice of appeal runs from the date when the district court dockets the first notice.

(3) When a defendant in a criminal case files a notice of appeal under this Rule 4(c), the 30–day period for the government to file its notice of appeal runs from the entry of the judgment or order appealed from or from the district court's docketing of the defendant's notice of appeal, whichever is later.

(d) Mistaken Filing in the Court of Appeals.
If a notice of appeal in either a civil or a criminal case is mistakenly filed in the court of appeals, the clerk of that court must note on the notice the date when it was received and send it to the district clerk. The notice is then considered filed in the district court on the date so noted.

[Amended April 30, 1979, effective August 1, 1979; amended by Pub.L. 100–690, Title VII, § 7111, November 18, 1988, 102 Stat. 4419; amended April 30, 1991, effective December 1, 1991; April 22, 1993, effective December 1, 1993; April 27, 1995, effective December 1, 1995; April 24, 1998, effective December 1, 1998; April 29, 2002, effective December 1, 2002.]

FRAP 5. APPEAL BY PERMISSION

(a) Petition for Permission to Appeal.

(1) To request permission to appeal when an appeal is within the court of appeals' discretion, a party must file a petition for permission to appeal. The petition must be filed with the circuit clerk with proof of service on all other parties to the district-court action.

(2) The petition must be filed within the time specified by the statute or rule authorizing the appeal or, if no such time is specified, within the time provided by Rule 4(a) for filing a notice of appeal.

(3) If a party cannot petition for appeal unless the district court first enters an order granting permission to do so or stating that the necessary conditions are met, the district court may amend its order, either on its own or in response to a party's motion, to include the required permission or statement. In that event, the time to petition runs from entry of the amended order.

(b) Contents of the Petition; Answer or Cross–Petition; Oral Argument.

(1) The petition must include the following:

(A) the facts necessary to understand the question presented;

(B) the question itself;

(C) the relief sought;

(D) the reasons why the appeal should be allowed and is authorized by a statute or rule; and

(E) an attached copy of:

(i) the order, decree, or judgment complained of and any related opinion or memorandum, and

(ii) any order stating the district court's permission to appeal or finding that the necessary conditions are met.

(2) A party may file an answer in opposition or a cross-petition within 7 days after the petition is served.

(3) The petition and answer will be submitted without oral argument unless the court of appeals orders otherwise.

(c) Form of Papers; Number of Copies.
All papers must conform to Rule 32(c)(2). Except by the court's permission, a paper must not exceed 20 pages, exclusive of the disclosure statement, the proof of service, and the accompanying documents required by Rule 5(b)(1)(E). An original and 3 copies must be filed unless the court requires a different number by local rule or by order in a particular case.

(d) Grant of Permission; Fees; Cost Bond; Filing the Record.

(1) Within 10 days after the entry of the order granting permission to appeal, the appellant must:

(A) pay the district clerk all required fees; and

(B) file a cost bond if required under Rule 7.

(2) A notice of appeal need not be filed. The date when the order granting permission to appeal is entered serves as the date of the notice of appeal for calculating time under these rules.

(3) The district clerk must notify the circuit clerk once the petitioner has paid the fees. Upon receiving this notice, the circuit clerk must enter the appeal on the docket. The record must be forwarded and filed in accordance with Rules 11 and 12(c).

[Amended April 30, 1979, effective August 1, 1979; April 29, 1994, effective December 1, 1994; April 24, 1998, effective December 1, 1998; April 29, 2002, effective December 1, 2002.]

FRAP 5.1 APPEAL BY PERMISSION UNDER 28 U.S.C. § 636(c)(5) [ABROGATED]

[Adopted March 10, 1986, effective July 1, 1986; amended April 22, 1993, effective December 1, 1993; April 29, 1994, effective December 1, 1994; abrogated effective December 1, 1998.]

FRAP 6. APPEAL IN A BANKRUPTCY CASE FROM A FINAL JUDGMENT, ORDER, OR DECREE OF A DISTRICT COURT OR BANKRUPTCY APPELLATE PANEL

(a) Appeal From a Judgment, Order, or Decree of a District Court Exercising Original Jurisdiction in a Bankruptcy Case.
An appeal to a court of appeals from a final judgment, order, or decree of a district court exercising jurisdiction under 28 U.S.C. § 1334 is taken as any other civil appeal under these rules.

(b) Appeal From a Judgment, Order, or Decree of a District Court or Bankruptcy Appellate Panel Exercising Appellate Jurisdiction in a Bankruptcy Case.

(1) *Applicability of Other Rules.* These rules apply to an appeal to a court of appeals under 28 U.S.C. § 158(d) from a final judgment, order, or decree of a district court or bankruptcy appellate panel exercising appellate jurisdiction under 28 U.S.C. § 158(a) or (b). But there are 3 exceptions:

(A) Rules 4(a)(4), 4(b), 9, 10, 11, 12(b), 13–20, 22–23, and 24(b) do not apply;

(B) the reference in Rule 3(c) to "Form 1 in the Appendix of Forms" must be read as a reference to Form 5; and

(C) when the appeal is from a bankruptcy appellate panel, the term "district court," as used in any applicable rule, means "appellate panel."

(2) *Additional Rules.* In addition to the rules made applicable by Rule 6(b)(1), the following rules apply:

(A) Motion for rehearing.

(i) If a timely motion for rehearing under Bankruptcy Rule 8015 is filed, the time to appeal for all parties runs from the entry of the order disposing of the motion. A notice of appeal filed after the district court or bankruptcy appellate panel announces or enters a judgment, order, or decree—but before disposition of the motion for rehearing—becomes effective when the order disposing of the motion for rehearing is entered.

(ii) Appellate review of the order disposing of the motion requires the party, in compliance with Rules 3(c) and 6(b)(1)(B), to amend a previously filed notice of appeal. A party intending to challenge an altered or amended judgment, order, or decree must file a notice of appeal or amended notice of appeal within the time prescribed by Rule 4—excluding Rules 4(a)(4) and 4(b)—measured from the entry of the order disposing of the motion.

(iii) No additional fee is required to file an amended notice.

(B) The record on appeal.

(i) Within 10 days after filing the notice of appeal, the appellant must file with the clerk possessing the record assembled in accordance with Bankruptcy Rule 8006—and serve on the appellee—a statement of the issues to be presented on appeal and a designation of the record to be certified and sent to the circuit clerk.

(ii) An appellee who believes that other parts of the record are necessary must, within 10 days after being served with the appellant's designation, file with the clerk and serve on the appellant a designation of additional parts to be included.

(iii) The record on appeal consists of:

• the redesignated record as provided above;

• the proceedings in the district court or bankruptcy appellate panel; and

• a certified copy of the docket entries prepared by the clerk under Rule 3(d).

(C) Forwarding the record.

(i) When the record is complete, the district clerk or bankruptcy appellate panel clerk must number the documents constituting the record and send them promptly to the circuit clerk together with a list of the documents correspondingly numbered and reasonably identified. Unless directed to do so by a party or the circuit clerk, the clerk will not send to the court of appeals documents of unusual bulk or weight, physical exhibits other than documents, or other parts of the record designated for omission by

local rule of the court of appeals. If the exhibits are unusually bulky or heavy, a party must arrange with the clerks in advance for their transportation and receipt.

(ii) All parties must do whatever else is necessary to enable the clerk to assemble and forward the record. The court of appeals may provide by rule or order that a certified copy of the docket entries be sent in place of the redesignated record, but any party may request at any time during the pendency of the appeal that the redesignated record be sent.

(D) Filing the record. Upon receiving the record—or a certified copy of the docket entries sent in place of the redesignated record—the circuit clerk must file it and immediately notify all parties of the filing date.

[Former Rule 6 amended April 30, 1979, effective August 1, 1979; repealed and new Rule 6 adopted April 25, 1989, effective December 1, 1989; caption amended April 30, 1991, effective December 1, 1991; caption and text amended April 22, 1993, effective December 1, 1993; April 24, 1998, effective December 1, 1998.]

FRAP 7. BOND FOR COSTS ON APPEAL IN A CIVIL CASE

In a civil case, the district court may require an appellant to file a bond or provide other security in any form and amount necessary to ensure payment of costs on appeal. Rule 8(b) applies to a surety on a bond given under this rule.

[Amended April 30, 1979, effective August 1, 1979; April 24, 1998, effective December 1, 1998.]

FRAP 8. STAY OR INJUNCTION PENDING APPEAL

(a) Motion for Stay.

(1) *Initial Motion in the District Court.* A party must ordinarily move first in the district court for the following relief:

(A) a stay of the judgment or order of a district court pending appeal;

(B) approval of a supersedeas bond; or

(C) an order suspending, modifying, restoring, or granting an injunction while an appeal is pending.

(2) *Motion in the Court of Appeals; Conditions on Relief.* A motion for the relief mentioned in Rule 8(a)(1) may be made to the court of appeals or to one of its judges.

(A) The motion must:

(i) show that moving first in the district court would be impracticable; or

(ii) state that, a motion having been made, the district court denied the motion or failed to afford the relief requested and state any reasons given by the district court for its action.

(B) The motion must also include:

(i) the reasons for granting the relief requested and the facts relied on;

(ii) originals or copies of affidavits or other sworn statements supporting facts subject to dispute; and

(iii) relevant parts of the record.

(C) The moving party must give reasonable notice of the motion to all parties.

(D) A motion under this Rule 8(a)(2) must be filed with the circuit clerk and normally will be considered by a panel of the court. But in an exceptional case in which time requirements make that procedure impracticable, the motion may be made to and considered by a single judge.

(E) The court may condition relief on a party's filing a bond or other appropriate security in the district court.

(b) Proceeding Against a Surety. If a party gives security in the form of a bond or stipulation or other undertaking with one or more sureties, each surety submits to the jurisdiction of the district court and irrevocably appoints the district clerk as the surety's agent on whom any papers affecting the surety's liability on the bond or undertaking may be served. On motion, a surety's liability may be enforced in the district court without the necessity of an independent action. The motion and any notice that the district court prescribes may be served on the district clerk, who must promptly mail a copy to each surety whose address is known.

(c) Stay in a Criminal Case. Rule 38 of the Federal Rules of Criminal Procedure governs a stay in a criminal case.

[Amended March 10, 1986, effective July 1, 1986; April 27, 1995, effective December 1, 1995; April 24, 1998, effective December 1, 1998.]

FRAP 9.　RELEASE IN A CRIMINAL CASE

(a) Release Before Judgment of Conviction.

(1) The district court must state in writing, or orally on the record, the reasons for an order regarding the release or detention of a defendant in a criminal case. A party appealing from the order must file with the court of appeals a copy of the district court's order and the court's statement of reasons as soon as practicable after filing the notice of appeal. An appellant who questions the factual basis for the district court's order must file a transcript of the release proceedings or an explanation of why a transcript was not obtained.

(2) After reasonable notice to the appellee, the court of appeals must promptly determine the appeal on the basis of the papers, affidavits, and parts of the record that the parties present or the court requires. Unless the court so orders, briefs need not be filed.

(3) The court of appeals or one of its judges may order the defendant's release pending the disposition of the appeal.

(b) Release After Judgment of Conviction. A party entitled to do so may obtain review of a district-court order regarding release after a judgment of conviction by filing a notice of appeal from that order in the district court, or by filing a motion in the court of appeals if the party has already filed a notice of appeal from the judgment of conviction. Both the order and the review are subject to Rule 9(a). The papers filed by the party seeking review must include a copy of the judgment of conviction.

(c) Criteria for Release. The court must make its decision regarding release in accordance with the applicable provisions of 18 U.S.C. §§ 3142, 3143, and 3145(c).

[Amended April 24, 1972, effective October 1, 1972; amended by Pub.L. 98–473, Title II, § 210, October 12, 1984, 98 Stat. 1987; April 29, 1994, effective December 1, 1994; April 24, 1998, effective December 1, 1998.]

LOC. R. 9.　RECALCITRANT WITNESSES

(a) A recalcitrant witness who is held in contempt for refusal to testify is entitled to disposition of the recalcitrant witness's appeal within thirty days if the recalcitrant witness is denied bail, and the government is entitled to equal promptness if bail is granted. The unsuccessful party on the bail issue may waive the thirty day statutory requirement by filing a written waiver with the clerk of this court.

(b) The district court shall allow bail, with or without surety, unless the appeal appears frivolous, but a condition shall be the filing of a notice of appeal forthwith, and obedience to all subsequent orders with respect to briefing and argument. Except for cause shown the district court shall not, in any case, order a witness committed for the first forty-eight hours after the date of the order.

(c) The appeal shall be docketed immediately, and the district court's order on bail may be reviewed by the court of appeals or a judge thereof.

Adopted effective Sept. 1, 1986.

FRAP 10.　THE RECORD ON APPEAL

(a) Composition of the Record on Appeal. The following items constitute the record on appeal:

(1) the original papers and exhibits filed in the district court;

(2) the transcript of proceedings, if any; and

(3) a certified copy of the docket entries prepared by the district clerk.

(b) The Transcript of Proceedings.

(1) *Appellant's Duty to Order.* Within 10 days after filing the notice of appeal or entry of an order disposing of the last timely remaining motion of a type specified in Rule 4(a)(4)(A), whichever is later, the appellant must do either of the following:

(A) order from the reporter a transcript of such parts of the proceedings not already on file as the appellant considers necessary, subject to a local rule of the court of appeals and with the following qualifications:

(i) the order must be in writing;

(ii) if the cost of the transcript is to be paid by the United States under the Criminal Justice Act, the order must so state; and

(iii) the appellant must, within the same period, file a copy of the order with the district clerk; or

(B) file a certificate stating that no transcript will be ordered.

(2) *Unsupported Finding or Conclusion.* If the appellant intends to urge on appeal that a finding or conclusion is unsupported by the evidence or is contrary to the evidence, the appellant must include in the record a transcript of all evidence relevant to that finding or conclusion.

(3) *Partial Transcript.* Unless the entire transcript is ordered:

(A) the appellant must—within the 10 days provided in Rule 10(b)(1)—file a statement of the issues that the appellant intends to present on the appeal and must serve on the appellee a copy of both the order or certificate and the statement;

(B) if the appellee considers it necessary to have a transcript of other parts of the proceedings, the appellee must, within 10 days after the service of the order or certificate and the statement of the issues, file and serve on the appellant a designation of additional parts to be ordered; and

(C) unless within 10 days after service of that designation the appellant has ordered all such parts, and has so notified the appellee, the appellee may within the following 10 days either order the parts or move in the district court for an order requiring the appellant to do so.

(4) *Payment.* At the time of ordering, a party must make satisfactory arrangements with the reporter for paying the cost of the transcript.

(c) Statement of the Evidence When the Proceedings Were Not Recorded or When a Transcript Is Unavailable. If the transcript of a hearing or trial is unavailable, the appellant may prepare a statement of the evidence or proceedings from the best available means, including the appellant's recollection. The

statement must be served on the appellee, who may serve objections or proposed amendments within 10 days after being served. The statement and any objections or proposed amendments must then be submitted to the district court for settlement and approval. As settled and approved, the statement must be included by the district clerk in the record on appeal.

(d) Agreed Statement as the Record on Appeal. In place of the record on appeal as defined in Rule 10(a), the parties may prepare, sign, and submit to the district court a statement of the case showing how the issues presented by the appeal arose and were decided in the district court. The statement must set forth only those facts averred and proved or sought to be proved that are essential to the court's resolution of the issues. If the statement is truthful, it—together with any additions that the district court may consider necessary to a full presentation of the issues on appeal—must be approved by the district court and must then be certified to the court of appeals as the record on appeal. The district clerk must then send it to the circuit clerk within the time provided by Rule 11. A copy of the agreed statement may be filed in place of the appendix required by Rule 30.

(e) Correction or Modification of the Record.

(1) If any difference arises about whether the record truly discloses what occurred in the district court, the difference must be submitted to and settled by that court and the record conformed accordingly.

(2) If anything material to either party is omitted from or misstated in the record by error or accident, the omission or misstatement may be corrected and a supplemental record may be certified and forwarded:

(A) on stipulation of the parties;

(B) by the district court before or after the record has been forwarded; or

(C) by the court of appeals.

(3) All other questions as to the form and content of the record must be presented to the court of appeals.

[Amended April 30, 1979, effective August 1, 1979; March 10, 1986, effective July 1, 1986; April 30, 1991, effective December 1, 1991; April 22, 1993, effective December 1, 1993; April 27, 1995, effective December 1, 1995; April 24, 1998, effective December 1, 1998.]

LOC. R. 10. *ORDERING TRANSCRIPTS*

(a) Timely Filing. Fed.R.App.P. 10(b) requires that the transcript be ordered within 10 days of the filing of the notice of appeal Parties are nevertheless urged to order any necessary transcript immediately after the filing of the notice. If the appellant fails to timely order a transcript in writing from the court reporter, the appeal may be dismissed for want of diligent prosecution.

(b) Transcript Order/Report. A Transcript Order/Report in the form prescribed by this court, shall be used to satisfy the requirements of Fed.R.App.P. 10(b).

(c) Transcripts under the Criminal Justice Act. If the cost of the transcript is to be paid by the United States under the Criminal Justice Act, counsel must complete and attach CJA form 24 to the Transcript Order/Report so as to satisfy the requirement of Fed. R.App.P 10(b)(4).

(d) Caveat. The court is of the opinion that in many cases a transcript is not really needed, and makes for delay and expense, as well as unnecessarily large records. The court urges counsel to endeavor, in appropriate cases, to enter into stipulations that will avoid or reduce transcripts. See Fed.R.App.P. 30(b). However, if an agreed statement of the evidence is contemplated, counsel are reminded of Fed. R.App.P. 10(c) requiring submission to the district court for approval The ten-day ordering rule will not be suspended because of such activity,-however, except by order of the court for good cause shown.

Adopted effective Sept. 1, 1986; amended effective Oct. 29, 1990; September, 1999.

FRAP 11. FORWARDING THE RECORD

(a) Appellant's Duty. An appellant filing a notice of appeal must comply with Rule 10(b) and must do whatever else is necessary to enable the clerk to assemble and forward the record. If there are multiple appeals from a judgment or order, the clerk must forward a single record.

(b) Duties of Reporter and District Clerk.

(1) *Reporter's Duty to Prepare and File a Transcript.* The reporter must prepare and file a transcript as follows:

(A) Upon receiving an order for a transcript, the reporter must enter at the foot of the order the date of its receipt and the expected completion date and send a copy, so endorsed, to the circuit clerk.

(B) If the transcript cannot be completed within 30 days of the reporter's receipt of the order, the reporter may request the circuit clerk to grant additional time to complete it. The clerk must note on the docket the action taken and notify the parties.

(C) When a transcript is complete, the reporter must file it with the district clerk and notify the circuit clerk of the filing.

(D) If the reporter fails to file the transcript on time, the circuit clerk must notify the district judge and do whatever else the court of appeals directs.

(2) *District Clerk's Duty to Forward.* When the record is complete, the district clerk must number the documents constituting the record and send them promptly to the circuit clerk together with a list of the documents correspondingly numbered and reasonably identified. Unless directed to do so by a party or the circuit clerk, the district clerk will not send to the court of appeals documents of unusual bulk or weight, physical exhibits other than documents, or other parts of the record designated for omission by local rule of the court of appeals. If the exhibits are unusually bulky or heavy, a party must arrange with the clerks in advance for their transportation and receipt.

(c) Retaining the Record Temporarily in the District Court for Use in Preparing the Appeal. The parties may stipulate, or the district court on motion may order, that the district clerk retain the record temporarily for the parties to use in preparing the papers on appeal. In that event the district clerk must certify to the circuit clerk that the record on appeal is complete. Upon receipt of the appellee's brief, or earlier if the court orders or the parties agree, the appellant must request the district clerk to forward the record.

(d) [Abrogated.]

(e) Retaining the Record by Court Order.

(1) The court of appeals may, by order or local rule, provide that a certified copy of the docket entries be forwarded instead of the entire record. But a party may at any time during the appeal request that designated parts of the record be forwarded.

(2) The district court may order the record or some part of it retained if the court needs it while the appeal is pending, subject, however, to call by the court of appeals.

(3) If part or all of the record is ordered retained, the district clerk must send to the court of appeals a copy of the order and the docket entries together with the parts of the original record allowed by the district court and copies of any parts of the record designated by the parties.

(f) Retaining Parts of the Record in the District Court by Stipulation of the Parties. The parties may agree by written stipulation filed in the district court that designated parts of the record be retained in the district court subject to call by the court of appeals or request by a party. The parts of the record so designated remain a part of the record on appeal.

(g) Record for a Preliminary Motion in the Court of Appeals. If, before the record is forwarded, a party makes any of the following motions in the court of appeals:

● for dismissal;

● for release;

● for a stay pending appeal;

● for additional security on the bond on appeal or on a supersedeas bond; or

● for any other intermediate order—

the district clerk must send the court of appeals any parts of the record designated by any party.

[Amended April 30, 1979, effective August 1, 1979; March 10, 1986, effective July 1, 1986; April 24, 1998, effective December 1, 1998.]

LOCAL RULE 11. TRANSMISSION OF THE RECORD, SEALED DOCUMENTS

(a) Duty of Appellant. *In addition to an appellant's duties under Fed. R. App. P. 11(a), it is an appellant's responsibility to see that the record, as certified, is complete.*

(b) Transmission of Original Papers and Exhibits. *The district courts are to transmit the original papers and exhibits when complete without waiting for the filing of the transcript.*

(c) Sealed Materials.

(1) Materials Sealed by District Court or Agency Order. *The court of appeals expects that ordinarily motions to seal all or part of a district court or agency record will be presented to, and resolved by, the lower court or agency. Motions, briefs, transcripts, and other materials which were filed with the district court or agency under seal and which constitute part of the record transmitted to the court of appeals shall be clearly labeled as sealed when transmitted to the court of appeals and will remain under seal until further order of court.*

(2) Motions to Seal in the Court of Appeals. *In order to seal in the court of appeals materials not already sealed in the district court or agency (e.g., a brief or unsealed portion of the record), a motion to seal must be filed in the court of appeals; parties cannot seal otherwise public documents merely by agreement or by labeling them "sealed." A motion to seal, which should not itself be filed under seal, must explain the basis for sealing and specify the desired duration of the sealing order. If discussion of confidential material is necessary to support the motion to seal, that discussion shall be confined to an affidavit or declaration, which may be filed provisionally under seal. A motion to seal may be filed before the sealed material is submitted or, alternatively the item to be sealed (e.g., the brief) may be tendered with the motion and, upon request, will be accepted provisionally under seal, subject to the court's subsequent ruling on the motion. Material submitted by a party under seal, provisionally or otherwise must be stamped or labeled by the party on the cover "FILED UNDER SEAL." If the court of appeals denies the movant's motion to seal, any materials tendered under provisional seal will be returned to the movant.*

(3) Limiting Sealed Filings. *Rather than automatically requesting the sealing of an entire brief, motion, or other filing, litigants should consider whether argument relating to sealed materials may be contained in separate supplemental brief, motion, or filing,*

which may then be sealed in accordance with the procedures in subsection (2).

(d) References to Sealed Materials.

(1) Records or materials sealed by district court, court of appeals, or agency order shall not be included in the regular appendix, but may be submitted in a separate, sealed supplemental volume of appendix. The sealed supplemental volume must be clearly and prominently labeled by the party on the cover "FILED UNDER SEAL."

(2) In addressing material under seal in an unsealed brief or motion or oral argument counsel are expected not to disclose the substance of the sealed material and to apprise the court that the material in question is sealed. If the record contains sealed materials of a sensitive character, counsel would be well advised to alert the court to the existence of such materials and their location by a footnote appended to the "Statement of facts" caption in the opening or answering brief.

Adopted effective Sept. 1, 1986; amended effective September, 1999.

FRAP 12. DOCKETING THE APPEAL; FILING A REPRESENTATION STATEMENT; FILING THE RECORD

(a) Docketing the Appeal. Upon receiving the copy of the notice of appeal and the docket entries from the district clerk under Rule 3(d), the circuit clerk must docket the appeal under the title of the district-court action and must identify the appellant, adding the appellant's name if necessary.

(b) Filing a Representation Statement. Unless the court of appeals designates another time, the attorney who filed the notice of appeal must, within 10 days after filing the notice, file a statement with the circuit clerk naming the parties that the attorney represents on appeal.

(c) Filing the Record, Partial Record, or Certificate. Upon receiving the record, partial record, or district clerk's certificate as provided in Rule 11, the circuit clerk must file it and immediately notify all parties of the filing date.

[Amended April 30, 1979, effective August 1, 1979; March 10, 1986, effective July 1, 1986; April 22, 1993, effective December 1, 1993; April 24, 1998, effective December 1, 1998.]

LOCAL RULE 12. APPEARANCE, WITHDRAWAL OF APPEARANCE

(a) Representation Statement, Appearance. *A representation statement must take the form of an appearance, in a form prescribed by this court. Attorneys for both appellant and appellee must file appear-*

ance forms within 10 days after the filing of the notice of appeal. See also Local Rule 46(a).

(b) Withdrawal of Appearance. No attorney who has entered an appearance in this court may withdraw without the consent of the court. An attorney who has represented a defendant in a criminal case in the district court will be responsible for representing the defendant on appeal, whether or not the *attorney has entered an appearance in the Court of Appeals, until the attorney is relieved of such duty by the court. Procedures for withdrawal in criminal cases are found in Local Rule 46.6. For requirements applying to court-appointed counsel, reference is made to Loc. R. 46.5, para. (c), the Criminal Justice Plan of this Circuit.*

Adopted effective Sept. 1, 1986; amended effective September, 1999.

TITLE III.　REVIEW OF A DECISION OF THE UNITED STATES TAX COURT

FRAP 13.　REVIEW OF A DECISION OF THE TAX COURT

(a) How Obtained; Time for Filing Notice of Appeal.

(1) Review of a decision of the United States Tax Court is commenced by filing a notice of appeal with the Tax Court clerk within 90 days after the entry of the Tax Court's decision. At the time of filing, the appellant must furnish the clerk with enough copies of the notice to enable the clerk to comply with Rule 3(d). If one party files a timely notice of appeal, any other party may file a notice of appeal within 120 days after the Tax Court's decision is entered.

(2) If, under Tax Court rules, a party makes a timely motion to vacate or revise the Tax Court's decision, the time to file a notice of appeal runs from the entry of the order disposing of the motion or from the entry of a new decision, whichever is later.

(b) Notice of Appeal; How Filed. The notice of appeal may be filed either at the Tax Court clerk's office in the District of Columbia or by mail addressed to the clerk. If sent by mail the notice is considered filed on the postmark date, subject to § 7502 of the Internal Revenue Code, as amended, and the applicable regulations.

(c) Contents of the Notice of Appeal; Service; Effect of Filing and Service. Rule 3 prescribes the contents of a notice of appeal, the manner of service, and the effect of its filing and service. Form 2 in the

Appendix of Forms is a suggested form of a notice of appeal.

(d) The Record on Appeal; Forwarding; Filing.

(1) An appeal from the Tax Court is governed by the parts of Rules 10, 11, and 12 regarding the record on appeal from a district court, the time and manner of forwarding and filing, and the docketing in the court of appeals. References in those rules and in Rule 3 to the district court and district clerk are to be read as referring to the Tax Court and its clerk.

(2) If an appeal from a Tax Court decision is taken to more than one court of appeals, the original record must be sent to the court named in the first notice of appeal filed. In an appeal to any other court of appeals, the appellant must apply to that other court to make provision for the record.

[Amended April 30, 1979, effective August 1, 1979; April 29, 1994, effective December 1, 1994; April 24, 1998, effective December 1, 1998.]

FRAP 14.　APPLICABILITY OF OTHER RULES TO THE REVIEW OF A TAX COURT DECISION

All provisions of these rules, except Rules 4–9, 15–20, and 22–23, apply to the review of a Tax Court decision.

[Amended April 24, 1998, effective December 1, 1998.]

TITLE IV.　REVIEW OR ENFORCEMENT OF AN ORDER OF AN ADMINISTRATIVE AGENCY, BOARD, COMMISSION, OR OFFICER

FRAP 15.　REVIEW OR ENFORCEMENT OF AN AGENCY ORDER—HOW OBTAINED; INTERVENTION

(a) Petition for Review; Joint Petition.

(1) Review of an agency order is commenced by filing, within the time prescribed by law, a petition for

review with the clerk of a court of appeals authorized to review the agency order. If their interests make joinder practicable, two or more persons may join in a petition to the same court to review the same order.

(2) The petition must:

(A) name each party seeking review either in the caption or the body of the petition—using such terms as "et al.," "petitioners," or "respondents" does not effectively name the parties;

(B) name the agency as a respondent (even though not named in the petition, the United States is a respondent if required by statute); and

(C) specify the order or part thereof to be reviewed.

(3) Form 3 in the Appendix of Forms is a suggested form of a petition for review.

(4) In this rule "agency" includes an agency, board, commission, or officer; "petition for review" includes a petition to enjoin, suspend, modify, or otherwise review, or a notice of appeal, whichever form is indicated by the applicable statute.

(b) Application or Cross–Application to Enforce an Order; Answer; Default.

(1) An application to enforce an agency order must be filed with the clerk of a court of appeals authorized to enforce the order. If a petition is filed to review an agency order that the court may enforce, a party opposing the petition may file a cross-application for enforcement.

(2) Within 20 days after the application for enforcement is filed, the respondent must serve on the applicant an answer to the application and file it with the clerk. If the respondent fails to answer in time, the court will enter judgment for the relief requested.

(3) The application must contain a concise statement of the proceedings in which the order was entered, the facts upon which venue is based, and the relief requested.

(c) Service of the Petition or Application. The circuit clerk must serve a copy of the petition for review, or an application or cross-application to enforce an agency order, on each respondent as prescribed by Rule 3(d), unless a different manner of service is prescribed by statute. At the time of filing, the petitioner must:

(1) serve, or have served, a copy on each party admitted to participate in the agency proceedings, except for the respondents;

(2) file with the clerk a list of those so served; and

(3) give the clerk enough copies of the petition or application to serve each respondent.

(d) Intervention. Unless a statute provides another method, a person who wants to intervene in a proceeding under this rule must file a motion for leave to intervene with the circuit clerk and serve a copy on all parties. The motion—or other notice of intervention authorized by statute—must be filed within 30 days after the petition for review is filed and must contain a concise statement of the interest of the moving party and the grounds for intervention.

(e) Payment of Fees. When filing any separate or joint petition for review in a court of appeals, the petitioner must pay the circuit clerk all required fees.

[Amended April 22, 1993, effective December 1, 1993; April 24, 1998, effective December 1, 1998.]

FRAP 15.1 BRIEFS AND ORAL ARGUMENT IN A NATIONAL LABOR RELATIONS BOARD PROCEEDING

In either an enforcement or a review proceeding, a party adverse to the National Labor Relations Board proceeds first on briefing and at oral argument, unless the court orders otherwise.

[Adopted March 10, 1986, effective July 1, 1986; April 24, 1998, effective December 1, 1998.]

FRAP 16. THE RECORD ON REVIEW OR ENFORCEMENT

(a) Composition of the Record. The record on review or enforcement of an agency order consists of:

(1) the order involved;

(2) any findings or report on which it is based; and

(3) the pleadings, evidence, and other parts of the proceedings before the agency.

(b) Omissions From or Misstatements in the Record. The parties may at any time, by stipulation, supply any omission from the record or correct a misstatement, or the court may so direct. If necessary, the court may direct that a supplemental record be prepared and filed.

[Amended April 24, 1998, effective December 1, 1998.]

FRAP 17. FILING THE RECORD

(a) Agency to File; Time for Filing; Notice of Filing. The agency must file the record with the circuit clerk within 40 days after being served with a petition for review, unless the statute authorizing review provides otherwise, or within 40 days after it files an application for enforcement unless the respondent fails to answer or the court orders otherwise. The court may shorten or extend the time to file the record. The clerk must notify all parties of the date when the record is filed.

(b) Filing—What Constitutes.

(1) The agency must file:

(A) the original or a certified copy of the entire record or parts designated by the parties; or

(B) a certified list adequately describing all documents, transcripts of testimony, exhibits, and other material constituting the record, or describing those parts designated by the parties.

(2) The parties may stipulate in writing that no record or certified list be filed. The date when the

stipulation is filed with the circuit clerk is treated as the date when the record is filed.

(3) The agency must retain any portion of the record not filed with the clerk. All parts of the record retained by the agency are a part of the record on review for all purposes and, if the court or a party so requests, must be sent to the court regardless of any prior stipulation.

[Amended April 24, 1998, effective December 1, 1998.]

FRAP 18. STAY PENDING REVIEW

(a) Motion for a Stay.

(1) *Initial Motion Before the Agency.* A petitioner must ordinarily move first before the agency for a stay pending review of its decision or order.

(2) *Motion in the Court of Appeals.* A motion for a stay may be made to the court of appeals or one of its judges.

(A) The motion must:

(i) show that moving first before the agency would be impracticable; or

(ii) state that, a motion having been made, the agency denied the motion or failed to afford the relief requested and state any reasons given by the agency for its action.

(B) The motion must also include:

(i) the reasons for granting the relief requested and the facts relied on;

(ii) originals or copies of affidavits or other sworn statements supporting facts subject to dispute; and

(iii) relevant parts of the record.

(C) The moving party must give reasonable notice of the motion to all parties.

(D) The motion must be filed with the circuit clerk and normally will be considered by a panel of the court. But in an exceptional case in which time requirements make that procedure impracticable, the motion may be made to and considered by a single judge.

(b) Bond. The court may condition relief on the filing of a bond or other appropriate security.

[Amended April 24, 1998, effective December 1, 1998.]

FRAP 19. SETTLEMENT OF A JUDGMENT ENFORCING AN AGENCY ORDER IN PART

When the court files an opinion directing entry of judgment enforcing the agency's order in part, the agency must within 14 days file with the clerk and serve on each other party a proposed judgment conforming to the opinion. A party who disagrees with the agency's proposed judgment must within 7 days file with the clerk and serve the agency with a proposed judgment that the party believes conforms to the opinion. The court will settle the judgment and direct entry without further hearing or argument.

[Amended March 10, 1986, effective July 1, 1986; April 24, 1998, effective December 1, 1998.]

FRAP 20. APPLICABILITY OF RULES TO THE REVIEW OR ENFORCEMENT OF AN AGENCY ORDER

All provisions of these rules, except Rules 3–14 and 22–23, apply to the review or enforcement of an agency order. In these rules, "appellant" includes a petitioner or applicant, and "appellee" includes a respondent.

[Amended April 24, 1998, effective December 1, 1998.]

TITLE V. EXTRAORDINARY WRITS

FRAP 21. WRITS OF MANDAMUS AND PROHIBITION, AND OTHER EXTRAORDINARY WRITS

(a) Mandamus or Prohibition to a Court: Petition, Filing, Service, and Docketing.

(1) A party petitioning for a writ of mandamus or prohibition directed to a court must file a petition with the circuit clerk with proof of service on all parties to the proceeding in the trial court. The party must also provide a copy to the trial-court judge. All parties to the proceeding in the trial court other than the petitioner are respondents for all purposes.

(2)(A) The petition must be titled "In re [name of petitioner]."

(B) The petition must state:

(i) the relief sought;

(ii) the issues presented;

(iii) the facts necessary to understand the issue presented by the petition; and

(iv) the reasons why the writ should issue.

(C) The petition must include a copy of any order or opinion or parts of the record that may be essential to understand the matters set forth in the petition.

(3) Upon receiving the prescribed docket fee, the clerk must docket the petition and submit it to the court.

(b) Denial; Order Directing Answer; Briefs; Precedence.

(1) The court may deny the petition without an answer. Otherwise, it must order the respondent, if any, to answer within a fixed time.

(2) The clerk must serve the order to respond on all persons directed to respond.

(3) Two or more respondents may answer jointly.

(4) The court of appeals may invite or order the trial-court judge to address the petition or may invite an amicus curiae to do so. The trial-court judge may request permission to address the petition but may not do so unless invited or ordered to do so by the court of appeals.

(5) If briefing or oral argument is required, the clerk must advise the parties, and when appropriate, the trial-court judge or amicus curiae.

(6) The proceeding must be given preference over ordinary civil cases.

(7) The circuit clerk must send a copy of the final disposition to the trial-court judge.

(c) Other Extraordinary Writs. An application for an extraordinary writ other than one provided for in Rule 21(a) must be made by filing a petition with the circuit clerk with proof of service on the respondents. Proceedings on the application must conform, so far as is practicable, to the procedures prescribed in Rule 21(a) and (b).

(d) Form of Papers; Number of Copies. All papers must conform to Rule 32(c)(2). Except by the court's permission, a paper must not exceed 30 pages, exclusive of the disclosure statement, the proof of service, and the accompanying documents required by Rule 21(a)(2)(C). An original and 3 copies must be filed unless the court requires the filing of a different number by local rule or by order in a particular case.

[Amended April 29, 1994, effective December 1, 1994; April 23, 1996, effective December 1, 1996; April 24, 1998, effective December 1, 1998; April 29, 2002, effective December 1, 2002.]

LOC. R. 21. PETITIONS FOR SPECIAL WRITS

A petition for a writ of mandamus or writ of prohibition shall be entitled simply "In re _____, Petitioner". To the extent that relief is requested of a particular judge, unless otherwise ordered, the judge shall be represented pro forma by counsel for the party opposing the relief, who shall appear in the name of the party and not that of the judge.

Adopted effective Sept. 1, 1986; amended effective Jan. 1, 1992; September, 1999.

TITLE VI. HABEAS CORPUS; PROCEEDINGS IN FORMA PAUPERIS

FRAP 22. HABEAS CORPUS AND SECTION 2255 PROCEEDINGS

(a) Application for the Original Writ. An application for a writ of habeas corpus must be made to the appropriate district court. If made to a circuit judge, the application must be transferred to the appropriate district court. If a district court denies an application made or transferred to it, renewal of the application before a circuit judge is not permitted. The applicant may, under 28 U.S.C. § 2253, appeal to the court of appeals from the district court's order denying the application.

(b) Certificate of Appealability.

(1) In a habeas corpus proceeding in which the detention complained of arises from process issued by a state court, or in a 28 U.S.C. § 2255 proceeding, the applicant cannot take an appeal unless a circuit justice or a circuit or district judge issues a certificate of appealability under 28 U.S.C. § 2253(c). If an applicant files a notice of appeal, the district judge who rendered the judgment must either issue a certificate of appealability or state why a certificate should not issue. The district clerk must send the certificate or statement to the court of appeals with the notice of appeal and the file of the district-court proceedings. If the district judge has denied the certificate, the applicant may request a circuit judge to issue the certificate.

(2) A request addressed to the court of appeals may be considered by a circuit judge or judges, as the court prescribes. If no express request for a certificate is filed, the notice of appeal constitutes a request addressed to the judges of the court of appeals.

(3) A certificate of appealability is not required when a state or its representative or the United States or its representative appeals.

[Amended by Pub.L. 104–32, § 103, April 24, 1996, 110 Stat. 1218; amended April 24, 1998, effective December 1, 1998.]

LOC. R. 22. HABEAS CORPUS; CERTIFICATE OF PROBABLE CAUSE

(Local Rule 22 is applicable to § 2254 petitions in which the appeal was initiated prior to April 24, 1996. See Slack v. McDaniel, 529 U.S. 473, 120 S.Ct. 1595 (2000).)

Certificate of Probable Cause. *In this circuit neither the court nor a judge thereof will initially receive or act on a request for a certificate of probable cause if the district judge who refused the writ is available. The request to the district judge should be made as promptly as possible. If the district judge denies the certificate, and a notice of appeal has been filed, this* *court will review the district court judge's decision. However, it may decline to make such review unless a memorandum has been filed by the petitioner, either in the district court, or in this court, giving specific reasons and not mere generalizations why such relief should be granted. Ten days after the district court file has been received in this court, the clerk will present the record to the court, with or without a separate request for a certificate of probable cause addressed to that court. If no sufficient memorandum has been filed by that time, the court may deny the certificate without further consideration. The effect of such denial is to terminate the appeal.*

Adopted effective Sept. 1, 1986; amended effective Jan. 1, 1992; rescinded effective September 10, 1996; reinstated July 22, 1997; September, 1999; September 26, 2000.

Publisher's Note

On July 22, 1997, the United States Court of Appeals for the First Circuit entered an order regarding Local Rule 22 and Interim Local Rules 22.1 and 22.2. Text of the order is as follows:

"In an Order effective September 10, 1996, this court adopted Interim Local Rules 22.1 and 22.2 in order to implement provisions of the Antiterrorism and Effective Death Penalty Act of 1996 ("AEDPA") relating to the processing of applications for certificates of appealability and motions to file second or successive petitions in proceedings arising under 28 U.S.C. §§ 2254 and 2255. The Order also rescinded Local Rule 22 relating to applications for certificates of probable cause in § 2254 proceedings.

"The Supreme Court's decision in *Lindh v. Murphy*, 117 S.Ct. 2059, 1997 WL 338568 (1997), indicates that the subject provisions of the AEDPA do not apply in non-capital cases that were pending in the district courts or courts of appeals prior to April 24, 1996, the effective date of the AEDPA.

"Accordingly, our Order effective September 10, 1996 is hereby <u>amended</u> as follows. Local Rule 22 is reinstated and is applicable to § 2254 proceedings which were pending prior to April 24, 1996. Interim Local Rules 22.1 and 22.2 shall be applied to the processing of non-capital § 2254 and § 2255 petitions, and to motions seeking permission to file second or successive petitions, which were filed on or after April 24, 1996."

LOC. R. 22.1 HABEAS CORPUS; CERTIFICATE OF APPEALABILITY

(Local Rule 22.1 is applicable to 28 U.S.C. §§ 2254 and 2255 petitions in which the appeal was initiated on or after April 24, 1996. Slack v. McDaniel, 529 U.S. 473, 120 S.Ct. 1595 (2000).)

(a) General Procedures. In this circuit, ordinarily neither the court nor a judge thereof will initially receive or act on a request for a certificate of appealability if the district judge who refused the writ is available, unless an application has first been made to the district court judge. A petitioner wishing to appeal from the denial of a § 2254 or § 2255 petition must timely file a notice of appeal and should

promptly apply to the district court for a certificate of appealability. If the district court grants a certificate of appealability, it must state which issue or issues satisfy the standard set forth in 28 U.S.C. § 2253 (c)(2). If the district court denies a certificate of appealability, it must state the reasons why the certificate should not issue.

(b) Denial in Full by District Court. If the district court denies a certificate of appealability, the petitioner should promptly apply within the time set by the clerk to the court of appeals for issuance of a certificate of appealability. The motion should be accompanied by a copy of the district court's order and a memorandum giving specific and substantial reasons, and not mere generalizations, why a certificate should be granted. If no sufficient memorandum has been filed by the time set by the clerk, the certificate may be denied without further consideration. The effect of a denial is to terminate the appeal.

(c) Partial Denial by District Court:

(1) If the district court grants a certificate of appealability as to one or more issues, the petitioner's appeal shall go forward only as to the issue or issues for which the district court granted the certificate. See Grant-Chase v. Commissioner, 145 F.3d 431 (1st Cir. 1998).

(2) If the petitioner wants appellate review of an issue or issues as to which the district court has denied a certificate of appealability, petitioner must apply promptly, within the time set by the clerk of the court of appeals, to the court of appeals for an expanded certificate of appealability. The request for an expanded certificate of appealability:

(A) must be explicit as to the additional issues the petitioner wishes the court to consider and

(B) should be accompanied by a copy of the district court order and a memorandum giving specific and substantial reasons, and not mere generalizations, why an expanded certificate of appealability should be granted.

If the petitioner fails to apply for an expanded certificate of appealability within the time designated by the clerk, the appeal will proceed only with respect to the issues on which the district court has granted a certificate; this court will not treat an inexplicit notice of appeal, without more, as a request for a certificate of appealability with respect to issues on which the district court has denied a certificate.

(d) Grant in Full by District Court. If the district court grants a certificate of appealability on all issues, the petitioner's appeal shall go forward. See Grant–Chase v. Commissioner, 145 F.3d 431 (1st Cir. 1998).

Adopted effective Sept. 10, 1996; July 22, 1997; amended effective September, 1999; September 26, 2000.

On July 22, 1997, the United States Court of Appeals for the First Circuit entered an order regarding Local Rule 22 and Interim Local Rules 22.1 and 22.2. Text of the order is as follows:

"In an Order effective September 10, 1996, this court adopted Interim Local Rules 22.1 and 22.2 in order to implement provisions of the Antiterrorism and Effective Death Penalty Act of 1996 ("AEDPA") relating to the processing of applications for certificates of appealability and motions to file second or successive petitions in proceedings arising under 28 U.S.C. §§ 2254 and 2255. The Order also rescinded Local Rule 22 relating to applications for certificates of probable cause in § 2254 proceedings.

"The Supreme Court's decision in *Lindh v. Murphy*, 117 S.Ct. 2059, 1997 WL 338568 (1997), indicates that the subject provisions of the AEDPA do not apply in non-capital cases that were pending in the district courts or courts of appeals prior to April 24, 1996, the effective date of the AEDPA.

"Accordingly, our Order effective September 10, 1996 is hereby amended as follows. Local Rule 22 is reinstated and is applicable to § 2254 proceedings which were pending prior to April 24, 1996. Interim Local Rules 22.1 and 22.2 shall be applied to the processing of non-capital § 2254 and § 2255 petitions, and to motions seeking permission to file second or successive petitions, which were filed on or after April 24, 1996."

LOC. R. 22.2 HABEAS CORPUS; SUCCESSIVE PETITIONS

(See *Appendix B: Order of the Court Regarding Section 2254, 2255 Petitions in the First Circuit*.)

(a) Motion for Authorization. Any petitioner seeking to file a second or successive petition for relief pursuant to 28 U.S.C. §§ 2254 or 2555 must first file a motion with this court for authorization. A motion for authorization to file a second or successive § 2254 or § 2255 petition must be sufficiently complete on filing to allow the court to assess whether the standard set forth in 28 U.S.C. §§ 2244(b) or 2255, as applicable, has been satisfied. The motion must be accompanied by both:

(1) a completed application form, available from this court, stating the new claims(s) presented and addressing how Section 2244(b) or Section 2255s standard is satisfied, *and*

(2) copies of all relevant portions of earlier court proceedings, which must ordinarily include:

(A) copies of all § 2254 or § 2255 petitions earlier filed,

(B) the respondent's answer to the earlier petitions (including any portion of the state record the respondent submitted to the district court),

(C) any magistrate-judge's report and recommendation in the earlier § 2254 or § 2255 proceedings,

(D) the district court's decision in the earlier proceedings, *and*

(E) the portions of the state court record needed to evaluate the claims presented and to show that movant has exhausted state court remedies.

(b) Incomplete Motion. Failure to provide the requisite application and attachments may result in the denial of the motion for authorization with or without prejudice to refiling. At its discretion, the court may instead treat the motion as lodged, the filing being deemed complete when the deficiency is remedied.

(c) Service. The movant shall serve a copy of the motion to file a second or successive petition and all accompanying attachments on the state attorney general (§ 2254 cases) or United States Attorney for the federal judicial district in which movant was convicted (§ 2255 cases) and shall comply with Fed.R.App.P. 25.

(d) Response. The state attorney general (§ 2254 cases) or United States Attorney (§ 2255 cases) is requested to file a response within 14 days of the filing of the motion.

(e) Transfer. If a second or successive § 2254 or § 2255 petition is filed in a district court without the requisite authorization by the court of appeals pursuant to 28 U.S.C. § 2244(b)(3), the district court will transfer the petition to the court of appeals pursuant to 28 U.S.C. § 1631 or dismiss the petition. If the petition is transferred the petitioner must file a motion meeting the substantive requirements of Loc. R. 22.2(a) within 45 days of the date of notice from the clerk of the court of appeals that said motion is required. If the motion is not timely filed, the court will enter an order denying authorization for the § 2254 or § 2255 petition.

Adopted effective Sept. 10, 1996; July 22, 1997; amended effective September, 1999.

On July 22, 1997, the United States Court of Appeals for the First Circuit entered an order regarding Local Rule 22 and Interim Local Rules 22.1 and 22.2. Text of the order is as follows:

"In an Order effective September 10, 1996, this court adopted Interim Local Rules 22.1 and 22.2 in order to implement provisions of the Antiterrorism and Effective Death Penalty Act of 1996 ("AEDPA") relating to the processing of applications for certificates of appealability and motions to file second or successive petitions in proceedings arising under 28 U.S.C. §§ 2254 and 2255. The Order also rescinded Local Rule 22 relating to applications for certificates of probable cause in § 2254 proceedings.

"The Supreme Court's decision in *Lindh v. Murphy*, 117 S.Ct. 2059, 1997 WL 338568 (1997), indicates that the subject provisions of the AEDPA do not apply in non-capital cases that were pending in the district courts or courts of appeals prior to April 24, 1996, the effective date of the AEDPA.

"Accordingly, our Order effective September 10, 1996 is hereby amended as follows. Local Rule 22 is reinstated and is applicable to § 2254 proceedings which were pending prior to April 24, 1996. Interim Local Rules 22.1 and 22.2 shall be applied to the processing of non-capital § 2254 and § 2255 petitions, and to motions seeking permission to file second or successive petitions, which were filed on or after April 24, 1996."

FRAP 23. CUSTODY OR RELEASE OF A PRISONER IN A HABEAS CORPUS PROCEEDING

(a) Transfer of Custody Pending Review. Pending review of a decision in a habeas corpus proceeding commenced before a court, justice, or judge of the United States for the release of a prisoner, the person having custody of the prisoner must not transfer custody to another unless a transfer is directed in accordance with this rule. When, upon application, a custodian shows the need for a transfer, the court, justice, or judge rendering the decision under review may authorize the transfer and substitute the successor custodian as a party.

(b) Detention or Release Pending Review of Decision Not to Release. While a decision not to release a prisoner is under review, the court or judge rendering the decision, or the court of appeals, or the Supreme Court, or a judge or justice of either court, may order that the prisoner be:

(1) detained in the custody from which release is sought;

(2) detained in other appropriate custody; or

(3) released on personal recognizance, with or without surety.

(c) Release Pending Review of Decision Ordering Release. While a decision ordering the release of a prisoner is under review, the prisoner must—unless the court or judge rendering the decision, or the court of appeals, or the Supreme Court, or a judge or justice of either court orders otherwise—be released on personal recognizance, with or without surety.

(d) Modification of the Initial Order on Custody. An initial order governing the prisoner's custody or release, including any recognizance or surety, continues in effect pending review unless for special reasons shown to the court of appeals or the Supreme Court, or to a judge or justice of either court, the order is modified or an independent order regarding custody, release, or surety is issued.

[Amended March 10, 1986, effective July 1, 1986; April 24, 1998, effective December 1, 1998.]

FRAP 24. PROCEEDING IN FORMA PAUPERIS

(a) Leave to Proceed In Forma Pauperis.

(1) *Motion in the District Court.* Except as stated in Rule 24(a)(3), a party to a district-court action who desires to appeal in forma pauperis must file a motion in the district court. The party must attach an affidavit that:

(A) shows in the detail prescribed by Form 4 of the Appendix of Forms the party's inability to pay or to give security for fees and costs;

(B) claims an entitlement to redress; and

(C) states the issues that the party intends to present on appeal.

(2) *Action on the Motion.* If the district court grants the motion, the party may proceed on appeal without prepaying or giving security for fees and costs, unless a statute provides otherwise. If the district court denies the motion, it must state its reasons in writing.

(3) *Prior Approval.* A party who was permitted to proceed in forma pauperis in the district-court action, or who was determined to be financially unable to obtain an adequate defense in a criminal case, may proceed on appeal in forma pauperis without further authorization, unless:

(A) the district court—before or after the notice of appeal is filed—certifies that the appeal is not taken in good faith or finds that the party is not otherwise entitled to proceed in forma pauperis and states in writing its reasons for the certification or finding; or

(B) a statute provides otherwise.

(4) *Notice of District Court's Denial.* The district clerk must immediately notify the parties and the court of appeals when the district court does any of the following:

(A) denies a motion to proceed on appeal in forma pauperis;

(B) certifies that the appeal is not taken in good faith; or

(C) finds that the party is not otherwise entitled to proceed in forma pauperis.

(5) *Motion in the Court of Appeals.* A party may file a motion to proceed on appeal in forma pauperis in the court of appeals within 30 days after service of the notice prescribed in Rule 24(a)(4). The motion must include a copy of the affidavit filed in the district court and the district court's statement of reasons for its action. If no affidavit was filed in the district court, the party must include the affidavit prescribed by Rule 24(a)(1).

(b) Leave to Proceed In Forma Pauperis on Appeal or Review of an Administrative Agency Proceeding. When an appeal or review of a proceeding before an administrative agency, board, commission, or officer (including for the purpose of this rule the United States Tax Court) proceeds directly in a court of appeals, a party may file in the court of appeals a motion for leave to proceed on appeal in forma pauperis with an affidavit prescribed by Rule 24(a)(1).

(c) Leave to Use Original Record. A party allowed to proceed on appeal in forma pauperis may request that the appeal be heard on the original record without reproducing any part.

[Amended April 30, 1979, effective August 1, 1979; March 10, 1986, effective July 1, 1986; April 24, 1998, effective December 1, 1998; April 29, 2002, effective December 1, 2002.]

TITLE VII. GENERAL PROVISIONS

FRAP 25. FILING AND SERVICE

(a) Filing.

(1) *Filing With the Clerk.* A paper required or permitted to be filed in a court of appeals must be filed with the clerk.

(2) *Filing: Method and Timeliness.*

(A) In general. Filing may be accomplished by mail addressed to the clerk, but filing is not timely unless the clerk receives the papers within the time fixed for filing.

(B) A brief or appendix. A brief or appendix is timely filed, however, if on or before the last day for filing, it is:

(i) mailed to the clerk by First–Class Mail, or other class of mail that is at least as expeditious, postage prepaid; or

(ii) dispatched to a third-party commercial carrier for delivery to the clerk within 3 calendar days.

(C) Inmate filing. A paper filed by an inmate confined in an institution is timely if deposited in the institution's internal mailing system on or before the last day for filing. If an institution has a system designed for legal mail, the inmate must use that system to receive the benefit of this rule. Timely filing may be shown by a declaration in compliance with 28 U.S.C. § 1746 or by a notarized statement, either of which must set forth the date of deposit and state that first-class postage has been prepaid.

(D) Electronic filing. A court of appeals may by local rule permit papers to be filed, signed, or verified by electronic means that are consistent with technical standards, if any, that the Judicial Conference of the United States establishes. A paper filed by electronic means in compliance with a local rule constitutes a written paper for the purpose of applying these rules.

(3) *Filing a Motion With a Judge.* If a motion requests relief that may be granted by a single judge, the judge may permit the motion to be filed with the judge; the judge must note the filing date on the motion and give it to the clerk.

(4) *Clerk's Refusal of Documents.* The clerk must not refuse to accept for filing any paper presented for that purpose solely because it is not presented in

proper form as required by these rules or by any local rule or practice.

(b) Service of All Papers Required. Unless a rule requires service by the clerk, a party must, at or before the time of filing a paper, serve a copy on the other parties to the appeal or review. Service on a party represented by counsel must be made on the party's counsel.

(c) Manner of Service.

(1) Service may be any of the following:

(A) personal, including delivery to a responsible person at the office of counsel;

(B) by mail;

(C) by third-party commercial carrier for delivery within 3 calendar days; or

(D) by electronic means, if the party being served consents in writing.

(2) If authorized by local rule, a party may use the court's transmission equipment to make electronic service under Rule 25(c)(1)(D).

(3) When reasonable considering such factors as the immediacy of the relief sought, distance, and cost, service on a party must be by a manner at least as expeditious as the manner used to file the paper with the court.

(4) Service by mail or by commercial carrier is complete on mailing or delivery to the carrier. Service by electronic means is complete on transmission, unless the party making service is notified that the paper was not received by the party served.

(d) Proof of Service.

(1) A paper presented for filing must contain either of the following:

(A) an acknowledgment of service by the person served; or

(B) proof of service consisting of a statement by the person who made service certifying:

(i) the date and manner of service;

(ii) the names of the persons served; and

(iii) their mail or electronic addresses, facsimile numbers, or the addresses of the places of delivery, as appropriate for the manner of service.

(2) When a brief or appendix is filed by mailing or dispatch in accordance with Rule 25(a)(2)(B), the proof of service must also state the date and manner by which the document was mailed or dispatched to the clerk.

(3) Proof of service may appear on or be affixed to the papers filed.

(e) Number of Copies. When these rules require the filing or furnishing of a number of copies, a court may require a different number by local rule or by order in a particular case.

[Amended March 10, 1986, effective July 1, 1986; April 30, 1991, effective December 1, 1991; April 22, 1993, effective December 1, 1993; April 29, 1994, effective December 1, 1994; April 23, 1996, effective December 1, 1996; April 24, 1998, effective December 1, 1998; April 29, 2002, effective December 1, 2002.]

LOC. R. 25.   FACSIMILE FILING

The Clerk of Court is authorized to accept for filing papers transmitted by facsimile equipment in situations determined by the Clerk to be of an emergency nature or other compelling circumstances, subject to such procedures for follow-up filing of hard copies, or otherwise, as the Clerk may from time to time specify.

Adopted effective March 18, 1992; amended effective September, 1999; December 1, 2000; December 16, 2003.

FRAP 26.   COMPUTING AND EXTENDING TIME

(a) Computing Time. The following rules apply in computing any period of time specified in these rules or in any local rule, court order, or applicable statute:

(1) Exclude the day of the act, event, or default that begins the period.

(2) Exclude intermediate Saturdays, Sundays, and legal holidays when the period is less than 11 days, unless stated in calendar days.

(3) Include the last day of the period unless it is a Saturday, Sunday, legal holiday, or—if the act to be done is filing a paper in court—a day on which the weather or other conditions make the clerk's office inaccessible.

(4) As used in this rule, "legal holiday" means New Year's Day, Martin Luther King, Jr.'s Birthday, Presidents' Day, Memorial Day, Independence Day, Labor Day, Columbus Day, Veterans' Day, Thanksgiving Day, Christmas Day, and any other day declared a holiday by the President, Congress, or the state in which is located either the district court that rendered the challenged judgment or order, or the circuit clerk's principal office.

(b) Extending Time. For good cause, the court may extend the time prescribed by these rules or by its order to perform any act, or may permit an act to be done after that time expires. But the court may not extend the time to file:

(1) a notice of appeal (except as authorized in Rule 4) or a petition for permission to appeal; or

(2) a notice of appeal from or a petition to enjoin, set aside, suspend, modify, enforce, or otherwise review an order of an administrative agency, board, commission, or officer of the United States, unless specifically authorized by law.

(c) Additional Time after Service. When a party is required or permitted to act within a prescribed period after a paper is served on that party, 3 calendar days are added to the prescribed period unless the paper is delivered on the date of service stated in the proof of service. For purposes of this Rule 26(c), a paper that is served electronically is not treated as delivered on the date of service stated in the proof of service.

[Amended March 1, 1971, effective July 1, 1971; March 10, 1986, effective July 1, 1986; April 25, 1989, effective December 1, 1989; April 30, 1991, effective December 1, 1991; April 23, 1996, effective December 1, 1996; April 24, 1998, effective December 1, 1998; April 29, 2002, effective December 1, 2002.]

FRAP 26.1   CORPORATE DISCLOSURE STATEMENT

(a) Who Must File. Any nongovernmental corporate party to a proceeding in a court of appeals must file a statement that identifies any parent corporation and any publicly held corporation that owns 10% or more of its stock or states that there is no such corporation.

(b) Time for Filing; Supplemental Filing. A party must file the Rule 26.1(a) statement with the principal brief or upon filing a motion, response, petition, or answer in the court of appeals, whichever occurs first, unless a local rule requires earlier filing. Even if the statement has already been filed, the party's principal brief must include the statement before the table of contents. A party must supplement its statement whenever the information that must be disclosed under Rule 26.1(a) changes.

(c) Number of Copies. If the Rule 26.1(a) statement is filed before the principal brief, or if a supplemental statement is filed, the party must file an original and 3 copies unless the court requires a different number by local rule or by order in a particular case.

[Adopted April 25, 1989, effective December 1, 1989; amended April 30, 1991, effective December 1, 1991; April 29, 1994, effective December 1, 1994; April 24, 1998, effective December 1, 1998; April 29, 2002, effective December 1, 2002.]

FRAP 27.   MOTIONS

(a) In General.

(1) *Application for Relief.* An application for an order or other relief is made by motion unless these rules prescribe another form. A motion must be in writing unless the court permits otherwise.

(2) *Contents of a Motion.*

(A) Grounds and relief sought. A motion must state with particularity the grounds for the motion, the relief sought, and the legal argument necessary to support it.

(B) Accompanying documents.

(i) Any affidavit or other paper necessary to support a motion must be served and filed with the motion.

(ii) An affidavit must contain only factual information, not legal argument.

(iii) A motion seeking substantive relief must include a copy of the trial court's opinion or agency's decision as a separate exhibit.

(C) Documents barred or not required.

(i) A separate brief supporting or responding to a motion must not be filed.

(ii) A notice of motion is not required.

(iii) A proposed order is not required.

(3) *Response.*

(A) Time to file. Any party may file a response to a motion; Rule 27(a)(2) governs its contents. The response must be filed within 8 days after service of the motion unless the court shortens or extends the time. A motion authorized by Rules 8, 9, 18, or 41 may be granted before the 8–day period runs only if the court gives reasonable notice to the parties that it intends to act sooner.

(B) Request for affirmative relief. A response may include a motion for affirmative relief. The time to respond to the new motion, and to reply to that response, are governed by Rule 27(a)(3)(A) and (a)(4). The title of the response must alert the court to the request for relief.

(4) *Reply to Response.* Any reply to a response must be filed within 5 days after service of the response. A reply must not present matters that do not relate to the response.

(b) Disposition of a Motion for a Procedural Order. The court may act on a motion for a procedural order—including a motion under Rule 26(b)—at any time without awaiting a response, and may, by rule or by order in a particular case, authorize its clerk to act on specified types of procedural motions. A party adversely affected by the court's, or the clerk's, action may file a motion to reconsider, vacate, or modify that action. Timely opposition filed after the motion is granted in whole or in part does not constitute a request to reconsider, vacate, or modify the disposition; a motion requesting that relief must be filed.

(c) Power of a Single Judge to Entertain a Motion. A circuit judge may act alone on any motion, but may not dismiss or otherwise determine an appeal or other proceeding. A court of appeals may provide by rule or by order in a particular case that only the court may act on any motion or class of motions. The court may review the action of a single judge.

(d) Form of Papers; Page Limits; and Number of Copies.

(1) *Format.*

(A) Reproduction. A motion, response, or reply may be reproduced by any process that yields a clear black image on light paper. The paper must be opaque and unglazed. Only one side of the paper may be used.

(B) Cover. A cover is not required, but there must be a caption that includes the case number, the name of the court, the title of the case, and a brief descriptive title indicating the purpose of the motion and identifying the party or parties for whom it is filed. If a cover is used, it must be white.

(C) Binding. The document must be bound in any manner that is secure, does not obscure the text, and permits the document to lie reasonably flat when open.

(D) Paper size, line spacing, and margins. The document must be on 8½ by 11 inch paper. The text must be double-spaced, but quotations more than two lines long may be indented and single-spaced. Headings and footnotes may be single-spaced. Margins must be at least one inch on all four sides. Page numbers may be placed in the margins, but no text may appear there.

(2) *Page Limits.* A motion or a response to a motion must not exceed 20 pages, exclusive of the corporate disclosure statement and accompanying documents authorized by Rule 27(a)(2)(B), unless the court permits or directs otherwise. A reply to a response must not exceed 10 pages.

(3) *Number of Copies.* An original and 3 copies must be filed unless the court requires a different number by local rule or by order in a particular case.

(e) Oral Argument. A motion will be decided without oral argument unless the court orders otherwise.

[Amended April 30, 1979, effective August 1, 1979; April 25, 1989, effective December 1, 1989; April 29, 1994, effective December 1, 1994; April 24, 1998, effective December 1, 1998; April 29, 2002, effective December 1, 2002.]

LOC. R. 27. MOTIONS

(a) *Assent. Motions will not necessarily be allowed even though assented to.*

(b) *Emergency Relief. Motions for stay, or other emergency relief, may be denied for failure to present promptly. Counsel who envisages a possible need for an emergency filing, or emergency action by the court, or both, during a period when the Clerk's Office is ordinarily closed should consult with the Clerk's Office at the earliest opportunity. Failure to consult* *with the Clerk's Office well in advance of the occasion may preclude such special arrangements.*

(c) Summary Disposition. At any time, on such notice as the court may order, on motion of appellee or sua sponte, the court may dismiss the appeal or other request for relief or affirm and enforce the judgment or order below if the court lacks jurisdiction, or if it shall clearly appear that no substantial question is presented. In case of obvious error the court may, similarly, reverse. Motions for such relief should be promptly filed when the occasion appears, and must be accompanied by four copies of a memorandum or brief.

Adopted effective Sept. 1, 1986; amended effective September, 1999; January 2, 2001.

FRAP 28. BRIEFS

(a) Appellant's Brief. The appellant's brief must contain, under appropriate headings and in the order indicated:

(1) a corporate disclosure statement if required by Rule 26.1;

(2) a table of contents, with page references;

(3) a table of authorities—cases (alphabetically arranged), statutes, and other authorities—with references to the pages of the brief where they are cited;

(4) a jurisdictional statement, including:

(A) the basis for the district court's or agency's subject-matter jurisdiction, with citations to applicable statutory provisions and stating relevant facts establishing jurisdiction;

(B) the basis for the court of appeals' jurisdiction, with citations to applicable statutory provisions and stating relevant facts establishing jurisdiction;

(C) the filing dates establishing the timeliness of the appeal or petition for review; and

(D) an assertion that the appeal is from a final order or judgment that disposes of all parties' claims, or information establishing the court of appeals' jurisdiction on some other basis;

(5) a statement of the issues presented for review;

(6) a statement of the case briefly indicating the nature of the case, the course of proceedings, and the disposition below;

(7) a statement of facts relevant to the issues submitted for review with appropriate references to the record (see Rule 28(e));

(8) a summary of the argument, which must contain a succinct, clear, and accurate statement of the arguments made in the body of the brief, and which must not merely repeat the argument headings;

(9) the argument, which must contain:

(A) appellant's contentions and the reasons for them, with citations to the authorities and parts of the record on which the appellant relies; and

(B) for each issue, a concise statement of the applicable standard of review (which may appear in the discussion of the issue or under a separate heading placed before the discussion of the issues);

(10) a short conclusion stating the precise relief sought; and

(11) the certificate of compliance, if required by Rule 32(a)(7).

(b) Appellee's Brief. The appellee's brief must conform to the requirements of Rule 28(a)(1)–(9) and (11), except that none of the following need appear unless the appellee is dissatisfied with the appellant's statement:

(1) the jurisdictional statement;

(2) the statement of the issues;

(3) the statement of the case;

(4) the statement of the facts; and

(5) the statement of the standard of review.

(c) Reply Brief. The appellant may file a brief in reply to the appellee's brief. An appellee who has cross-appealed may file a brief in reply to the appellant's response to the issues presented by the cross-appeal. Unless the court permits, no further briefs may be filed. A reply brief must contain a table of contents, with page references, and a table of authorities—cases (alphabetically arranged), statutes, and other authorities—with references to the pages of the reply brief where they are cited.

(d) References to Parties. In briefs and at oral argument, counsel should minimize use of the terms "appellant" and "appellee." To make briefs clear, counsel should use the parties' actual names or the designations used in the lower court or agency proceeding, or such descriptive terms as "the employee," "the injured person," "the taxpayer," "the ship," "the stevedore."

(e) References to the Record. References to the parts of the record contained in the appendix filed with the appellant's brief must be to the pages of the appendix. If the appendix is prepared after the briefs are filed, a party referring to the record must follow one of the methods detailed in Rule 30(c). If the original record is used under Rule 30(f) and is not consecutively paginated, or if the brief refers to an unreproduced part of the record, any reference must be to the page of the original document. For example:

- Answer p. 7;
- Motion for Judgment p. 2;
- Transcript p. 231.

Only clear abbreviations may be used. A party referring to evidence whose admissibility is in controversy must cite the pages of the appendix or of the transcript at which the evidence was identified, offered, and received or rejected.

(f) Reproduction of Statutes, Rules, Regulations, etc. If the court's determination of the issues presented requires the study of statutes, rules, regulations, etc., the relevant parts must be set out in the brief or in an addendum at the end, or may be supplied to the court in pamphlet form.

(g) [Reserved].

(h) Briefs in a Case Involving a Cross–Appeal. If a cross-appeal is filed, the party who files a notice of appeal first is the appellant for the purposes of this rule and Rules 30, 31, and 34. If notices are filed on the same day, the plaintiff in the proceeding below is the appellant. These designations may be modified by agreement of the parties or by court order. With respect to appellee's cross-appeal and response to appellant's brief, appellee's brief must conform to the requirements of Rule 28(a)(1)–(11). But an appellee who is satisfied with appellant's statement need not include a statement of the case or of the facts.

(i) Briefs in a Case Involving Multiple Appellants or Appellees. In a case involving more than one appellant or appellee, including consolidated cases, any number of appellants or appellees may join in a brief, and any party may adopt by reference a part of another's brief. Parties may also join in reply briefs.

(j) Citation of Supplemental Authorities. If pertinent and significant authorities come to a party's attention after the party's brief has been filed—or after oral argument but before decision—a party may promptly advise the circuit clerk by letter, with a copy to all other parties, setting forth the citations. The letter must state the reasons for the supplemental citations, referring either to the page of the brief or to a point argued orally. The body of the letter must not exceed 350 words. Any response must be made promptly and must be similarly limited.

[Amended April 30, 1979, effective August 1, 1979; March 10, 1986, effective July 1, 1986; April 25, 1989, effective December 1, 1989; April 30, 1991, effective December 1, 1991; April 22, 1993, effective December 1, 1993; April 29, 1994, effective December 1, 1994; April 24, 1998, effective December 1, 1998; April 29, 2002, effective December 1, 2002.]

LOC. R. 28. ADDENDUM TO BRIEFS REQUIRED

(a) Contents. In addition to the requirements of FRAP 28, for the court's convenience, the brief of the appellant must include an addendum containing the following items:

(1) The judgment, ruling or order appealed from and any supporting opinion, memorandum, or statement of reason;

(2) The portions of any instructions to the jury which are the subject of appeal;

(3) Pertinent portions of any document in the record that is the subject of an issue on appeal; and

(4) Other items or short excerpts from the record, if any, considered necessary for understanding the specific issues on appeal.

(b) Form. The addendum must be limited to 20 pages (exclusive of the judgment, order or opinion appealed from) and shall be bound at the rear of the appellant's brief

(1) The appellee's brief may include such an addendum to incorporate materials omitted from the appellant's addendum, subject to the same limitations on length and content.

(2) Material included in the addendum need not be reproduced in the appendix also.

Renumbered and amended effective October, 1999.

[Formerly Local Rule 28.2.]

LOC. R. 28.1 REFERENCES IN BRIEFS TO SEALED MATERIAL

Briefs filed with the court of appeals are a matter of public record. In order to have a brief sealed, counsel must file a specific and timely motion in compliance with Local Rule 11(c)(2) and (3) asking the court to seal a brief or supplemental brief. Counsel must also comply with Local Rule 11(d), when applicable.

Adopted 1999.

Former Local Rule 28.1 is renumbered 32.2.

FRAP 29. BRIEF OF AN AMICUS CURIAE

(a) When Permitted. The United States or its officer or agency, or a State, Territory, Commonwealth, or the District of Columbia may file an amicus-curiae brief without the consent of the parties or leave of court. Any other amicus curiae may file a brief only by leave of court or if the brief states that all parties have consented to its filing.

(b) Motion for Leave to File. The motion must be accompanied by the proposed brief and state:

(1) the movant's interest; and

(2) the reason why an amicus brief is desirable and why the matters asserted are relevant to the disposition of the case.

(c) Contents and Form. An amicus brief must comply with Rule 32. In addition to the requirements of Rule 32, the cover must identify the party or parties supported and indicate whether the brief supports affirmance or reversal. If an amicus curiae is a corporation, the brief must include a disclosure statement like that required of parties by Rule 26.1. An amicus brief need not comply with Rule 28, but must include the following:

(1) a table of contents, with page references;

(2) a table of authorities—cases (alphabetically arranged), statutes and other authorities—with references to the pages of the brief where they are cited;

(3) a concise statement of the identity of the amicus curiae, its interest in the case, and the source of its authority to file;

(4) an argument, which may be preceded by a summary and which need not include a statement of the applicable standard of review; and

(5) a certificate of compliance, if required by Rule 32(a)(7).

(d) Length. Except by the court's permission, an amicus brief may be no more than one-half the maximum length authorized by these rules for a party's principal brief. If the court grants a party permission to file a longer brief, that extension does not affect the length of an amicus brief.

(e) Time for Filing. An amicus curiae must file its brief, accompanied by a motion for filing when necessary, no later than 7 days after the principal brief of the party being supported is filed. An amicus curiae that does not support either party must file its brief no later than 7 days after the appellant's or petitioner's principal brief is filed. A court may grant leave for later filing, specifying the time within which an opposing party may answer.

(f) Reply Brief. Except by the court's permission, an amicus curiae may not file a reply brief.

(g) Oral Argument. An amicus curiae may participate in oral argument only with the court's permission.

[Amended April 24, 1998, effective December 1, 1998.]

FRAP 30. APPENDIX TO THE BRIEFS

(a) Appellant's Responsibility.

(1) *Contents of the Appendix.* The appellant must prepare and file an appendix to the briefs containing:

(A) the relevant docket entries in the proceeding below;

(B) the relevant portions of the pleadings, charge, findings, or opinion;

(C) the judgment, order, or decision in question; and

(D) other parts of the record to which the parties wish to direct the court's attention.

(2) *Excluded Material.* Memoranda of law in the district court should not be included in the appendix unless they have independent relevance. Parts of the record may be relied on by the court or the parties even though not included in the appendix.

(3) *Time to File; Number of Copies.* Unless filing is deferred under Rule 30(c), the appellant must file 10 copies of the appendix with the brief and must serve one copy on counsel for each party separately represented. An unrepresented party proceeding in forma pauperis must file 4 legible copies with the clerk, and one copy must be served on counsel for each separately represented party. The court may by local rule or by order in a particular case require the filing or service of a different number.

(b) All Parties' Responsibilities.

(1) *Determining the Contents of the Appendix.* The parties are encouraged to agree on the contents of the appendix. In the absence of an agreement, the appellant must, within 10 days after the record is filed, serve on the appellee a designation of the parts of the record the appellant intends to include in the appendix and a statement of the issues the appellant intends to present for review. The appellee may, within 10 days after receiving the designation, serve on the appellant a designation of additional parts to which it wishes to direct the court's attention. The appellant must include the designated parts in the appendix. The parties must not engage in unnecessary designation of parts of the record, because the entire record is available to the court. This paragraph applies also to a cross-appellant and a cross-appellee.

(2) *Costs of Appendix.* Unless the parties agree otherwise, the appellant must pay the cost of the appendix. If the appellant considers parts of the record designated by the appellee to be unnecessary, the appellant may advise the appellee, who must then advance the cost of including those parts. The cost of the appendix is a taxable cost. But if any party causes unnecessary parts of the record to be included in the appendix, the court may impose the cost of those parts on that party. Each circuit must, by local rule, provide for sanctions against attorneys who unreasonably and vexatiously increase litigation costs by including unnecessary material in the appendix.

(c) Deferred Appendix.

(1) *Deferral Until After Briefs Are Filed.* The court may provide by rule for classes of cases or by order in a particular case that preparation of the appendix may be deferred until after the briefs have been filed and that the appendix may be filed 21 days after the appellee's brief is served. Even though the filing of the appendix may be deferred, Rule 30(b) applies; except that a party must designate the parts of the record it wants included in the appendix when it serves its brief, and need not include a statement of the issues presented.

(2) *References to the Record.*

(A) If the deferred appendix is used, the parties may cite in their briefs the pertinent pages of the record. When the appendix is prepared, the record pages cited in the briefs must be indicated by inserting record page numbers, in brackets, at places in the appendix where those pages of the record appear.

(B) A party who wants to refer directly to pages of the appendix may serve and file copies of the brief within the time required by Rule 31(a), containing appropriate references to pertinent pages of the record. In that event, within 14 days after the appendix is filed, the party must serve and file copies of the brief, containing references to the pages of the appendix in place of or in addition to the references to the pertinent pages of the record. Except for the correction of typographical errors, no other changes may be made to the brief.

(d) Format of the Appendix. The appendix must begin with a table of contents identifying the page at which each part begins. The relevant docket entries must follow the table of contents. Other parts of the record must follow chronologically. When pages from the transcript of proceedings are placed in the appendix, the transcript page numbers must be shown in brackets immediately before the included pages. Omissions in the text of papers or of the transcript must be indicated by asterisks. Immaterial formal matters (captions, subscriptions, acknowledgments, etc.) should be omitted.

(e) Reproduction of Exhibits. Exhibits designated for inclusion in the appendix may be reproduced in a separate volume, or volumes, suitably indexed. Four copies must be filed with the appendix, and one copy must be served on counsel for each separately represented party. If a transcript of a proceeding before an administrative agency, board, commission, or officer was used in a district-court action and has been designated for inclusion in the appendix, the transcript must be placed in the appendix as an exhibit.

(f) Appeal on the Original Record Without an Appendix. The court may, either by rule for all cases or classes of cases or by order in a particular case, dispense with the appendix and permit an appeal to proceed on the original record with any copies of the record, or relevant parts, that the court may order the parties to file.

[Amended March 30, 1970, effective July 1, 1970; March 10, 1986, effective July 1, 1986; April 30, 1991, effective December 1, 1991; April 29, 1994, effective December 1, 1994; April 24, 1998, effective December 1, 1998.]

LOC. R. 30. APPENDIX TO THE BRIEFS

(a) Number of Copies. Pursuant to Fed. R. App. P. 30(a)(3), only five (5) copies of the appendix need be filed with the clerk and on motion, for cause shown, parties may be allowed to file even fewer copies.

(b) Filing of Designation. One copy of any designation, statement of issues, or counter-designation served pursuant to Fed. R. App. P. 30(b), or any notice of agreement thereunder, shall be simultaneously filed with the clerk.

(c) In Forma Pauperis. All appeals proceeding in forma pauperis shall be considered on the record on appeal as certified by the clerk of the district court without the necessity of filing an appendix unless otherwise ordered by this court in a specific case.

(d) Translations. The court will not receive documents not in the English language unless translations are furnished. Whenever an opinion of the Supreme Court of Puerto Rico is cited in a brief or oral argument which does not appear in the bound volumes in English, an official, certified or stipulated translation thereof with three conformed copies shall be filed. Partial translations will be accepted if stipulated by the parties or if submitted by one party not less than 30 days before the oral argument. Where partial translations are submitted by one party, opposing parties may, prior to oral argument, submit translations of such additional parts as they may deem necessary for a proper understanding of the holding.

(e) Sanctions. Not later than at the time of oral argument, on motion of a party to the action, or at any time upon this court's order to show cause why sanctions should not be imposed, the court may impose sanctions against attorneys who unreasonably and vexatiously increase the cost of litigation through the inclusion of unnecessary material in the appendix. Any party charged with misconduct under this rule shall be afforded an opportunity to respond within fifteen (15) days of service of a motion or an order to show cause before any sanctions are imposed by the court.

(f) Inclusion of Sealed Material in Appendices. Appendices filed with the court of appeals are a matter of public record. If counsel conclude that it is necessary to include sealed material in appendix form, then, in order to maintain the confidentiality of materials filed in the district court or agency under seal, counsel must designate the sealed material for inclusion in a supplemental appendix to be filed separately from the regular appendix and must file a specific and timely motion in compliance with Local Rules 11(c)(2), 11(c)(3), and 11(d) asking the court to seal the supplemental appendix.

Formerly Local Rules 30.2–30.8, renumbered and amended October, 1999.

FRAP 31. SERVING AND FILING BRIEFS

(a) Time to Serve and File a Brief.

(1) The appellant must serve and file a brief within 40 days after the record is filed. The appellee must

serve and file a brief within 30 days after the appellant's brief is served. The appellant may serve and file a reply brief within 14 days after service of the appellee's brief but a reply brief must be filed at least 3 days before argument, unless the court, for good cause, allows a later filing.

(2) A court of appeals that routinely considers cases on the merits promptly after the briefs are filed may shorten the time to serve and file briefs, either by local rule or by order in a particular case.

(b) Number of Copies. Twenty-five copies of each brief must be filed with the clerk and 2 copies must be served on each unrepresented party and on counsel for each separately represented party. An unrepresented party proceeding in forma pauperis must file 4 legible copies with the clerk, and one copy must be served on each unrepresented party and on counsel for each separately represented party. The court may by local rule or by order in a particular case require the filing or service of a different number.

(c) Consequence of Failure to File. If an appellant fails to file a brief within the time provided by this rule, or within an extended time, an appellee may move to dismiss the appeal. An appellee who fails to file a brief will not be heard at oral argument unless the court grants permission.

[Amended March 30, 1970, effective July 1, 1970; March 10, 1986, effective July 1, 1986; April 29, 1994, effective December 1, 1994; April 24, 1998, effective December 1, 1998; April 29, 2002, effective December 1, 2002.]

LOC. R. 31. FILING BRIEFS

(a) Time to File a Brief.

(1) Briefing schedules will be set in accordance with Fed. R. App. P. 31(a) except that a reply brief must be filed within 14 days after service of the brief of the appellee. A reply brief may be rejected by the court if it contains matter repetitive of the main brief, or which, in the opinion of the court, should have been in the main brief.

(2) Unavailability of the transcript shall constitute cause for granting extensions, subject, however, to the provisions of Local Rule 10, ante.

(b) Number of Copies. Only 10 copies of briefs need be filed with the clerk and on motion for cause shown, parties may be allowed to file even fewer copies. The disk required by Local Rule 32 constitutes one copy for the purpose of this rule.

Adopted effective Sept. 1, 1986; amended effective September, 1999.

FRAP 32. FORM OF BRIEFS, APPENDICES, AND OTHER PAPERS

(a) Form of a Brief.

(1) *Reproduction.*

(A) A brief may be reproduced by any process that yields a clear black image on light paper. The

paper must be opaque and unglazed. Only one side of the paper may be used.

(B) Text must be reproduced with a clarity that equals or exceeds the output of a laser printer.

(C) Photographs, illustrations, and tables may be reproduced by any method that results in a good copy of the original; a glossy finish is acceptable if the original is glossy.

(2) *Cover.* Except for filings by unrepresented parties, the cover of the appellant's brief must be blue; the appellee's, red; an intervenor's or amicus curiae's, green; any reply brief, gray; and any supplemental brief, tan. The front cover of a brief must contain:

(A) the number of the case centered at the top;

(B) the name of the court;

(C) the title of the case (see Rule 12(a));

(D) the nature of the proceeding (e.g., Appeal, Petition for Review) and the name of the court, agency, or board below;

(E) the title of the brief, identifying the party or parties for whom the brief is filed; and

(F) the name, office address, and telephone number of counsel representing the party for whom the brief is filed.

(3) *Binding.* The brief must be bound in any manner that is secure, does not obscure the text, and permits the brief to lie reasonably flat when open.

(4) *Paper Size, Line Spacing, and Margins.* The brief must be on 8½ by 11 inch paper. The text must be double-spaced, but quotations more than two lines long may be indented and single-spaced. Headings and footnotes may be single-spaced. Margins must be at least one inch on all four sides. Page numbers may be placed in the margins, but no text may appear there.

(5) *Typeface.* Either a proportionally spaced or a monospaced face may be used.

(A) A proportionally spaced face must include serifs, but sans-serif type may be used in headings and captions. A proportionally spaced face must be 14-point or larger.

(B) A monospaced face may not contain more than 10½ characters per inch.

(6) *Type Styles.* A brief must be set in a plain, roman style, although italics or boldface may be used for emphasis. Case names must be italicized or underlined.

(7) *Length.*

(A) Page limitation. A principal brief may not exceed 30 pages, or a reply brief 15 pages, unless it complies with Rule 32(a)(7)(B) and (C).

(B) Type-volume limitation.

(i) A principal brief is acceptable if:

● it contains no more than 14,000 words; or

● it uses a monospaced face and contains no more than 1,300 lines of text.

(ii) A reply brief is acceptable if it contains no more than half of the type volume specified in Rule 32(a)(7)(B)(i).

(iii) Headings, footnotes, and quotations count toward the word and line limitations. The corporate disclosure statement, table of contents, table of citations, statement with respect to oral argument, any addendum containing statutes, rules or regulations, and any certificates of counsel do not count toward the limitation.

(C) Certificate of Compliance.

(i) A brief submitted under Rule 32(a)(7)(B) must include a certificate by the attorney, or an unrepresented party, that the brief complies with the type-volume limitation. The person preparing the certificate may rely on the word or line count of the word-processing system used to prepare the brief. The certificate must state either:

● the number of words in the brief; or

● the number of lines of monospaced type in the brief.

(ii) Form 6 in the Appendix of Forms is a suggested form of a certificate of compliance. Use of Form 6 must be regarded as sufficient to meet the requirements of Rule 32(a)(7)(C)(i).

(b) **Form of an Appendix.** An appendix must comply with Rule 32(a)(1), (2), (3), and (4), with the following exceptions:

(1) The cover of a separately bound appendix must be white.

(2) An appendix may include a legible photocopy of any document found in the record or of a printed judicial or agency decision.

(3) When necessary to facilitate inclusion of odd-sized documents such as technical drawings, an appendix may be a size other than 8½ by 11 inches, and need not lie reasonably flat when opened.

(c) **Form of Other Papers.**

(1) *Motion.* The form of a motion is governed by Rule 27(d).

(2) *Other Papers.* Any other paper, including a petition for panel rehearing and a petition for hearing or rehearing en banc, and any response to such a petition, must be reproduced in the manner prescribed by Rule 32(a), with the following exceptions:

(A) A cover is not necessary if the caption and signature page of the paper together contain the information required by Rule 32(a)(2). If a cover is used, it must be white.

(B) Rule 32(a)(7) does not apply.

(d) **Signature.** Every brief, motion, or other paper filed with the court must be signed by the party filing the paper or, if the party is represented, by one of the party's attorneys.

(e) **Local Variation.** Every court of appeals must accept documents that comply with the form requirements of this rule. By local rule or order in a particular case a court of appeals may accept documents that do not meet all of the form requirements of this rule.

[Amended April 24, 1998, effective December 1, 1998; April 29, 2002, effective December 1, 2002.]

LOC. R. 32. BRIEFS, PETITIONS FOR RE-HEARING, AND OTHER PAPERS: COMPUTER GENERATED DISK REQUIRED

(a) Where a party is represented by counsel, one copy of its brief, petition for rehearing, and, in addition, all other papers exceeding 10 pages in length must be submitted on a computer readable disk. The disk shall be filed at the time the party's paper filing is made. The brief on disk must be accompanied by nine paper copies of the brief. The disk shall contain the entire brief exclusive of computer non-generated appendices. The label of the disk shall include the case name and docket number and identify the brief being filed (i.e. appellant's brief, appellee's brief, appellant's reply brief, etc.) and the file format utilized.

(b) The brief, petition for rehearing, and, in addition, all other papers exceeding 10 pages in length must be on a 3 1/2" disk in either DOS WordPerfect or WordPerfect for Windows, 5.1 or greater.

(c) One copy of the disk may be served on each party separately represented by counsel. If a party chooses to serve a copy of the disk, the certificate of service must indicate service of the brief, petition for rehearing, and, in addition, all other papers exceeding 10 pages in length in both paper and electronic format.

(d) A party may be relieved from filing and service under this rule by submitting a motion, within fourteen days after the date of the notice establishing the party's initial briefing schedule, certifying that compliance with the rule would impose undue hardship, that the text of the brief, petition for rehearing, and, in addition, all other papers exceeding 10 pages in length or other papers exceeding 10 pages in length is not available on disk, or that other unusual circumstances preclude compliance with this rule. The requirements of this rule shall not apply to parties appearing pro se. Briefs, petition for rehearing, and, in addition, all other papers exceeding 10 pages in length or other papers exceeding 10 pages in length tendered by counsel after January 1, 1998 without a computer disk copy or court-approved waiver of the

requirements of this rule may be rejected by the clerk's office.

Renumbered and amended effective October, 1999; amended effective January 2, 2001; December 16, 2003.

LOC. R. 32.1   CD–ROM SUBMISSION ALLOWED

In addition to filing paper briefs and the disk, a party may file a companion CD–ROM, called a CD–ROM submission. Except as specifically noted, filing of a CD–ROM submission does not affect the other requirements of this Court's rules.

(a) Conditions of Filing.

(1) If all parties are represented by counsel, a party may file a CD–ROM submission without prior notice to other parties.

(2) When a party is not represented by counsel, a CD–ROM submission may be filed

(A) by written consent of all parties;

(B) by leave of Court; or

(C) without leave or consent, if the submission includes all briefs and appendices filed by all parties to the appeal.

(b) Joint Submission.
Any two or more parties may file a joint submission. Inasmuch as the Court will realize the greatest benefit by working from a single CD–ROM, adversarial as well as allied parties are encouraged to file jointly.

(c) Time of Filing.
CD–ROM submissions shall be filed no later than ten days after the briefs or papers they accompany. Joint submissions by adversarial parties shall be filed no later than fourteen days after the final brief. Submissions under section (a)(2)(C) shall be filed no later than ten days after the final brief. This rule does not affect deadlines for paper briefs.

(d) Form of Filing.

(1) Parties shall file exactly nine copies of each CD–ROM submission. For all en banc filings, including petitions for rehearing en banc, responses to such petitions, and any filings on the grant of en banc hearing, parties shall file exactly nineteen copies of each submission. Parties filing a joint submission need file only one set of nine or nineteen copies.

(2) Parties shall serve one copy of each submission on each party represented by separate counsel and on each pro se party, except for parties participating in the submission. Each submission shall be accompanied by a certificate indicating such service.

(3) Each copy of a submission shall be packaged in a standard CD–ROM container, commonly known as a "jewel box." If a submission comprises more than one CD–ROM, each copy shall be packaged in a jewel box that holds, as a unit, the number of CD–ROMs in the submission.

(4) Each submission shall be labeled with the short name of the case, the docket number on appeal, the date of filing, and the most recent papers filed with the submission (e.g., appellant's brief, appellee's brief, appellant's reply brief). Joint submissions shall be labeled with the foregoing information as well as with a list of the parties participating in the submission. This label shall appear on the top surface of the CD–ROM itself, on the outside front cover of the jewel box, and on the front and back spines of the jewel box. If it is impractical to include the full label, a location may include an abbreviated label, but shall in all circumstances include the docket number, short name, and date of filing.

(5) For submissions including more than one CD–ROM, the label on each CD–ROM shall also indicate the number of the CD–ROM and the total number of CD–ROMs in the submission, e.g., "CD–ROM 1 of 2".

(e) Contents of Submission.

(1) Each submission shall contain the following:

(A) all briefs and motions filed in the current appeal by the party or parties to the submission, including addenda thereto;

(B) the appendix or appendices to such briefs; and

(C) any materials included in a prior submission that the filing party or parties made in the same appeal.

(2) Each submission may contain the following:

(A) briefs and appendices of parties not participating in the submission;

(B) briefs of amici curiae filing under Fed. R. App. P. 29;

(C) the entire record on appeal or portions of the record;

(D) materials cited by papers filed in the submission;

(E) any documents included by any party in a prior submission.

Parties are encouraged to file the entire record.

(3) All documents contained in a submission shall be precise copies of the corresponding paper documents filed with the Court, including, but not limited to, identical pagination. To satisfy this requirement as well as that of section (f)(6), parties should convert their word-processing documents to PDF format before printing, from the PDF-format document, the final paper versions of their filings.

(4) Documents filed under section (e) (2) (D), for which there are no corresponding papers filed with this Court, shall include unambiguous notation of their pagination in appropriate publications.

(5) If the documents required by sections (e)(1)(A)-(e)(1)(B) do not exceed the capacity of a single CD–ROM, they shall be included on the first CD–ROM of any submission comprising multiple CD–ROMs.

(6) To comply with section (e)(1)(C), parties may use files copied from their own prior submissions; under section (e)(2)(E), parties may copy files from prior submissions made by other parties. All such copies shall be verbatim copies, shall have the same file names, and shall reside in the same directories as in the submissions from which they were copied.

(7) All papers requiring a signature shall be signed on paper and in the CD–ROM submission. Signatures may appear on a separate signature page, which shall not be included in the page limits required by these rules. Section (f)(6) does not apply to such signature pages.

(f) Format.

(1) CD–ROMs in a submission shall be formatted according to ISO–9660, Level 1. Official copies of ISO–9660 are available for purchase at <http://www.iso.ch/cate/d17505.html>.

(2) Files on the submission shall be in Adobe PDF format, version 1.2 or later. The current PDF specification is available for download under "Developer Resources" at <http://www.adobe.com/prodindex/acrobat/adobepdf.html>.

(3) File names shall end with a period, followed by "pdf".

(4) Except as required by section (e)(6), no file or directory in a submission shall have the same path as a file or directory in a prior submission.

(5) Except for the table of contents required by section (h), all files on the submission shall reside in directories other than the root directory.

(6) Whenever possible, documents shall be prepared through direct conversion from the word processor, not through scanning.

(7) Files shall be configured to allow selecting and printing. All fonts used in a file shall be embedded in that file. Files shall be optimized.

(g) Hyperlinks. *Parties may insert hyperlinks corresponding to citations made by papers contained in the submission. Each hyperlink shall link to the document and page referenced by the corresponding citation. Hyperlinks shall be platform-independent and shall use relative file specifications, as discussed in the PDF specification. Hyperlinks shall link only to documents on the same CD–ROM, and not to any other location, including, but not limited to, other CD–ROMs or the Internet.*

(h) Table of Contents.

(1) Each CD–ROM shall contain a table of contents, which shall reside in its root directory. The table of contents shall be named "contents.pdf" unless

this name has been used for a prior submission, in which case the end of "contents" shall be replaced with an incrementing number (e.g., "content1.pdf", "content2.pdf", "content4.pdf").

(2) The table of contents shall contain hyperlinks to the first page of each document on the CD–ROM, and may contain hyperlinks to pages within documents. The table of contents shall be well organized and each hyperlink within it shall clearly identify the document it references.

(i) Indication of Filing. *Parties shall prominently indicate on their paper briefs their intention to file a CD–ROM submission. Papers to be included in a joint submission shall indicate the parties participating in the submission.*

(j) Quotation of Copyrighted Materials. *Counsel are responsible for obtaining any permission needed to quote copyrighted materials. The text of opinions released by a court are not copyrighted materials; law review articles typically are.*

Adopted effective October, 1999.

LOC. R. 32.2 CITATION OF STATE DECISIONS AND LAW REVIEW ARTICLES

All citations to State or Commonwealth Courts must include both the official state court citation and the National Reporter System citation when such decisions have been published in both reports; e.g., Coney v. Commonwealth, 364 Mass. 137, 301 N.E.2d 450 (1973). Law review or other articles unpublished at the time a brief or memorandum is filed may not be cited therein, except with permission of the court.

Renumbered and amended effective October, 1999.

[Formerly Local Rule 28.1.]

LOC. R. 32.3. CITATION OF UNPUBLISHED OPINIONS

(a) An unpublished opinion of this court may be cited in this court only in the following circumstances:

(1) When the earlier opinion is relevant to establish a fact about the case. An unpublished opinion of this court may be cited to establish a fact about the case before the court (for example, its procedural history) or when the binding or preclusive effect of the opinion, rather than its quality as precedent, is relevant to support a claim of res judicata, collateral estoppel, law of the case, double jeopardy, abuse of the writ, or other similar doctrine.

(2) Other circumstances. Citation of an unpublished opinion of this court is disfavored. Such an opinion may be cited only if (1) the party believes

that the opinion persuasively addresses a material issue in the appeal; and (2) there is no published opinion from this court that adequately addresses the issue. The court will consider such opinions for their persuasive value but not as binding precedent.

(3) Procedure. A party must note in its brief or other pleading that the opinion is unpublished, and a copy of the opinion or disposition must be included in an accompanying addendum or appendix.

(4) Definition. Almost all new opinions of this court are published in some form, whether in print or electronic medium. The phrase "unpublished opinion of this court" as used in this subsection and Local Rule 36(c) refers to an opinion (in the case of older opinions) that has not been published in the West Federal Reporter series, e.g., F., F.2d, and F.3d, or (in the case of recent opinions) bears the legend "not for publication" or some comparable phraseology indicating that citation is prohibited or limited.

(b) Unpublished or non-precedential opinions of other courts, as defined or understood by those courts, may be cited in the circumstances set forth in subsection (a)(1) above. Such opinions may also be cited in circumstances analogous to those set forth in subsection (a)(2) above, unless prohibited by the rules of the issuing court. If an unpublished or non-precedential opinion of another court is cited, the party must comply with the procedure set forth in subsection (a)(3) above.

Adopted effective December 16, 2003

FRAP 33. APPEAL CONFERENCES

The court may direct the attorneys—and, when appropriate, the parties to participate in one or more conferences to address any matter that may aid in disposing of the proceedings, including simplifying the issues and discussing settlement. A judge or other person designated by the court may preside over the conference, which may be conducted in person or by telephone. Before a settlement conference, the attorneys must consult with their clients and obtain as much authority as feasible to settle the case. The court may, as a result of the conference, enter an order controlling the course of the proceedings or implementing any settlement agreement.

[Amended April 29, 1994, effective December 1, 1994; April 24, 1998, effective December 1, 1998.]

LOC. R. 33. CIVIL APPEALS MANAGEMENT PLAN

Pursuant to Rule 47 of the Federal Rules of Appellate Procedure, the United States Court of Appeals for the First Circuit adopts the following plan to establish a Civil Appeals Management Program, said Program to have the force and effect of a local rule.

(a) Pre-argument Filing, Ordering Transcript.

(1) Upon receipt of the Notice of Appeal in the Court of Appeals, the Clerk of the Court of Appeals shall send notice of the Civil Appeals Management Plan to the appellant. Upon receipt of further notice from the Clerk of the Court of Appeals, appellant shall, within ten days:

(A) file with the Clerk of the Court of Appeals, and serve on Settlement Counsel and all other parties a statement, in the form of the Docketing Statement required by Local Rule 3(a), detailing information needed for the prompt disposition of an appeal;

(B) certify and file with the Clerk of the Court of Appeals a statement, in the form required by Local Rule 10(b), that satisfactory arrangements have been made with the court reporter for payment of the cost of the transcript.

The parties shall thereafter provide Settlement Counsel with such information about the appeals as Settlement Counsel may reasonably request.

(2) Nothing herein shall alter the duty to order from the court reporter, promptly upon filing of the Notice of Appeal in the District Court, a transcript of the proceedings pursuant to Fed. R. App. P. Rule 10(b).

(b) Pre-argument Conference; Pre-argument Conference Order.

(1) In cases where he may deem this desirable, the Settlement Counsel, who shall be appointed by the Court of Appeals, may direct the attorneys, and in certain cases the clients, to attend a pre-argument conference to be held as soon as practicable before him or a judge designated by the Chief Judge to consider the possibility of settlement, the simplification of the issues, and any other matters which the Settlement Counsel determines may aid in the handling or the disposition of the proceeding.

(2) At the conclusion of the conference, the Settlement Counsel shall consult with the Clerk concerning the Clerk's entry of a Conference Order which shall control the subsequent course of the proceeding.

(c) Confidentiality. The Settlement Counsel shall not disclose the substance of the Pre-argument Conference, nor report on the same, to any person or persons whomsoever (including, but not limited to, any judge). The attorneys are likewise prohibited from disclosing any substantive information emanating from the conference to anyone other than their clients or co-counsel, and then only upon receiving due assurance that the recipients will honor the confidentiality of the information. See In re Lake Utopia Paper Ltd., 608 F.2d 928 (1st Cir. 1979). The fact of the conference having taken place, and the bare result thereof (e.g., "settled," "not settled," "continued"), including any resulting Conference Order, shall not be considered to be confidential.

(d) Non–Compliance Sanctions. *If the appellant has not taken each of the actions set forth in section (a) of this Program, or in the Conference Order, within the time therein specified, the appeal may be dismissed by the Clerk without further notice.*

(e) Grievances. *Any grievances as to the handling of any case under the Program will be addressed by the Court of Appeals, and should be sent to the Circuit Executive, One Courthouse Way, Suite 3700, Boston, MA 02210, who will hold them confidential on behalf of the Court of Appeals unless release is authorized by the complainant.*

(f) Scope of Program. *The Program will include all civil appeals and review of administrative orders, except the following: It will not include original proceedings (such as petitions for mandamus), prisoner petitions, habeas corpus petitions, summary enforcement actions of the National Labor Relations Board or any pro se cases. Nothing herein shall prevent any judge or panel, upon motion or sua sponte, from referring any matter to the Settlement Counsel at any time.*

The foregoing Civil Appeals Management Program shall be applicable to all such cases as set forth above, arising from the District Courts in the Districts of Maine, New Hampshire, Massachusetts, and Rhode Island, in which the Notice of Appeal is received in the Court of Appeals on or after January 1, 1992; and all such cases arising from the District Court in the District of Puerto Rico, in which the Notice of Appeal is received in the Court of Appeals on or after January 1, 1993.

Adopted effective October 15, 1999.

FRAP 34.   ORAL ARGUMENT

(a) In General.

(1) *Party's Statement.* Any party may file, or a court may require by local rule, a statement explaining why oral argument should, or need not, be permitted.

(2) *Standards.* Oral argument must be allowed in every case unless a panel of three judges who have examined the briefs and record unanimously agrees that oral argument is unnecessary for any of the following reasons:

(A) the appeal is frivolous;

(B) the dispositive issue or issues have been authoritatively decided; or

(C) the facts and legal arguments are adequately presented in the briefs and record, and the decisional process would not be significantly aided by oral argument.

(b) Notice of Argument; Postponement. The clerk must advise all parties whether oral argument will be scheduled, and, if so, the date, time, and place for it, and the time allowed for each side. A motion to postpone the argument or to allow longer argument must be filed reasonably in advance of the hearing date.

(c) Order and Contents of Argument. The appellant opens and concludes the argument. Counsel must not read at length from briefs, records, or authorities.

(d) Cross–Appeals and Separate Appeals. If there is a cross-appeal, Rule 28(h) determines which party is the appellant and which is the appellee for purposes of oral argument. Unless the court directs otherwise, a cross-appeal or separate appeal must be argued when the initial appeal is argued. Separate parties should avoid duplicative argument.

(e) Non-appearance of a Party. If the appellee fails to appear for argument, the court must hear appellant's argument. If the appellant fails to appear for argument, the court may hear the appellee's argument. If neither party appears, the case will be decided on the briefs, unless the court orders otherwise.

(f) Submission on Briefs. The parties may agree to submit a case for decision on the briefs, but the court may direct that the case be argued.

(g) Use of Physical Exhibits at Argument; Removal. Counsel intending to use physical exhibits other than documents at the argument must arrange to place them in the courtroom on the day of the argument before the court convenes. After the argument, counsel must remove the exhibits from the courtroom, unless the court directs otherwise. The clerk may destroy or dispose of the exhibits if counsel does not reclaim them within a reasonable time after the clerk gives notice to remove them.

[Amended April 30, 1979, effective August 1, 1979; March 10, 1986, effective July 1, 1986; April 30, 1991, effective December 1, 1991; April 22, 1993, effective December 1, 1993; April 24, 1998, effective December 1, 1998.]

LOC. R. 34.   ORAL ARGUMENT

(a) Party's Statement. Any party who desires to do so may include, either in the opening or answering brief as the case may be, a statement limited to one-half page setting forth the reasons why oral argument should, or need not, be heard. If such a statement is included, it must be inserted in the brief immediately after the Table of Contents and Table of Authorities and immediately before the first page of the brief and must be captioned "REASONS WHY ORAL ARGUMENT SHOULD [NEED NOT] BE HEARD" as appropriate. The inclusion of this statement will not be counted in computing the maximum permitted length of the brief.

(b) Notice of Argument. If the court concludes that oral argument is unnecessary based on the standards set forth in Fed. R. App. P. 34(a)(2), counsel shall be

so advised. The court's decision to dispense with oral argument may be announced at the time that a decision on the merits is rendered.

(c) *Argument*.

(1) Presentation. *Parties may expect the court to have some familiarity with the briefs. Normally the court will permit no more than 15 minutes per side for oral argument. It is counsel's responsibility to keep track of time. Where more than one counsel argues on one side of a case, it is counsel's further responsibility to assure a fair division of the total time allotted. One or more cases posing the same issues, arising from the same factual context, will be treated as a single case for the purposes of this rule.*

(2) Rebuttal. *Although Fed. R. App. P. 34(c) permits an appellant both to open and conclude the argument, the court holds the view that seldom is counsel well served by an advance reservation of time for rebuttal. Not only does such action reduce the limited time allotted but is likely merely to allow repetitious argument. Counsel are expected to cover all anticipated issues in their arguments in chief. Should unexpected matters arise, such as the need for factual correction, the court is prepared to give counsel who have not reserved time a brief additional period for real rebuttal.*

Adopted effective Sept. 1, 1986; renumbered and amended effective October, 1999.

[Formerly Local Rule 34.1.]

LOC. R. 34.1 *TERMS AND SITTINGS*

(a) *Terms*. *The court shall not hold formal terms but shall be deemed always open for the purpose of docketing appeals and petitions, making motions, filing records, briefs and appendices, filing opinions and entering orders and judgments. Where a federal holiday falls on a Monday, the general order is that the court shall commence its sitting on Tuesday.*

(b) *Sittings*.

(1) Locations. *Sittings will be in Boston except that there will also be sittings in Puerto Rico in November and March and at such other times and places as the court orders. Cases arising in Puerto Rico which are assigned to other sessions may be reassigned to sessions scheduled to be conducted in Puerto Rico. All other cases will be assigned for hearing or submission to the next available session after the briefs have been filed or the time therefor has run.*

(2) Request for Assignment. *Requests for assignment to a specific session, including the March and November sessions, must state reasons justifying special treatment. Assignment to the November and March Puerto Rico session list, so long as space permits, will be made on the basis of statutory priority requirements, hardship that would result from travel to Boston, or other good cause shown.*

(c) *Calendaring*. *Approximately six weeks prior to hearing, the clerk will contact counsel concerning assignment of the case to a specific day, and request the name of the person who will present the oral argument. Two weeks before the monthly sitting commences the clerk will prepare and distribute an order assigning the cases for that session for hearing. The court reserves the privilege of reducing the allotted time for argument when the case is presented.*

(d) *Continuances*. *Once a case is scheduled for argument, continuances may be allowed only for grave cause.*

Adopted effective Sept. 1, 1986; amended effective April 1, 1988; renumbered and amended effective October, 1999; amended effective December 16, 2003.

[Formerly Local Rule 34.2.]

FRAP 35. EN BANC DETERMINATION

(a) When Hearing or Rehearing En Banc May Be Ordered. A majority of the circuit judges who are in regular active service may order that an appeal or other proceeding be heard or reheard by the court of appeals en banc. An en banc hearing or rehearing is not favored and ordinarily will not be ordered unless:

(1) en banc consideration is necessary to secure or maintain uniformity of the court's decisions; or

(2) the proceeding involves a question of exceptional importance.

(b) Petition for Hearing or Rehearing En Banc. A party may petition for a hearing or rehearing en banc.

(1) The petition must begin with a statement that either:

(A) the panel decision conflicts with a decision of the United States Supreme Court or of the court to which the petition is addressed (with citation to the conflicting case or cases) and consideration by the full court is therefore necessary to secure and maintain uniformity of the court's decisions; or

(B) the proceeding involves one or more questions of exceptional importance, each of which must be concisely stated; for example, a petition may assert that a proceeding presents a question of exceptional importance if it involves an issue on which the panel decision conflicts with the authoritative decisions of other United States Courts of Appeals that have addressed the issue.

(2) Except by the court's permission, a petition for an en banc hearing or rehearing must not exceed 15 pages, excluding material not counted under Rule 32.

(3) For purposes of the page limit in Rule 35(b)(2), if a party files both a petition for panel rehearing and a petition for rehearing en banc, they are considered a single document even if they are filed separately, unless separate filing is required by local rule.

(c) Time for Petition for Hearing or Rehearing En Banc. A petition that an appeal be heard initially en banc must be filed by the date when the appellee's brief is due. A petition for a rehearing en banc must be filed within the time prescribed by Rule 40 for filing a petition for rehearing.

(d) Number of Copies. The number of copies to be filed must be prescribed by local rule and may be altered by order in a particular case.

(e) Response. No response may be filed to a petition for an en banc consideration unless the court orders a response.

(f) Call for a Vote. A vote need not be taken to determine whether the case will be heard or reheard en banc unless a judge calls for a vote.

[Amended April 30, 1979, effective August 1, 1979; April 29, 1994, effective December 1, 1994; April 24, 1998, effective December 1, 1998.]

LOC. R. 35. EN BANC DETERMINATION

(a) Who May Vote, Composition of En Banc Court. The decision whether a case should be heard or reheard en banc is made solely by the circuit judges of this circuit who are in regular active service. Rehearing en banc shall be ordered only upon the affirmative votes of a majority of the judges of this court in regular active service who are not disqualified, provided that the judges who are not disqualified constitute a majority of the judges who are in regular active service. A court en banc consists solely of the circuit judges of this circuit in regular active service except that any senior circuit judge of this circuit shall be eligible to participate, at that judge's election, in the circumstances specified in 28 U.S.C. § 46(c).

(b) Petitions for Panel Hearing or Rehearing En Banc. If a petitioner files a petition for panel rehearing and a petition for rehearing en banc addressed to the same decisions or order of the court, the two petitions must be combined into a single document and the document is subject to the 15–page limitation contained in Fed. R. App. P. 35(b)(2), (3). However, the page limit may be enlarged on motion for good cause shown.

(c) Sanctions. If a petition for rehearing or for rehearing en banc is found on its face to be wholly without merit, vexatious, multifarious, or filed principally for delay, the court may tax a sum not exceeding $250 as additional costs, payable to the clerk of the court or the opposing party, as the court may direct. At the court's order, counsel may be required personally to pay all or any part of these costs.

(d) Number of Copies. Pursuant to Fed. R. App. P. 35(d), ten copies of a petition for a panel rehearing, rehearing en banc, or combined Fed. R. App. P. 35(b)(3) document must be filed with the clerk, including one copy on a computer generated disk. The disk

must be filed regardless of page length but otherwise in accordance with Local Rule 32.

Local Rule 35 adopted effective Sept. 1, 1986; renumbered as Local Rule 35.1 effective April 1, 1988; renumbered and amended effective October, 1999; amended effective January 2, 2001; amended effective December 16, 2003.

[Formerly Local Rules 35.1, 35.2, and 35.3.]

FRAP 36.   ENTRY OF JUDGMENT; NOTICE

(a) Entry. A judgment is entered when it is noted on the docket. The clerk must prepare, sign, and enter the judgment:

(1) after receiving the court's opinion—but if settlement of the judgment's form is required, after final settlement; or

(2) if a judgment is rendered without an opinion, as the court instructs.

(b) Notice. On the date when judgment is entered, the clerk must serve on all parties a copy of the opinion—or the judgment, if no opinion was written—and a notice of the date when the judgment was entered.

[Amended April 24, 1998, effective December 1, 1998; April 29, 2002, effective December 1, 2002.]

LOC. R. 36.   OPINIONS

(a) Opinions Generally. The volume of filings is such that the court cannot dispose of each case by opinion. Rather it makes a choice, reasonably accommodated to the particular case, whether to use an order, memorandum and order, or opinion. An opinion is used when the decision calls for more than summary explanation. However, in the interests both off expedition in the particular case, and of saving time and effort in research on the part of future litigants, some opinions are rendered in unpublished form; that is, the opinions are directed to the parties but are not otherwise published in the official West reporter, and may not be cited except as provided in Local Rule 32.3. As indicated in Local Rule 36(b), the court's policy, when opinions are used, is to prefer that they be published; but in limited situations, described in Local Rule 36(b), where opinions are likely not to break new legal ground or contribute otherwise to legal development, they are issued in unpublished form.

(b) Publication of Opinions. The United States Court of Appeals for the First Circuit has adopted the following plan for the publication of its opinions.

(1) Statement of Policy. In general, the court thinks it desirable that opinions be published and thus be available for citation. The policy may be overcome in some situations where an opinion does not articulate a new rule of law, modify an established rule, apply

an established rule to novel facts or serve otherwise as a significant guide to future litigants. (Most opinions dealing with claims for benefits under the Social Security Act, 42 U.S.C. § 205(g), will clearly fall within the exception.)

(2) Manner of Implementation.

(A) As members of a panel prepare for argument, they shall give thought to the appropriate mode of disposition (order, memorandum and order, unpublished opinion, published opinion). At conference the mode of disposition shall be discussed and, if feasible, agreed upon. Any agreement reached may be altered in the light of further research and reflection.

(B) With respect to cases decided by a unanimous panel with a single opinion, if the writer recommends that the opinion not be published, the writer shall so state in the cover letter or memorandum accompanying the draft. After an exchange of views, should any judge remain of the view that the opinion should be published, it must be.

(C) When a panel decides a case with a dissent, or with more than one opinion, the opinion or opinions shall be published unless all the participating judges decide against publication. In any case decided by the court en banc the opinion or opinions shall be published.

(D) Any party or other interested person may apply for good cause shown to the court for publication of an unpublished opinion.

(E) Periodically the court shall conduct a review in an effort to improve its publication policy and implementation.

(c) Precedential Value of Unpublished Opinions. While an unpublished opinion of this court may be cited to this court in accordance with Local Rule 32.3(a), a panel's decision to issue an unpublished opinion means that the panel sees no precedential value in that opinion.

(d) Copies of Opinions. Unless subject to a standing order which might apply to classes of subscribers, such as law schools, the charge for a copy of each opinion, after one free copy to counsel for each party is $5.00.

Renumbered and amended effective October, 1999. Par. (b)(2)(F) amended on an interim basis, effective September 24, 2001; amended effective December 16, 2003.

[Formerly Local Rules 36.1 and 36.2.]

LOC. R. 36.1   OPINIONS

[Renumbered Local Rule 36(a).]

Adopted effective Sept. 1, 1986; renumbered October, 1999.

LOC. R. 36.2   PUBLICATION OF OPINIONS

[Renumbered Local Rule 36(b).]

Adopted effective Sept. 1, 1986; renumbered effective October, 1999.

FRAP 37.   INTEREST ON JUDGMENT

(a) When the Court Affirms. Unless the law provides otherwise, if a money judgment in a civil case is affirmed, whatever interest is allowed by law is payable from the date when the district court's judgment was entered.

(b) When the Court Reverses. If the court modifies or reverses a judgment with a direction that a money judgment be entered in the district court, the mandate must contain instructions about the allowance of interest.

[Amended April 24, 1998, effective December 1, 1998.]

FRAP 38.   FRIVOLOUS APPEAL— DAMAGES AND COSTS

If a court of appeals determines that an appeal is frivolous, it may, after a separately filed motion or notice from the court and reasonable opportunity to respond, award just damages and single or double costs to the appellee.

[Amended April 29, 1994, effective December 1, 1994; April 24, 1998, effective December 1, 1998.]

FRAP 39.   COSTS

(a) Against Whom Assessed. The following rules apply unless the law provides or the court orders otherwise:

(1) if an appeal is dismissed, costs are taxed against the appellant, unless the parties agree otherwise;

(2) if a judgment is affirmed, costs are taxed against the appellant;

(3) if a judgment is reversed, costs are taxed against the appellee;

(4) if a judgment is affirmed in part, reversed in part, modified, or vacated, costs are taxed only as the court orders.

(b) Costs For and Against the United States. Costs for or against the United States, its agency, or officer will be assessed under Rule 39(a) only if authorized by law.

(c) Costs of Copies. Each court of appeals must, by local rule, fix the maximum rate for taxing the cost of producing necessary copies of a brief or appendix, or copies of records authorized by Rule 30(f). The rate must not exceed that generally charged for such work in the area where the clerk's office is located and should encourage economical methods of copying.

(d) Bill of Costs: Objections; Insertion in Mandate.

(1) A party who wants costs taxed must—within 14 days after entry of judgment—file with the circuit clerk, with proof of service, an itemized and verified bill of costs.

(2) Objections must be filed within 10 days after service of the bill of costs, unless the court extends the time.

(3) The clerk must prepare and certify an itemized statement of costs for insertion in the mandate, but issuance of the mandate must not be delayed for taxing costs. If the mandate issues before costs are finally determined, the district clerk must—upon the circuit clerk's request—add the statement of costs, or any amendment of it, to the mandate.

(e) Costs on Appeal Taxable in the District Court. The following costs on appeal are taxable in the district court for the benefit of the party entitled to costs under this rule:

(1) the preparation and transmission of the record;

(2) the reporter's transcript, if needed to determine the appeal;

(3) premiums paid for a supersedeas bond or other bond to preserve rights pending appeal; and

(4) the fee for filing the notice of appeal.

[Amended April 30, 1979, effective August 1, 1979; March 10, 1986, effective July 1, 1986; April 24, 1998, effective December 1, 1998.]

LOC. R. 39.   FEE APPLICATIONS

(a) Fee Applications under the Equal Access to Justice Act.

(1) Time for Filing. *An application to a court of appeals for an award of fees and other expenses pursuant to 28 U.S.C. § 2412, in connection with an appeal, must be filed with the clerk of the court of appeals, with proof of service on the United States, within 30 days of final judgment in the action. For purposes of the 30–day limit, a judgment must not be considered final until the time for filing an appeal or a petition for a writ of certiorari has expired, or the government has given written notice to the parties and to the court of appeals that it will not seek further review, or judgment is entered by the court of last resort.*

(2) Content. *The application shall:*

(A) identify the applicant and the proceeding for which the award is sought;

(B) show that the party seeking the award is a prevailing party and is eligible to receive an award;

(C) show the nature and extent of services rendered and the amount sought, including an item-

ized statement from an attorney representing the party or any agent or expert witness appearing on behalf of the party, stating the actual time expended and the rate at which fees are computed, together with a statement of expenses for which reimbursement is sought; and

(D) identify the specific position of the United States that the party alleges was not substantially justified. The court of appeals may, in its discretion, remit any such application to the district court for a determination.

(3) Objection. *If the United States has any objection to the application for fees and other expenses, such objection must be filed within 30 days of service of the application.*

(b) Fee Applications other than under 28 U.S.C. § 2412. *An application, under any statute, rule or custom other than 28 U.S.C. § 2412, for an award of fees and other expenses, in connection with an appeal, must be filed with the clerk of the court of appeals within 30 days of the date of entry of the final circuit judgment, whether or not attorney fees had been requested in the trial court, except in those circumstances where the court of appeals has ordered that the award of fees and other expenses be remanded to the district court for a determination. For purposes of the 30–day limit, a judgment must not be considered final until the time for filing an appeal or a petition for a writ of certiorari has expired, or judgment is entered by the court of last resort. If any party against whom an award of fees and other expenses is sought has any objection to the application, such objection must be filed within 30 days of service of the application. The court of appeals may, in its discretion, remit any such application to the district court for a determination.*

Renumbered and amended effective October, 1999.

[Formerly Local Rules 39.1 and 39.2.]

FRAP 40.   PETITION FOR PANEL REHEARING

(a) Time to File; Contents; Answer; Action by the Court if Granted.

(1) *Time.* Unless the time is shortened or extended by order or local rule, a petition for panel rehearing may be filed within 14 days after entry of judgment. But in a civil case, if the United States or its officer or agency is a party, the time within which any party may seek rehearing is 45 days after entry of judgment, unless an order shortens or extends the time.

(2) *Contents.* The petition must state with particularity each point of law or fact that the petitioner believes the court has overlooked or misapprehended and must argue in support of the petition. Oral argument is not permitted.

(3) *Answer.* Unless the court requests, no answer to a petition for panel rehearing is permitted. But ordinarily rehearing will not be granted in the absence of such a request.

(4) *Action by the Court.* If a petition for panel rehearing is granted, the court may do any of the following:

(A) make a final disposition of the case without reargument;

(B) restore the case to the calendar for reargument or resubmission; or

(C) issue any other appropriate order.

(b) Form of Petition; Length. The petition must comply in form with Rule 32. Copies must be served and filed as Rule 31 prescribes. Unless the court permits or a local rule provides otherwise, a petition for panel rehearing must not exceed 15 pages.

[Amended April 30, 1979, effective August 1, 1979; April 29, 1994, effective December 1, 1994; April 24, 1998, effective December 1, 1998.]

First Circuit Note: See Local Rule 35.1.

FRAP 41. MANDATE: CONTENTS; ISSUANCE AND EFFECTIVE DATE; STAY

(a) Contents. Unless the court directs that a formal mandate issue, the mandate consists of a certified copy of the judgment, a copy of the court's opinion, if any, and any direction about costs.

(b) When Issued. The court's mandate must issue 7 calendar days after the time to file a petition for rehearing expires, or 7 calendar days after entry of an order denying a timely petition for panel rehearing, petition for rehearing en banc, or motion for stay of mandate, whichever is later. The court may shorten or extend the time.

(c) Effective Date. The mandate is effective when issued.

(d) Staying the Mandate.

(1) *On Petition for Rehearing or Motion.* The timely filing of a petition for panel rehearing, petition for rehearing en banc, or motion for stay of mandate, stays the mandate until disposition of the petition or motion, unless the court orders otherwise.

(2) *Pending Petition for Certiorari.*

(A) A party may move to stay the mandate pending the filing of a petition for a writ of certiorari in the Supreme Court. The motion must be served on all parties and must show that the certiorari petition would present a substantial question and that there is good cause for a stay.

(B) The stay must not exceed 90 days, unless the period is extended for good cause or unless the party who obtained the stay files a petition for the writ and so notifies the circuit clerk in writing within the period of the stay. In that case, the stay continues until the Supreme Court's final disposition.

(C) The court may require a bond or other security as a condition to granting or continuing a stay of the mandate.

(D) The court of appeals must issue the mandate immediately when a copy of a Supreme Court order denying the petition for writ of certiorari is filed.

[Amended April 29, 1994, effective December 1, 1994; April 24, 1998, effective December 1, 1998; April 29, 2002, effective December 1, 2002.]

LOC. R. 41. STAY OF MANDATE

Whereas an increasingly large percentage of unsuccessful petitions for certiorari have been filed in this circuit in criminal cases in recent years, in the interests of minimizing unnecessary delay in the administration of justice mandate will not be stayed hereafter in criminal cases following the affirmance of a conviction simply upon request. On the contrary, mandate will issue and bail will be revoked at such time as the court shall order except upon a showing, or an independent finding by the court, of probable cause to believe that a petition would not be frivolous, or filed merely for delay. See 18 U.S.C. § 3148. The court will revoke bail even before mandate is due. A comparable principle will be applied in connection with affirmed orders of the NLRB, see NLRB v. Athbro Precision Engineering, 423 F.2d 573 (1st Cir. 1970), and in other cases where the court believes that the only effect of a petition for certiorari would be pointless delay.

Adopted effective Sept. 1, 1986.

FRAP 42. VOLUNTARY DISMISSAL

(a) Dismissal in the District Court. Before an appeal has been docketed by the circuit clerk, the district court may dismiss the appeal on the filing of a stipulation signed by all parties or on the appellant's motion with notice to all parties.

(b) Dismissal in the Court of Appeals. The circuit clerk may dismiss a docketed appeal if the parties file a signed dismissal agreement specifying how costs are to be paid and pay any fees that are due. But no mandate or other process may issue without a court order. An appeal may be dismissed on the appellant's motion on terms agreed to by the parties or fixed by the court.

[Amended April 24, 1998, effective December 1, 1998.]

FRAP 43. SUBSTITUTION OF PARTIES

(a) Death of a Party.

(1) *After Notice of Appeal Is Filed.* If a party dies after a notice of appeal has been filed or while a

proceeding is pending in the court of appeals, the decedent's personal representative may be substituted as a party on motion filed with the circuit clerk by the representative or by any party. A party's motion must be served on the representative in accordance with Rule 25. If the decedent has no representative, any party may suggest the death on the record, and the court of appeals may then direct appropriate proceedings.

(2) *Before Notice of Appeal Is Filed—Potential Appellant.* If a party entitled to appeal dies before filing a notice of appeal, the decedent's personal representative—or, if there is no personal representative, the decedent's attorney of record—may file a notice of appeal within the time prescribed by these rules. After the notice of appeal is filed, substitution must be in accordance with Rule 43(a)(1).

(3) *Before Notice of Appeal Is Filed—Potential Appellee.* If a party against whom an appeal may be taken dies after entry of a judgment or order in the district court, but before a notice of appeal is filed, an appellant may proceed as if the death had not occurred. After the notice of appeal is filed, substitution must be in accordance with Rule 43(a)(1).

(b) Substitution for a Reason Other Than Death. If a party needs to be substituted for any reason other than death, the procedure prescribed in Rule 43(a) applies.

(c) Public Officer: Identification; Substitution.

(1) *Identification of Party.* A public officer who is a party to an appeal or other proceeding in an official capacity may be described as a party by the public officer's official title rather than by name. But the court may require the public officer's name to be added.

(2) *Automatic Substitution of Officeholder.* When a public officer who is a party to an appeal or other proceeding in an official capacity dies, resigns, or otherwise ceases to hold office, the action does not abate. The public officer's successor is automatically substituted as a party. Proceedings following the substitution are to be in the name of the substituted party, but any misnomer that does not affect the substantial rights of the parties may be disregarded. An order of substitution may be entered at any time, but failure to enter an order does not affect the substitution.

[Amended March 10, 1986, effective July 1, 1986; April 24, 1998, effective December 1, 1998.]

FRAP 44. CASE INVOLVING A CONSTITUTIONAL QUESTION WHEN THE UNITED STATES OR THE RELEVANT STATE IS NOT A PARTY

(a) Constitutional Challenge to Federal Statute. If a party questions the constitutionality of an Act of Congress in a proceeding in which the United States or its agency, officer, or employee is not a party in an official capacity, the questioning party must give written notice to the circuit clerk immediately upon the filing of the record or as soon as the question is raised in the court of appeals. The clerk must then certify that fact to the Attorney General.

(b) Constitutional Challenge to State Statute. If a party questions the constitutionality of a statute of a State in a proceeding in which that State or its agency, officer, or employee is not a party in an official capacity, the questioning party must give written notice to the circuit clerk immediately upon the filing of the record or as soon as the question is raised in the court of appeals. The clerk must then certify that fact to the attorney general of the State.

[Amended April 24, 1998, effective December 1, 1998; April 29, 2002, effective December 1, 2002.]

FRAP 45.   CLERK'S DUTIES

(a) General Provisions.

(1) *Qualifications.* The circuit clerk must take the oath and post any bond required by law. Neither the clerk nor any deputy clerk may practice as an attorney or counselor in any court while in office.

(2) *When Court Is Open.* The court of appeals is always open for filing any paper, issuing and returning process, making a motion, and entering an order. The clerk's office with the clerk or a deputy in attendance must be open during business hours on all days except Saturdays, Sundays, and legal holidays. A court may provide by local rule or by order that the clerk's office be open for specified hours on Saturdays or on legal holidays other than New Year's Day, Martin Luther King, Jr.'s Birthday, Presidents' Day, Memorial Day, Independence Day, Labor Day, Columbus Day, Veterans' Day, Thanksgiving Day, and Christmas Day.

(b) Records.

(1) *The Docket.* The circuit clerk must maintain a docket and an index of all docketed cases in the manner prescribed by the Director of the Administrative Office of the United States Courts. The clerk must record all papers filed with the clerk and all process, orders, and judgments.

(2) *Calendar.* Under the court's direction, the clerk must prepare a calendar of cases awaiting argument. In placing cases on the calendar for argument, the clerk must give preference to appeals in criminal cases and to other proceedings and appeals entitled to preference by law.

(3) *Other Records.* The clerk must keep other books and records required by the Director of the Administrative Office of the United States Courts, with the approval of the Judicial Conference of the United States, or by the court.

(c) Notice of an Order or Judgment. Upon the entry of an order or judgment, the circuit clerk must immediately serve a notice of entry on each party, with a copy of any opinion, and must note the date of service on the docket. Service on a party represented by counsel must be made on counsel.

(d) Custody of Records and Papers. The circuit clerk has custody of the court's records and papers. Unless the court orders or instructs otherwise, the clerk must not permit an original record or paper to be taken from the clerk's office. Upon disposition of the case, original papers constituting the record on appeal or review must be returned to the court or agency from which they were received. The clerk must preserve a copy of any brief, appendix, or other paper that has been filed.

[Amended March 1, 1971, effective July 1, 1971; March 10, 1986, effective July 1, 1986; April 24, 1998, effective December 1, 1998; April 29, 2002, effective December 1, 2002.]

LOC. R. 45. DEFAULTS

(a) Appellant. When a cause is in default as to the filing of the brief for appellant or petitioner, and the appendix, if one is required, the clerk must enter an order dismissing the appeal for want of diligent prosecution. The party in default may have the appeal reinstated upon showing special circumstances justifying the failure to comply with the time limit. The motion to set aside the dismissal must be filed within ten days.

(b) Appellee. When a cause is in default as to the filing of the brief for appellee or respondent, the cause must be assigned to the next list and the appellee will not be heard at oral argument except by leave of the Court.

(c) Local Rule 3. Counsel are reminded of Local Rule 3 providing for the dismissal of the appeal for want of diligent prosecution if the docket fee is not paid within 7 days of the filing of the notice of appeal.

Adopted effective Sept. 1, 1986; amended effective Jan. 1, 1992; October 15, 1999.

LOC. R. 45.1 THE CLERK

(a) Business Hours. The office of the clerk shall be open for business from 8:30 a.m. to 5:00 p.m. except Saturdays, Sundays, and legal holidays.

(b) Fees and Costs. The clerk must charge the fees and costs which are fixed from time to time by the Judicial Conference of the United States, pursuant to 28 U.S.C. § 1913.

(c) Copies of Opinions. Unless subject to a standing order which might apply to classes of subscribers, such as law schools, the charge for a copy of each

opinion, after one free copy to counsel for each party is $5.00.

Adopted effective Sept. 1, 1986; amended effective October 15, 1999.

FRAP 46. ATTORNEYS

(a) Admission to the Bar.

(1) *Eligibility.* An attorney is eligible for admission to the bar of a court of appeals if that attorney is of good moral and professional character and is admitted to practice before the Supreme Court of the United States, the highest court of a state, another United States court of appeals, or a United States district court (including the district courts for Guam, the Northern Mariana Islands, and the Virgin Islands).

(2) *Application.* An applicant must file an application for admission, on a form approved by the court that contains the applicant's personal statement showing eligibility for membership. The applicant must subscribe to the following oath or affirmation:

> "I, _____, do solemnly swear [or affirm] that I will conduct myself as an attorney and counselor of this court, uprightly and according to law; and that I will support the Constitution of the United States."

(3) *Admission Procedures.* On written or oral motion of a member of the court's bar, the court will act on the application. An applicant may be admitted by oral motion in open court. But, unless the court orders otherwise, an applicant need not appear before the court to be admitted. Upon admission, an applicant must pay the clerk the fee prescribed by local rule or court order.

(b) Suspension or Disbarment.

(1) *Standard.* A member of the court's bar is subject to suspension or disbarment by the court if the member:

    (A) has been suspended or disbarred from practice in any other court; or

    (B) is guilty of conduct unbecoming a member of the court's bar.

(2) *Procedure.* The member must be given an opportunity to show good cause, within the time prescribed by the court, why the member should not be suspended or disbarred.

(3) *Order.* The court must enter an appropriate order after the member responds and a hearing is held, if requested, or after the time prescribed for a response expires, if no response is made.

(c) Discipline. A court of appeals may discipline an attorney who practices before it for conduct unbecoming a member of the bar or for failure to comply with any court rule. First, however, the court must afford the attorney reasonable notice, an opportunity to show cause to the contrary, and, if requested, a hearing.

[Amended March 10, 1986, effective July 1, 1986; April 24, 1998, effective December 1, 1998.]

LOC. R. 46. ATTORNEYS

(a) Admission.

(1) Admission Fee. *Upon being admitted to practice, an attorney other than government counsel, and court-appointed counsel, must pay a local admission fee of $50.00 to the clerk. The clerk must maintain the proceeds as a court's discretionary fund for the reimbursement of expenses of non-compensable court-appointed counsel and such other purposes as the court may order. This fee is in addition to the $150 national admission fee imposed by the Court of Appeals Miscellaneous Fee Schedule, promulgated under 28 U.S.C. § 1913. Attorneys may be admitted in open court on motion or otherwise as the court shall determine.*

(2) Admission as a Prerequisite to Practice. *In order to file motions, pleadings or briefs on behalf of a party or participate in oral argument, attorneys must be admitted to the bar of this court and file an appearance form. The appearance of a member of the bar of any court designated in Fed. R. App. P. 46(a) will be entered subject to filing an application and subsequent admission to practice in this court. Forms for admission and entry of appearance will be provided by the clerk.*

(3) Parties. *A party desiring to appear without counsel shall notify the clerk in writing by completing and filing an entry of appearance on a form approved by the court.*

(b) Temporary Suspension of Attorneys. *When it is shown to the Court of Appeals that any member of its bar has been suspended or disbarred from practice by a final decision issued by any other court of record, or has been found guilty of conduct unbecoming of a member of the bar of this court, the member may be temporarily suspended from representing parties before this court pending the completion of proceedings initiated under Fed. R. App. P. 46 and the Rules of Attorney Disciplinary Enforcement for the Court of Appeals for the First Circuit.*

(c) Disciplinary Rules. *The Rules of Attorney Disciplinary Enforcement for the Court of Appeals for the First Circuit are on file in the clerks's office. A copy may be obtained upon request addressed to the clerk of this court.*

(d) Library Access. *The law library of this court shall be open to members of the Bar, to the United States Attorney of the Circuit and their assistants, to other law officers of the government, and persons having a case in this court, but books may be removed only by government employees, who shall sign therefor.*

(e) Staff Attorneys and Law Clerks. *No one serving as a staff attorney to the court or as a law clerk to a member of this court or employed in any such capacity by this court shall engage in the practice of law while continuing in such position. Nor shall a staff attorney or law clerk after separating from that position practice as an attorney in connection with any case pending in this court during the term of service, or appear at the counsel table or on brief in connection with any case heard during a period of one year following separation from service with the court.*

(f) Standing Rule Governing Appearance and Argument by Eligible Law Students.

(1) Scope of Legal Assistance.

(A) An eligible law student with the written consent of an indigent and the indigent's attorney of record may appear in this court on behalf of that indigent in any case. The attorney of record, for purposes of this rule, must be a member of the bar of this court, the faculty member conducting the course in appellate advocacy described in paragraph (2)(c) of this section, and appointed as counsel on appeal for the indigent. The written consent must be filed with the clerk.

(B) An eligible law student may assist in the preparation of briefs and other documents to be filed in this court, but such briefs or documents must be signed by the attorney of record. Names of students participating in the preparation of briefs may, however, be added to the briefs. The law student may also participate in oral argument with leave of the court, but only in the presence of the attorney of record. The attorney of record must assume personal professional responsibility for the law student's work and for supervising the quality of the law student's work The attorney of record should be familiar with the case and prepared to supplement or correct any written or oral statements made by the student.

(2) Student Eligibility Requirements. *In order to appear, the student must:*

(A) Be enrolled in a law school approved by the American Bar Association;

(B) Have completed legal studies amounting to at least four (4) semesters, or the equivalent if the school is on some basis other than a semester basis;

(C) Be taking a course in appellate advocacy for academic credit;

(D) Be certified by the attorney of record as qualified to provide the legal representation permitted by this rule. This certification, which shall be filed with the clerk, may be withdrawn by the dean at any time by mailing a notice to the clerk or by termination by this court without notice or hearing and without any showing of cause;

(E) Neither ask for nor receive any compensation or remuneration of any kind for the student's services from the person on whose behalf the student renders services. This shall also prevent a law student from making charges for its services.;

(F) Certify in writing that the student has read and is familiar with the Code of Professional Responsibility of the American Bar Association, the Federal Rules of Appellate Procedure, and the rules of this court.

(3) Standards of Supervision. *The supervising attorney of record must:*

(A) File with this court the attorney's written consent to supervise the student;

(B) Assume personal professional responsibility for the student's work;

(C) Assist the student to the extent necessary;

(D) Appear with the student in all proceedings before this court and be prepared to supplement any written or oral statement made by the student to this court or opposing counsel.

(4) Forms Required by Rule.

(A) Form to be completed by the party for whom the law student is rendering services:

I authorize _____, a law student, to appear in court or at other proceedings on my behalf, and to prepare documents on my behalf.

_____
(Date)   (Signature of Client)

(If more than one client is involved, approvals from each shall be attached.)

(B) Form to be completed by the law student's supervising attorney:

I certify that this student has completed at least 4 semesters of law school work, and is, to the best of my knowledge, of good character and competent legal ability. I will carefully supervise all of this student's work. I authorize this student to appear in court or at other proceedings, and to prepare documents. I will accompany the student at such appearances, sign all documents prepared by the student, assume personal responsibility for the student's work, and be prepared to supplement, if necessary, any statements made by the student to the court or to opposing counsel.

_____
(Name of Student)   (Signature of Supervising Attorney)

_____

_____
*(Address & Phone of   (Address & Phone of
Above)   Above)*

_____
*Name of Law School
Attending*

(C) Form to be completed by law student:

I certify that I have completed at least 4 semesters of law school; that I am familiar and will comply with the Code of Professional Responsibility of the American Bar Association, the Federal Rules of Appellate Procedure, and the Rules of this Court; and that I am receiving no compensation from the party on whose behalf I am rendering services.

_____
(Date)   (Signature of Student)

Renumbered and amended effective October 15, 1999; amended effective December 16, 2003; January 1, 2005.

[Formerly Local Rules 45.2, 46, 46.2, 46.3 and 46.6.]

LOC. R. 46.5 APPOINTMENT OF COUNSEL IN CRIMINAL CASES

The United States Court of Appeals for the First Circuit adopts the following Plan to implement the Criminal Justice Act of 1964, 18 U.S.C. § 3006A, P.L. 88–455, as amended October 12, 1984, P.L. 98–473, and November 14, 1986, P.L. 99–651 to which references must be made. The purpose of this Plan is to provide adequate representation and defense of all persons to the extent provided therein including cases where a person faces loss of liberty or is in custody as a material witness. The court notes at the outset that the Act does not diminish the traditional responsibility of members of the Bar to accept appointments. It recognizes that compensation will, in most instances, be something less than full, and appreciates that service by counsel will represent a substantial measure of public dedication.

(a) Request for Counsel. Every person or eligible witness desiring counsel and that the government pay for the expense of appeal, whether or not the person had court-appointed counsel in the district court, shall address to this court a request in writing and a statement of the person's inability to pay. The court may make such further inquiry of the person's need as it may see fit. This inquiry may also be addressed to previously retained counsel, with the objective of ascertaining that present inability to pay is not a result of past excessive compensation. Such inquiry is not aimed at depriving an indigent of counsel but at the relatively few counsel who might reasonably be considered to have used up all of the available funds for doing only part of the work.

(b) Appointment of Counsel. The court may appoint counsel who represented the person in the dis-

trict court, or counsel from a panel maintained by the court, or otherwise. The addition or deletion of names from the panel and the selection of counsel shall be the sole and exclusive responsibility of the court but the actual administration thereof may be conducted by the clerk of this court. The person may ask for appointment of counsel who represented the defendant in the district court or for the non-appointment of such counsel, but shall not otherwise request any specific individual. The court shall give consideration to such request, but shall not be bound by it. A request for relief by trial counsel, upon a showing of cause, shall be given due consideration. It is recognized that counsel on appeal may require different qualifications than for trial. The substitution of counsel on appeal shall not in any way reflect upon the ability or upon the conduct of prior counsel. The Administration Office shall be notified promptly of each appointment, and of each order releasing counsel.

(c) Duration and Substitution of Counsel. The court notes, and incorporates herein, the provisions of section (c) of the Act, except the references therein to magistrates. Except when relieved by the court, counsel's appointment shall not terminate until, if the person loses the appeal, counsel informs the person of that fact and of the person's right to petition for certiorari and the time period, and has prepared and filed the petition if the person requests it and there are reasonable grounds for counsel properly to do so (see Rule 10 of the Rules of the Supreme Court of the United States). If counsel determines that there are no reasonable grounds and declines to file a petition for certiorari requested by the person, counsel shall so inform the Court and request leave to withdraw from the representation by written motion stating that counsel has reviewed the matter and determined that the petition would be frivolous, accompanied by counsel's certification of the date when a copy of the motion was furnished to the person. If the person does not wish to apply for certiorari or does not respond to the notification, counsel shall so inform the court by letter, which action shall terminate the representation. The clerk will inform the person in writing of the fact and effective date of the termination of counsel's appointment.

(d) Payment for Representation and Services other than Counsel. The court notes sections (d) and (e) of the Act and incorporates the pertinent portions herein. Expenses described in the Act do not include overhead and such matters as secretarial expenses not ordinarily billed to clients, but a reasonable charge for copying briefs may be allowed. For additional guidance, see the Guidelines for the Administration of the Criminal Justice Act and Related Statutes, *Volume VII*, Guide to Judiciary Policies and Procedures.

All claims, whether for compensation, or for expenditures, shall be submitted promptly after the completion of all duties, at the risk of disallowance. If counsel files a petition for a writ of certiorari, counsel's time and expenses involved in the preparation of the petition should be included on the voucher for services performed in this court. After court approval all orders for payment shall be processed through the Administrative Office.

(e) Receipt of Other Payments. The provisions of section (f) of the Act are incorporated herein. Appointed counsel shall be under a continuing duty to report to the court any circumstances indicating financial ability on behalf of the person to pay part or all of the person's counsel fees or expenses. The court shall in no instance permit counsel who receives payments under the Act to frustrate the intent of the limitations contained in sections (d) and (e) by the receipt of other payment, either during, before, or after such representation.

(f) Forms. For the appointment of counsel, the making of claims, and all other matters for which forms shall have been approved by the Administrative Office, such forms shall be used as a matter of course.

(g) Effective Date and Amendments. This amended Plan shall take effect on November 14, 1986. It may be amended at any time with the approval of the Judicial Council. The present plan incorporates an amendment made on December 16, 2002.

Adopted effective Sept. 1, 1986; amended effective Nov. 14, 1986; October, 1999; December 16, 2002.

LOC. R. 46.6 PROCEDURE FOR WITHDRAWAL IN CRIMINAL CASES

(a) Trial Counsel's Duty to Continue to Represent Defendant on Appeal Until Relieved by the Court of Appeals. An attorney who has represented a defendant in a criminal case in the district court will be responsible for representing the defendant on appeal, whether or not the attorney has entered an appearance in the court of appeals, until the attorney is relieved of such duty by the court of appeals. See Local Rule 12(b).

(b) Withdrawal by Counsel Appointed in the District Court. When a defendant has been represented in the district court by counsel appointed under the Criminal Justice Act, the clerk will usually send a "Form for Selection of Counsel on Appeal" to defendant, which asks defendant to select among the following:

(1) representing him or herself on appeal and proceeding pro se,

(2) requesting trial counsel to be appointed on appeal to represent defendant on appeal,

(3) requesting the appointment of new counsel on appeal, and

(4) retaining private counsel for appeal.

If the defendant returns the form and elects to proceed with new counsel to be appointed on appeal, then the court will ordinarily appoint new counsel and allow trial counsel to withdraw.

If counsel wishes to withdraw and either the defendant fails to complete the form or counsel wishes to terminate representation even though the defendant has selected (2) above, counsel may file an affidavit explaining the difficulty and move to withdraw.

An unsworn declaration under the penalty of perjury in the format set forth in 28 U.S.C. § 1746 will suffice in place of an affidavit.

(c) Procedure for Withdrawal in Situations not Governed by Local Rule 46.6(b). *Motions to withdraw as counsel on appeal in criminal cases must be accompanied by a notice of appearance of replacement counsel or, in the absence of replacement counsel, such motions must state the reasons for withdrawal and must be accompanied by one of the following:*

(1) The defendant's completed application for appointment of replacement counsel under the Criminal Justice Act or a showing that such application has already been filed with the court and, if defendant has not already been determined to be financially eligible, certification of compliance with Fed.R.App.P. 24; or

(2) An affidavit from the defendant showing that the defendant has been advised that the defendant may retain replacement counsel or apply for appointment of replacement counsel and expressly stating that the defendant does not wish to be represented by counsel but elects to appear pro se; or

(3) An affidavit from the defendant showing that the defendant has been advised of the defendant's rights with regard to the appeal and expressly stating that the defendant elects to withdraw the appeal; or

(4) If the reason for the motion is the frivolousness of the appeal, a brief following the procedure described in Anders v. California, *386 U.S. 738 (1967), must be filed with the court. [Counsel's attention is also directed to* McCoy v. Court of Appeals, *486 U.S. 429 (1988);* Penson v. Ohio, *488 U.S. 75 (1988)]. Any such brief shall be filed only after counsel has ordered and read all relevant transcripts, including trial, change of plea, and sentencing transcripts, as well as the presentence investigation report. Counsel shall serve a copy of the brief and motion on the defendant and advise the defendant that the defendant has thirty (30) days from the date of service in which to file a brief in support of reversal or modification of the judgment. The motion must be accompanied by proof of service on the defendant and certification that counsel has advised the defendant of the defendant's right to file a separate brief.*

If counsel is unable to comply with (1), (2), or (3) and does not think it appropriate to proceed in accor-

dance with (4), counsel may file an affidavit explaining the difficulty and move to withdraw.

An unsworn declaration under the penalty of perjury in the format set forth in 28 U.S.C. § 1746 will suffice in place of an affidavit.

(d) Service. *All motions must be accompanied by proof of service on the defendant and the Government and will be determined, without oral argument, by one or more judges.*

Renumbered and amended October, 1999. Amended effective December 16, 2002.

[Formerly Local Rule 46.4(a). Former Local Rule 46.6 renumbered Local Rule 46(b).]

FRAP 47. LOCAL RULES BY COURTS OF APPEALS

(a) Local Rules.

(1) Each court of appeals acting by a majority of its judges in regular active service may, after giving appropriate public notice and opportunity for comment, make and amend rules governing its practice. A generally applicable direction to parties or lawyers regarding practice before a court must be in a local rule rather than an internal operating procedure or standing order. A local rule must be consistent with—but not duplicative of—Acts of Congress and rules adopted under 28 U.S.C. § 2072 and must conform to any uniform numbering system prescribed by the Judicial Conference of the United States. Each circuit clerk must send the Administrative Office of the United States Courts a copy of each local rule and internal operating procedure when it is promulgated or amended.

(2) A local rule imposing a requirement of form must not be enforced in a manner that causes a party to lose rights because of a nonwillful failure to comply with the requirement.

(b) Procedure When There Is No Controlling Law. A court of appeals may regulate practice in a particular case in any manner consistent with federal law, these rules, and local rules of the circuit. No sanction or other disadvantage may be imposed for noncompliance with any requirement not in federal law, federal rules, or the local circuit rules unless the alleged violator has been furnished in the particular case with actual notice of the requirement.

[Amended April 27, 1995, effective December 1, 1995; April 24, 1998, effective December 1, 1998.]

LOC. R. 47. LOCAL RULES OF THE FIRST CIRCUIT

(a) Advisory Committee.

(1) Membership. *In accordance with 28 U.S.C. § 2077(b) an advisory committee on the rules of practice and internal operating procedures is hereby*

created for the court. This committee shall consist of members of the Bar of the court as follows: Three members from the District of Massachusetts, two members from the District of Puerto Rico and one each from the Districts of Maine, New Hampshire and Rhode Island.

(2) Duties. The advisory committee shall have an advisory role concerning the rules of practice and internal operating procedures of the court. The advisory committee shall, among other things,

(A) provide a forum for continuous study of the rules of practice and internal operating procedures of the court;

(B) serve as a conduit between the bar and the public and the court regarding procedural matters and suggestions for changes;

(C) consider and recommend rules and amendments for adoption; and

(D) render reports from time to time, on its own initiative and on request, to the court.

(3) Terms of Members. The members of the advisory committee shall serve three-year terms, which will be staggered commencing on October 1, 1986, so that three new members will be appointed every year in such order as the court decides. The court shall appoint one of the members of the committee to serve as chairman.

(b) Comments from Members of the Bar. Prior to the adoption of a proposed amendment to these Rules, if time permits, the court will seek the comments and recommendations of interested members of the bar through the office of the clerk and with the aid of the advisory committee created pursuant to 28 U.S.C. § 2077.

Renumbered and amended effective October 15, 1999; amended effective December 16, 2003.

[Formerly Local Rules 47.2, 47.3 and 47.4.]

LOC. R. 47.1 JUDICIAL CONFERENCE OF THE FIRST CIRCUIT

(a) There shall be held annually at such time and place as shall be designated by the chief judge of the circuit a Conference of all the circuit, district and bankruptcy judges of the circuit and of those magistrates designated by the chief judge of the circuit for the purpose of considering the state of business of the courts and advising ways and means of improving the administration of justice within the circuit. It shall be the duty of each circuit, district, and bankruptcy judge and designated magistrates in the circuit to attend the Conference and, unless excused by the chief judge, to remain throughout the Conference. The chief judge shall preside at the Conference.

(b) The chief judge of the circuit shall appoint a Planning Committee consisting of a circuit judge and/or district judge and such members of the Bar as

they may designate to plan and conduct the Conference.

(c) At least biennially, members of the Conference shall include the following:

(1) Presidents of the state bar associations of states and commonwealths within the circuit;

(2) The dean or member of the faculty designated by the dean of each accredited law school within the circuit;

(3) All United States Attorneys of the circuit;

(4) Lawyers to be appointed from each state in numbers to be determined by the Planning Committee, such appointment to be made by the district committee of each district; if such a committee does not exist, such appointments to be made by the district judges as determined by each district court. Such additional members of the Bar may also be invited as the chief circuit judge, in consultation with the other circuit judges, and the Planning Committee shall decide; and

(5) All federal defenders designated by the chief judge of the circuit.

(d) The Circuit Executive of this court shall be the Secretary of the Conference.

Adopted effective Sept. 1, 1986; amended effective October, 1999.

FRAP 48. MASTERS

(a) Appointment; Powers. A court of appeals may appoint a special master to hold hearings, if necessary, and to recommend factual findings and disposition in matters ancillary to proceedings in the court. Unless the order referring a matter to a master specifies or limits the master's powers, those powers include, but are not limited to, the following:

(1) regulating all aspects of a hearing;

(2) taking all appropriate action for the efficient performance of the master's duties under the order;

(3) requiring the production of evidence on all matters embraced in the reference; and

(4) administering oaths and examining witnesses and parties.

(b) Compensation. If the master is not a judge or court employee, the court must determine the master's compensation and whether the cost is to be charged to any party.

[Former Rule 48 renumbered as Rule 1(c) and new Rule 48 adopted April 29, 1994, effective December 1, 1994; April 24, 1998, effective December 1, 1998.]

LOC. R. 48. CAPITAL CASES

(a) Applicability of Rule. This rule shall govern all matters in which this Court is requested to rule in *any case where the death penalty has been imposed, including, but not limited to, the following:*

(1) direct criminal appeals;

(2) appeals from District Court rulings, such as on motions to vacate a sentence, petitions for a writ of habeas corpus, and requests for a stay or other injunction;

(3) original petitions for a writ of habeas corpus;

(4) motions for second or successive habeas corpus applications;

(5) any related civil proceedings challenging the conviction or sentence of death, or the time, place or manner of execution, as being in violation of federal law, whether filed by the prisoner or by someone else on his or her behalf.

Such cases shall be referred to herein as "capital cases" and shall be governed by this rule, except where otherwise specified in a written order by the Court. To the extent that any local rule of this Court is inconsistent with this rule, this rule shall govern. All local rules of this Court, including interim local rules, are otherwise as applicable to capital cases as they would have been absent this rule.

(b) Certificate of Death Penalty Case. *A special docket shall be maintained by the Clerk of this Court for all cases filed pursuant to this rule.*

(1) Filing. *Upon the filing of any proceeding in any District Court in this Circuit challenging a sentence of death imposed pursuant to a federal or a state court judgment, each party to such proceeding shall file a Certificate of Death Penalty Case with the Clerk of this Court. The U.S. Attorney shall file a Certificate of Death Penalty Case with the Clerk of this Court immediately upon notifying the District Court of intent to seek the death penalty in a federal criminal case. The U.S. Attorney shall also update the Certificate immediately upon return of a verdict imposing a sentence of death.*

(2) Content of the Certificate. *The Certificate shall set forth the names, telephones numbers and addresses of the parties and counsel, the proposed date and place of implementation of the sentence of death, if set, and the emergency nature of the proceedings, if appropriate. It shall be the responsibility of counsel for all parties to apprise the Clerk of this Court of any changes in the information provided on the Certificate as expeditiously as possible.*

(c) Certificates of Appealability and Stays.

(1) Certificates of Appealability and Motions for Stays. *Certificates of appealability for all habeas matters are addressed in Fed. R. App. P. 22. If no express request for a certificate of appealability has been filed in district or appellate court, a motion for stay of execution or a notice of appeal shall be deemed to constitute such a request.*

(2) Stays of Execution.

(A) Except where otherwise prohibited by 28 U.S.C. § 2262, a sentence of death shall automatically be stayed upon the filing of a notice of appeal. In cases where the petitioner is seeking leave to file a second or successive application under 28 U.S.C. § 2254 or § 2255, a stay of execution shall automatically be issued upon approval by the Court of Appeals of the filing of a second or successive application under 28 U.S.C. § 2244(b). The Clerk shall immediately notify all parties and the state or federal authorities responsible for implementing the defendant's sentence of death of the stay of execution. If notification is oral, it shall be followed as expeditiously as possible by written notice.

(B) Except where otherwise required by law or specified in a written order by the Court, an automatic stay of execution shall remain in effect until the Court issues its mandate, at which time the automatic stay shall expire. In the event that a motion requesting a stay of mandate is filed, the motion should also be accompanied by a motion requesting a case-specific stay of execution.

(C) The assigned panel may grant or modify or vacate any stay of execution at any time and will consider upon request motions for a case-specific stay of execution. All motions for a case-specific stay of execution must be accompanied by a memorandum of law, which must include at a minimum the prevailing standards of review and any relevant facts to advise the Court's decision.

(D) Upon making the necessary findings, the Court may enter a case-specific stay of execution which shall clearly specify the duration of the stay.

(E) The Clerk shall send notice to all the parties and state or federal authorities responsible for implementing the defendant's sentence of death when a stay imposed by this provision, be it automatic or case-specific, is no longer in effect.

Adopted effective October, 1999; amended effective December 16, 2003; amended effective October 6, 2004.

APPENDIX OF FORMS

FORM 1. NOTICE OF APPEAL TO A COURT OF APPEALS FROM A JUDGMENT OR ORDER OF A DISTRICT COURT

United States District Court for the
_____ District of _____

File Number _____

A. B., Plaintiff   )
v.   ) Notice of Appeal
C. D., Defendant   )

Notice is hereby given that ___(here name all parties taking the appeal)___, (plaintiffs) (defendants) in the above named case,* hereby appeal to the United States Court of Appeals for the _____ Circuit (from the final judgment) (from an order (describing it)) entered in this action on the ____ day of _____, 20___.

(s)_____

Attorney for _____

Address:_____

* See Rule 3(c) for permissible ways of identifying appellants.

[Amended April 22, 1993, effective December 1, 1993; amended March 27, 2003, effective December 1, 2003.]

FORM 2. NOTICE OF APPEAL TO A COURT OF APPEALS FROM A DECISION OF THE UNITED STATES TAX COURT

UNITED STATES TAX COURT
Washington, D.C.

A.B., Petitioner   )
)
v.   ) Docket No. _____
)
Commissioner of Internal)
Revenue, Respondent   )

Notice of Appeal

Notice is hereby given that ___(here name all parties taking the appeal)*___ hereby appeal to the United States Court of Appeals for the _____ Circuit from (that part of) the decision of this court entered in the above captioned proceeding on the ____ day of _____, 20___ (relating to _____).

(s)_____

Counsel for _____

Address:_____

* See Rule 3(c) for permissible ways of identifying appellants.

[Amended April 22, 1993, effective December 1, 1993; amended March 27, 2003, effective December 1, 2003.]

FORM 3. PETITION FOR REVIEW OF ORDER OF AN AGENCY, BOARD, COMMISSION OR OFFICER

United States Court of Appeals
for the _____ Circuit

A.B., Petitioner	)
	)
v.	) Petition for Review
XYZ Commission,	)
Respondent	)

(here name all parties bringing the petition)*   hereby petition the court for review of the Order of the XYZ Commission (describe the order) entered on _____, 20___.

(s)_____

Attorney for Petitioners

Address:_____

* See Rule 15.

[Amended April 22, 1993, effective December 1, 1993; amended March 27, 2003, effective December 1, 2003.]

FORM 4. AFFIDAVIT ACCOMPANYING MOTION FOR PERMISSION TO APPEAL IN FORMA PAUPERIS

United States District Court for the _____ District of _____

Appeal No. _____
v.   District Court or Agency No. _____

Affidavit in Support of Motion	Instructions
I swear or affirm under penalty of perjury that, because of my poverty, I cannot prepay the docket fees of my appeal or post a bond for them. I believe I am entitled to redress. I swear or affirm under penalty of perjury under United States laws that my answers on this form are true and correct. (28 U.S.C. § 1746; 18 U.S.C. § 1621.)	Complete all questions in this application and then sign it. Do not leave any blanks: if the answer to a question is "0," "none," or "not applicable (N/A)," write in that response. If you need more space to answer a question or to explain your answer, attach a separate sheet of paper identified with your name, your case's docket number, and the question number.
Signed: _____	Date: _____

My issues on appeal are:

1. For both you and your spouse estimate the average amount of money received from each of the following sources during the past 12 months. Adjust any amount that was received weekly, biweekly, quarterly, semiannually, or annually to show the monthly rate. Use gross amounts, that is, amounts before any deductions for taxes or otherwise.

Income source	Average monthly amount during the past 12 months		Amount expected next month	
	You	Spouse	You	Spouse
Employment	$_____	$_____	$_____	$_____
Self-employment	$_____	$_____	$_____	$_____
Income from real property (such as rental income)	$_____	$_____	$_____	$_____
Interest and dividends	$_____	$_____	$_____	$_____
Gifts	$_____	$_____	$_____	$_____
Alimony	$_____	$_____	$_____	$_____
Child support	$_____	$_____	$_____	$_____
Retirement (such as social security, pensions, annuities, insurance)	$_____	$_____	$_____	$_____
Disability (such as social security, insurance payments)	$_____	$_____	$_____	$_____
Unemployment payments	$_____	$_____	$_____	$_____
Public-assistance (such as welfare)	$_____	$_____	$_____	$_____
Other (specify): _____	$_____	$_____	$_____	$_____
Total monthly income:	$_____	$_____	$_____	$_____

2. *List your employment history, most recent employer first. (Gross monthly pay is before taxes or other deductions.)*

Employer	Address	Dates of employment	Gross monthly pay
_____	_____	_____	_____
_____	_____	_____	_____

3. *List your spouse's employment history, most recent employer first. (Gross monthly pay is before taxes or other deductions.)*

Employer	Address	Dates of employment	Gross monthly pay
_____	_____	_____	_____
_____	_____	_____	_____

4. *How much cash do you and your spouse have?* $_____

Below, state any money you or your spouse have in bank accounts or in any other financial institution.

Financial institution	Type of account	Amount you have	Amount your spouse has
_____	_____	$_____	$_____
_____	_____	$_____	$_____
_____	_____	$_____	$_____

If you are a prisoner, you must attach a statement certified by the appropriate institutional officer showing all receipts, expenditures, and balances during the last six months in your institutional accounts. If you have multiple accounts, perhaps because you have been in multiple institutions, attach one certified statement of each account.

5. *List the assets, and their values, which you own or your spouse owns. Do not list clothing and ordinary household furnishings.*

Home	(Value)	Other real estate	(Value)	Motor vehicle # 1	(Value)
				Make & year: _____	
_____		_____		Model: _____	
_____		_____		Registration # :_____	

Motor vehicle # 2	(Value)	Other assets	(Value)	Other assets	(Value)
Make & year: _____		_____		_____	
Model: _____		_____		_____	
Registration # :_____		_____		_____	

6. *State every person, business, or organization owing you or your spouse money, and the amount owed.*

Person owing you or your spouse money	Amount owed to you	Amount owed to your spouse
_____	_____	_____
_____	_____	_____
_____	_____	_____

7. *State the persons who rely on you or your spouse for support.*

Name	Relationship	Age
_____	_____	_____
_____	_____	_____
_____	_____	_____

8. *Estimate the average monthly expenses of you and your family. Show separately the amounts paid by your spouse. Adjust any payments that are made weekly, biweekly, quarterly, semiannually, or annually to show the monthly rate.*

	You	**Your Spouse**
Rent or home-mortgage payment (include lot rented for mobile home)	$_____	$_____
Are real-estate taxes included? ☐ Yes ☐ No		
Is property insurance included? ☐ Yes ☐ No		
Utilities (electricity, heating fuel, water, sewer, and Telephone)	$_____	$_____
Home maintenance (repairs and upkeep)	$_____	$_____
Food	$_____	$_____
Clothing	$_____	$_____
Laundry and dry-cleaning	$_____	$_____
Medical and dental expenses	$_____	$_____
Transportation (not including motor vehicle payments)	$_____	$_____
Recreation, entertainment, newspapers, magazines, etc.	$_____	$_____
Insurance (not deducted from wages or included in Mortgage payments)	$_____	$_____
Homeowner's or renter's	$_____	$_____
Life	$_____	$_____
Health	$_____	$_____
Motor Vehicle	$_____	$_____
Other: _____	$_____	$_____
Taxes (not deducted from wages or included in Mortgage payments) (specify): _____	$_____	$_____
Installment payments	$_____	$_____
Motor Vehicle	$_____	$_____
Credit card (name): _____	$_____	$_____
Department store (name): _____	$_____	$_____
Other: _____	$_____	$_____
Alimony, maintenance, and support paid to others	$_____	$_____
Regular expenses for operation of business, profession, or farm (attach detailed statement)	$_____	$_____
Other (specify): _____	$_____	$_____
Total monthly expenses:	$_____	$_____

9. *Do you expect any major changes to your monthly income or expenses or in your assets or liabilities during the next 12 months?*

☐ Yes ☐ No   If yes, describe on an attached sheet.

10. *Have you paid—or will you be paying—an attorney any money for services in connection with this case, including the completion of this form?* Yes No

If yes, how much? $_____

If yes, state the attorney's name, address, and telephone number:

_____

_____

_____

11. *Have you paid—or will you be paying—anyone other than an attorney (such as a paralegal or a typist) any money for services in connection with this case, including the completion of this form?*
☐ Yes ☐ No
If yes, how much? $_____
If yes, state the person's name, address, and telephone number:
_____
_____

12. *Provide any other information that will help explain why you cannot pay the docket fees for your appeal.*

13. State the address of your legal residence.
_____
_____

Your daytime phone number: (___) _____
Your age: _____ Your years of schooling: _____
Your social-security number: _____

[Amended April 24, 1998, effective December 1, 1998.]

FORM 5.   NOTICE OF APPEAL TO A COURT OF APPEALS FROM A JUDGMENT OR ORDER OF A DISTRICT COURT OR A BANKRUPTCY APPELLATE PANEL

United States District Court for the
_____ District of _____

In re

_____,)
Debtor   )
_____,)   File No. _____
A.B., Plaintiff   )
v.   )
_____,)
C.D., Defendant   )

Notice of Appeal to
United States Court of Appeals
for the _____ Circuit

_____, the plaintiff [or defendant or other party] appeals to the United States Court of Appeals for the _____ Circuit from the final judgment [or order or decree] of the district court for the district of _____ [or bankruptcy appellate panel of the _____ circuit], entered in this case on _____, 20__ [here describe the judgment, order, or decree] _____.

The parties to the judgment [or order or decree] appealed from and the names and addresses of their respective attorneys are as follows:

Dated _____

Signed _____

Attorney for Appellant

Address: _____

_____

[Adopted April 25, 1989, effective December 1, 1989; amended March 27, 2003, effective December 1, 2003.]

FORM 6.   CERTIFICATE OF COMPLIANCE WITH RULE 32(a)

Certificate of Compliance With Type–Volume Limitation,
Typeface Requirements, and Type Style Requirements

1.   This brief complies with the type-volume limitation of Fed. R. App. P. 32(a)(7)(B) because:

☐ this brief contains [*state the number of*] words, excluding the parts of the brief exempted by Fed. R. App. P. 32(a)(7)(B)(iii), *or*

☐ this brief uses a monospaced typeface and contains [*state the number of*] lines of text, excluding the parts of the brief exempted by Fed. R. App. P. 32(a)(7)(B)(iii).

2.   This brief complies with the typeface requirements of Fed. R. App. P. 32(a)(5) and the type style requirements of Fed. R. App. P. 32(a)(6) because:

☐ this brief has been prepared in a proportionally spaced typeface using [*state name and version of word processing program*] in [*state font size and name of type style*], *or*

☐ this brief has been prepared in a monospaced typeface using [*state name and version of word processing program*] with [*state number of characters per inch and name of type style*].

(s)_____

Attorney for _____

Dated: _____

[Adopted April 29, 2002, effective December 1, 2002.]

FIRST CIRCUIT APPEARANCE FORM

APPEARANCE FORM
(Please type or print all answers)

—————

No.

v.

COUNSEL *MUST* COMPLETE & RETURN THIS APPEARANCE FORM IN ORDER TO FILE PLEADINGS IN THIS COURT

Please review and complete the case caption form. If you represent a litigant who was a party below, *but who is not a party on appeal,* do not designate yourself as counsel for the appellant or the appellee.

The Clerk will enter my appearance as Counsel for the _____ appellant _____ appellee.

I do not represent a party to the appeal

_____

(Name of person or entity represented)

Name of Counsel: _____

Name of Firm: _____

Firm Address: _____

Tel.: _____

Fax: _____

_____
Signature
Court of Appeals Bar No. _____

Date: _____

Has this case or any related case previously been on appeal?

Yes ____
No ____

Court of Appeals No. _____

Appearances should be signed by a member of this Court. If you have not been admitted, you may file an appearance subject to subsequent admission to practice in this Court.

SEPARATE FORMS MUST BE COMPLETED FOR EACH PERSON OR ENTITY REPRESENTED

Effective October, 1999.

APPENDICES

APPENDIX A. SELECTED SECTIONS FROM TITLE 28 OF THE UNITED STATES CODE

§ 2253. APPEAL

(a) In a habeas corpus proceeding or a proceeding under section 2255 before a district judge, the final order shall be subject to review, on appeal, by the court of appeals for the circuit in which the proceeding is held.

(b) There shall be no right of appeal from a final order in a proceeding to test the validity of a warrant to remove to another district or place for commitment or trial a person charged with a criminal offense against the United States, or to test the validity of such person's detention pending removal proceedings.

(c)(1) Unless a circuit justice or judge issues a certificate of appealability, an appeal may not be taken to the court of appeals from–

(A) the final order in a habeas corpus proceeding in which the detention complained of arises out of process issued by a State court; or

(B) the final order in a proceeding under section 2255.

(2) A certificate of appealability may issue under paragraph (1) only if the applicant has made a substantial showing of the denial of a constitutional right.

(3) The certificate of appealability under paragraph (1) shall indicate which specific issue or issues satisfy the showing required by paragraph (2).

(June 25, 1948, c. 646, 62 Stat. 967; May 24, 1949, c. 139, § 113, 63 Stat. 105; Oct. 31 , 1951, c. 655, § 52, 65 Stat. 727. As amended Apr. 24, 1996, Pub.L. 104–132, Title 1, § 102, 110 Stat. 1217.)

§ 2254. STATE CUSTODY; REMEDIES IN FEDERAL COURTS

(a) The Supreme Court, a Justice thereof, a circuit judge, or a district court shall entertain an application for a writ of habeas corpus in behalf of a person in custody pursuant to the judgment of a State court only on the ground that he is in custody in violation of the Constitution or laws or treaties of the United States.

(b)(1) An application for a writ of habeas corpus on behalf of a person in custody pursuant to the judgment of a State court shall not be granted unless it appears that–

(A) the applicant has exhausted the remedies available in the courts of the State; or

(B)(i) there is an absence of available State corrective process; or

(ii) circumstances exist that render such process ineffective to protect the rights of the applicant.

(2) An application for a writ of habeas corpus may be denied on the merits, notwithstanding the failure of the applicant to exhaust the remedies available in the courts of the State.

(3) A State shall not be deemed to have waived the exhaustion requirement or be estopped from reliance upon the requirement unless the State, through counsel, expressly waives the requirement.

(c) An applicant shall not be deemed to have exhausted the remedies available in the courts of the State, within the meaning of this section, if he has the right under the law of the State to raise, by any available procedure, the question presented.

(d) An application for a writ of habeas corpus on behalf of a person in custody pursuant to the judgment of a State court shall not be granted with respect to any claim that was adjudicated on the merits in State court proceedings unless the adjudication of the claim–

(1) resulted in a decision that was contrary to, or involved an unreasonable application of, clearly established Federal law, as determined by the Supreme Court of the United States; or

(2) resulted in a decision that was based on an unreasonable determination of the facts in light of the evidence presented in the State court proceeding.

(e)(1) In a proceeding instituted by an application for a writ of habeas corpus by a person in custody pursuant to the judgment of a State court, a determination of a factual issue made by a State court shall be presumed to be correct. The applicant shall have the burden of rebutting the presumption of correctness by clear and convincing evidence.

(2) If the applicant has failed to develop the factual basis of a claim in State court proceedings, the court shall not hold an evidentiary hearing on the claim unless the applicant shows that–

(A) the claim relies on–

(i) a new rule of constitutional law, made retroactive to cases on collateral review by the Supreme Court, that was previously unavailable; or

(ii) a factual predicate that could not have been previously discovered through the exercise of due diligence; and

(B) the facts underlying the claim would be sufficient to establish by clear and convincing evidence that but for constitutional error, no reasonable fact-finder would have found the applicant guilty of the underlying offense.

(f) If the applicant challenges the sufficiency of the evidence adduced in such State court proceeding to support the State court's determination of a factual issue made therein, the applicant, if able, shall produce that part of the record pertinent to a determination of the sufficiency of the evidence to support such determination. If the applicant, because of indigency or other reason is unable to produce such part of the record, then the State shall produce such part of the record and the Federal court shall direct the State to do so by order directed to an appropriate State official. If the State cannot provide such pertinent part of the record, then the court shall determine under the existing facts and circumstances what weight shall be given to the State court's factual determination.

(g) A copy of the official records of the State court, duly certified by the clerk of such court to be a true and correct copy of a finding, judicial opinion, or other reliable written indicia showing such a factual determination by the State court shall be admissible in the Federal court proceeding.

(h) Except as provided in section 408 of the Controlled Substances Act, in all proceedings brought under this section, and any subsequent proceedings on review, the court may appoint counsel for an applicant who is or becomes financially unable to afford counsel, except as provided by a rule promulgated by the Supreme Court pursuant to statutory authority. Appointment of counsel under this section shall be governed by section 3006A of title 18.

(i) The ineffectiveness or incompetence of counsel during Federal or State collateral post-conviction proceedings shall not be a ground for relief in a proceeding arising under section 2254.

(June 25, 1948, c. 646, 62 Stat. 967; Nov. 2, 1966, Pub.L. 89–711, § 2, 80 Stat. 1105. As amended Apr. 24, 1996, Pub.L. 104–132, Title I, § 104, 110 Stat. 1218.)

§ 2255. FEDERAL CUSTODY; REMEDIES ON MOTION ATTACKING SENTENCE

A prisoner in custody under sentence of a court established by Act of Congress claiming the right to be released upon the ground that the sentence was imposed in violation of the Constitution or laws of the United States, or that the court was without jurisdiction to impose such sentence, or that the sentence was in excess of the maximum authorized by law, or is otherwise subject to collateral attack, may move the court which imposed the sentence to vacate, set aside or correct the sentence.

Unless the motion and the files and records of the case conclusively show that the prisoner is entitled to no relief, the court shall cause notice thereof to be served upon the United States attorney, grant a

prompt hearing thereon, determine the issues and make findings of fact and conclusions of law with respect thereto. If the court finds that the judgment was rendered without jurisdiction, or that the sentence imposed was not authorized by law or otherwise open to collateral attack, or that there has been such a denial or infringement of the constitutional rights of the prisoner as to render the judgment vulnerable to collateral attack, the court shall vacate and set the judgment aside and shall discharge the prisoner or resentence him or grant a new trial or correct the sentence as may appear appropriate.

A court may entertain and determine such motion without requiring the production of the prisoner at the hearing.

An appeal may be taken to the court of appeals from the order entered on the motion as from a final judgment on application for a writ of habeas corpus.

An application for a writ of habeas corpus in behalf of a prisoner who is authorized to apply for relief by motion pursuant to this section, shall not be entertained if it appears that the applicant has failed to apply for relief, by motion, to the court which sentenced him, or that such court has denied him relief, unless it also appears that the remedy by motion is inadequate or ineffective to test the legality of his detention.

A 1-year period of limitation shall apply to a motion under this section. The limitation period shall run from the latest of—

(1) the date on which the judgment of conviction becomes final;

(2) the date on which the impediment to making a motion created by governmental action in violation of the Constitution or laws of the United States is removed, if the movant was prevented from making a motion by such governmental action;

(3) the date on which the right asserted was initially recognized by the Supreme Court, if that right has been newly recognized by the Supreme Court and made retroactively applicable to cases on collateral review; or

(4) the date on which the facts supporting the claim or claims presented could have been discovered through the exercise of due diligence.

Except as provided in section 408 of the Controlled Substances Act, in all proceedings brought under this section, and any subsequent proceedings on review, the court may appoint counsel, except as provided by a rule promulgated by the Supreme Court pursuant to statutory authority. Appointment of counsel under this section shall be governed by section 3006A of title 18.

A second or successive motion must be certified as provided in section 2244 by a panel of the appropriate court of appeals to contain—

(1) newly discovered evidence that, if proven and viewed in light of the evidence as a whole, would be sufficient to establish by clear and convincing evidence that no reasonable factfinder would have found the movant guilty of the offense; or

(2) a new rule of constitutional law, made retroactive to cases on collateral review by the Supreme Court, that was previously unavailable.

(June 25, 1948, c. 646, 62 Stat. 967; May 24, 1949, c. 139, § 114, 63 Stat. 105. As amended Apr. 24, 1996, Pub.L. 104–132, Title I, § 105, 110 Stat. 1220.)

APPENDIX B. ORDER OF THE COURT REGARDING SECTION 2254, 2255 PETITIONS

ORDER OF COURT

This court has adopted Local Rules 22.1 and 22.2 in order to implement provisions of the Antiterrorism and Effective Death Penalty Act of 1996 ("AEDPA") relating to the processing of applications for certificates of appealability and motions to file second or successive petitions in proceedings arising under 28 U.S.C. §§ 2254 and 2255.

The Supreme Court's decision in Lindh v. Murphy, 117 S.Ct. 2059 (1997), indicates that the subject provisions of the AEDPA do not apply in non-capital cases that were filed in the district courts or courts of appeals prior to April 24, 1996, the effective date of the AEDPA.

Local Rule 22 is applicable to § 2254 proceedings which were pending prior to April 24, 1996. Local Rules 22.1 and 22.2 shall be applied to the processing of non-capital § 2254 and § 2255 petitions, and to motions seeking permission to file second or successive petitions, which were filed on or after April 24, 1996.

So ordered.

October 15, 1999

INTERNAL OPERATING PROCEDURES
OF THE FIRST CIRCUIT

Revised June 23, 2004

Including Amendments Received Through November 1, 2004

Table of Procedures

INTRODUCTION

This publication outlines the procedures followed in this Court, and its Clerk's Office, for the processing of appeals, petitions for review and other appellate matters in this Circuit. New techniques and procedures are continually tried and, when improvements are found, such procedures are adopted so that at any given time the procedures set forth herein may be in a state of change.

I. COURT ORGANIZATION

A. Facilities. The Clerk's Office and the appellate courtrooms are located in the United States Courthouse at 1 Courthouse Way in Boston. The staff attorneys, the Court of Appeals library, the Circuit Executive and some of the judges are located in the courthouse.

B. Clerk's Office. The office hours for the Clerk's Office are from 8:30 a.m. to 5:00 p.m., Monday through Friday. In case of an emergency, the Clerk or the Chief Deputy Clerk may be contacted after hours;

however, appropriate arrangements should be made with the Clerk's Office in advance.

C. Library. The Court of Appeals library is open from 8:30 a.m. to 5:00 p.m. and attorneys practicing in the federal courts may use the library, but books and materials may not be removed.

D. Staff Attorneys. The office of the staff attorneys assists the Court in many ways including research, drafting memoranda and other forms of legal assistance to the Court.

Effective January 1, 1992. Amended effective October, 1999.

II. ATTORNEYS

A. Admission. Attorneys seeking admission should obtain an application from the Court's web site at *www.ca1.uscourts.gov* or write to the Clerk's Office. The admission fee imposed by Local Rule 46 (a)(1) is $50.00. There is an additional $150 admission fee prescribed by the Court of Appeals Miscellaneous Fee Schedule, promulgated under 28 U.S.C. § 1913. The combined fee of $200 should be paid in a single check or money order, made payable to: "Clerk, United

States Court." Attorneys can mail the complete application along with the admission fee to the Clerk's Office for processing and a Certificate of Admission will be returned by mail. Attorneys may also apply for admission in person at the Clerk's Office and be sworn in prior to a Court session. See Federal Rule of Appellate Procedure 46 and Local Rule 46(a).

B. Discipline. Procedures to be followed in this Court are covered by Fed. R. App. P. 46(b) and the Rules of Attorney Disciplinary Enforcement for the Court of Appeals for the First Circuit. Copies of the latter rules may be obtained at the Clerk's Office.

Effective January 1, 1992. Amended effective October, 1999; January 1, 2005.

III. INITIAL PROCEDURES

A. Appeals, Petitions for Review and Fees. In cases appealed from the district court the notice of appeal is filed in the district court in accordance with the Fed. R. App. P. and the $255.00 combined docketing and filing fees are paid to the district court clerk. In administrative agency cases and petitions for mandamus, the $250.00 docketing fee is paid to the Clerk of the Court of Appeals at the time the petition is filed in the Court of Appeals.

B. Ordering Transcripts. The transcripts must be ordered from the court reporter(s) on the Transcript Order/Report Form which is available from the district court clerks and from the Clerk of the Court of Appeals. The order for the transcript must be given within 10 days after the filing of the notice of appeal and satisfactory financial arrangements must be made with the court reporter. See Fed. R. App. P. 10, 11; Local Rule 10. Counsel are required to complete these arrangements before the copy of the Transcript Order/Report is **filed** with the Court of Appeals. If counsel are being paid under the Criminal Justice Act ("CJA"), the CJA form must first be approved and then attached to the Transcript Order/Report Form.

C. Reporter's Duties. If the reporter cannot complete the transcript within 30 days after the order, then pursuant to Fed. R. App. P. 11(b) the reporter must file a motion in the Court of Appeals for an enlargement of time for filing the transcript. Counsel for appellants, however, would be well advised to check with the court reporter to see that the transcript will be timely filed and that the reporter is making such a request, if it will not be so completed.

Effective January 1, 1992. Amended effective October, 1999; June 23, 2004.

IV. DOCKETING PROCEDURES

A. Docketing. Pursuant to Fed. R. App. P. 12, appeals are docketed in the Court of Appeals upon receipt from the Clerk of the district court of copies of the notice of appeal and the district court docket entries. If the docketing fee has not been paid in the

district court, the failure to pay is grounds for dismissal of the appeal pursuant to Local Rule 3. Local Rule 3 also requires the filing of a Docketing Statement within 14 days of filing the Notice of Appeal.

B. Screening. In the First Circuit a preliminary screening takes place upon the docketing of the appeal and procedural defects are often called to the Court's attention for sua sponte action by the Court including dismissal of the appeal.

C. Briefing. Upon the filing of the record on appeal, including any transcripts required to complete the record, the Clerk's Office sends to counsel a notice advising appellant of the filing dates for the brief and the appendix. After the brief for appellant is filed, the Clerk's Office likewise gives notice to the appellee.

D. Civil Appeals Management Program. [See separately published Appendix]

Effective January 1, 1992. Amended effective October, 1999; June 23, 2004.

V. MOTION PROCEDURES

A. General. In accordance with Fed. R. App. P. 27(d)(3), all motions must be accompanied by 3 copies, and a proof of service showing the type of service that was made, i.e., by mail or by hand delivery. The date of service establishes the due date for filing the response per Fed. R. App. P. 27(a)(3).

B. Processing. All motions must be filed with the clerk. The single judge matters are transmitted to a single judge and the matters calling for three judge action are transmitted to a three judge panel. The motion judge and the motion panel duties are rotated among the judges of this Court. All motions are decided without oral argument, unless the Court orders otherwise. The motions are submitted to the Court after the return times provided in the Fed. R. App. P. have run except for (1) routine procedural motions which are usually processed forthwith, and (2) emergency motions which may be handled on an expedited basis.

C. Emergencies. If counsel anticipates that a matter may arise requiring emergency action by the court outside of ordinary business hours, the court's local rules advise counsel to contact the Clerk's Office at the earliest opportunity to discuss the matter. Depending on the circumstances, the Clerk's Office, in consultation with the duty judge and the Staff Attorney's Office, may make special arrangements for after hours filings and responses, issuance of orders after hours, and similar matters. Counsel are further advised that in all emergency matters, whether or not action outside of ordinary business hours is required, the process is facilitated if counsel contacts the Clerk's Office in advance and the motion seeking expedited relief clearly indicates the date by which a ruling is requested and the reasons supporting expedition.

Effective January 1, 1992. Amended effective October, 1999; January 2, 2001; June 23, 2004.

VI. BRIEFS AND APPENDICES

A. General. The court's website, *www.ca1.uscourts.gov*, contains guidelines and a checklist to assist counsel in preparing briefs. Counsel are advised that any brief that does not conform to the requirements of the rules may be rejected.

B. Modifications. The following modifications of the Fed. R. App. P. apply in the First Circuit:

1. One copy of the brief or petition must be filed on a computer generated disk. *See* Local Rule 32.

2. Only 10 copies, including the disk, need be filed.

C. Deferred Appendix. Note the Local Rules of this Court do not provide for the proceeding on a deferred appendix pursuant to Fed. R. App. P. 30(c). If special leave to proceed under this method is sought, and the Court grants such leave, the leave will be conditioned upon a shorter time schedule than the Fed. R. App. P. generally allow so that the processing of the appeal will not take any longer time than it would under the regular procedure.

D. Defaults. If the appellant fails to file the brief and appendix on time, the Clerk is authorized to enter an order dismissing the appeal, and when an appellee is in default as to filing a brief, the appellee will not be heard at oral argument. The party in default may remove the default by showing special circumstance justifying the failure to comply. Any motion to set aside a dismissal should be filed within ten days. See Local Rule 45.

Effective January 1, 1992. Amended effective October, 1999; June 23, 2004.

VII. SCREENING AND CALENDARING

A. General. Initially, the staff attorney reviews the briefs in the cases the Clerk has assigned for a particular session. If a panel of 3 judges, in accordance with Fed. R. App. P. 34 and after consultation with the staff attorney, is of the opinion that a case does not warrant oral argument, the Clerk so advises counsel. Shortly after the decision as to hearing is made, the amount of time to be allotted for oral argument is also set by the Court. Before the hearing list is finally established, the Clerk notifies the parties by letter of the proposed date for hearing the case so that counsel may contact the Clerk if it appears that a scheduling conflict exists.

B. Expedited Schedule. Expedited scheduling is provided automatically in those cases where it is required by statute, such as recalcitrant witness cases. In other cases a request for expedited processing may be filed, but the motion should be made shortly after the case is docketed in the Court of Appeals.

C. Dates of Sessions. In January through June, and October through December, the Court usually sits for one week starting on the first Monday of the month. In either July or August, the Court sits for one week. In September the Court starts on the Wednesday after Labor Day and sits for the 3 days in that week and the 5 days in the following week. In November and March the Court sits two weeks, with one week in Boston and one week in Puerto Rico.

D. Judges and Case Assignment. In accordance with long-standing practice, cases are assigned to panels on a random basis provided, however, that a case may be assigned to a particular panel or to a panel including a particular judge in the following circumstances:

(1) Where the case is a sequel to, or offshoot of, a case previously decided by the Court (e.g., following a remand);

(2) Where the case was presented to the duty panel in the regular course of duties, *see, e.g., Bui v. DiPaolo,* 170 F.3d 232, 238 (1st Cir. 1999)("[a]s an administrative measure, we advise litigants that, to the extent practicable, the panel that determines whether to issue a complementary COA also will be the panel that adjudicates the appeal on the merits"), *cert. denied,* 529 U.S. 1086 (2000);

(3) Where a case has been assigned to a panel, but scheduling changes (e.g., postponement of oral argument) or changes in the procedural handling of the case (e.g., a case intended for summary disposition is thereafter set for oral argument) require rescheduling;

(4) Where a case has been assigned to a panel, but the subsequent recusal of a judge (or other unavailability of a judge, e.g., due to illness) makes it appropriate to transfer the case to a different panel or to find a replacement judge. No other non–random assignments of cases shall be made except for special cause and with the concurrence of the duty judge.

E. Judges and Case Assignment in Capital Cases.

(1) Capital Case Panel. Capital cases, as defined in Local Rule 48, shall be randomly assigned to a panel of three judges, of whom at least one is an active judge of this Court, from the capital case pool. The capital case pool of judges shall consist of all active judges of this Court and those senior judges who have filed with the Clerk a statement of willingness to serve on capital case panels.

(2) Duties of Capital Case Panel. Notwithstanding the practices identified in Internal Operating Procedure V, the assigned capital case panel handles all matters relating to the case, including but not limited to, the merits of a direct appeal, all case management,

all petitions for collateral review, motions for stay of execution, motions to vacate a stay of execution, applications for a certificate of appealability, motions for an order authorizing the district court to consider a second or successive application for habeas corpus, appeals from subsequent petitions, and remands from the United States Supreme Court.

F. Timing. The Court will hear up to six cases per day. Generally, it is the practice of this Court to schedule cases in which the brief for appellee is filed by the fifteenth day of one month, so as to have the case screened and assigned to the list for hearing or submission on the second month thereafter.

Effective January 1, 1992. Amended effective October, 1999; October 6, 2004.

VIII. ORAL ARGUMENT

A. General. The Court establishes the times allotted for oral argument and the Clerk so notifies the parties at least one week before argument starts. Though the calendar is not called at the beginning of the court day, counsel should be present at the opening or make arrangements to ascertain whether there is any change in the order of the cases at the opening of Court. It is counsel's responsibility to be present and be prepared should earlier cases take less time for oral argument than was anticipated. See Local Rule 34.1.

B. Disclosure of Panel in Advance of Oral Argument. The names of the judges on each panel may be disclosed for a particular session seven (7) days in advance of the session. Once the panel is made public, the Court will not normally grant motions for continuances or for a change in argument date during the same session.

C. Lights. The signal lights are located on the Clerk's desk and they are set so that an amber light turns on when there are five minutes left and it remains on until the red light turns on indicating that the time for oral argument has ended.

D. Rebuttal. Extended rebuttal is not encouraged, and the court normally expects rebuttal to be used only where an unexpected matter has been raised and then usually not more than a minute is allowed.

E. Recording. Oral arguments in all cases are digitally recorded for the use of the Court and are not part of the permanent record of the case. A disk copy of the recording of an oral argument may be obtained by submitting a request in writing to the Clerk with a check for $20.00.

Effective January 1, 1992; revised November 24, 1992; June 9, 1997; June 23, 2004.

IX. OPINIONS AND JUDGMENTS

A. Processing. When the opinion of the Court (and concurring and dissenting opinions, if any) are

completed, they are turned over to the Clerk for reproducing and release. Copies of the opinion and copies of the judgment are sent to one counsel for each side. They are also released in electronic format on the same day.

B. Publication. The manner of deciding whether an opinion is to be published and the Court's policy with respect to publication are set forth in Local Rule 36.

C. Electronic Access. The Court's dockets and opinions are available electronically through the PACER network supported by the Administrative Office for the United States Courts. Details are available in the Clerk's Office.

Effective January 1, 1992. Amended effective October, 1999.

X. PETITIONS FOR PANEL REHEARING AND PETITIONS FOR HEARING OR REHEARING EN BANC

A. General. Fed. R. App. P. 40 and 35 should be consulted with respect to the procedures. Petitions for rehearing are intended to bring to the attention of the panel claimed errors in the opinion and they are not to be used for reargument of an issue previously presented.

B. No Response. Unless the court requests, no response to a petition is permitted.

C. En Banc Processing. A petition for a hearing or rehearing en banc is submitted by the Clerk to the panel that heard the case and to the other active First Circuit judges. A petition for rehearing en banc will also be treated as a petition for rehearing before the original panel.

D. Vacation of Previous Opinion and Judgment. Usually when an en banc rehearing is granted, the previous opinion and judgment will be vacated.

Effective January 1, 1992. Amended effective October, 1999.

XI. COMPLAINTS AGAINST JUDGES

The procedure for filing complaints against judges is set forth in the Rules of the Judicial Council of the First Circuit Governing Complaints of Judicial Misconduct or Disability. A copy of these Rules may be obtained from the Clerk of this Court.

Office of the Clerk
U.S. Court of Appeals for the First Circuit
John Joseph Moakley Courthouse
1 Courthouse Way, Suite 2500
Boston, Massachusetts 02210

Effective January 1, 1992. Amended effective June 23, 2004.

XII. CIRCUIT JUDICIAL CONFERENCES

In the First Circuit, generally Circuit Judicial Conferences are conducted in two different formats. Pursuant to 28 U.S.C. Sec. 333, the Chief Judge of the Circuit summons annually the Circuit, District, and Bankruptcy Judges of the Circuit in active service. Every judge summoned shall attend and, unless excused by the Chief Judge, shall remain throughout the conference. In the last few years, all conferences have been held in the fall of the year.

One type of conference, often called a "mini-conference", is designed primarily for judicial officers and certain court personnel. In addition to the judges and bankruptcy judges, others who attend are magistrates, the circuit executive, clerks, federal public defenders and representatives (usually one each) of the Administrative Office of the United States Courts, the Federal Judicial Center and the Attorney General of the United States. These conferences are conducted by the Court of Appeals judges under the leadership of the Chief Judge, or a committee of circuit judges appointed by the Chief Judge and the Circuit Executive.

The other format of conference is the full scale conference which usually is conducted every other year. Those who attend these conferences include those listed above in connection with the limited conferences and, pursuant to Local Rule 47.1, others such as presidents of the state and commonwealth bar associations, deans of accredited law schools, and the United States Attorneys. In addition, a substantial number of lawyers are invited to attend these full scale conferences. In this Circuit, there is no formal membership other than those who are required to attend pursuant to 28 U.S.C. Sec. 333.

In the case of the full scale conference, the Chief Judge of the Circuit, in consultation with the circuit judges, selects the approximate dates for the conference and assigns one of the districts in the circuit to act as a-host district for the conference. The Chief Judge of the host district appoints a Planning Committee to organize and conduct the Judicial Conference. This is usually done at least two years in advance of the holding of the conference. Thus, in June of 1987, Rhode Island was selected as the host district for the October 1989 full scale conference.

The selection of the attorney invitees to a full scale conference is handled in the following manner. After the Planning Committee has selected a site and received the approval of the Chief Judge of the circuit, the number of invitees that the facilities at the selected site can accommodate is determined, and a specific number of slots for attendees is assigned to each district (roughly based on the proportion of the number of judges in a given district to the total number of judges in the First Circuit, plus an allotment for the

Court of Appeals). The district court chief judges, in consultation with their respective judges, supply lists of nominees to receive invitations to attend. Based on these lists, invitations are then extended by the Chief Judge of the Circuit to the listed members of the Bar.

The office of the Circuit Executive assists the Planning Committees in all aspects of their work. The Circuit Executive also provides the point of contact for continuity purposes and is the custodian of the Judicial Conference Fund, as well as the secretary of the conferences.

Because of the many activities that must be planned for at a full scale conference, it is important that a Planning Committee consist of both members of the Bar and judges of the host court. Frequently, members of the Clerk's Office, as well as the judges' staffs can assist.

Effective January 1, 1992.

XIII. NOTIFICATION OF CHANGES OR NOTIFICATIONS OF THE COURT'S LOCAL RULES AND INTERNAL OPERATING PROCEDURES

Changes in the Local Rules of this Court or its Internal Operating Procedures will be publicized by circulating for comment the entire text of the proposed change to the following state legal publishers:

a. Massachusetts Lawyers Weekly,
   41 West Street,
   Boston, Massachusetts 02111.

b. Rhode Island Lawyers Weekly,
   c/o Massachusetts Lawyers Weekly,
   41 West Street,
   Boston, MA 02111.

c. New Hampshire Bar News,
   112 Pleasant Street,
   Concord, New Hampshire 03301.

d. Maine Bar Journal,
   P.O. Box 788,
   Augusta, Maine 04332.

e. Puerto Rico Bar Association,
   P.O. Box 1900,
   San Juan, PR 00903.

Notice of the changes will also be placed in all federal court bulletin boards and to all state bar associations within the Circuit. Comments should be forwarded to the Clerk's Office within thirty days from the date of the notice.

Effective January 1, 1992.

PUBLISHER'S APPENDIX

RULES OF THE JUDICIAL COUNCIL OF THE FIRST CIRCUIT GOVERNING COMPLAINTS OF JUDICIAL MISCONDUCT AND DISABILITY

Effective October 10, 1999

Including Amendments Received Through November 1, 2004

With Commentary
Prescribed under authority of
28 U.S.C. § 372(c)(11)

PREFACE TO THE RULES

Section 351(a) of title 28 of the United States Code provides a way for any person to complain about a federal judge who the person believes "has engaged in conduct prejudicial to the effective and expeditious administration of the business of the courts" or "is unable to discharge all the duties of office by reason of mental or physical disability."[1] Section 358 of title 28 of the United States Code permits the Judicial Councils of the circuits to adopt rules for the consideration of these complaints. These rules have been adopted under that authority.

Complaints are filed with the clerk of the court of appeals on a form that has been developed for that purpose. Each complaint is referred first to the chief judge of the circuit, who decides whether the complaint raises an issue that should be investigated. (If the complaint is about the chief judge, another judge will make this decision; see rule 18(f).)

The chief judge will dismiss a complaint if it does not properly raise a problem that is appropriate for consideration under section 351(a). The chief judge will also dismiss a complaint if the chief judge concludes that the complaint is directly related to the merits of a decision or procedural ruling or is frivolous.

The chief judge will also dismiss a complaint if, after a limited inquiry, the chief judge concludes that the allegations in the complaint lack any factual foundation or are conclusively refuted. The chief judge may also conclude the complaint proceeding if the problem has been corrected or if intervening events have made action on the complaint unnecessary. If the complaint is not disposed of in any of these ways, the chief judge will appoint a special committee to investigate the complaint. The special committee makes its report to the Judicial Council of the circuit, which decides what action, if any, should be taken.

The Judicial Council is a body that consists of all the judges of the court of appeals in active service and five district judges. The rules provide, in some circumstances, for review of decisions of the chief judge or the Judicial Council. The commentary to the rules is included for the purpose of assisting the bench, bar, and public in the understanding of the rules. Unlike the rules themselves, the Commentary has no official or binding status.

Effective October 10, 1999; amended effective April 24, 2003.

1. On November 2, 2002, the Judicial Reform and Judicial Conductc and Disability Act of 1980 (the "Act"), 28 U.S.C. § 372(c) was amended and recodified as Chapter 16 of the Judicial Improvements Act of 2002, Complaints Against Judges and Judicial Discipline, 28 U.S.C. § 351, et seq. The Act was reorganized as a separate chapter in order to "publicize its existence and . . . facilitate its use." Further, in amending the law, the legislature sought to define more clearly the "power of a circuit chief judge to conduct a 'limited inquiry'" and expand upon the "concept of dismissing a case for 'frivolousness.'" H.R. Rep. No. 107–459, 107th Cong., 2d Sess. (May 14, 2002). See 28 U.S.C. § 352(b). Finally, the statutory amendments provide a judicial council with the "explicit authority to refer a complaint to a five-member panel . . . ." H.R. Rep. No. 107–459, 107th Cong., 2d Sess. (May 14, 2002. See 28 U.S.C. § 352(d).

CHAPTER I. FILING A COMPLAINT

RULE 1. WHEN TO USE THE COMPLAINT PROCEDURE

a. **Purpose of the Procedure.** The purpose of the complaint procedure is to improve the administration of justice in the federal courts by taking action when judges have engaged in conduct that does not meet the standards expected of federal judicial officers or are physically or mentally unable to perform their duties. The law's purpose is essentially forward-looking and not punitive. The emphasis is on correction of conditions that interfere with the proper administration of justice in the courts.

b. **What May Me Complained About.** The law authorizes complaints about United States circuit judges, district judges, bankruptcy judges, or magistrate judges who have "engaged in conduct prejudicial to the effective and expeditious administration of the business of the courts" or who are "unable to discharge all the duties of office by reason of mental or physical disability."

"Conduct prejudicial to the effective and expeditious administration of the business of the courts" is not a precise term. It includes such things as use of the judge's office to obtain special treatment for friends and relatives, acceptance of bribes, improperly engaging in discussions with lawyers or parties to cases in the absence of representatives of opposing parties, and other abuses of judicial office. It does not include making wrong decisions—even very wrong decisions—in cases. The law provides that a complaint may be dismissed if it is "directly related to the merits of a decision or procedural ruling." "Mental or physical disability" may include temporary conditions as well as permanent disability.

c. Who May Be Complained About. The complaint procedure applies to judges of the United States court of appeals, judges of United States district courts, judges of United States bankruptcy courts, and United States magistrate judges. These rules apply, in particular, only to judges of the Court of Appeals for the First Circuit and to district judges, bankruptcy judges, and magistrate judges of federal courts within the circuit. The circuit includes the districts of Maine, Massachusetts, New Hampshire, Puerto Rico and Rhode Island.

Complaints about other officials of federal courts should be made to their supervisors in the various courts. If such a complaint cannot be satisfactorily resolved at lower levels, it may be referred to the chief judge of the court in which the official is employed. The circuit executive, whose address is United States Courthouse, 1 Courthouse Way, Suite 3700, Boston, Massachusetts 02210, is sometimes able to provide assistance in resolving such complaints.

d. Time for Filing Complaints. Complaints should be filed promptly. A complaint may be dismissed if it is filed so long after the events in question that the delay will make fair consideration of the matter impossible. A complaint may also be dismissed if it does not indicate the existence of a current problem with the administration of the business of the courts.

e. Limitations on Use of the Procedure. The complaint procedure is not intended to provide a means of obtaining review of a judge's decision or ruling in a case. The Judicial Council of the circuit, the body that takes action under the complaint procedure, does not have the power to change a decision or ruling. Only a court can do that.

The complaint procedure may not be used to have a judge disqualified from sitting on a particular case. A motion for disqualification should be made in the case.

Also, the complaint procedure may not be used to force a ruling on a particular motion or other matter that has been before the judge too long. A petition for mandamus can sometimes be used for that purpose.

f. Abuse of Complaint Procedure. A complainant who has filed vexatious, repetitive, harassing or frivolous complaints, or has otherwise abused the complaint procedure, may be restricted from filing further complaints. After affording the offending complainant an opportunity to show cause in writing why his or her ability to file further complaints should not be limited, the Judicial Council may restrict or impose conditions upon the complainant's use of the complaint procedure. Upon written request of the complainant, the Judicial Council may revise or withdraw any restrictions or conditions imposed.

Commentary on Rule 1

Advice to Prospective Complainants on Use of Complaint Procedure

As at least some members of Congress anticipated, a great many of the complaints that have been filed under the statute have been filed by litigants disappointed in the outcomes of their cases.[2] Some complaints allege nothing more than that the decision was in violation of established legal principles. Many of them allege that the judges are members of conspiracies to deprive the complainants of their rights, and offer the substance of the judicial decision as the only evidence of the conspiratorial behavior. A great many of the complaints seek various forms of relief in the underlying litigation.

Rule 1 is intended to provide prospective complainants with guidance about the appropriate uses of the complaint procedure. Paragraph (b) discusses cognizable subject matters, and paragraph (c) discusses cognizable persons. Paragraph (e) discusses remedies, and attempts to make it clear that the circuit council will not provide relief from a ruling or judgment of a court. It is hoped that such guidance will reduce the number of complaints filed that seek relief that cannot be given under the statute or deal with matters that are plainly not cognizable.

The last two paragraphs in rule 1(e), dealing with complaints alleging bias and those alleging undue delay, are in accord with Judicial Council decisions in some circuits. The use of the complaint procedure is not limited to cases in which a judge has committed an impropriety. For example, habitual failure to decide matters in a timely fashion may be the proper subject of a complaint where it is demonstrated that, over a period of years, the judge has persistently and unreasonably neglected to act on a substantial number of cases. Delay in a single case may be a proper subject for a complaint only in unusual cases, such as where the delay is improperly motivated or is the product of improper animus or prejudice toward a particular litigant, or, possibly, where the delay is of such an extraordinary or egregious character as to constitute a clear dereliction of judicial responsibilities suitable for discipline.

Venue

Rule 1(c) states that the complaint procedure applies to judges "of federal courts within the circuit." This language is intended to make it clear that the circuit in which a judge holds office is the appropriate circuit in which to file a complaint, regardless of where the alleged misconduct occurred.

Time Limitation

These rules do not contain a time limit for the filing of a complaint. However rule 1(d) indicates that a complaint may be dismissed, for reasons analogous to laches, if the delay in filing the complaint would prejudice the ability of the Judicial Council to give fair consideration to the matter.

Effective October 10, 1999; amended effective April 24, 2003.

2. *See* 125 Cong. Rec. 30,093–94 (1979) (remarks of Sen. Bellmon); 126 Cong. Rec. 28,091 (1980) (remarks of Sen. DeConcini); H.R. Rep. No. 1313, 96th. Cong., 2d Sess. 18–19 (1980).

RULE 2.   HOW TO FILE A COMPLAINT

a.   Form. Complaints should be filed on the official form for filing complaints in the First Circuit, which is reproduced in the appendix to these rules. Forms may be obtained by writing or telephoning the Office of the Circuit Executive, United States Courthouse, 1 Courthouse Way, Suite 3700, Boston, Massachusetts 02210, (617) 748–9330. Forms may be picked up in person at the Office of the Clerk of the Court of Appeals or any district court or bankruptcy court within the circuit.

b.   Statements of Facts. A statement should be attached to the complaint form, setting forth the particular facts on which the claim of misconduct or disability is based. The statement should not be longer than five pages (five sides), and the paper size should not be larger than the paper the form is printed on. Normally, the statement of facts will include—

(1) A statement of what occurred;

(2) The time and place of the occurrence or occurrences;

(3) Any other information that would assist an investigator in checking the facts, such as the presence of a court reporter or other witnesses and their names and addresses.

c.   Legibility. Complaints should be typewritten if possible. If not typewritten, they must be legible.

d.   Submission of Documents. Documents such as excerpts from transcripts may be submitted as evidence of the behavior complained about; if they are, the statement of facts should refer to the specific pages in the documents on which relevant materials appears.

e.   Number of Copies. If the complaint is about a single judge of the court of appeals, three copies of the complaint form, the statement of facts, and any documents submitted must be filed. If it is about a single district judge or magistrate judge, four copies must be filed; if about a single bankruptcy judge, five copies. If the complaint is about more than one judge, enough copies must be filed to provide one for the circuit executive, one for the chief judge of the circuit, one for each judge complained about, and one for each judge to whom the circuit executive must send a copy under rule 3(a)(2).

f.   Signature and Oath. The form must be signed and the truth of the statements verified in writing under oath. As an alternative to taking an oath, the complainant may declare under penalty of perjury that the statements are true. The complainant's address must also be provided.

g.   Anonymous Complaints. Anonymous complaints are not handled under these rules. However, anonymous complaints received by the clerk will be forwarded to the chief judge of the circuit for such action as the chief judge considers appropriate, including identifying a complaint. *See* rules 2(k) and 20.

h.   Where to File. Complaints should be sent to: Clerk, United States Court of Appeals, United States Courthouse, 1 Courthouse Way, Suite 2500, Boston, Massachusetts 02210. The envelope should be marked "Complaint of Misconduct" or "Complaint of Disability." The name of the judge complained about should not appear on the envelope.

i.   No fee required. There is no filing fee for complaints of misconduct or disability.

j.   Intervention. No person shall be granted the right to intervene or to appear as amicus curiae in connection with any complaint filed under these rules.

k.   Chief Judge's Authority to Initiate Complaint. In the interest of effective and expeditious administration of the business of the courts and on the basis of information available to the chief judge of the circuit, the chief judge may, by written order stating reasons therefor, identify a complaint as authorized by 28 U.S.C. § 351(b) and thereby dispense with the filing of a written complaint. A chief judge who has identified a complaint under this rule will not be considered a complainant and, subject to the second sentence of rule 18(a), will perform all the functions assigned to the chief judge under these rules for the determination of complaints filed by a complainant.

Commentary on Rule 2

Use of Complaint Form

Paragraph (a) of rule 2 provides that complaints be filed on a form. Use of a complaint form provides a simple means of eliciting some fairly standard information that is helpful in administering the act. The use of a complaint form will also resolve ambiguities that sometimes arise about whether the author of a complaining letter intends to invoke the procedures of section 372(c). With the use of the form, the 351(c) procedure will be used only if the complainant clearly invokes it.

Limitation on Length of Complaint

Paragraph (b) of rule 2 provides a five-page limit on the statement of facts. Paragraph (d), however, does not restrict the volume of documents that may be submitted as evidence of the behavior complained about. It is hoped that a five-page limit will get rid of the long, rambling complaints that do not clearly identify the conduct complained of without unduly restricting the ability to communicate the facts supporting a complaint.

The provision allowing submission of documentary evidence is partly motivated by the concern that a complainant not be unduly restricted in presenting the factual basis of the complaint, but also reflects a sense that prohibiting the submission of documents with the complaint tends to make the procedure unnecessarily complex. In many cases, a chief judge will have to ask for documents if they haven't been submitted.

Complaints Against More than One Judicial Officer

A separate complaint relating to the same underlying matter for each judicial officer complained about is not required under these rules. However, a complaint should provide sufficient facts alleging misconduct for each officer named in the complaint.

Oath or Declaration

Rule 2(f) includes a requirement that complaints be signed and verified under oath or declaration. This requirement is designed to deter occasional abuse of the complaint process. In view of the ease with which a complainant can make a declaration under penalty of perjury, the requirement should not be burdensome. As is indicated below, anonymous complaints should not be handled under the section 351 procedure; the requirement of an oath or declaration would be inconsistent with a policy of accepting such complaints.

Under 28 U.S.C. § 1746, any statement required by rule to be made under an oath in writing may be subscribed instead with a written declaration under penalty of perjury that the statement is true and correct. 18 U.S.C. § 1621 includes in the definition of perjury a willfully false statement subscribed pursuant to 18 U.S.C. § 1746. Rule 2(f) prescribes an oath but informs prospective complainants of the availability of the alternative. The complaint form permits either method.

Anonymous Complaints

Rule 2(g) requires that complaints under section 351(a) be signed but makes it clear that the chief judge, as chair of the circuit judicial council, can, as he or she always has, consider information from any source, anonymous or otherwise. This solution is consistent with congressional expressions of intention that informal methods of resolving problems, traditionally used under section 332, should continue to be used in many cases.[3] Hence, under these rules, the formalities of the statute would not be invoked by an anonymous complaint, but the chief judge and the circuit council may nevertheless consider it. Information obtained from an anonymous complaint could also provide a basis for identification of a complaint by the chief judge under rule 2(k).

Identification of Complaints

Section 351(b) authorizes the chief judge, by written order stating reasons therefor, to identify a complaint and thereby dispense with the filing of a written complaint. Because the identification of a complaint is within the discretion of the chief judge, a chief judge's failure to identify a complaint will not ordinarily constitute a proper basis for the filing of a complaint of misconduct against the chief judge under section 351(a).

Once the chief judge has identified a complaint, the chief judge (subject to the disqualification provisions of rule 18(a)) will perform all functions assigned to the chief judge for the determination of complaints filed by a complainant. The

identified complaint will be treated in a manner identical to a filed complaint under these rules.

Effective October 10, 1999; amended effective April 24, 2003.

3. *See* S. Rep. No. 362, 96th. Cong., 1st. Sess. 3–4, 6 (1979); 126 Cong. Rec. 28,092 (1980) (remarks of Sen. DeConcini on final passage).

RULE 3. ACTION BY CIRCUIT EXECUTIVE UPON RECEIPT OF A COMPLAINT

a. Receipt of Complaint in Proper Form.

(1) Upon receipt of a complaint against a judge filed in proper form under these rules, the clerk of court of appeals will promptly file such complaint and transmit it to the circuit executive. The circuit executive will have custody of the complaint and all related papers and see that the complaint is expeditiously processed. The circuit executive will open a file, assign a docket number, and acknowledge receipt of the complaint. The circuit executive will promptly send copies of the complaint to the chief judge of the circuit (or the judge authorized to act as chief judge under rule 18(f)) and to each judge whose conduct is the subject of the complaint. The original of the complaint will be retained by the circuit executive.

When the chief judge issues an order identifying a complaint under rule 2(k), the circuit executive will process such complaint as otherwise provided by these rules.

(2) If a district judge or magistrate judge is complained about, the circuit executive will also send a copy of the complaint to the chief judge of the district court in which the judge or magistrate judge holds his or her appointment. If a bankruptcy judge is complained about, the circuit executive will send copies to the chief judges of the district court and the bankruptcy court. However, if the chief judge of the district court or bankruptcy court is a subject of a complaint, the chief judge's copy will be sent to the judge of such court in regular active service who is most senior in date of commission among those who are not subjects of the complaint.

b. Receipt of Complaint About Official Other Than a Judge of the First Circuit. If the circuit executive receives a complaint about an official other than a judge of the First Circuit, the circuit executive will not accept the complaint for filing and will advise the complainant in writing of the procedure for processing such complaints.

c. Receipt of Complaint About a Judge of the First Circuit and Another Official. If a complaint is received about a judge of the First Circuit and another official, the circuit executive will accept the complaint for filing only with regard to the judge, and will advise the complainant accordingly.

d. Receipt of a Complaint Not in Proper Form. If the circuit executive receives a complaint against a judge of this circuit that uses the complaint form but does not comply with the requirements of rule 2, the circuit executive will normally not accept the complaint for filing and will advise the complainant of the appropriate procedures. If a complaint against a judge is received in letter form, the circuit executive will normally not accept the letter for filing as a complaint, will advise the writer of the right to file a formal complaint under these rules, and will enclose a copy of these rules and the accompanying forms.

Commentary on Rule 3

Role of Staff

Rule 2(h) follows the statutory language and provides that complaints are to be filed with the clerk of the court of appeals. Rule 3(a) provides that any complaint or related

document filed with the clerk of the court of appeals will be forwarded promptly to the circuit executive who will thereafter have custody of the complaint and related papers and see that the complaint is expeditiously processed.

Distribution of Complaint to Chief Judge of District Court or Bankruptcy Court

The statute requires that the complaint be transmitted to the chief judge of the circuit and the judge complained about. If the complaint is about a district judge, bankruptcy judge, or magistrate judge, rule 3(a)(2) requires in addition that a copy be transmitted to the chief judge of the district court and, where a bankruptcy judge is the subject, the chief judge of the bankruptcy court. This provision is included in recognition of the responsibility of every chief judge of the administration of his or her court.

Effective October 10, 1999.

CHAPTER II. REVIEW OF A COMPLAINT BY THE CHIEF JUDGE

RULE 4. REVIEW BY THE CHIEF JUDGE

a. Procedure for Review by the Chief Judge. When a complaint in proper form is sent to the chief judge by the circuit executive's office or identified under section 351(b), the chief judge will review the complaint. In determining what action to take, the chief judge may conduct a limited inquiry for the purpose of determining: (1) whether appropriate corrective action has been or can be taken without the necessity for a formal investigation, (2) whether intervening events have made action on the complaint unnecessary, and (3) whether the facts stated in the complaint are either plainly untrue or are incapable of being established through investigation. For this purpose, the chief judge may request the judge whose conduct is complained of to file a written response to the complaint. The chief judge may also communicate orally or in writing with the complainant, the judge whose conduct is complained of, and other people who may have knowledge of the matter, and may review any transcripts or other relevant documents. The chief judge will not undertake to make findings of fact about any matter that, after an initial limited inquiry, remains reasonably in dispute.

b. Actions Available to the Chief Judge. After reviewing a complaint, under subsection (a), the chief judge, by written order stating his or her reasons, may:

(1) Dismiss the complaint if the chief judge concludes—

(A) that the claimed conduct, even if the claim is true, is not "conduct prejudicial to the effective and expeditious administration of the business of the courts" and does not indicate a mental or physical disability resulting in inability to discharge the duties of office;

(B) that the complaint is directly related to the merits of a decision or procedural ruling; or

(C) that the complaint is frivolous, a term that includes making charges that are wholly unsupported or which are incapable of being established through investigation; or

(D) that a limited inquiry conducted under subsection (a) demonstrates that the allegations in the complaint lack any factual foundation or are conclusively refuted by objective evidence; or

(E) that, under the statute, the complaint is otherwise not appropriate for consideration; or

(2) Conclude the proceeding if the chief judge determines that appropriate action has been taken to remedy the problem raised by the complaint, or that action on the complaint is no longer necessary because of intervening events; or

(3) Appoint a special committee, constituted as provided in rule 9, to investigate the complaint and make recommendations to the Judicial Council. However, ordinarily a special committee will not be appointed until the judge complained about has been invited to respond to the complaint and has been allowed a reasonable time to do so. In the discretion of the chief judge, separate complaints may be joined and assigned to a single special committee; similarly, a single complaint about more than one judge may be severed and more than one special committee appointed.

c. Notice of the Chief Judge's Action.

(1) If the complaint is dismissed or the proceeding concluded on the basis of corrective action taken or because intervening events have made action on the complaint unnecessary, the chief judge will prepare a supporting memorandum that sets forth the allegations of the complaint and the reasons for the disposition. The memorandum will not include the name of the complainant or of the judge whose conduct is complained of. The order and the supporting memorandum will be provided to the complainant, the

judge, and any judge entitled to receive a copy of the complaint pursuant to rule 3(a)(2). The complainant will be notified of the right to petition of the Judicial Council for review of the decisions and of the deadline for filing a petition.

(2) If a special committee is appointed, the chief judge will notify the complainant, the judge of whose conduct is complained, and any judge entitled to receive a copy of the complaint pursuant to rule 3(a)(2) that the matter has been referred and will inform them of the membership of the committee.

d. Public Availability of the Chief Judge's Decision. Materials related to the chief judge's decision will be made public at the time and in the matter set forth in rule 17.

e. Report to the Judicial Council. The chief judge will from time to time report to the Judicial Council of the circuit on actions taken under this rule.

f. Allegations of Criminal Conduct. If a chief judge dismisses, solely for lack of jurisdiction under 28 U.S.C. § 351(a), non-frivolous allegations of criminal conduct by a judge, the chief judge's order of dismissal shall inform the complainant that the dismissal does not prevent the complainant from bringing any allegations of criminal conduct to the attention of appropriate federal or state criminal authorities. If, in this situation, the allegations of criminal conduct were originally referred to the circuit by a congressional committee or member of Congress, the chief judge—if no petition for review of the dismissal is filed within the thirty-day period specified by rule 6(a)—shall notify the congressional committee or member that the judiciary has concluded that it lacks jurisdiction under § 351(a).

Commentary on Rule 4

Expeditious Review

The statute requires the chief judge to review a complaint "expeditiously." It should be a rare case in which more than sixty days are permitted to elapse from the filing of the complaint to the chief judge's action on it.

Purpose of Chief Judge's Review

Although the statute permits the chief judge to conclude the proceeding "if the chief judge finds that appropriate corrective action has been taken," it seems clear that the chief judge, in cases in which a complaint appears to have merit, should make every effort to determine whether it is possible to fashion a remedy without the necessity of appointing a special committee. The formal investigatory procedures are to be regarded as a last resort; the remedial purpose of the statute is on the whole better and more promptly served if an informal solution can be found that will correct the problem giving rise to a complaint.

Inquiry by Chief Judge

The chief judge is not required to act solely on the face of the complaint. The power to conclude a complaint proceeding on the basis that corrective action has been taken implies some power to determine whether the facts alleged are true. See Report of the National Commission on Judicial Discipline and Removal (1993), at 102 [hereafter National Commission

Report] ("such power is necessarily contemplated by the Act's provision authorizing a chief judge to conclude a proceeding"). But the boundary line of that power—the point at which a chief judge invades the territory reserved for special committees—is unclear. Rule 4(a) addresses that issue by stating that the chief judge may conduct a limited inquiry to determine whether the facts of the complaint are "either plainly untrue or are incapable of being established through investigation," and that the chief judge "will not undertake to make findings of fact about any matter that, after an initial limited inquiry, remains reasonably in dispute." Offered here, as commentary, are some hypothetical situations demonstrating the implementation of this principle:

(1) The complainant alleges an impropriety and asserts that he knows of it because his voices told him. It would appear clearly appropriate to treat such a complaint as frivolous.

(2) The complainant alleges an impropriety and asserts that he knows of it because it was observed and reported to her by a person whom the complainant is not free to identify. The judge denies that the event occurred. The statutory basis for dismissal does not seem strong, but dismissal seems eminently sensible unless it is appropriate for special committee to subpoena the complainant and insist on the identity of the source. On balance, it would appear that the complaint should be dismissed as unsupported pursuant to 28 U.S.C. § 352(b)(1)(B).

(3) The complainant alleges an impropriety and asserts that he knows of it because it was observed and reported to him by a person who is identified. The judge denies that the event occurred. When contacted, the source also denies it. In such a case, the chief judge's proper course of action may well turn on whether the source had any role in the allegedly improper conduct. If the complaint were based on a lawyer's statement that he had an improper ex parte contact with a judge, the lawyer's denial of the impropriety might not be taken as wholly persuasive, and it seems appropriate to conclude that a real factual issue is raised. On the other hand, if the complaint quoted a disinterested third party and the disinterested party denied that the statement had been made, there would not appear to be any value in opening a formal investigation. In such a case, it would seem appropriate to dismiss the complaint under 28 U.S.C. § 352(b)(1)(B) on the basis that there is no support for the allegation of misconduct.

(4) The complainant alleges an impropriety and alleges that he observed it and there were no other witnesses; the judge denies that the event occurred. This situation presents the possibility of a simple credibility conflict. Unless the complainant's allegations are wholly implausible, it would appear that a special committee must be appointed because there is a factual question that is reasonably in dispute.

(5) The complainant alleges an impropriety, which the judge complained of denies. Unlike example (4) (supra), where there are no witnesses, in this case the chief judge conducts a preliminary investigation and finds that the record clearly contradicts the complainant's allegations. The chief judge should dismiss the complaint.

Grounds for Dismissal of Complaints

It has been the accepted practice in many circuits to dismiss as "frivolous" a complaint that is shown to be unfounded by the chief judge's limited inquiry pursuant to rule 4(b). The 2002 statutory amendments clarify that the term "frivolous", however, may be more commonly understood by complainants to refer to complaints that contain insufficient factual allegations to warrant inquiry, as opposed to complaints adequate on their face that are found clearly unsupported after a limited inquiry. See 28 U.S.C. § 352(b)(1)(A)(iii). In contrast, where a complaint raises serious or sensitive allegations that are found unsupported after inquiry, the chief judge may indicate in the order of dismissal that the complaint, while not inadequate on its face, has been shown by a limited inquiry pursuant to rule 4(a) to be plainly untrue or lacking any factual foundation. See 28 U.S.C. § 352(b)(1)(B). Rule 4(b)(1)(E) provides that a complaint may be dismissed as "otherwise not appropriate for consideration." This language is intended to accommodate dismissals of complaints for reasons such as untimeliness (see rule 1(d)) or mootness.

Opportunity of Judge to Respond

Rule 4(d) states that a judge will ordinarily be invited to respond to the complaint before a special committee is appointed.

Judges, of course, receive copies of complaints at the same time that they are referred to the chief judge, and they are free to volunteer responses to them. Under rule 4(b), the chief judge may request a response if it is thought necessary. However, many complaints are clear candidates for dismissal even if their allegations are accepted as true, and there is no need for the judge complained about to devote time to a defense. By stating that ordinarily a chief judge will issue an invitation to respond before a special committee is appointed, the rule should encourage officials not to respond unnecessarily.

Notification to Complainant and Judge

Section 352(b) requires that the order dismissing a complaint or concluding the proceeding contain a statement of reasons and that a copy of the order be sent to the complainant. Rule 4(f) contemplates that a formal order disposing of the complaint and a memorandum of reasons, either included in the order or issued separately, will be provided to the complainant, the judge complained against, and any other judge entitled to receive a copy of the complaint. Rule 17, dealing with availability of information to the public, contemplates that the memorandum would be made public, usually without disclosing the names of the complainant or the judge

involved. However, if the chief judge concludes a proceeding because corrective action was taken, the order should explain the corrective action taken so the complainant will be better able to assess the adequacy of the decision and decide whether or not to file a petition for review.

Rule 4(f) also provides that a complainant will be notified, in the case of a disposition by the chief judge, of the right to petition the Judicial Council for review. Although the complainant should in all cases have a copy of the circuit rules at the time the complaint is filed, it seems appropriate to provide a reminder at the time of dismissal of the complaint.

Allegations of Criminal Conduct

In the course of implementing § 351, some circuits have ruled that certain instances of alleged criminal conduct did not fall within the definition of misconduct set out in 28 U.S.C. § 351(a), i.e, "conduct prejudicial to the effective and expeditious administration of the business of the courts." Generally speaking, the rationale of these rulings is that there is some range of purely personal behavior of the judge—in some conceivable circumstances even criminal behavior—that his so little relationship to the performance of judicial duties as to be not cognizable under § 351. These rulings raise the concern that dismissal by a circuit, solely on jurisdictional grounds, of non-frivolous allegations of criminal conduct—without at least informing the complainant that he or she may bring those allegations to the attention of criminal authorities—entails a risk that no one will undertake whatever investigation of those allegations may be appropriate. Actual criminal conduct might then go unpunished. Rule 4(i) resolves the problem by requiring a chief judge in that situation to inform the complainant that the dismissal does not prevent the complainant from bringing any allegations of criminal conduct to the attention of appropriate federal or state criminal authorities. If the allegations were originally referred to the circuit by a congressional committee or member of Congress, the chief judge shall also notify the congressional committee or member that the judiciary has concluded that it lacks jurisdiction under § 351. Rule 14(k) imposes similar requirements for a Judicial Council's dismissal, solely on jurisdictional grounds, of a complaint alleging criminal conduct.

Effective October 10, 1999; amended effective April 24, 2003.

CHAPTER III. REVIEW OF CHIEF JUDGE'S DISPOSITION OF A COMPLAINT

RULE 5. PETITION FOR REVIEW OF CHIEF JUDGE'S DISPOSITION

If the chief judge dismisses a complaint or concludes the proceeding on the ground that corrective action has been taken or that intervening events have made action unnecessary, a petition for review may be addressed to the Judicial Council of the circuit. The Judicial Council may affirm the order of the chief judge, return the matter to the chief judge for further action, or, in exceptional cases, take other appropriate action.

Commentary on Rule 5
Petition to the Judicial Council for Review

Section 352(c) provides that a complainant or judge aggrieved by a chief judge's order dismissing a complaint or

concluding a proceeding on the basis of correction action may "petition the Judicial Council for review thereof."

There is some suggestion in the legislative history that the draftsmen contemplated a two-step procedure, under which the council would first determine whether to grant or deny review and would then, if the petition were granted, proceed to the merits. Senator DeConcini, explaining the bill just before final Senate passage, said the "the Judicial Council may exercise its discretion in granting ... review."[4] Moreover, the "petition ... for review" formulation was used in the very next sentence of the legislation to describe the procedure for obtaining Judicial Conference review of an order of a Judicial Council, and in that context congressional leaders indicated that they contemplated a procedure analogous to the certiorari procedure in the Supreme Court.[5]

The analogy to the writ of certiorari raises more questions than it answers, however. The essence of the certiorari procedure is that the standards used for deciding whether to hear a case are different from the standards used for deciding a case on the merits. In the context of the petition for review to the Judicial Council from a chief judge's disposition of a complaint, it is not at all clear what different standards might apply to decisions whether or not to grant review. Indeed, Senator DeConcini, immediately after stating that the Judicial Council would have discretion, said, "It is to be expected that it is only in those rare cases where the chief judge has not recognized the merit of a complaint, that the council will reexamine a dismissed complaint about the conduct of a judge."[6] That statement seems to imply that the decision whether to grant review is to be a decision on the merits.

Therefore, the council ordinarily will review the decision of the chief judge on the merits, treating the petition for review for all practical purposes as an appeal. This view has been carried into the rules, which state that the circuit council may respond to a petition by affirming the chief judge's order, remanding the matter, or, in exceptional cases, taking other appropriate action. The "exceptional cases" language would permit the council to deny review rather than affirm in a case in which the process was obviously being abused.

Effective October 10, 1999; amended effective April 24, 2003.

4. 126 Cong. Rec. 28.086 (1980).

5. *Id.* at 28,092–93 (remarks of Sen. DeConcini); *id.* at 28,616 (remarks of Rep. Kastenmeier).

6. *Id.* at 28,086.

RULE 6. HOW TO PETITION FOR REVIEW OF A DISPOSITION BY THE CHIEF JUDGE

a. Time. A petition for review must be received in the office of the clerk of the court of appeals within 30 days of the date of the circuit executive's letter to the complainant transmitting the chief judge's order.

b. Form. A petition should be in the form of a letter, addressed to the clerk of the court of appeals, beginning "I hereby petition the Judicial Council for review of the chief judge's order ... " There is no need to enclose a copy of the original complaint.

c. Legibility. Petitions should be typewritten, if possible. If not typewritten, they must be legible.

d. Number of Copies. Only an original is required.

e. Statement of Grounds for Petition. The letter should set forth a *brief* statement of the reasons why the petitioner believes that the chief judge should not have dismissed the complaint or concluded the proceeding. It should not repeat the complaint; the complaint will be available to members of the circuit council considering the petition.

f. Signature. The letter must be signed.

g. Where to File. Petition letters should be sent to Clerk, United States Court of Appeals, United States Courthouse, 1 Courthouse Way, Suite 2500, Boston, Massachusetts 02210. The envelope should be marked "Misconduct Petition" or "Disability Petition." The name of the judge complained about should *not* appear on the envelope.

h. No Fee Required. There is no fee for filing a petition under this procedure.

i. Intervention. No person shall be granted the right to intervene or to appear as amicus curiae in connection with any petition filed with the Judicial Council.

Commentary on Rule 6

Time for Filing Petition for Review

Rule 6(a) contains a limit of thirty days for the filing of a petition for review. It seems appropriate that there should be some time limit on petitions for review of the chief judge's dispositions in order to provide finality to the process. If the complaint requires an investigation, the investigation should proceed; if it does not, the judge complained about should know at some point that the matter is closed. The thirty-day limit is relatively generous in recognition of the fact that most complainants are unrepresented and many are not well organized to maintain the discipline of court deadlines.

In accordance with this approach, rule 7(c) of the rules provides for an automatic extension of the time if a person files a petition that is rejected for failure to comply with formal requirements.

Effective October 10, 1999.

RULE 7. ACTION BY CIRCUIT EXECUTIVE UPON RECEIPT OF A PETITION FOR REVIEW

a. Receipt of Timely Petition in Proper Form. Upon receipt of a petition for review filed within the time allowed and in proper form under these rules, the clerk of the court of appeals will promptly transmit such petition to the circuit executive, who will acknowledge receipt of the petition. The circuit executive will promptly send to each member of the Judicial Council review panel, as set forth in rule 8(a), except for any member disqualified under rule 18, copies of: (1) the complaint form and statement of facts; (2) any response filed by the judge; (3) any record of information received by the chief judge in connection with the chief judge's consideration of the complaint; (4) the chief judge's order disposing of the complaint; (5) any memorandum in support of the chief judge's order; (6) the petition for review; (7) any other documents in the files of the circuit executive that appear to be relevant and material to the petition; (8) a list of any documents in the circuit executive's files that are not being sent because they are not considered relevant and material; and (9) a ballot that conforms with rule 8(a). The circuit executive will also send the same materials, except for the ballot, to the chief judge of the circuit and each judge whose conduct is at issue, except the materials previously sent to a person may be omitted.

b. Receipt of Untimely Petition. The circuit executive will refuse to accept a petition that is received after the deadline set forth in rule 6(a).

c. Receipt of Timely Petition Not in Proper Form. Upon receipt of a petition filed within the time allowed but not in proper form under these rules (including a document that is ambiguous about whether a petition for review is intended), the circuit executive will acknowledge receipt of the petition, call the petitioner's attention to the deficiencies, and give the petitioner the opportunity to correct the deficiencies within fifteen days of the date of the circuit executive's letter or within the original deadline for filing the petition, whichever is later. If the deficiencies are corrected within the time allowed, the circuit executive will proceed in accordance with paragraph (a) of this rule. If the deficiencies are not corrected, the circuit executive will reject the petition.

Commentary on Rule 7

Transmittal of Documents by Circuit Executive

The rules include no limit on the volume of documents that may be submitted in support of a complaint. One of the problems created by this liberality is that some complaint files may get very thick with attachments. Hence, the circuit executive should have some discretion to decide what portions of the file should be duplicated and transmitted to the members of the circuit council. Rule 7(a) provides such discretion but requires the circuit executive to furnish a list of the documents not transmitted. Rule 8(c) enables each member of the council, as well as the judge complained about, to obtain a copy of any document not originally transmitted by the circuit executive.

Effective October 10, 1999. Amended effective April 24, 2003.

RULE 8. REVIEW BY THE JUDICIAL COUNCIL OF A CHIEF JUDGE'S ORDER

a. Review Panel. The chief judge shall annually designate two review panels to act for the Judicial Council on all petitions for review of the chief judge's dismissal order, except for those petitions referred to the full membership of the Judicial Council pursuant to Rule 8(b). Each review panel will serve alternating six-month terms and shall be comprised of five members of the Judicial Council, excluding the chief judge. In order of seniority, each circuit judge council member shall be alternately assigned to each of the two review panels. The district judge council members shall also be alternately assigned in order of seniority to each of the two panels so as to ensure that at least two of the members of each review panel shall be district judges. In the event of the absence of a panel member, or the recusal or disqualification of a panel member under Rule 18 from ruling on a particular petition for review, the circuit executive will select a judge in order of seniority from the other review panel to replace the unavailable panel member. An unavailable circuit judge will be replaced by the next

available circuit judge in rotation. An unavailable district judge will be replaced by the next available district judge in rotation. If necessary, an unavailable circuit judge may be replaced by a district judge and an unavailable district judge may be replaced by a circuit judge but in no event will the panel be composed of fewer than two district judges. In the event of a change in Judicial Council membership, the new council member shall take the place of his or her predecessor pending the review panels' annual reorganization.

b. Mail Ballot. Each member of the review panel to whom a ballot was sent will return a signed ballot, or otherwise communicate the member's vote, to the circuit executive. The ballot form will provide opportunities to vote to: (1) affirm the chief judge's disposition, or (2) refer the petition to the full membership of the Judicial Council. The form will also provide an opportunity for members to indicate that they have disqualified themselves from participating in consideration of the petition. Upon the vote of any member of the review panel, the petition for review shall be referred to the full membership of the Judicial Council. Any member of the review panel who votes to refer the petition to the full council shall include a brief statement of the reasons for the referral with the ballot. The review panel may act only by vote of all five members. If, because of absence, recusal or disqualification, all five members of the panel cannot participate, the petition shall be referred to the full membership of the Judicial Council. Upon referral of a petition to the full membership of the Judicial Council, the circuit executive shall send the referring judge's ballot and brief statement to each member of the Judicial Council. The circuit executive will also transmit the documents specified in Rule 7(a) to council members not then serving on the reviewing panel, unless disqualified under Rule 18. Every voting member of the Judicial Council will return a signed ballot, or otherwise communicate the member's vote, to the circuit executive. The ballot form will provide opportunities to vote to: (1) affirm the chief judge's disposition, (2) suggest an alternative disposition, or (3) discuss the matter further. The form will also provide an opportunity for members to indicate that they have disqualified themselves from participating in consideration of the petition. Any member of the Judicial Council who suggests an alternative disposition or votes to discuss the matter further shall include a brief statement of the reasons for the vote with the ballot.

c. Availability of Documents. Upon request, the circuit executive will make available to any member of the Judicial Council or to the judge complained about any document from the files that was not sent to the council members pursuant to rule 7(a).

d. Vote by Full Judicial Council. If a petition is referred to the full Judicial Council, a majority of council members eligible to participate (see rule 18) shall constitute a quorum and is required for any effective council action. Council action may be taken by majority of the members voting.

e. Rights of Judge Complained about.

(1) At any time after the filing of a petition for review by a complainant, the judge complained about may file a written response with the circuit executive. The circuit executive will promptly distribute copies of the response to each member of the Judicial Council review panel who is not disqualified, to the chief judge, and to the complainant. The judge may not communicate with individual council members about the matter, either orally or in writing.

(2) The judge complained about will be provided with copies of any communications that may be addressed to the members of the Judicial Council by the complainant.

f. Notice of Council Decision.

(1) The order of the Judicial Council shall state the names of the judges who participated in the matter, as well as any disqualifications. The council order, together with any accompanying memorandum in support of the order, will be provided to the complainant, the judge, and any judge entitled to receive a copy of the complaint pursuant to rule 3(a)(2).

(2) If the decision is unfavorable to the complainant, the complainant will be notified that the law provides for no further review of the decision.

(3) A memorandum supporting a council order will not include the name of the complainant or the judge whose conduct was complained of. If the order of the council affirms the chief judge's disposition, a supporting memorandum will be prepared only if the Judicial Council concludes that there is a need to supplement the chief judge's explanation.

g. Public Availability of Council Decision.

Materials related to the council's decision will be made public at the time and in the manner set forth in rule 17.

Commentary on Rule 8

Voting Procedures

Rule 8(a) has been amended to provide for the referral of petitions for review to a panel of the Judicial Council. See 28 U.S.C. § 352(d). The second paragraph of Rule 8(a), as amended, ensures that, in the event of the unavailability of one or more panel members, the composition of the council review panel remains consistent with the statutory requirements. Rule 8(b) adopts the use of mail ballots on petitions for review. The mail ballot procedure specified here assures that there will be full discussion in the council if any member of the reviewing panel believes that summary affirmance may not be appropriate. It should be emphasized that the "rule of one" on the mail ballot is not intended to invoke the analogy of the Supreme Court's certiorari jurisdiction. A vote to affirm on the mail ballot is intended to be a vote on the merits. The "rule of one" is intended to guarantee an opportunity for discussion and a vote following discussion if any member of the council is uncomfortable with a summary affirmance.

Effective October 10, 1999. Amended effective April 24, 2003.

CHAPTER IV. INVESTIGATION AND RECOMMENDATION BY SPECIAL COMMITTEE

RULE 9. APPOINTMENT OF SPECIAL COMMITTEE

a. Membership. A special committee appointed pursuant to rule 4(e) will consist of the chief judge of the circuit and equal numbers of circuit and district judges. If the complaint is about a district judge, bankruptcy judge, or magistrate judge, the district judge members of the committee will be from districts other than the district of the judge or magistrate judge complained about.

b. Presiding officer. At the time of appointing the committee, the chief judge will designate one of its members (who may be the chief judge) as the presiding officer. When designating another member of the committee as the presiding officer, the chief judge may also delegate to such member the authority to direct the clerk of the court of appeals to issue subpoenas related to proceedings of the committee.

c. Bankruptcy Judge or Magistrate Judge as Adviser. If the judicial officer complained about is a bankruptcy judge or magistrate judge, the chief judge

may also designate a bankruptcy judge or magistrate judge, as the case may be, to serve as an adviser to the committee. The chief judge will designate such an adviser if, within ten days of notification of the appointment of the committee, the bankruptcy judge or magistrate judge complained about requests that an adviser be designated. The adviser will be from a district other than the district of the bankruptcy judge or magistrate judge complained about. The adviser will not vote but will have the other privileges of a member of the committee.

d. Provision of Documents. The chief judge will certify to each other member of the committee and to the adviser, if any, copies of (1) the complaint form and statement of facts, and (2) any other documents on file pertaining to the complaint (or to that portion of the complaint referred to the special committee).

e. Continuing Qualification of Committee Members. A member of a special committee who was qualified at the time of appointment may continue to serve on the committee even though the member relinquishes the position of chief judge, active circuit judge, or active district judge, as the case may be, but only if the member continues to hold office under Article III, Section 1, of the Constitution of the United States.

f. Inability of Committee Member to Complete Service. In the event that a member of a special committee can no longer serve because of death, disability, disqualification, resignation, retirement from office, or other reason, the chief judge of the circuit will determine whether to appoint a replacement member, either a circuit or district judge as the case may be. However, no special committee appointed under these rules will function with only a single member, and the quorum and voting requirements for a two-member committee will be applied as if the committee had three members.

Commentary on Rule 9

Membership and Presiding Officer

Rule 9 leaves the size of a special committee flexible, to be determined on a case-by-case basis.

There is good reason to preserve the statutory flexibility in this regard. The question of the committee size is one that should be weighed with some care in view of the potential for consuming the members' time; a large committee should be appointed only if there is a special reason to do so.

Although the statute requires that the chief judge be a member of each special committee, it does not require that the chief judge preside.[7] Once again, the rules leave the decision for case-by-case determination at the time the committee is appointed.

Section 356(a) provides that a special committee will have subpoena powers as provided in 28 U.S.C. § 332(d). The latter section provides that subpoenas shall be issued on behalf of circuit councils by the clerk of the court of appeals "at the direction of the chief judge of the circuit or his designee." While it might be regarded as implicit that a special committee can exercise it subpoena power through its own presiding officer, strict compliance with the letter of section 332(d) would appear to be the safer course. Rule 9(b) therefore permits the chief judge, when designating someone else as presiding officer, to make an explicit delegation of the authority to direct the issuance of subpoenas related to committee proceedings.

The rule does not specifically address the case in which, because of disqualification of the chief judge, another judge is exercising the powers of the chief judge in the proceeding. Under such circumstances, the designation to direct the issuance of subpoenas should nevertheless come from the chief judge.

Bankruptcy Judge or Magistrate Judge as Adviser

The rule provides that, if a bankruptcy judge or magistrate judge is the judicial officer complained about, a bankruptcy judge or magistrate judge, respectively, will be named as an adviser to the special committee upon request of the judge complained about. Absent such a request the chief judge may appoint an adviser sua sponte.

The adviser will have all the privileges of a member of a committee except the franchise. That would include participating in all deliberations of the committee, questioning witnesses at hearing, and even writing a separate statement

to accompany the report of the special committee to the Judicial Council.

Continuing Qualification

Rule 9(e) provides that a member of a special committee who remains an article III judge may continue to serve on the committee even though the member's status changes. Thus, a committee that originally consisted of the chief judge and an equal number of circuit and district judges, as required by the law, may continue to function even though changes of status alter that composition. This provision reflects the belief that stability of membership will make an important contribution to the quality of the work of such committees.

Inability of Committee Member to Complete Service

Stability of membership is also the principal concern animating rule 9(f), which deals with the case in which a special committee loses a member before its work is complete. The rule would permit the chief judge to determine whether a replacement member should be appointed. Generally, the appointment of a replacement member is desirable in these situations unless the committee has conducted evidentiary hearings before the vacancy occurs. However, other cases may also arise in which a committee is in the late stages of its work, and in which it would be difficult for a new member to play a meaningful role. The rule protects the collegial character of the committee process by prohibiting a single surviving member from serving as a committee and by providing that a committee of two surviving members will, in essence, operate under a unanimity rule.

Effective October 10, 1999; amended effective April 24, 2003.

7. *See* H.R. Rep. No. 1313, 96th. Cong., 2d Sess. 11 (1980) (chief judge may appoint another judge as presiding officer).

RULE 10. CONDUCT OF AN INVESTIGATION

a. Extent and Methods to Be Determined by Committee. Each special committee will determine the extent of the investigation and the methods of conducting it that are appropriate in the light of the allegations of the complaint. If, in the course of the investigation, the committee develops reason to believe that the judge may have engaged in misconduct that is beyond the scope of the complaint, the committee may, with written notice to the judge expand the scope of the investigation to encompass such misconduct.

b. Criminal Matters. In the event that the complaint alleges criminal conduct on the part of a judge, or in the event that the committee becomes aware of possible criminal conduct, the committee will consult with the appropriate prosecuting authorities to the extent permitted by 28 U.S.C. § 360 in an effort to avoid compromising any criminal investigation. However, the committee will make its own determination about the timing of its activities, having in mind the importance of ensuring the proper administration of the business of the courts.

c. Staff. The committee may arrange for staff assistance in the conduct of the investigation. It may use existing staff of the judicial branch or may arrange, through the Administrative Office of the United States Courts, for the hiring of special staff to assist in the investigation.

d. Delegation. The committee may delegate duties in its discretion to subcommittees, to staff members, to individual committee members, or to an adviser designated under rule 9(c). The authority to exercise the committee's subpoena powers may be delegated only to the presiding officer. In the case of failure to comply with such subpoena, the Judicial Council or special committee may institute a contempt proceeding consistent with 28 U.S.C. § 332(d).

e. Report. The committee will file with the Judicial Council a comprehensive report of its investigation, including findings of the investigation and the committee's recommendations for council action. Any findings adverse to the judge will be based on evidence in the record. The report will be accompanied by a statement of the vote by which it was adopted, any separate or dissenting statements of committee members, and the record of any hearings held pursuant to rule 11.

f. Voting. All actions of the committee will be by vote of a majority of all of the members of the committee.

Commentary on Rule 10

Nature of the Process

Rule 10 and the three rules that follow are all concerned with the way in which a special committee carries out its mission. They reflect the view that a special committee has what are generally regarded in our jurisprudence as two distinct roles. The committee will often be performing an investigative role of the kind that is characteristically given to executive branch agencies in our system of justice and, in some stages, a more formalized fact-finding role. Even though the same body has responsibility for both roles, it is important to distinguish between them in order to ensure that due process rights are afforded at appropriate times to the judge complained about.

Criminal Matters

One of the difficult questions that can arise under the judicial discipline statute is the relationship between proceedings under this statute and criminal investigations. Rule 10(b) assigns coordinating responsibility to the special committee in cases in which criminal conduct is suspected and gives the committee the authority to decide what the appropriate pace of its activity should be in light of any criminal investigation. However, a special committee should not abdicate its responsibility by assenting to indefinite deferral of its own work.

It is noted that a special committee may be barred from disclosing some information to a prosecutor or grand jury under 28 U.S.C. § 360. This provision is discussed in the commentary under rule 16.

Delegation

Rule 10(d) permits the committee, in its discretion, to delegate any of its duties to subcommittees, individual committee members, or staff. This is consistent with the general principle, expressed in rule 10(a), that each special committee will determine the methods of conducting the investigation that are appropriate in the light of the allegations of the

complaint. It is, of course, not contemplated that the ultimate duty of adopting a report would be delegable.

Rule 9(b) suggests that, where the chief judge designates someone else as presiding officer of a special committee, the presiding officer also be delegated the authority to direct the clerk of the court of appeals to issue subpoenas related to committee proceedings. That is not intended to imply, however, that the decision to direct the issuance of a subpoena is necessarily exercisable by the presiding officer alone. Under rule 10(d), it is up to the committee to decide whether to delegate that decision-making authority.

Basis of Findings

Rule 10(e) requires that findings adverse to the judge complained about be based on evidence in the record. There is no similar requirement in the rules for determinations favorable to the judge. A committee may, in some circumstances, recommend dismissal of a complaint on the ground that preliminary investigation reveals no basis for going forward with hearings on the record.

Voting in the Special Committee

Rule 10(f) provides that actions of a special committee will be by vote of a majority of all the members. It seems reasonable to expect that, almost always, all the members of a committee will participate in committee decisions. In that circumstance, it seems reasonable to require that committee decisions be made by a majority of the membership, rather than a majority of some smaller quorum.

Effective October 10, 1999; amended effective April 24, 2003.

RULE 11. CONDUCT OF HEARINGS BY SPECIAL COMMITTEE

a. Purpose of Hearings. The committee may hold hearings to take testimony and receive other evidence, to hear argument, or both. If the committee is investigating allegations against more than one judge it may, in its discretion, hold joint hearings or separate hearings.

b. Notice to Judge Complained About. The judge complained about will be given adequate notice in writing of any hearing held, its purposes, the names of any witnesses whom the committee intends to call, and the text of any statements that have been taken from such witnesses. The judge may at any time suggest additional witnesses to the committee.

c. Committee Witnesses. All persons who are believed to have substantial information to offer will be called as committee witnesses. Such witnesses may include the complainant and the judge complained about. The witnesses will be questioned by committee members, staff, or both. The judge will be afforded the opportunity to cross-examine committee witnesses, personally or through counsel.

d. Witnesses Called by the Judge. The judge complained about may also call witnesses and may examine them personally or through counsel. Such witnesses may also be examined by committee members, staff, or both.

e. Witness Fees. Witness fees will be paid as provided in 28 U.S.C. § 1821.

f. Rules of Evidence; Oath. The Federal Rules of Evidence will apply to any evidentiary hearing except to the extent that departures from the adversarial format of a trial make them inappropriate. All testimony taken at such a hearing will be given under oath or affirmation.

g. Record and Transcript. A record and transcript will be made of any hearing held.

Commentary on Rule 11

The Role of Hearings in the Investigation Process

The roles of a special committee include an investigative role and a fact-finding role. In conformity with this concept of roles, hearings ordinarily will be held only after the investigative work has been done and the committee has concluded that there is sufficient evidence to warrant a formal fact-finding proceeding. Rule 11 is concerned only with the conduct of hearings, and does not govern the earlier investigative stages of a special committee's work.

Inevitably, a hearing will have something of an adversarial character. The judge who has been complained about will surely feel threatened if the matter has reached this stage. Even though there are two roles and an investigation will commonly have two distinct stages, committee members should not regard themselves as prosecutors one day and judges the next. Their duty—and that of their staff—is at all times to be impartial.

In conformity with this view, rule 11(c) contemplates that witnesses at hearings should generally be called as committee witnesses, regardless of whether their testimony will be favorable or unfavorable to the judge complained about. Staff or others who are organizing the hearings should regard it as their role to present the entire picture, and not to act as prosecutors. Even the judge complained about should normally be called as a committee witnesses. Although rule 11(d) preserves the statutory right of the judge to call witnesses on his or her own behalf, we believe that this should not often be necessary.

Testimony of the Judge

It is appropriate to call the judge complained about as a committee witness. This assumes that the judge would wish to testify in most cases. The special committee should be the sponsor of that testimony as well as other testimony favorable to the judge. Cases may arise in which the judge will not testify voluntarily. In such cases, subpoena power appears to be available, subject to the normal testimonial privileges.

Applicability of Rules of Evidence

Rule 11(f) provides that the Federal Rules of Evidence will apply to evidentiary hearings conducted by special committees "except to the extent that departures from the adversarial format of a trial make them inappropriate."

Effective October 10, 1999.

RULE 12. RIGHTS OF A JUDGE IN INVESTIGATION

a. Notice. The judge complained about is entitled to written notice of the investigation (rule 4(f)), to written notice of the expansion of the scope of an investigation (rule 10(a)), and to written notice of any hearing (rule 11(b)).

b. Presentation of Evidence. The judge is entitled to a hearing, and has the right to present evidence and to compel the attendance of witnesses and the production of documents at the hearing. Upon request of the judge, the chief judge or the chief judge's designee, will direct the clerk of the court of appeals to issue a subpoena in accordance with 28 U.S.C. § 332(d)(1).

c. Presentation of Argument. The judge may submit written argument to the special committee at any time, and will be given a reasonable opportunity to present oral argument at an appropriate stage of the investigation.

d. Attendance at Hearings. The judge will have the right to attend any hearing held by the special committee and to receive copies of the transcript and any documents introduced, as well as copies of any written arguments submitted by the complainant to the committee.

e. Receipt of Committee's Report. The judge will have the right to receive the report of the special committee at the time it is filed with the Judicial Council.

f. Representation by Counsel. The judge may be represented by counsel in the exercise of any of the rights enumerated in this rule. The costs of such representation may be borne by the United states as provided in rule 14(h).

Commentary on Rule 12

Right to Attend Hearings

The statute states that rules adopted by Judicial Councils shall contain provisions requiring that "the judge whose conduct is the subject of the complaint be afforded an opportunity to appear (in person or by counsel) at proceedings conducted by the investigating panel, to present oral and documentary evidence, to compel the attendance of witnesses or the production of documents, to cross-examine witnesses, and to present argument orally or in writing." To implement this provision, rule 12(d) gives the judge the right to attend any hearing held by the committee. The word "hearings" is used in the rules to include sessions held for the purpose of receiving evidence of record or hearing argument.

The statute does not require that the judge be permitted to attend **all** proceedings of the special committee. Hence, the rules do not accord a right to attend such proceedings as meetings at which the committee is engaged in investigative activity (such as interviewing a possible witness or examining documents delivered pursuant to a subpoena duces tecum to determine if they contain relevant evidence) or meetings at which the committee is deliberating on the evidence.

Effective October 10, 1999.

RULE 13. RIGHTS OF COMPLAINANT IN INVESTIGATION

a. Notice. The complainant is entitled to written notice of the investigation as provided in rule 4(f). Upon the filing of the special committee's report to the Judicial Council, the complainant will be notified that the report has been filed and is before the council for decision. Although the complainant is not entitled to a copy of the report of the special committee, the Judicial Council may, in its discretion, release a copy of the report of the special committee to the complainant.

b. Opportunity to Provide Evidence. The complainant is entitled to be interviewed by a representative of the committee. If it is believed that the complainant has substantial information to offer, the complainant will be called as a witness at a hearing.

c. Presentation of Argument. The complainant may submit written argument to the special committee at any time. In the discretion of the special committee, the complainant may be permitted to offer oral argument.

d. Representation by Counsel. A complainant may submit written argument through counsel and, if permitted to offer oral argument, may do so through counsel.

Commentary on Rule 13

In accordance with the view of the process as fundamentally administrative, these rules do not give the complainant the rights of a party to litigation, and leave the complainant's role largely within the discretion of the special committee. However, rule 13(b) promises complainants that, where a special committee has been appointed, the complainant will at a minimum be interviewed by a representative of the committee. Such an interview may, of course, be in person or by telephone, and the representative of the committee may be either a member or staff. In almost every case, such an interview would be regarded by the committee as essential in the performance of its task. Complainants should have an opportunity to tell their stories orally.

Rule 13 does not contemplate that the complainant will be permitted to attend proceedings of the special committee except when testifying or presenting argument.

The special committee may exercise its discretion to permit the complainant to be present at its proceedings, or to permit the complainant, individually or through counsel, to participate in the examination or cross-examination of witnesses.

Section 360(a)(1) authorizes an exception to the confidentiality provisions of section 360(a) where the Judicial Council has in its discretion released a copy of the report of the special committee to the complainant and to the judge who is the subject of the complaint. Since these rules view the disciplinary process as fundamentally administrative rather than adversarial, the rules do not accord the complainant the rights of a litigant and do not entitle the complainant to receipt of a copy of the report of the special committee. Therefore, it remains a matter within the discretion of the Judicial Council whether to release a copy of the special committee's report to the complainant, and whether to impose conditions upon any such release, including that the complainant must keep the report confidential.

Effective October 10, 1999; amended effective April 24, 2003.

CHAPTER V. JUDICIAL COUNCIL CONSIDERATION OF RECOMMENDATIONS OF SPECIAL COMMITTEE

RULE 14. ACTION BY JUDICIAL COUNCIL

a. Purpose of Judicial Council Consideration. After receipt of a report of a special committee, the Judicial Council will determine whether to dismiss the complaint, conclude the proceeding on the ground that corrective action has been taken or that intervening events make action unnecessary, refer the complaint to the Judicial Conference of the United States, or order corrective action.

b. Basis of Council Action. Subject to the rights of the judge to submit argument to the council as provided in rule 15(a), the council may take action on the basis of the report of the special committee and the record of any hearings held. If the council finds the report and record provide an inadequate basis for decision, it may (1) order further investigation and a further report by the special committee, or (2) conduct such additional investigation as it deems appropriate.

c. Dismissal. The council will dismiss a complaint if it concludes—

(1) that the claimed conduct, even if the claim is true, is not "conduct prejudicial to the effective and expeditious administration of the business of the courts" and does not indicate a mental or physical disability resulting in inability to discharge the duties of office;

(2) that the complaint is directly related to the merits of a decision or procedural ruling;

(3) that the facts on which the complaint is based have not been demonstrated; or

(4) that, under the statute, the complaint is otherwise not appropriate for consideration.

d. Conclusion of the Proceeding on the Basis of Corrective Action Taken. The council will conclude the complaint proceeding if it determines that appropriate action has already been taken to remedy the problem identified in the complaint, or that intervening events make such action unnecessary.

e. Referral to the Judicial Conference of the United States. The Judicial Council may, in its discretion, refer a complaint to the Judicial Conference of the United States with the council's recommendations for action. It is required to refer such a complaint to the Judicial Conference of the United States if the council determines that a circuit judge or district judge may have engaged in conduct—

(1) that might constitute ground for impeachment; or

(2) that, in the interest of justice, is not amenable to resolution by the Judicial Council.

f. Order of Corrective Action. If the complaint is not disposed of under paragraphs (c) through (e) of this rule, the Judicial Council will take other action to assure the effective and expeditious administration of the business of the courts. Such action may include, among other measures—

(1) censuring or reprimanding the judge, either by private communication or by public announcement;

(2) ordering that, for a fixed temporary period, no new cases be assigned to the judge;

(3) in the case of a magistrate judge, ordering the chief judge of the district court to take action specified by the council, including the initiation of removal proceedings pursuant to 28 U.S.C. § 631(i);

(4) in the case of a bankruptcy judge, removing the judge from office pursuant to 28 U.S.C. § 152;

(5) in the case of a circuit or district judge, requesting the judge to retire voluntarily with the provision (if necessary) that ordinary length-of-service requirements will be waived; or

(6) in the case of a circuit or district judge who is eligible to retire but does not do so, certifying the disability of the judge under 28 U.S.C. § 372(b) so that an additional judge may be appointed.

g. Combination of Actions. Referral of a complaint to the Judicial Conference of the United States under paragraph (e) or to a district court under paragraph (f)(3) of this rule will not preclude the council from simultaneously taking such other action under paragraph (f) as is within its power.

h. Recommendation About Fees. Upon the request of a judge whose conduct is the subject of a complaint, the Judicial Council may, if the complaint has been finally dismissed, recommend that the Director of the Administrative Office of the United States Courts award reimbursement, from funds appropriated to the judiciary, for those reasonable expenses, including attorneys' fees, incurred by that judge during the investigation, which would not have been incurred but for the requirements of 28 U.S.C. § 351, et seq., and these rules.

i. Notice of Action of Judicial Council. Council action will be by written order. Unless the council finds that, for extraordinary reasons, it would be contrary to the interests of justice, the order will be accompanied by a memorandum setting forth the fac-

tual determinations on which it is based and the reasons for the council action. The memorandum will not include the name of the complainant or of the judge whose conduct was complained about. The order and the supporting memorandum will be provided to the complainant, the judge, and any judge entitled to receive a copy of the complaint pursuant to rule 3(a)(2). However, if the complaint has been referred to the Judicial Conference of the United States pursuant to paragraph (e) of this rule and the council determines that disclosure would be contrary to the interests of justice, such disclosure need not be made. The complainant and the judge will be notified of the right to seek review of the Judicial Council's decision by the Judicial Conference of the United States and of the procedures for filing a petition for review.

j. Public Availability of Council Action. Materials related to the council's action will be made public at the time and in the matter set forth in rule 17.

k. Allegations of Criminal Conduct. If the Judicial Council dismisses, solely for lack of jurisdiction under 28 U.S.C. § 351(a), non-frivolous allegations of criminal conduct by a judge, the Judicial Council's order of dismissal shall inform the complainant that the dismissal does not prevent the complainant from bringing any allegation of criminal conduct to the attention of appropriate federal or state criminal authorities. If, in this situation, the allegations of criminal conduct were originally referred to the circuit by a congressional committee or member of Congress, the Judicial Council—if no petition for review of the dismissal by the Judicial Council lies under 28 U.S.C. § 357(a), or if no petition for review is filed—shall notify the congressional committee or member that the judiciary has concluded that it lacks jurisdiction under § 351(a).

Commentary on Rule 14

Basis of Council Action

Section 354(a)(1)(A) states that, upon receipt of a report from a special committee, the Judicial Council may conduct additional investigation that it considers to be necessary. While the statute does not explicitly refer to an authority to ask the special committee to do further work and file a supplemental report, it appears that such a procedure is so inherently a part of a committee process that the authority for it may safely be assumed. An investigation of any magnitude by the entire Judicial Council would be warranted in only the rarest cases, since it would constitute a substantial drain on judicial resources of the circuit. There may be some cases, however, in which a loose end can be tied up without the necessity of a remand.

Council Action

Paragraphs (2)(A), (2)(B) and (2)(c) of section 354(a) enumerate actions that the council may take after receipt of the report of a special committee in order to assure the effective and expeditious administration of the business of the courts within the circuit. See 28 U.S.C. § 354(a). Paragraphs (3)(A) and (3)(B) of section 354(a) limit the judicial council's authority to order the removal of a judge. There are two notable omissions from this statutory enumeration: conclusion of the proceedings on the ground that corrective action has been taken, and conclusion of the proceedings on the ground that action on the complaint is no longer necessary because of intervening events. The authority to take these actions implicitly derives from the judicial council's ability to "take such action as is appropriate to assure the effective and expeditious administration of the business of the courts within the circuit." 28 U.S.C. § 354(a)(1)(C). These rules include these two options for concluding the proceedings in the enumerated alternatives for council action.

Combination of Actions

Rule 14(g) states that referral of a complaint to the Judicial Conference of the United States, or to a district court in a case involving a magistrate judge, will not preclude the Judicial Council from simultaneously taking other action to assure the effective and expeditious administration of the business of the courts.

Referral to the Judicial Conference of the United States may take place under either clause (1) or clause (2) of section 354(b). Clause (1) states that, "[i]n addition to the authority granted under subsection (a)," Judicial Councils may, in their discretion, refer matters to the Judicial Conference of the United States with recommendations for action by the Conference. Clause (2) mandates Judicial Council referral of complaints to the Judicial Conference in certain circumstances; it is not introduced with the phrase, "[i]n addition to the authority granted under subsection (a)." This distinction in the introductory language was not intended to suggest a difference in the authority of the Judicial Council to take corrective action simultaneously with referral of a matter to the Conference. The phrase "[i]n addition to" in clause (1) says no more than that referral is another action within the council's authority, in addition to those actions listed in subsection (a).

Attorneys' Fees

Section 361 makes explicit the authority of the Judicial Council, upon the request of the judge who is the subject of the complaint, to recommend to the Director of the Administrative Office of the United States Courts that the judge who is the subject of the complaint be reimbursed for reasonable expenses, including attorneys' fees, incurred during the investigation. Under the statutory provision, the Judicial Council has the authority to recommend such reimbursement only where, after investigation by a special committee, the complaint has been finally dismissed under § 354(a)(1)(B). Accordingly, there is no basis in the statute for a recommendation of reimbursement for attorneys' fees where the Judicial Council, after an investigation, concludes the proceeding on the ground that corrective action has been taken or that intervening events have made action on the complaint unnecessary.

Notice of Council Action

Rule 14(i) requires that council action normally be supported with a memorandum of factual determinations and reasons and that notice of the action be given to the complainant and the judge complained about. The two "interests of justice" exceptions are derived from 28 U.S.C. §§ 354(b)(3) and 360(b).

Right to Petition for Review of Judicial Council Action

The right to petition for review of judicial council action applies to any action of the judicial council under section 354. Rule 14(i) requires that the notification to the complainant and the judge complained about include notice of the right to petition the Judicial Conference of the United States for review of the council's decision.

Effective October 10, 1999; amended effective April 24, 2003.

RULE 15. PROCEDURES FOR JUDICIAL COUNCIL CONSIDERATION OF A SPECIAL COMMITTEE'S REPORT

a. Rights of Judge Complained About. Within ten days after the filing of the report of a special committee, the judge complained about may address a written response to all of the members of the Judicial Council. The judge will also be given an opportunity to present oral argument to the council, personally or through counsel. The judge may not communicate with individual council members about the matter, either orally or in writing, except that the council may designate a member or members to receive communications from the judge or to initiate communications with the judge.

b. Conduct of Additional Investigation by the Council. If the Judicial Council decides to conduct additional investigation, the judge complained about will be given adequate prior notice in writing of that decision and of the general scope and purpose of the additional investigation. The conduct of the investigation will be generally in accordance with the procedures set forth in rules 10 through 13 for the conduct of an investigation by a special committee. However, if hearings are held, the council may limit testimony to avoid unnecessary repetition of testimony presented before the special committee.

c. Voting. Council action will be taken by a majority of those members of the council who are not disqualified, except that a decision to remove a bankruptcy judge from office requires a majority of all the members of the council.

Commentary on Rule 15

Voting

Section 372(c)(6)(B)(vii) requires that removal of a bankruptcy judge be in accordance with 28 U.S.C. § 152. Subsection (e) of that section requires the concurrence of a majority of all the members of the council in the order of removal. It is not appropriate to apply a similar rule to the less severe actions that a Judicial Council may take under the act. If some members of the council are disqualified in the matter, their disqualification should not be given the effect of a vote against council action.

Effective October 10, 1999.

CHAPTER VI. MISCELLANEOUS RULES

RULE 16. CONFIDENTIALITY

a. General Rule. Consideration of a complaint by the chief judge, a special committee, or the Judicial Council will be treated as confidential business, and information about such consideration will not be disclosed by any judge, or employee of the judicial branch, or any person who records or transcribes testimony, except in accordance with these rules.

b. Files. All files related to complaints of misconduct or disability, whether maintained by the circuit executive, the chief judge, members of a special committee, members of the Judicial Council, or staff, and whether or not the complaint was accepted for filing, will be maintained separate and apart from all other files and records, with appropriate security precautions to ensure confidentiality.

c. Disclosure in Memoranda of Reasons. Memoranda supporting orders of the chief judge or the Judicial Council, and dissenting opinions or separate statements of members of the council, may contain such information and exhibits as the authors deem appropriate, and such information and exhibits may be made public pursuant to rule 17.

d. Availability to Judicial Conference. In the event that a complaint is referred under rule 14(e) to the Judicial Conference of the United States, the circuit executive will provide the Judicial Conference with copies of the report of the special committee and any other documents and records that were before the Judicial Council at the time of its determination. Upon request of the Judicial Conference or its Committee to Review Circuit Council Conduct and Disability Orders, in connection with their consideration of a referred complaint or a petition under 28 U.S.C. § 372(c)(10) for review of a council order, the circuit executive will furnish any other records related to the investigation.

e. Availability to District Court. In the event that the Judicial Council directs the initiation of proceedings for removal of a magistrate judge under rule 14(f)(3), the circuit executive will provide to the chief judge of the district court copies of the report of the special committee and any other documents and records that were before the Judicial Council at the time of its determination. Upon request of the chief judge of the district court, the Judicial Council may authorize release of any other records relating to the investigation.

f. Impeachment Proceedings. The Judicial Council may release to the legislative branch any materials that are believed necessary to an impeachment investigation of a judge or a trial on articles of impeachment.

g. Consent of Judge Complained About. Any materials from the files may be disclosed to any person upon the written consent of both the judge complained about and the chief judge of the circuit. The chief judge may require that the identity of the complainant, of witnesses in an investigation conducted by a special committee or the Judicial Council, or of judges other than the judge complained about, be shielded in any materials disclosed.

h. Disclosure by Judicial Council in Special Circumstances. The Judicial Council may authorize disclosure of information about the consideration of a complaint, including the papers, documents, and transcripts relating to the investigation, to the extent that the council concludes that such disclosure is justified by special circumstances and is not prohibited by 28 U.S.C. § 372(c)(14).

Such disclosure may be made to judiciary researchers engaged in the study or evaluation of experience under 28 U.S.C. § 372(c) and related modes of judicial discipline, but only where such study or evaluation has been specifically approved by the Judicial Conference or by the Judicial Conference Committee to Review Circuit Council Conduct and Disability Orders. The Judicial Council should take appropriate steps (to the extent the Judicial Conference or its committee has not already done so) to shield the identities of the judge complained about, the complainant, and witnesses from public disclosure, and may impose other appropriate safeguards to protect against the dissemination of confidential information.

i. Disclosure of Identity by Judge Complained About. Nothing in this rule will preclude the judge complained about from acknowledging that he or she is the judge referred to in documents made public pursuant to rule 17.

j. Assistance and Consultation. Nothing in this rule precludes the chief judge or Judicial Council, for purposes of acting on a complaint filed under 28 U.S.C. § 372(c), from seeking the assistance of qualified staff, or from consulting other judges who may be helpful in the process of complaint disposition.

Commentary on Rule 16

Scope of Confidentiality Requirement

Section 372(c)(14) applies a rule of confidentiality to "papers, documents, and records of proceedings related to investigations conducted under this subsection" and states that they shall not be disclosed "by any person in any proceeding," with enumerated exceptions. Three questions arise: Who is bound by the confidentiality rule, what proceedings are subject to the rule, and who is within the circle of people who may have access to information without breaching the rule?

With regard to the first question, rule 16(a) provides that judges, employees of the judicial branch, and people involved in recording proceedings and preparing transcripts are obliged to respect the confidentiality requirement. This of course includes judges who may be the subjects of complaints.

With regard to the second question, the reference to "investigations" suggests that section 372(c)(14) technically applies only in cases in which a special committee has been appointed. However, rule 16(a) applies the rule of confidentiality more broadly, covering consideration of a complaint at any stage.

With regard to the third question, it seems clear that there is no barrier of confidentiality between a Judicial Council and the Judicial Conference, and that members of the Judicial Conference or its standing committee may have access to any of the confidential records for use in their consideration of a referred matter or a petition for review. It is implicit that a district court may have similar access if the Judicial Council orders in response to a complaint that the district court initiate proceedings to remove a magistrate judge from office, and rule 16(e) so provides. It would be absurd if the district court were in this circumstance denied access to the evidence on which the order was based.

The confidentiality requirement does not, of course, prevent the chief judge from "communicat[ing] orally or in writing with ... people who may have knowledge of the matter," rule 4(b), as part of a limited inquiry conducted by the chief judge under that rule.

In addition, we find it implicit that chief judges and Judicial Councils may seek staff assistance or consult with other judges who may be helpful in the process of complaint disposition. Rule 16(j) provides that the confidentiality requirement does not preclude this. See National Commission Report at 103 (finding that "[t]he Act, including its provision on confidentiality does not constitute a barrier to such assistance or consultation"). The chief judge, for example, may properly seek the advice and assistance of another judge whom the chief judge deems to be in the best position to speak with the judge named in the complaint in an attempt to bring about corrective action to remedy the problem raised in the complaint. As another example, a new chief judge may wish to confer with a predecessor to learn how similar complaints have been handled. In consulting with other judges, of course, the chief judge should disclose information regarding the complaint only to the extent the chief judge deems necessary under the circumstances.

On the other hand, the statute makes it clear that there is a barrier of confidentiality between the judicial branch and the legislative; it provides, as an exception to the rule of confidentiality, that material is to be disclosed to Congress only if it is "believed necessary to an impeachment investigation or trial of a judge under article I."

Exceptions to Confidentiality Rule

With regard to the exception for impeachment proceedings, rule 16(f) tracks the statutory language, and deliberately preserves the ambiguity about who must believe that disclosure is necessary to an impeachment investigation or trial. There is some possibility of conflict between the legislative and judicial branches about this issue. It may never arise in fact, and it does not seem appropriate to try to resolve it in advance by rule.

Another exception to the rule of confidentiality is provided by section 372(c)(14)(B), which states that confidential materials may be disclosed if authorized in writing by the judge complained about and by the chief judge of the circuit.

Accordingly, the report of a special committee, or a summary of investigative findings in such form as the Judicial Council or the special committee may choose, may be disclosed upon the written consent of both the judge complained about and the chief judge of the circuit.

Rule 16 also recognizes that there must be some implicit exceptions to the confidentiality requirement. For example, 28 U.S.C. § 372(c)(15) requires that certain orders and the reasons for them shall be made public; it would be a barren collection of reasons that could not refer to the evidence. Rule 16(c) thus makes it explicit that memoranda supporting chief judge and council orders, as well as dissenting opinions and separate statements, may contain references to information that would otherwise be confidential and that such information may be made public.

Rule 16(h) permits disclosure of additional information by order of the council in circumstances not enumerated. Unfortunately, the statutory language does not explicitly authorize exceptions, so many cases will present issues of statutory interpretation. A strong case could be made for disclosure to permit a prosecution for perjury based on testimony given before a special committee. A more difficult case would be presented if a special committee turned up evidence of criminal conduct by a judge and wanted to refer the matter to a grand jury. The rule refers to the statutory prohibition but does not attempt to resolve such questions.

Rule 16(h) specifically permits the Judicial Council to authorize disclosure of information about the consideration of a complaint, including papers, documents, and transcripts relating to the investigation, to judiciary researchers engaged in the study or evaluation of experience under 28 U.S.C. § 372(c) and related modes of judicial discipline. This provision responds to the recommendation of the National Commission on Judicial Discipline and Removal that council rules should authorize the "release [of] information, with appropriate safeguards, to government entities or properly accredited individuals engaged in the study or evaluation of experience under the 1980 Act." National Commission Report at 108.

The rule envisions disclosure of information from the official record of complaint proceedings to a limited category of persons for appropriately authorized research purposes only, and with appropriate safeguards to protect individual identities in any published research results that ensue. In authorizing disclosure, the Judicial Council may refuse to release particular materials whose release would be contrary to the interests of justice, or that constitutes purely internal communications. The rule does not envision any disclosure of purely internal communications between judges and their colleagues and staff.

Disclosure of Materials upon Consent

Once the judge complained about has consented to the disclosure of confidential materials pursuant to section 372(c)(14)(C) and rule 16(g), the chief judge ordinarily will refuse to consent only to the extent necessary to protect the confidentiality interest (1) of the complainant, or (2) of witnesses who have testified in investigatory proceedings or who have provided information in response to a limited inquiry undertaken pursuant to rule 4(b). It will generally be necessary, therefore, for the chief judge to require that the identities of the complainant or of such witnesses, as well as any identifying information, be shielded in any materials disclosed, except insofar as (1) the chief judge has secured the consent of the complainant or of the particular witness to disclosure, or (2) there is a demonstrated need for disclosure of the information that, in the judgment of the chief judge, outweighs the confidentiality interests of the complainant or of a particular witness (as may be the case where the complainant or particular witness has already demonstrated a lack of concern about maintaining the confidentiality of the proceedings).

Effective October 10, 1999.

RULE 17. PUBLIC AVAILABILITY OF DECISIONS

a. **General Rule**. A docket-sheet record of orders of the chief judge and the Judicial Council and the texts of any memoranda supporting such orders and any dissenting opinions or separate statements by members of the Judicial Council will be made public when final action on the complaint has been taken and is no longer subject to review.

(1) If the complaint is finally disposed of without appointment of a special committee, or if it is disposed of by council order dismissing the complaint for reasons other than mootness or because intervening events have made action on the complaint unnecessary, the publicly available materials will not disclose the name of the judge complained about without his or her consent.

(2) If the complaint is finally disposed of by censure or reprimand by means of private communication, the publicly available materials will not disclose either the name of the judge complained about or the text of the reprimand.

(3) If the complaint is finally disposed of by any other action taken pursuant to rule 14(d) or (f), the text of the dispositive order will be included in the materials made public, and the name of the judge will be disclosed.

(4) If the complaint is dismissed as moot, or because intervening events have made action on the complaint unnecessary, at any time after the appointment of a special committee, the Judicial Council will determine whether the name of the judge is to be disclosed.

The name of the complainant will not be disclosed in materials made public under this rule unless the chief judge orders such disclosure.

b. **Manner of Making Public**. The records referred to in paragraph (a) will be made public by placing them in a publicly accessible file in the office of the circuit executive, United States Courthouse, 1 Courthouse Way, Suite 3700, Boston, Massachusetts 02210. The circuit executive will send copies of the publicly available materials to the Federal Judicial Center, Thurgood Marshall Federal Judiciary Building, One Columbus Circuit, N.E., Washington, DC 20002, where such materials will also be available for public inspection. In cases in which memoranda appear to have precedential value, the chief judge may cause them to be published.

c. **Decisions of Judicial Conference Standing Committee**. To the extent consistent with the policy of the Judicial Conference Committee to Review Circuit Council Conduct and Disability Orders, opinions of the committee about complaints arising from this circuit will also be made available to the public in the office of the circuit executive.

d. **Complaints Referred to the Judicial Conference of the United States**. If a complaint is referred to the Judicial Conference of the United States pursuant to rule 14(e), materials relating to the complaint will be made public only as may be ordered by the Judicial Conference.

Commentary on Rule 17

Section 360(b) provides that "[e]ach written order to implement any action under paragraph (6)(B) of section 354(a)(1)(C)" shall be made publicly available and that, "[u]nless contrary to the interest of justice," each such order shall be accompanied by written reasons. Section 360(a) states that "papers, documents, and records of proceedings related to investigations" shall be confidential. Section 354(a)(2)(A) lists, among possible council actions following an investigation, censure or reprimand "by means of private communication" or "by means of public announcement." These three provisions exhaust the statutory guidance with respect to public availability of decisions on complaints.

The statute and its legislative history exhibit a strong policy goal of protecting judges from the damage that could be done by publicizing unfounded allegations of misconduct. Except in cases in which the proposed Court on Judicial Conduct and Disability held a de novo hearing, the Senate-passed bill specifically provided for confidentiality at all states of the complaint procedure "unless final adverse action is taken against a judge, not including an order of dismissal."[8] Although the language of the final legislation is derived from the House bill[9] and is limited to materials "related to investigations," there is no indication that non-confidential treatment of other materials was contemplated.

It is consistent with the congressional intent to protect a judge from public disclosure of a complaint, both while it is pending and after it has been dismissed if that should be the outcome. On the other hand, the goal of assuring the public that the disciplinary mechanism is operating satisfactorily is better served by making the process more open. Also, publication of some of the chief judges' dismissal orders—as contrasted with mere public availability—would surely improve the operation of the mechanism.

Rule 17 attempts to accommodate these conflicting interests. It provides for public availability of decisions of the chief judge and the Judicial Council, and the texts of any memoranda supporting their orders, together with any dissenting opinions of separate statements by members of the Judicial Council. However, these orders and memoranda are to be made public only when final action on the complaint has been taken and any right of review has been exhausted. Whether the name of the judge is disclosed will then depend upon the nature of the final action. If the final action is an order predicated on a finding of misconduct or disability (other than censure or reprimand by means of private communication), the name of the judge will be made public. If the final action is dismissal of the complaint, or a conclusion of the proceeding by the chief judge on the basis of corrective action taken, the name of the judge will not be disclosed. However, if the chief judge or Judicial Council concludes a proceeding because corrective action was taken, the order should explain the corrective action taken so the complainant will be better able to assess the adequacy of the decision and decide whether or not to file an appeal.

If a complaint is dismissed as moot, or because intervening events have made action on the complaint unnecessary, after appointment of a special committee, rule 17(a)(4) leaves it to the Judicial Council to determine whether the judge will be identified. In such a case, no final decision has been reached on the merits, but it may be the public interest—particularly if a judicial officer resigns in the course of an investigation— to make the identity of the judge known.

It should be noted that rule 17 provides for different treatment where a proceeding is concluded on the basis of corrective action taken, depending on whether the proceeding is concluded by the chief judge or by the council following investigation by a special committee. If a chief judge concludes a proceeding on the basis, rule 17(a)(1) provides that the name of the judge will not be disclosed. Shielding the name of the judge in this circumstance should contribute to the frequency of this kind of informal disposition. Once a special committee has been appointed, and a proceeding is concluded by the full council on the basis of corrective action taken, rule 17(a)(3) provides for disclosure of the name of the judge. An "informal" resolution of the complaint at this stage is likely to look very much like any other council order, and should be disclosed in the same manner.

The proposal that decisions be made public only after final action has been taken is designed in part to avoid disclosure of the existence of pending proceedings. Because the Judicial Conference has not established a deadline for filing petitions for review with the Committee to Review Judicial Council Conduct and Disability Orders, rule 17(d) provides for making decisions public if thirty days have elapsed without the filing of a petition for review.

Public availability of orders under 28 U.S.C. § 354(a)(1)(C) is a statutory requirement. The statute does not prescribe the time at which these orders must be made public, and it might be thought implicit that it should be without delay. Similarly, the statute does not state whether the name of the judge must be disclosed, but it could be argued that such disclosure is implicit. In view of the legislative interest in protecting a judge from public airing of unfounded charges, rule 17 adopts an interpretation permitting non-disclosure of the identity of a judicial officer who is ultimately exonerated and also permitting delay in disclosure until the ultimate outcome is known. In this connection congressional leaders described the public availability requirement as applying to "sanctioning orders."[10]

Finally, the rule provides that the identity of the complainant will be disclosed only if the chief judge so orders. Identifying the complainant when the judge is not identified would of course increase the likelihood that the identity of the judge would become publicly known, thus thwarting the policy of non-disclosure. If the identity of the complainant is not to be made public in such cases, there is no particular reason to change the rule and make it public routinely in cases in which the judge is identified. However, it may not always be practicable to shield the complainant's identity while making public disclosure of the Judicial Council's order

and supporting memoranda; in some circumstances, moreover, the complainant may consent to public identification.

Effective October 10, 1999; April 24, 2003.

8. S. 1873, 96th. Cong., 1st. Sess. § 2(a) (1979) (proposed 28 U.S.C. § 372(n)(1)(C)); see S. Rep. No. 362, 96th. Cong., 1st. Sess. 16 (1979).

9. H.R. 7974, 96th. Cong., 2d Sess. § 3(a) (1980) (proposed 28 U.S.C. § 372(c)(14)).

10. 126 Cong. Rec. 28,093 (1980) (remarks of Sen. DeConcini); id. at 28,617 (remarks of Rep. Kastenmeier).

RULE 18. DISQUALIFICATION

a. Complainant. If the complaint is filed by a judge, that judge will be disqualified from participation in any consideration of the complaint except to the extent that these rules provide for participation by a complainant. A chief judge who has identified a complaint under rule 2(k) will not be automatically disqualified from participating in the consideration of the complaint, but may consider in his or her discretion whether the circumstances warrant disqualification.

b. Judge Complained About. A judge whose conduct is the subject of a complaint will be disqualified from participating in any consideration of the complaint except to the extent that these rules provide for participation by a judge who is complained about.

c. Disqualification of Chief Judge on Consideration of a Petition for Review of a Chief Judge's Order. If a petition for review of a chief judge's order dismissing a complaint or concluding a proceeding is filed with the Judicial Council pursuant to rule 5, the chief judge will not participate in the council's consideration of the petition. In such a case, the chief judge may address a written communication to all of the members of the Judicial Council, with copies provided to the complainant and to the judge complained about. The chief judge may not communicate with individual council members about the matter, either orally or in writing.

d. Member of Special Committee Not Disqualified. A member of the Judicial Council who is appointed to a special committee will not be disqualified from participating in council consideration of the committee's report.

e. Judge Under Investigation. Upon appointment of a special committee, the judge complained about will automatically be disqualified from serving on (1) any special committee appointed under rule 4(e); (2) the Judicial Council of the circuit; (3) the Judicial Conference of the United States; and (4) the Committee to Review Circuit Council Conduct and Disability Orders of the Judicial Conference of the United States. The disqualification will continue until all proceedings regarding the complaint are finally terminated, with no further right of review. The proceedings will be deemed terminated thirty days after the final action of the Judicial Council if no petition for review has at that time been filed with the Judicial Conference.

f. Substitute for Disqualified Chief Judge. If the chief judge of the circuit is disqualified from participating in consideration of the complaint, the duties and responsibilities of the chief judge under these rules will be assigned to the circuit judge in regular active service who is the most senior in date of commission of those who are not disqualified. If no such circuit judge is available, these duties and responsibilities will be assigned to the district judge member of the Judicial Council who is the most senior in date of commission of those who are not disqualified. If no such judge is available, the complaint may be referred to a circuit judge from another circuit pursuant to 28 U.S.C. § 291(a). The Judicial Council could also decide that it is necessary, appropriate, and in the interest of sound judicial administration to permit the chief judge to dispose of the complaint on the merits. Members of the Judicial Council who are named in the complaint may participate in this determination if necessary to obtain a quorum of the Judicial Council.

g. Judicial Council Action Where Multiple Judges Are Disqualified. Notwithstanding any other provision in these rules to the contrary, a member of the Judicial Council who is a subject of the complaint may participate in the disposition thereof if (1) participation by members who are subjects of the complaint is necessary to obtain a quorum of the Judicial Council, and (2) the Judicial Council votes that it is necessary, appropriate, and in the interest of sound judicial administration that such complained-against members be eligible to act. Members of the Judicial Council who are subjects of the complaint may participate in this determination if necessary to obtain a quorum of the Judicial Council. Under no circumstances, however, shall the judge who acted as chief judge of the circuit in ruling on the complaint under rule 4 be permitted to participate in this determination.

Commentary on Rule 18

Disqualification of Chief Judge on Review of Chief Judge's Order

Rule 18(c) would bar participation by the chief judge in decisions on petitions to the circuit council. Such a policy is best calculated to assure complainants that their petitions will receive fair consideration.

Disqualification of Judge Under Investigation

28 U.S.C. § 359(a) states that a judge under investigation will be disqualified from certain activities "until all related proceedings under this chapter relating to such investigation have been finally terminated." In the absence of Judicial Conference rules regulating the time within which a petition for review must be filed, rule 18(e) provides that the proceedings will be deemed terminated if no petition for review is filed within thirty days after the final action of the Judicial Council.

Substitute for Disqualified Chief Judge

Under 28 U.S.C. § 351(c), a complaint against the chief judge is to be handled by "that circuit judge in regular active

service next senior in date of commission." Rule 18(f) interprets the statutory language to mean that seniority among judges other than the chief is to be determined by date of commission, with the result that complaints against the chief judge may be routed to a former chief judge or other judge who was appointed earlier than the chief judge. No evidence exists that Congress intended to depart from the normal order of precedence.

If the presiding member of the Judicial Council is disqualified from participating under these rules, the most senior active circuit judge, or if all circuit judges are disqualified, the most senior active district judge who is a member of the Judicial Council will preside.

Disqualification when Multiple Judges are Complained Against

Sometimes a single complaint is filed against a large group of judges. Complaints have been filed against all the members of the court of appeals and at least one has been filed against all circuit and district court judges of the circuit. If the normal disqualification rules are observed in the former case, no court of appeals judge can serve as acting chief judge of the circuit, and the Judicial Council will be without appellate members. In the latter case—where the complainant is against all circuit and district judges—no member of the Judicial Council can perform the duties assigned to the council under the statute. A similar problem is created by successive complaints arising out of the same underlying grievance.

Although these multiple-judge complaints are virtually always meritless, the appearance of justice is best served by adherence to traditional principles that matters should be decided by disinterested judges. If no circuit judge or district judge member of the Judicial Council is available to serve as acting chief judge of the circuit, intercircuit assignment procedures under 28 U.S.C. § 291(a) can be used to assign a circuit judge from another circuit to perform the statutory duties of the chief judge. If a quorum of the Judicial Council cannot be obtained to act on a petition for review of a chief judge's order, it would be appropriate to assign the matter to another body. Among other alternatives, the council might ask the Judicial Council of another circuit to consider the petition or might ask the chief justice to assign the matter to either the Judicial Council of another circuit or the Judicial Conference Committee to Review Judicial Conduct and Disability Orders. In the unlikely event that a quorum of the Judicial Council cannot be obtained to consider the report of a special committee, there is legislative history suggesting that the council should use the authority provided in section 354(b)(1) to refer the complaint to the Judicial Conference for consideration.[11]

With recognition that these multiple-judge complaints are virtually always meritless, we have concluded that the Judicial Council should be accorded authority to determine (1) whether it is necessary, appropriate, and in the interest of sound judicial administration to permit the chief judge to dispose of a complaint where it would otherwise be impossible for any active circuit or district judge on the Judicial Council to act, and (2) whether it is necessary, appropriate, and in the interest of sound judicial administration to permit complained-against members of the Judicial Council to participate in the disposition of a petition for review where it would otherwise be impossible to obtain a quorum.

We do not believe that any reasonable observer will view invocation of a rule of necessity in these situations to be inconsistent with the appearance of justice. See, e.g., In Re Complaint of Doe, 2 F.3d 308 (8th Cir. Jud. Council 1993) (invoking the rule of necessity); In Re Complaint of Judicial Misconduct, No. 91–80464 (9th Cir. Jud. Council 6/24/92 (same)); National Commission Report at 105. There is no unfairness in permitting the chief judge to dispose of a patently insubstantial complaint that names all active circuit judges in the circuit.

The remaining option is to use intercircuit assignment procedures under 28 U.S.C. § 291(a) to assign a circuit judge from another circuit to perform the statutory duties of the chief judge. Given the administrative inconvenience and delay involved in this alternative, we have concluded that it is desirable to use intercircuit assignment procedures only if the Judicial Council determines that the complaint is substantial enough to warrant such action.

Similarly, there is no unfairness in permitting complained-against judges, in these circumstances, to participate in the review of a chief judge's dismissal of an insubstantial complaint. The remaining option is to assign the matter to another body. Among other alternatives, the council might ask the Judicial Council of another circuit to consider the petition or might ask the chief justice to assign the matter to either the Judicial Council of another circuit or the Judicial Conference Committee to Review Circuit Council Conduct and Disability Orders. Given the administrative inconveniences and delay involved in these alternatives, we have concluded that it is desirable to refer the petition to another body only if the Judicial Council determines that the petition is substantial enough to warrant such action.

In the unlikely event that a quorum of the Judicial Council cannot be obtained to consider the report of a special committee, it would normally be necessary to refer the matter to another body. There is legislative history suggesting that in such a circumstance the council should use the authority provided in section 354(b)(1) to refer the complaint to the Judicial Conference for consideration.[12]

Effective October 10, 1999; amended effective April 24, 2003.

11. H.R. Rep. No. 1313, 96th. Cong., 2d Sess. 12 (1980).

12. H.R. Rep. No. 1313, 96th. Cong., 2d Sess. 12 (1980).

RULE 19. WITHDRAWAL OF COMPLAINTS AND PETITIONS FOR REVIEW

a. Complaint Pending Before Chief Judge. A complaint that is before the chief judge for a decision under rule 4 may be withdrawn by the complainant with the consent of the chief judge.

b. Complaint Pending Before Special Committee or Judicial Council. After a complaint has been referred to a special committee for investigation, the complaint may be withdrawn by the complainant only with the consent of both (1) the judge complained about, and (2) the special committee (before its report has been filed) or the Judicial Council.

c. Petition for Review of Chief Judge's Disposition. A petition to the Judicial Council for review of the chief judge's disposition of a complaint may be withdrawn by the petitioner at any time before the Judicial Council acts on the petition.

Commentary on Rule 19

Rule 19 treats the complaint proceeding, once begun, as a matter of public business rather than as the property of the complainant. The complainant is denied the unrestricted power to terminate the proceeding by withdrawing the complaint.

Under rule 19(a), a complaint pending before the chief judge may be withdrawn if the chief judge consents. In appropriate cases, the chief judge consents. In appropriate cases, the chief judge may accordingly be saved the burden of preparing a formal order and supporting memorandum.

If the chief judge appoints a special committee, however, rule 19(b) provides that the complaint may be withdrawn only with the consent of both the body before which it is pending (the special committee or the Judicial Council) and the judge complained about. Once a complaint has reached the stage of appointment of a special committee, the judge complained about is thus given the right to insist that the matter be resolved on the merits, thereby escaping the ambiguity that might remain if the proceeding were terminated by withdrawal of the complaint.

With regard to petitions for Judicial Council review, rule 19(c) grants the petitioner unrestricted authority to withdraw the petition. The public's interest in the proceeding is adequately protected, since there will necessarily have been a decision by the chief judge in such a case.

Effective October 10, 1999.

RULE 20. AVAILABILITY OF OTHER PROCEDURES

The availability of the complaint procedure under these rules and 28 U.S.C. § 351, et seq., will not preclude the chief judge of the circuit or the Judicial Council of the circuit from considering any information that may come to their attention suggesting that a judge has engaged in conduct prejudicial to the effective and expeditious administration of the business of the courts or is unable to discharge all the duties of office by reason of disability.

Commentary on Rule 20

Rule 20 reflects the fact that the enactment of the statutory complaint procedure was not intended to displace the historic functions of the chief judge and the Circuit Judicial Council to respond to problems that come to their attention. As stated by Senator DeConcini in his remarks upon final Senate passage of the 1980 act, "the informal, collegial resolution of the great majority of meritorious disability or disciplinary matters is to be the rule rather than the exception. Only in the rare case will it be deemed necessary to invoke the formal statutory procedures and sanctions provided for in the act."[13]

Effective October 10, 1999; amended effective April 24, 2003.

13. 126 Cong. Rec. 28, 092 (1980).

RULE 21. AVAILABILITY OF RULES AND FORMS

These rules and copies of the complaint form prescribed by rule 2 will be available without charge in the Office of the Clerk of the Court of Appeals, United States Courthouse, 1 Courthouse Way, Suite 2500, Boston, Massachusetts 02210, and in each office of the clerk of a district court or bankruptcy court within this circuit.

Effective October 10, 1999.

RULE 22. EFFECTIVE DATE

These rules apply to complaints filed on or after April 24, 2003. The handling of complaints filed before that date will be governed by the rules previously in effect.

Effective October 10, 1999; amended effective April 24, 2003.

RULE 23. ADVISORY COMMITTEE

The advisory committee appointed by the Court of Appeals for the First Circuit for the study of rules of practice and internal operating procedures shall also constitute the advisory committee for the study of these rules, as provided by 28 U.S.C. § 2077(b), and shall make any appropriate recommendations to the circuit council concerning these rules.

Effective October 10, 1999.

APPENDIX A. 28 U.S.C. §§ 351–364

See Sections 351 through 364 of Title 28 of the United States Code.

APPENDIX B. COMPLAINT FORM

JUDICIAL COUNCIL OF THE FIRST CIRCUIT
COMPLAINT OF JUDICIAL MISCONDUCT OR DISABILITY

Mail this form to the Clerk, United States Court of Appeals for the First Circuit, United States Courthouse, Suite 2500, 1 Courthouse Way, Boston, Massachusetts 02210. Mark the envelope JUDICIAL MISCONDUCT COMPLAINT or JUDICIAL DISABILITY COMPLAINT. Do not put the name of the judge or magistrate on the envelope.

See Rule 2(e) For the number of copies required.

1. **Complainant's name**:
   Address:

   Daytime telephone: (   )
2. **Judge or magistrate complained about**:
   Name:
   Court:
3. Does this complaint concern the behavior of the judge or magistrate in a particular lawsuit or lawsuits?
   ☐ Yes   ☐ No
   If yes, give the following information about each lawsuit (use the reverse side if there is more than one):
   Court:
   Docket Number:
   Are (were) you a party or lawyer in the lawsuit?
   ☐ Party ☐ Lawyer ☐ Neither
   If a party, give the name, address and telephone number of your lawyer:

   Docket numbers of any appeals to the First Circuit:
4. Have you filed any lawsuits against the judge or magistrate?
   ☐ Yes   ☐ No
   If yes, give the following information about each lawsuit (use the reverse side if there is more than one):
   Court:
   Docket number:
   Present status of suit:
   Name, address, and telephone number of your lawyer: _____

Court to which any appeal has been taken:
Docket number of the appeal:
Present status of the appeal:

5. On separate sheets of paper, not larger than the paper this form is printed on, describe the conduct or the evidence of disability that is the subject of this complaint. *See* Rule 2(b) and 2(d). Do not use more than 5 pages (5 sides).

6. You should either:
   (1) check the first box below and sign this form in the presence of a notary public; or
   (2) check the second box and sign the form. You do not need a notary public if you check the second box.
   ( ) I swear (affirm) that —
   ( ) I declare under penalty of perjury that —
      (1) **I have read Rules 1 and 2 of the Rules of the Judicial Council of the First Circuit Governing Complaints of Judicial Misconduct or Disability, and**
      (2) The statements made in this complaint are true and correct to the best of my knowledge.

Signature   _____

Date executed: _____

Sworn and subscribed to before me

Date: _____

Notary Public: _____

My commission expires: _____

Effective October 10, 1999.

RULES OF DISCIPLINARY ENFORCEMENT FOR THE COURT OF APPEALS FOR THE FIRST CIRCUIT

Effective August 1, 2002

INTRODUCTION

The Court of Appeals for the First Circuit, in furtherance of its inherent power and responsibility to supervise the conduct of attorneys who are admitted to practice before it, or admitted for the purpose of a particular proceeding (pro hac vice), promulgates the following Rules of Disciplinary Enforcement superseding all of its other Rules pertaining to disciplinary enforcement heretofore promulgated.

[August 1, 2002.]

RULE I. ATTORNEYS CONVICTED OF CRIMES

A. Upon filing with this Court of a certified copy of a judgment of conviction demonstrating that any attorney admitted to practice before the Court has been convicted in any Court of the United States, or the District of Columbia, or of any state, territory, commonwealth or possession of the United States of a serious crime as hereinafter defined, the Chief Judge shall refer the matter to a disciplinary panel. The disciplinary panel shall enter an order immediately suspending that attorney, whether the conviction resulted from a plea of guilty or nolo contendere or from a verdict after trial or otherwise, and regardless of the pendency of any appeal, until final disposition of a disciplinary proceeding to be commenced upon such conviction. A copy of such order shall immediately be served by the Clerk of this Court upon the attorney personally or by certified or registered mail. Upon motion and good cause shown, the disciplinary panel may set aside such order when it appears in the interest of justice to do so.

B. The term "serious crime" shall include any felony and any lesser crime, a necessary element of which, as determined by the statutory or common law definition of such crime in the jurisdiction where the judgment was entered, involves false swearing, misrepresentation, fraud, willful failure to file income tax returns, deceit, bribery, extortion, misappropriation, theft, or an attempt or a conspiracy or solicitation of another to commit a "serious crime."

C. Upon the filing of a certified copy of a judgment of conviction of an attorney for a serious crime, the disciplinary panel shall, in addition to suspending that attorney in accordance with the provisions of this Rule, also initiate disciplinary proceedings in which the sole issue to be determined shall be the extent of the final discipline to be imposed as a result of the conduct resulting in the conviction, provided that no

final disposition will be rendered until all direct appeals from the conviction are concluded. The certified copy of the judgment of conviction shall be conclusive evidence of the commission of that crime by the attorney in question.

D. Upon the filing of a certified copy of a judgment of conviction of an attorney for any crime not constituting a "serious crime," the Chief Judge may refer the matter to a disciplinary panel for disciplinary proceedings or may exercise discretion to make no reference with respect to convictions for minor offenses for which discipline would not be appropriate.

E. Any attorney suspended under the first paragraph of this Rule will be reinstated immediately upon the filing of a certificate demonstrating that the underlying conviction has been vacated or reversed on direct appeal, but the reinstatement shall not terminate any disciplinary proceeding then pending against the attorney, the disposition of which shall be determined by the disciplinary panel on the basis of all available evidence pertaining to both guilt and the extent of discipline to be imposed.

RULE II. DISCIPLINE IMPOSED BY OTHER COURTS

A. Any attorney admitted to practice before this Court shall, upon being subject to public discipline by any other Court of the United States, or the District of Columbia, or of any state, territory, commonwealth or possession of the United States, promptly inform the Clerk of this Court of such action.

B. Upon filing of a certified copy of a judgment, order, or other official document demonstrating that an attorney admitted to practice before this Court has been publicly disciplined by another court, the Chief Judge shall refer the matter to a disciplinary panel and the Clerk of this Court shall serve on the attorney, personally or by certified or registered mail, a notice containing:

1. a copy of the judgment or order from the other court; and

2. an order to show cause directing that the attorney inform this Court within 30 days after service of the order of any claim predicated upon the grounds set forth in paragraph (C) of this Rule that the imposition of substantially similar discipline on the attorney would be unwarranted and the reasons therefor. The order shall also state that a hearing on such a claim must be requested within 30 days after service of the order.

C. Upon the expiration of the time to show cause, if no response has been filed, then the disciplinary panel shall enter an order imposing substantially similar discipline. If a timely response is filed, the disciplinary panel shall, after any applicable hearing or other proceedings, impose substantially the same discipline imposed by the other court unless the attorney demonstrates, and the disciplinary panel is persuaded:

1. that the procedure used by the other court was so lacking in notice or opportunity to be heard as to constitute a deprivation of due process; or

2. that there was such an infirmity of proof establishing the misconduct as to give rise to the clear conviction that this Court could not, consistent with its duty, accept as final the conclusion on that subject; or

3. that the imposition of substantially similar discipline by this Court would result in grave injustice; or

4. that the misconduct established is deemed by this Court to warrant different discipline.

Where the disciplinary panel determines that any of these elements exist, it shall enter such other order as it deems appropriate.

D. In all other respects, a final adjudication in another court that an attorney has been guilty of misconduct shall establish conclusively the misconduct for purposes of any disciplinary proceeding in this Court.

RULE III. DISBARMENT ON CONSENT OR RESIGNATION IN OTHER COURTS

A. Any attorney admitted to practice before this Court who shall be disbarred on consent or resign from the bar of any other court of the United States or the District of Columbia, or from the Bar of any state, territory, commonwealth or possession of the United States while an investigation into allegations of misconduct is pending, shall, upon the filing with this Court of a certified or exemplified copy of the judgment or order accepting such disbarment on consent or resignation, cease to be permitted to practice before this Court and be stricken from the roll of attorneys admitted to practice before this Court.

B. Any attorney admitted to practice before this Court shall, upon being disbarred on consent or resigning from the bar of any other court of the United States or the District of Columbia, or from the Bar of any state, territory, commonwealth or possession of the United States while an investigation into allegations of misconduct is pending, promptly inform the Clerk of this Court of such disbarment on consent or resignation.

RULE IV. STANDARDS FOR PROFESSIONAL CONDUCT

A. For misconduct defined in these Rules, and for good cause shown, and after notice and opportunity to be heard, any attorney admitted to practice before this Court may be disbarred, suspended from practice before this Court, reprimanded or subjected to such other disciplinary action as the circumstances may warrant.

B. Acts or omissions by an attorney admitted to practice before this Court, individually or in concert with any other person or persons, which violate the Code of Professional Responsibility, either of the state, territory, commonwealth or possession of the United States in which the attorney maintains his principal office; or of the state, territory, commonwealth or possession of the United States in which the attorney is acting at the time of the misconduct; or of the state in which the circuit maintains its Clerk's Office, shall constitute misconduct and shall be grounds for discipline, whether or not the act or omission occurred in the course of the attorney-client relationship. The Code of Professional Responsibility means that code adopted by the highest court of the state, territory, commonwealth or possession of the United States, as amended from time to time by that court, except as otherwise provided by specific Rule of this Court after consideration of comments by representatives of bar associations within the state, territory, commonwealth or possession of the United States. Failure to comply with the Federal Rules of Appellate Procedure, the Local Rules of this Court, or the orders of this Court may also constitute misconduct and be grounds for discipline.

RULE V. DISCIPLINARY PROCEEDINGS

A. When misconduct or allegations of misconduct on the part of an attorney admitted to practice before this Court shall come to the attention of a Judge or officer of this Court, whether by complaint or otherwise, and the applicable procedure is not otherwise mandated by these rules, the Judge or officer shall refer the matter to the Chief Judge for initial review. If the Chief Judge determines that misconduct is alleged which, if substantiated, would warrant discipline by this Court, the Chief Judge shall refer the matter to a disciplinary panel; if not, the Chief Judge may dismiss the matter. A disciplinary panel shall consist of three judges of this Court, whether active or senior, appointed by the Chief Judge. The Chief Judge may serve as a member of the disciplinary panel. In the absence of the Chief Judge, the active judge most senior in service on the Court serves as chair. If no active judge is on the disciplinary panel, the Chief Judge shall appoint the chair. The disciplinary panel may at any time appoint counsel to investigate or to prosecute any disciplinary matter. In a matter in which the Chief Judge is recused, references to "Chief Judge" shall mean the senior active judge who is not recused.

B. If the disciplinary panel determines that cause may exist for disciplinary action, the disciplinary panel will direct the Clerk of the Court to issue an order to the attorney in question to show cause why (1) specified discipline should not be imposed or (2) discipline to be determined later should not be imposed. The order shall be served on the attorney personally or by certified or registered mail, shall notify the attorney of the alleged conduct and the reason the conduct may justify disciplinary action, and shall direct that 5 copies of a response, including any supporting evidence or request for a hearing, be filed within 30 days of service of the order or such other time as the order may specify. The Clerk shall also append a copy of these rules to the order. In any response to the order, the attorney must also (a) include an affidavit listing the other bars to which the attorney is admitted, (b) note which if any of the facts alleged are controverted, and (c) specify the basis on which any controverted facts are disputed. If the disciplinary panel determines on initial investigation and review that cause does not exist for disciplinary action, the disciplinary panel may dismiss the matter.

C. If the attorney fails to timely respond to an order to show cause, or if the attorney's timely response to the order to show cause does not specifically request to be heard in person, the disciplinary panel may direct entry of an order imposing discipline or take any other appropriate action. If the attorney specifically requests to be heard in person, either in defense or in mitigation, the disciplinary panel shall set the matter for such hearing as is appropriate under the circumstances. The disciplinary panel may itself order a hearing whether or not one is requested. Following such a hearing and the receipt of any findings or recommendation that may be required and any further submissions that the disciplinary panel may invite, the disciplinary panel may direct entry of an order imposing discipline or take any other appropriate action.

D. If a hearing is ordered, the disciplinary panel may conduct the hearing itself or designate a special master (including but not limited to a district judge or magistrate judge serving within the circuit) for purposes of conducting any hearing. The disciplinary panel (or the special master, subject to the instruction of the disciplinary panel) may in its discretion adopt appropriate procedural and evidentiary rules for any such hearing. At the conclusion of a hearing held before a special master, the special master shall promptly make a report of findings and—if directed by the disciplinary panel—recommendations to the disciplinary panel. A copy of the report and any recommendations shall be made available to the attorney under investigation. The disciplinary panel may

reject or adopt the findings and/or recommendations of the special master in whole or part.

E. Any attorney may file a petition for rehearing by the disciplinary panel or a combined petition for rehearing by the disciplinary panel and suggestion for rehearing en banc by the active judges of the Court. Similarly, the attorney may seek a stay of any disciplinary order entered by the disciplinary panel, the stay to be sought from the disciplinary panel in the first instance and thereafter if desired by the attorney from the Court en banc. The procedures for any such petition will be in accordance with the Federal Rules of Appellate Procedure and the Local Rules of this Court. If en banc review is granted, any senior judge shall be eligible to be a member of the en banc Court, at that judge's election, in the circumstances specified in 28 U.S.C. § 46(c).

F. At any time, the disciplinary panel may in its discretion refer a disciplinary matter pending before it to an appropriate state bar association or state disciplinary board. In such a case, the disciplinary panel is free to dismiss the matter or hold its own proceedings in abeyance pending the completion of the state disciplinary proceedings. Nothing in these rules prevents any disciplinary panel, Judge, or officer of this Court from bringing disciplinary matters to the attention of the appropriate state disciplinary authorities.

G. The provisions of this Rule shall govern disciplinary proceedings addressed to misconduct as defined in Rule IV, and shall also apply to any proceedings under Rule I (Attorneys Convicted of Crimes), Rule II (Discipline Imposed by Other Courts), and Rule VII (Reinstatement) to the extent not inconsistent with the express provisions of those rules.

RULE VI. DISBARMENT ON CONSENT WHILE UNDER DISCIPLINARY INVESTIGATION OR PROSECUTION

A. Any attorney admitted to practice before this Court who is the subject of an investigation into, or a pending proceeding involving, allegations or misconduct may consent to disbarment, but only by delivering to this Court an affidavit stating that the attorney desires to consent to disbarment and that:

1. the attorney's consent is freely and voluntarily rendered; the attorney is not being subjected to coercion or duress; the attorney is fully aware of the implications of so consenting;

2. the attorney is aware that there is a presently pending investigation or proceeding involving allegation that there exist grounds for the attorney's discipline the nature of which the attorney shall specifically set forth;

3. the attorney acknowledges that the material facts so alleged are true; and

4. the attorney so consents because the attorney knows that if charges were predicted upon the matters under investigation, or if the proceeding were prosecuted, the attorney could not successfully defend himself.

B. Upon receipt of the required affidavit, this Court shall enter an order disbarring the attorney.

C. The order disbarring the attorney on consent shall be a matter of public record. However, the affidavit required under the provisions of this Rule shall not be publicly disclosed or made available for use in any other proceeding except upon order of this Court.

RULE VII. REINSTATEMENT

A. Unless the suspension order provides otherwise, an attorney who is suspended shall be automatically reinstated at the end of the period of suspension upon filing with this Court of an affidavit of compliance with the provisions of the order. An attorney who is suspended indefinitely or disbarred may not resume practice until reinstated by order of this Court. Suspensions may be directed to run concurrently with a suspension mandated by other state or federal courts, in which event the attorney shall be eligible for reinstatement in this Court when said suspension expires and will be automatically reinstated upon filing with this Court an affidavit indicating that the period of suspension has run.

B. Petitions for reinstatement by an attorney disbarred or indefinitely suspended under these rules shall be filed with the Clerk of this Court and contain a concise statement of the circumstances of the disciplinary proceeding, the discipline imposed by this Court, and the grounds that justify reinstatement of the attorney in question. In accordance with Rule V, the Chief Judge shall conduct an initial review, and, as warranted, dismiss the petition or refer it to a disciplinary panel. After whatever investigation it sees fit, the disciplinary panel may set the matter for whatever hearing it deems appropriate under the circumstances.

C. The petitioner shall have the burden of demonstrating by clear and convincing evidence that he or she has the moral qualifications, competency, and learning in the law required for admission to practice law before this Court and that the resumption of the practice of law will not be detrimental to the integrity and standing of the bar or to the administration of justice, or subversive to the public interest.

D. If the disciplinary panel finds that the petitioner is unfit to resume the practice of law, the petition shall be dismissed. If the petitioner is found fit to resume the practice of law, the disciplinary panel shall enter an order of reinstatement, provided that the disciplinary panel may make reinstatement conditional upon the payment of all or part of the costs of the proceedings, and upon the making of partial or complete restitution to parties harmed by the petitioner whose conduct led to the suspension or disbarment, and the disciplinary panel may impose such other reasonable conditions as it deems meet. Further, if the petitioner has been suspended or disbarred for five or more years, the disciplinary panel may in its discretion condition reinstatement upon the furnishing of proof of competency and learning in the law, which proof may include successful completion of an examination for admission to practice subsequent to the date of suspension or disbarment.

E. No petition for reinstatement under this Rule shall be filed within one year following an adverse final judgment upon a petition for reinstatement filed by or on behalf of the same attorney.

RULE VIII. ATTORNEYS SPECIALLY ADMITTED

Whenever an attorney applies to be admitted or is admitted to this Court for purposes of a particular proceeding (pro hac vice), the attorney shall be deemed thereby to have conferred disciplinary jurisdiction upon this Court for any alleged misconduct of that attorney arising in the course of or in the preparation for such proceeding.

RULE IX. APPOINTMENT OF COUNSEL

Whenever counsel is appointed pursuant to these rules to investigate allegations of misconduct or prosecute disciplinary proceedings or in conjunction with a reinstatement petition filed by a disciplined attorney, a member of the Bar of this Court shall be appointed. Counsel, once appointed, shall not resign without the consent of the disciplinary panel.

RULE X. DUTIES AND POWERS OF THE CLERK

A. The Clerk of this Court shall promptly notify the National Discipline Data Bank operated by the American Bar Association of any order imposing public discipline upon any attorney admitted to practice before this Court.

B. The Clerk of this Court is empowered, upon being informed that any attorney admitted to practice before this Court has been convicted of any crime or has been subjected to discipline by another court, to obtain and file with this Court a certified or exemplified copy of such conviction or disciplinary judgment or order.

C. Whenever it appears that any person who is disbarred or suspended or censured or disbarred on consent by this Court is admitted to practice law in any other jurisdiction or before any other court, the Clerk of this Court is empowered, to the extent he deems it desirable and necessary to supplement the action taken under clause A, above, to so advise the disciplinary authority in such other jurisdiction or such other court.

RULE XI. JURISDICTION

Nothing contained in these Rules shall be construed to deny to this Court such powers as are necessary for the Court to maintain control over proceedings conducted before it, such as proceedings for contempt under Title 18 of the United States Code or under Rule 42 of the Federal Rules of Criminal Procedure.

RULE XII. EFFECTIVE DATE

These Rules shall become effective on August 1, 2002, provided that any formal disciplinary proceedings then pending before the Court shall (unless the Court otherwise directs) be concluded under the Rules existing prior to that date.

INDEX TO
FEDERAL RULES OF APPELLATE PROCEDURE WITH LOCAL RULES AND INTERNAL OPERATING PROCEDURES OF THE FIRST CIRCUIT

FRAP ....Federal Rule of Appellate Procedure
Loc. Rule.............................First Circuit Local Rule
DER ....Rules of Disciplinary Enforcement
IOP ....First Circuit Internal Operating Procedures
JMD.................................Rules Governing Complaints of Judicial Misconduct or Disability

OFFICIAL BONDS
Bonds (Officers and Fiduciaries), generally, this index

OMISSIONS
Administrative bodies and proceedings, record on review or enforcement, **FRAP 16**
Briefs, arrangement of appendices, **FRAP 30**

OPINIONS
Generally, **Loc. Rule 36; IOP 9**
Mailing copies, parties, **FRAP 36**

ORAL ARGUMENTS
Generally, **FRAP 34; Loc. Rule 34; IOP 8**
Amicus curiae participation, **FRAP 29**
Appeal by permission, **FRAP 5**
Extraordinary writs, **FRAP 21**
Law students, **Loc. Rule 46**
Mandamus, **FRAP 21**
National Labor Relations Board hearings, **FRAP 15.1**
Petition for rehearing, **FRAP 40**
Prohibition, **FRAP 21**
Rehearing, petition for, **FRAP 40**

ORGANIZATION OF COURT
Generally, **IOP 1**

ORDERS
Administrative Bodies and Proceedings, generally, this index
Discipline, attorneys, orders to show cause, **DER 5**

ORDERS OF COURT
Appeal conferences, **FRAP 33**
Attorneys, suspension or disbarment, **FRAP 46**
Bankruptcy cases, appeal from, **FRAP 6**
Clerk of court of appeals,
   Duties, **FRAP 45**
   Office hours, **FRAP 45**
Conferences, appeal conferences, **FRAP 33**
Determination of motions for procedural orders, **FRAP 27**
Dismissal in court of appeals, **FRAP 42**
District courts, retention of record, **FRAP 11**
Extraordinary writs, directing answer, **FRAP 21**
Hearings in banc, **FRAP 35**
Mandamus, directing answer, **FRAP 21**
Prohibition, directing answer, **FRAP 21**
Rehearing in banc, **FRAP 35**
Relief from, motion, effect on time for appeal, **FRAP 4**
Substitution of parties, **FRAP 43**

ORGANIZATION OF COURT
Generally, **IOP 1**

ORIGINAL WRIT
Habeas corpus, application, **FRAP 22; Loc. Rule 22**

PAPERS
Books and Papers, generally, this index

PARTIAL TRANSCRIPT
District courts, record on appeal, notice, **FRAP 10**

PARTIES
Administrative Bodies and Proceedings, this index
Appeal conferences, **FRAP 33**
Appearances, **Loc. Rules 12, 46**
Briefs, references to parties, **FRAP 28**
Constitutional questions, United States or state not a party, **FRAP 44**
Conferences, appeal conferences, **FRAP 33**

PARTIES—Cont'd
Costs, persons entitled, **FRAP 39**
Judgments and decrees, mailing copies, **FRAP 36**
Nonappearance, arguments, **FRAP 34**
Opinions, mailing, **FRAP 36**
References in briefs, **FRAP 28**
Representation statement, attorneys, **FRAP 12; Loc. Rule 12**
Substitution of parties, **FRAP 43**

PAUPERS
Indigent Persons, generally, this index

PENAL INSTITUTIONS
Correctional Institutions, generally, this index

PENITENTIARIES
Correctional Institutions, generally, this index

PERMISSION
Appeals by permission, district courts, **FRAP 5**

PERSONAL REPRESENTATIVES
Death of party, substitution, **FRAP 43**

PETITIONS
Administrative bodies and proceedings, review of order, **FRAP 15**
   Petition for, **FRAP Appendix Form 3**
Appeals by permission, **FRAP 5**
Corporate disclosure statements, **FRAP 26.1**
Covers, **FRAP 32**
Discipline, attorneys, reinstatement, **DER 7**
District courts, appeals by permission, **FRAP 5**
Extraordinary writs, **FRAP 21**
Forms,
   Briefs, appendices and other papers, **FRAP 32**
Habeas corpus, **FRAP 22; Loc. Rule 22 et seq.**
Judicial misconduct or disability, complaints, review, **JMD**
Mandamus, **FRAP 21**
   Filing and fees, **IOP 3**
   Special writs, **Loc. Rule 21**
Permission to appeal, **FRAP 5**
Prohibition writs, **FRAP 21**
   Special writs, **Loc. Rule 21**
Rehearing, **FRAP 40; Loc. Rule 32; IOP 10**
Reinstatement, attorneys, **DER 7**
Signatures, **FRAP 32**
Special writs, **Loc. Rule 21**
Writs, extraordinary writs, **FRAP 21; Loc. Rule 21**

POOR PERSONS
Indigent Persons, generally, this index

POSTPONEMENT
Arguments, **FRAP 34**

PRELIMINARY HEARINGS
Court of appeals, transmission of record from district court, **FRAP 11**
Record for preliminary hearing in court of appeals, district courts, transmission of record, **FRAP 11**

PRINTING
Briefs,
   Costs, **FRAP 39**
   Form of briefs and appendices, **FRAP 32**

PRISONS AND PRISONERS
Correctional Institutions, generally, this index

PRO HAC VICE
Discipline, jurisdiction, **DER 8**

LOCAL RULES FOR THE FIRST CIRCUIT BANKRUPTCY APPELLATE PANEL

Effective November 3, 1997

Research Note

Use WESTLAW ® *to find cases citing a rule.* WESTLAW *may also be used to search for specific terms or to update a rule; see the US–RULES and US–ORDERS Scope Screens for further information.*

Amendments to these rules are published, as received, in Federal Reporter 3d, Bankruptcy Reporter *and* Mass.Dec. *advance sheets.*

Table of Rules

INTRODUCTION

Purpose of the Local Rules for the Bankruptcy Appellate Panel for the First Circuit. The following Local Rules for the First Circuit Bankruptcy Appellate Panel (BAP) govern practice before the BAP.

Scope and Function. The Local Rules for the First Circuit BAP supplement Part VIII of the Federal Rules of Bankruptcy Procedure.

Form of Citation. The First Circuit BAP Rules shall be cited as:

"1st Cir.BAP R. ____"

[Effective November 3, 1997.]

RULE 8001–1. NOTICE OF APPEAL

(a) Notice of Appeal: Filing and Fees.

(1) *Where to File; Fee.* Notices of appeal shall be filed, with the filing fee, in the appropriate bankruptcy court. The filing fee is $105.00, or such other amount as may be prescribed by statute.

(2) *Mistaken Filing.* If a notice of appeal is mistakenly filed with the BAP, the Clerk shall follow the procedures set forth in Rule 8002(a) of the Federal Rules of Bankruptcy Procedure.

(b) Notice of Appeal: Form.

(1) *Format.* The notice of appeal must conform in substance to Official Form 17. The notice of appeal shall be accompanied by a filed, stamped copy of the bankruptcy court order or judgment from which the appeal is taken.

(2) *Designation of Parties.* The notice of appeal shall set forth the names of all parties to the judgment, order or decree appealed from as well as the names, addresses and telephone numbers of their respective attorneys. [The term "et al." may not be used in the caption of the notice of appeal.]

(3) *Signature.* Every notice of appeal shall be signed by counsel for the appellant or, if unrepresented, by the appellant personally.

(c) Voluntary Dismissal of Appeal.

(1) *Before Docketing.* If an appeal has not yet been docketed in the BAP, it may be dismissed in the bankruptcy court upon the filing of a stipulation signed by all parties or on a proper motion and notice by all appellants.

(2) *After Docketing.* If an appeal has been docketed in the BAP, it may be dismissed by the parties in the manner set forth in Rule 8001(c)(2) of the Federal Rules of Bankruptcy Procedure. An appeal may also be dismissed on motion of all appellants, if no response or opposition is filed within ten (10) days after service of the motion, on terms and conditions determined by the BAP.

(d) Forum for Appeal: BAP and Opt–Out to District Court.

(1) *Appeals to the First Circuit Bankruptcy Appellate Panel.* All appeals from bankruptcy courts are to the BAP, unless an election is made under sub-section (2) of this Rule.

(2) *Election to Have Appeal Heard by District Court.*

(i) Election by Appellant. An appellant electing to have an appeal heard by the district court pursuant to 28 U.S.C. § 158(c)(1) must file, with the notice of appeal, a separate written statement of election to have the appeal heard by the district court. The separate written statement shall include the case caption and be clearly entitled "Election to Proceed to District Court," and be accompanied by sufficient copies of the statement to enable the bankruptcy court clerk to effect the notice required under subpart (d)(3) of this Rule. Failure to so elect at the time of filing the notice of appeal waives the right of election under 28 U.S.C. 158(c)(1) and Rule 8001(e) of the Federal Rules of Bankruptcy Procedure.

(ii) Election by Appellee. An appellee electing to have an appeal heard by the district court must file, within thirty (30) days from service of the notice of appeal, a separate written statement of election to have the appeal heard by the district court. The separate written statement shall include the case caption and shall be clearly entitled "Election to Proceed to District Court," and be accompanied by sufficient copies of the separate statement to enable the BAP Clerk to effect the notice required under subpart (d)(3) of this Rule. Except as otherwise ordered by the BAP, the filing of any paper [other than a notice of appearance] with the BAP or with the bankruptcy court by an appellee or any other party in interest prior to making an Election to Proceed to District Court shall be deemed a waiver of any time remaining in the thirty (30) day election period.

(iii) Consent. Failure to file a timely written election to have an appeal heard by the district court shall be deemed consent that the appeal be heard by the BAP.

(3) *Procedure Upon Opt–Out.*

(i) If an appellant timely elects to have its appeal heard by the district court, the clerk of the bankruptcy court shall so notify the parties, the United States trustee and the BAP Clerk, by serving each with a copy of the separate written statement of election at the time service of the notice of the appeal is effected pursuant to Fed.R.Bankr.P. 8004. If an appellee so elects, the BAP Clerk shall notify the parties, the United States trustee, and the clerk of the bankruptcy court, by serving each with a copy of the separate statement of election immediately upon its filing.

(ii) Upon an effective election by an appellant, the bankruptcy court clerk shall direct the appeal to the district court in accordance with any established rules in the district. Upon an effective election by an appellee, the BAP Clerk shall transfer to the bankruptcy court all pleadings filed with the BAP and a certified copy of the BAP docket sheet.

(4) *Challenges to Election.* Challenges to the effectiveness of an election to proceed before the district court shall, in the case of an appellant's election, be referred to the district court for determination. In

the case of an election by an appellee, such challenges shall be referred to the appropriate BAP judge(s).

[Effective November 3, 1997.]

RULE 8003–1. MOTION FOR LEAVE TO FILE INTERLOCUTORY APPEAL

(a) **Motion Required.** Grant of leave to appeal from an interlocutory judgment, order or decree is discretionary with the BAP. Parties seeking leave to bring an interlocutory appeal must file in the bankruptcy court clerk's office a motion, containing the matters set forth in Fed.R.Bankr.P. 8003(a), together with a notice of appeal. The moving party shall serve its motion upon all other parties named in the notice of appeal accompanying its motion and upon the United States trustee. A party seeking leave to appeal to the district court must make an affirmative election to have the motion and the interlocutory appeal heard by the district court in the same manner required by 1st Cir. BAP R. 8001–1(d).

(b) **Response.** Unless otherwise ordered, any party opposing a motion for leave to bring an interlocutory appeal before the district court must file its response with the bankruptcy court clerk within 10 days. A party opposing a motion for leave to bring an interlocutory appeal must elect to have the appeal heard by the district court in the same manner as an appellee, and file a separate written statement of such selection within thirty (30) days of service of the motion for leave to appeal. Except as otherwise ordered by the BAP the filing of any paper prior to making the election, including a response to the motion for leave to bring an interlocutory appeal, terminates the time remaining in the thirty (30) day period to elect to have the appeal heard in the district court.

(c) **Decision on Motion.** Unless there is an election to have the interlocutory appeal heard by the district court, the bankruptcy court clerk shall forward the motion and any responses to the BAP for decision. The BAP may render its decision on the motion, with or without a hearing. Upon the entry of the BAP decision or order, the BAP Clerk shall serve the same on the parties and the bankruptcy court clerk.

[Effective November 3, 1997.]

RULE 8005–1. STAY PENDING APPEAL TO BANKRUPTCY APPELLATE PANEL

All parties shall strictly comply with Fed. R.Bankr.P. 8005 upon the filing of a motion for a stay pending appeal of an order, judgment or decree of a bankruptcy judge.

[Effective November 3, 1997.]

RULE 8006–1. RECORD AND ISSUES ON APPEAL

(a) **Copy of Designation of Record.** Within ten days of filing its designation of record with the bankruptcy court, a party shall provide the Bankruptcy Appellate Panel with three copies of its designation and each item designated.

[Effective April 2, 2002.]

RULE 8007–1. DOCKETING OF APPEAL

Upon receipt of the designated record on appeal, the BAP Clerk shall docket and file the designation and the record with the notice of appeal and immediately issue a notice thereof to all parties appearing on the notice of appeal. Unless otherwise ordered by the BAP, appellant briefs shall be due 15 days from the date of the notice of the *filing* of the designated record. Appellee briefs shall be due 15 days from *service* of opening appellant briefs. *See* Fed. R.Bankr.P. 8009(a).

[Effective November 3, 1997.]

RULE 8008–1. FILING AND SERVICE OF OTHER PAPERS

(a) **Filing Upon Receipt.** All other papers shall be considered timely if received in the office of the BAP Clerk on or before the due date. All papers shall be received, filed and docketed by the BAP Clerk, whether or not timely filed.

(b) **Copies.** Unless otherwise ordered by the BAP, all papers required or permitted to be filed shall include an original and three copies.

(c) **Service.** Copies of all papers filed with the BAP, with the exception of the designated record, must be served by the filing party on all other parties to the appeal in the same manner and form as filed. A signed certificate of service shall be attached to the papers. Although the BAP Clerk shall accept for filing papers lacking a certificate of service, failure to effect service properly or to file such certificate shall be grounds for such sanctions as the BAP may deem appropriate.

(d) **Facsimile Filing.** The BAP Clerk is authorized to accept, for filing, papers transmitted by facsimile equipment in situations determined by the Clerk [or designee] to be of an emergency nature or in other compelling circumstances, subject to such procedures for follow-up filing of hard copies, or otherwise, as the Clerk may from time to time prescribe.

[Effective November 3, 1997.]

RULE 8009–1. TIME FOR FILING BRIEFS AND RELATED PAPERS

(a) **Filing of Briefs.** Unless otherwise ordered by the BAP, the briefing schedule shall be governed by

Fed.R.Bankr.P. 8009(a). All parties shall file briefs in accordance with the governing rule, or affirmatively move for modification of the briefing schedule. Briefs and appendices are considered filed on the date mailed. Fed.R.Bankr.P. 8008(a).

(b) Appendix. Appellant briefs shall be accompanied by relevant appendices containing the matter set forth in Fed.R.Bankr.P. 8009(b). An appellee may serve and file a supplemental appendix as provided in Fed.R.Bankr.P. 8009(b).

(c) Transcript. Appellant shall include in its appendix a transcript or portion thereof of the order or judgment from which the appeal is taken, and/or the findings of fact and conclusions of law orally delivered by the Bankruptcy Court. The parties shall include in their respective appendices all portions of the transcript required for adequate review of the issues before the BAP.

[Effective November 3, 1997.]

RULE 8010–1. FORM OF BRIEFS AND RELATED PAPERS

(a) Length and Content. Opening briefs may not exceed 30 pages and reply briefs may not exceed 20 pages. A party may include copies of relevant statutes, rules and regulations either in an addendum to its brief or in pamphlet form, which shall not be included in the page limit.

(1) *Translations Required.* The Bankruptcy Appellate Panel will reject documents not in the English language unless translations are furnished. Whenever a party cites to a statute, rule or regulation, or an opinion of the Supreme Court of Puerto Rico or other court of Puerto Rico in an appendix, brief or at oral argument and the cited authority is not available in the bound English language volumes, an official, certified or stipulated translation thereof, with three conformed copies, shall be filed. Partial translations are acceptable if stipulated to by the parties or submitted by a party not less than 30 days before oral argument. Where partial translations are submitted by a party, opposing parties may submit, prior to oral argument, translations of such additional parts as they deem necessary for a proper understanding of the substance of any such statute, rule, regulation or holding.

(b) Paper and Margins. Briefs shall be printed on 8½″ by 11″ paper with a one-inch margin on all four sides of text, to include pagination and footnotes.

(c) Spacing, Type and Font Minimal. Briefs shall use the following line format: single spacing for the caption and footnotes, and double-spacing for the main text. All printed matter must appear in at least 11 point type.

(d) Colors of Covers. All briefs shall have a color cover depending on the respective party. Appellant's brief shall have a blue cover; appellee's brief shall have a red cover; and appellant's reply brief shall have a gray cover. The cover of the appendix shall be white.

[Effective November 3, 1997. Amended effective April 2, 2002.]

RULE 8011–1. MOTION PRACTICE

(a) Written Motion Required; Responses. All motions to the BAP shall be in writing and filed with the BAP Clerk and accompanied by a signed certificate of service. Briefs, affidavits and other papers permitted to accompany a motion must be filed with the motion. Unless otherwise directed or ordered, responses or opposition to a motion must be filed within 10 days after *service* of the motion.

(b) Procedural Motions. The BAP Clerk may act on the following motions, if unopposed, without submission to a BAP panel or judge:

(1) Motions relating to the production or filing of the record, transcripts, appendices or briefs on appeal;

(2) Motions for voluntary dismissal of appeals;

(3) Motions to dismiss for want of prosecution;

(4) Motions for extension of time;

(5) Motions for leave to consolidate appeals; and

(6) Such other motions as the BAP may designate the BAP Clerk to act upon and that are subject to disposition by a single judge under Federal Rule of Bankruptcy Procedure 8011(e).

Dispositive orders by the BAP Clerk shall reflect their entry pursuant to this rule. An order entered by the BAP Clerk shall be subject to reconsideration by a single judge or a BAP panel if, within ten (10) days of service of notice of the entry of the order, a party adversely affected thereby moves for reconsideration.

(c) Expedited or Emergency Motions. A party requesting an expedited or emergency determination shall plainly title its motion as one for emergency or expedited relief; clearly setting forth a date or period within which it seeks such determination and requesting that the period for response be reduced to a specified date or period. The circumstances warranting emergency or expedited consideration shall be fully disclosed and explained by a *verified* statement of counsel accompanying the motion, or by the party if not represented by counsel.

(d) Motions During Election Period.

(1) *Place for Filing.* If an appellant has not elected to proceed before the district court at the time its notice of appeal is filed, all motions relating to the appeal shall be filed with the BAP Clerk unless and until the case has been transferred to the district court. *The BAP may not dismiss or finally dispose of an appeal within thirty (30) days from the date of service of the notice of appeal,* but otherwise may fully

consider and dispose of all motions filed within the thirty day period or until an election to proceed before the district court is made.

(2) *Substantive Motions.* Substantive motions (e.g., motions for leave to appeal, to dismiss an appeal, to reduce bond, etc.) shall be forwarded by the BAP Clerk to the full panel for determination. Unless specifically directed by the panel, oral argument will not be held on motions.

(e) Summary Disposition. At any time, on such notice as the Bankruptcy Appellate Panel may direct, on motion of any appellant, any appellee, or sua sponte, the Panel may (i) dismiss the appeal if the Panel lacks jurisdiction, (ii) dismiss the appeal, grant any other request for relief, or affirm and enforce the judgment or order below if it shall clearly appear that no substantial question is presented or (iii) reverse in the case of obvious error. Motions for such relief should be promptly filed when the occasion appears, and must be accompanied by an original and three copies of a memorandum or brief.

[Effective November 3, 1997. Amended effective April 2, 2002.]

RULE 8012–1. ORAL ARGUMENT

(a) Party's Statement. Any party may include, either in the opening or answering brief, a statement limited to one-half page setting forth the reasons oral argument should, or need not, be heard. Any such statement shall be inserted immediately after the Table of Contents and Table of Authorities, and before the first page of the brief, and shall bear the caption "REASONS ORAL ARGUMENT SHOULD [NEED NOT] BE HEARD" as appropriate. This statement shall not be considered in determining the maximum number of pages in the brief.

(b) Notice of Argument. If the Bankruptcy Appellate Panel concludes that oral argument is unnecessary based on the standards set forth in Fed. R.Bankr.P. 8012 counsel shall be so advised. The Panel's decision to dispense with oral argument may be announced by the Panel at the time the decision on the merits is rendered.

(c) Argument.

(1) *Presentation.* At oral argument the parties may expect the Panel to have some familiarity with the briefs and the record on appeal. The Panel will permit no more than 15 minutes per side for oral argument unless a different time is announced by the Panel at the commencement of argument. Counsel shall adhere to the prescribed time limit by their own devices. Where more than one counsel argues on one side of a case, it is their responsibility to assure a fair division of the total time allotted. One or more cases posing

the same issues arising from the same factual context may be treated as a single case for the purposes of this rule.

(2) *Consequence of Failure to File Brief.* A party who fails to file a brief is not entitled to be heard at oral argument, unless the Panel determines otherwise.

[Effective April 2, 2002.]

RULE 8018–1. OPINIONS

(a) Opinions Generally. The Bankruptcy Appellate Panel normally issues a formal opinion which is published and may be cited in future cases. Where an opinion is issued "not for publication" it may be cited only in related cases.

(b) Statement of Policy. Normally, opinions are published in the official printed West reporter so as to be available for citation. This policy may be overcome in situations where an opinion does not articulate a new rule of law, modify an established rule, apply an established rule to novel facts or develop issues sufficiently to serve as a significant guide for future litigants or the Panel.

(c) Opinions and Dispositions Not to Be Used for Citation. Unpublished opinions and dispositions may not be used for citation except to establish res judicata, estoppel, or the law of the case. Otherwise only published opinions may be cited.

(1) If counsel believes that an unpublished disposition has precedential value in relation to a material issue in a case and that no published opinion would serve as well, such disposition may be cited provided a copy is served on all other parties in the case, as well as on the Panel.

[Effective April 2, 2002.]

RULE 8070–1. DISMISSAL OF APPEAL FOR FAILURE TO PROSECUTE

If no party has elected to proceed before the district court and no appellant prosecutes the appeal in accordance with the requirements of the Federal Rules of Bankruptcy Procedure and these rules, the BAP Clerk may enter an order dismissing the appeal for failure to prosecute. The BAP may reinstate the appeal upon motion by a defaulting party, within ten (10) days of service of the order. Such a motion shall not be allowed absent a verified statement by counsel for the defaulting party or by the defaulting party, if pro se, showing special circumstances justifying the failure to comply with the requirements of the Federal Rules of Bankruptcy Procedure or these rules.

[Effective November 3, 1997.]

UNITED STATES DISTRICT COURT FOR THE DISTRICT OF MASSACHUSETTS

Summary of Contents

Local Rules of the United States District Court for the District of Massachusetts.

Expense and Delay Reduction Plan.

Rules for United States Magistrates in the United States District Court for the District of Massachusetts.

Electronic Case Filing

Index.

LOCAL RULES OF THE UNITED STATES DISTRICT COURT FOR THE DISTRICT OF MASSACHUSETTS

Effective September 1, 1990

Including Amendments Received Through January 1, 2005

Research Note

Use WESTLAW® *to find cases citing or applying specific rules.* WESTLAW *may also be used to search for specific terms in court rules or to update court rules. See the* MA–RULES *and* MA–ORDERS *Scope Screens for detailed descriptive information and search tips.*

Amendments to these rules are published, as received, in the North Eastern 2d *and the* Massachusetts Decisions *advance sheets.*

Table of Rules

PREFACE

At the request of the Committee on Rules and Practice of the Judicial Conference of the United States, local rules dealing with civil practice have been renumbered to key them to the Federal Rules of Civil Procedure. Accordingly, the numbering is not sequential. Criminal Rules will be numbered from 100 to 199, and district court rules relating to bankruptcy from 200 to 299.

RULE 1.1   TITLE

These rules shall be known as Local Rules of the United States District Court for the District of Massachusetts and cited as "LR, D.Mass." or "LR."

Effective September 1, 1990.

RULE 1.2   APPLICATION

(a) **In General.** These rules shall apply to all proceedings in the United States District Court for the District of Massachusetts.

(b) Cases Pending When Rules Adopted and Amended. These rules became effective in this form on September 1, 1990, and have been amended from time to time thereafter. They shall, except as applicable time periods may have run, govern all actions and proceedings pending on or commenced after the date of adoption or amendment. Where justice so requires, proceedings in designated cases or other matters before the court on the effective date of the adoption or amendment of these rules shall be governed by the practice of the court before the adoption of these rules.

Effective September 1, 1990; amended effective October 1, 1992.

RULE 1.3   SANCTIONS

Failure to comply with any of the directions or obligations set forth in, or authorized by, these Local Rules may result in dismissal, default, or the imposition of other sanctions as deemed appropriate by the judicial officer.

Adopted effective October 1, 1992.

RULE 3.1   CIVIL COVER SHEET

The party filing the initial pleading shall also file a civil cover sheet in the form prescribed by the Judicial Conference of the United States (JS 44) and the local category sheet.

Effective September 1, 1990.

RULE 4.1   SERVICE OF PROCESS— DISMISSAL FOR FAILURE TO MAKE SERVICE

(A) Any summons not returned with proof that it was served within one-hundred twenty (120) days of the filing of the complaint is deemed to be unserved for the purpose of Fed.R.Civ.P. 4(m).

(B) Counsel and parties appearing pro se who seek to show good cause for the failure to make service within the 120 day period prescribed by Fed.R.Civ.P. 4(m) shall do so by filing a motion for enlargement of time under Fed.R.Civ.P. 6(b), together with a supporting affidavit. If on the tenth day following the expiration of the 120 day period good cause has not been shown as provided herein, the clerk shall forthwith automatically enter an order of dismissal for failure to effect service of process, without awaiting any further order of the court. The clerk shall furnish a copy of this local rule to counsel or pro se plaintiffs, together with the summons, and delivery of this copy by the clerk will constitute the notice required by Rule 4(m) Federal Rules of Civil Procedure. Such notice shall constitute the notice required by Fed.R.Civ.P. 4(m). No further notice need be given by the court.

(C) In those cases where the Federal Rules of Civil Procedure authorize service of process to be made in accordance with state practice, it shall be the duty of counsel for the party seeking such service to furnish to the Clerk of Court forms of all necessary orders and sufficient copies of all papers to comply with the requirements of the state practice, together with specific instructions for the making of such service, if such service is to be made by the United States marshal.

Effective September 1, 1990; amended effective January 2, 1995.

RULE 4.5   FEES

(a) Except as otherwise provided by law, the clerk and other officers and employees of the court shall not be required to perform any service for a party other than the United States for which a fee is lawfully prescribed, unless the amount of the fee, if it is known, or an amount sufficient to cover the fee reasonably expected by the officer to come due for performance of the service has been deposited with the court.

(b) This provision shall not apply to the United States or a party who is proceeding in forma pauperis, or in any other situation where, in the judgment of the officer entitled to a fee, it is unnecessary to ensure payment of the fee and would work hardship or an injustice.

(c) The clerk shall receive for filing all complaints accompanied by a request to proceed in forma pauperis, and note the date thereon. If the request is denied, the matter will be noted on the miscellaneous business docket. If the request is allowed, or the denial is reversed, the clerk shall file the complaint on the civil docket. Requests to proceed in forma pauperis shall be accompanied by an affidavit containing details of the individual's financial status. (The recommended form is available without charge from the clerk's office.)

(d) In seamen's cases, or cases in which the plaintiff is granted leave to proceed in forma pauperis, the plaintiff remains liable for filing and other fees in the event he is the prevailing party at settlement or otherwise, and he collects a money judgment or any costs taxed by the court or clerk. These fees are payable forthwith upon collection of any sums from the defendant.

(e) The clerk shall on request file notices of appeal whether or not accompanied by the required filing fee.

Effective September 1, 1990.

[Publisher's Note: See also, "Appendix A. Local Rule 4.5 Supplement."]

RULE 5.1   FORM AND FILING OF PAPERS

(a) Form and Signing of Papers.

(1) The provisions of the Federal Rules of Civil Procedure pertaining to the form and signing of plead-

ings, motions, and other papers shall be applicable to all papers filed in any proceeding in this court. The board of bar overseers registration number of each attorney signing such documents, except the United States Attorney and his staff, shall be inscribed below the signature.

(2) All papers filed in the court shall be adapted for flat filing, be filed on 8½″ × 11″ paper without backers and be bound firmly by staple or some such other means (excluding paper or binder clip or rubber band). All papers, except discovery requests and responses, shall be double-spaced except for the identification of counsel, title of the case, footnotes, quotations and exhibits. Discovery requests and responses shall be single-spaced. Except for complaints and notices of appeal, papers that do not conform to the requirements of this subsection shall be returned by the clerk.

(b) Time and Place of Filing. Except as noted in Rule 33–36(f), the original of all papers required to be served under Fed.R.Civ.P. 5(d) shall, unless otherwise submitted to the court, be filed in the office of the clerk within three (3) days after service has been made.

(c) Requests for Special Action. When any pleading or other paper filed in the court includes a request for special process or relief, or any other request such that, if granted, the court will proceed other than in the ordinary course, the request shall, unless it is noted on the category sheet [*see* Rule 40.1(a)(1)], be noted on the first page to the right of or immediately beneath the caption.

(d) Additional Copies. Whenever, because of the nature of a proceeding, such as a proceeding before a three-judge district court under 28 U.S.C. § 2284, additional copies of a paper required to be filed are necessary either for the use of the court or to enable the clerk to carry out his duties, it is the responsibility of the party filing or having filed the paper to provide the necessary copies.

(e) Removal of Papers. Except as otherwise provided, papers filed in the office of the clerk shall not be removed from the office except by a judge, official, or employee of the court using the papers in official capacity, or by order of the court. All other persons removing papers from the office of the clerk shall prepare, sign and furnish to the clerk a descriptive receipt therefor in a form satisfactory to the clerk.

Effective September 1, 1990.

RULE 5.2   SERVICE AND FILING OF PLEADINGS AND OTHER PAPERS

(a) Manner of Service. Service of all pleadings subsequent to the original complaint and of all other papers required to be served shall be made in the manner specified by Rule 5, Federal Rules of Civil Procedure.

(b) Proof of Service.

(1) Except as otherwise provided by the Federal Rules of Civil Procedure, proof of service of all pleadings and other papers required to be served (except discovery papers that in accordance with Rule 33–36(f) are not to be filed) shall be filed in the office of the clerk promptly after service has been made. The proof shall show the time and manner of service, and may be made by written acknowledgment of service, a certificate of a member of the bar of this court, or an affidavit of the person who served the paper.

(2) A certificate of service of a member of the bar shall appear at the bottom of or on the margin of the last page of the paper to which it relates. The certificate shall be a brief, single-spaced statement and may be in the following form:

I hereby certify that a true copy of the above document was served upon (each party appearing pro se and) the attorney of record for each other party by mail (by hand) on (date). (Signature)

On or after the effective date of these local rules, documents not conforming to the requirements of this rule (except notices of appeal) shall be returned by the clerk.

(3) Failure to make proof of service does not affect the validity of the service.

(c) Service on Nonresident Attorney or Party Acting Pro Se.

(1) *Nonresident Attorney.* On application of a party, the court may order an attorney who represents any other party and who does not maintain an office within this district where service can be made on him by delivery as provided by Rule 5(b), Federal Rules of Civil Procedure, to designate a member of the bar of this court who does maintain such an office to receive service of all pleadings and other papers in his behalf.

(2) *Party Acting Pro Se.* On application of a party, the court may order any other party who is appearing without an attorney and who does not maintain an office or residence within this district where service can be made on him by delivery as provided by Rule 5(b), Federal Rules of Civil Procedure, to designate an address within the district at which service can be made on him by delivery.

Effective September 1, 1990.

RULE 5.3   PERSONAL DATA IDENTIFIERS

(A) Restrictions on Personal Identifiers in Filings. In compliance with the policy of the Judicial Conference of the United States, and the E-Government Act of 2002, and in order to promote electronic access to case files while also protecting personal privacy and other legitimate interests, parties shall refrain from including, or shall partially redact where inclusion is necessary, the following personal data identifiers from all filings submitted to the court, including exhibits thereto, whether filed electronically or in paper, unless otherwise ordered by the Court.

(1) *Social Security Numbers.* If an individual's social security number must be included in a filing, only the last four digits of that number should be used.

(2) *Names of Minor Children.* If the involvement of a minor child must be mentioned, only the initials of that child should be used.

(3) *Dates of Birth.* If an individual's date of birth must be included in a pleading, only the year should be used.

(4) *Financial Account Numbers.* If financial account numbers are relevant, only the last four digits of these numbers should be used.

(B) Non-Redacted Filings Under Seal. In compliance with the E-Government Act of 2002, a party wishing to file a document containing the personal data identifiers listed above may file an unredacted document under seal, pursuant to Local Rule 7.2. This document shall be retained by the court as part of the record. The court may, however, still require the party to file a redacted copy for the public file.

(C) Responsibility for Redaction. The responsibility for redacting these personal identifiers rests solely with counsel and the parties. The Clerk will not review each pleading for compliance with this rule.

Effective May 6, 2003.

RULE 7.1   MOTION PRACTICE

(A) Control of Motion Practice.

(1) *Plan for the Disposition of Motions.* At the earliest practicable time, the judicial officer shall establish a framework for the disposition of motions, which, at the discretion of the judicial officer, may include specific deadlines or general time guidelines for filing motions. This framework may be amended from time to time by the judicial officer as required by the progress of the case.

(2) *Motion Practice.* No motion shall be filed unless counsel certify that they have conferred and have attempted in good faith to resolve or narrow the issue.

(3) *Unresolved Motions.* The court shall rule on motions as soon as practicable, having in mind the reporting requirements set forth in the Civil Justice Reform Act.

(B) Submission of Motion and Opposition to Motion.

(1) *Submission of Motion.* A party filing a motion shall at the same time file a memorandum of reasons, including citation of supporting authorities, why the

motion should be granted. Affidavits and other documents setting forth or evidencing facts on which the motion is based shall be filed with the motion.

(2) *Submission of Opposition to a Motion.* A party opposing a motion, shall file an opposition to the motion within fourteen (14) days after service of the motion, unless another period is fixed by rule or statute, or by order of the court, and in the same (rather than a separate), document a memorandum of reasons, including citation of supporting authorities, why the motion should not be granted. Affidavits and other documents setting forth or evidencing facts on which the opposition is based shall be filed with the opposition. The fourteen day period is intended to include the period specified by the civil rules for mailing time and provide for a uniform period regardless of the use of the mails.

(3) *Additional Papers.* All other papers not filed as indicated in subsections (B)(1) and (2), whether in the form of a reply brief or otherwise, may be submitted only with leave of court.

(4) Memoranda supporting or opposing allowance of motions shall not, without leave of court, exceed twenty (20) pages, double-spaced.

(C) Service. All papers filed pursuant to section (B) shall be served unless the moving party indicates in writing on the face of the motion that ex parte consideration is requested. Motions filed "ex parte" and related papers need not be served until the motion has been ruled upon or the court orders that service be made.

(D) Request for Hearing. Any party making or opposing a motion who believes that oral argument may assist the court and wishes to be heard shall include a request for oral argument in a separate paragraph of the motion or opposition. The request should be set off with a centered caption, "REQUEST FOR ORAL ARGUMENT."

(E) Hearing. If the court concludes that there should be a hearing on a motion, the motion will be set down for hearing at such time as the court determines.

(F) Decision of Motion Without Hearing. Motions that are not set down for hearing as provided in subsection (E) will be decided on the papers submitted after an opposition to the motion has been filed, or, if no opposition is filed, after the time for filing an opposition has elapsed.

Effective September 1, 1990; amended effective October 1, 1992.

RULE 7.2   IMPOUNDED
AND CONFIDENTIAL
MATERIALS

(a) Whenever a party files a motion to impound, the motion shall contain a statement of the earliest date on which the impounding order may be lifted, or a statement, supported by good cause, that the material should be impounded until further order of the court. The motion shall contain suggested custody arrangements for the post-impoundment period.

(b) The clerk shall attach a copy of the order to the envelope or other container holding the impounded material.

(c) If the impoundment order provides a cut-off date but no arrangements for custody, the clerk (without further notice to the court or the parties) shall place the material in the public information file upon expiration of the impoundment period. If the order provides for post-impoundment custody by counsel or the parties, the materials must be retrieved immediately upon expiration of the order, or the clerk (without further notice to the court or the parties) shall place the material in the public file.

(d) Motions for impoundment must be filed and ruled upon prior to submission of the actual material sought to be impounded, unless the court orders otherwise.

(e) The court will not enter blanket orders that counsel for a party may at any time file material with the clerk, marked confidential, with instructions that the clerk withhold the material from public inspection. A motion for impoundment must be presented each time a document or group of documents is to be filed.

Effective September 1, 1990.

RULE 7.3 CORPORATE DISCLOSURE STATEMENT

(A) A nongovernmental corporate party to a civil action or proceeding in this court must file a statement identifying any parent corporation and any publicly held company that owns 10% or more of the party's stock.

(B) A party must file the Local Rule 7.3(A) statement upon its first appearance, pleading, petition, motion, response, or other request addressed to the court and must promptly supplement the statement upon any change in the information that the statement requires.

Adopted effective January 1, 2001.

RULE 10.1 SOCIAL SECURITY APPEALS [STRICKEN]

Effective September 1, 1990. Stricken effective May 6, 2003.

RULE 15.1 ADDITION OF NEW PARTIES

(A) Amendments Adding Parties. Amendments adding parties shall be sought as soon as an attorney reasonably can be expected to have become aware of the identity of the proposed new party.

(B) Service on New Party. A party moving to amend a pleading to add a new party shall serve, in the manner contemplated by Fed.R.Civ.P. 5(b), the motion to amend upon the proposed new party at least ten (10) days in advance of filing the motion, together with a separate document stating the date on which the motion will be filed. A motion to amend a pleading to add a new party shall be accompanied by a certificate stating that it has been served in advance on the new party as required by this rule.

Adopted effective October 1, 1992; amended effective January 2, 1995.

RULE 16.1 EARLY ASSESSMENT OF CASES

(A) Scheduling Conference in Civil Cases. In every civil action, except in categories of actions exempted by LR 16.2 as inappropriate for scheduling procedures, the judge or, in the interests of the efficient administration of justice, a designated magistrate judge shall convene a scheduling conference as soon as practicable, but in any event within ninety (90) days after the appearance of a defendant and within one hundred twenty (120) days after the complaint has been served on a defendant. In cases removed to this court from a state court or transferred from any other federal court, the judge or designated magistrate judge shall convene a scheduling conference within sixty (60) days after removal or transfer.

(B) Obligation of Counsel to Confer. Unless otherwise ordered by the judge, counsel for the parties must, pursuant to Fed.R.Civ.P. 26(f), confer at least 21 days before the date for the scheduling conference for the purpose of:

(1) preparing an agenda of matters to be discussed at the scheduling conference,

(2) preparing a proposed pretrial schedule for the case that includes a plan for discovery, and

(3) considering whether they will consent to trial by magistrate judge.

(C) Settlement Proposals. Unless otherwise ordered by the judge, the plaintiff shall present written settlement proposals to all defendants no later than ten (10) days before the date for the scheduling conference. Defense counsel shall have conferred with their clients on the subject of settlement before the scheduling conference and be prepared to respond to the proposals at the scheduling conference.

(D) Joint Statement. Unless otherwise ordered by the judge, the parties are required to file, no later than five (5) business days before the scheduling conference and after consideration of the topics contemplated by Fed.R.Civ.P. 16(b) & (c) and 26(f), a joint statement containing a proposed pretrial schedule, which shall include:

(1) a joint discovery plan scheduling the time and length for all discovery events, that shall

(a) conform to the obligation to limit discovery set forth in Fed.R.Civ.P. 26(b), and

(b) take into account the desirability of conducting phased discovery in which the first phase is limited to developing information needed for a realistic assessment of the case and, if the case does not terminate, the second phase is directed at information needed to prepare for trial; and

(2) a proposed schedule for the filing of motions; and

(3) certifications signed by counsel and by an authorized representative of each party affirming that each party and that party's counsel have conferred:

(a) with a view to establishing a budget for the costs of conducting the full course—and various alternative courses—of the litigation; and

(b) to consider the resolution of the litigation through the use of alternative dispute resolution programs such as those outlined in LR 16.4

To the extent that all parties are able to reach agreement on a proposed pretrial schedule, they shall so indicate. To the extent that the parties differ on what the pretrial schedule should be, they shall set forth separately the items on which they differ and indicate the nature of that difference. The purpose of the parties' proposed pretrial schedule or schedules shall be to advise the judge of the parties' best estimates of the amounts of time they will need to accomplish specified pretrial steps. The parties' proposed agenda for the scheduling conference, and their proposed pretrial schedule or schedules, shall be considered by the judge as advisory only.

(E) Conduct of Scheduling Conference. At or following the scheduling conference, the judge shall make an early determination of whether the case is "complex" or otherwise appropriate for careful and deliberate monitoring in an individualized and case-specific manner. The judge shall consider assigning any case so categorized to a case management conference or series of conferences under LR 16.3. The factors to be considered by the judge in making this decision include:

(1) the complexity of the case (the number of parties, claims, and defenses raised, the legal difficulty of the issues presented, and the factual difficulty of the subject matter);

(2) the amount of time reasonably needed by the litigants and their attorneys to prepare the case for trial;

(3) the judicial and other resources required and available for the preparation and disposition of the case;

(4) whether the case belongs to those categories of cases that:

(a) involve little or no discovery,

(b) ordinarily require little or no additional judicial intervention, or

(c) generally fall into identifiable and easily managed patterns;

(5) the extent to which individualized and case-specific treatment will promote the goal of reducing cost and delay in civil litigation; and

(6) whether the public interest requires that the case receive intense judicial attention.

In other respects, the scheduling conference shall be conducted according to the provisions for a pretrial conference under Federal Rule of Civil Procedure 16 and for a case management conference under LR 16.3.

(F) Scheduling Orders. Following the conference, the judge shall enter a scheduling order that will govern the pretrial phase of the case. Unless the judge determines otherwise, the scheduling order shall include specific deadlines or general time frameworks for:

(1) amendments to the pleadings;

(2) service of, and compliance with, written discovery requests;

(3) the completion of depositions, including, if applicable, the terms for taking and using videotape depositions;

(4) the identification of trial experts;

(5) the sequence of disclosure of information regarding experts contemplated by Fed.R.Civ.P. 26(b);

(6) the filing of motions;

(7) a settlement conference, to be attended by trial counsel and, in the discretion of the judge, their clients;

(8) one or more case management conferences and/or the final pretrial conference;

(9) a final pretrial conference, which shall occur within eighteen months after the filing of the complaint;

(10) the joinder of any additional parties;

(11) any other procedural matter that the judge determines is appropriate for the fair and efficient management of the litigation.

(G) Modification of Scheduling Order. The scheduling order shall specify that its provisions, including any deadlines, having been established with the participation of all parties, can be modified only by order of the judge, or the magistrate judge if so authorized by the judge, and only upon a showing of good cause supported by affidavits, other evidentiary materials, or references to pertinent portions of the record.

(H) Definition of Judge. As used in this rule, "judge" refers to the United States District Judge to whom the case is assigned or to the United States Magistrate Judge who has been assigned the case pursuant to 28 U.S.C. § 636(c), if the Magistrate Judge has been assigned the case prior to the convening of the scheduling conference mandated by this rule.

Adopted effective October 1, 1992; amended effective January 2, 1995; December 10, 1996; December 1, 2000; January 2, 2001.

Publisher's Note

See "Attachment C," infra, for the form "Notice of Scheduling Conference" which Judges of the District Court utilize in connection with the conference mandated by LR 16.1.

RULE 16.2　EXEMPTIONS FROM FED.R.CIV.P. 16(b)

Pursuant to Rule 16(b), Federal Rules of Civil Procedure, as amended, the following categories of actions (based upon the numbered "Nature of Suit" list on form JS 44) are exempted in this district from the scheduling and planning provisions of Rule 16(b), Federal Rules of Civil Procedure, as inappropriate actions for such scheduling and planning:

CONTRACT
    150   Recovery of Overpayment & Enforcement of Judgment
    152   Recovery of Defaulted Student Loans
    153   Recovery of Overpayment of Veterans Benefits

REAL PROPERTY
    210   Condemnation
    220   Foreclosure
    230   Rent Lease & Ejectment
    245   Asbestos Cases Only

PRISONER PETITIONS
    510   Vacate Sentence (2255)
    530   Habeas Corpus
    540   Mandamus & Other
    535   Death Penalty
    550   Other

FORFEITURE/PENALTY
    610   Agriculture
    620   Food & Drug
    625   Drug Related Seizure
    630   Liquor Laws
    640   R.R. & Truck
    650   Airline Regs.

BANKRUPTCY
    422   Appeal (22 U.S.C. 158)
    423   Withdrawal (28 U.S.C. 157)

SOCIAL SECURITY
    861   HIA (1395ff)
    862   Black Lung (923)
    863   DIWC (405(g))
    863   DIWW (405(g))
    864   SSID Title XVI
    865   RSI (405(g))

TAX SUITS
    871   IRS–Third Party (26 U.S.C. 7609)

OTHER STATUTES
    400   State Reapportionment
    450   Interstate Freight Damage Claims Only
    875   Customer Challenge (12 U.S.C. 3410)
    900   Appeal of Fee Determination Under Equal Access to Justice Act

Effective September 1, 1990.

RULE 16.3　CASE MANAGEMENT CONFERENCES

(A) Conduct of Case Management Conferences. Case management conferences shall be presided over by a judicial officer who, in furtherance of the scheduling order required by LR 16.1(f) may:

(1) explore the possibility of settlement;

(2) identify or formulate (or order the attorneys to formulate) the principal issues in contention;

(3) prepare (or order the attorneys to prepare) a specific discovery schedule and discovery plan that, if the presiding judicial officer deems appropriate, might:

    (a) identify and limit the volume of discovery available in order to avoid unnecessary or unduly burdensome or expensive discovery;

    (b) sequence discovery into two or more stages; and

    (c) include time limits set for the completion of discovery;

(4) establish deadlines for filing motions and a time framework for their disposition;

(5) provide for the "phased resolution" or "bifurcation of issues for trial" consistent with Federal Rule 42(b); and

(6) explore any other matter that the judicial officer determines is appropriate for the fair and efficient management of the litigation.

(B) Obligation of Counsel to Confer. The judicial officer may require counsel for the parties to confer before the case management conference for the purpose of preparing a joint statement containing:

(1) an agenda of matters that one or more parties believe should be addressed at the conference; and

(2) a report advising the judicial officer whether the case is progressing within the allotted time limits and in accord with the specified pretrial steps.

This statement is to be filed with the court no later than five (5) business days before the case management conference.

(C) Additional Case Management Conferences. Nothing in this rule shall be construed to prevent the convening of additional case management conferences by the judicial officer as may be thought appropriate in the circumstances of the particular case. In any event, a conference should not terminate without the parties being instructed as to when and for what purpose they are to return to the court.

Adopted effective October 1, 1992.

RULE 16.4 ALTERNATIVE DISPUTE RESOLUTION

(A) The judicial officer shall encourage the resolution of disputes by settlement or other alternative dispute resolution programs.

(B) Settlement. At every conference conducted under these rules, the judicial officer shall inquire as to the utility of the parties' conducting settlement negotiations, explore means of facilitating those negotiations, and offer whatever assistance may be appropriate in the circumstances. Assistance may include a reference of the case to another judicial officer for settlement purposes. Whenever a settlement conference is held, a representative of each party who has settlement authority shall attend or be available by telephone.

(C) Other Alternative Dispute Resolution Programs.

(1) *Discretion of Judicial Officer.* The judicial officer, following an exploration of the matter with all counsel, may refer appropriate cases to alternative dispute resolution programs that have been designated for use in the district court or that the judicial officer may make available. The dispute resolution programs described in subdivisions (2) through (4) are illustrative, not exclusive.

(2) *Mini-Trial.*

(a) The judicial officer may convene a mini-trial upon the agreement of all parties, either by written motion or their oral motion in open court entered upon the record.

(b) Each party, with or without the assistance of counsel, shall present his or her position before:

(1) selected representatives for each party, or

(2) an impartial third party, or

(3) both selected representatives for each party and an impartial third party.

(c) An impartial third party may issue an advisory opinion regarding the merits of the case.

(d) Unless the parties agree otherwise, the advisory opinion of the impartial third party is not binding.

(e) The impartial third party's advisory opinion is not appealable.

(f) Neither the advisory opinion of an impartial third party nor the presentations of the parties shall be admissible as evidence in any subsequent proceeding, unless otherwise admissible under the rules of evidence. Also, the occurrence of the mini-trial shall not be admissible.

(3) *Summary Jury Trial.*

(a) The judicial officer may convene a summary jury trial:

(1) with the agreement of all parties, either by written motion or their oral motion in court entered upon the record, or

(2) upon the judicial officer's determination that a summary jury trial would be appropriate, even in the absence of the agreement of all the parties.

(b) There shall be six (6) jurors on the panel, unless the parties agree otherwise.

(c) The panel may issue an advisory opinion regarding:

(1) the respective liability of the parties, or

(2) the damages of the parties, or

(3) both the respective liability and the damages of the parties.

Unless the parties agree otherwise, the advisory opinion is not binding and it shall not be appealable.

(d) Neither the panel's advisory opinion nor its verdict, nor the presentations of the parties shall be admissible as evidence in any subsequent proceeding, unless otherwise admissible under the rules of evidence. Also, the occurrence of the summary jury trial shall not be admissible.

(4) *Mediation.*

(a) The judicial officer may grant mediation upon the agreement of all parties.

(b) The mediator selected may be an individual, group of individuals or institution. The mediator shall be compensated as agreed by the parties.

(c) The mediator shall meet, either jointly or separately, with each party and counsel for each party and shall take any other steps that may appear appropriate in order to assist the parties to resolve the impasse or controversy.

(d) If mediation does not result in a resolution of the dispute, the parties shall promptly report the termination of mediation to the judicial officer.

(e) If an agreement is reached between the parties on any issues, the mediator shall make appropriate note of that agreement and refer the parties to the judicial officer for entry of a court order.

(f) Any communication related to the subject matter of the dispute made during the mediation by any participant, mediator, or any other person present at the mediation shall be a confidential communication to the full extent contemplated by Fed. R.Evid. 408. No admission, representation, statement, or other confidential communication made in setting up or conducting the proceedings not otherwise discoverable or obtainable shall be admissible as evidence or subject to discovery.

Adopted effective October 1, 1992.

RULE 16.5 FINAL PRETRIAL CONFERENCE

(A) **Schedule of Conference.** The judicial officer to whom the case is assigned for trial may set a new date for the final pretrial conference if that judicial officer determines that resolution of the case through settlement or some other form of alternative dispute resolution is imminent.

(B) **Representation by Counsel; Settlement.** Unless excused by the judicial officer to whom the case is assigned for trial, each party shall be represented at the final pretrial conference by counsel who will conduct the trial. Counsel shall have full authority from their clients with respect to settlement and shall be prepared to advise that judicial officer as to the prospects of settlement.

(C) **Disclosures Preliminary to the Pretrial Conference.** As provided in LR 26.4(A), the disclosure regarding experts required by Fed.R.Civ.P. 26(a)(2) shall be made at least 90 days before the final pretrial conference. No later than 30 days before the date of the pretrial conference the parties shall make the pretrial disclosures required by Fed.R.Civ.P. 26(a)(3). Any objections to the use of the evidence identified in the pretrial disclosure required by Fed.R.Civ.P. 26(a)(3) shall be made before counsel confer regarding the pretrial memorandum, shall be a subject of their conference and shall not be filed with the court unless the objections cannot be resolved. Filing of such objections shall be made pursuant to subsection (D)(12) of this rule.

(D) **Obligation of Counsel to Confer and Prepare Pretrial Memorandum.** Unless otherwise ordered by the judicial officer to whom the case is assigned for trial, counsel for the parties shall confer no later than fifteen (15) days before the date of the final pretrial conference for the purpose of jointly preparing a pretrial memorandum for submission to the judicial officer. Unless otherwise ordered by the judicial officer to whom the case is assigned for trial, the parties are required to file, no later than five (5) business days prior to the pre-trial conference, a joint pretrial memorandum which shall set forth:

(1) a concise summary of the evidence that will be offered by:

    (a) plaintiff;

    (b) defendant; and

    (c) other parties;

with respect to both liability and damages (including special damages, if any);

(2) the facts established by pleadings or by stipulations or admissions of counsel;

(3) contested issues of fact;

(4) any jurisdictional questions;

(5) any questions raised by pending motions;

(6) issues of law, including evidentiary questions, together with supporting authority;

(7) any requested amendments to the pleadings;

(8) any additional matters to aid in the disposition of the action;

(9) the probable length of the trial;

(10) the names, addresses and telephone numbers of witnesses to be called (expert and others) and whether the testimony of any such witness is intended to be presented by deposition;

(11) the proposed exhibits; and

(12) the parties' respective positions on any remaining objections to the evidence identified in the pretrial disclosure required by Fed.R.Civ.P. 26(a)(3).

(E) **Conduct of Conference.** The agenda of the final pretrial conference, when possible and appropriate, shall include:

(1) a final and binding definition of the issues to be tried;

(2) the disclosure of expected and potential witnesses and the substance of their testimony;

(3) the exchange of all proposed exhibits;

(4) a pretrial ruling on objections to evidence;

(5) the elimination of unnecessary or redundant proof, including the limitation of expert witnesses;

(6) a consideration of the bifurcation of the issues to be tried;

(7) the establishment of time limits and any other restrictions on the trial;

(8) a consideration of methods for expediting jury selection;

(9) a consideration of means for enhancing jury comprehension and simplifying and expediting the trial;

(10) a consideration of the feasibility of presenting direct testimony by written statement;

(11) the exploration of possible agreement among the parties on various issues and encouragement of a stipulation from the parties, when that will serve the ends of justice, including:

(a) that direct testimony of some or all witnesses will be taken in narrative or affidavit form, with right of cross-examination reserved;

(b) that evidence in affidavit form will be read to the jury by the witnesses, or by counsel or another reader with court approval; and (c) that time limits shorter than those set forth in Rule 43.1 be used for trial; and

(12) a consideration of any other means to facilitate and expedite trial.

(F) Trial Brief. A trial brief, including requests for rulings or instructions, shall be filed by each party five (5) calendar days before the commencement of trial. Each party may supplement these requests at the trial if the evidence develops otherwise than as anticipated.

Adopted effective October 1, 1992; amended effective January 2, 1995.

RULE 26.1 CONTROL OF DISCOVERY

(A) Cooperative Discovery. The judicial officer should encourage cost effective discovery by means of voluntary exchange of information among litigants and their attorneys. This may be accomplished through the use of:

(1) informal, cooperative discovery practices in which counsel provide information to opposing counsel without resort to formal discovery procedures; or

(2) stipulations entered into by the parties with respect to deposition notices, waiver of signing, and other matters, except that the parties may not enter into stipulations extending the time for responding to discovery requests or otherwise modify discovery procedures ordered by the judicial officer.

(B) Disclosure Orders. The judicial officer may order the parties to submit at the scheduling conference, or at any subsequent time the officer deems appropriate, sworn statements disclosing certain information to every other party. At the discretion of the judicial officer, this order may direct the submission of:

(1) a sworn statement from a claimant, whether plaintiff, third-party plaintiff, cross-claimant, or counter-claimant, that:

(a) itemizes all economic loss and provides a computation of damages for which recovery is sought, if any, sustained before the date of service of process;

(b) identifies all persons then known to the claimant or the claimant's attorney who witnessed or

participated in the transaction or occurrence giving rise to the claim or otherwise known or believed to have substantial discoverable information about the claim or defenses, together with a statement of the subject and a brief summary of that information;

(c) identifies all opposing parties, and all officers, directors, and employees of opposing parties, from whom statements have been obtained by or on behalf of the claimant regarding the subject matter of the claim; and

(d) identifies all governmental agencies or officials then known to the claimant or the claimant's attorney to have investigated the transaction or occurrence giving rise to the claim; and

(2) a sworn statement from a defendant, whether the direct defendant, third-party defendant, cross-claim defendant, or counterclaim defendant, that identifies:

(a) all persons then known to the defendant or the defendant's attorneys who witnessed the transaction or occurrence giving rise to the claim or otherwise is known or believed to have substantial discoverable information about the claims or defenses, together with a statement of the subject and a brief summary of that information;

(b) all opposing parties, and all officers, directors, and employees of opposing parties, from whom statements have been obtained by or on behalf of the defendant regarding the subject matter of the claims or defenses; and

(c) all government agencies or officials then known to the defendant or the defendant's attorneys to have investigated the transaction or occurrence giving rise to the claims or defenses.

Noncompliance may be excused only by order of the judicial officer.

(C) Discovery Event Limitations. Unless the judicial officer orders otherwise, the number of discovery events shall be limited for each side (or group of parties with a common interest) to ten (10) depositions, twenty-five (25) interrogatories, twenty-five (25) requests for admissions, and two (2) separate sets of requests for production. For purposes of determining the number of interrogatories propounded, subparts of a basic interrogatory which are logical extensions of the basic interrogatory and seek only to obtain specified additional particularized information with respect to the basic interrogatory shall not be counted separately from the basic interrogatory.

Adopted effective October 1, 1992; amended effective January 2, 1995.

RULE 26.2 SEQUENCES OF DISCOVERY

(A) Automatic Required Disclosure. Unless otherwise ordered by the judge, or by the United States Magistrate Judge who has been assigned the case pursuant to 28 U.S.C. § 636(c), disclosure required by Fed.R.Civ.P. 26(a)(1) should be made as soon as practicable and in any event must be made at or within 14 days after the meeting required by Fed.R.Civ.P. 26(f) and LR 16.1(B). Unless otherwise ordered by such a judicial officer, before a party may initiate discovery, that party must provide to other parties disclosure of the information and materials called for by Fed. R.Civ.P. 26(a)(1).

(B) Further Discovery. Should a party exhaust the opportunities for any type of discovery events under LR 26.1(C), any requests that such party may make for additional interrogatories, depositions, admissions or the production of documents beyond that allowed pursuant to LR 26.1(C) shall be by discovery motion. All requests for additional discovery events, extensions of deadlines, for the completion of discovery or for postponement of the trial must be signed by the attorney and the party making the request.

(C) Certification of Discovery Motions. The judicial officer shall not consider any discovery motion that is not accompanied by a certification, as required by LR 7.1(A)(2) and LR 37.1(B), that the moving party has made a reasonable and good-faith effort to reach agreement with opposing counsel on the matters set forth in the motion. In evaluating any discovery motion, the judicial officer may consider the desirability of conducting phased discovery, as contemplated by LR 26.3.

(D) Removed and Transferred Actions. In all actions removed to this court or transferred to this court from another federal court, the submission required by subdivision (A) shall be made as prescribed in that subdivision, and if discovery was initiated before the action being removed or transferred to this court, then the submission required by subdivision (A) shall be made within twenty (20) days of the date of removal or transfer.

Adopted effective October 1, 1992; amended effective January 2, 1995; December 10, 1996; December 1, 2000.

RULE 26.3   PHASING OF DISCOVERY

In order to facilitate settlement and the efficient completion of discovery, the judicial officer has discretion to structure discovery activities by phasing and sequencing the topics which are the subject of discovery. For example, an order may be framed limiting the first phase to developing information needed for a realistic assessment of the case. If the case does not terminate, the second phase would be directed at information needed to prepare for trial.

Adopted effective October 1, 1992; amended effective January 2, 1995.

RULE 26.4   SPECIAL PROCEDURES FOR HANDLING EXPERTS

(A) Objections to Expert Witnesses. Unless otherwise directed by the judicial officer, the disclosure

regarding experts required by Fed.R.Civ.P. 26(a)(2) shall be made at least 90 days before the final pretrial conference. A party who intends to object to the qualifications of an expert witness, or to the introduction of any proposed exhibit related to that expert's testimony, shall give written notice of the grounds of objection, together with supporting authority, to all other parties no later than the time for such objections provided in LR 16.5(c).

(B) Setting Terms and Conditions. At the final pretrial conference, the judge shall consider:

(1) precluding the appearance of expert witnesses not timely identified;

(2) precluding use of any trial testimony by an expert at variance with any written statement or any deposition testimony;

(3) making a ruling concerning the use of expert depositions, including videotaped depositions at trial; and

(4) making any other ruling on the admissibility of expert testimony at the trial.

Adopted effective October 1, 1992; amended effective January 2, 1995.

RULE 26.5   UNIFORM DEFINITIONS IN DISCOVERY REQUESTS

(A) Incorporation by Reference and Limitations. The full text of the definitions set forth in paragraph (C) is deemed incorporated by reference into all discovery requests, but shall not preclude

(1) the definition of other terms specific to the particular litigation;

(2) the use of abbreviations; or

(3) a narrower definition of a term defined in paragraph (C).

(B) Effect on Scope of Discovery. This rule is not intended to broaden or narrow the scope of discovery permitted by the Federal Rules of Civil Procedure.

(C) Definitions. The following definitions apply to all discovery requests:

(1) *Communication.* The term "communication" means the transmittal of information (in the form of facts, ideas, inquiries, or otherwise).

(2) *Document.* The term "document" is defined to be synonymous in meaning and equal in scope to the usage of this term in Fed.R.Civ.P. 34(a). A draft or non-identical copy is a separate document within the meaning of this term.

(3) *Identify (With Respect to Persons).* When referring to a person, "to identify" means to give, to the extent known, the person's full name, present or last

known address, and, when referring to a natural person, the present or last known place of employment. Once a person has been identified in accordance with this subparagraph, only the name of that person need be listed in response to subsequent discovery requesting the identification of that person.

(4) *Identify (With Respect to Documents).* When referring to documents, "to identify" means to give, to the extent known, the

(a) type of document;

(b) general subject matter;

(c) date of the document; and

(d) author(s), addressee(s), and recipient(s).

(5) *Parties.* The terms "plaintiff" and "defendant" as well as a party's full or abbreviated name or a pronoun referring to a party mean the party and, where applicable, its officers, directors, employees, partners, corporate parent, subsidiaries, or affiliates. This definition is not intended to impose a discovery obligation on any person who is not a party to the litigation.

(6) *Person.* The term "person" is defined as any natural person or any business, legal, or governmental entity or association.

(7) *Concerning.* The term "concerning" means referring to, describing, evidencing, or constituting.

(8) *State the Basis.* When an interrogatory calls upon a party to "state the basis" of or for a particular claim, assertion, allegation, or contention, the party shall

(a) identify each and every document (and, where pertinent, the section, article, or subparagraph thereof), which forms any part of the source of the party's information regarding the alleged facts or legal conclusions referred to by the interrogatory;

(b) identify each and every communication which forms any part of the source of the party's information regarding the alleged facts or legal conclusions referred to by the interrogatory;

(c) state separately the acts or omissions to act on the part of any person (identifying the acts or omissions to act by stating their nature, time, and place and identifying the persons involved) which form any part of the party's information regarding the alleged facts or legal conclusions referred to in the interrogatory; and

(d) state separately any other fact which forms the basis of the party's information regarding the alleged facts or conclusions referred to in the interrogatory.

Adopted effective October 1, 1992.

RULE 26.6 COURT FILINGS AND COSTS

(A) Nonfiling of Discovery Materials. Automatic or voluntary disclosure materials, depositions upon oral examinations and notices thereof, depositions upon written questions, interrogatories, requests for documents, requests for admissions, answers and responses thereto, and any other requests for or products of the discovery process shall not be filed unless so ordered by the court or for use in the proceeding. The party taking a deposition or obtaining any material through discovery is responsible for its preservation and delivery to the court if needed or so ordered. If for any reason a party or concerned citizen believes that any of the named documents should be filed, an ex parte request may be made that such document be filed, stating the reasons therefor. The court may also order filing sua sponte. If relief is sought under Fed.R.Civ.P. 26(c) or 37, copies of the relevant portions of disputed documents shall be filed with the court contemporaneously with any motion. If the moving party under Fed.R.Civ.P. 56 or the opponent relies on discovery documents, copies of the pertinent parts thereof shall be filed with the motion or opposition.

(B) Copying Expense for Discovery Materials.

(1) *Inspection of Documents.* Except as otherwise provided in an order entered pursuant to Fed.R.Civ.P. 26(c), all parties to an action shall be entitled to inspect documents produced by another party pursuant to Fed.R.Civ.P. 33(c) or 34 at the location where they are produced.

(2) *Copies of Documents.* Except as otherwise provided in an order entered pursuant to Fed.R.Civ.P. 26(c), upon request of any party, and upon that party's agreement to pay the copying costs at the time of delivery, a party who produces documents pursuant to Fed.R.Civ.P. 33(c) or 34 shall provide copies of all or any specified part of the documents. No party shall be entitled to obtain copies of documents produced by another party pursuant to Fed.R.Civ.P. 33(c) or 34 without paying the costs thereof.

Adopted effective October 1, 1992; amended effective January 2, 1995.

RULE 30.1 PLACE FOR TAKING DEPOSITIONS

For purposes of Rule 45(d)(2), Federal Rules of Civil Procedure, without further order of the court:

(a) Boston shall be deemed a convenient place for taking of a deposition of any person who resides, is employed, or transacts business in person in any of the following counties: Suffolk, Bristol, Essex, Middlesex, Norfolk, Plymouth and Worcester.

(b) Springfield shall be deemed a convenient place for taking of a deposition of any person who resides, is employed, or transacts business in person in any of the following counties: Berkshire, Franklin, Hampden and Hampshire.

Effective September 1, 1990.

RULE 30.2 OPENING OF DEPOSITIONS

(a) If filed, unless the court directs otherwise, depositions taken pursuant to Rule 26, Federal Rules of Civil Procedure, in a pending action shall be opened by the clerk and made available for inspection and copying on request of any party or counsel for any party to the proceeding.

(b) Depositions before action or pending appeal taken pursuant to Rule 27, Federal Rules of Civil Procedure, shall be opened by the clerk and made available for inspection and copying on request of any person served with notice pursuant to subsection (a)(2) of that rule, or by counsel for such person.

Effective September 1, 1990.

RULE 33.1 INTERROGATORIES

(A) **Form of Response.**

(1) Answers and objections in response to interrogatories, served pursuant to Fed.R.Civ.P. 33 shall be made in the order of the interrogatories propounded.

(2) Each answer, statement, or objection shall be preceded by the interrogatory to which it responds.

(3) Each objection and the grounds therefor shall be stated separately.

(B) **Reference to Records.** Whenever a party answers any interrogatory by reference to records from which the answer may be derived or ascertained, as permitted in Federal Rule of Civil Procedure 33(c):

(1) the specification of documents to be produced shall be in sufficient detail to permit the interrogating party to locate and identify the records and to ascertain the answer as readily as could the party from whom discovery is sought;

(2) the producing party shall make available any computerized information or summaries thereof that it either has, or can adduce by a relatively simple procedure, unless these materials are privileged or otherwise immune from discovery;

(3) the producing party shall provide any relevant compilations, abstracts, or summaries in its custody or readily obtainable by it, unless these materials are privileged or otherwise immune from discovery; and

(4) the documents shall be made available for inspection and copying within fourteen (14) days after service of the answers to interrogatories or at a date agreed upon by the parties.

(C) **Objections to Interrogatories.**

(1) When an objection is made to any interrogatory, or subpart thereof, it shall state with specificity all grounds upon which the objecting party relies. Any ground not stated in an objection within the time provided by the Federal Rules of Civil Procedure, or any extensions thereof, shall be deemed waived.

(2) No part of an interrogatory shall be left unanswered merely because an objection is interposed to another part of the interrogatory.

(D) **Answers to Interrogatories Following Objections.** Answers to interrogatories with respect to which objections were served and which are subsequently required to be answered shall be served within fourteen (14) days after it is determined that they should be answered, unless the court directs otherwise.

(E) **Claims of Privilege.** When a claim of privilege is asserted in objection to any interrogatory, or any sub-part thereof, and an answer is not provided on the basis of that assertion, the attorney asserting the privilege shall identify in the objection the nature of the privilege that is being claimed. If the privilege is being asserted in connection with a claim or defense governed by state law, the attorney asserting the privilege shall indicate the particular privilege rule that is being invoked.

Adopted effective October 1, 1992; amended effective January 2, 1995.

RULE 34.1 DOCUMENT PRODUCTION

(A) **Form of Response.**

(1) Answers and objections in response to requests for document production, served pursuant to Fed. R.Civ.P. 34 shall be made in the order of the requests propounded.

(2) Each answer, statement, or objection shall be preceded by the request to which it responds.

(3) Each objection and the grounds therefor shall be stated separately.

(B) [RESERVED].

(C) **Objections to Document Request.**

(1) When an objection is made to any document request, or sub-part thereof, it shall state with specificity all grounds upon which the objecting party relies. Any ground not stated in an objection within the time provided by the Federal Rules of Civil Procedure, or any extensions thereof, shall be deemed waived.

(2) No part of a document request shall be left unanswered merely because an objection is interposed to another part of the document request.

(D) **Answers to Document Request Following Objections.** Answers to a document request with respect to which objections were served and which are subsequently required to be answered shall be served within fourteen (14) days after it is determined that they should be answered, unless the court directs otherwise.

(E) **Claims of Privilege.** When a claim of privilege is asserted in objection to any document request, or any sub-part thereof, and any document is not provided on the basis of that assertion, the attorney asserting the privilege shall identify in the objection the nature of the privilege that is being claimed with respect to each such document. If the privilege is being asserted in connection with a claim or defense governed by state law, the attorney asserting the privilege shall indicate the particular privilege rule that is being invoked.

Adopted effective October 1, 1992; amended effective January 2, 1995.

RULE 35.1 DISCLOSURE OF MEDICAL INFORMATION IN PERSONAL INJURY CASES

(A) Disclosure by Claimants. Fourteen (14) days after an issue is joined by a responsive pleading, a claimant, whether plaintiff, third-party plaintiff, cross-claimant, or counter-claimant, who asserts a claim for personal injuries shall serve defendant, whether the direct defendant, third-party defendant, cross-claim defendant, or counterclaim defendant with

(1) an itemization of all medical expenses incurred before the date of service of the pleading containing the claim for which recovery is sought. If the claimant anticipates that recovery will be sought for future medical expenses, the itemization shall so state, but need not set forth an amount for the anticipated future medical expenses;

(2) a statement that either:

(a) identifies a reasonably convenient location and date, within no more than fourteen (14) days, at which the defendant may inspect and copy, at the defendant's expense, all non-privileged medical records pertaining to the diagnosis, care, or treatment of injuries for which recovery is sought; or

(b) identifies all health care providers from which the claimant has received diagnosis, care, or treatment of injuries for which recovery is sought together with executed releases directed at each provider authorizing disclosure to the defendant or its counsel of all non-privileged medical records in the provider's possession.

(B) Assertion of Privilege. Insofar as medical records are not produced in accordance with subdivision (a)(2) on the ground of privilege, the claimant shall identify the privileged documents and state the privilege pursuant to which they are withheld.

(C) Removed and Transferred Actions. In all actions removed to this court from a state court or transferred to this court from another federal court, claimants seeking recovery for personal injuries shall provide the information and materials described in subdivision (A) within twenty (20) days after the date of removal or transfer.

Adopted effective October 1, 1992.

RULE 36.1 ADMISSIONS

(A) Requests for Admission—Form of Response.

(1) Statements and objections in response to requests for admission served pursuant to Fed.R.Civ.P. 36 shall be made in the order of the requests for admission propounded.

(2) Each answer, statement, or objection shall be preceded by the request for admission to which it responds.

(3) Each objection and the grounds therefor shall be stated separately.

(B) Statements in Response to Requests for Admission Following Objections. When there is objection to a request for admission and it is subsequently determined that the request is proper, the matter, the admission of which is requested, shall be deemed admitted unless within fifteen (15) days after such determination such party to whom the request was directed serves a statement denying the matter or setting forth the reasons why that party cannot admit or deny the matter, as provided in Fed.R.Civ.P. 36.

Adopted effective October 1, 1992; amended effective January 2, 1995.

RULE 37.1 DISCOVERY DISPUTES

(A) Before filing any discovery motion, including any motion for sanctions or for a protective order, counsel for each of the parties shall confer in good faith to narrow the areas of disagreement to the greatest possible extent. It shall be the responsibility of counsel for the moving party to arrange for the conference. Conferences may be conducted over the telephone. Failure of opposing counsel to respond to a request for a discovery conference within seven (7) days of the request shall be grounds for sanctions, which may include automatic allowance of the motion.

(B) If (I) opposing counsel has failed to respond to a request for a discovery conference within the seven day period set forth in subdivision (A), (II) opposing counsel has failed to attend a discovery conference within fourteen (14) calendar days of the request, or (III) if disputed issues are not resolved at the discovery conference, a dissatisfied party may file a motion and supporting memorandum. The motion shall include a certificate in the margin of the last page that the provisions of this rule have been complied with. The memorandum shall state with particularity the following:

(1) If a discovery conference was not held, the reasons why it was not;

(2) If a discovery conference was held, the time, date, location and duration of the conference; who was present for each party; the matters on which the parties reached agreement; and the issues remaining to be decided by the court;

(3) The nature of the case and the facts relevant to the discovery matters to be decided;

(4) Each interrogatory, deposition question, request for production, request for admission or other discovery matter raising an issue to be decided by the court, and the response thereto; and

(5) A statement of the moving party's position as to each contested issue, with supporting legal authority, which statement shall be set forth separately immediately following each contested item.

(C) The opposing party may respond to the memorandum within fourteen (14) calendar days after service thereof. The response, if any, shall conform to the requirements of subdivision (B)(5) of this Rule.

Adopted effective October 1, 1992.

RULE 40.1   ASSIGNMENT OF CASES

(A) Civil Cases.

(1) *Categories of Cases.* All civil cases shall be divided into the following five categories for purposes of assignment, based upon the numbered Nature of the Suit listed in the civil cover sheet used by the clerk in initiating the civil docket:

I —   160, 410, 470, 535, R.23, regardless of nature of suit.

II —   195, 368, 400, 440, 441–444, 540, 550, 555, 625, 710, 720, 730, 740, 790, 791, 820, 830, 840, 850, 890, 892–894, 895, 950.

III —   110, 120, 130, 140, 151, 190, 210, 230, 240, 245, 290, 310, 315, 320, 330, 340, 345, 350, 355, 360, 362, 365, 370, 371, 380, 385, 450, 891.

IV —   220, 422, 423, 430, 460, 510, 530, 610, 620, 630, 640, 650, 660, 690, 810, 861–865, 870, 871, 875, 900.

V —   150, 152, 153.

A copy of the civil cover sheet form referred to is attached as an appendix to this rule.*

(2) *Designation of Nature of Suit.* The party filing the initial pleading shall complete a civil cover sheet, Form JS 44**, or any successor forms, and file it with the initial pleading. If the clerk should determine that the designation of Nature of Suit is in error, the clerk shall correctly classify the suit and notify the party filing the initial pleading. A designation shall not thereafter be changed except by order of the Chief Judge or the judge to whom the case is assigned.

(3) *Assignment.* The clerk shall place a case in one of the five categories described in subsection (A)(1) and, unless otherwise ordered by the Court, assign it by lot among the judges of the court in active service at their respective duty stations in accordance with this rule in such manner that each such judge shall be assigned as nearly as possible the same number of

cases in each category. A senior judge may limit the category of case and nature of suit assigned to that judge and, within the categories of cases or suits that senior judge will accept, assignment shall be by lot in accordance with this rule.

   * See Appendix C following the rules.
   ** See Appendix B following the rules.

(B) Criminal Cases.

(1) *Categories of Cases.* All criminal cases shall be divided into the following three categories:

I —   Felony cases expected to require a combined total of fifteen (15) days or more for pretrial hearings and trial before a district judge.

II —   All other felony cases.

III —   All misdemeanor and petty offense cases where a district judge has been requested; Rule 20 cases; cases involving waivers of indictment; and all matters involving alleged violations of conditions of release by persons transferred to this District for supervision.

(2) *Designation of Category.* The attorney for the United States shall identify the appropriate category on Form AO 45, as modified for the district of Massachusetts, or any successor form, and submit the form contemporaneously with the document that initiates the case. If the clerk should determine that the designation of category is in error, the clerk shall correctly classify the case and notify the attorney for the United States. The designation shall not thereafter be changed except by order of the Chief Judge or the judge to whom the case is assigned.

(3) *Assignment.* The clerk shall place a case in one of the three categories described in subsection (B)(1) and, unless otherwise ordered by the Court, assign it by lot among the judges of the court in active service at their respective active duty stations within the divisions of the court in accordance with this rules in such manner that each judge shall be assigned as nearly as possible the same number of cases in each category. A senior judge may limit the category of cases or types of alleged criminal offenses assigned to that judge and within the categories of cases or offenses that senior judge will accept, assignment shall be in accordance with this rule.

(C) Designation of Divisions. The District of Massachusetts constitutes one judicial district comprising three divisions.

(1) *Eastern Division.* The Eastern Division of the District of Massachusetts comprises the counties of Barnstable, Bristol, Dukes, Essex, Middlesex, Nantucket, Norfolk, Plymouth, and Suffolk. Cases assigned to the Eastern Division and all pleadings and documents therein shall be filed in the clerk's office in Boston.

(2) *Central Division.* The Central Division of the District of Massachusetts is Worcester County. Cases assigned to the Central Division and all pleadings and documents therein shall be filed in the clerk's office in Worcester.

(3) *Western Division.* The Western Division of the District of Massachusetts comprises the counties of Berkshire, Franklin, Hampden and Hampshire. Cases shall be assigned to the Western Division and all pleadings and documents therein shall be filed at the clerk's office in Springfield.

(D) Assignment of Civil Cases.

(1) Civil cases shall be assigned to the respective divisions if:

(a) All of the parties reside in that division.

(b) All of the parties reside in the District of Massachusetts and the majority of the plaintiff(s) reside(s) in that division.

(c) The only parties residing in the District of Massachusetts reside in that division; or

(d) Any of the parties are the United States, the Commonwealth of Massachusetts, or any governmental agency of either the United States or the Commonwealth of Massachusetts and all other parties resident in the District of Massachusetts reside in that division.

(2) Except as otherwise ordered by the Court, cases not governed by section (D)(1) may be filed, subject to reassignment and transfer, in the division chosen by the plaintiff.

(E) Assignment of Criminal Cases. Criminal cases shall be assigned to that division in which the most significant criminal conduct related to the alleged violations occurred within the District of Massachusetts. All documents in each criminal case shall be filed in the clerk's office administering cases for the division to which that case is assigned.

(F) Transfer Between Divisions. Any case may be transferred from one division to another division on motion of any party for good cause shown or sua sponte for good cause by the judge to whom the case is assigned.

(G) Related Civil Cases.

(1) For purposes of this rule, a civil case is related to one previously filed in this court if some or all of the parties are the same and if one or more of the following similarities exist also: the cases involve the same or similar claims or defenses; or the cases involve the same property, transaction or event; or the cases involve insurance coverage for the same property, transaction or event; or the cases involve substantially the same questions of fact and law. In addition, two cases, one criminal and one civil, are related if the civil case involves forfeiture of property from a transaction or event which is the subject of a previously filed criminal case, or the civil case seeks enforcement of a restitution order or fine imposed in a previously filed criminal case. This rule shall not apply if more than two (2) years have elapsed since the closing of the previous action.

(2) If the party filing the initial pleading believes that the case is related to a case already assigned, whether or not the case is then pending, that party shall notify the clerk by notation on the local civil category sheet indicating the title and number of each such earlier case.

(3) The clerk shall assign related cases to the same judge without regard to the number of other cases in that category previously assigned to that judge. Related cases shall be counted as cases assigned, except as the Chief Judge may otherwise direct.

(4) The assignment of cases as related by the clerk shall be subject to correction only by the judge to whom they have been assigned, who shall return cases erroneously assigned on that basis to the clerk for reassignment.

(5) The treatment of a case as not related to another case shall be subject to correction only by the joint decision of the judge to whom it has been assigned and the judge to whom it should be assigned, if related to another case. The judges may then transfer the case pursuant to section (I) of this rule, and shall notify the clerk of the reason for the transfer.

(H) Proceedings After Assignment. Unless otherwise ordered by the court, all proceedings in a case after its assignment shall be conducted before the judge to whom it has been assigned, except as otherwise provided in these rules. This section does not preclude reassignment of cases by the court or the clerk, at the direction of the court, without prior notice to the parties.

(I) Reassignment and Transfer of Cases. In the interest of justice or to further the efficient performance of the business of the court, a judge may return a case to the clerk for reassignment, whether or not the case is related to any other case, with the approval of the Chief Judge, or, with respect to civil cases only, may transfer the case to another judge, if the other judge consents to the transfer.

(J) Motion for Consolidation of Cases. A motion for consolidation of two or more cases shall be made in the case first filed in this court.

(K) Proceedings After Appeal.

(1) When an appellate court remands a case to this court for a new trial, the case shall be reassigned to a judge other than the judge before whom the first trial was held.

(2) In all other cases in which the mandate of the appellate court requires further proceedings in this court, such proceedings shall not be conducted before the judge before whom the prior proceedings were

conducted unless the terms of the remand require that further proceedings be conducted before the original judge or unless the judge determines that there will result a substantial saving in the time of the whole court and that there is no reason why, in the interest of justice, further proceedings should be conducted before another judge. If the judge before whom the prior proceedings were conducted does not retain the case for further proceedings, that judge shall return it to the clerk for reassignment.

Effective September 1, 1990. Amended effective January 1, 2001.

RULE 40.2　CONFLICT OF COURT APPEARANCES

(A) Order of Preference and Notice to Clerks. In situations where counsel, including Assistant United States Attorneys, have conflicting court appearances among cases pending before different judges or magistrates of this court, the following order of preference shall apply, except as otherwise provided by law:

(1) Trials shall take precedence over all other hearings, and jury trials shall take precedence over nonjury trials.

(2) Criminal cases shall take precedence over civil cases.

(3) Criminal cases involving defendants who are in custody pending trial in the particular case shall take precedence over other criminal cases.

(4) Among civil cases or among criminal cases not involving defendants in custody, the case having the earliest docket number shall take precedence over the others.

When such conflicts appear, the counsel involved shall notify the deputy clerk assigned to each judge concerned, in writing, not later than three (3) days after the receipt of the notice or calendar giving rise to such conflict. The notice shall contain the names and docket number of each case, the time of the scheduled hearings in each case, the purpose thereof, and advise which case has precedence and the reason therefor. Upon receipt of such notice and a determination that a conflict in fact exists, the case or cases not having precedence shall be rescheduled.

(B) Substitution of Counsel. Counsel, in lieu of giving a notice of conflict, may elect to have a colleague, including another Assistant United States Attorney, handle the matter for the counsel involved. This shall not apply to any appointed defense counsel in the trial of criminal cases, unless the judicial officer orders otherwise.

(C) Primacy of Speedy Trial Plan. In the event of any conflict between the provisions of this rule and the provisions of the Speedy Trial Plan for the District of Massachusetts, the Speedy Trial Plan shall control.

(D) Scheduling Policy Regarding Superior Court Cases. When counsel have engagement conflicts with respect to cases pending in the Massachusetts Superior Court and The United States District Court for the District of Massachusetts, the following scheduling policy shall apply:

(1) Trials shall take precedence over all other hearings.

(2) Jury trials shall take precedence over nonjury trials.

(3) Criminal cases shall take precedence over civil cases.

(4) Criminal cases involving defendants who are in custody pending trial shall take precedence over other criminal cases.

(5) Among civil cases, or among criminal cases not involving defendants in custody, the case having the earliest docket number shall take precedence over the others, except that a trial setting involving numerous parties and counsel will ordinarily take precedence over other trials.

Counsel shall notify the presiding Superior Court Justice and U.S. District Judge of the scheduling conflict, in writing, not later than three (3) days after the receipt of the scheduling order giving rise to the conflict. Counsel's notification shall include: a) the names and docket numbers of each case, b) the date and time of the scheduled proceedings in each case, and c) a brief statement as to which case has precedence under this policy. The case or cases not having precedence shall be rescheduled, unless the presiding Justice and Judge agree otherwise. In the event of any conflict between the provisions of this policy and the provisions of the Speedy Trial Plan for the United States District of Massachusetts, the Speedy Trial Plan shall have precedence.

Effective September 1, 1990; amended effective January 2, 1995.

RULE 40.3　CONTINUANCES

(A) A motion for the continuance of a trial, evidentiary hearing, or any other proceeding, will be granted only for good cause.

(B) Motions to continue discovery and pretrial conferences will not be entertained unless the date and time of the pretrial conference are set out in the motion as well as a statement of how many other requests, if any, for continuances have been sought and granted.

(C) Illness of parties and material witnesses shall be substantiated by a current medical certificate.

(D) The judicial officer may condition a continuance upon the payment of expenses caused to the other parties and of jury fees incurred by the court.

Effective September 1, 1990; amended effective October 1, 1992.

RULE 40.4 EMERGENCIES AND SPECIAL PROCEEDINGS

(a) Matters and Proceedings Heard by Miscellaneous Business Docket (MBD) Judge. There will be designated an MBD judge to hear and determine:

(1) Emergency matters requiring immediate action in cases already assigned to any judge of the court, if the judge to whom a case had been assigned is unavailable or otherwise unable to hear the matter.

(2) Special proceedings, the nature of which precludes their assignment in the ordinary course, e.g., motions relating to grand jury investigations, discovery in cases pending in other districts, enforcement of administrative subpoenas; and

(3) Any other proceedings, including an admission to the bar and a naturalization, which are not part of or related to a case that should be assigned in the ordinary course.

(b) Disposition of "Emergency" Matters. The MBD judge will dispose of matters pursuant to subsection (a)(1), only to the extent necessary to meet the emergency. So far as practicable, consistent with justice and the efficient performance of the business of the court, the matter will be continued for disposition by the judge to whom the case is assigned.

(c) Subsequent "Emergency" Proceedings. If the MBD judge before whom the proceeding is brought concludes that, for lack of an emergency or otherwise, the proceeding should not be determined under this rule, the party who brought the proceeding shall not thereafter present the same matter to any other judge sitting as MBD judge, unless relevant circumstances change in the interim, in which case he shall bring to the attention of such other judge the prior proceeding and the changed circumstances which warrant resubmission of the matter under this rule.

(d) Special and Other Proceedings. Proceedings pursuant to subsections (a)(2) and (3) shall continue before the judge first handling the matter until conclusion.

Effective September 1, 1990.

RULE 41.1 DISMISSAL FOR WANT OF PROSECUTION

(a)(1) Whenever in any civil action the clerk shall ascertain that no proceeding has been docketed therein for a period of one (1) year, he shall then mail notice to all persons who have entered an appearance in such a case that, subject to the provisions of subsection (a)(3), the case will be dismissed without further notice thirty (30) days after the sending of the notice.

(2) After the thirtieth day following the sending of the notice, without order of the court the clerk shall, subject to the provisions of subsection (a)(3), enter an order of dismissal for all cases on the list. It shall not be necessary for the clerk to send additional notice of the dismissal to any counsel or party.

(3) A case shall not be dismissed for lack of prosecution if within thirty (30) days of the sending of notice an explanation for the lack of proceedings is filed and the judge to whom the case is assigned orders that it not be dismissed.

(b)(1) Additionally, each judge may from time to time give notice of not less than twenty (20) business days of hearing on a dismissal calendar for actions or proceedings assigned to that judge that appear not to have been diligently prosecuted. Unless otherwise ordered by the assigned judge, each party shall, not less than ten (10) business days prior to the noticed hearing date, serve and file a certificate describing the status of the action or proceeding and showing that good cause exists for the court to retain the case on the docket. Nothing in this rule precludes the filing of a motion for dismissal under Rule 41(b) of the Federal Rules of Civil Procedure.

(2) Failure on the part of the plaintiff to file the required statement or his failure to appear at the scheduled hearing shall be grounds for the dismissal of the action.

(c) The dismissal of a case pursuant to this rule shall not operate as an adjudication on the merits unless the court on motion of a party directs otherwise.

Effective September 1, 1990.

RULE 43.1 TRIAL

(A) Time Limits for Evidentiary Hearing.

(1) Absent agreement of the parties as to the time limits for the trial acceptable to the judicial officer, the judicial officer may order a presumptive limit of a specified number of hours. This time shall be allocated equally between opposing parties, or groups of aligned parties, unless otherwise ordered for good cause.

(2) A request for added time will be allowed only for good cause. In determining whether to grant a motion for an increased allotment of time, the court will take into account:

(a) whether or not the moving party has

(1) used the time since the commencement of trial in a reasonable and proper way, and

(2) complied with all orders regulating the trial;

(b) the moving party's explanation as to the way in which the requested added time would be used and why it is essential to assure a fair trial; and

(c) any other relevant and material facts the moving party may wish to present in support of the motion.

The court will be receptive to motions for reducing or increasing the allotted time to assure that the distribution is fair among the parties and adequate for developing the evidence.

(B) Evidence at the Evidentiary Hearing.

(1) Each party shall give advance notice to the judicial officer and the other parties, before jury selection, of the identity of all witnesses whose testimony it may offer during trial, whether by affidavit, deposition, or oral testimony.

(2) Not later than two (2) court days before it seeks to use the testimony of any witness, or on shorter notice for good cause shown, a party shall advise the judicial officer and all other parties of its intent to use the testimony of the witness on a specified day.

(3) Except for good cause shown, no party shall be allowed to:

(a) use the testimony of a witness other than the witnesses already listed on the filing with the court before trial commences; or

(b) introduce documentary evidence, during direct examination, other than those exhibits already listed with the judicial officer and furnished to the other parties before trial commences.

Adopted effective October 1, 1992.

RULE 48.1 [DELETED]

Deleted effective January 2, 1995.

RULE 54.3 [DELETED]

Deleted effective January 2, 1995.

RULE 56.1 MOTIONS FOR SUMMARY JUDGMENT

Motions for summary judgment shall include a concise statement of the material facts of record as to which the moving party contends there is no genuine issue to be tried, with page references to affidavits, depositions and other documentation. Failure to include such a statement constitutes grounds for denial of the motion. Opposition to motions for summary judgment shall include a concise statement of the material facts of record as to which it is contended that there exists a genuine issue to be tried, with page references to affidavits, depositions and other documentation. Copies of all referenced documentation

shall be filed as exhibits to the motion or opposition. Material facts of record set forth in the statement required to be served by the moving party will be deemed for purposes of the motion to be admitted by opposing parties unless controverted by the statement required to be served by opposing parties.

Effective September 1, 1990.

RULE 58.2 SATISFACTION OF JUDGMENTS

(a) Satisfaction of a money judgment shall be entered by the clerk without order of the court:

(i) On payment into court of the amount of the judgment including costs taxed, plus interest, and the amount of any fees due; or

(ii) On the filing of a satisfaction of judgment executed by the judgment creditor, or his legal representative or assignees with evidence of their authority, or his attorney in the proceeding in which judgment has been entered; or

(iii) On the filing of a satisfaction of judgment executed by the United States Attorney, if the judgment is in favor of the United States; or

(iv) On registration of a certified copy of a satisfaction of judgment entered in another district court.

(b) When satisfaction is made by payment of money into court, that fact shall be noted in the entry of satisfaction.

(c) Entry of judgment shall constitute sufficient authorization for the clerk to accept payment into court.

(d) **Mandate of an Appellate Court.** An order or judgment of an appellate court in a case appealed from this court shall, if further proceedings are not required, become the order or judgment of this court and be entered as such on receipt of the mandate of the appellate court.

Effective September 1, 1990.

RULE 62.2 SUPERSEDEAS BOND

A supersedeas bond staying execution of a money judgment shall be in the amount of the judgment plus ten (10%) percent of the amount to cover interest and any award of damages for delay plus Five Hundred and no/100 ($500.00) Dollars to cover costs, unless the court directs otherwise.

Effective September 1, 1990.

RULE 67.1 SURETIES

(a) **Members of the Bar and Court Officers.** No judge, clerk, marshal, member of the bar or other officer or employee of the court may be surety or guarantor of any bond or undertaking in any proceeding in this court.

(b) Form of Bond. Surety bonds shall be signed and acknowledged by the party and his surety or sureties. They shall refer to the statute, rule, or court order under which given, state the conditions of the obligation, and contain a provision expressly subjecting them to all applicable federal statutes and rules.

(c) Security. Except as otherwise provided by law or by order of the court, a bond or similar undertaking must be secured by:

(1) The deposit of cash or obligations of the United States in the amount of the bond (note Rule 67.4 with regard to the court's cash policy); or

(2) The guaranty of a company or corporation holding a certificate of authority from the Secretary of the Treasury pursuant to 6 U.S.C. § 8; or

(3) The guaranty of two (2) individual residents of this district each of whom owns unencumbered real or personal property within the district worth the amount of the bond, in excess of legal obligations and exemptions.

(d) Deposits of cash or obligations of the United States shall be accompanied by a written statement, duly acknowledged, that the signer is owner thereof, that the same is subject to the conditions of the bond, and that the clerk may collect or sell the obligations and apply the proceeds, or the cash deposited, in case of default as provided in the bond. Upon satisfaction of the conditions of the bond, the monies or obligations shall be returned to the owner on the order of a magistrate or district judge.

(e) Individual Sureties. An individual acting as surety, pursuant to subsection (c)(3), shall file an affidavit:

(1) Giving his name, occupation, and residential and business address;

(2) Showing that he is qualified to act as surety; and

(3) [In criminal cases] stating that he will not encumber or dispose of the property on which his qualification as surety depends while the bond remains in effect.

(f) Approval of Bond. Except as otherwise provided by law, the Clerk of Court may approve a bond in the amount fixed by the court or by statute or rule, and secured in the manner provided by subsections (c)(1) or (2). All other bonds must be approved by the court.

(g) Service. The party on whose behalf a bond is given shall promptly, after approval and filing of the bond, serve a copy of it on all other parties to the proceeding, but such service need not be made on the United States in a criminal case.

(h) Modification of Bond. The amount or terms of a bond or similar undertaking may be changed at any time as justice requires, by order of the court on its own motion or on motion of a party.

(i) Further Security. The court may order a party to furnish further or different security, or require personal sureties to furnish further justification.

Effective September 1, 1990.

RULE 67.2 REGISTRY FUNDS

(a) Deposit of Money in the Registry of the Court. Except as otherwise provided or authorized by law, no money shall be sent to the Clerk of Court or deposited in the registry of the court without a prior order of the court specifically directing such deposit, as provided by Rule 67 of the Federal Rules of Civil Procedure. Orders for deposits of funds covered by Rule 67 must recite that fact. In the absence of a reference to Rule 67, the clerk is relieved of any obligation to comply with that rule.

(The clerk may temporarily retain funds received under Fed.R.Civ.P. 67 in noninterest-bearing accounts while arrangements for deposit to interest bearing accounts are made and/or pending distribution.)

(b) Authorized Depository Bank. Unless otherwise ordered by the court or required by law, all funds deposited with the clerk for the registry of the court are placed in the court's account at the United States Treasury Department and bear no interest. The clerk is relieved of any responsibility to deposit funds covered by Fed.R.Civ.P. 67 into interest-bearing accounts if the party depositing the funds fails to obtain an order for deposit or investment that complies with the provisions of this local rule.

(c) Deposit of Registry Funds Into Interest–Bearing Accounts. Unless required to do so by law, the court shall not routinely order funds to be deposited in an interest-bearing account for less than ninety (90) days.

When, on motion or stipulation, an interested party requests that specific funds be used to purchase a certificate of deposit or deposited in an interest-bearing account with accrued interest to be accumulated for the benefit of the ultimate owners of the funds or otherwise as determined by court order, counsel shall obtain the certification of the clerk on a proposed order setting forth the following information:

(i) The amount to be invested and the type of account instrument;

(ii) The terms of the investment, including the rate of interest to be applied;

(iii) The name and address of the financial institution approved by the clerk where the funds are to be invested or certificate is to be purchased;

(iv) The amount of collateral or additional collateral to be posted by the private institution in the event standard FDIC coverage is insufficient to insure the total deposit; and

(v) Other appropriate information which is applicable under the facts and circumstances of the particular case.

The proposed order shall state that the plaintiff(s), defendant(s), their counsel, or other non-court employees, shall be responsible for making the investment and any reinvestments, which shall be accomplished by the same procedure followed for the original investment.

The proposed order shall also direct the clerk to deduct from the income earned on the investment a fee, not exceeding that authorized by the Judicial Conference of the United States and set by the Director of the Administrative Office at equal to the first 45 days income earned on the investment, whenever such income becomes available for deduction in the investment so held and without further order of the court.

The investment shall be made in the name of "Clerk, United States District Court" and bear the case number. A copy of the court order is required to be filed with the bank when the account is opened or certificate is purchased. The party making the investment shall bring such savings account passbook or certificate of deposit to the Clerk of Court who shall keep these documents in a safe place, subject to further order of the court.

(d) Signature Cards. Two signature cards are required for an interest-bearing account. They must be signed by the Clerk of Court personally and his designee and returned to the bank.

(e) Action by Clerk. If the investment or reinvestment order requires the clerk to take any action, the moving party shall deliver a copy of said order either personally or by certified mail to the clerk. The clerk shall have fifteen (15) days to comply with the order, not including the day of service. The party or parties obtaining the order directing the investment of funds at interest will verify that the clerk has taken the required action within the fifteen (15) day period. Absent the aforesaid service and verification, the clerk shall be relieved of any personal liability relative to compliance with the order respecting the particular registry funds.

(f) Disposition of Funds at Maturity. It shall be the responsibility of counsel to notice the clerk regarding disposition of funds at maturity of a timed instrument. In the absence of such notice, or if the parties fail to comply with any court order for renewal or other disposition, the clerk will redeposit said funds, together with any interest thereon, into the noninterest-bearing registry account of the court.

Service of notice by counsel as required in this section will be in accordance with the requirements as provided by section (e) no later than fifteen (15) days prior to maturity.

Effective September 1, 1990.

RULE 67.3 DISBURSEMENT OF REGISTRY FUNDS

The clerk shall not distribute any registry funds without an order of a district judge of this court. All orders for distribution, unless prepared by a deputy clerk assigned to the financial section of the clerk's office, must be approved by the clerk before presentation to a district judge.

All checks drawn by the Clerk of Court on deposits made in the registry of the court shall be made payable to the order of the payee(s) as the name(s) thereof appear in the orders of this court providing for distribution.

Disbursement from the registry of the court shall be made in accordance with the terms and at the time provided in the order for disbursement, or immediately upon receipt of the order if no time is specified, except in cases where it is necessary to allow time for a check or draft to clear. Prior to distribution, any party claiming an interest in the funds may move the court for a stay of the disbursement order pending appeal.

(a) Payees. If more than one check is to be issued on a single order, the portion due to each payee must be set out separately. In all cases, counsel must furnish the clerk with the address and social security number or taxpayer identification number of each recipient, and this number shall be included in the court order for release of funds.

(b) Disbursement of Monies Other Than Registry Funds. All disbursements to individuals made by the clerk of this court of monies received in his official capacity, other than registry funds, when made by check of the clerk on the Treasury of the United States, shall be made to the payee as the name shall appear in the disbursement voucher certified by the clerk or his designated certifying officer. The name of the payee in the disbursement voucher shall conform to the name appearing in the clerk's records of the case to which the disbursement relates. The clerk shall endeavor to note of record the given name of all individuals making deposits of monies with the clerk, and in those cases where the given name appears of record, disbursement vouchers and checks thereunder shall show the full given name, additional initials, if any, and the surname of the payee.

(c) Escrow Agents. In lieu of these provisions, an interested party may apply to the court for appointment of escrow agents. Such agents may deposit funds in a financial institution in an interest-bearing account and provide for the disposition of interest so earned, as approved by the court.

Effective September 1, 1990.

RULE 67.4 PAYMENTS AND DEPOSITS MADE WITH THE CLERK

(a) The clerk will not routinely accept payments or deposits in cash; but the court, on motion of any party, may order that the clerk accept cash in a particular instance.

(b) All checks must be made payable to "Clerk, United States District Court." The clerk is authorized to refuse any check not so made payable.

(c) The clerk may, in his discretion, require any payment to be made by certified check or its equivalent. The clerk shall require payment of bail to be made by certified check or its equivalent, unless otherwise ordered by the court.

Effective September 1, 1990.

RULE 68.2 SETTLEMENT

When a case is settled, the parties shall file in the office of the clerk a signed agreement for judgment or stipulation for dismissal, as appropriate, within thirty (30) days, unless the court otherwise orders.

Effective September 1, 1990.

RULE 77.1 SITTINGS

(A) The court shall be in continuous session for transacting judicial business on all business days throughout the year at Boston, Worcester and Springfield.

(B) Any judge of the court may, in the interest of justice or to further efficient performance of the business of the court, conduct proceedings at a special session at any time, anywhere in the district, on request of a party or otherwise.

Effective September 1, 1990; amended effective January 1, 2001.

RULE 77.2 OFFICE OF THE CLERK

The offices of the Clerk of Court at Boston, Worcester and Springfield shall be open from 8:30 a.m. until 5:00 p.m. on all days except Saturdays, Sundays, legal holidays and other days so ordered by the court and announced in advance, if feasible.

Effective September 1, 1990.

RULE 79.1 EXHIBITS

(a) Custody. Unless otherwise ordered by the court, all exhibits marked in evidence or for identification shall remain in the custody of the party that introduced them. Exhibits shall be preserved in the form in which they were offered until the proceeding is finally concluded. The party having custody shall make the exhibits available to all parties.

(b) Any party may move the court for custody arrangements that differ from those in section (a) upon a showing of good cause. The court may, on its own motion, provide for different custody arrangements or modify existing arrangements at any time.

(c) A court order that the clerk take custody of any exhibit shall specify the period during which the clerk shall maintain custody, the party to whom the exhibit shall be returned at the end of the period, and provision for destruction by the clerk without further notice to the parties at a set time after expiration of the custody period, if the party to whom the exhibit is to be returned fails to remove it from the custody of the clerk. Such court order shall constitute the only notice required for the purpose of exhibit disposal.

(d) It shall be sufficient if orders under the above sections are in writing, signed by the court or the clerk at the direction of the court, or are entered orally on the record and the substance of the order is reproduced on the docket sheet.

(e) Photographs of Chalks. In order to make a record of a chalk, the court may permit a party to photograph it or otherwise copy it, on such terms as are just. Unless otherwise ordered by the court, in jury cases chalks may be destroyed by the clerk as soon as the jury verdict has been recorded; in nonjury cases, chalks may be destroyed as soon as the evidence is closed.

Effective September 1, 1990.

RULE 81.1 REMOVAL

(a) Within thirty (30) days after filing a notice for removal of an action from a state court to this court pursuant to 28 U.S.C. § 1446, the party filing the notice shall file certified or attested copies of all records and proceedings in the state court and a certified or attested copy of all docket entries in the state court.

(b) If the clerk of this court has not received the papers required to be filed under section (a) within forty-five (45) days of the filing of the notice for removal, the case shall be remanded to the state court from which it was removed, unless this court directs otherwise.

(c) When a case is remanded to a state court, the clerk shall mail certified copies of the docket and order of remand, together with the remainder of the original file, to the clerk of the state court.

Effective September 1, 1990.

RULE 81.2 DEFINITION OF A JUDICIAL OFFICER

As used in these rules, "judicial officer" refers to either a United States District Court Judge or a United States Magistrate Judge. For purposes of LR 83.6(5)(A), the term "judicial officer" also refers to a United Stated Bankruptcy Judge.

Adopted effective October 1, 1992; amended effective August 1, 1997.

RULE 83.1A PROCEDURE FOR ADOPTING, RESCINDING AND AMENDING RULES

(a) These rules may be amended or rescinded by a majority of the active judges of this court.

(b) The clerk will maintain in suitable form an updated master copy of the rules.

Effective September 1, 1990.

RULE 83.1B GENERAL ORDER DOCKET

(a) Effective upon the adoption of these local rules, the clerk shall establish and maintain one (1) general order docket for each calendar year.

(b) All rules, administrative orders or directives of the court and amendments thereto shall bear a general order number assigned by the clerk, and be entered on the general order docket.

(c) The clerk shall place all prior administrative orders and directives, if they remain in effect at the time of adoption of these rules, on the general order docket for the year in which these rules are adopted.

(d) Any judge of this court may enter standing orders for his session, and may direct the clerk to maintain a docket therefor in accordance with sections (a) through (c).

Effective September 1, 1990.

RULE 83.2A RELEASE OF INFORMATION BY ATTORNEYS

No lawyer or law firm shall release or authorize the release of information or opinion which a reasonable person would expect to be disseminated by means of public communication, in connection with pending or imminent criminal litigation with which he or the firm is associated, if there is a reasonable likelihood that such dissemination will interfere with a fair trial or otherwise prejudice the due administration of justice.

With respect to a grand jury or other pending investigation of any criminal matter, a lawyer participating in or associated with the investigation shall refrain from making any extrajudicial statement, which a reasonable person would expect to be disseminated by means of public communication, that goes beyond the public record or that is not necessary to inform the public that the investigation is underway, to describe the general scope of the investigation, to obtain assistance in the apprehension of a suspect, to warn the public of any dangers, or otherwise to aid in the investigation.

From the time of arrest, issuance of an arrest warrant, or the filing of a complaint, information, or indictment in any criminal matter until the commencement of trial or disposition without trial, a lawyer or law firm associated with the prosecution or defense shall not release or authorize the release of any extrajudicial statement, which a reasonable person would expect to be disseminated by means of public communication, relating to that matter and concerning:

(1) The prior criminal record (including arrests, indictments, or other charges of crime), or the character or reputation of the accused, except that the lawyer or law firm may make a factual statement of the accused's name, age, residence, occupation, and family status, and if the accused has not been apprehended, a lawyer associated with the prosecution may release any information necessary to aid in his apprehension or to warn the public of any dangers he may present;

(2) The existence or contents of any confession, admission, or statement given by the accused, or the refusal or failure of the accused to make any statement;

(3) The performance of any examinations or tests or the accused's refusal or failure to submit to an examination or test;

(4) The identity, testimony, or credibility of prospective witnesses, except that the lawyer or law firm may announce the identity of the victim if the announcement is not otherwise prohibited by law;

(5) The possibility of a plea of guilty to the offense charged or a lesser offense; and

(6) Any opinion as to the accused's guilt or innocence as to the merits of the case or the evidence in the case.

The foregoing shall not be construed to preclude the lawyer or law firm during this period, in the proper discharge of his or its official or professional obligations, from announcing the facts and circumstances of arrest (including time and place of arrest, resistance, pursuit, and use of weapons), the identity of the investigating and arresting officer or agency, and the length of the investigation; from making an announcement, at the time of seizure of any physical evidence other than a confession, admission or statement, which is limited to a description of the evidence seized; from disclosing the nature, substance, or text of the charge, including a brief description of the offense charged; from quoting or referring without comment to public records of the court in the case; from announcing the scheduling or result of any stage in the judicial process; from requesting assistance in obtaining evidence; or from announcing without further comment that the accused denies the charges made against him.

During the trial of any criminal matter, including the period of selection of the jury, no lawyer or law firm associated with the prosecution or defense shall give or authorize any extrajudicial statement or interview relating to the trial or the parties or issues in the trial which a reasonable person would expect to be disseminated by means of public communication, except that the lawyer or law firm may quote from or refer without comment to public records of the court in the case.

After the completion of a trial or disposition without trial of any criminal matter, and prior to the imposition of sentence, a lawyer or law firm associated with the prosecution or defense shall refrain from making or authorizing any extrajudicial statement which a reasonable person would expect to be disseminated by means of public communication if there is a reasonable likelihood that such dissemination will affect the imposition of sentence.

Nothing in this rule is intended to preclude the formulation or application of more restrictive rules relating to the release of information about juvenile or other offenders, to preclude the holding of hearings or the lawful issuance of reports by legislative, administrative, or investigative bodies, or to preclude any lawyer from replying to charges of misconduct that are publicly made against him.

A lawyer or law firm associated with a civil action shall not during its investigation or litigation make or participate in making an extrajudicial statement, other than a quotation from or reference to public records, which a reasonable person would expect to be disseminated by means of public communication if there is a reasonable likelihood that such dissemination will interfere with a fair trial and which relates to:

(1) Evidence regarding the occurrence or transaction involved.

(2) The character, credibility, or criminal record of a party, witness, or prospective witness.

(3) The performance or results of any examination or tests or the refusal or failure of a party to submit to such.

(4) His opinion as to the merits of the claims or defenses of a party, except as required by law or administrative rule.

(5) Any other matter reasonably likely to interfere with a fair trial of the action.

Effective September 1, 1990.

RULE 83.2B SPECIAL ORDERS FOR THE PROTECTION OF THE ACCUSED OR THE LITIGANTS IN WIDELY PUBLICIZED OR SENSATIONAL CRIMINAL OR CIVIL CASES

In a widely publicized or sensational criminal or civil case, the court, on motion of either party or on its

own motion, may issue a special order governing such matters as extrajudicial statements by parties and witnesses likely to interfere with the rights of the accused or the litigants to a fair trial by an impartial jury, the seating and conduct in the courtroom of spectators and news media representatives, the management and sequestration of jurors and witnesses, and any other matters which the court may deem appropriate for inclusion in such an order.

Effective September 1, 1990.

RULE 83.3 PHOTOGRAPHING, RECORDING AND BROADCASTING

(a) **Recording and Broadcasting Prohibited.** Except as specifically provided in these rules or by order of the court, no person shall take any photograph, make any recording, or make any broadcast by radio, television, or other means, in the course of or in connection with any proceedings in this court, on any floor of any building on which proceedings of this court are or, in the regular course of the business of the court, may be held. This prohibition shall apply specifically but shall not be limited to the second, third, ninth, eleventh, twelfth, thirteenth, fifteenth, sixteenth, eighteenth, nineteenth and twentieth floors of the John W. McCormack Post Office and Courthouse Building in Boston and the fifth floor of the Courthouse Building in Springfield.

(b) **Voice Recordings by Court Reporters.** Official court reporters are not prohibited by section (a) from making voice recordings for the sole purpose of discharging their official duties. No recording made for that purpose shall be used for any other purpose by any person.

(c) The court may permit (1) the use of electronic or photographic means for the preservation of evidence or the perpetuation of a record, and (2) the broadcasting, televising, recording, or photographing of investitive, ceremonial, or naturalization proceedings.

(d) The use of dictation equipment is permitted in the clerk's office of this court by persons reviewing files in that office.

Effective September 1, 1990.

RULE 83.3.1 RULE GOVERNING THE PILOT PROGRAM ON PHOTOGRAPHING, RECORDING AND BROADCASTING CIVIL PROCEEDINGS IN THE COURTROOM

(A) **General Provisions.**

(1) This rule applies to all civil proceedings in any session of the United States District Court and the

Bankruptcy Court of the District of Massachusetts. The term "presiding judicial officer" applies to the judicial officer presiding in any such session.

(2) Reasonable advance notice is required from the media of a request to be present to broadcast, televise, record electronically, or take photographs at a particular session. Where possible, such notice should be given prior to the end of the preceding business day, but in no event later than one hour prior to the commencement of the proceedings. In the absence of such notice, the presiding judicial officer may refuse to permit media coverage. The presiding judicial officer may also waive such notice requirement.

(3) A presiding judicial officer may refuse, limit, or terminate media coverage of an entire case, portions thereof, or testimony of particular witnesses, in the interests of justice to protect the rights of the parties, witnesses, and the dignity of the court; to assure the orderly conduct of the proceedings; or for any other reason considered necessary or appropriate by the presiding judicial officer.

(4) No direct public expense is to be incurred for equipment, wiring, or personnel needed to provide media coverage.

(5) Nothing in this rule shall prevent the court from placing additional restrictions, or prohibiting altogether, photographing, recording, or broadcasting in designated areas of the courthouse. The provisions of this experimental rule pertain only to photographing, recording, and broadcasting in the courtroom. In all other areas of the courthouse, the provisions of Local Rule 83.3 remain in full force and effect.

(6) This rule takes effect July 1, 1991, and expires June 30, 1994.

(B) Limitations.

(1) Coverage of criminal proceedings is prohibited.

(2) There shall be no audio pickup or broadcast of conferences which occur in a court facility between attorneys and their clients, between co-counsel of a client, or between counsel and the presiding judicial officer, at the bench or in chambers.

(3) No coverage of the jury, or of any juror or alternate juror, while in the jury box, in the courtroom, in the jury deliberation room, or during recess, or while going to or from the deliberation room at any time, shall be permitted. Coverage of the prospective jury during voir dire is also prohibited.

(C) Equipment and Personnel.

(1) Not more than one television camera, operated by not more than one camera person and related equipment at any one time, shall be permitted in any court proceeding.

(2) Not more than one still photographer, utilizing not more than one camera and related equipment at any one time, shall be permitted in any court proceed-

ing. More than one camera may be brought into the courtroom, provided that only one camera may be used at any one time.

(3) If two or more media representatives apply to cover a proceeding, no such coverage may begin until all such representatives have agreed upon a pooling arrangement for their respective news media. Such pooling arrangements shall include the designation of pool operators, procedures for cost sharing, access to and dissemination of material and selection of a pool representative if appropriate. The presiding judicial officer may not be called upon to mediate or resolve any dispute as to such arrangements.

(4) Equipment or clothing shall not bear the insignia or marking of a media agency. Camera operators shall wear appropriate business attire.

(D) Sound and Light Criteria.

(1) Equipment shall not produce distracting sound or light. Signal lights or devices to show when equipment is operating shall not be visible. Motorized drives, moving lights, flash attachments, or sudden light changes shall not be used. All equipment shall use existing light only.

(2) Except as otherwise approved by the presiding judicial officer, existing courtroom sound and light systems shall be used without modification. Audio pickup for all media purposes shall be accomplished from existing audio systems present in the court facility, or from a television camera's built-in microphone. If no technically suitable audio system exists in the court facility, microphones and related wiring essential for media purposes shall be unobtrusive and shall be located in places designated in advance of any proceeding by the presiding judicial officer.

(E) Location of Equipment and Personnel.

(1) The presiding judicial officer shall designate the location in the courtroom for the camera equipment and operators. Such location may be designated in advance of any request, and where possible, should be outside of the direct line of sight between the jury box and the witness stand.

(2) During the proceedings, operating personnel shall not move about nor shall there be placement, movement, or removal of equipment. All such activities shall take place each day before the proceeding begins, after it ends, or during a recess.

(F) Compliance. Any media representative who fails to comply with the rule shall be subject to appropriate sanction, as determined by the presiding judicial officer.

(G) Review. This rule shall not be construed to create any litigable rights or right to appellate review. Accordingly, a grant or denial of media coverage shall not be litigable or appealable, except as otherwise provided by law.

(H) Compliance With Rule 83.3. Except as specifically provided in this rule, the prohibitions contained in LR 83.3 shall remain in full force and effect.

Adopted September 3, 1991; expired December 1994.

RULE 83.4 COURTROOM SEARCHES; COURTROOM SEATING

(a) All persons entering a courtroom are subject to search by the United States Marshal, a Deputy United States Marshal, or any other officer authorized by the court, as are all briefcases, parcels or other containers carried by persons entering a courtroom.

(b) Except by leave of the judge or magistrate presiding at a particular session of this court, only members of the bar of this court may be seated within the bar enclosure.

(c) With the exception of weapons carried by the United States Marshal, Deputy United States Marshals, or Federal Protective Officers, no weapons, other than exhibits, are permitted in any courtroom. No other person, including any federal law enforcement agent, shall bring a weapon other than an exhibit into any courtroom, except as specifically set forth below with respect to the courtrooms of the United States District Judges or United States Magistrates. No firearms intended for introduction as an exhibit may be brought into any courtroom unless it is first presented to the marshal for a safety check and the marshal reports to the clerk that the check has been completed.

Nothing in this rule shall be construed as precluding a federal law enforcement officer having custody or being in charge of the transportation of a federal prisoner from carrying a firearm in a courtroom assigned to a United States District Judge or United States Magistrate on the occasion of proceedings under Rule 5, Federal Rules of Criminal Procedure, or as precluding a duly authorized Correctional Officer of the Commonwealth of Massachusetts, entrusted with responsibility of transporting a state prisoner to proceedings before a United States Magistrate for civil or criminal proceedings where a Deputy United States Marshal is unavailable for such purpose, provided that the judge or magistrate is first advised of that fact.

Effective September 1, 1990.

RULE 83.5.1 BAR OF THE DISTRICT COURT

(a) Admission to the District Bar.

(1) An attorney is qualified for admission to the district bar of this district if the attorney (i) is currently in good standing as an attorney admitted to practice before the Supreme Judicial Court of Massachusetts; (ii) has satisfied the examination requirements as defined by the District Committee on Admissions relating to familiarity with the Federal Rules of Civil Procedure, the Federal Rules of Evidence, principles of federal jurisdiction and venue, and rules relating to professional responsibility; and (iii) has filed a certificate in a form approved by the District Committee on Admissions attesting to familiarity with the local rules of this district. For so long as the Rules of the Board of Bar Examiners of the Commonwealth of Massachusetts include for examination the subjects named in this rule, proof of good standing as an attorney admitted to practice before the Supreme Judicial Court of Massachusetts satisfies the examination requirement set out in this rule. An attorney admitted to practice in this court before the effective date of this rule and in good standing upon that date is a member of this district bar as of that date without further action on the attorney's part.

(2) All applicants for admission to practice before this court shall complete, verify, and file an application on an official form provided by the clerk.

(3) The clerk shall examine the application and if it is in order transmit it to the United States Attorney.

(4) Within twenty (20) days after the application is transmitted to the United States Attorney, if concluding on the basis of the information contained in the application that the application should be granted, the United States Attorney shall return the application to the clerk with written approval. The clerk shall place the name of the applicant on the list for the first available admissions ceremony.

(5) The United States Attorney, if concluding on the basis of the information contained in the application or otherwise that the application should not be granted, shall return the application to the clerk with written objection. The clerk shall deny the application without prejudice and send notice of the denial together with a copy of the United States Attorney's objection to the applicant.

(6) Any applicant denied admission may ask the court by motion to approve the application. The motion shall be presented to the Miscellaneous Business Docket (MBD) judge, who may rule on the motion ex parte, invite a response from the United States Attorney and the clerk, or schedule the matter for hearing. If the court approves the application, the clerk shall proceed as under subsection (a)(4).

(7) Approved applicants must appear at an admissions ceremony and make the following oath or affirmation before the judge presiding over the admissions ceremony:

I solemnly swear (affirm) that I shall conduct myself as a member of the bar of the United States District Court for the District of Massachusetts uprightly and according to the law.

Approved applicants shall be admitted to the district bar of this district upon signing the register of attorneys and paying to the "Clerk, United States District Court" the approved attorney admission fee.

(b) Student Practice Rule.

(1) A senior law student in a law school who has successfully completed a course for credit or who is enrolled in a course for credit in evidence or trial practice, with the written recommendation of the dean of such school of the law student's character, legal ability, and training, may appear without compensation (i) on behalf of the government or any governmental agency, if the conduct of the case is under the supervision of a member of the district bar; (ii) on behalf of indigent defendants in criminal proceedings, if the defendant consents (as provided in subsection (b)(6)) and if the conduct of the case is under the supervision of a member of the district bar assigned by the court or employed by a nonprofit program of legal aid, legal assistance or defense, or a law school clinical instruction program; and (iii) on behalf of indigent parties in civil proceedings, if the party consents (as provided in subsection (b)(6)), and if the conduct of the case is under the supervision of a member of the district bar assigned by the court or employed by a nonprofit program of legal aid, legal assistance or defense, or a law school clinical instruction program.

(2) A student may not appear in a criminal proceeding, either for the defense or for the prosecution, unless the dean's recommendation indicates that the student, in addition to satisfying all other requisites of this rule, has also successfully completed for credit a course in criminal procedure.

(3) The expression "supervision" shall be construed to require the attendance in court of the supervising member of the district bar. The term "senior law student" shall mean a student who has completed successfully the next-to-the-last year of law school study.

(4) The written recommendation described in subsection (b)(1) shall be filed with the Clerk of Court and shall be in effect, unless withdrawn earlier, until the date of the student's graduation from law school.

(5) A student who has begun the next-to-the-last year of law study in a law school, qualified and supervised as provided in subsections (b)(1), (3) and (4), may appear in civil proceedings under the same conditions as a senior law student, if the written approval referred to in subsections (b)(1) and (4) states that the law student is currently participating in a law school clinical instruction program.

(6) Before acting or appearing for any client, the student shall: (i) file with the clerk a certificate stating that the student has read and will abide by the standards of professional conduct set out in Rules 3:07 and 3:08 of the Rules of the Supreme Judicial Court of Massachusetts and is familiar with the local rules of this district; (ii) disclose to the client the student's

status as a law student; (iii) obtain from the client a signed document in which the client acknowledges having been informed of the student's status and authorizes the named student to appear for and represent the client in the litigation or proceedings identified in the document; (iv) have the document approved by the supervising attorney; and (v) file the document and the written appearance of the supervising attorney with the Clerk of Court.

(7) The rules of law and of evidence relating to communications between attorney and client shall govern communications made or received by any student acting under the provisions of this rule.

(8) A student acting under this rule shall comply with the standards of professional conduct set out in Rules 3:07 and 3:08 of the Rules of the Supreme Judicial Court of Massachusetts. Failure of an attorney supervising students to provide proper training or supervision may be grounds for disciplinary action or revocation or restriction of the attorney's authority to supervise students.

(9) The expression "without compensation" used in this rule shall not be construed to prohibit the receipt of a fixed compensation paid regularly by a governmental agency or legal assistance program or law school clinical instruction program acting as the employer of a law student. It shall, however, be construed to prohibit the receipt of a fee by a law student from a client for work on a particular case.

Effective September 1, 1990.

RULE 83.5.2 APPEARANCES

(a) Generally. The filing of the complaint shall constitute an appearance by the attorney who signs it. All other appearances in a case shall be made by filing a notice of appearance containing the docket number of the case, name, address and telephone number of the person entering an appearance, in compliance with Rule 5.1(a)(1).

(b) Appearance Pro Se. A party who appears pro se shall so state in the initial pleading or other paper filed by him or in his notice of appearance. The words "pro se" shall follow his signature on all papers subsequently filed by him in the same case.

(c) Withdrawal of Appearance. An attorney may withdraw from a case by serving notice of his withdrawal on his client and all other parties and filing the notice, provided that (1) such notice is preceded or accompanied by notice of the appearance of other counsel; (2) there are no motions pending before the court; (3) no trial date has been set; and (4) no hearings or conferences are scheduled, and no reports, oral or written, are due. Unless these conditions are met, an attorney (including one whose services have been terminated by his client) may withdraw from a case only by leave of court.

(d) Firms and Corporations. The court will not recognize the appearance of a firm or professional corporation unless it is accompanied by the appearance of at least one (1) attorney. In the event that a party is represented by more than one (1) attorney, whether or not from the same firm, the clerk shall not be required to send notice of orders, judgments, trial settings, etc., to more than one (1) attorney for any party, unless the attorneys represent different interests and this fact is noted on the record.

(e) Change of Address. Each attorney appearing and each party appearing pro se is under a continuing duty to notify the clerk of any change of address and telephone number. Notice under this rule shall be filed in every case. Any attorney or party appearing pro se who has not filed an appearance or provided the clerk with his current address in accordance with this rule shall not be entitled to notice. Notice mailed to an attorney's or party's last address of record shall constitute due notice contestable only upon proof of a failure to mail delivery.

Effective September 1, 1990.

RULE 83.5.3 PRACTICE BY PERSONS NOT MEMBERS OF THE BAR

(a) Attorneys for the United States. An attorney in good standing as a member of the bar in every jurisdiction where he has been admitted to practice and not subject to pending disciplinary proceedings as a member of the bar of any United States District Court may appear and practice in this court as the attorney for the United States or any agency of the United States or an officer of the United States in his official capacity.

(b) Other Attorneys. An attorney who is a member of the bar of any United States District Court or the bar of the highest court of any state may appear and practice in this court in a particular case by leave granted in the discretion of the court, provided he files a certificate that (1) he is a member of the bar in good standing in every jurisdiction where he has been admitted to practice; (2) there are no disciplinary proceedings pending against him as a member of the bar in any jurisdiction; and (3) he is familiar with the Local Rules of the United States District Court for the District of Massachusetts; and provided, further, his application for leave to practice in this court is on motion of a member of the bar of this court, who shall also file an appearance. An attorney seeking admission under this subsection may not enter an appearance or sign any papers until his application has been granted, except that the attorney may sign a complaint or any paper necessary to prevent entry of default for failure to answer or otherwise plead, provided such complaint or other paper is accompanied by his application for admission in proper form.

(c) Other Persons. A person who is not a member of the bar of this court, and to whom sections (a) and

(b) are not applicable, will be allowed to appear and practice before the court only in his own behalf.

Effective September 1, 1990.

RULE 83.6 RULES OF DISCIPLINARY ENFORCEMENT

(1) Attorneys Convicted of Crimes.

(A) Upon the filing with this court of a certified copy of a judgment of conviction demonstrating that any attorney admitted to practice before the court has been convicted in any court of the United States, or of any state, the District of Columbia, territory, commonwealth, or possession of the United States of a serious crime as hereinafter defined, the court shall enter an order immediately suspending that attorney, whether the conviction resulted from a plea of guilty, or nolo contendere, or from a verdict after trial or otherwise, and regardless of the pendency of any appeal, until final disposition of a disciplinary proceeding to be commenced upon such conviction. A copy of such order shall immediately be served upon the attorney. Upon good cause shown, the court may set aside such order when it appears in the interest of justice to do so.

(B) The term "serious crime" shall include any felony and any lesser crime, a necessary element of which, as determined by the statutory or common law definition of such crime in the jurisdiction where the judgment was entered, involves false swearing, misrepresentation, fraud, willful failure to file income tax returns, deceit, bribery, extortion, misappropriation, theft, or an attempt of a conspiracy or solicitation of another to commit a "serious crime."

(C) A certified copy of a judgment of conviction of an attorney for any crime shall be conclusive evidence of the commission of that crime in any disciplinary proceeding instituted against that attorney based upon the conviction.

(D) Upon the filing of a certified copy of a judgment of conviction of an attorney for a serious crime, the court shall, in addition to suspending that attorney in accordance with the provisions of this rule, also refer the matter to counsel for the institution of a disciplinary proceeding before the court in which the sole issue to be determined shall be the extent of the final discipline to be imposed as a result of the conduct resulting in the conviction, provided that a disciplinary proceeding so instituted will not be brought to final hearing until all appeals from the conviction are concluded.

(E) Upon the filing of a certified copy of a judgment of conviction of an attorney for a crime not constituting a "serious crime," the court may refer the matter to counsel for whatever action counsel may deem warranted, including the institution of a disciplinary proceeding before the court; provided, however, that the court may in its discretion make no reference with respect to convictions for minor offenses.

(F) An attorney suspended under the provisions of this rule will be reinstated immediately upon the filing of a certificate demonstrating that the underlying conviction of a serious crime has been reversed but the reinstatement will not terminate any disciplinary proceeding then pending against the attorney, the disposition of which shall be determined by the court on the basis of all available evidence pertaining to both guilt and the extent of discipline to be imposed.

(2) Discipline Imposed by Other Courts.

(A) Any attorney admitted to practice before this court shall, upon being subject to public discipline by any other court of the United States, or by a court of any state, the District of Columbia, territory, commonwealth, or possession of the United States, promptly inform the clerk of this court of such action.

(B) Upon the filing of a certified or exemplified copy of a judgment or order demonstrating that an attorney admitted to practice before this court has been disciplined by another court, this court shall forthwith issue a notice directed to the attorney containing:

(i) a copy of the judgment or order from the other court; and

(ii) an order to show cause directing that the attorney inform this court within thirty (30) days after service of that order upon the attorney, personally or by mail, of any claim by the attorney predicated upon the grounds set forth in subsection (2)(D) hereof that the imposition of the identical discipline by this court would be unwarranted and the reasons therefor. The order shall state that a hearing on such a claim may be had if requested within fifteen (15) days after service of the order; otherwise the matter will be determined on the papers without hearing.

(C) In the event the discipline imposed in the other jurisdiction has been stayed there, any reciprocal discipline imposed in this court shall be deferred until such stay expires.

(D) Upon the expiration of thirty (30) days from service of the notice issued pursuant to the provisions of subsection (2)(B), or any longer period needed for a hearing and consideration by the court, this court shall impose the identical discipline unless the respondent-attorney demonstrates, or this court finds, that upon the face of the record upon which the discipline in another jurisdiction is predicated it clearly appears:

(i) that the procedure was so lacking in notice or opportunity to be heard as to constitute a deprivation of due process; or

(ii) that there was such an infirmity of proof establishing the misconduct as to give rise to the

clear conviction that this court could not, consistent with its duty, accept as final the conclusion on that subject; or

(iii) that the imposition of the same discipline by this court would result in grave injustice; or

(iv) that the misconduct established is deemed by this court to warrant substantially different discipline. Where this court determines that any of said elements exist, it shall enter such other order as it deems appropriate.

(E) In all other respects, a final adjudication in another court that an attorney has been guilty of misconduct shall establish conclusively the misconduct for purposes of a disciplinary proceeding in this court.

(F) This court may at any stage appoint counsel to prosecute the disciplinary proceedings.

(3) Disbarment on Consent or Resignation in Other Courts.

(A) Any attorney admitted to practice before this court who shall be disbarred on consent or resign from the bar of any other court of the United States, or from the bar of any state, the District of Columbia, territory, commonwealth, or possession of the United States while an investigation into allegations of misconduct is pending, shall, upon the filing with this court of a certified or exemplified copy of the judgment or order accepting such disbarment on consent or resignation, cease to be permitted to practice before this court and be stricken from the roll of attorneys admitted to practice before this court.

(B) Any attorney admitted to practice before this court shall, upon being disbarred on consent or resigning from the bar of any other court of the United States, or from the bar of any state, the District of Columbia, territory, commonwealth, or possession of the United States while an investigation into allegations of misconduct is pending, promptly inform the clerk of this court of such disbarment on consent or resignation.

(4) Standards for Professional Conduct.

(A) For misconduct defined in these rules, and for good cause shown, and after notice and opportunity to be heard, any attorney admitted to practice before this court may be disbarred, suspended from practice before this court, reprimanded or subjected to such other disciplinary action as the circumstances may warrant.

(B) Acts or omissions by an attorney admitted to practice before this court pursuant to this Rule 83.6, or appearing and practicing before this court pursuant to Rule 83.7, individually or in concert with any other person or persons, that violate the ethical requirements and rules concerning the practice of law of the Commonwealth of Massachusetts, shall constitute misconduct and shall be grounds for discipline, whether or not the act or omission occurred in the course of an attorney-client relationship. The ethical requirements and rules concerning the practice of law mean those canons and rules adopted by the Supreme Judicial Court of Massachusetts, embodied in Rules 3:05, 3:07 and 3:08 of said court, as they may be amended from time to time by said court, except as otherwise provided by specific rule of this court after consideration of comments by representatives of bar associations within the Commonwealth.

(5) Disciplinary Proceedings.

(A) When misconduct or allegations of misconduct that, if substantiated, would warrant discipline as to an attorney admitted to practice before this court, is brought to the attention of a judicial officer, whether by complaint or otherwise, and the applicable procedure is not otherwise mandated by these rules, the judicial officer may refer the matter to counsel for investigation, the prosecution of a formal disciplinary proceeding or the formulation of such other recommendation as may be appropriate.

(B) Should counsel conclude after investigation and review that a formal disciplinary proceeding should not be initiated against the respondent-attorney because sufficient evidence is not present, or because there is pending another proceeding against the respondent-attorney, the disposition of which in the judgment of counsel should be awaited before further action by this court is considered or for any other valid reason, counsel shall file with the court a recommendation for disposition of the matter, whether by dismissal, admonition, deferral, or otherwise, setting forth the reasons therefor.

(C) To initiate formal disciplinary proceedings, counsel shall obtain an order of this court upon a showing of probable cause, requiring the respondent-attorney to show cause within thirty (30) days after service of that order upon that attorney, personally or by mail, why the attorney should not be disciplined. The order to show cause shall include a certification of all courts before which the respondent-attorney is admitted to practice, as specified in the form appended to these rules.

(D) Upon the respondent-attorney's answer to the order to show cause, if any issue of fact is raised or the respondent-attorney wishes to be heard in mitigation, the Chief Judge of this court or, in his absence, the next senior district judge shall set the matter for prompt hearing before three (3) judges of this court, provided however that if the disciplinary proceeding is predicated upon the complaint of a judge of this court the complaining judge shall not sit, and if the Chief Judge is the complainant, the member of the court who is next senior shall assume his responsibilities in the matter. An en banc hearing may be granted on the affirmative vote of five (5) judges. Nothing herein shall prevent the court from using a master for purposes of fact finding and to make recommendations in a suitable case. The respondent-attorney shall exe-

cute the certification of all courts before which that respondent-attorney is admitted to practice, and file the certification with the answer.

(6) Disbarment on Consent While Under Disciplinary Investigation or Prosecution.

(A) Any attorney admitted to practice before this court who is the subject of an investigation into, or a pending proceeding involving, allegations of misconduct may consent to disbarment, but only by delivering to this court an affidavit stating that the attorney desires to consent to disbarment and that:

(i) the attorney's consent is freely and voluntarily rendered; the attorney is not being subjected to coercion or duress; the attorney is fully aware of the implications of so consenting;

(ii) the attorney is aware that there is a presently pending investigation or proceeding involving allegation that there exist grounds for the attorney's discipline, the nature of which the attorney shall specifically set forth;

(iii) the attorney acknowledges that the material facts so alleged are true; and

(iv) the attorney so consents because the attorney knows that if charges were predicated upon the matters under investigation, or if the proceedings were prosecuted, the attorney could not successfully defend himself.

(B) Upon receipt of the required affidavit, this court shall enter an order disbarring the attorney.

(C) The order disbarring the attorney on consent shall be a matter of public record. However, the affidavit required under the provisions of this rule shall not be publicly disclosed or made available for use in any other proceeding except upon order of this court.

(7) Reinstatement.

(A) *After Disbarment or Suspension.* An attorney who is suspended shall be automatically reinstated at the end of the period of suspension upon the filing with the court of an affidavit of compliance with the provisions of the order. An attorney who is suspended indefinitely or disbarred may not resume practice until reinstated by order of this court. Suspensions may be directed to run concurrently with a suspension mandated by other state or federal courts, in which event the attorney shall be eligible for reinstatement in this court when said suspension expires, and will be automatically reinstated upon filing with this court an affidavit indicating that the period of suspension has run.

(B) *Hearing on Application.* Petitions for reinstatement by a disbarred or indefinitely suspended attorney under this rule shall be filed with the Chief Judge of this court. Upon receipt of the petition, the Chief Judge shall promptly refer the petition to counsel and shall assign the matter for prompt hearing before one or more judges of this court provided, however, that if the disciplinary proceeding was predicated upon the complaint of a judge of this court, the complaining judge shall not sit, and if the Chief Judge is the complainant, the judge next senior shall assume his responsibilities in the matter. The judge or judges assigned to the matter shall within thirty (30) days after referral schedule a hearing at which the petitioner shall have the burden of demonstrating by clear and convincing evidence that he has the moral qualifications, competency and learning in the law required for admission to practice law before this court and that his resumption of the practice of law will not be detrimental to the integrity and standing of the bar or to the administration of justice, or subversive of the public interest.

(C) *Duty of Counsel.* In all proceedings upon a petition for reinstatement, cross-examination of the witnesses of the respondent-attorney and the submission of evidence, if any, in opposition to the petition shall be conducted by counsel.

(D) *Conditions of Reinstatement.* If the petitioner is found unfit to resume the practice of law, the petition shall be dismissed. If the petitioner is found fit to resume the practice of law, the judgment shall reinstate him, provided that the judgment may make reinstatement conditional upon the payment of all or part of the costs of the proceedings, and upon the making of partial or complete restitution to parties harmed by the disbarment. Provided further, that if the petitioner has been suspended or disbarred for five (5) years or more, reinstatement may be conditioned, in the discretion of the judge or judges before whom the matter is heard, upon furnishing proof of competency and learning in the law, which proof may include certification by the bar examiners of a state or other jurisdiction of the attorney's successful completion of an examination for admission to practice subsequent to the date of suspension or disbarment.

(E) *Successive Petitions.* No petition for reinstatement under this rule shall be filed within one (1) year following an adverse judgment upon a petition for reinstatement filed by or on behalf of the same person.

(8) Attorneys Specially Admitted.

(A) Whenever an attorney applies to be admitted or is admitted to this court for purposes of a particular proceeding (pro hac vice), the attorney shall be deemed thereby to have conferred disciplinary jurisdiction upon this court for any alleged misconduct of that attorney arising in the course of or in preparation for such proceeding.

(9) Appointment of Counsel.

(A) Whenever counsel is to be appointed pursuant to these rules to investigate allegations of misconduct or prosecute disciplinary proceedings or in conjunction with a reinstatement petition filed by a disciplined

attorney, this court shall appoint as counsel the disciplinary agency of the highest court of the state or commonwealth in which the attorney is maintaining his principal office, or other disciplinary agency which the court deems suitable, including the United States Attorney for this district. If no such disciplinary agency exists or such disciplinary agency declines appointment, or such appointment is clearly inappropriate, this court shall appoint as counsel one or more members of the bar of this court to investigate allegations of misconduct or to prosecute disciplinary proceedings under these rules, provided, however, that the respondent-attorney may move to disqualify an attorney so appointed who is or has been engaged as an adversary of the respondent-attorney in any matter. Counsel, once appointed, may not resign without permission of this court.

(10) Duties and Powers of the Clerk.

(A) The clerk of this court shall promptly notify the National Discipline Data Bank operated by the American Bar Association of any order imposing public discipline upon any attorney admitted to practice before this court.

(B) The clerk of this court shall, upon being informed that any attorney admitted to practice before this court has been convicted of any crime or has been subjected to discipline by another court, obtain and file with this court a certified or exemplified copy of such conviction or disciplinary judgment or order.

(C) Whenever it appears that any person who is disbarred or suspended or censured or disbarred on consent by this court is admitted to practice law in any other jurisdiction or before any other court, the clerk of this court may, if necessary to supplement the action taken under subsection (10)(A), so advise the disciplinary authority in such other jurisdiction or such other court.

(11) Jurisdiction.

(A) Nothing contained in these rules shall be construed to deny to the court such powers as are necessary for the court to maintain control over proceedings conducted before it, such as proceedings for contempt under Title 18 of the United States Code or under Rule 42 of the Federal Rules of Criminal Procedure.

Effective September 1, 1990; amended effective August 1, 1997.

RULE 106.1   GRAND JURIES

(a) The names of any jurors drawn from the qualified jury wheel and selected to sit on a grand jury shall be kept confidential and not made public or disclosed to any person not employed by the district court, except as otherwise authorized by a court order in an individual case pursuant to 28 U.S.C. § 1867(f).

(b) All subpoenas, motions, pleadings, and other documents filed with the clerk concerning or contesting grand jury proceedings shall be sealed and impounded unless otherwise ordered by the court based upon a showing of particularized need. Impoundment under this rule shall not preclude necessary service of papers on opposing parties or their counsel nor prohibit the clerk from providing copies of papers to the party or counsel filing same.

Effective September 1, 1990.

RULE 106.2 RELEASE OF INFORMATION BY COURTHOUSE PERSONNEL IN CRIMINAL CASES

All court supporting personnel, including the United States Marshal, Deputy United States Marshals, the Clerk of Court, deputy clerks, probation officers, assistant probation officers, bailiffs, court reporters, and employees or subcontractors retained by the court-appointed official reporters, judges' secretaries and law clerks and student assistants, and other employees are prohibited from disclosing without authorization by the court, information relating to a pending grand jury proceeding or criminal case that is not part of the public records of the court. Divulging information concerning in camera hearings is also prohibited.

Effective September 1, 1990.

[LOCAL RULES CONCERNING CRIMINAL CASES]

RULE 112.1 MOTION PRACTICE

Unless otherwise specified in these Local Rules or by order of the court, motion practice in criminal cases shall be subject to L.R. 7.1.

Adopted September 8, 1998, effective December 1, 1998.

RULE 112.2 EXCLUDABLE DELAY PURSUANT TO THE SPEEDY TRIAL ACT

(A) The Court, having found that a fair and prompt resolution of criminal cases is best served by the minimizing of formal motion practice and the establishment of the system of discovery set forth in these Local Rules, has determined that the following periods of time may be excluded, under 18 U.S.C. § 3161(h)(8)(A), to serve the ends of justice in order to accomplish such discovery:

(1) No more than fourteen (14) days from arraignment, the time period available to the defendant for consideration whether to participate in the automatic discovery process, if the defendant files the Waiver provided under L.R. 116.1(B).

(2) No more than twenty-eight (28) days from arraignment, during which time period the parties are developing their discovery plans and producing discovery under the automatic discovery process, if the defendant does not file the Waiver provided under L.R. 116.1(B).

(3) No more than fourteen (14) days from the filing of a copy of any letter requesting discovery under L.R. 116.3(A).

(B) The parties shall inform the court upon agreement or in connection with any Status Conference convened under L.R. 116.5 and any Pretrial Conference convened under L.R. 117.1 of the periods for which orders of excludable time should be entered. The time periods indicated above will not be automatically excluded. All periods of excludable delay must be included in a separate order issued by the district judge or magistrate judge detailing the time period to be covered.

Adopted September 8, 1998, effective December 1, 1998.

RULE 112.4 CORPORATE DISCLOSURE STATEMENT

(A) A nongovernmental corporate party to a criminal proceeding in this court must file a statement that identifies any parent corporation and any publicly held corporation that owns 10% or more of its stock or states there is no such corporation.

(B) If an organization is a victim of the alleged criminal activity, the government must file a statement identifying the victim. If the organizational victim is a corporation, the statement must also disclose the information required by Local Rule 112.4(A) charged in any indictment or information.

(C) A party must file the Local Rule 112.4(A) statement upon its first appearance, pleading, petition, motion, response or other request addressed to the court and must promptly supplement the statement upon any change in the identification that the statement requires.

Adopted effective January 1, 2001.

RULE 116.1 DISCOVERY IN CRIMINAL CASES

(A) Discovery Alternatives.

(1) *Automatic Discovery.* In all felony cases, unless a defendant waives automatic discovery, all discoverable material and information in the possession, custody, or control of the government and that defendant, the existence of which is known, or by the exercise of due diligence may become known, to the attorneys for those parties, must be disclosed to the opposing party without formal motion practice at the times and under

the automatic discovery procedures specified in this Local Rule.

(2) *Non-automatic Discovery.* In felony cases, if the defendant waives automatic discovery, and in non-felony cases the defendant must obtain discovery directly through the provisions of the Federal Rules of Criminal Procedure in the manner provided under Local Rule 116.3.

(B) Waiver. A defendant shall be deemed to have requested all the discovery authorized by Fed. R. Crim. P. 16(a)(1)(A)–(D) unless that defendant files a Waiver of Request for Disclosure (the "Waiver") at, or within fourteen (14) days after, arraignment. If the Waiver is not timely filed, the defendant shall be subject to the correlative reciprocal discovery obligations of Fed. R. Crim. P. 16(b) and of this Local Rule and shall be deemed to have consented to the exclusion of time for Speedy Trial Act purposes as provided in L.R. 112.2(A)(2).

(C) Automatic Discovery Provided By The Government.

(1) *Following Arraignment.* Unless a defendant has filed the Waiver, within twenty-eight (28) days of arraignment—or within fourteen (14) days of receipt by the government of a written statement by the defendant that no Waiver will be filed—the government must produce to the defendant:

(a) Fed. R. Crim. P. 16 Materials. All of the information to which the defendant would be entitled under Fed. R. Crim. P. 16(a)(1)(A)–(D).

(b) Search Materials. A copy of any search warrant (with supporting application, affidavit, and return) and a written description of any consent search or warrantless search (including an inventory of evidence seized):

(i) which resulted in the seizure of evidence or led to the discovery of evidence that the government intends to offer as part of its case-in-chief; or

(ii) was obtained for or conducted of the defendant's property, residence, place of business, or person, in connection with investigation of the charges contained in the indictment.

(c) Electronic Surveillance.

(i) A written description of any interception of wire, oral, or electronic communications as defined in 18 U.S.C. § 2510, relating to the charges in the indictment in which the defendant was intercepted and a statement whether the government intends to offer any such communications as evidence in its case-in-chief; and

(ii) A copy of any application for authorization to intercept such communications relating to the charges contained in the indictment in which the defendant was named as an interceptee or pursuant to which the defendant was intercepted, together with all supporting affidavits, the court orders authorizing such interceptions, and the court orders directing the sealing of intercepted communications under 18 U.S.C. § 2518(a).

(d) Consensual Interceptions.

(i) A written description of any interception of wire, oral, or electronic communications, relating to the charges contained in the indictment, made with the consent of one of the parties to the communication ("consensual interceptions"), in which the defendant was intercepted or which the government intends to offer as evidence in its case-in-chief.

(ii) Nothing in this subsection is intended to determine the circumstances, if any, under which, or the time at which, the attorney for the government must review and produce communications of a defendant in custody consensually recorded by the institution in which that defendant is held.

(e) Unindicted Coconspirators. As to each conspiracy charged in the indictment, the name of any person asserted to be a known unindicted coconspirator. If subsequent litigation requires that the name of any such unindicted coconspirator be referenced in any filing directly with the court, that information must be redacted from any public filing and be filed under L.R. 7.2 pending further order of the court.

(f) Identifications.

(i) A written statement whether the defendant was a subject of an investigative identification procedure used with a witness the government anticipates calling in its case-in-chief involving a line-up, show-up, photospread or other display of an image of the defendant.

(ii) If the defendant was a subject of such a procedure, a copy of any videotape, photospread, image or other tangible evidence reflecting, used in or memorializing the identification procedure.

(2) *Exculpatory Information.* The timing and substance of the disclosure of exculpatory evidence is specifically provided in L.R. 116.2.

(D) Automatic Discovery Provided by the Defendant. In felony cases if the defendant has not filed the Waiver, within twenty-eight (28) days after arraignment, the defendant must produce to the government all material described in Fed. R. Crim. P. 16(b)(1)(A) and (B).

Effective September 1, 1990; amended September 8, 1998, effective December 1, 1998.

RULE 116.2   DISCLOSURE OF EXCULPATORY EVIDENCE

(A) Definition. Exculpatory information includes, but may not be limited to, all information that is material and favorable to the accused because it tends to:

(1) Cast doubt on defendant's guilt as to any essential element in any count in the indictment or information;

(2) Cast doubt on the admissibility of evidence that the government anticipates offering in its case-in-chief, that might be subject to a motion to suppress or exclude, which would, if allowed, be appealable pursuant to 18 U.S.C. § 3731;

(3) Cast doubt on the credibility or accuracy of any evidence that the government anticipates offering in its case-in-chief; or

(4) Diminish the degree of the defendant's culpability or the defendant's Offense Level under the United States Sentencing Guidelines.

(B) Timing of Disclosure by the Government. Unless the defendant has filed the Waiver or the government invokes the declination procedure under Rule 116.6, the government must produce to that defendant exculpatory information in accordance with the following schedule:

(1) Within the time period designated in L.R. 116.1(C)(1):

(a) Information that would tend directly to negate the defendant's guilt concerning any count in the indictment or information.

(b) Information that would cast doubt on the admissibility of evidence that the government anticipates offering in its case-in-chief and that could be subject to a motion to suppress or exclude, which would, if allowed, be appealable under 18 U.S.C. § 3731.

(c) A statement whether any promise, reward, or inducement has been given to any witness whom the government anticipates calling in its case-in-chief, identifying by name each such witness and each promise, reward, or inducement, and a copy of any promise, reward, or inducement reduced to writing.

(d) A copy of any criminal record of any witness identified by name whom the government anticipates calling in its case-in-chief.

(e) A written description of any criminal cases pending against any witness identified by name whom the government anticipates calling in its case-in-chief.

(f) A written description of the failure of any percipient witness identified by name to make a positive identification of a defendant, if any identification procedure has been held with such a witness with respect to the crime at issue.

(2) Not later than twenty-one (21) days before the trial date established by the judge who will preside:

(a) Any information that tends to cast doubt on the credibility or accuracy of any witness whom or

evidence that the government anticipates calling or offering in its case-in-chief.

(b) Any inconsistent statement, or a description of such a statement, made orally or in writing by any witness whom the government anticipates calling in its case-in-chief, regarding the alleged criminal conduct of the defendant.

(c) Any statement or a description of such a statement, made orally or in writing by any person, that is inconsistent with any statement made orally or in writing by any witness the government anticipates calling in its case-in-chief, regarding the alleged criminal conduct of the defendant.

(d) Information reflecting bias or prejudice against the defendant by any witness whom the government anticipates calling in its case-in-chief.

(e) A written description of any prosecutable federal offense known by the government to have been committed by any witness whom the government anticipates calling in its case-in-chief.

(f) A written description of any conduct that may be admissible under Fed. R. Evid. 608(b) known by the government to have been committed by a witness whom the government anticipates calling in its case-in-chief.

(g) Information known to the government of any mental or physical impairment of any witness whom the government anticipates calling in its case-in chief, that may cast doubt on the ability of that witness to testify accurately or truthfully at trial as to any relevant event.

(3) No later than the close of the defendant's case: Exculpatory information regarding any witness or evidence that the government intends to offer in rebuttal.

(4) Before any plea or to the submission by the defendant of any objections to the Pre-Sentence Report, whichever first occurs: A written summary of any information in the government's possession that tends to diminish the degree of the defendant's culpability or the defendant's Offense Level under the United States Sentencing Guidelines.

(5) If an item of exculpatory information can reasonably be deemed to fall into more than one of the foregoing categories, it shall be deemed for purposes of determining when it must be produced to fall into the category which requires the earliest production.

Adopted September 8, 1998, effective December 1, 1998.

RULE 116.3 DISCOVERY MOTION PRACTICE

(A) Within forty-two (42) days of arraignment, any party by letter to the opposing party may request discovery. The opposing party shall reply in writing to the requests contained in such letter, no later than fourteen (14) days after its receipt, stating whether that party agrees or does not agree to furnish the requested discovery and, if that party agrees, when the party will furnish the requested discovery. A copy of the discovery request letter and any response must also be filed with the Clerk's Office.

(B) If a party agrees in writing to provide the requested discovery, the agreement shall be enforceable to the same extent as a court order requiring the agreed-upon disclosure.

(C) If a party does not agree to provide the requested information, that party must provide a written statement of the basis for its position.

(D) A defendant participating in automatic discovery must not request information expressly required to be produced under L.R. 116.1; all such information is by these Local Rules deemed ordered by the court to be produced.

(E) Except in an emergency, no discovery motion, or request for a bill of particulars, shall be filed until the opposing party has declined in writing to provide the requested discovery or has failed to respond in writing within fourteen (14) days of receipt to a written request.

(F) Except in an emergency, before filing any discovery motion, the moving party shall confer with opposing counsel to attempt to eliminate or narrow the areas of disagreement. In the motion, the moving party shall certify that a good faith attempt was made to eliminate or narrow the issues raised in the motion through a conference with opposing counsel or that a good faith attempt to comply with this requirement was precluded by the opposing party's unwillingness to confer.

(G) Any discovery motion shall be filed within fourteen (14) days of receipt of the opposing party's written reply to the letter requesting discovery described in subdivision (A) of this Local Rule or the passage of the period within which the opposing party has the obligation to reply pursuant to subdivision (A). The discovery motion shall state with particularity each request for discovery, followed by a concise statement of the moving party's position with respect to such request, including citations of authority.

(H) In multi-defendant cases, except with leave of court, the defendant parties must confer and, to the maximum extent possible in view of any potentially differing positions of the defendants, consolidate their written requests to the government for any discovery. If a discovery motion is to be filed, the defendant parties must endeavor to the maximum extent possible to file a single consolidated motion. Each defendant need not join in every written request submitted to the government or filed in a consolidated motion, but all defense requests and motions, whether or not joined in by each defendant, must to the maximum extent possible be contained within a single document or filing.

(I) The opposing party must file its response to all discovery motions within fourteen (14) days of receipt. In its response, the opposing party, as to each request, shall make a concise statement of the opposing party's basis for opposing that request, including citations to authority.

(J) The procedure set forth in this section shall apply to subsequent requests for discovery after the initial forty-two (42) day period. When filing a discovery motion based on a subsequent discovery request, the moving party must additionally certify that the discovery request resulting in the motion was prompted by information not known, or issues not reasonably foreseeable, to the moving party before the deadline for discovery motions, or that the delay in making the request was for other good cause, which the moving party must describe with particularity.

Adopted September 8, 1998, effective December 1, 1998.

RULE 116.4   SPECIAL PROCEDURES FOR TAPE RECORDINGS

(A) Availability of Tape Recordings.

(1) The government must provide at least one copy of all tape recordings in its possession that are discoverable for examination and review by the defendant parties.

(2) If a defendant requests additional copies, the government must make arrangements to provide or to enable that defendant to make such copies at that defendant's expense.

(3) If in a multi-defendant case any defendant is in custody, the government must insure that an extra copy of all tape recordings is available for review by the defendant(s) in custody.

(B) Composite Tapes, Preliminary Transcripts and Final Transcripts. The parties must make arrangements promptly to provide or make available for inspection and copying by opposing counsel all:

(1) Composite electronic surveillance or consensual interception tapes to be used in that party's case-in-chief at trial, once prepared;

(2) Preliminary transcripts, once prepared. A preliminary transcript may not be used at trial or in any hearing on a pretrial motion without the prior approval of the court based on a finding that the preliminary transcript is accurate in material respects and it is in the interests of the administration of justice to use it.

(3) Final transcripts, once prepared.

(4) Nothing in this Local Rule shall be construed to require a party to prepare composite tapes, or preliminary or final transcripts, of any tape recording.

Adopted September 8, 1998, effective December 1, 1998.

RULE 116.5 STATUS CONFERENCES AND STATUS REPORTS PROCEDURE

(A) Initial Status Conference. Unless all parties advise the Magistrate Judge that such a conference is not necessary, and the Magistrate Judge concurs, on or about the 42nd day following arraignment, the Magistrate Judge shall convene an Initial Status Conference with the attorneys for the parties who will conduct the trial in any felony or Class A misdemeanor case to be decided by a district judge. The discussion at the conference must include the following issues, and any other issues relevant to the progress of the case:

(1) Whether relief should be granted from the otherwise applicable timing requirements imposed by L.R. 116.3.

(2) Whether the defendant requests discovery concerning expert witnesses under Fed. R. Crim. P. 16(a)(1)(E). If the defendant requests the disclosure required by Fed. R. Crim. P. 16(a)(1)(E), what date should be established for response by the government and what date should be established for reciprocal discovery from the defendant concerning expert witnesses required under Fed. R. Crim. P. 16(b)(1)(C).

(3) Whether a party anticipates providing additional discovery as a result of its future receipt of information, documents, or reports of examinations or tests.

(4) Whether a motion date should be established under Fed. R. Crim. P. 12(c).

(5) What periods of excludable delay should be ordered under the Speedy Trial Act at the time of the conference.

(6) Whether a trial is anticipated and, if so, its anticipated length.

(7) What date should be established for the Final Status Conference and/or any Interim Status Conferences.

(B) Scheduling and Status Report. After any Status Conference, the Magistrate Judge shall file for the District Judge who will preside at trial an Interim Status and Scheduling Report which:

(1) Outlines the scheduling and completion of discovery and filing of motions;

(2) Identifies whether the case involves unusual or complex issues by reason of which an early joint conference of the District Judge and Magistrate Judge with all attorneys would be useful;

(3) Identifies any features of the case that may deserve special attention or modification of the standard schedule.

(4) Identifies and orders periods of excludable delay that are applicable at the time of the report.

(5) Identifies and returns the file to the district judge upon an indication that the defendant intends to plead guilty.

(C) Final Status Conference. Before the Magistrate Judge issues the Final Status Report required by subdivision (D) of this Local Rule, the Magistrate Judge shall convene a Final Status Conference with the attorneys for the parties who will conduct the trial. Prior to this conference, counsel shall confer and, not later than three (3) business days before the conference, prepare and file a joint memorandum addressing the following issues, and any other issue relevant to the progress of the case, which counsel must be prepared to discuss at the conference:

(1) Whether there are outstanding discovery issues not yet presented or resolved by the Court;

(2) Whether a party anticipates providing additional discovery as a result of its future receipt of information, documents, or reports of examinations or tests;

(3) Whether the defendant intends to raise a defense of insanity or public authority;

(4) Whether the government has requested notice of alibi by the defendant and, if so, whether the defendant has timely responded;

(5) Whether the defendant has filed, or intends to file, any motion to sever, dismiss, or suppress, or any other motion requiring a ruling by the District Court before trial;

(6) Whether a schedule should be set concerning any matter in the case other than trial;

(7) Whether the parties have discussed the possibility of an early resolution of the case without trial and, if so, the results of that discussion;

(8) Whether there are periods of excludable delay under the Speedy Trial Act as to which the parties agree, and what they are, and whether there are any disagreements, and what they are, to enable the Magistrate Judge to rule on periods of excludable delay at the Final Status Conference; and

(9) The estimated length of trial.

(D) Final Status Report. After the Final Discovery Conference, and any continuation of it necessary to assure that the discovery to have been provided prior to the conference is complete, the Magistrate Judge shall file for the District Judge who will preside at trial a Final Status Report that addresses:

(1) Whether a trial will be necessary;

(2) Whether all discovery to be provided under this Local Rule before the Initial Pretrial Conference with the trial judge is complete and, if not, why the case should not remain before the Magistrate Judge until discovery is complete;

(3) Whether the defendant has filed, or intends to file, any motion to sever, dismiss, or suppress and, if

so, the briefing schedule established by the Magistrate Judge;

(4) The total amount of time that has been ordered excluded thus far and the amount of time remaining under the Speedy Trial Act before trial must commence, and whether there are any pending or anticipated motions that will cause additional excludable time for Speedy Trial Act purposes;

(5) The estimated length of trial;

(6) Any other matters relevant to the progress or resolution of the case.

Adopted September 8, 1998, effective December 1, 1998.

RULE 116.6 DECLINATION OF DISCLOSURE AND PROTECTIVE ORDERS

(A) **Declination.** If in the judgment of a party it would be detrimental to the interests of justice to make any of the disclosures required by these Local Rules, such disclosures may be declined, before or at the time that disclosure is due, and the opposing party advised in writing, with a copy filed in the Clerk's Office, of the specific matters on which disclosure is declined and the reasons for declining. If the opposing party seeks to challenge the declination, that party shall file a motion to compel that states the reasons why disclosure is sought. Upon the filing of such motion, except to the extent otherwise provided by law, the burden shall be on the party declining disclosure to demonstrate, by affidavit and supporting memorandum citing legal authority, why such disclosure should not be made. The declining party may file its submissions in support of declination under seal pursuant to L.R. 7.2 for the Court's in camera consideration. Unless otherwise ordered by the Court, a redacted version of each such submission shall be served on the moving party, which may reply.

(B) **Ex Parte Motions for Protective Orders.** This Local Rule does not preclude any party from moving under L.R. 7.2 and ex parte (i.e. without serving the opposing party) for leave to file an ex parte motion for a protective order with respect to any discovery matter. Nor does this Local Rule limit the Court's power to accept or reject an ex parte motion or to decide such a motion in any manner it deems appropriate.

Adopted September 8, 1998, effective December 1, 1998.

RULE 116.7 DUTY TO SUPPLEMENT

The duties established by these Local Rules are continuing. Each party is under a duty, when it learns that a prior disclosure was in some respect inaccurate or incomplete to supplement promptly any disclosure required by these Local Rules or by the Federal Rules of Criminal Procedure.

Adopted September 8, 1998, effective December 1, 1998.

RULE 116.8 NOTIFICATION TO RELEVANT LAW ENFORCEMENT AGENCIES OF DISCOVERY OBLIGATIONS

The attorney for the government shall inform all federal, state, and local law enforcement agencies formally participating in the criminal investigation that resulted in the case of the discovery obligations set forth in these Local Rules and obtain any information subject to disclosure from each such agency.

Adopted September 8, 1998, effective December 1, 1998.

RULE 116.9 PRESERVATION OF NOTES

(A) All contemporaneous notes, memoranda, statements, reports, surveillance logs, tape recordings, and other documents memorializing matters relevant to the charges contained in the indictment made by or in the custody of any law enforcement officer whose agency at the time was formally participating in an investigation intended, in whole or in part, to result in a federal indictment shall be preserved until the entry of judgment unless otherwise ordered by the Court.

(B) These Local Rules do not require the preservation of rough drafts of reports after a subsequent draft of final report is prepared.

(C) These Local Rules do not require modification of a government agency's established procedure for the retention and disposal of documents when the agency does not reasonably anticipate a criminal prosecution.

Adopted September 8, 1998, effective December 1, 1998.

RULE 117.1 PRETRIAL CONFERENCES

(A) **Initial Pretrial Conference.** After receiving the Magistrate Judge's Final Status Report, and at least thirty (30) days before trial, or at the earliest practicable shorter time before trial consistent with the Speedy Trial Act, the judge who will preside at trial must conduct an Initial Pretrial Conference, which counsel who will conduct the trial must attend. At the Initial Pretrial Conference the judge must:

(1) Attempt to determine if the case will be resolved by a guilty plea, a plea of nolo contendere, or dismissal.

(2) If necessary, schedule a hearing on any motion to dismiss, suppress, or sever or any other motion requiring pretrial resolution.

(3) Establish a reliable trial date.

(4) Unless the declination procedure provided by L.R. 116.6 has previously been invoked, order the government to disclose to the defendant no later than twenty-one (21) days before the trial date:

(a) The exculpatory information identified in L.R. 116.2.

(b) A general description (including the approximate date, time and place) of any crime, wrong, or act the government proposes to offer pursuant to Fed. R. Evid. 404(b).

(5) Determine whether the parties have furnished statements, as defined by 18 U.S.C. § 3500(e) and Fed. R. Crim. P. 26.2(f), of witnesses they intend to call in their cases-in-chief and, if not, when they propose to do so.

(6) Determine whether any party objects to complying with the presumptive timing directives of L.R. 117.1(A)(8) and (A)(9) for the disclosure of witnesses and identification of exhibits and materials. If any party expresses an objection, the court may decide the issue(s) presented at the Initial Pretrial Conference or may order briefing and/or later argument on such issue(s).

(7) Establish a schedule for the filing and briefing of possible motions in limine and for the filing of proposed voir dire questions, proposed jury instructions, and, if appropriate, trial briefs.

(8) Unless an objection has been made pursuant to L.R. 117.1(A)(6), order that at least seven (7) days before the trial date the government must:

(a) Provide the defendant with the names and addresses of witnesses the government intends to call at trial in its case-in-chief. If the government subsequently forms an intent to call any other witness, the government shall promptly notify the defendant of the name and address of that prospective witness.

(b) Provide the defendant with copies of the exhibits and a premarked list of the exhibits the government intends to offer in its case-in-chief. If the government subsequently decides to offer any additional exhibit in its case-in-chief, the government shall promptly provide the opposing party with a copy of the exhibit and a supplemental exhibit list.

(9) Unless an objection has been made pursuant to L.R. 117.1(A)(6), order that at least three (3) days before the trial the defendant must provide the government with witness and exhibit identification and materials to the same extent the government is obligated to do so under L.R. 117.1(A)(8).

(10) Determine whether the parties will stipulate to any facts that may not be in dispute.

(11) Establish a date for a Second Pretrial Conference, to be held not more than seven (7) days before the trial date, to resolve any matters that must be decided before trial.

(12) Resolve any issues concerning excludable delay under the Speedy Trial Act.

(B) Special Orders. The judge who will preside at trial may, upon motion of a party or on the judge's own initiative, modify any of the requirements of paragraph (A) of this Local Rule if the judge determines that there are factors in the particular case that make it in the interests of justice to do so.

(C) Subsequent Pretrial Conferences. At least one subsequent Pretrial Conference shall be held unless all parties advise the court that such a conference is not necessary and the judge concurs.

Adopted September 8, 1998, effective December 1, 1998.

RULE 118.1 EFFECTIVE DATE

These Local Rules shall become effective on December 1, 1998. They shall, except as applicable time periods may have run, govern all actions pending or commenced after the effective date. Where justice so requires, proceedings in cases on the effective date shall be governed by the practice of the court before the adoption of these Local Rules.

Adopted September 8, 1998, effective December 1, 1998.

RULE 201. REFERENCE TO BANKRUPTCY COURT

Pursuant to 28 U.S.C. § 157(a), any and all cases arising under Title 11 United States Code and any and all proceedings arising under Title 11 or arising in or related to a case under Title 11 shall be referred to the judges of the bankruptcy court for the District of Massachusetts.

Adopted effective January 2, 1995.

RULE 202. BANKRUPTCY COURT JURY TRIALS

Pursuant to 28 U.S.C. § 157(e), the judges of the bankruptcy court for the District of Massachusetts are specially designated to conduct jury trials with the express consent of the parties in any proceeding which may be heard by a bankruptcy judge to which a right to jury trial applies.

Adopted effective January 2, 1995.

RULE 203. BANKRUPTCY APPEALS

(A) The bankruptcy court is authorized and directed to dismiss an appeal filed after the time specified in Bankruptcy Rule 8002 or an appeal in which the appellant has failed to file a designation of the items for the record or a statement of the issues as required by Bankruptcy Rule 8006. The bankruptcy court is also authorized and directed to decide motions to extend the foregoing deadlines and to consolidate appeals which present similar issues from a common record. Bankruptcy court orders entered under this subsection may be reviewed by the district court on motion filed within ten days of the entry of the order.

(B) The briefing schedule specified by Bankruptcy Rule 8009 may be altered only by order of the district court. If the clerk of the district court does not receive appellant's brief within the time specified by said Rule 8009, he shall forthwith provide the district judge to whom the appeal has been assigned with a proposed order for dismissal of the appeal.

(C) Upon receipt of the district court's opinion disposing of the appeal, the district court clerk shall enter judgment in accordance with Bankruptcy Rule 8016(a) and shall immediately transmit to each party and to the clerk of the Bankruptcy court a notice of entry together with a copy of the court's opinion.

(D) The bankruptcy court clerk shall enclose a copy of this rule with the notice of appeal given to each party in accordance with Bankruptcy Rule 8004; pro-vided, however, that failure of the clerk to enclose a copy of this rule shall not suspend its operation.

(E) This rule is not intended to restrict the district court's discretion as to any aspect of any appeal.

Effective September 1, 1990; amended effective January 2, 1995.

RULE 204. BANKRUPTCY COURT LOCAL RULES

Pursuant to Rule 9029(a) of the Federal Rules of Bankruptcy Procedure, the judges of the bankruptcy court for the District of Massachusetts are authorized to make and amend rules of practice and procedure. Such rules and any amendments thereto shall become effective 45 days after the receipt by the Clerk of the District Court of a certified copy of any such proposed rule or amendment as adopted by the judges of the bankruptcy court, together with a copy of the notice and all comments received regarding the rule.

Adopted effective August 1, 1997.

RULE 205. DISCIPLINARY REFERRALS BY BANKRUPTCY JUDGES

A judge of the bankruptcy court for the District of Massachusetts is authorized as a judicial officer to make referrals for disciplinary proceedings as provided under LR 83.6(5)(a).

Adopted effective August 1, 1997.

APPENDICES

APPENDIX A. LOCAL RULE 4.5 SUPPLEMENT

(A) Filing Fees—New Civil Action.

(1) The filing fee for a complaint is $150.00.*

* Publishers note: Effective February 7, 2005, the filing fee is increased to $250.00, pursuant to the Consolidated Appropriations Act of 2005 (Pub. L. 108–447).

(2) The filing fee for a notice of removal is $150.00.

(3) The filing fee for an application for writ of habeas corpus is $5.00.

(B) Miscellaneous Fees.

(1) The fee for a notice of appeal is $5.00. The fee for docketing a case on appeal is $100.00. These fees are payable to the Clerk of the District Court at the time of filing of the notice of appeal and may be paid in a single check.

(2) The fee for filing or indexing any miscellaneous matter or paper not in a case or proceeding for which a case filing fee has been paid is $20.00.

(3) The fee for a search of the records conducted by the clerk or a deputy clerk is $15.00.

(4) The fee for certifying any document or paper, whether the certification is made directly on the document or by separate instrument, is $5.00. The fee for exemplification of any document or paper is twice the amount of the fee for certification.

(5) The fee for reproducing (copying) any document is $.50 per page.

(6) The fee for reproducing a magnetic tape recording is $15.00.

(7) The fee for each microfiche sheet of film or microfilm jacket copy of any court record, where available, is $3.00.

(8) The fee for retrieving a record from the Federal Records Center is $25.00.

(9) The fee for an appeal to a district judge from a judgment of conviction by a magistrate in a misdemeanor case is $25.00.

(10) The fee for admission to practice before this court is $100.00 each, including a certificate of admission. The fee for a duplicate certificate of admission or certificate of good standing is $15.00. The fee for

filing a motion for leave to appear and practice in a particular case in the District of Massachusetts is $50.00

(11) The fee to a payor for any check paid into the court which is returned for lack of funds is $25.00.

Effective September 1, 1990. Amended effective December 18, 1996; January 1, 1998; June 1, 1999.

UNITED STATES DISTRICT COURT

APPENDIX B. CIVIL COVER SHEET

JS 44 (Rev. 3/99)

CIVIL COVER SHEET

The JS-44 civil cover sheet and the information contained herein neither replace nor supplement the filing and service of pleadings or other papers as required by law, except as provided by local rules of court. This form, approved by the Judicial Conference of the United States in September 1974, is required for the use of the Clerk of Court for the purpose of initiating the civil docket sheet. (SEE INSTRUCTIONS ON THE REVERSE OF THE FORM.)

I. (a) PLAINTIFFS

DEFENDANTS

APPENDIX B   CIVIL COVER SHEET

(b) County of Residence of First Listed Plaintiff _____
(EXCEPT IN U.S. PLAINTIFF CASES)

County of Residence of First Listed _____
(IN U.S. PLAINTIFF CASES ONLY)
NOTE: IN LAND CONDEMNATION CASES, USE THE LOCATION OF THE LAND INVOLVED.

(c) Attorney's (Firm Name, Address, and Telephone Number)

Attorneys (If Known)

II. BASIS OF JURISDICTION   (Place an "X" in One Box Only)

G 1 U.S. Government
Plaintiff

G 2 U.S. Government
Defendant

G 3 Federal Question
(U.S. Government Not a Party)

G 4 Diversity
(Indicate Citizenship of Parties
in Item III)

III. CITIZENSHIP OF PRINCIPAL PARTIES (Place an "X" in One Box for Plaintiff
(For Diversity Cases Only)   and One Box for Defendant)

	PLF	DEF		PLF	DEF
Citizen of This State	G 1	G 1	Incorporated or Principal Place of Business In This State	G 4	G 4
Citizen of Another State	G 2	G 2	Incorporated and Principal Place of Business In Another State	G 5	G 5
Citizen or Subject of a Foreign Country	G 3	G 3	Foreign Nation	G 6	G 6

IV. NATURE OF SUIT   (Place an "X" in One Box Only)

CONTRACT	TORTS		FORFEITURE/PENALTY	BANKRUPTCY	OTHER STATUTES
G 110 Insurance	**PERSONAL INJURY**	**PERSONAL INJURY**	G 610 Agriculture	G 422 Appeal 28 USC 158	G 400 State Reapportionment
G 120 Marine	G 310 Airplane	G 362 Personal Injury—	G 620 Other Food & Drug		G 410 Antitrust
G 130 Miller Act	G 315 Airplane Product	Med. Malpractice	G 625 Drug Related Seizure	G 423 Withdrawal	G 430 Banks and Banking
G 140 Negotiable Instrument	Liability	G 365 Personal Injury —	of Property 21 USC	28 USC 157	G 450 Commerce/ICC Rates/etc.
G 150 Recovery of Overpayment	G 320 Assault, Libel &	Product Liability	G 630 Liquor Laws		G 460 Deportation
& Enforcement of Judgment	Slander	G 368 Asbestos Personal	G 640 R.R. & Truck	**PROPERTY RIGHTS**	G 470 Racketeer Influenced and
G 151 Medicare Act	G 330 Federal Employers'	Injury Product	G 650 Airline Regs.	G 820 Copyrights	Corrupt Organizations
G 152 Recovery of Defaulted	Liability	Liability	G 660 Occupational	G 830 Patent	G 810 Selective Service
Student Loans	G 340 Marine	**PERSONAL PROPERTY**	Safety/Health	G 840 Trademark	G 850 Securities/Commodities/
(Excl. Veterans)	G 345 Marine Product	G 370 Other Fraud	G 690 Other		Exchange
G 153 Recovery of Overpayment	Liability	G 371 Truth in Lending			G 875 Customer Challenge
of Veteran's Benefits	G 350 Motor Vehicle	G 380 Other Personal	**LABOR**	**SOCIAL SECURITY**	12 USC 3410
G 160 Stockholders' Suits	G 355 Motor Vehicle	Property Damage	G 710 Fair Labor Standards	G 861 HIA (1395ff)	G 891 Agricultural Acts
G 190 Other Contract	Product Liability	G 385 Property Damage	Act	G 862 Black Lung (923)	G 892 Economic Stabilization Act
G 195 Contract Product Liability	G 360 Other Personal	Product Liability	G 720 Labor/Mgmt. Relations	G 863 DIWC/DIWW (405(g))	G 893 Environmental Matters
	Injury			G 864 SSID Title XVI	G 894 Energy Allocation Act
REAL PROPERTY	**CIVIL RIGHTS**	**PRISONER PETITIONS**	G 730 Labor/Mgmt.Reporting	G 865 RSI (405(g))	G 895 Freedom of
G 210 Land Condemnation	G 441 Voting	G 510 Motions to Vacate	& Disclosure Act		Information Act
G 220 Foreclosure	G 442 Employment	Sentence	G 740 Railway Labor Act	**FEDERAL TAX SUITS**	G 900 Appeal of Fee
G 230 Rent Lease & Ejectment	G 443 Housing/	Habeas Corpus:			Determination Equal Access to
G 240 Torts to Land	Accommodations	G 530 General	G 790 Other Labor Litigation	G 870 Taxes (U.S. Plaintiff	Justice
G 245 Tort Product Liability	G 444 Welfare	G 535 Death Penalty		or Defendant)	G 950 Constitutionality of
G 290 All Other Real Property	G 440 Other Civil Rights	G 540 Mandamus & Other	G 791 Empl. Ret. Inc.	G 871 IRS – Third Party	State Statutes
		G 550 Civil Rights	Security Act	26 USC 7609	G 890 Other Statutory Actions
		G 555 Prison Condition			

V. ORIGIN   (PLACE AN "X" IN ONE BOX ONLY)

G 1 Original
Proceeding

G 2 Removed from
State Court

G 3 Remanded from
Appellate Court

G 4 Reinstated or
Reopened

G 5 Transferred from
another district
(specify)

G 6 Multidistrict
Litigation

G 7 Appeal to
District
Judge from
Magistrate
Judgment

VI. CAUSE OF ACTION   (Cite the U.S. Civil Statute under which you are filing and write brief statement of cause.
Do not cite jurisdictional statutes unless diversity.)

**VII. REQUESTED IN
COMPLAINT:**   G CHECK IF THIS IS A CLASS ACTION
UNDER F.R.C.P. 23

DEMAND $

CHECK YES only if demanded in complaint:
JURY DEMAND: G Yes   G No

**VIII. RELATED CASE(S)
IF ANY**   (See instructions):

JUDGE _____

DOCKET NUMBER _____

DATE

SIGNATURE OF ATTORNEY OF RECORD

FOR OFFICE USE ONLY

RECEIPT # _____   AMOUN _____   APPLYING IFP _____   JUDGE _____   MAG. JUDGE _____

JS 44 Reverse (Rev. 12/96)

INSTRUCTIONS FOR ATTORNEYS COMPLETING CIVIL COVER SHEET FORM JS-44

Authority For Civil Cover Sheet

The JS-44 civil cover sheet and the information contained herein neither replaces nor supplements the filings and service of pleading or other papers as required by law, except as provided by local rules of court. This form, approved by the Judicial Conference of the United States in September 1974, is required for the use of the Clerk of Court for the purpose of initiating the civil docket sheet. Consequently, a civil cover sheet is submitted to the Clerk of Court for each civil complaint filed. The attorney filing a case should complete the form as follows:

I.   (a) Plaintiffs-Defendants. Enter names (last, first, middle initial) of plaintiff and defendant. If the plaintiff or defendant is a government agency, use only the full name or standard abbreviations. If the plaintiff or defendant is an official within a government agency, identify first the agency and then the official, giving both name and title.

(b.) County of Residence. For each civil case filed, except U.S. plaintiff cases, enter the name of the county where the first listed plaintiff resides at the time of filing. In U.S. plaintiff cases, enter the name of the county in which the first listed defendant resides at the time of filing. (NOTE: In land condemnation cases, the county of residence of the "defendant" is the location of the tract of land involved.)

(c) Attorneys. Enter the firm name, address, telephone number, and attorney of record. If there are several attorneys, list them on an attachment, noting in this section "(see attachment)".

II.   Jurisdiction. The basis of jurisdiction is set forth under Rule 8(a), F.R.C.P., which requires that jurisdictions be shown in pleadings. Place an "X" in one of the boxes. If there is more than one basis of jurisdiction, precedence is given in the order shown below.

United States plaintiff. (1) Jurisdiction based on 28 U.S.C. 1345 and 1348. Suits by agencies and officers of the United States, are included here.

United States defendant. (2) When the plaintiff is suing the United States, its officers or agencies, place an "X" in this box.

Federal question. (3) This refers to suits under 28 U.S.C. 1331, where jurisdiction arises under the Constitution of the United States, an amendment to the Constitution, an act of Congress or a treaty of the United States. In cases where the U.S. is a party, the U.S. plaintiff or defendant code takes precedence, and box 1 or 2 should be marked.

Diversity of citizenship. (4) This refers to suits under 28 U.S.C. 1332, where parties are citizens of different states. When Box 4 is checked, the citizenship of the different parties must be checked. (See Section III below; federal question actions take precedence over diversity cases.)

III.   Residence (citizenship) of Principal Parties. This section of the JS-44 is to be completed if diversity of citizenship was indicated above. Mark this section for each principal party.

IV.   Nature of Suit. Place an "X" in the appropriate box. If the nature of suit cannot be determined, be sure the cause of action, in Section IV below, is sufficient to enable the deputy clerk or the statistical clerks in the Administrative Office to determine the nature of suit. If the cause fits more than one nature of suit, select the most definitive.

V.   Origin. Place an "X" in one of the seven boxes.

Original Proceedings. (1) Cases which originate in the United States district courts.

Removed from State Court. (2) Proceedings initiated in state courts may be removed to the district courts under Title 28 U.S.C., Section 1441. When the petition for removal is granted, check this box.

Remanded from Appellate Court. (3) Check this box for cases remanded to the district court for further action. Use the date of remand as the filing date.

Reinstated or Reopened. (4) Check this box for cases reinstated or reopened in the district court. Use the reopening date as the filing date.

Transferred from Another District. (5) For cases transferred under Title 28 U.S.C. Section 1404(a) Do not use this for within district transfers or multidistrict litigation transfers.

Multidistrict Litigation. (6) Check this box when a multidistrict case is transferred into the district under authority of Title 28 U.S.C. Section 1407. When this box is checked, do not check (5) above.

Appeal to District Judge from Magistrate Judgment. (7) Check this box for an appeal from a magistrate judge's decision.

VI.   Cause of Action. Report the civil statute directly related to the cause of action and give a brief description of the cause.

VII.   Requested in Complaint. Class Action. Place an "X" in this box if you are filing a class action under Rule 23, F.R.Cv.P.

Demand. In this space enter the dollar amount (in thousands of dollars) being demanded or indicate other demand such as a preliminary injunction.

Jury Demand. Check the appropriate box to indicate whether or not a jury is being demanded.

VIII.   Related Cases. This section of the JS-44 is used to reference related pending cases if any. If there are related pending cases, insert the docket numbers and the corresponding judge names for such cases.

Date and Attorney Signature. Date and sign the civil cover sheet.

APPENDIX C. CIVIL CATEGORY SHEET

UNITED STATES DISTRICT COURT
DISTRICT OF MASSACHUSETTS

1. TITLE OF CASE (NAME OF FIRST PARTY ON EACH SIDE ONLY) —————

——

2. CATEGORY IN WHICH THE CASE BELONGS BASED UPON THE NUMBERED NATURE OF SUIT CODE LISTED ON THE CIVIL COVER SHEET. (SEE LOCAL RULE 40.1(A)(1)).
   —— I.   160, 410, 470, R.23, REGARDLESS
           OF NATURE OF SUIT.
   —— II. 195, 368, 400, 440, 441-444, 540, 550,   *Also complete AO 120 or AO 121 for
           555, 625, 710, 720, 730, 740, 790, 791,   patent, trademark or copyright cases
           820*, 830*, 840*, 850, 890, 892-894,
           895, 950.
   —— III. 110, 120, 130, 140, 151, 190, 210, 230,
           240, 245, 290, 310, 315, 320, 330, 340,
           345, 350, 355, 360, 362, 365, 370, 371,
           380, 385, 450, 891.
   —— IV. 220, 422, 423, 430, 460, 510, 530, 610,
           620, 630, 640, 650, 660, 690, 810,
           861-865, 870, 871, 875, 900.
   —— V.   150, 152, 153.

3. TITLE AND NUMBER, IF ANY, OF RELATED CASES. (SEE LOCAL RULE 40.1(G)). IF MORE THAN ONE PRIOR RELATED CASE HAS BEEN FILED IN THIS DISTRICT PLEASE INDICATE THE TITLE AND NUMBER OF THE FIRST FILED CASE IN THIS COURT.

——

4. HAS A PRIOR ACTION BETWEEN THE SAME PARTIES AND BASED ON THE SAME CLAIM EVER BEEN FILED IN THIS COURT?
   YES ☐   NO ☐

5. DOES THE COMPLAINT IN THIS CASE QUESTION THE CONSTITUTIONALITY OF AN ACT OF CONGRESS AFFECTING THE PUBLIC INTEREST? (SEE 28 USC § 2403)
   YES ☐   NO ☐
   IF SO, IS THE U.S.A. OR AN OFFICER, AGENT OR EMPLOYEE OF THE U.S.A. PARTY?
   YES ☐   NO ☐

6. IS THIS CASE REQUIRED TO BE HEARD AND DETERMINED BY A DISTRICT COURT OF THREE JUDGES PURSUANT TO TITLE 28 USC § 2284?
   YES ☐   NO ☐

7. DO ALL OF ALL THE PARTIES IN THIS ACTION, EXCLUDING GOVERNMEN-TAL AGENCIES OF THE UNITED STATES AND THE COMMONWEALTH OF MASSACHUSETTS ("GOVERNMENTAL AGENCIES"), RESIDING IN MASSACHU-SETTS RESIDE IN THE SAME DIVISION?—(SEE LOCAL RULE 40.1(D)).
   YES ☐   NO ☐
   A. IF YES, IN WHICH DIVISION DO ALL OF THE NON–GPVERNMENTAL PARTIES RESIDE?
      EASTERN DIVISION☐   CENTRAL DIVISION☐   WESTERN DIVISION☐
   B. IF NO, IN WHICH DIVISION DO THE MAJORITY OF THE PLAINTIFFS OR THE ONLY PARTIES, EXCLUDING GOVERNMENTAL AGENCIES, RESID-ING IN MASSACHUSETTS RESIDE?
      EASTERN DIVISION☐   CENTRAL DIVISION☐   WESTERN DIVISION☐

(PLEASE TYPE OR PRINT)
ATTORNEY'S NAME ————————————————————————————
ADDRESS ——————————————————————————————————
TELEPHONE NO. ————————————————————————————————
(Categfrm.rev - 11/00)

APPENDIX D. NOTICE OF SCHEDULING CONFERENCE

UNITED STATES DISTRICT COURT
DISTRICT OF MASSACHUSETTS

_____
         v.   Civil Action No._____
_____

NOTICE OF SCHEDULING CONFERENCE

An initial scheduling conference will be held in Courtroom No. ___ on the ___ floor at ____.m. on _____, 19___, in accordance with Fed.R.Civ.P. 16(b) and Local Rule 16.1. The court considers attendance of the senior lawyers ultimately responsible for the case and compliance with sections (B), (C), and (D) of Local Rule 16.1[1] to be of the utmost importance. Counsel may be given a continuance only if actually engaged on trial. Failure to comply fully with this notice and with sections (B), (C), and (D) of Local Rule 16.1 may result in sanctions under Local Rule 1.3. Counsel for the plaintiff is responsible for ensuring that all parties and/or their attorneys, who have not filed an answer or appearance with the court, are notified of the scheduling conference date.

_____
Date

                    United States District Judge

          By: _____
                    Deputy Clerk

_____

1. These sections of Local Rule 16.1 provide:

(B) Obligations or counsel to confer. Unless otherwise ordered by the judge, counsel for the parties shall, pursuant to Fed.R.Civ.P. 26(f), confer no later than fourteen (14) days before the date for the scheduling conference for the purpose of:

(1) preparing an agenda of matters to be discussed at the scheduling conference,

(2) preparing a proposed pretrial schedule for the case that includes a plan for discovery, and

(3) considering whether they will consent to trial by magistrate judge.

(C) Settlement proposing. Unless otherwise ordered by the judge, the plaintiff shall present written settlement proposals to all defendants no later than ten (10) days before the date for the scheduling conference. Defense counsel shall have conferred with their clients on the subject of settlement before the scheduling conference and be prepared to respond to the proposals at the scheduling conference.

(D) Joint statement. Unless otherwise ordered by the judge, the parties are required to file, no later than five (5) business days before the scheduling conference and after consideration of the topics contemplated by Fed.R.Civ.P. 16(b) and 26(f), a joint statement containing a proposed pretrial schedule, which shall include:

(1) a joint discovery plan scheduling the time and length for all discovery events, that shall

(a) conform to the obligation to limit discovery set forth in Fed.R.Civ.P. 26(b), and

(b) take into account the desirability of conducting phased discovery in which the first phase is limited to developing information needed for a realistic assessment of the case and, if the case does not terminate, the second phase is directed at information needed to prepare for trial: and

(2) a proposal schedule for the filing of motions; and

(3) certifications signed by counsel and by an authorized representative of each party affirming that each party and that party's counsel have conferred:

(a) with a view to establishing a budget for the costs of conducting the full course—and various alternative courses—of the litigation; and

(b) to consider the resolution of the litigation through the use of alternative dispute resolution programs such as those outlined in Local Rule 16.4.

To the extent that all parties are able to reach agreement on a proposal pretrial schedule, they shall so indicate. To the extent that the parties differ on what the pretrial schedule should be, they shall set forth separately the items on which they differ and indicate the nature of that difference. The purpose of the parties' proposed pretrial schedule or schedules shall be to advise the judge of the parties' best estimates of the amounts of time they will need to accomplish specified pretrial steps. The parties' proposed agenda for the scheduling conference, and their proposed pretrial schedule or schedules, shall be considered by the judge as advisory only.

ATTACHMENTS

ATTACHMENT A. CORRELATOR—EXPENSE AND DELAY PLAN PROVISION TO LOCAL RULE

Publisher's Note

The Expense and Delay Reduction Plan appears, infra.

Article I, Rule 1.01 is the basis for L.R. 81.2—Definition of Judicial Officer.

Article I, Rule 1.02 is the basis for L.R. 16.1—Early Assessment of Cases.

Article I, Rule 1.03 is the basis for L.R. 16.3—Case Management Conferences.

Article II, Rule 2.01 is the basis for L.R. 26.1—Control of Discovery.

Article II, Rule 2.02 is the basis for L.R. 26.2—Sequencing of Discovery.

Article II, Rule 2.03 is the basis for L.R. 35.1—Disclosure of Medical Information in Personal Injury Cases.

Article II, Rule 2.04 is the basis for L.R. 26.6—Court Filings and Costs.

Article II, Rule 2.05(c) and (d) is the basis for Rules 33.1, 34.1 and 36.1—Interrogatories, Document Requests and Request for Admissions.

Article II, Rule 2.05(a) and (b) is the basis for L.R. 26.3—Subsequent Stages of Discovery.

Article II, Rule 2.06 is the basis for L.R. 26.5—Uniform Definitions in Discovery Requests.

Article III of the Plan, Rule 3.01 is the basis for L.R. 7.1(A)—Motion Practice.

Article III of the Plan, Rule 3.02 is the basis for L.R. 15.1—Addition of New Parties.

Article IV, Rules 4.01, 4.02 and 4.03 is the basis for L.R. 16.4—Alternative Dispute Resolution.

Article V, Rule 5.01 is the basis for L.R. 16.5—Final Pretrial Conference.

Article V, Rule 5.01(e) is the basis for L.R. 40.3—Continuances.

Article V, Rule 5.02 is the basis for L.R. 26.4—Procedures for Handling Experts.

Article V, Rule 5.03 is the basis for L.R. 43.1—Trial.

Article VI, Rule 6.01 is the basis for L.R. 1.3—Sanctions.

Adopted effective October 1, 1992.

ATTACHMENT B. CORRELATOR—LOCAL RULE TO EXPENSE AND DELAY PLAN

Publisher's Note

The Expense and Delay Reduction Plan appears, infra.

L.R. 1.2—Application—is designed to provide a transition plan for these and other amendments.

L.R. 1.3—Sanctions—is drawn from Article VI, Rule 6.01 and the reporter's commentary and notes thereto.

L.R. 7.1(A)—Motion Practice—is drawn from Article III of the Plan, Rule 3.01.

L.R. 15.1—Addition of New Parties—is drawn from Article III of the Plan, Rule 3.02.

L.R. 16.1—Early Assessment of Cases—is essentially drawn from Article I, Rule 1.02.

L.R. 16.3—Case Management Conferences—is drawn from Article I, Rule 1.03.

L.R. 16.4—Alternative Dispute Resolution—is drawn from Article IV, Rules 4.01, 4.02 and 4.03.

L.R. 16.5—Final Pretrial Conference—is drawn from Article V, Rule 5.01.

L.R. 26.1—Control of Discovery—is drawn from Article II, Rule 2.01.

L.R. 26.2—Sequencing of Discovery—is drawn from Article II, Rule 2.02.

L.R. 26.3—Subsequent Stages of Discovery—is drawn from Article II, Rule 2.05.

L.R. 26.4—Procedures for Handling Experts—is drawn from Article V, Rule 5.02.

L.R. 26.5—Uniform Definitions in Discovery Requests—is drawn from Article II, Rule 2.06.

L.R. 26.6—Court Filings and Costs—is drawn from Article II, Rule 2.04.

Rule 33.1—Interrogatories and Requests—is drawn from Article II, Rule 2.05(c) and (d).

Rule 34.1—Document Production—is drawn from Article II, Rule 2.05(c) and (d).

Rule 35.1—Disclosure of Medical Information in Personal Injury Cases—is drawn from Article II, Rule 2.03.

Rule 36.1—Request for Admissions—is drawn from Article II, Rule 2.05(c) and (d).

L.R. 37.1—Imposition of Sanctions—is drawn from Article VI, Rule 6.01.

L.R. 40.3—Continuances—is drawn from Article V, Rule 5.01(e).

L.R. 43.1—Trial—is drawn from Article V, Rule 5.03.

L.R. 81.2—Definition of Judicial Officer—is drawn from Article I, Rule 1.01.

Adopted effective October 1, 1992.

EXPENSE AND DELAY REDUCTION PLAN

Adopted November 18, 1991

Including Amendments Received Through
January 1, 2005

Research Note

Use WESTLAW ® *to find cases citing or applying specific rules.* WESTLAW *may also be used to search for specific terms in court rules or to update court rules. See the MA–RULES and MA–ORDERS Scope Screens for detailed descriptive information and search tips.*

Amendments to these rules are published, as received, in the North Eastern 2d *and the* Massachusetts Decisions *advance sheets.*

Table of Rules

ARTICLE I.   PRETRIAL DIFFERENTIAL CASE MANAGEMENT

RULE 1.01   DEFINITION OF A JUDICIAL OFFICER

As used in this Plan, "judicial officer" refers to either a United States District Court Judge or a United States Magistrate Judge.

Comment

The definition of "judicial officer" used in this Rule is derived from the definition set forth in the Civil Justice Reform Act, 28 U.S.C. § 482.

RULE 1.02   EARLY ASSESSMENT OF CASES

(a) Scheduling Conference in Civil Cases. In every civil action, except in categories of actions exempted by district court rule as inappropriate, the judge shall convene a scheduling conference as soon as practicable, but in no event more than ninety (90) days after the appearance of a defendant or the time that is specified in Federal Rule of Civil Procedure 16, if it is shorter. In cases removed to this court from a state court or transferred from any other federal court, the judge shall convene a scheduling conference within sixty (60) days after removal or transfer.

(b) Obligation of Counsel to Confer. Unless otherwise ordered by the judge, counsel for the parties shall confer no later than ten (10) days prior to the date for the scheduling conference for the purpose of:

(1) preparing an agenda of matters to be discussed at the scheduling conference,

(2) preparing a proposed pretrial schedule for the case that includes a plan for discovery, and

(3) considering whether they will consent to trial by magistrate judge.

(c) Settlement Proposals. Unless otherwise ordered by the judge, the plaintiff shall present written settlement proposals to all defendants no later than ten (10) days prior to the date for the scheduling conference. Defense counsel shall have conferred with their clients on the subject of settlement prior to

the scheduling conference and be prepared to respond to the proposals at the scheduling conference.

(d) Joint Statement. Unless otherwise ordered by the judge, the parties are required to file, no later than five (5) business days prior to the scheduling conference, a joint statement containing a proposed pretrial schedule, which shall include:

(1) a joint discovery plan scheduling the time and length for all discovery events, that shall

    (A) conform to the obligation to limit discovery set forth in Federal Rule 26(b), and

    (B) consider the desirability of conducting phased discovery in which the first phase is limited to developing information needed for a realistic assessment of the case and, if the case does not terminate, the second phase is directed at information needed to prepare for trial; and

(2) a proposed schedule for the filing of motions.

(3) certifications signed by counsel and by an authorized representative of each party affirming that each party and that party's counsel have conferred with a view to establishing a budget for the costs of conducting the full course—and various alternative course—of the litigation.

To the extent that all parties are able to reach agreement on a proposed pretrial schedule, they shall so indicate. To the extent that the parties differ on what the pretrial schedule should be, they shall set forth separately the items on which they differ and indicate the nature of that difference. The purpose of the parties' proposed pretrial schedule or schedules shall be to advise the judge of the parties' best estimates of the amounts of time they will need to accomplish specified pretrial steps. The parties' proposed agenda for the scheduling conference, and their proposed pretrial schedule or schedules, shall be considered by the judge as advisory only.

(e) Conduct of Scheduling Conference. At or following the scheduling conference, the judge shall make an early determination of whether the case is "complex" or otherwise appropriate for careful and deliberate monitoring in an individualized and case-specific manner. The judge shall consider assigning any case so categorized to a case management conference or series of conferences under Rule 1.03. The factors to be considered by the judge in making this decision include:

(1) the complexity of the case (the number of parties, claims, and defenses raised, the legal difficulty of the issues presented, and the factual difficulty of the subject matter);

(2) the amount of time reasonably needed by the litigants and their attorneys to prepare the case for trial;

(3) the judicial and other resources required and available for the preparation and disposition of the case;

(4) whether the case belongs to those categories of cases that:

(A) involve little or no discovery,

(B) ordinarily require little or no additional judicial intervention, or

(C) generally fall into identifiable and easily managed patterns;

(5) the extent to which individualized and case-specific treatment will promote the goal of reducing cost and delay in civil litigation; and

(6) whether the public interest requires that the case receive intense judicial attention.

In other respects, the scheduling conference shall be conducted according to the provisions for a pretrial conference under Federal Rule of Civil Procedure 16 and for a case management conference under Rule 1.03.

(f) Scheduling Orders. Following the conference, the judge shall enter a scheduling order that will govern the pretrial phase of the case. Unless the judge determines otherwise, the scheduling order shall include specific deadlines or general time frameworks for:

(1) amendments to the pleadings;

(2) service of, and compliance with, written discovery requests;

(3) the completion of depositions, including, if applicable, the terms for taking and using videotape depositions;

(4) the identification of trial experts;

(5) the disclosure of the information regarding experts, as contemplated by Federal Rule of Civil Procedure 26(b)(4)(A)(i);

(6) the filing of motions;

(7) a date for a settlement conference, to be attended by trial counsel and, in the discretion of the judge, their clients;

(8) one or more case management conferences and/or the final pretrial conference;

(9) a date for a final pretrial conference, which shall occur within eighteen months after the filing of the complaint;

(10) the joinder of any additional parties;

(11) early and binding disclosure of expert witnesses;

(12) submission of an affidavit of the expert witness' statement in advance of his or her deposition; and

(13) any other procedural matter that the judge determines is appropriate for the fair and efficient management of the litigation.

(g) Modification of Scheduling Order. The scheduling order shall specify that its provisions, including any deadlines, having been established with the participation of all parties, can be modified only by order of the judge, or the magistrate judge if so authorized by the judge, and only upon a showing of good cause supported by affidavits, other evidentiary materials, or references to pertinent portions of the record.

Comment

The most effectively managed cases often are those in which a relatively early scheduling conference is convened by the judge, and in which a case-specific scheduling order is worked out with substantial input from the parties. Experience demonstrates that scheduling orders can not be expected to work well if one or both litigants do not seriously believe that the order will be enforced. If a routine form order is issued, without actual participation by the parties, it is quite likely that it will have to be modified later to suit the particular characteristics of the case. To make it clear to all participants that the scheduling procedure is to be taken seriously, Rule 1.02 calls for the conference to be conducted and the order to be issued by a district judge. This was thought more likely to produce a more reliable schedule because if the process were handled by a magistrate judge, the district judge, whose schedule ultimately will determine when the case is tried, might be more likely to revise it or be more receptive to an application for modification by a party who is unhappy with it.

The Civil Justice Reform Act requires the court to consider including a method of "systematic, differential treatment of civil cases that tailors the level of individualized and case specific management" to the needs of the particular case. This may be accomplished by flexible scheduling that relies on judicial discretion. Although emphasizing the use of judicial discretion will require the expenditure of a judge's time, it is felt that resort to a practice of standard procedures and deadlines actually could increase costs and delay by generating additional hearings and conferences concerning the fairness of the application of the deadlines and procedures to the individual case.

Even a schedule of presumptive deadlines and procedures that may be rebutted upon the showing of good cause would be too restrictive. Some cases need more judicial management than others, and some may need none at all. The procedures adopted by the court should be designed to allow the judicial officer to make an early assessment of each case filed and to identify those actions that may be amenable to settlement or other alternative disposition techniques. Arguably, a schedule of presumptive deadlines would put counsel on notice of a general time framework for resolving a dispute deemed to be "complex" or otherwise appropriate for particularized management. But it also would tend to decrease the valuable exercise of a judge's discretion and insight with respect to a particular case. Presumptive deadlines should not be necessary if the scheduling conference and case management conferences are used wisely.

A scheduling conference is required for every civil action filed, with the exception of those categories of cases that expressly are exempted by local rule because they do not warrant the use of any automatic management procedures. Over-management is as undesirable as under-management. Rule 1.02 is the only procedure mandated by these rules. Further management by a judicial officer is a matter of discretion to be exercised on the basis of the circumstances of individual cases.

An individual judge may make greater or lesser use of the options provided by Rule 1.02. Some judges may elect to assign a large number of cases to a case management program. Others might employ a higher threshold, assigning only those cases that they anticipate would benefit most from specific, tailored, individual attention. Subdivision (e) lists six factors that a judge may consider in deciding whether to assign a given case to further case management.

The attorneys must take seriously their pre-conference obligations under subdivisions (b), (c) and (d) of Rule 1.02. This is critical to the success of the scheduling conference procedure. Unless they come to the conference prepared, as prescribed by this Rule, time will be wasted and the conference will not be fully effective. The court must enforce the performance of these obligations by counsel.

The four core objectives that the Civil Justice Reform Act identifies for effective case management are (1) to explore the parties' receptivity to and the propriety of settlement, (2) to identify or formulate the principal issues in contention, thereby narrowing the contested legal or factual issues, and possibly paving the way for more expedited discovery and even settlement, (3) to prepare a discovery schedule and plan that sets out concisely and firmly the requirements of litigants, counsel, and the court, and (4) to set time limits for the completion of discovery. The purpose of the Rule 1.02 conference is to provide the judge with sufficient information to meet these objectives, and to tailor an appropriate scheduling order.

Subdivision (f) lists thirteen specific items to be included in the scheduling order. However, a judge may determine that certain of these measures are unnecessary or are premature or may suggest the use of other case management procedures. Therefore, the options listed should not be applied in a rote manner in the order. The exercise of case specific judicial discretion should be the foundation of the scheduling order.

The date for the final pretrial conference, or the trial itself, should be set as early as possible. By moving cases toward trial, the court meets its basic obligation to litigants seeking relief in the federal court system. Further, it is recognized widely that establishing firm completion dates is among the most effective methods for prompting settlement. The final

pretrial conference or trial date may be set according to such criteria as case complexity (with simple cases having time priority) or specific "case events" that signal the trial date. The Civil Justice Reform Act suggests a standard of eighteen months after the filing of the complaint. Exceptions to the eighteen month time limit may be necessary if the judge determines that it is impossible to schedule the case within that time because of its complexity, or because of other special circumstances.

Rule 1.02(f) requires that a date for a final pretrial conference be set at the time of the scheduling order. Setting a firm trial date early in the case can be beneficial. Realistically, however, it may not be possible to fix trial dates with any certainty only two or three months after the case has been instituted. Perhaps the most important characteristic of scheduling orders is that they be reliable, so that they are unlikely to be modified at a later date. This rule reflects the view that, in some cases, it is better to set a reliable date for a final pretrial conference and then to establish a practice of setting actual trial dates as soon after the final pretrial conference or, close of discovery, as reasonably as possible. If attorneys understand that it is the practice in this district for cases to be tried within a month or two after the final pretrial conference, setting a reliable date for that conference will have many of the same beneficial effects as would setting a trial date at the scheduling conference.

Reporter's Notes to Rule 1.02

1. The Federal Rules of Civil Procedure establish consistent and uniform time limits for several relevant procedures:

Federal Rule 4(e)—requires that process be served within 120 days after the filing of the complaint.

Federal Rule 6—sets time limits generally.

Federal Rule 12(a)—establishes the time limit for answering.

Federal Rule 15(a)—prescribes the time limit for amending pleadings.

Federal Rule 56—provides the time limit for summary judgment.

There is no Federal Rule, however, that establishes a consistent and uniform time limit for discovery or pretrial management.

2. Relevant Local Rules of the United States District Court for the District of Massachusetts currently provide for the categorization of actions, time limits, and other differential case management techniques.

(a) Local rules that provide for the categorization of actions include:

Local Rule 3.1—requires the party filing the initial pleading also to file a civil cover sheet and the local category sheet.

Local Rule 16.2—identifies certain categories of actions that are exempt from the scheduling and planning provisions of Federal Rule 16(b).

Local Rule 40.1—divides all civil cases filed into five categories based upon the "nature of the suit," for purposes of assignment, and divides criminal cases into three categories based on "complexity" and "nature of suit."

(b) Local rules that provide for time limits include:

Local Rule 4.1—provides that process must be served within 120 days (consistent with Federal Rule 4(e)).

Local Rule 7.1—provides that opposition to a motion must be submitted within 14 days.

Local Rule 41.1—calls for dismissal for want of prosecution after 1 year of inactivity.

Local Rule 81.1—sets forth time limits with respect to removal of an action from state to federal court.

(c) Local rules that provide for miscellaneous differential management techniques include:

Local Rule 40.1—provides that "related" civil cases are assigned to the same judge.

RULE 1.03 CASE MANAGEMENT CONFERENCE

(a) **Conduct of Case Management Conference.** The case management conference shall be presided over by a judicial officer who, in furtherance of the scheduling order required by Rule 1.02, may:

(1) explore the possibility of settlement;

(2) identify or formulate (or order the attorneys to formulate) the principal issues in contention;

(3) prepare (or order the attorneys to prepare) a discovery schedule and discovery plan that, if the presiding judicial officer deems appropriate, might:

(A) identify and limit the volume of discovery available in order to avoid unnecessary or unduly burdensome or expensive discovery;

(B) sequence discovery into two or more stages; and

(C) include time limits set for the completion of discovery;

(4) establish deadlines for filing motions and a time framework for their disposition;

(5) provide for the "staged resolution" or "bifurcation of issues for trial" consistent with Federal Rule 42(b); and

(6) explore any other matter that the judicial officer determines is appropriate for the fair and efficient management of the litigation.

(b) **Obligation of Counsel to Confer.** Prior to the case management conference, the judicial officer may require counsel for the parties to confer for the purpose of preparing a joint statement containing

(1) an agenda of matters that one or more parties believe should be addressed at the conference; and

(2) a report advising the judicial officer whether the case is progressing within the allotted time limits and in accord with the specified pretrial steps.

This statement is to be filed with the court no later than five (5) business days prior to the case management conference.

(c) **Additional Case Management Conferences.** Nothing in this rule shall be construed to prevent the convening of additional case management conferences by the judicial officer as may be thought appropriate

in the circumstances of the particular case. In any event, a conference should not terminate without the parties being instructed as to when and for what purpose they are to return to the court. Any conference under this rule designated as final shall be conducted pursuant to Federal Rule of Civil Procedure 16(d).

Comment

Rule 1.03 gives the court general authority to continue its management of a case, providing for one or more pretrial conferences along the lines prescribed by Federal Rule 16. Whether, when, and how frequently to employ this procedure is left to the judicial officer in charge of the pretrial processing of the case. No mandatory case management conference is prescribed by Rule 1.03. Many cases simply will not require any formal judicial control beyond the scheduling conference.

In arriving at a case management plan, the judicial officer should recognize that, although cases may be classified according to general notions of complexity, each case is unique and may require procedures tailored to fit its specific characteristics. The strategy developed by the judge for each case should be "event-oriented," with certain litigation events viewed as important benchmarks in ascertaining case progress, limit the periods of time between case events, and incorporate methods to supervise and control these intervals in order to make them more productive.

The scheduling conference is intended to provide an early opportunity for the litigants and their attorneys to narrow the areas of inquiry to those that truly are relevant and material, to establish priorities for completion of the most important tasks as quickly as possible, particularly any that might be dispositive of the action, and to devote attention to weighing the value of uncovering every single item of "relevant" material against the value of resolving the dispute more fairly, more quickly, and less expensively.

In many instances, it will be desirable for the judicial officer to convene a case management conference after the parties have conducted some discovery. That will enable the judicial officer to ascertain the progress that is being made and the kinds of problems the case is likely to present. In advance of the conference, the judicial officer should become familiar with the case file in order to be able to discuss scheduling and other issues with counsel on an informed basis. In that setting, any resulting order will be credible and recognized by counsel as being firm, absent a demonstration of good cause for its modification. The judge should be willing to modify an order to accommodate any legitimate problems it may create, but should be unwilling to do so merely because one side or the other, or even all the parties, file a motion alleging in some conclusory fashion that they "need more time."

The Civil Justice Reform Act suggests certain methods by which the judicial officer, at an early date, may become involved in and manage the pretrial process, assessing and planning the progress of the case. These are "setting early, firm trial dates," "authority to control motion practice," "authority to control discovery." Of course, it is imperative that the case be kept moving toward trial.

It should be a guiding principle that, before any meeting between the judicial officer and the parties is adjourned, the judicial officer should give counsel a date to return, with clear instructions as to what will be expected of them at the time. This practice should be observed whether the "meeting" is denominated a case management conference, a status conference, or occurs for any other purpose.

One objective of the Civil Justice Reform Act is to thwart attempts by wealthy or powerful litigants to impede appropriate discovery by litigants with more modest resources. Federal Rule 26 already provides considerable authority to control discovery. The Civil Justice Reform Act gives district judges and magistrate judges the additional authority to control the extent of discovery, the time for its completion, and to ensure compliance with appropriate requested discovery in a timely fashion.

The Civil Justice Reform Act also provides the judicial officer with the authority to streamline motion practice by setting deadlines for filing motions as well as target dates for deciding them. That should be part of the objective of any case management effort under Rule 1.03.

Reporter's Notes to Rule 1.03

1. Relevant Local Rules of the United States District Court for the District of Massachusetts include:

Local Rule 16.2—states that a motion for the continuance of a trial, evidentiary hearing, or any other proceeding, will be granted only for good cause.

Local Rule 37—provides that prior to filing any discovery motion, counsel for each of the parties shall confer in good faith to narrow the areas of disagreement to the greatest possible extent.

2. It may be desirable for the judicial officer to require in advance of the case management conference that, in addition to preparing a suggested case management plan, the counsel complete and submit a Case Disclosure Form ("CDF") to the judicial officer. (*See* Appendix A: "Plaintiff Case Disclosure Form" and Appendix B: "Defendant Case Disclosure Form.") Like the case management plan, the purpose of the CDF would be to require the lawyers to analyze and explain their case with considerable care. But, the CDF also requires the lawyers to disclose additional information that may be of use to the judicial officer in evaluating and managing the case that may not appear in counsels' suggested case management plans.

3. For a discussion of the managerial techniques that have been incorporated into local court rules, *see generally Pretrial Conference: A Critical Examination of Local Rules Adopted by Federal Courts*, 64 Va.L.Rev. 467 (1978).

4. The *Manual for Complex Litigation, Second* (1985) suggests a series of four pretrial conferences: the first to assume control of the case and to handle preliminary matters such as pleading and the joinder of parties and claims; the second to plan discovery; the third to control the discovery process and provide for pretrial briefs; and the last to plan the details of the trial. The original *Manual* did the same. The *Manual* also recognizes that these procedures must be altered to fit the needs of each case.

5. For an analysis of the successes and problems faced by the courts in cases in which some of the Manual's procedures have been utilized, *see* Note, *The Judicial Panel and the Conduct of Multidistrict Litigation*, 87 Harv.L.Rev. 1001 (1974).

ARTICLE II. DISCOVERY

RULE 2.01　CONTROL OF DISCOVERY

(a) Cooperative Discovery. The judicial officer should encourage cost effective discovery by means of the voluntary exchange of information among litigants and their attorneys. This may be accomplished through the use of:

(1) informal, cooperative discovery practices in which counsel provide information to opposing counsel without resort to formal discovery procedures; or

(2) stipulations entered into by the parties with respect to deposition notices, waiver of signing, and other matters, except that the parties may not enter into stipulations extending the time for responding to discovery requests or otherwise modify discovery procedures ordered by the judicial officer.

(b) Disclosure Orders. The judicial officer may order the parties to submit at the scheduling conference, or at any subsequent time the officer deems appropriate, sworn statements disclosing certain information to every other party. At the discretion of the judicial officer, this order may direct the submission of:

(1) a sworn statement from a claimant, whether plaintiff, third-party plaintiff, cross-claimant, or counterclaimant, that:

(A) itemizes all economic loss and provides a computation of damages for which recovery is sought, if any, sustained prior to the date of service of process;

(B) identifies all persons then known to the claimant or the claimant's attorney who witnessed or participated in the transaction or occurrence giving rise to the claim or otherwise known or believed to have substantial discoverable information about the claim or defenses, together with a statement of the subject and a brief summary of that information;

(C) identifies all opposing parties, and all officers, directors, and employees of opposing parties, from whom statements have been obtained by or on behalf of the claimant regarding the subject matter of the claim; and

(D) identifies all governmental agencies or officials then known to the claimant or the claimant's attorney to have investigated the transaction or occurrence giving rise to the claim; and

(2) a sworn statement from a defendant, whether the direct defendant, third-party defendant, cross-claim defendant, or counterclaim defendant, that identifies:

(A) all persons then known to the defendant or the defendant's attorneys who witnessed the transaction or occurrence giving rise to the claim or otherwise is known or believed to have substantial discoverable information about the claims, or defenses, together with a statement of the subject and a brief summary of that information;

(B) all opposing parties, and all officers, directors, and employees of opposing parties, from whom statements have been obtained by or on behalf of the defendant regarding the subject matter of the claims or defenses; and

(C) all government agencies or officials then known to the defendant or the defendant's attorneys to have investigated the transaction or occurrence giving rise to the claims or defenses.

Noncompliance may be excused only by order of the judicial officer.

(c) Discovery Event Limitations. Unless the judicial officer orders otherwise, the number of discovery events shall be limited for each side (or group of parties with a common interest) to five (5) depositions, thirty (30) interrogatories, and two (2) requests for production.

Comment

Discovery costs often account for a significant portion of the expense of litigation. The Civil Justice Reform Act requests that the district court consider alternative methods of obtaining effective discovery to reduce cost and delay in civil litigation. The Reform Act also indicates that each district's Plan should include procedures that encourage (i) cost-effective discovery and (ii) conservation of judicial resources.

The provisions of Rule 2.01 allow the judicial officer to exert early control over the discovery process. Specifically, the judicial officer should (1) encourage the parties to exchange voluntarily certain items on an informal basis, (2) obtain a joint discovery plan from counsel, (3) consider discovery motions only after the moving party first has attempted to deal with opposing counsel, and (4) determine whether the suggested numerical limits on discovery events are appropriate for the particular case. As more fully set forth in Rule 2.02, the judicial officer also has control over the sequencing of discovery.

Many aspects of cooperative discovery also are being considered by the Federal Rules Advisory Committee at this time and proposed rule changes have been published for comment. Proposals for forms of automatic disclosure also have been made by others. Because the notion may appear revolutionary to some members of the bar, the judicial officer may have to make clear that compliance is expected.

In a given situation, a fixed number of interrogatories and requests for production of documents may be too arbitrary to be workable or fair. Subdivision (c), therefore provides for judicial discretion with respect to modification. Some cases will require more than five depositions and thirty interrogatories. The judicial officer should maintain control over discovery and exercise discretion on a case-by-case basis and should not automatically impose the constraints set out in Rule 2.01(c). Rather, decisions about limiting the number of discovery events, questions regarding any further discovery,

and the manner for resolving any discovery disputes should be addressed by the judicial officer at the case management conference.

Delays caused by discovery abuse may be remedied by effective enforcement of the 1983 revisions to Federal Rule 26. Delays also will be reduced if the deadlines contained in tailored scheduling orders are enforced, and if litigants and their attorneys come to understand that the provisions of the discovery rules and of discovery orders ordinarily will be enforced as written.

Reporter's Notes to Rule 2.01

1. Relevant Local Rules of the United States District Court for the District of Massachusetts include:

Local Rules 33–36—indicates that the maximum number of interrogatories that may be served by a party during the course of discovery shall be thirty (30) unless leave to file a specified larger number is granted by the court.

Local Rule 37—provides that prior to filing any discovery motion, counsel for each of the parties shall confer in good faith to narrow the areas of disagreement to the greatest possible extent.

2. The local rules of fifty-two federal district courts, including the District of Massachusetts, require a conference between the parties prior to their making any discovery motions.

3. Some incremental benefit might be achieved by amending current Local Rules 33–36 to impose numerical restrictions on the number of Federal Rule 34 requests for documents and tangible items as presently are imposed on interrogatories. But, it is important that unreasonably low numerical restrictions on discovery requests be avoided since they might well result in delay caused by the need for routine motions for leave to serve additional discovery.

RULE 2.02 SEQUENCING OF DISCOVERY

(a) Automatic Document Disclosure. Before any party may initiate any discovery, that party must submit to the opposing party a description, including the location, of all documents that reasonably are likely to bear substantially on any of the claims or defenses in the action. By agreement of the parties, copies of documents may be submitted to the opposing party in lieu of a description. Documents subject to automatic disclosure shall include:

(1) any contract between the party and any other party to the action that concerns the dispute;

(2) any insurance agreement under which any person carrying on an insurance business may be liable to satisfy part or all of a judgment that may be entered in the action or to indemnify or reimburse for payments made to satisfy the judgment;

(3) any report of an expert who may be called at trial;

(4) any report by an insurance agent or investigator not protected by Federal Rule 26(b)(3); and

(5) any other documents that the judicial officer determines are appropriate.

The disclosure obligation provided for in this rule is reciprocal and continues throughout the case.

(b) Further Discovery. After the automatic document discovery required by subdivision (a) has been completed, any requests that the parties may make for interrogatories, depositions, or the production of additional documents shall be by discovery motion. All requests for extensions of deadlines for the completion of discovery or for postponement of the trial must be signed by the attorney and, if the judicial officer should elect, the party making the request.

(c) Certification of Discovery Motions. The judicial officer shall not consider any discovery motion that is not accompanied by a certification that the moving party has made a reasonable and good-faith effort to reach agreement with opposing counsel on the matters set forth in the motion. In evaluating any discovery motion, the judicial officer may consider the desirability of conducting phased discovery, limiting the first phase to developing information needed for a realistic assessment of the case. If the case does not terminate, the second phase would be directed at information needed to prepare for trial.

(d) Resolution of Discovery Disputes. Counsel shall confer in order to resolve all discovery disputes. Any dispute not so resolved shall be presented to a judicial officer.

(e) Removed and Transferred Actions. In all actions removed to this court from a state court or transferred to this court from another federal court, the filing required by subdivision (a) shall be made as prescribed in that subdivision, and if discovery was initiated prior to the action being removed or transferred to this court, then the filing required by subdivision (a) shall be made within twenty (20) days of the date of removal or transfer.

Comment

There are certain basic types of information that are discovered in virtually every case and ordinarily must be disclosed before the parties can enter serious settlement negotiations. This material usually should be readily available to the respective parties without need for formal discovery proceedings, and should be provided automatically at the outset of the litigation. For example, discovery may proceed in a more orderly fashion, and be less time-consuming and expensive, if counsel are able to determine the types and locations of documents early in the process. This initial discovery phase should be conducted automatically, without need for a request.

After this first wave has been completed, additional "waves" of discovery on various aspects of the case may be conducted. The judicial officer may order additional discovery or disclosure of a basic and preliminary nature that may include, the identify and location of witnesses to be examined, the production of certain physical evidence, or a computation of damages. This may avoid the possibility that a great deal

of very expensive discovery is conducted on issues that never have to be tried.

Defendants in actions for damages always are entitled to learn the out-of-pocket losses for which recovery is sought. Indeed, they cannot seriously consider settlement until they are given this information. Similarly, plaintiffs seeking damages typically are entitled to learn how much liability insurance is available, and often need that information to form an idea of what they can realistically expect in settlement.

There rarely is a valid justification for a plaintiff to resist quantifying economic loss before or shortly after bringing suit, or for needing months of discovery proceedings to get them to disclose that information. Requiring plaintiffs and their counsel to compile this information, even though it is preliminary, before bringing suit or very shortly thereafter will save time and expense. Disclosure of insurance coverage also will have the salutary effect in some cases of making plaintiffs more realistic about what to expect from their lawsuit.

Similarly, a litigant almost always is entitled to learn the identity of witnesses to or participants in the events that are central to the litigation, the identity of officials who were involved, and whether the opposing party has received statements from any agents or employees. Rule 2.02 authorizes the court to order these matters disclosed.

Securing this type of basic information is the essential first step in a litigant's investigation of the merits of the claims and defenses. Rather than having to go through months of needless discovery in order to learn who the witnesses are and what public documents are available, the parties should disclose that information, to the extent they have it, at the outset of the process. This early disclosure approach is valuable in preventing ineffectual discovery early in the action and in avoiding postponements that otherwise may result from belated discovery of witnesses and documents during the final phase of the pretrial process.

Of course, there is always the possibility that a rule requiring pre-discovery disclosure would be counterproductive to the purposes of the Cost and Delay Reduction Act, which is why Rule 2.02 does not mandate it in all actions. There is no reason to require extensive disclosure when it is not necessary. The careful exercise of discretion is essential.

Along the same lines, the parties should be permitted to define the scope of the discovery they want and can afford by tailoring their own discovery requests, which can be calibrated to the circumstances of individual cases. Any "automatic" discovery is likely to overreach in some cases. It therefore may be to everyone's benefit if counsel can agree to produce certain categories of documents, without taking the time to decide which ones are "reasonably likely to bear substantially on the claim or defenses," and without going through the time consuming process of describing each one. Furthermore, parties should be allowed to agree to curtail the amount of discovery that otherwise might occur under a no-exception automatic discovery process.

Subdivisions (c), (d), and (e) deal with procedural matters and are largely self-explanatory. As indicated in subdivision (d), it is hoped that disputes can be worked out without recourse to the court. Otherwise the basic objective of Rule 2.02 will be undermined.

Reporter's Notes to Rule 2.02

1. The procedures described in the *Manual for Complex Litigation, Second* (1985) should be consulted for guidance in

the application of the principles of waves of discovery in complex litigation. (*See generally* id. at § 21.4).

RULE 2.03 DISCLOSURE OF MEDICAL RECORDS IN PERSONAL INJURY CASES

(a) **Disclosure by Claimants.** Fourteen (14) days after an issue is joined by a responsive pleading, a claimant, whether plaintiff, third-party plaintiff, cross-claimant, or counterclaimant, who asserts a claim for personal injuries shall serve defendant, whether the direct defendant, third-party defendant, cross-claim defendant, or counterclaim defendant with

(1) an itemization of all medical expenses incurred prior to the date of service of the pleading containing the claim for which recovery is sought. If the claimant anticipates that recovery will be sought for future medical expenses, the itemization shall so state, but need not set forth an amount for the anticipated future medical expenses;

(2) a statement that either

(A) identifies a reasonably convenient location and date, within no more than fourteen (14) days, at which the defendant may inspect and copy, at the defendant's expense, all non-privileged medical records pertaining to the diagnosis, care, or treatment of injuries for which recovery is sought; or

(B) identifies all health care providers from which the claimant has received diagnosis, care, or treatment of injuries for which recovery is sought together with executed releases directed to each provider authorizing disclosure to the defendant or its counsel of all nonprivileged medical records in the provider's possession.

(b) **Assertion of Privilege.** Insofar as medical records are not produced in accordance with subdivision (a)(2) on the ground of privilege, the claimant shall identify the privileged documents and state the privilege pursuant to which they are withheld.

(c) **Removed and Transferred Actions.** In all actions removed to this court from a state court or transferred to this court from another federal court, claimants seeking recovery for personal injuries shall provide the information and materials described in subdivision (a) within thirty (30) days after the date of removal or transfer.

Comment

In personal injury cases, effective settlement analysis usually cannot begin until the claimant's medical bills and pertinent medical records have been made available to the defendant. Good practice dictates that suit not be filed until a personal injury plaintiff's counsel has assembled and reviewed the relevant medical records and bills. Certainly, the plaintiff's attorney should not wait to examine the medical records until the defendants have issued subpoenas seeking their production to the health care providers.

In order to obtain medical information under present practice, a defendant first must identify through interrogatories or deposition the persons and the institutions that have treated the plaintiff for the injuries allegedly sustained from the defendant's conduct and then issue "keeper of records" deposition notices to those persons and institutions in order to obtain their records. The process often is complicated by the keepers' refusal to comply with the subpoena until a court has issued an order directing them to do so. Frequently, additional delay results because the plaintiff's attorney insists that their production be postponed until he has had a chance to review them to determine if any portions are privileged. As a result, it can take several months for the defendant to obtain the medical records that are needed for meaningful settlement analysis.

Rule 2.03 is designed to eliminate delays in the commencement of settlement analysis. Plaintiffs and their attorneys typically are entitled to see and copy records upon request. It is not unreasonable, therefore, to require that exchange of information at the beginning of the litigation rather than months later. Rule 2.03 should have the effect of advancing the date at which settlement realistically can be considered, reduce the number of formal discovery requests that have to be served and answered in personal injury cases, limit the number of discovery motions that have to made, and secure the disclosure of obviously relevant and discoverable information earlier rather than later.

Reporter's Notes to Rule 2.03

1. The "Suggested Local Rule" entitled "Pretrial Disclosure" set forth at page 16 of the Federal Judicial Center's January 16, 1991 memorandum entitled *Implementation of the Civil Justice Reform Act of 1990* may be unrealistic in the type of pleading system called for by Federal Rule 8 and likely to generate litigation about the adequacy of a party's compliance with the rule, motions for leave to serve discovery notwithstanding non-compliance with the rule, or motions to dismiss complaints or for more definite statements of claims or defenses. In view of these potential difficulties with rules contemplating automatic discovery, an effort has been made to draft Rule 2.03 so that the parties can know easily whether or not they have complied with it and to limit its scope to what realistically can be accomplished in the context of real-world litigation.

RULE 2.04 COPYING EXPENSE FOR DISCOVERY MATERIALS

(a) **Inspection of Documents.** Except as otherwise provided in an order entered pursuant to Federal Rule of Civil Procedure 26(c), all parties to an action shall be entitled to inspect documents produced by another party pursuant to Federal Rule of Civil Procedure 33(c) or 34 at the location where they are produced.

(b) **Copies of Documents.** Except as otherwise provided in an order entered pursuant to Federal Rule of Civil Procedure 26(c), upon request of any party, and upon that party's agreement to pay the copying costs at the time of delivery, a party who produces documents pursuant to Federal Rule of Civil Procedure 33(c) or 34 shall provide copies of all or any specified part of the documents. No party shall be entitled to obtain copies of documents produced by another party pursuant to Federal Rule of Civil Procedure 33(c) or 34 without paying the costs thereof.

Comment

This provision is declaratory of present practice and is designed to emphasize to attorneys their responsibility in drafting discovery requests and the economic consequences of doing so carelessly. It reflects a simple proposition. Parties who except to bear none of the expense attendant upon their discovery requests are more likely to draft overly broad and needlessly expensive requests than those who know that some of the cost will be imposed on them.

Reporter's Notes to Rule 2.04

1. In cases involving voluminous discovery documents that are to be shared among numerous parties, it may be to the parties' benefit to establish a document depository as suggested in the *Manual for Complex Litigation, Second* (1985). The depository should provide the parties with efficient and economical access to the documents for examination and duplication. Especially in cases in which problems associated with production and use of the documentary materials have developed, the judicial officer may recommend a central depository to the parties. The document depository need not be located at the courthouse or be supervised by the court. Each side may decide to keep its own depository or the parties may arrange to have the depository located at some other convenient site and share expenses. Costs may be defrayed by charging for photoduplication and facsimile transmission equipment use at the depository site.

RULE 2.05　SUBSEQUENT STAGES OF DISCOVERY

(a) **In General.** In order to facilitate settlement and the efficient completion of discovery, the judicial officer has discretion to structure the remaining discovery in the action.

(b) **Phasing of Interrogatories and Document Requests.** After the initial document and disclosure phase of discovery, use of interrogatories and demands for production of documents by parties shall be phased by the judicial officer so that:

(1) at the commencement of discovery, interrogatories will be restricted to those seeking the names of witnesses with knowledge or information relevant to the subject matter of the action, the computation of each category of damages alleged, and the existence, custodian, location, and general description of relevant documents and other physical evidence, or information of a similar nature;

(2) during discovery, interrogatories other than those seeking information described in subparagraph (1) may be served only if they represent a more practical method of obtaining the information sought than a request for production or a deposition; and

(3) interrogatories seeking information about the claims and contentions of the opposing party may be served unless the court has ordered otherwise, but interrogatories seeking the names of expert witnesses and the substance of their opinions also may be

served, if this information has not been obtained previously.

(c) **Objections to Interrogatories.** When an objection is made to any interrogatory, or sub-part thereof, or to any document request under Federal Rule of Civil Procedure 34, it shall state with specificity all grounds upon which the objecting party relies. Any ground not stated in an objection within the time provided by the Federal Rules of Civil Procedure, or any extensions thereof, shall be deemed waived. No part of an interrogatory shall be left unanswered merely because an objection is interposed to another part of the interrogatory.

(d) **Answers to Interrogatories.** Whenever a party answers any interrogatory by reference to records from which the answer may be derived or ascertained, as permitted in Federal Rule of Civil Procedure 33(c):

(1) the specification of documents to be produced shall be in sufficient detail to permit the interrogating party to locate and identify the records and to ascertain the answer as readily as could the party from whom discovery is sought;

(2) the producing party shall make available any computerized information or summaries thereof that it either has, or can adduce by a relatively simple procedure, unless these materials are privileged or otherwise immune from discovery;

(3) the producing party shall provide any relevant compilations, abstracts, or summaries in its custody or readily obtainable by it, unless these materials are privileged or otherwise immune from discovery; and

(4) the documents shall be made available for inspection and copying within ten (10) days after service of the answers to interrogatories or at a date agreed upon by the parties.

(e) **Claims of Privilege.** When a claim of privilege is asserted in objection to any interrogatory, or any sub-part thereof, or any request for production of a document, and an answer is not provided on the basis of that assertion, the attorney asserting the privilege shall identify in the objection the nature of the privilege that is being claimed. If the privilege is being asserted in connection with a claim or defense governed by state law, the attorney asserting the privilege shall indicate the particular privilege rule that is being invoked.

Comment

After completion of the mandatory document/disclosure phase, the judicial officer and counsel may find it useful to participate in defining two or more subsequent stages of discovery. The first of these is whatever additional discovery is needed for assessment of the case before any realistic settlement efforts can occur. Since the majority of cases settle before trial, it may be desirable to defer costly discovery not necessary to promote the settlement process. Subsequent stages of discovery should be undertaken only if efforts have failed to dispose of the case. Thus, the discovery following the disclosure called for under Rules 2.02 and

2.03 should be tailored to allow the parties to obtain information that has become necessary as the case has evolved. Should the case not be settled, the final phase of discovery would be directed at that additional information needed to prepare for trial.

In accord with these guiding principles, this Rule allows a judicial officer to "phase" discovery. Additional provisions relate to streamlining the discovery process—as the case progresses. For example, interrogatories will be limited to those instances when no "more practical method" exists for obtaining the same information and objections to interrogatories not stated will be deemed waived. The Rule also requires that when interrogatories are answered by referring to other parts of the record, that these references be clear, precise, and responsive so that the other side is able to locate the answer to the question posed quickly, and that any document referred can be produced and made available for inspection and copying with a minimum of delay.

Reporter's Notes to Rule 2.05

1. For a discussion of the considerations motivating the decision to separate discovery into two stages, *see* Peckham, *A Judicial Response to the Cost of Litigation: Case Management, Two-Stage Discovery Planning and Alternative Dispute Resolution*, 37 Rutgers L.Rev. 253, 253–77 (1985).

2. For highly technical disputes that are likely to involve divergent viewpoints from experts retained by the parties, it may be desirable to appoint an expert to help define discovery issues. Federal Rule of Evidence 706 gives courts the inherent authority to appoint experts to assist in carrying out court functions, and authorizes payment to be allocated to the parties. This device especially might be useful for some patent or antitrust suits. The judicial officer may issue an order appointing a court expert and instructing each side to define the technical questions and to meet with the expert to decide what the discovery process should entail. After gathering the necessary information from the parties, the expert could establish specifications for tests, and otherwise shape the foundations for reports by all experts and the development of those documents. The court appointed expert might prepare a statement of his or her opinion on the technical issues for the parties.

3. In order to avoid some discovery disputes, for example, over the form and content of interrogatories and requests for production of documents, the court might endorse "form interrogatories" and "form requests" that could be used by parties in particular types of cases.

RULE 2.06 UNIFORM DEFINITIONS IN DISCOVERY REQUESTS

(a) Incorporation by Reference and Limitations. The full text of the definitions set forth in paragraph (c) is deemed incorporated by reference into all discovery requests, but shall not preclude

(1) the definition of other terms specific to the particular litigation;

(2) the use of abbreviations; or

(3) a more narrow definition of a term defined in paragraph (c).

(b) Effect on Scope of Discovery. This rule is not intended to broaden or narrow the scope of discovery permitted by the Federal Rules of Civil Procedure.

(c) Definitions. The following definitions apply to all discovery requests:

(1) *Communication.* The term "communication" means the transmittal of information (in the form of facts, ideas, inquiries, or otherwise).

(2) *Document.* The term "document" is defined to be synonymous in meaning and equal in scope to the usage of this term in Federal Rule of Civil Procedure 34(a). A draft or non-identical copy is a separate document within the meaning of this term.

(3) *Identify (With Respect to Persons).* When referring to a person, "to identify" means to give, to the extent known, the person's full name, present or last known address, and when referring to a natural person, additionally, the present or last known place of employment. Once a person has been identified in accordance with this subparagraph, only the name of that person need be listed in response to subsequent discovery requesting the identification of that person.

(4) *Identify (With Respect to Documents).* When referring to documents, "to identify" means to give, to the extent known, the

(A) type of document;

(B) general subject matter;

(C) date of the document; and

(D) author(s), addressee(s), and recipient(s).

(5) *Parties.* The terms "plaintiff" and "defendant" as well as a party's full or abbreviated name or a pronoun referring to a party mean the party and, where applicable, its officers, directors, employees, partners, corporate parent, subsidiaries, or affiliates. This definition is not intended to impose a discovery obligation on any person who is not a party to the litigation.

(6) *Person.* The term "person" is defined as any natural person or any business, legal, or governmental entity or association.

(7) *Concerning.* The term "concerning" means referring to, describing, evidencing, or constituting.

(8) *State the Basis.* When an interrogatory calls upon a party to "state the basis" of or for a particular claim, assertion, allegation, or contention, the party shall:

(A) identify each and every document (and, where pertinent, the section, article, or subparagraph thereof), which forms any part of the source of the party's information regarding the alleged facts or legal conclusions referred to by the interrogatory;

(B) identify each and every communication which forms any part of the source of the party's information regarding the alleged facts or legal conclusions referred to by the interrogatory;

(C) state separately the acts or omissions to act on the part of any person (identifying the acts or omissions to act by stating their nature, time, and place and identifying the persons involved) which form any part of the party's information regarding the alleged facts or legal conclusions referred to in the interrogatory; and

(D) state separately any other fact which forms the basis of the party's information regarding the alleged facts or conclusions referred to in the interrogatory.

Comment

The definitions in Rule 2.06 are to be used to standardize to some extent the language of discovery requests by defining carefully terms that are used frequently—"communication," "document," "identify," "parties," "person," "concerning," and "state the basis." One of the basic problems with

discovery is that too little effort is made to serve properly drafted and well-thought-out requests. Indeed, in many instances, the best way to avoid needless discovery disputes might be for the party seeking discovery to serve several narrowly worded but well-focused discovery requests instead of a single global request intended to "cover all bases." The latter type of request often ends up being so ambiguous and broad that no adequate response can be made and it virtually invites objection. Counsel must recognize that properly drafted and painstakingly tailored discovery requests are the very foundation of successful pretrial processing of the case.

Reporter's Notes to Rule 2.06

1. This Rule has been adapted from the Southern and Eastern Districts of New York's Local Rule on Uniform Definition of Discovery requests. Uniform instructions and definitions for use in responding to interrogatories and document request have proved successful in those districts.

2. It is envisaged that Rule 2.06 will be enlarged from time to time as other standard terms are identified.

ARTICLE III. MOTION AND PARTY PRACTICE

RULE 3.01   CONTROL OF MOTION PRACTICE

(a) **Plan for the Disposition of Motions.** At the earliest practicable time, the judicial officer shall establish a framework for the disposition of motions, which, at the discretion of the judicial officer, may include specific deadlines or general time guidelines for filing motions. In arriving at this framework, the judicial officer may consider the parties' proposals for the filing of motions contained in the joint statement required by Rule 1.02(d). In accordance with the framework established by the judicial officer, counsel shall submit an agreed schedule for the filing of motions, which may be amended from time to time by the judicial officer as required by the progress of the case.

(b) **Motion Practice.** No motion shall be filed unless counsel certify that they have conferred and have attempted in good faith to resolve or narrow the issue. Any memorandum in support of a motion or in response thereto shall not exceed twenty (20) pages, unless otherwise ordered. Motions may be decided without oral hearing.

(c) **Unresolved Motions.** The court shall rule on motions as soon as practicable, having in mind the reporting requirements set forth in the Civil Justice Reform Act.

Comment

The guiding principle expressed in Rule 3.01 is that be setting target dates, the delay associated with motion practice is likely to be reduced. Thus, this Rule is consistent philosophically with the earlier Rules relating to scheduling and case management conferences and discovery. The deadlines do not have to be established at the outset of the case, but may be set at appropriate times throughout the litigation

as motions are filed and decided. Furthermore, it is not necessary that all motions of a certain type be considered to require identical time frames. Once again, the complete cooperation of counsel is critical and must be assured by the court. Rule 3.01(c) is designed to reduce the delay and cost that is a necessary consequence of the inability to resolve motions in timely fashion. This may be the result of the number of motions filed, the length or complexity of individual motions, motions that are not dispositive of an issue, untimely motions, or occasional delay in the resolution of motions.

Reporter's Notes to Rule 3.01

1. A possible alternative proposals is to require that all motions be conferenced briefly before they can be filed. This is the rule in the Southern District of New York. The ten to fifteen minute conference that the procedure entails may resolve matters often enough to be worth the expenditure of parties' and judges' time. Pre-motion conferences on discovery motions can be handled slightly differently from other motions (e.g., heard only on one afternoon with the parties simply writing or calling chambers to get on a list and then appearing that afternoon and waiting their turn).

RULE 3.02   ADDITION OF NEW PARTIES

(a) **Amendments Adding Parties.** Amendments adding parties shall be sought as soon as an attorney reasonably can be expected to have become aware of the identity of the proposed new party.

(b) **Service on New Party.** A party moving to amend a pleading to add a new party shall serve the motion to amend upon the proposed new party at lest ten days in advance of filing the motion, together with a separate document certifying that the motion has been so served and stating the date on which the motion will be filed. No motion to amend a pleading to add a new party shall be accepted for filing unless it is accompanied by a certificate of the type described in this provision.

(c) Limitation on Amendment by Consent. An amendment of a party's pleading to add a new party may not be made by written consent of the adverse party more than three months after the filing of the party's initial pleading, unless the proposed new party also consents in writing and the judicial officer approves the proposed amendment.

Comment

It is becoming more common for plaintiffs to bring suit against defendants seriatim. One defendant will be sued. The litigation will progress. Another defendant will be added. The litigation will progress some more. Another defendant will be added. And the pattern will continue. This may occur because the plaintiff cannot ascertain the identity of all the defendants before bringing suit, or simply because the plaintiff's attorney has undertaken only minimal pre-suit efforts to identify potential defendants. It also may be used tactically as a way of intentionally building a case against "target" defendants, without allowing them an opportunity to participate in discovery proceedings.

Whether planned or not, however, the late addition of parties inevitably delays the case and generates unnecessary procedural litigation. Each time a new defendant is added, that party must be given time to "get up to speed" and then to prepare a defense. A newly added defendant often must repeat much of the pretrial discovery that already has been conducted by other parties having interests diverse from those of the added party's interest. In addition, the process of adding parties generates litigation issues—for example, the proper use that may be made of discovery taken prior to

the addition of the late defendant, the amount of time needed to give the new defendant fair opportunity to prepare, and the need for modification of previously entered orders.

Sometimes, information readily available to the plaintiffs or their attorneys is fully adequate to permit them to know well in advance of initiating suit who the potential defendants were and to determine whether or not each should be sued. Yet, cases that are quite uncomplicated may take inordinate amounts of time to bring to resolution. Rule 3.02 establishes a procedure for controlling the adding of parties in a way that permits the practice when needed but without excessive delay.

Except in extraordinary circumstances, no motion to amend a party's pleading to add a new party should be allowed more than three months after the party's initial pleading was filed unless a showing is made, by affidavit or otherwise, that the moving party: (1) was not aware, and with due diligence reasonably could not have been aware, of the identity of the proposed new party, or (2) was not aware, and with due diligence reasonably could not have been aware, of facts sufficient to put that party on notice of the claim against the proposed new party. For these purposes, the expiration of the applicable statute of limitations on claims against the proposed new party should not in and of itself constitute extraordinary circumstances.

Reporter's Notes to Rule 3.02

1. Rule 3.02 is not designed to undermine the liberal amendment policy of Federal Rule of Civil Procedure 15, but to provide some guidance as to when leave to amend should be "freely given" and to encourage the early addition of parties. *See generally* Donnici, *The Amendment of Pleadings—A Study of the Operation of Judicial Discretion in the Federal Courts,* 37 S.Cal.L.Rev. 529 (1964).

ARTICLE IV.   ALTERNATIVE DISPUTE RESOLUTION

RULE 4.01   ALTERNATIVE DISPUTE RESOLUTION

The judicial officer shall encourage the resolution of disputes by settlement or other alternative dispute resolution programs.

RULE 4.02   SETTLEMENT

At every conference conducted under these rules, the judicial officer shall inquire as to the utility of the parties conducting settlement negotiations, explore means of facilitating those negotiations, and offer whatever assistance that may be appropriate in the circumstances. Assistance may include a reference of the case to another judicial officer for settlement purposes. Whenever a settlement conference is held, a representative of each party who has settlement authority shall attend or be available by telephone.

RULE 4.03   OTHER ALTERNATIVE DISPUTE RESOLUTION PROGRAMS

(a) Discretion of Judicial Officer. The judicial officer, following an exploration of the matter with all

counsel, may refer appropriate cases to alternative dispute resolution programs that have been designated for use in the district court or that the judicial officer may make available. The dispute resolution programs described in subdivisions (b) through (d) are illustrative, not exclusive.

(b) Mini-Trial.

(1) The judicial officer may convene a mini-trial upon the agreement of all parties, either by written motion or their oral motion in open court entered upon the record.

(2) Each party, with or without the assistance of counsel, shall present his or her position before:

(A) selected representatives for each party, or

(B) an impartial third party, or

(C) both selected representatives for each party and an impartial third party.

(3) An impartial third party may issue an advisory opinion regarding the merits of the case.

(4) Unless the parties agree otherwise, the advisory opinion of the impartial third party is not binding.

(5) The impartial third party's advisory opinion is not appealable.

(6) Neither the advisory opinion of an impartial third party nor the presentations of the parties shall be admissible as evidence in any subsequent proceeding, unless otherwise admissible under the rules of evidence. Additionally, the occurrence of the minitrial shall not be admissible.

(c) Summary Jury Trials.

(1) The judicial officer may convene a summary jury trial:

(A) with the agreement of all parties, either by written motion or their oral motion in court entered upon the record, or

(B) upon the judicial officer's determination that a summary jury trial would be appropriate, even in the absence of the agreement of all the parties.

(2) There shall be six (6) jurors on the panel, unless the parties agree otherwise.

(3) The panel may issue an advisory opinion regarding:

(A) the respective liability of the parties, or

(B) the damages of the parties, or

(C) both the respective liability and damages of the parties.

Unless the parties agree otherwise, the advisory opinion is not binding and it shall not be appealable.

(4) Neither the panel's advisory opinion nor its verdict, nor the presentations of the parties shall be admissible as evidence in any subsequent proceeding, unless otherwise admissible under the rules of evidence. Additionally, the occurrence of the summary jury trial shall not be admissible.

(d) Mediation.

(1) The judicial officer may grant mediation upon the agreement of all parties, either by written motion or their oral motion in court entered upon the record.

(2) A mediator may be selected and assigned to the case who shall be qualified and knowledgeable about the subject matter of the dispute, but have no specific knowledge about the case. The mediator shall be compensated as agreed by the parties, subject to the approval of the judicial officer.

(3) The mediator shall meet, either jointly or separately, with each party and counsel for each party and shall take any other steps that may appear appropriate in order to assist the parties to resolve the impasse or controversy.

(4) The mediation shall be terminated if, after the seven (7) day period immediately following the appointment of the mediator, any party, or the mediator, determines that mediation has failed or no longer wishes to participate in mediation.

(5) If an agreement is reached between the parties on any issues, the mediator shall make appropriate note of that agreement and refer the parties to the judicial officer for entry of a court order.

(6) Mediation proceedings shall be regarded as settlement proceedings and any communication related to the subject matter of the dispute made during the mediation by any participant, mediator, or any other person present at the mediation shall be a confidential communication. No admission, representation, statement, or other confidential communication made in setting up or conducting the proceedings not otherwise discoverable or obtainable shall be admissible as evidence or subject to discovery.

Comment

Active judicial case management should include the ability to explore alternative means of resolving disputes. The Civil Justice Reform Act, therefore, suggests that authorization be granted to refer appropriate cases to alternative dispute resolution programs. These programs may include those already designated for use in this district, or programs that the judicial officer, in his or her discretion, believes hold promise of success. The most commonly employed approaches are set out in Rules 4.02 and 4.03.

Rule 4.03 expressly authorizes the use of three widely used modes of alternative dispute resolution. Their specification is not intended to suggest that they are exclusive; as indicated in subdivision (a) of the Rule, the court has plenary discretion in this matter.

In a mini-trial, selected representatives for each party, or an impartial third party, are presented with an abbreviated version of the parties' positions. After hearing the presentations, the merits of the dispute are discussed, and a nonbinding advisory opinion is issued. Like the summary jury trial, a mini-trial is a means of providing the disputants with an early evaluation of their respective cases, and thereby fosters the development of a basis for realistic settlement negotiations.

The summary jury trial provides a procedure in which an informal verdict is rendered by mock jurors who have heard the parties' arguments. A summary jury trial, therefore, is essentially a device for early case evaluation and the development of realistic settlement negotiations.

Mediation calls for the appointment of an impartial third party by the court in an effort to assist in reconciling a civil dispute. The impartial mediator, working with the parties and their representatives, may offer interpretation and advice and allow the parties to reach a mutually acceptable agreement as to particular issues, or the entire controversy.

The value of mediation, unlike summary jury trials, is that mediators bring professional experience to bear that can compensate for the abridged nature of the proceedings. More important, good mediators can be persuasive advocates of settlement, unlike a summary jury trial, which does not directly further the negotiation process. The court should be more active in encouraging the use of the Boston Bar Association's federal mediation program. Perhaps parties could be asked at an early case management conference to agree to submit to the process. Although mediation works best after basic discovery is completed, a case management conference might be used to encourage voluntary and prompt document production and to identify a limited number of depositions essential to the mediation process. That could place mediation on an accelerated track, and possibly result in early settlement.

Reporter's Notes to Rules 4.01–4.03

1. Some doubt previously had been raised whether summary jury trial is a permissible procedure in the federal courts. *See Hume v. M & C Management,* No. C87–3104 (N.D.Ill., Feb. 15, 1990). The authority for a summary jury trial does appear to be embraced in Federal Rules of Civil Procedure 1 and 16 and in the court's "inherent power to

manage and control its docket." The specific reference to summary jury trial in Section 473(a)(6) of the Civil Justice Reform Act should eliminate any doubt that has existed.

2. The literature on alternative dispute resolution has become voluminous. For observations on the subject by one of the original proponents of the movement, *see* e.g., Sander, *Varieties of Dispute Processing,* 70 F.R.D. 111, 119–33 (1976). *See also Recent Developments in Alternative Forms of Dispute Resolution,* 100 F.R.D. 512 (1984); Lambros, *Summary Jury Trial and Other Methods of Dispute Resolution,* 103 F.R.D. 461 (1984).

ARTICLE V. CONTROL OF TRIAL

RULE 5.01 FINAL PRETRIAL CONFERENCE

(a) Schedule of Conference. The judicial officer may set a new date for the final pretrial conference if that officer determines that resolution of the case through settlement or some other form of alternative dispute resolution is imminent.

(b) Representation by Counsel; Settlement. Unless excused by the judicial officer, each party shall be represented at the final pretrial conference by counsel who will conduct the trial. Counsel shall have full authority from their clients with respect to settlement and shall be prepared to advise the judicial officer as to the prospects of settlement.

(c) Obligation of Counsel to Confer. Unless otherwise ordered by the judicial officer, counsel for the parties shall confer no later than fifteen (15) days prior to the date of the final pretrial conference for the purpose of preparing, either jointly or separately, a pretrial memorandum for submission to the judicial officer.

(d) Pretrial Memorandum. Unless otherwise ordered by the judicial officer, the parties are required to file, no later than five (5) business days prior to the scheduling conference, a pretrial memorandum which shall set forth:

(1) a concise summary of the evidence that will be offered by:

  (A) plaintiff;

  (B) defendant; and

  (C) other parties;

with respect to both liability and damages (including special damages, if any);

(2) the facts established by pleadings or by stipulations or admissions of counsel;

(3) contested issues of fact;

(4) any jurisdictional questions;

(5) any questions raised by pending motions;

(6) issues of law, including evidentiary questions, together with supporting authority;

(7) any requested amendments to the pleadings;

(8) any additional matters to aid in the disposition of the action;

(9) the probable length of the trial;

(10) the names of witnesses to be called (expert and others); and

(11) the proposed exhibits.

(e) Motions to Continue. Motions to continue discovery and pretrial conferences will not be entertained unless the date and time of the pretrial conference is set out in the motion as well as a statement of how many other requests, if any, for continuances have been sought and granted.

(f) Conduct of Conference. The agenda of the final pretrial conference, when possible and appropriate, shall include:

(1) a final and binding definition of the issues to be tried;

(2) the disclosure of expected and potential witnesses and the substance of their testimony;

(3) the exchange of all proposed exhibits;

(4) a pretrial ruling on objections to evidence;

(5) the elimination of unnecessary or redundant proof, including the limitation of expert witnesses;

(6) a consideration of the bifurcation of the issues to be tried;

(7) the establishment of time limits and any other restrictions on the trial;

(8) a consideration of methods for expediting jury selection;

(9) a consideration of means for enhancing jury comprehension and simplifying and expediting the trial;

(10) a consideration of the feasibility of presenting direct testimony by written statement;

(11) the exploration of possible agreement among the parties on various issues and encouragement of a

stipulation from the parties, when that will serve the ends of justice, including:

(A) that direct testimony of some or all witnesses will be taken in narrative or affidavit form, with right of cross-examination reserved, rather than "orally in open court" as is the right of each party under Federal Rule of Civil Procedure 43(a);

(B) that evidence in affidavit form will be read to the jury by the witnesses, or by counsel or another reader with court approval; and

(C) that time limits shorter than those set forth in Rule 5.03 be used for trial; and

(12) a consideration of any other means to facilitate and expedite trial.

(g) **Trial Brief.** A trial brief, including requests for rulings or instructions, shall be filed by each party five (5) calendar days prior to the commencement of trial. Each party may supplement these requests at the trial if the evidence develops otherwise than as anticipated.

Comment

The Civil Justice Reform Act does not expressly require a final pretrial conference. But to be effective in controlling cost and delay, a comprehensive plan should cover this aspect of case management. This Rule is an elaboration on Federal Rule of Civil Procedure 16(f). It provides that an elective final pretrial conference be held in any case that has not been resolved fifteen days in advance of the scheduled trial date, unless the judicial officer finds that settlement is imminent.

The focus of the final pretrial conference will be different than that of the scheduling conference and any subsequent case management conferences. The emphasis will be on "nailing down" the practical elements of trial—the facts that have been established and those that remain to be established, the issues to be tried, the evidence to be offered, the relevant time limitations, and, if necessary, the details of selection of a jury.

The agenda of the final pretrial conference must be tailored to the individual case. Toward this end, the parties should meet to prepare a "Pretrial Memorandum." This joint statement, analogous to the joint statement required before the scheduling conference (*see* Rule 1.02(d)), shall set forth the basic information needed to prepare for trial. The joint statement is advisory, but should assist the judicial officer to set the agenda of the final pretrial conference.

The issues to be addressed at the final pretrial conference are left to the discretion of the judicial officer, but subsection (f) of this Rule sets out twelve agenda items that potentially may be relevant. Acknowledging the conventional wisdom that firm trial dates are the most effective method for prompting settlement, motions to continue discovery and delay the final pretrial conference should not be allowed except for the most exceptional reasons.

Reporter's Notes to Rule 5.01

1. A large body of literature and experience exists that can be tapped for concrete methods and techniques that judges have used and found effective in specific situations or particular cases. A judicial officer may experiment with specialized techniques at trial. They may be provided with notebooks containing key exhibits. Jurors may be permitted to take notes, pictures of each witness may be mounted in front of the jury box as she or he testifies, and pictures then may be permitted to be taken into the jury room so jurors can recall each witness.

2. For a discussion of innovative trial techniques, *see*, e.g., H. Reasoner, J. Murchison, Jr. & W. Tomlin, *Innovative Judicial Techniques in Complex Litigation*, The American College of Trial Lawyer's 40th Annual Spring Meeting 2 (Palm Desert, California, March 1990); Bilecki, *A More Efficient Method of Jury Selection for Lengthy Trials*, 73 Judicature 43 (1989); G. Bermant, J. Cecil, A. Chaset, E. Lind & P. Lombard, *Protracted Civil Trials: Views from the Bench and the Bar* 47–53 (Federal Judicial Center 1981).

RULE 5.02 SPECIAL PROCEDURES FOR HANDLING EXPERTS

(a) **Setting Terms and Conditions.** At the final pretrial conference, the judicial officer shall consider:

(1) precluding the appearance of witnesses not identified previously;

(2) precluding use of any trial testimony by an expert at variance with the written statement and any deposition testimony;

(3) making a ruling concerning the use of depositions, including videotaped depositions; and

(4) making a ruling on the admissibility of expert testimony at the trial.

(b) **Objections to Expert Witnesses.** A party who intends to object to the qualifications of an expert witness, or to the introduction of any proposed exhibit, shall give written notice of the grounds of objection, together with supporting authority, to all other parties within three (3) days following the final pretrial conference.

Comment

Experts play a very significant role in many of today's cases and for a number of reasons expert testimony frequently may present special challenges. This might be true, for instance, in some patent cases, antitrust suits, or other disputes involving evidence of a highly technical nature. Rule 5.02(a) provides four techniques for handling expert testimony at trial that the judicial officer may consider employing. They expressly authorize the judicial officer to set terms and conditions for handling experts, and to address matters that appropriately may be dealt with before trial, including making sure that any objections to expert testimony on the basis of qualifications are heard beforehand.

Reporter' Notes to Rule 5.02

1. Some consideration might be given to limiting the number of experts to be heard at trial and to appointing an expert to act as special advisor to the court during trial, especially when it is anticipated that there will be divergent expert testimony in highly technical or complex litigation. See *Manual for Complex Litigation, Second* (1985). The court has considerable flexibility in deciding how to use the expert. For example, if employed early in the process, the expert can work with counsel in shaping discovery. The

expert, therefore, could continue to function as an advisor to the judicial officer, subject, of course, to limitations that assure the parties a fair hearing on the expert's advice to the court.

RULE 5.03 TRIAL

(a) Time Limits for Evidentiary Hearing.

(1) Absent agreement of the parties as to the time limits for the trial acceptable to the court, the court may order a presumptive limit of a specified number of hours. This time shall be allocated equally between opposing parties, or groups of aligned parties, unless otherwise ordered for good cause.

(2) A request for added time will be allowed only for good cause. In determining whether to grant a motion for an increased allotment of time, the court will take into account:

(A) whether or not the moving party has

(i) used the time since the commencement of trial in a reasonable and proper way, and

(ii) has complied with all orders regulating the trial;

(B) the moving party's explanation as to the way in which the requested added time would be used and why it is essential to assure a fair trial; and

(C) any other relevant and material facts the moving party may wish to present in support of the motion.

The court will be receptive to motions for reducing or increasing the allotted time to assure that the distribution is fair among the parties and adequate for developing the evidence.

(b) Evidence at the Evidentiary Hearing.

(1) Each party shall give advance notice to the judicial officer and the other parties, before jury selection, of the identity of all witnesses whose testimony it may offer during trial, whether by affidavit, deposition, or oral testimony.

(2) Not later than two (2) court days before it seeks to use the testimony of any witness, or on shorter notice for good cause shown, a party shall advise the court and all other parties of its intent to use the testimony of the witness on a specified day.

(3) Except for good cause shown, no party shall be allowed to:

(A) use the testimony of a witness other than the witnesses already listed on the filing with the court before trial commences; or

(B) introduce documentary evidence, during direct examination, other than those exhibits already listed with the court and furnished to the other parties before trial commences.

Comment

Time limits provide an incentive to make the best possible use of the limited time allowed for trial of the case. If the parties are not able to agree upon time limits for the trial, the court, after inviting submissions from the parties, may prescribe presumptive limits that are subject to modification for good cause shown. The parties will have an incentive to agree upon a schedule of time limits since those that the court otherwise will impose may not serve the parties' mutual interests in achieving a shorter, less expensive, and better quality trial.

Because presumptive allotments of time probably will be stated as a total number of hours, each party will be free to allocate time as that party chooses among different uses as long as its total allotment is not exceeded. By not allocating times for particular witnesses or proceedings, the proposal avoids the increased cost and delay associated with proceedings to reallocate time whenever the presumptive allotments are not appropriate to the case.

An explicit purpose of this provision is to create an incentive for using trial time exclusively on issues material to a disposition on the merits. The court should construe Rule 5.03 equitably and flexibly so that any party who makes proper use of time throughout the trial should be assured that an extension will be allowed if more time is needed to present all its evidence adequately.

Reporter's Notes to Rule 5.03

1. Judge Keeton has advocated a number of nontraditional trial practices. He sets out the general considerations underlying some of his innovative suggestions in Keeton, *The Functioning of Local Rules and the Tension with Uniformity,* 854 U.Pitt.L.Rev. 853 (1989) and includes model orders covering every phase of litigation.

ARTICLE VI. SANCTIONS

RULE 6.01 IMPOSITION OF SANCTIONS

Failure to comply with any of the directions or obligations set forth in, or authorized by, this Plan may result in dismissal, default, or the imposition of other sanctions consistent with the provisions of Federal Rule of Civil Procedure 16(f) deemed appropriate by the judicial officer.

Comment

District courts have broad discretion, within the limits prescribed by the Federal Rules of Civil Procedure and Title 28, to impose sanctions when a party fails to comply with its obligations. Rule 6.01 is a general provision expressly authorizing the imposition of sanctions for noncompliance with any of the rules contained in the Plan. The Rule does not provide a schedule of penalties corresponding to types of sanctionable conduct, but relies on the sound discretion of the judicial officer to determine when a sanction is appropriate and to tailor the sanction to the particular situation.

Essentially declaratory of present practice, Rule 6.01 is designed to emphasize to parties and their counsel that they have a duty to act in a timely and responsible manner and to indicate that there may be consequences for not doing so.

Because it is based on the fact of noncompliance with the Plan, Rule 6.01 authorizes sanctions whether the noncompliance was the result of neglect or willful misconduct.

It is anticipated that, if all participants know that the court will impose sanctions when warranted, it will provide an incentive for them to act in an appropriately responsible manner. If the sanctions authorized by this Rule are used as a means for assuring compliance with the procedures and techniques set forth in this Plan, rather than as a substitute for the planning process, it should advance the Plan's purpose to reduce expense and delay in litigation.

Rule 6.01 is not intended to confer any additional power on the presiding judicial officer—it is merely an explicit statement of the court's inherent power to enforce its rules. Accordingly, Rule 6.01 is not intended to be inconsistent with any federal law or the Federal Rules of Civil Procedure nor is it intended to change any party's substantive rights.

Reporter's Notes to Rule 6.01

1. The procedures described in the *Manual for Complex Litigation, Second* (1985) should be consulted for guidance in the application of the principles for imposing sanctions in complex cases. (*See generally* id. at § 42.2).

2. An analysis of the use of monetary penalties for noncompliance with pretrial orders can be found in Brazil, *Improving Judicial Controls over the Pretrial Development of Civil Actions: Model Rules for Case Management and Sanctions,* 1981 Am.B.Found.Research J. 873, 921–55; Peckham, *The Federal Judge as Case Manager: The New Rule of Guiding a Case from Filing to Disposition,* 69 Calif.L.Rev. 770, 800–04 (1981). *See also* 5A Wright & Miller, *Federal Practice and Procedure: Civil 2d* §§ 1331–1338 (1990); Rodes, Ripple & Mooney, *Sanctions Imposable for Violations of the Federal Rules of Civil Procedure* (Federal Judicial Center 1981).

3. For a discussion of the imposition of sanctions based on authority granted in a district court's local rules, *see Miranda v. Southern Pacific Trans. Co.,* 710 F.2d 516 (9th Cir.1983) (upholding district court's authority to impose sanctions against the parties and attorneys for violation of court rules. The local rule at issue, C.D.Cal.R. 28, provided that: "[t]he violation of or failure to conform to any of these local rules shall subject the offending party and his attorney, at the discretion of the court, to appropriate discipline, including the imposition of costs and such attorney's fees as the court may deem proper under the circumstances.").

APPENDICES

APPENDIX A. PLAINTIFF CASE DISCLOSURE FORM

1. Describe in 200 words or less the basis of your lawsuit.

2. Identify all legal theories of recovery and for each legal theory specify the facts that support your claim.

3. Describe all damages you claim to have suffered, the cause of the alleged damages and how the amount of the damages was calculated.

4. If you cannot describe any portion of your damages, state what information you need and from whom you need it to make such a determination.

5. Identify all individuals with knowledge of the facts alleged in the complaint.

6. Attach copies of any and all contracts or other documents that form the basis of your lawsuit.

7. Attach all documents that contain any admissions of the defendant(s).

8. Identify any depositions you now believe are necessary in this matter.

9. Identify all documents in the possession of the defendants you need to prepare your case. Documents must be described with specificity and requests that "relate or pertain to" are unacceptable.

10. State when you will be ready for trial.

11. State whether you are willing to waive or limit discovery in exchange for an earlier trial date.

12. State any facts you believe are not in dispute.

13. State your settlement demand.

APPENDIX B. DEFENDANT CASE DISCLOSURE FORM

1. Describe in 200 words or less the basis of your defense to plaintiff's lawsuit.

2. Identify each defense to plaintiff's lawsuit and for each defense, specify the facts that support your position.

3. Identify all individuals with knowledge of the facts alleged in the Complaint.

4. Attach copies of any and all contracts or other documents that form the basis of your defenses.

5. Attach all documents that contain any admissions of the plaintiff.

6. Identify any depositions you now believe are necessary in this matter.

7. Identify all documents in the possession of the plaintiffs you need to prepare your case. Documents must be described with specificity and requests that "relate or pertain to" are unacceptable.

8. State when you will be ready for trial.

9. State whether you would be willing to waive or limit discovery in exchange for an earlier trial date.

10. State any facts you are willing to stipulate to.

11. What do you offer, if anything, to settle this case or any portion of it.

RULES FOR UNITED STATES MAGISTRATE JUDGES IN THE UNITED STATES DISTRICT COURT FOR THE DISTRICT OF MASSACHUSETTS

Adopted January 15, 1981

Including Amendments Received Through January 1, 2005

Research Note

Use WESTLAW ® *to find cases citing or applying specific rules.* WESTLAW *may also be used to search for specific terms in court rules or to update court rules. See the MA–RULES and MA–ORDERS Scope Screens for detailed descriptive information and search tips.*

Amendments to these rules are published, as received, in the North Eastern 2d *and the* Massachusetts Decisions *advance sheets.*

Table of Rules

I. TITLE AND EFFECT

These rules shall be known as the Rules for United States Magistrates Judges in the United States District Court for the District of Massachusetts.

Proceedings in cases or other matters before the court on the effective date of these Rules will be governed by these Rules unless, in a particular case, the court determines that application of the Rules in that case would be impracticable or unjust.

Amended effective Jan. 8, 2002.

323

II. AUTHORITY OF UNITED STATES MAGISTRATE JUDGES

RULE 1. DUTIES UNDER 28 U.S.C. SECTION 636(a)

Each United States Magistrate Judge appointed by this court is authorized to perform the duties prescribed by 28 U.S.C. Section 636(a) as hereinafter specified and may–

(a) Exercise all the powers and duties conferred or imposed upon United States Commissioners by law or the Federal Rules of Criminal Procedure;

(b) Administer oaths and affirmations, impose conditions of release or detention under 18 U.S.C. Section 3142 et seq., and take acknowledgments, affidavits, and depositions;

(c) When specially designated to exercise such jurisdiction by the district court, try persons accused of, and sentence persons convicted of, misdemeanors (including petty offenses) committed within this district in accordance with 18 U.S.C. Section 3401, Fed. R. Crim P. 58, and Rules 10 through 12 of these Rules, conduct a jury trial in any misdemeanor case (including petty offenses) where the defendant so requests and is entitled to trial by jury under the Constitution and laws of the United States, order a presentence investigative report on any such person who is convicted or pleads guilty or nolo contendere, and sentence such person;

(d) Conduct removal proceedings and issue warrants of removal in accordance with Fed. R. Crim. P. 40;

(e) Conduct extradition proceedings, in accordance with 18 U.S.C. Section 3184; and

(f) Supervise proceedings conducted pursuant to letters rogatory, in accordance with 28 U.S.C. Section 1782.

Amended effective Jan. 8, 2002.

RULE 2. NON–DISPOSITIVE PRE–TRIAL MATTERS

(a) A magistrate judge may hear and determine any pretrial motion or other pretrial matter, in accordance with 28 U.S.C. Section 636(b)(1)(A), other than those motions specified in Rule 3 of these Rules.

(b) A party may not assign as error any aspect of the magistrate judge's order made under subsection (a) hereof, unless a timely objection is made. A party must serve and file any objections to the magistrate judge's order within 10 days of being served with a copy of that order unless a different time is prescribed by the magistrate judge or a district judge. The district judge to whom the case is assigned will consider such objections and will modify or set aside any portion of the magistrate judge's order determined to be clearly erroneous or contrary to law.

(c) The ruling or order of a magistrate judge in a matter that is heard and determined under subsection (a) hereof is the ruling of the Court and is final unless reversed, vacated or modified by a district judge as provided in Fed. R. Civ. P. 72(a) and subsection (b) hereof. The filing of objections under subsection (b) hereof does not operate as a stay of a magistrate judge's ruling or order unless so ordered by the magistrate judge or a district judge, and then only to the extent specifically ordered by the magistrate judge or district judge. Any party desiring a stay of a magistrate judge's ruling or order, or any part thereof, pending ruling on objections filed under subsection (b) hereof, must first apply therefor to the magistrate judge from whose ruling the objection is taken. If the magistrate judge denies a stay, written application therefor may then be made to the district judge to whom the case is assigned. Any application to the district judge for a stay must have appended to it the certificate of counsel that application for the stay sought has been made to the magistrate judge and denied by the magistrate judge, together with a copy of the magistrate judge's denial.

Amended effective Jan. 8, 2002.

RULE 3. DISPOSITIVE PRE–TRIAL MOTIONS AND PRISONER CASES

(a) In accordance with 28 U.S.C. Section 636(b)-(1)-(B) and -(C), a magistrate judge upon a specific referral by the district judge assigned to the case may conduct such evidentiary hearings as are necessary or appropriate, and submit to a district judge proposed findings of fact and recommendations for the disposition of:

(1) applications for post-trial relief made by individuals convicted of criminal offenses;

(2) prisoner petitions challenging conditions of confinement;

(3) motions for injunctive relief (including preliminary injunctions but excluding motions for temporary restraining orders);

(4) motions for judgment on the pleadings;

(5) motions for summary judgment;

(6) motions to dismiss or quash an indictment or information made by a defendant;

(7) motions to suppress evidence in a criminal case;

(8) motions to dismiss or permit the maintenance of a class action;

(9) motions to dismiss for failure to state a claim upon which relief may be granted;

(10) motions to dismiss an action involuntarily;

(11) motions for judicial review of administrative determinations;

(12) motions for review of default judgments;

(13) motions to dismiss or for judgment by default under Fed. R. Civ. P. 37(b);

(14) motions to revoke or modify probation or supervised release under the provisions of Fed. R. Crim. P. 32.1(b), in cases not within the consent jurisdiction of a magistrate judge; and

(15) Such other pretrial matters as are dispositive of a claim or a defense.

(b) The procedures set forth in Fed. R. Civ. P. 72(b) are applicable to all reports and recommendations made and filed under the provisions of subsection (a) hereof, whether made and filed in civil or criminal cases. In each such report and recommendation the magistrate judge must incorporate therein clear notice to the parties that failure to file timely and appropriate objections to that report and recommendation under the provisions of this Rule will result in preclusion of the right to appeal the district court's order to the United States Court of Appeals. That notice may consist of the following language—

The parties are hereby advised that under the provisions of Rule 72, Fed. R. Civ. P., any party who objects to these proposed findings and recommendations must file specific written objections thereto with the Clerk of this Court within 10 days of the party's receipt of this Report and Recommendation. The written objections must specifically identify the portion of the proposed findings, recommendations, or report to which objection is made and the basis for such objections. The parties are further advised that the United States Court of Appeals for this Circuit has repeatedly indicated that failure to comply with Fed. R. Civ. P. 72(b), will preclude further appellate review of the District Court's order based on this Report and Recommendation. See Keating v. Secretary of Health and Human Services, 848 F.2d 271 (1st Cir. 1988); United States v. Emiliano Valencia–Copete, 792 F.2d 4 (1st Cir. 1986); Park Motor Mart, Inc. v. Ford Motor Co., 616 F.2d 603 (1st Cir. 1980); United States v. Vega, 678 F.2d 376, 378–379 (1st Cir. 1982); Scott v. Schweiker, 702 F.2d 13, 14 (1st Cir. 1983); see also, Thomas v. Arn, 474 U.S. 140, 106 S.Ct. 466 (1985).

The notice will be effective if stated in other language that clearly communicates the effect of failure to comply with the provisions of Fed. R. Civ. P. 72(b), as set forth by the United States Court of Appeals for this Circuit in United States v. Emiliano Valencia–Copete, 792 F.2d 4 (1st Cir. 1986).

(c) Within 10 days of being served with a copy of the recommended disposition, a party may serve and file specific, written objections to the proposed findings and recommendations. The written objections must specifically identify the portions of the proposed findings and recommendations or report to which objection is made and the basis for each objection. A party may respond to another party's objections within 10 days after being served with a copy thereof.

The district judge to whom the case is assigned must make a de novo determination upon the record, or after additional evidence, of any portion of the magistrate judge's recommended disposition to which specific written objection has been made in accordance with this Rule. The district judge, however, need not conduct a new hearing and may consider the record developed before the magistrate judge, making a determination on the basis of that record. The district judge may accept, reject or modify the recommended disposition, receive further evidence or recommit the matter to the magistrate judge with instructions.

(d) A magistrate judge may exercise the powers enumerated in Rules 2, 3, 6 and 7 of the Rules Governing Section 2254 and 2255 Proceedings, in accordance with the standards and criteria established in 28 U.S.C. Section 636(b)(1), and may recommend to the district judge appropriate orders under Rules 4, 5, 8 and 9 of the Rules Governing Section 2254 and 2255 Proceedings.

Amended effective Jan. 8, 2002.

RULE 4. SPECIAL MASTER REFERENCES AND TRIALS BY CONSENT

(a) A magistrate judge may serve as a special master subject to the procedures and limitations of 28 U.S.C. Section 636(b)(2) and Fed. R. Civ. P. 53. Unless the district judge orders that a transcript of the proceedings not be filed, any order of reference under this subsection or under Section 4(b) of these Rules must include a directive that the parties, in such proportionate share as the district judge determines to be appropriate, will bear the expense of preparing the transcript required to be filed under Fed. R. Civ. P. 53(e).

(b) With the consent of the parties and the approval of the district judge to whom the case has been assigned, a magistrate judge may serve as special master in any civil case without regard to the provisions of Fed. R. Civ. P. 53(b). The entry of final judgment under this subsection, however, must be ordered by a district judge of the court, or at the direction of a district judge.

(c) Notwithstanding any provision of law to the contrary–

(1) Upon the consent of the parties (including added parties), a magistrate judge, when specially designated to exercise such jurisdiction by the district court, may conduct any and all proceedings in a jury or non-jury civil case and order judgment in the case. A record of the proceedings must be made in accordance with the requirements of 28 U.S.C. § 636(c)(5).

(2) The Clerk of the Court will notify the parties in all civil cases that they may consent to have a magistrate judge conduct any or all proceedings in the case and order the entry of the final judgment. Such notice will be handed or mailed to the plaintiff or plaintiff's representative at the time an action is filed and to the other parties as attachments to copies of the complaint and summons, when served. Additional notices may be furnished to the parties at later stages of the proceedings, and may be included with pretrial notices. If new parties are added after the initial filing, the plaintiff is responsible for obtaining an executed consent form from the new parties.

(3) The Clerk must not accept a consent form unless it has been signed by all the parties in a case. The plaintiff is responsible for obtaining the executed consent form from the parties and filing the form with the Clerk of the Court within 20 days of the filing of an answer or other responsive pleading by the parties, unless the time is enlarged by order of the court. Thereafter, either a district judge or a magistrate judge may again advise the parties of the availability of trial by consent before a magistrate judge, but in so doing, must also advise the parties that they are free to withhold consent without adverse substantive consequences.

(4) Upon entry of judgment of any case reassigned under paragraph (1) of subsection (c) of this Rule, an aggrieved party may appeal directly to the United States Court of Appeals for the First Circuit from the judgment of the magistrate judge in the same manner as if appealing from any other judgment of a district court. Nothing in this paragraph is to be construed as a limitation of any party's right to seek review by the Supreme Court of the United States.

(5) The district court may, for good cause, on its own initiative or under extraordinary circumstances shown by any party, vacate a referral of a civil matter to a magistrate judge under this subsection.

Amended effective Jan. 8, 2002.

RULE 5. OTHER DUTIES

A magistrate judge is also authorized to–

(a) Conduct pretrial conferences, settlement conferences, alternative dispute resolution procedures, and related pretrial proceedings;

(b) Conduct arraignments in cases not triable by the magistrate judge to the extent of taking a not guilty plea or noting a defendant's intention to plead guilty or nolo contendere; and order the preparation of a presentence report when the defendant has expressed a firm intention of entering a plea of guilty and requests that the report be promptly prepared;

(c) Receive grand jury returns in accordance with Fed. R. Crim. P. 6(f);

(d) Conduct a preliminary hearing, if a hearing is required, before revocation of probation or supervised release by a district judge; and may conduct necessary proceedings leading to potential revocation of probation or supervised release imposed by a magistrate judge;

(e) Issue subpoenas, writs of habeas corpus ad testificandum or habeas corpus ad prosequendum, or other orders necessary to obtain the presence of parties or witnesses or evidence needed for court proceedings;

(f) Order the exoneration or forfeiture of bonds;

(g) Conduct examinations of judgment debtors, in accordance with Fed. R. Civ. P. 69;

(h) Conduct evidentiary hearings and prepare findings in employment discrimination cases as a master under Title VII of the Civil Rights Act of 1964, as amended, whenever a district judge cannot schedule a case for trial within 120 days after issue has been joined (42 U.S.C. Section 2000e–5(f)(5));

(i) Administer oath of allegiance to new citizens at naturalization hearings and administer oath of admission to attorneys at admission ceremony;

(j) Conduct evidentiary hearings and prepare recommended findings in civil rights cases brought by prisoners in penal institutions;

(k) Accept petit jury verdicts in civil cases in the absence of a district judge with the consent of the parties;

(l) Conduct proceedings consistent with the provisions of Fed. R. Civ. P. 16(b);

(m) Accept a waiver of indictment pursuant to Fed. R. Crim. P. 7(b); and

(n) Perform any additional duty not inconsistent with the Constitution and laws of the United States.

The enumeration of specific duties in this section is not to be construed as limiting the referral of any other matter otherwise not inconsistent with the Constitution and laws of the United States.

Amended effective Jan. 8, 2002.

III. ASSIGNMENT OF DUTIES TO MAGISTRATE JUDGES

RULE 6. GENERALLY

(a) Assignment By Division.

(1) *Eastern Division.* Except as set forth in Rule 8 of these Rules, the Clerk or deputy clerk must assign cases referred in the Eastern Division to the magistrate judges sitting in Boston by lot in such a manner that each magistrate judge is assigned as nearly as possible the same number of cases, except that when a magistrate judge has already ruled on a matter in a particular case, a subsequent referral in that case must be assigned to the same magistrate judge.

(2) *Central Division.* The Clerk or deputy clerk must assign cases referred in the Central Division to the magistrate judge sitting in Worcester.

(3) *Western Division.* The Clerk or deputy clerk must assign cases referred in the Western Division to the magistrate judge sitting in Springfield.

(b) The Clerk must maintain a list of all cases assigned to the magistrate judges.

(c) Each magistrate judge will place assigned cases on a calendar as required by law and in such manner as is most consistent with the just, efficient performance of the business of the court.

(d) The Clerk must designate each referral to a magistrate judge as falling within one of the following categories:

(1) Civil Rule 16(b)/Pretrial Proceedings

(2) Civil and MBD Discovery

(3) Service as a Special Master

(4) Civil Dispositive Motions

(5) Miscellaneous

(6) Criminal Dispositive Motions

(7) Criminal Pretrial or Discovery

(8) Criminal Ex Parte Motions

(9) Post-conviction proceedings

(e) The Clerk must maintain a daily schedule that shows the regular place of business of a magistrate judge during the hours of each business day, and the place where business may be brought to the attention of a magistrate judge at all other times.

(f) It is the continuing duty of each magistrate judge to give the Clerk the information required to maintain the schedule identified in paragraph (e) above.

(g) Every order and decision of a magistrate judge must be entered on the docket of the case in the same manner as orders and decisions of the district judge.

(h) No ex parte motion or ex parte matter in a criminal or civil case will be assigned to a magistrate judge except upon a separate Order of Reference specifically referring the ex parte motion or ex parte matter to a magistrate judge for disposition.

Amended effective Jan. 8, 2002.

RULE 7. CRIMINAL CASES

(a) Method of Assignment.

(1) For purposes of assignment of criminal cases to magistrate judges for proceedings consistent with the provisions of Rule 2 of these Rules, all criminal cases are divided into the following categories based upon the category for assignment of the case to the district judge on the JS–45 form:

Category A—Felony cases in which eight (8) or more defendants are named.

Category B—Felony cases in which seven (7) or fewer defendants are named.

Category C—All misdemeanor and petty offense cases; cases involving waivers of indictment; and all matters involving alleged violations of conditions of release by persons transferred to this District for supervision.

(2) Upon the return of an indictment, all criminal cases charging a felony or felonies are automatically assigned by the clerk of the court to a magistrate judge for the conduct of an arraignment and the appointment of counsel to the extent authorized by law, unless the district judge assigned to the case orders otherwise. Upon such referral, the magistrate judge must also conduct such scheduling and status conferences as are necessary and must hear and determine all pretrial procedural and discovery motions, in accordance with Rule 2. Unless such an assignment is made under the provisions of subsection (a)(3) hereof, the Clerk must place a case in one of the categories described in subsection (a)(1) above, and must assign it by lot among the magistrate judges in such manner that each magistrate judge is assigned as nearly as possible the same number of cases in each category, taking into account assignments made under this subsection as well as subsection (a)(3) hereof.

(3) Upon referral by specific order of the district judge to whom the case has been assigned, the magistrate judge may hear motions to suppress evidence and motions to dismiss or quash an indictment or information made by the defendant and must submit a report and recommended disposition of such a motion to the district judge, in accordance with Rule 3 of these Rules. In conducting such proceedings, the magistrate judge must conform to the general procedural

Rules of this court and the instructions of the district judge to whom a case is assigned.

(4) For purposes of referral under paragraphs (a)(1) and (a)(2) of this Rule, if a magistrate judge has conducted previous proceedings in connection with the case, including, but not limited to, the receipt of a complaint under Fed. R. Crim. P. 3, or the issuance of a search warrant pursuant to Fed. R. Crim. P. 41, except in the situation described in the second paragraph of Rule 15(d)(1) of these Rules, the United States Attorney must, in a form accompanying the indictment or information, notify the Clerk as to the identity of the magistrate judge conducting such previous proceedings. The Clerk must thereupon refer the matter to the magistrate judge who conducted the previous proceedings. For purposes of this subsection, previous proceedings do not include the approval of applications for pen registers or traps and traces. In all other cases, the referral must be consistent with the provisions set forth in Rule 6(a) of these Rules.

(b) Misdemeanor Cases.

(1) *Initiating Document.* A misdemeanor (other than a petty offense) may be prosecuted by indictment, information, or complaint. A petty offense may be prosecuted by an indictment, information, complaint, citation or violation notice.

(2) An indictment or information charging a misdemeanor other than a petty offense must be filed with the Clerk of the Court, who shall assign the case a docket number, without assigning the case to a district judge until such time as the defendant elects to be tried before a district judge of the district court pursuant to 18 U.S.C. Section 3401(b), or until such time as the case is ordered retained or transferred to a district judge pursuant to the provisions of Fed. R. Crim. P. 58(b)(3)(B).

(3) Upon assigning the case a docket number, the Clerk must thereupon refer the case to the district judge then assigned to the miscellaneous business docket who must, within 48 hours of the referral, review the case and order that the case be continued before the district court, or referred to a magistrate judge.

(4) If the district judge then assigned to the miscellaneous business docket determines that the case is to be retained by the district court, then the Clerk must assign the case to a district judge in accordance with Rule 40.1(B) of the Local Rules of this court and then may be referred to a magistrate judge under the provisions of subsection (a) hereof concerning method of assignment.

(5) If the district judge then assigned to the miscellaneous business docket determines that the case is to be referred to a magistrate judge, then the Clerk must refer the case to a magistrate judge in the same manner as in felony cases under the provisions of subsection (a) above.

(6) Upon receipt of the case, the magistrate judge must proceed under the provisions of Rules 10 through 12 of these Rules.

(7) In the event that the attorney for the government, because of the novelty, importance, or complexity of the case, or other pertinent factors, seeks an order of the district court prohibiting referral of a misdemeanor case pursuant to the provisions of paragraph (5) of this subsection, a petition for such relief, filed in accordance with regulations promulgated by the Attorney General, must be filed at the same time the initiating document is filed with the Clerk.

Amended effective Jan. 8, 2002.

RULE 8. CIVIL CASES

(a) Method of Assignment.

(1) *Eastern Division.*

(A) Cases filed After January 1, 2003. Civil cases filed on or after January 1, 2003 shall be randomly assigned to both a district judge and a magistrate judge. The manner of referral to the magistrate judge of specific matter in a case shall be in accordance with the provisions of Rule 8(b) below.

(B) Cases Filed Before January 1, 2003. Effective January 1, 1993 until December 31, 2002, each Eastern Division magistrate judge was paired with two or more district judges for purposes of referral of matters and proceedings in civil cases, with pairing rotating every two years. The pairings in effect on December 31, 2002 shall continue to apply to cases filed before January 1, 2003 except where there has been a prior ruling by a magistrate judge as described in section 1(C) below.

In the event that one or more district judges were not paired, cases referred by those district judges were and will continue to be randomly drawn.

(C) Effect of Prior ruling. When a magistrate judge has already ruled on a matter in a particular case, a subsequent referral in that case is assigned to the same magistrate judge.

(D) Effect of Recusal. In the event that a magistrate judge is recused on a particular matter referred under the provisions of these Rules, the case must be returned to the Clerk to be redrawn to another magistrate judge on a random basis.

(2) *Central and Western Divisions.* All civil and miscellaneous cases as described above are referred in the Central and Western Division to the magistrate judge sitting respectively in Worcester and Springfield.

(b) Manner of Referral.

(1) The following civil matters may be automatically referred to the magistrate judges by the Clerk, if and

when timely opposition is filed or the time for opposition has expired, for hearing and decision by a magistrate judge in accordance with Rule 2, unless the district judge orders otherwise in a particular case:

(A) Motions for enlargement of time to file pleadings or complete discovery, except when the time for the completion of discovery has been established after a pretrial conference by order of the district judge;

(B) Motions for more definite statement;

(C) All motions for discovery and for enforcement of discovery orders under Fed. R. Civ. P. 26 through 37, except motions to dismiss or for a judgment by default under Rule 37, and motions for proceedings under Fed. R. Civ. P. 26(f).

(2) The following civil matters may be referred to the magistrate judges by the Clerk for hearing and determination by a magistrate judge as soon as they are filed and docketed, whether opposed or not, in accordance with Rule 2 of these Rules:

(A) Applications to proceed in forma pauperis filed under the provisions of 28 U.S.C. Section 1915 that are not referred to the Pro Se Staff Attorney;

(B) Motions for appointment of counsel in civil cases that are not referred to the Pro Se Staff Attorney;

(C) Supplementary proceedings to enforce a money judgment under Fed. R. Civ. P. 69.

(3) Unopposed non-dispositive motions as defined in 28 U.S.C. Section 636(b)(1)(A) may be decided on the merits by the magistrate judge if referred to the magistrate judge by the Clerk.

(4) All other civil matters may be referred to the magistrate judges only by order of a district judge. The order must specify the matters to be considered and the action to be taken by the magistrate judge.
Amended effective Jan. 8, 2002; amended effective July 8, 2003.

RULE 9. EMERGENCY REVIEW

The miscellaneous business judge may review matters that arise in the administration of the duties of the magistrate judges under these Rules only to the extent necessary to meet an "emergency" as defined by Rule 40.4 of the Local Rules of this court. Unless manifest prejudice to a party will result, the matter will be continued for disposition by the district judge to whom the case is assigned.
Amended effective Jan. 8, 2002.

IV. TRIAL OF MISDEMEANORS

RULE 10. SCOPE

Magistrate Judges in the District of Massachusetts shall have all powers granted to magistrate judges by the provisions of 18 U.S.C. Section 3401 and proceedings conducted pursuant to those powers must be exercised in conformity with Fed. R. Crim. P. 58.
Amended effective Jan. 8, 2002.

RULE 11. PRETRIAL PROCEDURES FOR CLASS A MISDEMEANORS

(a) **Consent and Arraignment**. If the defendant consents, either in writing or orally on the record, to be tried before the magistrate judge and the consent specifically waives trial before a district judge, the magistrate judge will take the defendant's plea to the Class A misdemeanor charge. The defendant may plead not guilty, guilty, or, with the consent of the magistrate judge, nolo contendere. If the defendant pleads not guilty, the magistrate judge must either conduct the trial within 30 days upon written consent of the defendant or fix a time for trial, giving due regard to the needs of the parties to consult with counsel and prepare for trial.

(b) **Failure to Consent**. If the defendant does not, within ten days of arraignment (or other reasonable time set by the magistrate judge), indicate an intention to waive the right to a trial before a district

judge, then the case must be tried by a district judge unless the defendant shows good cause why the case should be sent back to the magistrate judge for trial. In the event that the defendant does not, in the form and manner prescribed by the magistrate judge at the time of defendant's initial appearance before the magistrate judge, file an intention to waive the right to a trial before a district judge within ten days of the arraignment (or other such reasonable time prescribed by the magistrate judge), the case must be returned immediately to the Clerk to be randomly drawn to a district judge. The magistrate judge must explain the terms of this subsection to the defendant at the time of arraignment.
Amended effective Jan. 8, 2002.

RULE 12. RECORD OF PROCEEDINGS

Proceedings under Rules 10 through 11 must be taken down by a court reporter or recorded by suitable sound recording equipment. In the discretion of the magistrate judge or, in the case of a misdemeanor other than a petty offense, on timely request of either party made not later than ten days before the scheduled trial, the proceedings must be taken down by a court reporter. With the consent of the defendant, the keeping of a verbatim record may be waived in petty offense cases.
Amended effective Jan. 8, 2002.

RULE 13. REVOCATION PROCEEDINGS

In any case in which the government seeks revocation or modification of probation or supervised release, consistent with the provisions of Fed. R. Crim. P. 32.1(b), after a defendant has been sentenced by a magistrate judge consistent with these Rules, that application must be determined by the magistrate judge who imposed the sentence; and, in the case of the unavailability of that magistrate judge, by another magistrate judge designated by the Chief Magistrate Judge.

Amended effective Jan. 8, 2002.

RULE 14. FORFEITURE OF COLLATERAL IN LIEU OF APPEARANCE

(a) **Forfeiture of Collateral–Generally.** A person who is charged with a petty offense may, in lieu of appearance, post collateral in the amount indicated for the offense, waive appearance before a magistrate judge, and consent to forfeiture of collateral, unless either the charging document makes appearance mandatory or the offense charged is not posted on the Forfeiture of Collateral Schedule approved by the Court.

(b) **Forfeiture of Collateral Schedule.** The offenses for which collateral may be posted and forfeited in lieu of appearance by the person charged, together with the amounts of collateral to be posted, are set forth in APPENDIX A FOR SCHEDULE OF FINES.

(c) **Excluded Offenses.** Under no circumstances may a person charged with operating a motor vehicle under the influence of alcohol or controlled substances in violation of any federal regulation or Massachusetts General Laws ch. 90, Section 24, or other governing statutes, be permitted to post collateral, waive appearance before a magistrate judge, and consent to forfeiture of collateral.

(d) **Maximum Penalties in Lieu of Forfeiture of Collateral.** If a person charged with an offense under subsection (a) hereof fails to post and forfeit collateral, a punishment, including fine, imprisonment or probation, may be imposed within the limits established by law upon conviction by plea or after trial.

(e) **Failure to Appear.** If a person charged with an offense under subsection (a) hereof fails to post and forfeit collateral, and then fails to appear for a duly scheduled hearing on the offense charged, and a showing is made consistent with the provisions of Fed. R. Crim. P. 58(d)(3), then the magistrate judge may issue a warrant of arrest for that person. Upon receipt of the warrant of arrest, the United States Marshal for this District may, in lieu of execution thereof, give written notice to the person that a warrant of arrest has issued for his or her arrest, and must state in the notice that the warrant of arrest will not be executed if, within seven (7) days of the notice, (1) the person voluntarily presents himself or herself before the magistrate judge during usual business hours for the purpose of scheduling a hearing on the petty offense; or (2) the person remits as collateral to be posted and forfeited an amount twice that authorized for the violations as set forth in subsection (b) hereof, or the maximum allowable by the applicable statute, whichever is smaller. In the event that the person properly appears before the magistrate judge, or properly remits and forfeits the collateral, as hereabove set forth, then the magistrate judge must vacate the warrant of arrest; if the person fails to appear or remit as stated above, the United States Marshal must execute the warrant of arrest consistently with applicable law.

(f) **Amendments to Forfeiture of Collateral Schedules.** A federal agency authorized to issue violation notices for violations within its jurisdiction may petition the United States District Court for the District of Massachusetts for an order authorizing a schedule for forfeiture of collateral or amendments to such schedules under subsection (a) hereof. Such petitions seeking such schedules or amendments thereto must be initiated in the following manner:

(1) *Submission of Proposed Schedule.* The federal agency must first submit the schedule, or proposed amendments to the schedule, to the United States Attorney for the District of Massachusetts for such consideration as the United States Attorney deems appropriate. Upon approval by the United States Attorney or the authorized designee of the United States Attorney, that schedule, or amendments thereto, must be forwarded to the Chief Magistrate Judge for consideration and approval by the magistrate judges. When and if approved by the magistrate judges, the Chief Magistrate Judge must transmit the schedule, and amendments to it, to the district judges for approval of an order authorizing that schedule or amendments thereto.

(2) *New Federal Agencies.* If a federal agency that is not currently authorized by the orders of this court to participate in the forfeiture of collateral provisions seeks authorization for adoption of a schedule, that federal agency is responsible for initiating contact and making arrangements with the Central Violations Bureau in San Antonio, Texas. That federal agency shall also be responsible for obtaining all necessary authorizations from the United States Attorney for this District designating one or more persons within that agency to prosecute matters before magistrate judges in the District of Massachusetts.

(3) *Authority to Prosecute.* In no event will a federal agency be permitted to prosecute a Central Violations Bureau matter before a magistrate judge unless the prosecution is by a member of that agency specifically authorized to do so by the United States Attorney for the District of Massachusetts.

(4) *Agency Preparation of Forfeiture of Collateral Schedules*. In all instances in which a federal agency seeks authorization of a schedule of forfeiture of collateral, or amendments thereto, that agency is responsible for preparation of that schedule in the format prescribed by the Clerk of this Court. In addition to the submission of a hard copy of that proposed sched-ule or amendments thereto, the federal agency is responsible for the submission to the Clerk of this Court of that schedule, or amendments to it, on electronic media in the manner prescribed by the Clerk of this Court.

Amended effective Jan. 8, 2002.

V. MISCELLANEOUS

RULE 15. EMERGENCY MAGISTRATE JUDGE

(a) Generally. One of the magistrate judges is designated as the emergency magistrate judge at Boston for each month of the calendar year. The magistrate judge designated as emergency magistrate judge at Boston during a particular month is the emergency magistrate judge for all emergency matters arising during that month within the territorial jurisdiction of the Eastern Division. The magistrate judge sitting in Worcester is the emergency magistrate judge for all emergency matters within the territorial jurisdiction of the Central Division. The magistrate judge sitting in Springfield is the emergency magistrate judge for all emergency matters within the territorial jurisdiction of the Western Division.

It is the duty of the Chief Magistrate Judge to advise the Clerk of the Court as to which magistrate judge has been designated as the emergency magistrate judge in Boston for any given month of the calendar year.

(b) Original Proceedings. All new original matters within the territorial jurisdiction of the magistrate judges involving the filing of criminal complaints, issuance of warrants of arrest and search warrants, seizure warrants, warrants to permit inspections of worksites sought by or on behalf of OSHA, warrants to inspect sites under CERCLA, presentations for bail or detention, conduct of preliminary examinations pursuant to Fed. R. Crim. P. 5.1, removal proceedings under Fed. R. Crim. P. 40, grand jury returns under Fed. R. Crim. P. 6(f), appointment of counsel in criminal cases in connection with original matters, applications for pen registers, traps and traces, electronic tracking devices, and other matters within the original jurisdiction of magistrate judges, must be filed with the magistrate judge then designated as the emergency magistrate judge.

(c) Referred Proceedings. The following matters not within the original jurisdiction of magistrate judges, or within the concurrent jurisdiction of district judges and magistrate judges, unless otherwise directed by the district judge, must be automatically referred to the emergency magistrate judge:

(1) Applications to proceed in forma pauperis filed under the provisions of 28 U.S.C. section 1915 not otherwise referred to the Pro Se Staff Attorney;

(2) Applications for writs of entry filed by or on behalf of the Internal Revenue Service (see subsection (d)(2), infra);

(3) Motions for appointment of counsel filed in connection with grand jury proceedings;

(4) Applications for tax returns and tax returns information filed under the provisions of 26 U.S.C. section 6103(i)(1)(B)(see subsection (d)(2), infra);

(5) Any other civil motion that the trial judge (or, in the absence of the trial judge, the district judge assigned to the miscellaneous business docket) determines should be resolved before the time that the magistrate judge previously assigned to the case, or in the absence of such previous assignment, the magistrate judge who would normally be assigned the case, could otherwise hear the motion.

(d) Related Procedures.

(1) *Previous Proceedings*. If, on a previous occasion, an emergency magistrate judge has received a criminal complaint or has issued a search warrant under the provisions of Fed. R. Crim. P. 41, in connection with an ongoing investigation, subsequent applications for warrants or arrest, search warrants, or other matters within the original jurisdiction of a magistrate judge, must be made to the magistrate judge who had conducted previous proceedings in the case, unless the new application or matter is not directly related to the previous investigation. If, as a result of that continuing investigation, an indictment is returned, or an information is filed, the attorney for the government must, before the return of the indictment or the filing of the information, record the docket or case number(s) of those prior proceedings before the magistrate judge on the required Form JS 45.

If the United States Attorney seeks the issuance of a search warrant on the day an indictment is returned in Boston in a case in which no previous proceedings before a magistrate judge have occurred, the United States Attorney must present the application for a search warrant to the magistrate judge to whom the indictment is drawn after the indictment is returned. If the presentation of the application for the search warrant cannot be delayed until the indictment is returned and the indictment is drawn to a magistrate judge, the United States Attorney may present the application for the search warrant to the emergency magistrate judge for issuance. In that instance, the issuance of the search warrant is not treated as a previous proceeding so as to cause the case to be drawn to that magistrate judge when the indictment is returned.

(2) *Applications for Writs of Entry and Tax Information.* Applications for writs of entry filed by or on behalf of the Internal Revenue Service referred to in subsection (c)(2) hereof , motions for appointment of counsel filed in connection with grand jury proceedings referred to in subsection (c)(3) hereof, and applications for returns and returns information filed under the provisions of 26 U.S.C. Section 6103(i)(1)(B) referred to in subsection (c)(4) hereof, must first be filed with the Clerk of the Court to be docketed on the miscellaneous business docket of the court. All such matters must then be referred, unless otherwise directed by the district judge then serving as the miscellaneous business judge, to the magistrate judge who was designated as the emergency magistrate judge at the time of the filing of the application or motion.

(3) *Pen Registers, Traps and Traces, Orders for Telephone Subscriber Information and Electronic Tracking Devices.* Renewals of applications for pen registers, traps and traces, telephone subscriber information, and electronic tracking devices, must be made to the magistrate judge who issued the original order allowing the requested relief. For the purposes of this Rule, however, a renewal does not include an application made after the expiration or termination of the original order. If an order authorizing a pen register, trap and trace, telephone subscriber information, or electronic tracking device, has expired by its terms, a subsequent application must be made to the current emergency magistrate judge.

(4) *Violations of Conditions.* If a person has been arrested for violation of a condition of release, a violation of a condition of probation, or a violation of a condition of supervised release, that matter must be presented to the magistrate judge who conducted previous proceedings in connection with that case; otherwise, the matter must be presented to the current emergency magistrate judge.

(5) *Unavailability of Emergency Magistrate Judge.* For all matters referred under Rule 15(c) above, if the emergency magistrate judge is not available, and the matter so referred requires appropriate action before the emergency magistrate judge, the matter must be referred to another magistrate judge sitting in Boston by random draw.

(6) *Internal Revenue Service Summons Enforcement.* Applications for Orders to Show Cause in matters related to Internal Revenue Service Summonses are **not** emergency matters within the meaning of these Rules. Those applications must be filed with the Clerk of the Miscellaneous Business Docket and must,

if ordered referred to a magistrate judge, be drawn to a magistrate judge on a random basis.

(e) Matters Ancillary to Proceedings in Other Districts. The emergency magistrate judge is responsible for all matters in this district ancillary to proceedings in other districts. Such proceedings include the appearance of a Massachusetts resident before a magistrate judge in this district to co-sign a surety bond or post property for a defendant who is being prosecuted in another district. In all such cases, the emergency magistrate judge must assign a Magistrate Judge Docket number to the ancillary proceeding and open a file; the file must be maintained in the same manner as a file maintained in connection with an application for a search warrant.

Amended effective Jan. 8, 2002.

RULE 16. CONTEMPT OF COURT

Magistrate judges in the District of Massachusetts have all powers granted to magistrate judges by the provisions of 28 U.S.C. Section 636(e) with respect to contempt of court, and all proceedings they conduct pursuant to these powers must be in conformity with these statutory provisions.

Amended effective Jan. 8, 2002.

RULE 17. TIMING OF REFERRAL OF CIVIL MOTION

The rule stated here does not apply to those motions referred to in Rule 8(b) of these Rules. In the absence of any extraordinary circumstances warranting prompt referral, no civil motion can be referred to a magistrate judge until such time as the non-moving parties are required to file an opposition under Rule 7.1(B)(2) of the Local Rules of this Court. The order of reference must state whether or not an opposition to the motion or motions has been filed.

Amended effective Jan. 8, 2002.

RULE 18. TRANSMITTAL OF PAPERS TO A MAGISTRATE JUDGE

After referral of a case to a magistrate judge, the docket clerk must promptly docket all subsequently filed papers relating to that case and promptly must transmit the filed papers to the magistrate judge for consideration.

Amended effective Jan. 8, 2002.

RULE 19. RECORD OF SUBSEQUENT PROCEEDINGS

In any case in which a party has filed objections to a magistrate judge's determination under Rule 2(b) of these Rules, or to a magistrate judge's proposed findings, recommendations or report under Rule 3(b) of these Rules, or has filed an appeal under Fed. R. Crim. P. 58(g)(2), the docket clerk assigned to the district judge to whom the motion for reconsideration, objections, or appeal, has been assigned must promptly transmit to the magistrate judge who conducted the previous proceedings all records and opinions relating to the subsequent action taken by the district judge.

Amended effective Jan. 8, 2002.

RULE 20. FORM OF REFERRAL

All referrals to magistrate judges must be made by uniform orders of reference in civil, criminal, miscella-neous, and post-conviction cases in the form annexed to these Rules. In those civil cases referred to a magistrate judge for proceedings consistent with the provisions of Fed. R. Civ. P. 16, however, and in other pretrial management functions, non-dispositive motions may be referred to a magistrate judge under the provisions of Rule 17 of these Rules without a form of reference.

Amended effective Jan. 8, 2002.

ORDER OF REFERENCE
UNITED STATES DISTRICT COURT
DISTRICT OF MASSACHUSETTS

ORDER OF REFERENCE

Check if previously referred _____

_____

        V.   CA/CR No. _____

_____   Criminal Category _____

In accordance with 28 U.S.C. §636 and the Rules for United States Magistrates in the United States District Court for the District of Massachusetts, the above-entitled case is referred to Magistrate Judge _____ for the following proceedings:

(A)   Determination (Order) on:
         ( ) Rule 16(b) and/or Pretrial proceedings *(except ex parte motions in criminal cases)*
         ( ) Nondispositive pretrial and discovery motions(s) not listed in Paragraph (B) below
            See Documents Numbered : _____
         ( ) Ex Parte Motions in criminal cases - See Documents Numbered: _____

         Action taken by the Magistrate Judge on matters referred for determination shall constitute the Order of the Court and shall be reconsidered only where shown to be clearly erroneous in fact or contrary to law.   28 U.S.C. §636(b)(1)(A)

(B)   Findings and Recommendations pursuant to 28 U.S.C. §636(b)(1)(B) on:
         ( ) Motion(s) for injunctive relief
         ( ) Motion(s) for judgment on the pleadings
         ( ) Motion(s) for summary judgment
         ( ) Motion(s) to permit maintenance of a class action
         ( ) Motion(s) to suppress evidence
         ( ) Motion(s) to dismiss
            See Documents Numbered: _____

(C)   Service as a special master for hearing, determination and report, subject to the terms of the special order filed herewith:
         ( ) In accordance with Rule 53, F.R.Civ.P.
         ( ) In accordance with 42 U.S.C. §2000e-5(f)(5)

(D)   Special instructions _____
_____

_____   By :_____
      DATE   Deputy Clerk

( ) Civil Rule 16(b) /Pretrial Proceedings   ( ) Criminal Dispositive Motions
( ) Civil and MBD Discovery   ( ) Criminal Pretrial or Discovery
( ) Service as Special Master   ( ) Criminal Ex Parte Motions
( ) Civil Dispositive Motions   ( ) Post Conviction Proceedings[1]
( ) Miscellaneous

(Order of Ref to MJ.wpd - 12/98)   [oref., koref.]

---

[1]   See reverse side of order for instructions

INSTRUCTIONS FOR POST-CONVICTION PROCEEDINGS

In accordance with all rules governing §2254 and §2255 cases the magistrate judge to whom this post-conviction proceeding is referred shall:

_____   Make a recommendation as to summary dismissal under Rule 4 of the Rules for §2254 and §2255 cases

_____   Appoint counsel if the interests of justice so require

_____   Order issuance of appropriate process, if necessary

_____   Hold a hearing to determine whether or not an evidentiary hearing must be held and make a recommendation to the district judge

_____   If the magistrate judge expects to recommend that an evidentiary hearing be held, the magistrate judge shall hold a pretrial conference for the purpose of narrowing the issue to be tried and submit a memo to the district judge setting forth:

       (a)   a concise summary of the ultimate facts claimed by
                     (1) petitioner   (2) respondent   (3) other parties;

       (b)   the facts established by the pleadings or by stipulations of the parties which may be incorporated by reference;

       (c)   any jurisdictional questions;

       (d)   issues of law, including evidentiary questions;

       (e)   the probable length of the evidentiary hearing.

The magistrate judge may also require the parties to submit the names of witnesses whom they intend to produce, and to exhibit to one another, and submit a schedule of, exhibits which they expect to offer in evidence.

_____   As to any issue concerning which the magistrate judge does not intend to recommend an evidentiary hearing, the magistrate judge shall submit a memo which shall:

       (a)   identify the relevant portions of the record or transcript of prior proceedings;

       (b)   summarize the relevant facts;

       (c)   summarize the parties' contentions of law with appropriate citations;

       (d)   state the recommendations as to the disposition of such contentions of law, and the grounds therefore.

(Postconv.ins - 09/92)

(Order of Ref to MJ.wpd - 12/98)

APPENDIX A. SCHEDULE OF FINES

Forfeiture of Collateral Schedule

Description of Violation	CFR Title	CFR Section	Agency Initials	Collateral Amount
Closure and public use restrictions	36	1.5(f)	NPS	$50.00
Permit violations	36	1.6(g)	NPS	$75.00
Wildlife and plant resources, possession or destruction	36	2.1(a)(1)(i), (ii) & (iv)	NFS	$75.00
Archeological resources, possession or destruction	36	2.1(a)(1)(iii)	NPS	$150.00
Wildlife or plants, introduction into park	36	2.1(a)(2)	NPS	$50.00
Rocks or other items, throwing or tossing	36	2.1(a)(3)	NPS	$25.00
Gathered wood, use or possession	36	2.1(a)(4)	NPS	$50.00
Archeological or cultural resource, monument or statute, interference with	36	2.1(a)(5)	NPS	$50.00
Structure or cultural or archeological resource, interference with	36	2.1(a)(6)	NPS	$150.00
Metal or mineral detector, possession or use	36	2.1(a)(7)	NPS	$75.00
Trails and walkways, shortcutting	36	2.1(b)	NPS	$25.00
Natural product violations	36	2.1(c)(3)	NPS	$50.00
Wildlife, unauthorized taking	36	2.2(a)(1)	NPS	$150.00
Wildlife, molesting or disturbing	36	2.2(a)(2)	NPS	$50.00
Wildlife, possession of unlawfully taken wildlife	36	2.2(a)(3)	NPS	$150.00
Hunting, MGL c. 131, §§ 1–92 assimilated	36	2.2(b)(4)	NPS	$50.00/ $100.00
Hunting, 321 CMR § 3 assimilated	36	2.2(b)(4)	NPS	$50.00/ $150.00
Animals, spotlighting	36	2.2(e)	NPS	$50.00
Fishing, state law assimilated	36	2.3(a)	NPS	$50.00
Fishing, violations	36	2.3(d) (1)-(3), (6)-(8)	NPS	$50.00
Weapons, traps or nets, violations	36	2.4(a)-(c), and (f)	NPS	$100.00
Wildlife, plant or animal specimens, taking	36	2.5(a)	NPS	$100.00
Camping or food storage, violations	36	2.10(b)(1)-(10)	NPS	$50.00
Picnicking, violations	36	2.11	NPS	$25.00
Audio disturbances	36	2.12(a)	NPS	$25.00
Fire, in undesignated areas	36	2.13(a)(1)	NPS	$50.00
Fires, prohibited acts	36	2.13(a)(2)-(5)	NPS	$50.00
Fires, failure to extinguish	36	2.13(b)	NPS	$50.00
Sanitation and refuse, violations	36	2.14	NPS	$75.00
Pets, prohibited acts	36	2.15(a)(1)-(3)	NPS	$50.00
Pets, noise and excrement disposal	36	2.15(a)(4), (5)	NPS	$50.00
Horses and pack animals, prohibited acts	36	2.16	NPS	$50.00
Aircraft and air delivery, prohibited acts	36	2.17	NPS	$100.00
Snowmobiles, violations	36	2.18(a)-(d)	NPS	$50.00

Description of Violation	CFR Title	CFR Section	Agency Initials	Collateral Amount
Winter activities, area restrictions	36	2.19(c)	NPS	$50.00
Skating and skateboards, use restrictions	36	2.2	NPS	$50.00
Smoking, prohibited acts	36	2.21	NPS	$25.00
Property, abandoned	36	2.22(a)(1)	NPS	$50.00
Property, leaving unattended	36	2.22(a)(2)	NPS	$50.00
Property, failure to turn in found property	36	2.22(a)(3)	NPS	$50.00
Fee area, entering without payment	36	2.23(b)	NPS	$50.00
Property, misappropriation	36	2.30(a)(1)-(5)	NPS	$150.00
Trespassing	36	2.31(a)(1)	NPS	$75.00
Tampering, or attempting	36	2.31(a)(2)	NPS	$100.00
Vandalism	36	2.31(a)(3)	NPS	$100.00
Interference with agency function	36	2.32(a)(1)	NPS	$100.00
Failure to obey lawful order	36	2.32(a)(2)	NPS	$100.00
False report or information	36	2.32(a)(3), (4)	NPS	$100.00
Failure to report injury or damage	36	2.33(b)	NPS	$100.00
Disorderly conduct	36	2.34(1)-(4)	NPS	$150.00
Alcohol, sale to underage person	36	2.35(a)(2)(i)	NPS	$100.00
Alcohol, possession violations	36	2.35(a)(2)(ii)-(iv)	NPS	$50.00
Alcohol, consumption violations	36	2.35(a)(3)	NPS	$50.00
Controlled substances, possession	36	2.35(b)(2)	NPS	$100.00
Alcohol or controlled substances, presence in park under the influence	36	2.35(c)	NPS	$100.00
Gambling	36	2.36(a)	NPS	$50.00
Soliciting, non-commercial	36	2.37	NPS	$50.00
Fireworks, possession	36	2.38(b)	NPS	$50.00
Permit, violation of terms	36	2.50(e)	NPS	$75.00
Public assemblies and meetings, prohibited acts	36	2.51(h)	NPS	$50.00
Printed matter, sale and distribution, prohibited acts	36	2.52(h)	NPS	$75.00
Livestock and agriculture, prohibited acts	36	2.60(a)	NPS	$50.00
Residing on federal lands, prohibited acts	36	2.61(a)	NPS	$100.00
Memorialization	36	2.62	NPS	$50.00
U.S. Coast Guard, state regulations	36	3.1	NPS	$25.00
Accidents, failure to report	36	3.4	NPS	$50.00
Vessel inspections, violations	36	3.5	NPS	$50.00
Vessel operation, negligent or reckless operation	36	3.6(a)	NPS	$100.00
Vessel operation, prohibited acts	36	3.6(c)-(1)	NPS	$50.00
Vessel, noise abatement violations	36	3.7	NPS	$50.00
Swimming, surfing, scuba and water skiing, violations	36	3.20–23	NPS	$50.00
Personal water craft, prohibited operations	36	3.24	NPS	$50.00
Assimilative crimes	36	4.2(b)	NPS	$50.00
Traffic, failure to report accident	36	4.4(c)	NPS	$25.00
Traffic, travel on roads and designated routes	36	4.10(a) and (c)	NPS	$50.00
Traffic, load, weight and size violations	36	4.11(b)	NPS	$50.00
Traffic, control devices	36	4.12	NPS	$50.00

Description of Violation	CFR Title	CFR Section	Agency Initials	Collateral Amount
Traffic, unauthorized parking, or parking contrary to signs	36	4.12	NPS	$25.00
Traffic, parking in handicapped spot	36	4.12	NPS	$50.00
Traffic, obstructing	36	4.13	NPS	$50.00
Traffic, open container of alcohol	36	4.14(b)	NPS	$50.00
Traffic, seat belts	36	4.15(c)	NPS	$25.00
Traffic, right of way	36	4.2	NPS	$25.00
Traffic, speeding (1–10 mph over)	36	4.21(c)	NPS	$50.00
Traffic, speeding(11–20 mph over)	36	4.21(c)	NPS	$100.00
Traffic, speeding(21 plus mph over)	36	4.21(c)	NPS	$150.00
Traffic, unsafe operation	36	4.22(b)(1,3–4)	NPS	$100.00
Traffic, skidding and squealing tires	36	4.22(b)(2)	NPS	$50.00
Bicycles, prohibited acts	36	4.3	NPS	$25.00
Hitchhiking	36	4.31	NPS	$25.00
Advertisements and postings, violations	36	5.1	NPS	$75.00
Business operations, prohibited acts	36	5.3	NPS	$75.00
Traffic, commercial vehicle prohibited use	36	5.6(b)	NPS	$75.00
Traffic, driving off route	36	7.67(a)(5)(i)	CCNS	$75.00
Traffic, exceeding speed limit	36	7.67(a)(5)(ii)	CCNS	$50.00
Traffic, parking in route	36	7.67(a)(5)(iii)	CCNS	$50.00
Traffic, riding on outside of vehicle	36	7.67(a)(5)(iv)	CCNS	$50.00
Traffic, driving on protected beach	36	7.67(a)(5)(v)	CCNS	$100.00
Traffic, operating a motorcycle	36	7.67(a)(5)(vi)	CCNS	$50.00
Equipment, required equipment	36	7.67(a)(6)	CCNS	$50.00
Permit, violations	36	7.67(a)(7)	CCNS	$100.00
Camping, ORV violations	36	7.67(a)(9)	CCNS	$75.00
Aircraft	36	7.67(b)	CCNS	$100.00
Motorboats	36	7.67(c)	CCNS	$50.00
Nudity	36	7.67(e)	CCNS	$50.00
Closed areas, entry into (trespass)	41	101–20.302	GSA/FPS	$75.00
Rubbish, improper disposal	41	101–20.303	GSA/FPS	$75.00
Buildings, throwing objects at or climbing on	41	101–20.303	GSA/FPS	$50.00
Property, theft, destruction, damage or removal	41	101–20.303	GSA/FPS	$150.00
Failure to obey signs	41	101–20.304	GSA/FPS	$50.00
Failure to obey lawful order	41	101–20.304	GSA/FPS	$100.00
Loitering, unauthorized	41	101–20.305	GSA/FPS	$50.00
Disorderly conduct	41	101–20.305	GSA/FPS	$150.00
Gambling	41	101–20.306	GSA/FPS	$50.00
Alcohol, entering premises under the influence of alcohol or controlled substances	41	101–20.307	GSA/FPS	$100.00
Alcohol, unauthorized use on property of alcohol or controlled substances	41	101–20.307	GSA/FPS	$100.00
Solicitation, unauthorized	41	101–20.308	GSA/FPS	$50.00
Solicitation, unauthorized commercial or political solicitation or advertising	41	101–20.308	GSA/FPS	$50.00
Advertising, posting or distributing	41	101–20.309	GSA/FPS	$50.00
Photography, unauthorized	41	101–20.310	GSA/FPS	$50.00
Traffic, failure to obey signs	41	101–20.312	GSA/FPS	$25.00

Description of Violation	CFR Title	CFR Section	Agency Initials	Collateral Amount
Traffic, reckless or unsafe operation	41	101–20.312	GSA/FPS	$100.00
Traffic, unauthorized parking	41	101–20.312	GSA/FPS	$25.00
Traffic, parking contrary to signs or in reserved or restricted areas	41	101–20.312	GSA/FPS	$25.00
Traffic, parking in handicapped spots	41	101–20.312	GSA/FPS	$50.00
Traffic, parking in emergency spots, fire lanes or near fire hydrant	41	101–20.312	GSA/FPS	$50.00
Traffic, failure to park in marked space	41	101–20.312	GSA/FPS	$25.00
Traffic, blocking roadway, entrance, driveway or walk	41	101–20.312	GSA/FPS	$25.00
Rubbish, improper disposal	38	1.218(b)(1)	VA	$75.00
Spitting, on property	38	1.218(b)(2)	VA	$10.00
Buildings, throwing from or climbing on	38	1.218(b)(3)	VA	$25.00
Property, destruction, damage or removal	38	1.218(b)(4)	VA	$150.00
Grave marker, destruction, defacement or removal	38	1.218(b)(5)	VA	$150.00
Failure to obey signs	38	1.218(b)(6)	VA	$25.00
Signs, tampering with or removal	38	1.218(b)(7)	VA	$75.00
Trespass into posted or closed areas	38	1.218(b)(8)	VA	$25.00
Demonstration, unauthorized	38	1.218(b)(9)	VA	$50.00
Disturbance, during burial ceremony	38	1.218(b)(10)	VA	$75.00
Disorderly conduct	38	1.218(b)(11)	VA	$150.00
Failure to depart premises	38	1.218(b)(12)	VA	$25.00
Loitering, unauthorized	38	1.218(b)(13)	VA	$25.00
Gambling	38	1.218(b)(14)	VA	$50.00
Alcohol/drugs, entering premises under influence of alcohol or controlled substances	38	1.218(b)(16)	VA	$100.00
Alcohol/drugs, unauthorized use of alcohol or controlled substances	38	1.218(b)(17)	VA	$100.00
Alcohol/drugs, unauthorized introduction onto property or giving to patient	38	1.218(b)(18)	VA	$100.00
Solicitation, unauthorized	38	1.218(b)(19)	VA	$25.00
Solicitation, commercial	38	1.218(b)(20)	VA	$25.00
Advertisements, distributing	38	1.218(b)(21)	VA	$15.00
Advertisements, postings or display	38	1.218(b)(22)	VA	$15.00
Photography, unauthorized	38	1.218(b)(23)	VA	$25.00
Traffic, failure to comply with traffic directions of police	38	1.218(b)(24)	VA	$25.00
Traffic, parking in handicapped spot	38	1.218(b)(25)	VA	$35.00
Traffic, parking in no-parking areas	38	1.218(b)(26)	VA	$25.00
Traffic, parking in emergency spaces, fire lanes or near fire hydrant	38	1.218(b)(27)	VA	$35.00
Traffic, parking in intersection or blocking an entrance or exit lane	38	1.218(b)(28)	VA	$25.00
Traffic, parking in reserved spots or in excess of time limit	38	1.218(b)(29)	VA	$15.00
Traffic, failure to make full stop	38	1.218(b)(30)	VA	$25.00
Traffic, failure to yield to pedestrian in crosswalk	38	1.218(b)(31)	VA	$25.00

Description of Violation	CFR Title	CFR Section	Agency Initials	Collateral Amount
Traffic, driving in wrong direction on one-way street	38	1.218(b)(32)	VA	$25.00
Traffic, reckless or unsafe operation	38	1.218(b)(33)	VA	$75.00
Traffic, speeding (1–10 mph over)	38	1.218(b)(34)	VA	$25.00
Traffic, speeding (11–20 mph over)	38	1.218(b)(34)	VA	$35.00
Traffic, speeding (21 plus mph over)	38	1.218(b)(34)	VA	$75.00
Traffic, excessive noise in hospital or cemetery zone	38	1.218(b)(35)	VA	$25.00
Traffic, right of way	38	1.218(b)(36)	VA	$25.00
Firearms, possession	38	1.218(b)(37)	VA	$250.00
Explosives, possession	38	1.218(b)(38)	VA	$250.00
Dangerous weapons, knives, possession	38	1.218(b)(39)	VA	$150.00
Dangerous weapons, liquid or gas emitting, possession	38	1.218(b)(40)	VA	$100.00
Room keys, unauthorized possession, manufacture or use	38	1.218(b)(41)	VA	$100.00
Unauthorized opening of locks or barrier mechanisms	38	1.218(b)(42)	VA	$150.00
Prostitution, act or solicitation	38	1.218(b)(43)	VA	$100.00
Sexual activity, unlawful	38	1.218(b)(44)	VA	$100.00
Cemetery grounds, bicycling, jogging prohibited	38	1.218(b)(45)	VA	$25.00
Traffic, unauthorized parking or without permit	39	232.1(k)	PS	$25.00
Traffic, parking contrary to signs or in restricted zone	39	232.1(k)	PS	$25.00
Traffic, failure to park within marked spaces	39	232.1(k)	PS	$25.00
Traffic, blocking entrances, driveways, walks, and fire hydrants	39	232.1(k)	PS	$50.00
Failure to obey lawful order	39	232.1(d)	PS	$100.00
Trespassing	39	232.1(d)	PS	$75.00
Failure to present identification upon request	39	232.1(b)	PS	$75.00
Rubbish, improper disposal	39	232.1(c)	PS	$75.00
Buildings, throwing from or climbing on	39	232.1(c)	PS	$50.00
Property, destroying, damaging or removal	39	232.1(d)	PS	$150.00
Disorderly conduct	39	232.1(e)	PS	$150.00
Traffic, parking in handicapped spot	39	232.1(k)	PS	$100.00
Alcohol, entering property under influence of alcohol or controlled substance	39	232.1(g)	PS	$100.00
Vessels, non-compliance with special regulations	33	207.20(a)-(m)	USACE	$250.00
Waste, non-authorized disposal	33	207.20(n)	USACE	$250.00
Trespassing	33	207.20(o)	USACE	$75.00
Bridges,	33	207.20(p)	USACE	$50.00
Traffic, unauthorized parking	33	207.20(q)(2)	USACE	$50.00
Traffic, speeding (1–10 mph over)	33	207.20(q)(2)	USACE	$50.00
Traffic, speeding (11–20 mph over)	33	207.20(q)(2)	USACE	$100.00
Traffic, speeding (20 plus mph over)	33	207.20(q)(2)	USACE	$150.00
Traffic, motorized vehicles in non-authorized areas	33	207.20(q)(2)	USACE	$100.00
Swimming, scuba diving	33	207.20(q)(3)	USACE	$50.00
Camping	33	207.20(q)(4)	USACE	$100.00

Description of Violation	CFR Title	CFR Section	Agency Initials	Collateral Amount
Fishing	33	207.20(q)(5)	USACE	$50.00
Hunting	33	207.20(q)(6)	USACE	$100.00
Fires	33	207.20(q)(7)	USACE	$50.00
Animals, control of	33	207.20(q)(8)	USACE	$50.00
Posted restrictions	33	207.20(q)(9)	USACE	$50.00
Explosives	33	207.20(q)(10)	USACE	$100.00
Property, destruction or removal	33	207.20(q)(11)	USACE	$150.00
Plant and animal life, disturbing, injuring or damaging	33	207.20(q)(11)	USACE	$50.00
Property, abandonment	33	207.20(q)(12)	USACE	$50.00
Property, lost and found	33	207.20(q)(13)	USACE	$50.00
Advertising	33	207.2	USACE	$50.00
Commercial activities	33	207.20(q)(15)	USACE	$100.00
Structures, unauthorized	33	207.20(q)(16)	USACE	$100.00
Special events	33	207.20(q)(17)	USACE	$100.00
Interference with employees	33	207.20(q)(18)	USACE	$100.00
Traffic, parking in violation of posted restrictions	36	327.2(b)	USACE	$25.00
Traffic, operating off roadways	36	327.2(c)	USACE	$100.00
Traffic, violating posted regulations	36	327.2(d)	USACE	$50.00
Traffic, careless, negligent, reckless operation	36	327.2(e)	USACE	$100.00
Traffic, operating in developed areas	36	327.2(f)	USACE	$50.00
Traffic, exhaust system violations	36	327.2(g)	USACE	$25.00
Vessels, placement and/or operation	36	327.3(b)	USACE	$50.00
Vessels, violating posted regulations	36	327.3(c)	USACE	$50.00
Vessels, careless, negligent, reckless operation	36	327.3(d)	USACE	$100.00
Vessels, safety equipment violations	36	327.3(e)	USACE	$50.00
Vessels, habitation	36	327.3(f)	USACE	$50.00
Vessels, water skis, parasails	36	327.3(g)	USACE	$50.00
Vessels, navigational aids violations	36	327.3(h)	USACE	$50.00
Vessels, Safe Boating Act violations	36	327.3(i)	USACE	$50.00
Vessels, exhaust system violations	36	327.3(j)	USACE	$25.00
Aircraft	36	327.4	USACE	$100.00
Swimming	36	327.5	USACE	$50.00
Picnicking	36	327.6	USACE	$25.00
Camping	36	327.7	USACE	$100.00
Hunting, fishing, trapping	36	327.8	USACE	$100.00
Sanitation, violations	36	327.9	USACE	$100.00
Fires	36	327.1	USACE	$50.00
Animals, control of	36	327.11	USACE	$50.00
Restrictions, closure and public use	36	327.12(a)	USACE	$50.00
Restrictions, quiet hours and noise violations	36	327.12(b) and (d)	USACE	$50.00
Restrictions, disorderly or unsafe conduct	36	327.12(c)	USACE	$150.00
Restrictions, possession or use of alcohol	36	327.12(e)	USACE	$50.00
Restrictions, smoking violations	36	327.12(f)	USACE	$25.00
Explosives, fireworks	36	327.13	USACE	$50.00
Property, public	36	327.14	USACE	$100.00
Property, abandonment	36	327.15	USACE	$50.00
Property, lost and found	36	327.16	USACE	$50.00
Advertising	36	327.17	USACE	$50.00
Commercial activity	36	327.18	USACE	$100.00

Description of Violation	CFR Title	CFR Section	Agency Initials	Collateral Amount
Permits, violations	36	327.19	USACE	$50.00
Structures, unauthorized	36	327.2	USACE	$100.00
Special events, violations	36	327.21	USACE	$100.00
Occupation or agricultural use, unauthorized	36	327.22	USACE	$100.00
Recreation use fees, violations	36	327.23	USACE	$50.00
Interference with federal employee	36	327.24(a)	USACE	$150.00
Failure to comply with lawful order	36	327.24(b)	USACE	$100.00
Traffic, improper overtaking	MGLc 89	2	ACA/HAFB	$25.00
Traffic, failure to yield to emergency vehicles	MGLc 89	7A	ACA/HAFB	$50.00
Traffic, failure to stop for posted sign	MGL c 89	9	ACA/HAFB	$25.00
Traffic, yield sign violation	MGLc 89	9	ACA/HAFB	$25.00
Traffic, failure to yield to pedestrian in crosswalk	MGLc 89	11	ACA/HAFB	$50.00
Traffic, leaving vehicle running and unattended	MGLc 89	13	ACA/HAFB	$25.00
Traffic, failure to stop for school bus	MGLc 90	14	ACA/HAFB	$100.00
Traffic, failure to yield to pedestrian	MGLc 90	14	ACA/HAFB	$25.00
Traffic, improper use of traffic lane	MGLc 90	14	ACA/HAFB	$25.00
Traffic, failure to use turn signal	MGLc 90	14	ACA/HAFB	$25.00
Traffic, use of automobile in unauthorized area	MGLc 90	16	ACA/HAFB	$25.00
Traffic, speeding	MGLc 90	17	ACA/HAFB	$35.00 plus $10.00 for each mph over 10 mph over the limit
Traffic, improper display of license plate	MGLc 90	6	ACA/HAFB	$25.00
Traffic, defective equipment	MGLc 90	7	ACA/HAFB	$25.00
Traffic, failure to wear protective headgear	MGLc 90	7	ACA/HAFB	$25.00
Traffic, no state inspection	MGLc 90	7A	ACA/HAFB	$25.00
Traffic, child under 5 years without restraint	MGLc 90	7AA	ACA/HAFB	$25.00
Traffic, operating an unregistered vehicle	MGLc 90	9	ACA/HAFB	$50.00
Traffic, operating a vehicle without license	MGLc 90	10	ACA/HAFB	$500.00
Traffic, failure to have license or registration in possession	MGLc 90	11	ACA/HAFB	$25.00
Traffic, objectionable/ unreasonable noise	MGLc 90	16	ACA/HAFB	$25.00
Traffic, operating after suspension or revocation of license	MGLc 90	23	ACA/HAFB	$500.00
Traffic, attaching wrong plates	MGLc 90	23	ACA/HAFB	$50.00
Traffic, open containers of alcohol	MGLc 90	24I	ACA/HAFB	$100.00
Traffic, failure to obey lawful order of authorized official	MGLc 90	25	ACA/HAFB	$100.00
Traffic, failure to exhibit identification/ providing false identification	MGLc 90	25	ACA/HAFB	$100.00
Traffic, failure to submit identification to officer	MGLc 90	25	ACA/HAFB	$100.00
Traffic, failure to report accident in excess of $1000	MGLc 90	26	ACA/HAFB	$25.00

Description of Violation	CFR Title	CFR Section	Agency Initials	Collateral Amount
Traffic, failure to report personal injury accident	MGLc 90	26	ACA/HAFB	$25.00
Traffic, transportation of alcohol by minor	MGLc 138	34C	ACA/HAFB	$35.00
Alcohol, possession by minor	MGLc 138	34C	ACA/HAFB	$35.00
Animals, domestic, trespassing	MGLc 266	118	ACA/HAFB	$5.00
Disorderly conduct, indecent exposure, nudism	MGLc 272	53	ACA/HAFB	$150.00
Trespassing, military base	18 USC	1382	HAFB	$75.00
Property, failure to turn in lost property	50	25.22	F & W	$50.00
Permits, failure to exhibit permit or license	50	25.42	F & W	$75.00
Entrance fee violations	50	25.56	F & W	$50.00
Property or injury, failure to report accidents	50	25.72	F & W	$50.00
Trespassing	50	26.21(a)	F & W	$75.00
Trespassing, domestic animals	50	26.21(b)	F & W	$50.00
Regulations, non-compliance	50	26.22	F & W	$50.00
Special regulations, non-compliance	50	26.33	F & W	$50.00
Permit violations, assemblies and demonstrations	50	26.36	F & W	$75.00
Animals and plants, taking without authorization	50	27.21	F & W	$100.00/ $50.00
Traffic, motorized vehicles in restricted areas	50	27.31	F & W	$75.00
Traffic, unlawful operation	50	27.31(a)	F & W	$50.00
Traffic, operation to endanger	50	27.31(b)	F & W	$100.00
Traffic, speeding (1–10 mph over)	50	27.31(d)	F & W	$50.00
Traffic, speeding (11–20 mph over)	50	27.31(d)	F & W	$100.00
Traffic, speeding (21 plus mph over)	50	27.31(d)	F & W	$150.00
Traffic, faulty muffler	50	27.31(e)(1)	F & W	$25.00
Traffic, unauthorized parking	50	27.31(h)	F & W	$25.00
Failure to obey order of officer	50	27.31(i)	F & W	$100.00
Traffic, moving auto involved in accident	50	27.31(k)	F & W	$50.00
Boating, violation of regulations	50	27.32	F & W	$50.00
Water skiing, violation of regulations	50	27.33	F & W	$50.00
Aircraft, low-level operation of unauthorized landing or take-off	50	27.34	F & W	$100.00
Firearms, fireworks or explosives, carrying, possessing or discharging	50	27.41	F & W	$100.00
Firearms, unlawful possession, use or transportation	50	27.42	F & W	$100.00
Weapons, other than firearms, unauthorized possession or use	50	27.43	F & W	$100.00
Plant or animals, disturbing or injuring	50	27.51	F & W	$50.00
Plant or animals, introducing from elsewhere	50	27.52	F & W	$50.00
Public property, destruction or removal	50	27.61	F & W	$100.00
Objects of antiquity, searching for or removing	50	27.62	F & W	$100.00
Valued objects, unauthorized searching or removal	50	27.63	F & W	$100.00
Prospecting or mining, unlawful	50	27.64	F & W	$100.00
Motor vehicles or equipment, unauthorized entry or starting	50	27.65	F & W	$100.00

Description of Violation	CFR Title	CFR Section	Agency Initials	Collateral Amount
Commercial film making without authorization	50	27.71	F & W	$100.00
Unreasonable operation of audio equipment	50	27.72	F & W	$25.00
Hunting, unauthorized spotting of wildlife	50	27.73	F & W	$100.00
Alcohol, entering or remaining while under influence	50	27.81	F & W	$100.00
Drugs, presence under the influence	50	27.82	F & W	$100.00
Indecent or disorderly conduct	50	27.83	F & W	$150.00
Interference with authorized activities	50	27.84	F & W	$100.00
Gambling	50	27.85	F & W	$50.00
Begging, food solicitation	50	27.86	F & W	$50.00
Field dog trials, unauthorized	50	27.91	F & W	$50.00
Private structures, unauthorized	50	27.92	F & W	$100.00
Personal property, abandoning	50	27.93	F & W	$100.00
Unauthorized garbage disposal, polluting waters or other areas	50	27.94	F & W	$150.00
Fire, unauthorized use	50	27.95	F & W	$50.00
Advertising, unauthorized	50	27.96	F & W	$50.00
Soliciting business, conducting commercial enterprise, unauthorized	50	27.97	F & W	$50.00
Trapping, non-compliance with conditions	50	28.16	F & W	$50.00
Hunting, non-compliance with general provisions	50	32.2	F & W	$100.00
Alcohol, use or possession while hunting	50	32.2(j)	F & W	$100.00
Big game, non-compliance with specific regulations	50	32.32	F & W	$100.00
Sport fishing, non-compliance with general provisions	50	32.5	F & W	$100.00
Sport fishing, each violating fish	50	32.5	F & W	$25.00
MBTA, taking with illegal device or substance	50	20.21(a)	F & W	$200.00
MBTA, taking with shotgun capable of holding more than 3 shells	50	20.21(b)	F & W	$50.00
MBTA, taking by means, aid or use of sinkbox	50	20.21(c)	F & W	$100.00
MBTA, taking by means or use of motorized vehicle or aircraft	50	20.21(d)	F & W	$150.00
MBTA, taking by means of motorized boat under power	50	20.21(e)	F & W	$150.00
MBTA, taking by use or aid of live birds	50	20.21(f)	F & W	$250.00
MBTA, taking by means or use of recorded or amplified bird calls	50	20.21(g)	F & W	$250.00
MBTA, taking by means or aid of motorized conveyance to drive, rally or stir up waterfowl	50	20.21(h)	F & W	$150.00
MBTA, taking by use of bait	50	20.21(i)	F & W	$300.00
MBTA, taking waterfowl or coots while possessing prohibited shot shells	50	20.21(j)	F & W	$75.00
MBTA, taking during closed season	50	20.22	F & W	$150.00
MBTA, each bird taken during closed season	50	20.22	F & W	$25.00

Description of Violation	CFR Title	CFR Section	Agency Initials	Collateral Amount
MBTA, taking before or after legal shooting hours, first 15 minutes	50	20.23	F & W	$50.00
MBTA, taking before or after legal shooting hours, each additional 15 minutes	50	20.23	F & W	$25.00
MBTA, taking more than daily bag limit	50	20.24	F & W	$150.00
MBTA, each bird in excess of daily bag limit	50	20.24	F & W	$25.00
MBTA, wanton waste	50	20.25	F & W	$150.00
MBTA, possession of birds taken in violation of 20.21 through 20.24	50	20.31	F & W	$150.00
MBTA, each bird possessed that was taken in violation of 20.21 through 20.24	50	20.31	F & W	$25.00
MBTA, possession of freshly killed bird during closed season	50	20.32	F & W	$150.00
MBTA, each freshly killed bird possessed during closed season	50	20.32	F & W	$25.00
MBTA, exceeding possession limit taken in United States	50	20.33	F & W	$150.00
MBTA, each bird possessed over limit taken in United States	50	20.33	F & W	$25.00
MBTA, possession in excess of daily bag limit on opening day	50	20.34	F & W	$150.00
MBTA, each bird possessed in excess of daily bag limit on opening day	50	20.34	F & W	$25.00
MBTA, possession or transportation in excess of daily bag limit	50	20.35	F & W	$150.00
MBTA, each bird possessed or transported in excess of daily bag limit	50	20.35	F & W	$25.00
MBTA, violation of tagging regulations	50	20.36	F & W	$50.00
MBTA, possession of untagged birds of another person	50	20.37	F & W	$50.00
MBTA, possession of live wounded bird	50	20.38	F & W	$50.00
MBTA, transportation of birds taken in violation of 20.21 through 20.24	50	20.41	F & W	$150.00
MBTA, each bird transported that was taken in violation of 20.21 through 20.24	50	20.41	F & W	$25.00
MBTA, transportation of untagged birds of another person	50	20.42	F & W	$50.00
MBTA, transportation of birds with species identification removed	50	20.43	F & W	$100.00
MBTA, mis-marking or non-marking of bird containers via Postal or common carrier	50	20.44	F & W	$50.00
MBTA, exportation of birds taken in violation of 20.21 through 20.24	50	20.51	F & W	$150.00
MBTA, each bird exported that was taken in violation of 20.21 through 20.24	50	20.51	F & W	$25.00
MBTA, export of birds with species identification removed	50	20.52	F & W	$100.00

Description of Violation	CFR Title	CFR Section	Agency Initials	Collateral Amount
MBTA, mis-marking or non-marking of bird containers via Postal or common carrier	50	20.53	F & W	$50.00
MBTA, importing in excess of importation limits	50	20.61	F & W	$100.00
MBTA, each bird imported in excess of importation limits	50	20.61	F & W	$25.00
MBTA, importing birds of another	50	20.62	F & W	$50.00
MBTA, importing birds with species identification removed	50	20.63	F & W	$100.00
MBTA, import, possess, transport or ship birds without export permits, tags and other documentation	50	20.64	F & W	$100.00
MBTA, importing birds not drawn or dressed as required	50	20.65	F & W	$50.00
MBTA, mis-marking or non-marking bird containers via Postal or common carrier	50	20.66	F & W	$50.00
MBTA, taking, possession, transportation or exporting migratory birds, parts, eggs or nests in violation of any other federal regulation	50	20.71	F & W	$150.00
MBTA, each bird taken, possessed, transported or exported in violation of any other federal regulation	50	20.71	F & W	$25.00
MBTA, taking, possession, transportation or exporting migratory birds, parts, eggs, or nests in violation of any state regulation	50	20.72	F & W	$150.00
MBTA, importing, possession, or transportation of any migratory bird, parts, eggs or nests if taken, bought, sold, transported, possessed or exported contrary to law or regulation of the foreign country or state or province thereof	50	20.73	F & W	$150.00
MBTA, each bird imported, possessed, or transported if taken, bout/bought, sold, transported, possessed or exported contrary to law or regulation of the foreign country, state or province thereof	50	20.73	F & W	$25.00
MBTA, commercial facility with untagged migratory birds of another	50	20.81	F & W	$100.00
MBTA, commercial facility, violation of record keeping requirements	50	20.82	F & W	$100.00
MBTA, commercial facility, not permitting inspection of records or premises	50	20.83	F & W	$200.00
MBTA, purchase, sell or barter, or offer thereof, of feathers of migratory game birds for millinery or ornamental use	50	20.91(a)	F & W	$200.00
MBTA, purchase, sell or barter, or offer thereof, of mounted specimens taken by hunting	50	20.91(b)	F & W	$200.00
MBTA, violation of crow hunting regulations	50	20.133	F & W	$50.00

Description of Violation	CFR Title	CFR Section	Agency Initials	Collateral Amount
MBTA, each crow illegally taken	50	20.133	F & W	$25.00
MBTA, taking, possession, transportation, selling, purchasing, barter, or offering thereof, exporting or importing migratory birds, parts, eggs or nests without authorization	50	21.11	F & W	$150.00
MBTA, each specimen taken, possessed, transported, sold, purchased, bartered, exported or imported without authorization	50	21.11	F & W	$25.00
MBTA, acquisition or disposition of migratory birds from or to unauthorized persons	50	21.12(b)	F & W	$100.00
MBTA, each specimen acquired or disposed of from or to unauthorized persons	50	21.12(b)	F & W	$25.00
MBTA, taking mallard ducks or eggs from wild without permit	50	21.13(a)	F & W	$150.00
MBTA, each mallard duck or egg taken from wild without permit	50	21.13(a)	F & W	$25.00
MBTA, possession of unmarked mallard ducks without permit	50	21.13(b)	F & W	$75.00
MBTA, sale or disposal of unmarked mallard ducks	50	21.13(c)	F & W	$75.00
MBTA, shooting captive-reared mallard ducks when unauthorized	50	21.13(d)	F & W	$75.00
MBTA, possession of unmarked mallard ducks prior to final processing for consumption	50	21.13(e)	F & W	$75.00
MBTA, acquisition of captive-reared migratory waterfowl from unauthorized person	50	21.14(a)	F & W	$75.00
MBTA, possession of unmarked waterfowl after 6 weeks of age	50	21.14(b)	F & W	$100.00
MBTA, disposal of captive migratory waterfowl without permit	50	21.14(c)	F & W	$100.00
MBTA, shooting of captive migratory waterfowl without authorization	50	21.14(d)	F & W	$75.00
MBTA, possession of unmarked captive migratory waterfowl prior to final processing for consumption	50	21.14(e)	F & W	$75.00
MBTA, failure to furnish or retain form 3–186	50	21.14(f)	F & W	$75.00
MBTA, importing migratory birds, parts, eggs or nests without import permit	50	21.21(a)(1)	F & W	$150.00
MBTA, each specimen imported without permit	50	21.21(a)(1)	F & W	$25.00
MBTA, exporting migratory birds, parts, eggs or nests without export permit	50	21.21(a)(2)	F & W	$150.00
MBTA, each specimen exported without permit	50	21.2(a)(2)	F & W	$25.00
MBTA, capturing and/or banding migratory birds without a permit	50	21.22	F & W	$100.00
MBTA, performing taxidermy of migratory birds for another without permit	50	21.24	F & W	$150.00

Description of Violation	CFR Title	CFR Section	Agency Initials	Collateral Amount
MBTA, failure to keep accurate records of taxidermy operations	50	21.24(d)(1)	F & W	$150.00
MBTA, failure to properly tag migratory birds for taxidermy purposes	50	21.24(d)(2)	F & W	$100.00
MBTA, taking, possession, transportation, selling, purchasing, bartering or transferring any raptor for falconry purposes in violation of federal falconry standards	50	21.28	F & W	$250.00
MBTA, each bird taken, possessed, transported, sold, purchased, bartered or transferred in violation of federal falconry standards	50	21.28	F & W	$50.00
MBTA, taking, possession, transportation, selling, purchasing or bartering any raptor for falconry purposes in violation of state laws	50	21.29	F & W	$250.00
MBTA, each bird taken, possessed, transported, sold, purchased or bartered in violation of state laws pertaining to falconry	50	21.29	F & W	$50.00
Permit, engaging in activity without required permit	50	13.1	F & W	$150.00
Permit, unauthorized transfer	50	13.25	F & W	$100.00
Wildlife, possession maintained under inhumane and unhealthful conditions	50	13.41	F & W	$150.00
Wildlife, each specimen possessed under inhumane and unhealthful conditions	50	13.41	F & W	$25.00
Permit, failure to adhere to specific authorizations	50	13.42	F & W	$100.00
Permit, alter or misuse of permit	50	13.43	F & W	$150.00
Permit, failure to display as required	50	13.44	F & W	$50.00
Permit, failure to report permit activities	50	13.45	F & W	$100.00
Permit, failure to keep or retain permit records	50	13.46	F & W	$100.00
Permit, failure to permit inspections	50	13.47	F & W	$200.00
Permit, non-compliance with conditions of permit and all laws and regulations governing activity	50	13.48	F & W	$100.00
Wildlife, import or transport to U.S. any wild mammal or bird under inhumane or unhealthful conditions	50	14.103	F & W	$300.00
Exotic birds, violation of import regulations or issued permits	50	15.11(a)-(e)	F & W	$250.00
Exotic birds, each bird imported contrary to regulations or permits	50	15.11(a)-(e)	F & W	$50.00
Wildlife, unauthorized importing or shipping in interstate commerce of prohibited fish or wildlife species	50	16.3 through 16.15	F & W	$250.00
Wildlife, each specimen imported or transported in violation of 16.3 through 16.15	50	16.3 through 16.15	F & W	$50.00

Description of Violation	CFR Title	CFR Section	Agency Initials	Collateral Amount
Wildlife, violation of permit	50	16.22	F & W	$100.00
Wildlife, violation of threatened wildlife prohibitions, short of taking threatened wildlife or violating captive-bred threatened wildlife regulations	50	17.31	F & W	$250.00
Wildlife, taking of any threatened wildlife	50	17.31	F & W	$500.00
Wildlife, violation of captive-breed threatened wildlife regulations	50	17.31	F & W	$150.00
Wildlife, each specimen of threatened wildlife for which threatened wildlife prohibitions have been violated	50	17.31	F & W	$50.00
Wildlife, violation of special regulations pertaining to threatened wildlife	50	17.40 through 17.48	F & W	$150.00
Wildlife, each specimen for which special threatened wildlife regulations are violated	50	17.40 through 17.48	F & W	$50.00
Fish hatchery, violation of 50 CFR 27, as they pertain to Wildlife Refuges	50	70.4(a)	F & W	same amounts as listed for violation of 50 CFR 27
Fish hatchery, unauthorized taking (or attempt) of fish or aquatic animal	50	70.4(b)	F & W	$150.00
Fish hatchery, each unauthorized specimen taken (or attempt)	50	70.4(b)	F & W	$25.00
Fish hatchery, unauthorized taking (or attempt) of any animal	50	70.4(c)	F & W	$150.00
Fish hatchery, each unauthorized specimen taken (or attempt)	50	70.4(c)	F & W	$25.00
Fish hatchery, disturbing spawning fish	50	70.4(d)	F & W	$250.00
Fish hatchery, violation of 50 CFR 26, as they pertain to Wildlife Refuges	50	70.6	F & W	same amounts as listed for violation of 50 CFR 26
Hunting, without federal duck stamp	16 USC	718a	F & W	$75.00
Hunting, with invalid federal duck stamp	16 USC	718b	F & W	$50.00
Hunting, loan of federal duck stamp to another	16 USC	718e(a)	F & W	$75.00

[Effective January 8, 2002.]

ELECTRONIC CASE FILING

GENERAL ORDER RE: ELECTRONIC CASE FILING

September 2, 2003

GENERAL ORDER RE: ELECTRONIC CASE FILING

Fed. R. Civ. P. 5(e) authorizes this Court to establish practices and procedures for the filing, signing and verification of documents by electronic means.

Accordingly, the United States District Court for the District of Massachusetts hereby orders that all cases filed within this District are eligible for electronic case filing according to the rules and procedures outlined in the following:

A) The Electronic Case Filing Administrative Procedures

B) Electronic Case Filing User's Manual

C) Standing Orders concerning ECF implementation and the provision of courtesy copies.* Unless otherwise specified by the particular court in its session order, each session will adopt a standing order of the form attached.

Please Note: Counsel should pay particular attention to the rules with regard to sealed documents and ex parte submissions. Under ECF, if sealed documents or ex parte submissions are inadvertently filed electronically, they become immediately available to the public.

After September 8, 2003, counsel who have registered for ECF and who have received information concerning login and passwords will receive electronic notice of court orders and decisions. After October 1, 2003, counsel who have registered for ECF and have received login and password information will be eligible to file documents electronically, according to the rules and procedures outlined above.

* Publishers note: Counsel should consult specific Sessions of Court for Standing Order requirements on CM/ECF that may apply in practice before a specific judge.

ELECTRONIC CASE FILING ADMINISTRATIVE PROCEDURES

ELECTRONIC FILING and PDF

Electronic Filing is the process of uploading a document from the registered user's computer, using the court's Internet-based Electronic Case Files (ECF) system, to file the document in the court's case file. The ECF system only accepts documents in a portable document format (PDF). There are two types of PDF documents–electronically converted PDF's and scanned PDF's. Although either type is acceptable, PDF documents converted electronically are preferred over scanned PDF files due to the size differences and ability to search text.

Electronically converted PDF's are created from word processing documents (MS Word, WordPerfect, etc) using Adobe Acrobat or similar software. They are text searchable and their file size is small.

Scanned PDF's are created from paper documents run through an optical scanner. Scanned PDF's are not searchable and have a large file size.

ADMINISTRATIVE PROCEDURES

A. General Information

1.   Effective **October 1, 2003,** documents submitted for filing in all pending civil and criminal cases, except those documents specifically exempted in subsection (H) of these procedures, may be filed either electronically using the Electronic Case Filing System (ECF) or on a properly labeled 3.5" floppy or compact disk in portable document format (PDF) so that the document can be added to the electronic case file. **Attorneys should be guided by the standing orders of each judge to determine when it is appropriate to begin electronically filing documents in their cases and whether courtesy copies of documents need to be provided.** Magistrate Judges may issue standing orders for electronic filing in their consent cases on a case by case basis.

2.   The Clerk's Office will not maintain a paper court file in any civil or criminal case commenced after October 1, 2003, except as otherwise provided herein or as ordered by the Judge in a particular session. (The case files in actions commenced prior to October 1, 2003 may contain paper versions of those documents filed prior to October 1, 2003 and electronic files of the documents filed on or after October 1, 2003). The official court record in ECF cases shall be the electronic file maintained on the court's servers together with any paper documents, attachments and exhibits filed in accordance with these procedures.

3.   The Clerk's Office may discard the PDF disk after it has been uploaded to ECF or the original document after it has been scanned and uploaded to ECF.

4. All documents filed by electronic means must comply with technical standards, if any, established by the Judicial Conference of the United States or by this Court.

B. Registration

1. Attorneys admitted to the bar of this court, including attorneys admitted pro hac vice, must register as filing users of the court's ECF system prior to filing any pleadings electronically. Registration can be accomplished by filling in the online ECF registration or by completing an ECF Registration Form, a copy of which is on the Court's web page (*www.mad.us-courts.gov*). If not submitted on-line, completed ECF Registration Forms should be mailed or hand delivered to:

Clerk, United States District Court
Attn: CM/ECF Registration
John Joseph Moakley United States Courthouse
1 Courthouse Way, Suite 2300
Boston, MA 02210

2. Anyone who is a party to a civil action, and not a prisoner, and who is not represented by an attorney may register as a filing user in the ECF system. If during the course of the action the person retains an attorney who appears on the person's behalf, the Clerk shall terminate the person's registration upon the attorney's appearance.

3. A registered user shall not allow another person to file a document using the user's log-in and password, except for an authorized agent of the filing user. Use of a user's log-in and password by a staff member shall be deemed to be the act of the registered user.

4. Registration constitutes consent to service of all documents by electronic means as provided in these procedures and Federal Rule of Civil Procedure (Fed. R.Civ.P) 5(b) and 77(d), and Federal Rule of Criminal Procedure (Fed.R.Crim.P.) 49(b).

5. Once an account has been established by the court, your login and password will be sent to you by the Office of the Clerk via e-mail.

C. Filing and Service of Civil Case Opening Documents

1. Civil case opening documents, such as a complaint, petition, or notice of removal, together with a summons and civil cover sheet and category sheet, shall be filed in the traditional manner by United States mail or delivered in person to the Clerk's Office accompanied by the required filing fee. Case opening documents may also be provided in PDF format on a properly labeled 3.5" floppy or compact disk, so that the documents can be added to ECF. Otherwise, the Clerk's Office will scan the complaint and cover sheets and upload them to the System.

2. New cases are deemed filed the day the Clerk's Office receives the complaint and any required filing fee.

3. Via mail, the Clerk's Office will return a signed and sealed summons for service of process to plaintiff's counsel. A party may not electronically serve a civil complaint but shall effect service in the manner required by Fed.R.Civ.P.4.

D. Electronic Filing

1. Electronic transmission of a document to the ECF system, together with the transmission of a Notice of Electronic Filing (NEF) from the court, constitutes filing of the document for all purposes of the Federal Rules of Civil Procedure and constitutes entry of the document on the docket maintained by the Clerk pursuant to Fed.R.Civ.P.58, Fed.R.Civ.P.79 and Fed.R.Crim.P.55.

2. A document filed electronically shall be deemed filed at the time and date stated on the Notice of Electronic Filing received from the court.

3. All pleadings filed electronically shall be titled in accordance with the approved dictionary of civil or criminal events of the ECF system of this court.

4. E-mailing or faxing a document to the Clerk's Office or to the assigned judge does not constitute "filing" of the document. A document shall not be considered filed until the System generates a notice of electronic filing.

E. Service of Electronically Filed Documents

1. Whenever a pleading or other document is filed electronically, the ECF system will automatically generate and send a Notice of Electronic Filing (NEF) to the filing user and registered users of record in the case. The user filing the document shall retain a paper or digital copy of the NEF, which shall serve as the court's date-stamp and proof of filing.

2. Transmission of the NEF shall constitute service of the filed document and shall be deemed to satisfy the requirements of Fed.R.Civ.P.5(b)(2)(D), Fed.R.Civ.P.77(d) and Fed.R.Crim.P.49(b). A certificate of service is not necessary on electronically filed documents. The attorney filing the document electronically is responsible for serving a paper copy of the document by mail in accordance with Fed.R.Civ.P.5(b) to those attorneys or pro se litigants who have not been identified on the NEF as electronic recipients.

3. Service by electronic means shall be treated the same as service by mail for the purpose of adding three (3) days to the prescribed period to respond. In accordance with Local Rule 7.1, a party opposing a motion, shall file an opposition to the motion within fourteen (14) days after service of the motion unless another period is fixed by rule or statute, or by order of the court. The fourteen day period is intended to include the period specified by the civil rules for mailing time and provide for a uniform period regardless of the use of the mails.

F. Subsequent Documents with Fee Requirement

Subsequent documents filed in a case which require a fee, such as notice of appeal, motion for leave to appear pro hac vice, etc., may be electronically filed. However, the required fee must be paid within 24 hours after the document is submitted electronically. A copy of the Notice of Electronic Filing should be submitted with the fee to the Clerk's Office.

G. Deadlines

Filing documents electronically does not in any way alter any filing deadlines. All electronic transmissions of documents must be completed **prior to 6:00 p.m., Eastern Standard Time, in order to be considered timely filed that day.** Where a specific time of day deadline is set by Court order or stipulation, the electronic filing must be completed by that time.

H. Special Filing Requirements and Exceptions

1. The following documents **shall be filed only on paper and will not be scanned into ECF by the Clerk's Office:**

a. Documents filed under seal;

b. Administrative records in social security cases and in other administrative review proceedings;

c. The state court record and other Rule 5 materials in habeas corpus cases filed in 28 U.S.C. § 2254 proceedings;

d. Ex parte motions and applications;

e. Pretrial hearing and trial exhibits; and

f. Medical Records

2. The following documents **shall be filed on paper,** which **may also be scanned** into ECF by the Clerk's Office:

a. The state court record filed in 28 U.S.C. § 1446 removal proceedings;

b. All handwritten pleadings;

c. All pleadings and documents filed by pro se litigants who are incarcerated or who are not registered filing users in ECF;

d. The charging document in a criminal case, such as the complaint, indictment, and information, as well as the criminal JS45 form for the District of Massachusetts;

e. Affidavits for search and arrest warrants and related papers;

f. Fed.R.Crim.P.20 and Fed.R.Crim.P.40 papers received from another court;

g. Appearance bonds;

h. Any pleading or document in a criminal case containing the signature of a defendant, such as a waiver of indictment or plea agreement; and

i. Petitions for violations of supervised release.

3. The following documents **may be scanned by counsel** and filed using ECF, **or filed** on paper:

a. Rule 4 executed service of process documents, and

b. Attachments to filings (See subsections L and M).

4. The following documents may be received by the Clerk's Office in criminal cases, but are not filed, electronically or otherwise, unless ordered by the Court:

a. Pretrial service reports;

b. Psychiatric and psychological reports;

c. Pre-sentencing reports and other papers submitted prior to sentencing; and

d. Letters from defendants

I. Documents Not Filed Electronically

1. *Sealed Documents/Cases*: At this time, the Court will not permit the electronic filing of sealed documents. These documents should be filed as always, clearly labeled as a sealed document, with the appropriate accompanying motion to seal pursuant to Local Rule 7.2.

a. A party may electronically file a motion to file a document under seal. If the motion is granted, the assigned judge will electronically file an order authorizing the filing of the document under seal. The filing party shall then deliver the document to the Clerk's Office for conventional filing under seal. A paper copy of the order must be attached to the documents filed under seal and delivered to the clerk.

2. *Ex Parte Motions, Motions by CJA Attorneys for Funds, etc.*: These motions should be filed as hard copies. These will be handled in the same fashion as sealed documents (except for the requirement to file a separate motion to seal for each document).

3. *Alternative Dispute Resolution (ADR) Documents*: Other than the Order of Reference to ADR and subsequent reports from the ADR Provider, all documents generated by the parties in the ADR process should be sent or delivered to the ADR Provider directly as a hard copy, clearly identified as a document for the ADR Provider. ADR documents are not part of the public case file.

J. Signature

1. *Attorneys*. The user log-in and password required to submit documents to the ECF system shall serve as that user's signature for purposes of Fed. R.Civ.P.11 and for all other purposes under the Federal Rules of Civil Procedure and the Local Rules of this Court. All electronically filed documents must include a signature block and must set forth the attorney's name, Bar number, address, telephone number and e-mail address. The name of the ECF user under whose log-in and password the document

is submitted must be preceded by a "/s/" and typed in the space where the signature would otherwise appear.

2. *Multiple Signatures.* The filer of any document requiring more than one signature (e.g, stipulations, joint motions, joint status reports, Magistrate Judge consent forms, etc.) must list thereon all the names of other signatories by means of a   "/s/"   block for each. By submitting such a document, the filing attorney certifies that each of the other signatories has expressly agreed to the form and substance of the document and that the filing attorney has their actual authority to submit the document electronically. The filing attorney shall retain any records evidencing this concurrence for future production, if necessary, until two (2) years after the expiration of the time for filing a timely appeal. A non-filing signatory or party who disputes the authenticity of an electronically filed document containing multiple signatures must file an objection to the document within fourteen (14) days of the date on the Notice of Electronic Filing.

3. *Affidavits.* Except as provided in subsection H(2)(e), affidavits shall be filed electronically; however, the electronically filed version must contain a "/s/ "   block indicating that the paper document bears an original signature. The filing attorney shall retain the original for future production, if necessary, for two (2) years after the expiration of the time for filing a timely appeal.

K. Privacy

To address the privacy concerns created by Internet access to court documents, unless otherwise ordered by the Court, the filing attorney shall modify certain personal data identifiers in pleadings and other papers as follows:

1. Minors' names: Use of the minors' initials only;

2. Social security numbers: Use of the last four numbers only;

3. Dates of birth: Use of the year of birth only;

4. Financial account numbers: Identify the type of account and the financial institution, but use only the last four numbers of the account number.

It is not the responsibility of the Clerk's Office to review each document to determine if pleadings have been modified and are in the proper form.

SPECIAL NOTICE TO ATTORNEYS INVOLVED IN SOCIAL SECURITY CASES—It is your responsibility to provide the U.S. Attorneys' Office with the social security number of the plaintiff upon the filing of a new social security case.

L. Attachments to Filings and Exhibits (other than hearing and trial exhibits)

1. Attachments to filings and exhibits must be filed in accordance with the Court's ECF User Manual, unless otherwise ordered by the court.

2. A filing user must submit as attachments only those excerpts of the referenced documents that are directly germane to the matter under consideration by the court. Excerpted material must be clearly and prominently identified as such. Users who file excerpts of documents do so without prejudice to their right to timely file additional excerpts or the complete document, as may be allowed by the Court. Responding parties may timely file additional excerpts or the complete document that they believe are directly germane.

3. Filers shall not attach as an exhibit any pleading or other paper already on file with the Court in that case, but shall merely refer to that document.

M. File Size Limitations and Conventional Filing of Documents

1. Whether documents are submitted electronically or on paper, they are still subject to page limitations set by LR 7.1(B)(4) or by order of the court.

2. A filing party must limit the size of the PDF file to no more than 2 megabytes which may be approximately equivalent to a 30 page scanned document. Filing parties should take into consideration that scanned images take up considerably more space on the system than PDF files containing electronically generated documents converted to PDF. However, larger documents or exhibits may be submitted electronically if they are broken up into separate two megabyte segments and attached to the main document.

3. Because documents scanned in color or containing a graphic take much longer to upload, filing parties must configure their scanners to scan documents at 200 dpi and in black and white rather than in color. Documents appearing in color in their original form, such as color photographs, may be scanned in color and then uploaded to the System.

4. The filing party is required to verify the readability of scanned documents before filing them electronically with the court.

5. Documents or exhibits submitted conventionally shall be served on other parties as if not subject to these procedures.

6. When documents or exhibits are submitted conventionally, a Notice of Filing with Clerk's Office shall be filed electronically or shall be attached to the main document. The Notice of Filing with Clerk's Office (see Appendix A) shall describe each of the documents that will be retained as paper copies in the Clerk's Office files, or include an index of the documents if they are voluminous.

N. Orders and Judgments

1. The assigned judge, chambers staff or deputy clerk shall electronically file all signed orders. Any order signed electronically has the same force and effect as if the judge had affixed his/her signature to a

paper copy of the order and it had been entered on the docket conventionally.

2. When mailing paper copies of an electronically filed order to a party who is not a registered participant in ECF, the Clerk's Office will include the Notice of Electronic Filing to provide the non-participant with proof of the filing.

3. A judge, or deputy clerk, if appropriate, may grant routine orders by a text-only entry upon the docket entitled "Electronic Order". In such cases, no PDF document will issue; the text-only entry shall constitute the court's only order on the matter and counsel will receive a system generated NEF.

O. Motions for Leave to File

In any case of an electronic filing in which a party seeks leave of court to file a document or to amend a document previously filed, the party must attach electronically to the motion seeking leave a copy of the document which the party proposes to file. That document must be marked "Proposed [document designation]." If leave to file the document is granted, the party proposing the document must then file the original of that document (which may be done electronically), indicating in the caption of the document that leave has been granted.

P. Submitting Redacted Documents

The parties may request or the Court may require the submission of redacted documents which have sensitive or confidential information removed from them. When filing the original document electronically, the actual document should not be attached to the entry. In its place attach a PDF file which includes the caption of the document and the notation "Document Sealed". If the Court requires the filing of a redacted version of the document, under the Other Filings/Other Documents menu option select Redacted Document and link it back to the original entry but attach the redacted version to this entry.

Q. Submitting Proposed Order

Proposed orders may be submitted electronically in PDF. All proposed orders, other than those filed by the Government pursuant to 18 U.S.C.§ 3161(h)(8)(A), must be either attached as an exhibit to a motion or stipulation or contained within the body of a stipulation. The court may request proposed orders in word processing format by submission to the court on a disk or by e-mail.

R. Transcripts

Proceedings of this Court. A transcript of a proceeding of this court shall be filed in the traditional manner by the court reporter. The transcript will be maintained in the case file in the Clerk's Office.

1. *Transcripts from other Courts.* A transcript of a proceeding of another court shall be filed electronically in PDF, if so available, otherwise on paper.

2. *Depositions.* Transcripts of depositions, when required to be filed, shall be filed electronically using ECF or on either a 3.5" floppy disk or compact disk in PDF, if so available, otherwise on paper.

S. Correcting Docket Entries

1. Once a document is submitted and becomes part of the case docket, corrections to the docket are made only by the Clerk's Office. The System will not permit the filing party to make changes to the document(s) or docket entry filed in error once the transaction has been accepted.

2. A document incorrectly filed in a case may be the result of posting the wrong PDF file to a docket entry, or selecting the wrong document type from the menu, or entering the wrong case number and not catching the error before the transaction is completed. **The filing party should not attempt to refile the document.**

3. As soon as possible after an error is discovered, the filing party should contact the Clerk's Office with the case number and document number for which the correction is being requested. If appropriate, the court will make an entry indicating that the document was filed in error. The filing party will be advised *if* the document needs to be refiled.

T. Technical Failures

1. Known systems outages will be posted on the web site, if possible. A filing user whose filing is made untimely as the result of a technical failure of the Court's ECF system may seek appropriate relief from the Court.

2. Problems on the filer's end, such as phone line problems, problems with the filer's Internet Service Provider (ISP), or hardware or software problems, will not constitute a technical failure under these procedures nor excuse an untimely filing. A filer who cannot file a document electronically because of a problem on the filer's end must file the document conventionally with the document in PDF format on a 3.5" floppy or compact disk or contact the Clerk's Office for permission to file the PDF document via e-mail. Since help desk support will only be available during normal business hours, filers are strongly urged to electronically file any documents due on a given day during normal business hours.

U. Pro Se Litigation

Non-prisoner pro se litigants in civil actions may register with ECF or may file (and serve) all pleadings and other documents on paper. The Clerk's Office will scan into ECF any pleadings and documents filed on paper in accordance with section H of these procedures.

V. Access to Electronically Stored Documents

The public may review at the Clerk's Office all filings that have not been sealed. The public may access civil and criminal files in ECF through the court's Internet site (*www.mad.uscourts.gov*) by obtaining a PACER log-in and password. Documents in criminal cases are available through remote public access, as the District of Massachusetts is part of a pilot program adopted by the Judicial Conference of the United States in March 2002 to provide public access to electronic files in criminal cases in a selected number of courts.

W. Retention

Unless otherwise ordered by the Court, documents that are filed on paper and subsequently uploaded to the ECF system may be destroyed and need not be maintained in paper form by the Clerk's Office. Any document requiring an original signature shall be maintained by the attorney until two (2) years after the expiration of the time for filing a timely appeal. (See subsection J(2) and (3))

UNITED STATES DISTRICT COURT
DISTRICT OF MASSACHUSETTS

APPENDIX A

_____

V.   CASE NO. _____
_____

NOTICE OF FILING WITH CLERK'S OFFICE

Notice is hereby given that the documents, exhibits or attachments listed below have been manually filed with the Court and are available in paper form only:

The original documents are maintained in the case file in the Clerk's Office.

_____

Date

_____

Attorney for

_____

_____

_____

_____

October 24, 2003

POLICY REGARDING ELECTRONIC DEVICES

February 8, 2004

The general public is prohibited from bringing cameras, beepers, cellular telephones, personal data assistants (PDA's), laptop computers, tape recorders, and other electronic devices into any United States courthouse in the District of Massachusetts. Persons bringing these devices on to court property must check them at the security screening station in order to gain access to the building. Attorneys who present a valid bar card from any jurisdiction, together with two valid forms of identification, at least one with a photograph, are permitted to bring PDA's, laptop computers, and cellular telephones into the courthouse for business use. Attorneys carrying these items will be required to submit them for x-ray and such other examination as deemed appropriate by court security personnel. Laptop computers with silent keyboards may be used in the courtroom with the permission of the presiding judge. Cellular telephones and PDA's must be turned off or placed in silent vibrator mode while in the courtroom. Violation of this provision may result in severe sanctions. Cellular telephones may only be used in public areas of the courthouse no less than twenty feet from the entrance to any courtroom. Attorneys are reminded that the recording of court proceedings by any electronic or photographic means is strictly forbidden.

INDEX TO THE LOCAL RULES OF THE UNITED STATES DISTRICT COURT FOR THE DISTRICT OF MASSACHUSETTS

356

LOCAL BANKRUPTCY RULES OF THE UNITED STATES BANKRUPTCY COURT FOR THE DISTRICT OF MASSACHUSETTS

Effective August 1, 1997

Including Amendments Received Through January 1, 2005

Research Note

Use WESTLAW ® *to find cases citing or applying specific rules. WESTLAW may also be used to search for specific terms in court rules or to update court rules. See the MA–RULES and MA–ORDERS Scope Screens for detailed descriptive information and search tips.*

Amendments to these rules are published, as received, in the North Eastern 2d *and the* Massachusetts Decisions *advance sheets.*

Table of Rules

App.
  Rule
  9.   Service of Document by Electronic Means.
  10. Notice of Court Orders and Judgments.
  11. Technical Failures.
  12. Public Access.

OFFICIAL LOCAL FORMS

Form
1.   Matrix List of Creditors.
2A. Notice of Intended Private Sale.

Form
2B. Notice of Intended Public Sale of Estate Property.
3.   Chapter 13 Plan and Cover Sheet.
4.   Order Confirming Chapter 13 Plan.
5.   Order and Notice Fixing Deadline for Filing Proofs of
     Claim in Chapter 11 Cases.
6.   Reaffirmation Agreement.
7.   Declaration Re: Electronic Filing.
8.   Chapter 13 Agreement Between Debtor and Counsel—
     Rights and Responsibilities of Chapter 13 Debtors
     and Their Attorneys.

LOCAL RULES AND FORMS

RULE 1001–1. TITLE

These Local Bankruptcy Rules, promulgated under Fed.R.Bankr.P. 9029, shall be known as the Local Bankruptcy Rules of the United States Bankruptcy Court for the District of Massachusetts, a unit of the United States District Court for the District of Massachusetts, and shall be referred to in abbreviation as MLBR. These rules shall take effect on January 1, 2005 with respect to pending cases and those filed thereafter, and shall govern all proceedings in bankruptcy cases insofar as is just and practicable.

Effective August 1, 1997. Amended effective September 1, 1999; January 1, 2002; March 1, 2003; January 1, 2005.

RULE 1002–1. CASE COMMENCEMENT [DELETED]

Effective August 1, 1997; Deleted effective January 1, 2005.

RULE 1006–1. FILING FEES

Applicable filing fees are set forth in Appendix 3.

Effective August 1, 1997.

RULE 1006–2. FEES–INSTALLMENT PAYMENTS

The Court, upon motion of an individual debtor or joint debtors, may permit payment of the case filing fee in installments. Such debtor(s) shall pay $40.00 at the time of filing, and, except for cause shown upon motion of the debtor, the balance shall be paid in three (3) equal payments in intervals of not greater than thirty (30) days. Failure to make payments shall result in dismissal of the case. No discharge shall enter until all filing fees are paid in full.

Effective August 1, 1997.

RULE 1007–1. LISTS, SCHEDULES AND STATEMENTS

(a) **Separate List of Creditors/Social Security Number.** Each petition shall be accompanied by an original matrix of all creditors and their last known complete addresses and shall conform to the specifications of MLBR Official Local Form 1. Any creditors subsequently added to the matrix shall be included in an amended matrix filed in compliance with MLBR 1009–1 which amended matrix shall be served simultaneously on the United States trustee. A matrix or Statement of Debtor's Social Security Number (Form B21) not filed with the original petition shall be filed no later than three (3) court days from the date of the filing of the petition. Failure to timely comply with this requirement shall result in dismissal of the case without further notice.

(b) **Answer "None" to Be Stated.** Each item in the schedules and statement of affairs shall be completed. Items for which no other entry can be made shall be completed by the entry "none" or "not applicable," whichever response is appropriate.

(c) **Corporate, Partnership or Trust Petitions.**

(1) A petition by a corporation shall be signed or verified by an officer or agent of the corporation and shall be accompanied by a copy of the resolution of the board of directors or other evidence of the officer's or agent's authority to file the petition on behalf of the corporation.

(2) A petition by a partnership or a trust shall be signed or verified by a general partner, trustee or appropriate agent and shall be accompanied by evidence of the signing party's authority to file the petition.

(3) A petition filed on behalf of a corporation, partnership or trust shall indicate that the debtor is represented by counsel and shall state the attorney's name, address and telephone number.

(4) Failure to comply with this rule shall result in dismissal of the case within seven (7) days after the Court issues a notice of defective filing.

Effective August 1, 1997; amended effective January 1, 2005.

RULE 1009–1. AMENDMENTS

A party filing a document amending a voluntary petition, list, schedule, statement of financial affairs, or statement of executory contracts shall do so by notice as set forth in Fed.R.Bankr.P. 1009(a), except with respect to the following: 1) amendments to the debtor's schedule of liabilities, adding a creditor after the deadline for filing complaints under 11 U.S.C. §§ 523 or 727; and 2) amendments to the schedule of exemptions after the deadline for objecting to the exemptions. If either of these exceptions apply, the debtor shall file a motion with the Court for approval of the amendment. A copy of the amended document shall be attached to the notice or motion and clearly state in the caption that it is an amendment. An amendment to a matrix which adds creditors shall contain the names and addresses of all added creditors in compliance with MLBR Official Local Form 1.

Effective August 1, 1997. Amended effective September 1, 1999.

RULE 1015–1. JOINT ADMINISTRATION OF CASES PENDING IN THE SAME COURT

(a) Motion for Joint Administration. A request for an order allowing joint administration of two or more related cases pursuant to Fed.R.Bankr.P. 1015–b shall be made by motion. In the motion for joint administration, the moving party shall 10 designate the name and number of the lead case for conducting proceedings in the jointly administered cases; 2) state the cause warranting joint administration, including the reasons supporting the proposed lead case designation; and 3) state any known facts which may give rise to actual or potential conflicts of interest warranting protection of the interests of creditors of the various estates. A motion for joint administration shall be filed in each case for which joint administration is proposed. A motion for joint administration shall be served by the moving party on all creditors and equity security holders who have requested notice in accordance with Fed.R.Bankr.P. 2002(i), any committee elected under § 705 or appointed under § 1102 of the Bankruptcy Code, the twenty largest unsecured creditors in each case as listed on Official Form 4, all secured creditors and taxing authorities, all attorneys of record, any appointed trustee, and the United States trustee. The court shall grant the motion for joint administration if it is likely to ease the administrative burden on the parties and the court.

(b) Notice and Effect of Order. Upon entry of an order authorizing joint administration of cases, or upon the automatic allowance of a motion for joint administration in accordance with (c) below, the moving party shall serve notice of said order upon all creditors and interested parties of all debtors that are the subject of the motion. The court shall enter the order in each of the other related cases in addition to the designated lead case. An order approving joint administration shall not effect substantive consolidation of the respective debtors' estates.

(c) Automatic Joint Administration of Chapter 11 Cases. If a motion for joint administration of debtors, other than individual debtors, is filed at the same time as the filing of the petitions commencing the cases proposed to be jointly administered, the motion for joint administration shall be treated as an emergency motion and shall be allowed effective upon filing, subject to reconsideration as set forth in (d) below.

(d) Reconsideration. The Court may reconsider an order allowing joint administration upon motion of any party in interest or sua sponte.

Adopted effective January 1, 2005

RULE 2002–1. NOTICE TO PARTIES

(a) Unless the Court orders otherwise, the moving party shall give notice to all parties entitled to notice under the Bankruptcy Code, the Federal Rules of Bankruptcy Procedure, MLBR, or an order of the Court, of the following events:

(1) the proposed use, sale or lease of property of the estate;

(2) a proposed compromise or settlement;

(3) a motion for conversion or dismissal;

(4) objections to and the hearing on the adequacy of a disclosure statement;

(5) the order approving a disclosure statement;

(6) a proposed modification of a plan in a chapter 9, 11, or 12 case;

(7) applications for compensation in a chapter 9, 11, or 12 case or a chapter 13 case, except as provided in the chapter 13 rules at paragraph 13–7(b);

(8) the time for filing claims in a chapter 9 or 11 case;

(9) the time for filing objections to and the hearing on confirmation of a chapter 9, 11 or 12 plan; and

(10) the order confirming a plan in a chapter 9, 11, or 12 case.

(b) Unless the Court orders otherwise, motions to limit notice may be served only upon parties who have filed appearances and requested service of all notices and pleadings, any trustee and trustee's counsel, the debtor and debtor's counsel, the twenty (20) largest creditors, the United States trustee and any creditors' committee and its counsel.

Effective August 1, 1997.

RULE 2002-2. NOTICES TO THE UNITED STATES OF AMERICA AND THE COMMONWEALTH OF MASSACHUSETTS

The addresses for service upon federal, and state governmental agencies are set forth in MLBR Appendix 4.

Effective August 1, 1997.

RULE 2002-4. ADDRESSES

(a) The debtor or debtor's counsel must notify the Clerk, all creditors, parties in interest and all attorneys who have filed appearances in the case or any proceeding of a mailing address change for the debtor or debtor's counsel within ten (10) days of such change.

(b) The Clerk shall direct all returned notices of a § 341(a) meeting of creditors and discharge orders to the debtor's attorney or the debtor, if pro se, to enable that party to locate the correct address and to forward the notice or order to that address. The responsible party must file a certificate of service of the new mailing with the Clerk and must request, in writing, that the Clerk change the creditor's address on the matrix.

(c) The debtor or debtor's counsel shall maintain, be responsible for the accuracy of, and remit to any party immediately upon request, the master mailing matrix and any amendments to it. The master mailing matrix shall include parties who have filed appearances and requested service of all notices and pleadings, any trustee and trustee's counsel, the debtor and debtor's counsel, all creditors, the United States trustee and any creditors' committee and its counsel. When serving notices, the Clerk and any party may rely exclusively on the master mailing matrix, or amended master mailing matrix.

Effective August 1, 1997.

RULE 2002-5. CONTENT OF NOTICES OF SALE

(a) Subject to the requirements of Fed.R.Bankr.P. 6004 and MLBR 6004-1, a notice of proposed private sale of property shall: conform substantially to Official Local Form 2A suited to the particular circumstances of the case; include the name and address of the purchaser; the consideration for the purchase; the time and place of the proposed sale; the terms and conditions of the proposed sale; the time fixed for filing higher offers and/or objections to the proposed sale; the hearing date fixed by the Court; a general description of the property to be sold; an itemized list of the asset or assets; the relationship, if any, of the buyer and the seller; a statement as to the fair market value of the property to be sold; the opinion of any professional appraiser or broker as to the value of the property to be sold, if available; a statement of the

basis for the seller's opinion that the purchase price is reasonable; and a statement as to the marketing efforts undertaken by the seller.

(b) Unless the Court orders otherwise, the estate representative shall give not less than twenty (20) days written notice by mail to all creditors and interested parties of any sale or use of estate assets out of the ordinary course of business. The notice shall state that any objection, higher offer, or request for hearing must be filed and served within the time established by the Court, which time shall be conspicuously stated in the notice.

Effective August 1, 1997.

RULE 2014-1. APPLICATION TO EMPLOY PROFESSIONAL PERSONS

(a) **Application and Statement.** An application of a debtor (other than a chapter 7 debtor), debtor in possession, estate representative, or committee to employ any professional person, including an attorney, accountant, appraiser, broker, auctioneer, consultant or agent, shall include all of the information required to be provided by Fed.R.Bankr.P. 2014(a). In addition, in the statement accompanying the application, the person to be employed (hereinafter the "professional") shall make the following representations and disclosures under penalty of perjury in accordance with section (c):

(1) Neither I nor any member of my firm holds or represents any interest adverse to the estate of the above-named debtor.

(2) My and my firm's connections with the debtor, any creditor, or other party in interest, their respective attorneys and accountants are as follows:

_____

_____

_____

I am and each member of my firm is a "disinterested person" as that term is defined in 11 U.S.C. § 101(14).

(3) I have not agreed to share with any person (except members of my firm) the compensation to be paid for the services rendered in this case, except as follows:

_____

_____

(4) I have received a retainer in this case in the amount of $_____, which sum, upon information and belief, was generated by the debtor from: _____.

(5) I shall amend this statement immediately upon my learning that (A) any of the within representations

are incorrect or (B) there is any change of circumstance relating thereto.

(6) I have reviewed the provisions of MLBR 2016–1.

(b) Clarifying Terms.

(1) *Connections and Relationships.* For the purposes of subsection (a)(2) and 11 U.S.C. § 101(14), "connections" and "relationships" shall include, without limitation:

(A) the professional's representation of the debtor or any affiliate of the debtor as that term is defined in 11 U.S.C. § 101(2), or any insider of the debtor as that term is defined in 11 U.S.C. § 101(31), at any time;

(B) the professional's representation of a creditor against the debtor, or any insider or affiliate of the debtor, at any time;

(C) the professional's representation of a creditor on a regular basis or in connection with a substantial matter;

(D) the professional's representation of or by, or employment of or by, another authorized professional specifically in connection with this case or on a regular basis or in connection with a substantial matter in another case; and

(E) a family affiliation to the third degree of consanguinity or marital relationship between the professional or the member(s) of the professional's firm who will actually render services and any party in interest (or officer, director, or shareholder of such party) or other professional authorized to be employed in the case.

It shall be the duty of the professional to make a preliminary inquiry as to such connections and relationships among the members and employees of the professional's firm.

(2) *Source of Funds.* For the purposes of subsection (a)(4), the professional should disclose whether the funds were generated by the debtor from operations, salary, wages, other income, a loan or capital contribution. If the source is a loan or capital contribution and such loan (other than an advance on a continuing line of credit) or capital contribution was made to the debtor within ninety (90) days prior to the filing of the petition, the identity of the lender or investor/stockholder and the terms of repayment shall be disclosed, as well as any claims by and between the debtor and the lender or investor/stockholder.

(c) Form of Statement. The statement accompanying the application to employ a professional person shall take the form of an affidavit dated and signed under penalty of perjury by the person to be employed, and above such signature the affiant shall include a sworn declaration as provided in 28 U.S.C. § 1746, which states: "I declare (or certify, or verify,

or state) under penalty of perjury that the foregoing is true and correct."

(d) Effective Date. If a court approves an application for the employment of a professional person, such approval shall be deemed effective as of the date of the filing of the application. However, if such application is filed within fourteen (14) days from the later of case commencement or the date the professional commenced rendering services, court approval shall be deemed effective commencing the date that services were first rendered. Approval shall not be otherwise retroactive absent extraordinary circumstances.

Effective August 1, 1997. Amended effective September 1, 1999.

RULE 2016–1.   APPLICATION FOR COMPENSATION

(a) Any professional seeking interim or final compensation for services and reimbursement of expenses under 11 U.S.C. §§ 330, 331, 503(b)(2), 503(b)(4) or 506(b) shall file an application for compensation and reimbursement. The application shall conform generally to Fed.R.Bankr.P. 2016.

(1) The application and any attachments shall:

(A) be legible and understandable;

(B) identify the time period or periods during which services were rendered;

(C) describe the specific services performed each day by each person with the time broken down into units of tenths of one hour devoted to such services;

(D) include a copy of any contract or agreement reciting the terms and conditions of employment and compensation;

(E) include a copy of the order authorizing the employment;

(F) include the date and amount of any retainer, partial payment or prior interim allowances;

(G) include a brief narrative description of services performed and a summary of hours by professionals and other personnel;

(H) if the trustee is also serving as his or her own attorney, the trustee's attorney's application must contain a certification that no compensation has been or will be sought for services as an attorney which are properly trustee services; and

(I) include a brief biography of each person included in the fee application, stating his or her background and experience.

(2) All applications by professionals shall include a summary chart, which clearly sets forth in columns:

(A) the full names of the attorneys, paralegals and clerks performing services;

(B) the initials used for each person;

(C) the hourly rate charged by each person and, if there is a change in the hourly rate for any such person during the covered period, then that person's name shall be listed as many times as there are changes in the hourly rate and each entry shall show the number of hours at each rate and the date each change became effective; and

(D) the total amount of fees for each person and a column showing a grand total figure (See MLBR Appendix 6 as an example).

(E) the total amount of each type of out-of-pocket expense for which reimbursement is sought, which amounts, subject to subsection (F), shall not exceed the actual cost to the applicant.

(F) In lieu of calculating the actual cost of the expenses set forth below, the applicant may request the rates of reimbursement set forth in MLBR Appendix 2 for:

(i) copies;

(ii) incoming telecopier transmissions; and

(iii) auto mileage.

(b) Any application for compensation by co-counsel shall specify the separate services rendered by each counsel and contain a certification that no compensation is sought for duplicate services.

(c) If an application for compensation and reimbursement by a chapter 7, 11 or 12 trustee exceeds $5,000.00, the trustee shall state:

(1) the total amount received in the estate;

(2) the amount of money disbursed and to be disbursed by the trustee to parties in interest (excluding the debtor) and a calculation of the maximum fee allowable under 11 U.S.C. § 326;

(3) a brief narrative description of services performed;

(4) if the payment sought is interim compensation, why the payment of interim compensation is reasonable and appropriate;

(5) the dividend, expressed as a percentage of funds to be distributed to creditors, if the requested compensation and other requested administrative expenses are allowed in the amounts requested. If a trustee has served both as a chapter 7 and a chapter 11 trustee, separate itemizations must be provided for each period. The amount of compensation shall be stated as a dollar amount, regardless of the calculation of the maximum compensation allowable under 11 U.S.C. § 326(a).

(d)(1) All applications which seek more than $35,000.00 in compensation, or are otherwise very lengthy, must be divided into narrative sections and must utilize the project categories set forth in subsection (2) below. Each narrative section within each project category must represent a task, must describe the task and the benefit to the estate, and must

identify the work done by each professional. There shall be attached to each narrative section a specific description of services performed under such project category each day by each person and the time devoted to such services on that day by each person. The end of each narrative section must include a summary chart that conforms to the requirements of section (a)(2)(A)-(F) of this rule.

(2) The following project categories (as described below) are to be utilized in all applications submitted pursuant to this rule. Applications may contain additional categories as may be required in a particular case:

(A) Asset Analysis and Recover: identification and review of potential assets including causes of action and non–litigation recoveries and appraisals of assets;

(B) Asset Disposition: sales, leases, matters under 11 U.S.C. § 365, abandonment and related transaction work;

(C) Business Operations: issues related to debtor–in–possession operating in Chapter 11 cases, such as employee issues, vendor issues, lease and contract issues, and other similar matters, as well as analysis of tax issues and preparation of tax returns;

(D) Case Administration: coordination and compliance activities (including preparation of statements of financial affairs, schedules, lists of contracts, and United States Trustee interim statements and operating reports), contacts with the United States Trustee, and general creditor inquiries;

(E) Claims Administration and Objections: specific claim inquiries, bar date motions, analyses, objections and allowance of claims;

(F) Employee Benefits and Pensions: issues such as severance, retention, 401(k) coverage and continuance of pension plans;

(G) Employment Applications and Objections: preparation of employment applications, motions to establish interim compensation procedures, and review of and objections to employment applications of others;

(H) Fee Applications and Objections: preparation of fee applications and review of and objections to fee applications of others;

(I) Financing: matters under 11 U.S.C. §§ 361, 363 and 364, including cash collateral and secured claims, and analysis of loan documents;

(J) Litigation: a separate category should be utilized for each litigation matter;

(K) Meetings of Creditors: preparing for and attending conference of creditors, meetings held pursuant to 11 U.S.C. § 341, and other creditors' committee meetings;

(L) Plan and Disclosure Statement: formulation, presentation and confirmation, compliance with confirmation order, related orders and rules, disbursements and case closing activities (except those relating to allowance of any objections to claims); and

(M) Relief from Stay Proceedings: matters relating to termination or continuation of automatic stay under 11 U.S.C. § 362.

Effective August 1, 1997; amended effective January 1, 2005.

RULE 2082-1. CONFIRMATION OF CHAPTER 12 PLANS

(a) The Clerk, in conjunction with issuing a notice of the initial meeting of creditors, shall issue a notice of the deadline for the filing of claims as established by Fed.R.Bankr.P. 3002.

(b) The Clerk shall schedule the confirmation hearing and establish a plan objection deadline upon the filing of the debtor's plan and notify the debtor of these dates. The debtor shall give at least fifteen (15) days notice of the hearing and the deadline for filing objections and shall serve a copy of the plan upon all creditors, equity security holders, and the chapter 12 trustee, and the United States trustee. The debtor shall file a certificate of service with the Court indicating that service has been made.

Effective August 1, 1997.

RULE 2090-2. DISCIPLINARY PROCEEDINGS

(a) An attorney who appears for any purpose in any case or proceeding submits himself or herself to the Court's disciplinary jurisdiction and shall be held to the standards of professional conduct set forth in District Court Local Rule 83.6.

(b) In any matter in which a bankruptcy judge has reasonable cause to believe that an attorney has committed a violation of any canon or ethical rule, the bankruptcy judge may refer the attorney for disciplinary proceedings to the District Court pursuant to District Court Local Rule 83.6 and to any state disciplinary authority. In connection with any such referral, the bankruptcy judge may recommend expedited interim action by the District Court and the state disciplinary authority if in the opinion of the bankruptcy judge such action is necessary to avoid an imminent risk of harm to the public.

(c) A bankruptcy judge may impose any other sanction the judge deems necessary under the circumstances in accordance with the relevant statutes, rules of this Court and the District Court, or applicable law.

Effective August 1, 1997. Amended effective September 1, 1999.

RULE 2091-1. WITHDRAWAL OF APPEARANCE

(a) An attorney may withdraw from a case or proceeding without leave of the Court by serving a notice of withdrawal on the client and all other parties in interest and filing the notice, provided that:

(1) such notice is accompanied by the filing of a notice of appearance of successor counsel;

(2) there are no motions pending before the Court; and

(3) no trial date has been set.

Unless these conditions are met, an attorney may withdraw from a case or proceeding only with leave of the Court.

(b) An attorney granted leave to withdraw shall immediately serve on the client and all other parties in interest the order permitting withdrawal. If the client is a corporation, the order shall contain a provision directing that new counsel file a notice of appearance within twenty (20) days from the date of the order or such shorter period as the Court may direct. If a party who has been served with notice of an attorney's withdrawal fails to appear in the case or proceeding either through a newly appointed attorney or, if such party is an individual, in person, within the period prescribed, such failure shall be grounds for entry of a default judgment, dismissal or other appropriate action by the Court.

Effective August 1, 1997.

RULE 3001-1. PROOFS OF CLAIM IN NO ASSET CASES

In any case in which creditors have been advised that there are insufficient assets to pay a dividend, and the trustee, in accordance with Fed.R.Bankr.P. 3002(a)(5), subsequently notifies the Court that payment of a dividend is anticipated, the Clerk shall issue a bar date for the filing of claims and a notice that creditors who previously filed proofs of claims need not file claims again in order to receive a distribution.

Effective August 1, 1997.

RULE 3007-1. OBJECTIONS TO CLAIMS

(a) A party who files an objection to the allowance of any proof of claim shall state in the objection, with particularity, the factual and legal grounds for the objection, and shall make a recommendation to the Court as to whether the claim should be disallowed or allowed in an amount or with a priority other than as filed. A party may file multiple objections to claims in one pleading. The provisions of this rule shall apply to single as well as multiple objections to claims.

(b) The procedures for motion practice and contested matters set forth in Fed.R.Bankr.P. 9013 and 9014 and MLBR 9013-1 shall govern objections to claims.

Upon the filing of an objection to a proof of claim, the Clerk shall assign a deadline for a claimant to file a response to the objection and a hearing date. The party objecting to the claim shall serve upon the claimant and any other party entitled to notice a copy of the objection and the notice of response deadline and hearing date, and shall file a certificate of service with respect to the notice.

(c) If a claimant contests an objection to claim, the claimant shall file with the Clerk a written response to the objection, which response shall state with particularity why the objection to the claim should be overruled. The response shall be served on the party objecting to the claim and any other party entitled to notice of the response. In addition, at the time of the service of the response, the claimant should also serve on the party objecting to the claim documentation in support of the allowance of the claim. A claimant who does not file a timely response to a properly served objection to claim will be deemed to have agreed that the objection to claim may be sustained. The Court, in its discretion, may cancel the hearing on any properly served objection to claim to which a timely response has not been filed and may sustain the objection to claim without further notice or hearing.

(d) In the event of one or more timely responses to objections to claims, within ten (10) days after the deadline for responses, and at least two (2) days prior to the hearing on objections to claims, the party filing the objection(s) to claims shall file a "Report and Hearing Agenda", setting forth 1) a list of the objections to claims to which no timely responses were filed and the objecting party's recommendations with respect to those claims; 2) a report on the settlement of any objections to claims; 3) the status of any objection to claim to which a timely response was filed and which remains unresolved; 4) whether the objection is likely to be resolved; and 5) the objecting party's recommendation for further proceedings on the objection to claim. If a creditor timely files a response to an objection to claim, the initial hearing on the objection shall be a preliminary nonevidentiary hearing, at which the parties shall appear and be prepared to discuss the need for an evidentiary hearing, discovery, scheduling and settlement.

(e) Within seven (7) days after the Court's action on any objection to claim, the objecting party shall submit a proposed order on the objections to claims.

Effective August 1, 1997; amended effective January 1, 2005.

RULE 3011–1. PROCEDURE FOLLOWING FINAL DISTRIBUTION

(a) One hundred and fifty (150) days after final distribution in a chapter 7 or chapter 13 case, the trustee shall forward to the Clerk:

(1) a list of names and addresses of persons whose checks were not negotiated and the amounts to which they are entitled; and

(2) a check payable to the Clerk in the full amount of all outstanding unpaid checks.

(b) In chapter 7 cases, the trustee shall close out the estate's bank account(s) relating to the case and file with the Clerk a copy of the final bank statement(s) indicating that the bank account(s) has (have) been closed with a zero (0) balance. In chapter 13 cases, the chapter 13 trustee shall file with the Clerk a statement indicating the amount of monies distributed to creditors, the amount of the trustee's commission, the amount of monies being turned over to the Clerk under section (a), and a representation that there is a zero (0) balance in the debtor(s)' account in the records of the chapter 13 trustee.

(c) The trustee shall retain custody of all of the estate's cancelled checks and bank statements for no less than two (2) years from the date the case is closed.

(d) Any check issued by a trustee shall contain a legend stating that the check will not be paid more than ninety (90) days after it is issued.

(e) Prior to the closing of the case, the trustee shall file with the Clerk the Trustee's Final Distribution Report, in such form as may be approved by the United States trustee.

Effective August 1, 1997.

RULE 3015–1. CHAPTER 13 CASES

The chapter 13 rules attached hereto as MLBR Appendix 1 are adopted and incorporated herein by reference.

Effective August 1, 1997.

RULE 3017–1. APPROVAL OF DISCLOSURE STATEMENTS IN CHAPTER 11 CASES

(a) Objections and Hearing on Approval. Notice of the time fixed for filing objections and of the hearing to consider final approval of the disclosure statement shall be given in accordance with Fed. R.Bankr.P. 2002(b). Upon motion and for cause shown, the Court may issue an order combining the hearing on the approval of the disclosure statement with the notice of the hearing on confirmation of the plan.

(b) Prior to filing an objection to a disclosure statement, counsel to the party who intends to object to the adequacy of the disclosure statement shall contact counsel to the plan proponent and confer by telephone or in person in a good faith effort to narrow areas of disagreement.

(c) An objection to the disclosure statement shall be filed and served on the debtor, the United States trustee, the plan proponent, any chapter 11 trustee, any examiner, all members of any committee appointed under the Bankruptcy Code and its counsel and any other entity that has requested service of pleadings in the case or which has been designated by the Court. Any objection to the adequacy of a disclosure statement shall contain a certificate stating that the conference required by section (b) was held, the date and time of the conference and the names of the participating parties, or a statement detailing the reasons why the conference was not held. The Court may overrule without a hearing objections that are not accompanied by the conference certificate.

Effective August 1, 1997.

RULE 3017–2. FILING OF PLAN AND DISCLOSURE STATEMENT IN SMALL BUSINESS CHAPTER 11 REORGANIZATION CASES

(a) **Election to be Considered a Small Business in a Chapter 11 Case.** In a chapter 11 case, a debtor that is a small business may elect to be considered a small business within the meaning of 11 U.S.C. § 1121(e) by filing a written statement of election no later than sixty (60) days after the date of the order for relief or at such later date as the Court, for cause, may fix. If the debtor seeks to extend the time period within which it may make the election, the debtor shall file an appropriate motion with the Court before the expiration of the election time period.

(b) **Approval of Disclosure Statement to Chapter 11 Plan in Small Business Case.**

(1) *Conditional Approval.* If the debtor is a small business and has made a timely election to be considered a small business in a chapter 11 case, the Court may, on application of the debtor, conditionally approve a disclosure statement filed in accordance with Fed.R.Bankr.P. 3016. On or before conditional approval of the disclosure statement, the Court shall:

(A) fix a time within which the holders of claims and interests may accept or reject the plan;

(B) fix a time for filing objections to the disclosure statement;

(C) fix a date for the hearing on final approval of the disclosure statement to be held if a timely objection is filed; and

(D) fix a date for the hearing on confirmation.

(2) *Application of Fed.R.Bankr.P. 3017.* If the disclosure statement is conditionally approved, Fed.R.Bankr.P. 3017(a), (b), (c), and (e) shall not apply. Conditional approval of the disclosure statement is considered approval of the disclosure statement for the purpose of applying Fed.R.Bankr.P. 3017(d).

Effective August 1, 1997.

RULE 3022–1. CLOSING CHAPTER 11 CASES

(a) **Definitions.** For purposes of this rule, 11 U.S.C. § 350 and Fed.R.Bankr.P. 3022, a chapter 11 case is "fully administered" unless a matter is pending sixty (60) days following the entry of a final order confirming a plan of reorganization.

(b) **Motion for Final Decree.** Counsel for the plan proponent shall prepare and file a motion for final decree closing the chapter 11 case within sixty (60) days of the date on which it is fully administered. Preparation and filing of the motion for final decree shall be a continuing post-confirmation duty of counsel to the plan proponent.

(c) **Form of Motion for Final Decree.** The motion for final decree shall contain the following statements made under oath by an individual with personal knowledge:

(1) that the plan has been substantially consummated in accordance with 11 U.S.C. § 1101(2) and the provisions of the plan and the confirmation order; that any subsequent orders of the Court have been complied with; and that the case may be closed in accordance with Fed.R.Bankr.P. 3022;

(2) that the debtor, trustee or agent has paid all administrative expenses, including court-authorized professional compensation and costs (unless otherwise agreed in writing by the parties or unless otherwise provided for by the confirmed plan), as evidenced by an attached Exhibit "A" listing the names, addresses and amounts paid to each of the recipients;

(3) that the debtor, trustee or agent has commenced making distributions prescribed by the plan, as evidenced by an attached Exhibit "B" listing the names, addresses and amounts paid to each of the recipients;

(4) that all remaining distributions prescribed by the plan shall be made in accordance with an attached Exhibit "C" listing the names, addresses and amounts to be paid to each of the recipients; and

(5) if applicable, that distributions have not been made to recipients set forth on an attached Exhibit "D" listing the names, addresses and amounts tendered but returned and the reasons why payments have not been made, despite reasonable attempts.

(d) **Interim Report on Administration Progress.** If counsel for the plan proponent cannot file a motion for final decree on or before sixty (60) days after the entry of an order confirming the plan, counsel shall prepare and file an interim report on administration progress, describing the actions taken to consummate the plan and fully administer and close the case. The report shall contain detailed accounts, under subsections (c) (2), (3), and (4), of all amounts paid under the plan, if any, since the entry of the confirmation order. The Court, in its discretion, may direct the filing of additional reports and/or issue an order setting forth a schedule of future reporting.

(e) Service of Motion for Final Decree and Interim Report on Administration Progress. Counsel for the plan proponent shall serve copies of any motion for a final decree or interim report on administration progress, together with all supporting documentation, on any committee appointed by the United States trustee, counsel to any committee, and any party who filed an appearance in the case and requested service of all notices and pleadings, the United States trustee and any other parties as the Court may direct.

(f) Objections to Motion for Final Decree. Any party in interest, including the United States trustee, may object to any motion for final decree or interim report on administration progress.

(g) Hearings. The Court, in its discretion, may schedule a hearing on any motion for final decree or interim report on administration progress or any objection thereto.

(h) Entry of Final Decree. The Court may enter a final decree closing the case with or without a hearing.

(i) Reopening of Case. Nothing in this rule shall be interpreted as limiting the Court's ability to reopen a case pursuant to 11 U.S.C. § 350 and Fed. R.Bankr.P. 5010.

Effective August 1, 1997.

RULE 4001–1. MOTIONS FOR RELIEF FROM STAY; SUBMISSION OF MOTIONS AND OPPOSITIONS TO MOTIONS

(a) A party seeking relief from the automatic stay provided by 11 U.S.C. § 362(a) shall file, in accordance with Fed.R.Bankr.P. 9014, a motion and a proposed order.

(b) If the motion contains a request for authority to foreclose pursuant to a mortgage or security interest, the movant shall provide the following information:

(1) If the movant seeks relief for cause pursuant to 11 U.S.C. § 362(d)(1), then the cause shall be specifically stated in the motion.

(2) If the movant seeks relief with respect to a stay of an act against property pursuant to 11 U.S.C. § 362(d)(1) or (d)(2), then the motion shall state:

(A) the amount and priority of the debt alleged to be owed to the movant;

(B) the identification, amount, and priority of each other encumbrance affecting the property, including real estate taxes and other municipal charges;

(C) the total of the amounts set forth in subsections (a) and (b);

(D) the fair market value and liquidation value of the collateral, with any available appraisal(s) attached;

(E) either that (i) there is no other collateral securing the obligation, or (ii) there is other collateral securing the obligation, indicating the identity, value and valuation method and attaching any available appraisal(s);

(F) the original holder of the obligations secured by the security interest and/or mortgage and every subsequent transferee, if known to the movant, and whether the movant is the holder of that obligation or an agent of the holder; and

(G) if known to the movant, whether and where any declaration of homestead has been recorded against the property;

(3) If the movant seeks relief from stay pursuant to 11 U.S.C. § 362(d)(3), the motion shall state:

(A) whether a plan of reorganization has been filed in the case;

(B) whether the debtor has commenced monthly payments to creditors with interests in the real estate pursuant to 11 U.S.C. § 363(d)(3)(B); and

(C) the original holder of the obligations secured by the security interest and/or mortgage and every subsequent transferee, if known to the movant, and whether the movant is the holder of that obligation or an agent of the holder.

(c) A party opposing a motion for relief from the automatic stay must file an opposition to the motion within ten (10) days, inclusive of the three (3) day mailing period provided in Fed.R.Bankr.P. 9006(f), after service of the motion. The opponent shall either admit, deny or state that the opponent has insufficient knowledge to admit or deny each and every allegation of the motion, shall state specifically why the motion should not be granted, and shall state the terms of any offer of adequate protection made by the debtor or trustee. If the value alleged by the movant is disputed, any appraisal available to the opponent shall be attached to the opposition. If the motion is scheduled for an expedited hearing before the expiration of the ten (10) day period, then the opposition shall be filed before the expedited hearing.

(d) Documents not filed with the motion or opposition to the motion, whether in the form of a reply memorandum or otherwise, may be submitted only by leave of Court.

(e) In the absence of a timely filed opposition and upon evidence of proper service, the Court, without a hearing, may allow or deny the motion after the expiration of the ten (10) day opposition period. The Court may deny a motion for relief from stay without a hearing if the moving party fails to comply with section (b).

(f) All documents filed pursuant to this rule shall be served in accordance with Fed.R.Bankr.P. 4001(a) and 9006(d)–(f) upon all parties who have filed appearances and requested service of all notices and pleadings, and on any other party that the Court may designate. If the motion seeks relief with respect to an act against property, the motion shall also be served on all entities that claim an interest in the property, including all co-owners, lienholders and taxing authorities.

(g) A preliminary hearing on a motion for relief from the automatic stay will be a consolidated preliminary and final nonevidentiary hearing unless at the conclusion of the preliminary hearing the Court schedules a final evidentiary or nonevidentiary hearing.

(h) If the estate representative fails to file a response within the time prescribed in section (c), then the estate representative shall be deemed to have assented to the motion.

Effective August 1, 1997; amended effective January 1, 2005.

RULE 4001–2. USE OF CASH COLLATERAL, OBTAINING CREDIT AND STIPULATIONS RELATING TO SAME

(a) A motion for use of cash collateral, for authority to obtain credit, or a stipulation relating to same shall set forth the total dollar amount of the request for use of funds, the specific uses to which the funds will be put, the debtor's proposed budget for the use of the funds, pricing and economic terms including interest rates and fees, maturity, termination and default provisions, disclosure by the debtor as to whether it has reason to believe that the budget will be adequate to pay all administrative expenses due and payable during the period covered by the budget, the amount of debt asserted to be owed to any creditor claiming an interest in the collateral, the value of the collateral which secures the creditor's asserted interest, any proposal for providing adequate protection including any priority or superpriority provisions, including the effect thereof on existing liens and any carve–outs from liens or superpriorities, and any choice of law provision. If the credit is to be extended pursuant to a loan agreement or similar agreement, the agreement must be attached to the motion, together with a separate summary of its terms. If the debtor seeks authority to use cash collateral or to obtain credit on an emergency or expedited basis, the debtor shall state the nature of the emergency requiring an emergency or expedited determination.

(b) A motion for use of cash collateral, for authority to obtain credit, or a stipulation relating to same as well as any proposed orders for which entry is sought shall be served on all creditors who assert an interest in the cash collateral and their attorneys, if known, any taxing authority that has a claim against the debtor, the debtor's twenty (20) largest unsecured creditors, the members of any committee appointed in the case and counsel to any committee, any parties who have filed a request for service of all pleadings and notices and the United States trustee.

(c) Subject to section (d), the following provisions contained in an agreement between the debtor and the holder of a secured claim as to use of cash collateral, obtaining credit, or adequate protection, or any interim or final order approving or authorizing the use of cash collateral, obtaining credit, or adequate protection, shall be unenforceable:

(1) Cross-collateralization clauses: Provisions that elevate prepetition debt to administrative expense or higher status or secure the repayment of prepetition debt with postpetition assets, other than (i) a claim arising from postpetition advances which constitute an additional non-replacement extension of credit; or (ii) a claim representing the diminution in value of the secured claim after the commencement of the case;

(2) Concessions as to the status of prepetition lien or debt: Provisions or findings of fact that bind the debtor, the estate representative or other parties in interest with respect to the validity, perfection, priority, enforceability or amount of the secured creditor's prepetition lien or debt;

(3) Provisions creating liens on bankruptcy causes of action: Provisions that grant liens on the estate's claims arising under 11 U.S.C. sections 506(c), 544, 545, 547, 548 or 549;

(4) Waivers: Provisions that seek a waiver of or restrict in any way rights that the debtor or estate representative may have under sections 506(c), 544, 545, 547, 548 or 549; or that purport to release, waive or restrict alleged prepetition claims by the debtor or the estate against the secured creditor; or that in any way restrict the ability of the debtor or the estate representative to file a plan or that prohibit or restrict any proposed treatment of a creditor in that plan;

(5) Right to relief from stay: Provisions that grant automatic relief from stay upon the occurrence of any event; or that purport to bind the court to an expedited or emergency hearing on a request for such relief; or that limit in any way the court's consideration of issues that may arise under section 362(d) or the debtor's or estate representative's rights to bring those issues before the court;

(6) Rollups: provisions that deem prepetition secured debt to be postpetition debt or that use postpetition loans from a prepetition secured creditor to pay part or all of a secured creditor's prepetition debt;

(7) Non-consensual priming: Provisions that create a lien senior or equal to any existing lien without the consent of that lienholder;

(8) Disparate carveouts: Provisions that provide fee or expense carveouts for any professional disparate from those provided to any and all professionals whose employment is approved by the court;

(9) Waiver of right to seek use of cash collateral: Provisions that limit the right of the debtor or the estate representative to move for an order authorizing the use of cash collateral or that seek to prime the secured position of any other secured party under Section 364(d) in the absence of the secured creditor's consent;

(10) Waiver of procedural requirements for foreclosure: provisions that waive the procedural requirements for foreclosure required under applicable non-bankruptcy law;

(11) Venue in foreign jurisdiction: Provisions that place venue in a jurisdiction other than this court in the event of a dispute under any agreement;

(12) Payment of secured creditor's expenses: Provisions that require the debtor to pay a secured creditor's expenses and attorney's fees in connection with a proposed financing or use of cash collateral without any notice or review by the office of the United States Trustee and the court;

(13) Termination; Default; Remedies: Provisions that provide that the use of cash collateral will cease or the financing agreement will default, on (i) the filing of a challenge to lender's prepetition lien or lender's prepetition conduct; (ii) entry of an order granting relief from automatic stay (except as to material assets); (iii) grant of a change of venue with respect to the case or any adversary proceeding; (iv) the making of a motion by a party in interest seeking any relief (as distinct from an order granting such relief); (v) management changes or the departure, from the debtor, of any identified employees;

(14) Release of Liability: Provisions that purport to release the prepetition lender's liability for alleged pre-petition torts, breaches of contract, or lender liability, releases of pre-petition defenses and/or counterclaims, and provisions that shorten the period of limitations within which any party in interest (including a successor trustee) may bring causes of action against the lender.

(d) Notwithstanding section (c), the Court may order the enforcement of any terms and conditions on the use of cash collateral or obtaining credit, provided that (i) the proposed order or agreement specifically states that the proposed terms and conditions vary from the requirements of section (c), and (ii) any such proposed terms and conditions are conspicuously and specifically set forth in the proposed agreement or order.

(e) Preliminary and Final Orders; Notice

(1) A single motion may be filed seeking entry of an interim and final order authorizing use of cash collateral or a borrowing or approving a stipulation relating to same. The motion shall be accompanied by any proposed order for which entry is sought. Notice of

the motion and any notice of any hearing shall be served on the United States trustee, as well as those parties required by Fed. R. Bankr. P. 4001(b)(1) and (c)(1).

(2) The Court may enter an Interim Preliminary Order authorizing use of cash collateral or borrowing, or a stipulation relating to same only to the extent necessary to avoid immediate and irreparable harm to the estate pending a final hearing. Any provision of an Interim Preliminary Order may be reconsidered at the Final Hearing. Provisions in an Interim Preliminary Order shall not be binding on the Court with respect to the provisions of the Final Order, except that a lender: (a) will be afforded the benefits and protections of the Interim Preliminary Order for funds advanced during the term of the Interim Preliminary Order, and (b) will not be required to advance funds under a Final Order which contains provisions contrary to or inconsistent with the Interim Preliminary Order.

(3) A final hearing on a motion authorizing use of cash collateral or a borrowing, or a stipulation relating to same shall not be held earlier than 15 days after service of the notice of hearing.

Effective August 1, 1997. Amended January 1, 2002; January 1, 2005.

RULE 4003-1. AVOIDANCE OF JUDICIAL LIENS

(a) A motion to avoid a judicial lien pursuant to 11 U.S.C. § 522(f)(1) shall:

(1) identify the holder of the judicial lien sought to be avoided and provide the name and address of the lien holder;

(2) state the date the judicial lien was granted and identify the court that issued the lien;

(3) state the amount of the judicial lien as of the date of the filing of the petition;

(4) identify the holders of all other liens on the property listed in order of their priority;

(5) state the amount of each other lien on the property and provide a total of same;

(6) state the amount of the exemption that is allegedly impaired and provide the applicable statute for the debtor's claim of exemption;

(7) state the value of the debtor's interest in the property and attach any available appraisal report;

(8) apply the formula under 11 U.S.C. § 522(f)(2)(A); and

(9) state whether the debtor contends that the entire lien is voidable, or if the lien can only be partially avoided, the amount of the surviving lien.

(b) Any opposition to a motion to avoid a judicial lien shall admit or deny each and every allegation of the motion, specifically state why the motion should not be granted, and apply the formula under 11 U.S.C. § 522(f)(2)(A). If the opposing party intends to rely on an appraisal report, the report shall be attached to the opposition.

Effective September 1, 1999.

RULE 4008–1. REAFFIRMATION AGREEMENTS

(a) A reaffirmation agreement that does not comply with 11 U.S.C. § 524(c) or (d) shall be unenforceable. Fed.R.Bankr.P. 9011 shall apply to an attorney's declaration under 11 U.S.C. § 524(c).

(b) If a debtor is unrepresented by counsel during the course of negotiating of a reaffirmation agreement, the Court shall hold a hearing on the approval of the reaffirmation agreement pursuant to 11 U.S.C. § 524(d). The Court, in its discretion, may schedule a hearing sua sponte on the validity or approval of any other reaffirmation agreement and/or may require that any reaffirmation agreement conform to Official Form 6.

Effective August 1, 1997. Amended effective January 1, 2002.

RULE 5001–1. DIVISIONS OF COURT, CASE ASSIGNMENTS AND FILING OF PAPERS

(a) The District of Massachusetts shall contain the divisions comprised of the counties, cities and towns set forth in MLBR Appendix 5.

(b) All documents related to cases and proceedings for the Eastern division shall be filed in the Clerk's Office in Boston. All documents in cases and proceedings for the Western division shall be filed in the Clerk's Office in Worcester.

(c) The debtor or petitioning creditor(s) shall file an original petition only in the appropriate division office. Venue for a division shall be determined in the same fashion as venue for a district under 28 U.S.C. § 1408 and applicable case law. In the event of an emergency, either division office may accept for filing on behalf of the other division office an original petition under any chapter of the Bankruptcy Code, if accompanied by a written request for transfer to the appropriate division.

(d) Any bankruptcy judge may, in the interest of justice or to further the efficient performance of the business of the Court, reassign a case or proceeding to any other bankruptcy judge, except that when reassignment is required by reason of recusal, the Clerk shall reassign the case or proceeding to another judge in the same division (and if there is more than one available judge in that division, on a random basis) or,

if there is no available judge in the division, on a random basis to an available judge within the district.

(e) In the absence of a judge before whom a case or proceeding is pending, emergency matters submitted to the Court may be acted upon by any available judge as determined by the Clerk or as provided for by the absent judge.

(f) The Clerk shall transfer any document pertaining to a case or proceeding mistakenly filed in the wrong division office to the proper division office and any such document shall be deemed to have been filed on the date first received in either office of the Clerk.

(g) Any party filing a document in the Clerk's Office which relates to a matter scheduled for hearing within twenty four (24) hours of the filing shall specifically bring to the attention of the Clerk, through an accompanying cover letter, the fact that the matter is scheduled for a hearing within 24 hours of the filing, and request that it be delivered to the judge immediately. Failure to comply with this rule may result in the document being deemed filed late and not being considered by the Court.

(h) Pleadings and other documents filed in a case or adversary proceeding may be removed from the Clerk's Office only if the Court has allowed a motion to remove the documents.

Effective August 1, 1997. Amended effective January 1, 2002.

RULE 5001–2. OFFICE OF THE CLERK

(a) The offices of the Clerk of the Court at Boston and Worcester shall be open Monday through Friday with the Clerk or Deputy Clerk in attendance in accordance with Fed.R.Bankr.P. 5001(c).

(b) All pleadings, including petitions, motions, and complaints, shall be received for filing in the office of the Clerk between the hours of 8:30 AM and 4:30 PM. Filings before 8:30 AM or after 4:30 PM on court days or on weekends or holidays can be made, for cause, by prior arrangements or in emergency circumstances, as determined by the Clerk or his or her designee, by contacting the Clerk at the telephone numbers set forth in Appendix 5.

Effective August 1, 1997.

RULE 5003–1. CLERK'S AUTHORITY TO ENTER MINISTERIAL ORDERS

The clerk and his/her deputies are authorized to sign and enter without further direction by the Court the following orders, deemed to be of a ministerial nature:

1) Orders permitting the payment of the petition filing fee in installments and fixing the number, amounts and dates of payment;

2) Orders deferring the payment of an adversary proceeding filing fee;

3) Orders to correct defects in the documents accompanying the original petition or orders to file or update such documents;

4) Orders discharging a Chapter 7, 11, 12, or 13 trustee and closing a case after the case has been fully administered;

5) Orders granting a discharge;

6) Orders reopening a case that has been closed due to administrative error; and

7) Orders to show cause regarding inactivity in bankruptcy cases and adversary proceedings and orders dismissing cases for failure to comply with or to respond to an order to show cause.

This rule is not intended to limit a bankruptcy judge's discretion regarding the governance of a case in any way whatsoever. The above orders may, in particular cases, be subject to modification by a bankruptcy judge.

Effective September 1, 1999.

RULE 5005-4. FACSIMILE FILINGS

(a) The Court will accept for filing documents transmitted by facsimile machine only if the documents are permitted to be filed non–electronically pursuant to Rule 1 of Appendix 8, except that the following documents may be filed by facsimile machine only with the prior permission of the Clerk, the Deputy Clerk or their designee:

(1) documents constituting a pleading for which a filing fee is required; and

(2) documents which exceed 35 pages, exclusive of the certificate of service.

(b) All documents filed in accordance with subsection (a) shall be deemed originally filed within the meaning of Fed.R.Civ.P. 5(e) and 11, as made applicable by Fed.R.Bankr.P. 9014 and within the meaning of Fed.R.Bankr.P. 9011. No subsequent original shall be filed after the document is filed by facsimile.

(c) Documents received by the Clerk by facsimile after 4:30 P.M. on a court day shall be deemed received as of the following court day.

Effective August 1, 1997. Amended effective September 1, 1999; January 1, 2005.

RULE 5009-1. CLOSING CHAPTER 7 CASES

No chapter 7 case in which dividends will be paid to creditors will be closed until the trustee has filed with the Court a statement indicating the following:

(a) there are no pending adversary proceedings;

(b) all claims have been examined and any objections to claims have been resolved;

(c) all applications by any professionals for compensation have been filed and acted upon, including an application by debtor's counsel to approve application of a retainer; and

(d) the United States trustee has approved the final account, unless the Court determines that such approval is not necessary.

Effective August 1, 1997.

RULE 5011-1. WITHDRAWAL OF THE REFERENCE

A motion for withdrawal of the reference shall be filed with the Clerk of the Bankruptcy Court, accompanied by a properly completed United States District Court cover sheet and the prescribed filing fee. Upon the filing of such a motion, the Clerk shall docket receipt of the motion and promptly transmit the original motion and cover sheet to the Clerk of the United States District Court for disposition.

Effective August 1, 1997.

RULE 5071-1. CONTINUANCES

(a) No continuance shall be effective unless the Court approves it in writing or in open court. Counsel shall not be excused from appearing before the Court absent such approval or an unexpected emergency.

(b) If a matter or proceeding is resolved between the parties prior to the day of the hearing, any motion for the continuation of a trial or nonevidentiary hearing or for the approval of a settlement of any contested matter or adversary proceeding, or any withdrawal of a motion or opposition, shall be filed and served at least one (1) business day prior to the hearing date.

(c) A motion to continue a hearing or withdraw a motion or opposition must be filed and served upon all previously served parties in a manner reasonably sufficient to reach said parties prior to their attendance at the subject hearing.

(d) Sections (a) and (b) shall not apply to motions filed by the chapter 13 trustee to dismiss a case.

Effective August 1, 1997.

RULE 6004-1. SALE OF ESTATE PROPERTY

(a) Private Sales.

(1) *Motion to Sell.*

(A) Every notice of private sale shall be accompanied by a motion for authority to sell, whether or not the sale is to be free and clear of liens or interests. The motion shall identify the holder of any lien or interest, shall state the efforts made by the estate representative in exploring the market for the property, shall state whether the proposed sale is to be free and clear of liens or interests, shall seek approval of any proposed distribution of proceeds, and shall state why a private sale, rather than a public sale, is in the estate's best interest. If all or substantially all of a chapter 11 debtor's assets are to be sold, the motion shall state why the sale is proposed under 11 U.S.C. § 363 rather than through a chapter 11 plan and shall contain a practical and abbreviated equivalent of the adequate information required in a disclosure statement to a chapter 11 plan.

(B) By motion served on the debtor or debtor's counsel, the United States trustee, any secured creditor or its counsel, the 20 largest unsecured creditors, the members and counsel of any approved creditors or equity committee and any attorneys who have filed appearances in the case, the estate representative:

(i) may obtain prior approval of any term of the proposed sale; and

(ii) must obtain prior approval from the Court of any terms for the proposed sale protecting the initial proposed purchaser, including the amount of a break-up fee or the minimum increase required for a higher offer, unless (1) the proposed breakup fee does not exceed the lesser of 5% of the proposed original purchase price or $50,000 and is subject to final court approval upon application by the bidder; and (2) the minimum increase required for a higher offer does not exceed 5% of the proposed original purchase price.

(2) *Contents of Notice of Sale.*

(A) The notice of private sale shall be substantially similar to MLBR Official Form 2A. The proposed notice shall be attached to the motion to sell filed with the Court and shall contain blank spaces for the deadline for filing objections and higher offers, as well as a blank space for the date and time of the hearing on the sale. Higher offers, together with any requisite deposit required by the notice, shall be submitted to the estate representative by the deadline established by the Court and a copy of any higher offer shall be filed with the Court. The notice shall state whether the sale shall be free and clear of liens or interests, the method of auction proposed by the estate representative, including without limitation by sealed bid or open auction, and that the method for auction shall be determined by the Court at or prior to the hearing on the proposed sale. Upon receipt of the proposed notice, the Clerk shall assign a deadline for filing objections and making higher offers, schedule a hearing date, and transmit such dates to the moving party by telephone or such other means as the Clerk deems appropriate. The estate representative shall then serve the motion to sell and the completed notice as required by subsection (a)(3) of this rule.

(B) Unless the movant requests or is required to obtain advance approval of the form of notice and/or the terms of the proposed sale pursuant to subsection 2(B) of this rule, the proposed notice need not be served on any party.

(3) *Service of Motion to Sell and Completed Notice.*

(A) Unless the Court orders otherwise, the motion to sell and the completed notice of proposed private sale shall be served upon the following parties: all creditors, parties in interest, including the United States trustee, parties who have filed appearances and requested service of all pleadings and notices. A copy of the completed notice should also be served on parties regarded by the estate representative as potential purchasers, including, if appropriate, dealers in the property and competitors of the debtor. The motion and completed notice shall be served no less than twenty (20) days (plus such additional time as may be provided in Fed. R. Bankr. P. 9006(f)) prior to the deadline for filing objections or higher offers. The motion to sell need not be served on any party until the Clerk has provided the information necessary to serve the completed notice.

(B) The estate representative shall file a certificate of service within seven (7) days of service of the motion to sell and the completed notice.

(4) *Court Approval of Sale.*

(A) If there are no objections or higher offers timely filed with the Court by the deadline, the Court may approve the sale without holding the scheduled hearing.

(B) Within three (3) days of receipt of a written request by the debtor, estate representative, or other party in interest, the Clerk shall issue a certificate of no objections concerning the sale of property of the estate.

(b) Public Auctions.

(1) *Court Authorization.* The estate representative, with prior Court approval, may sell estate property by public auction. Subsequent confirmation by the Court of the auction is not required unless such confirmation is a condition of the Court's approval. The notice of public sale shall be substantially similar to MLBR Official Form 2B. The estate representative shall file a motion to sell the estate assets, and state why a public, rather than a private, sale is requested. Any auction advertisement placed by an auctioneer or estate representative shall conspicuously state the bankruptcy case name and number. The proposed notice shall be attached to the motion to sell but need not be served on any party. Upon receipt of the proposed notice, the Clerk shall assign a deadline for filing objections, fix a hearing date, and transmit such dates to the moving party by telephone or such other means as the Clerk deems appropriate. The estate representative shall then serve the motion to sell and

the completed notice in the manner provided in subsection (a)(3) of this rule or other order of the Court and shall file a certificate of service within seven (7) days of service.

(2) *Restrictions.* An auctioneer shall not introduce non-bankruptcy estate items at an auction without the Court's prior approval. An auctioneer employed by an estate representative shall not bid on property of the estate. No buyer's premium shall be charged. Failure to comply with this subsection shall result in denial of all compensation and/or the issuance of sanctions.

(3) *Qualification of Auctioneer.*

(A) An auctioneer shall not be authorized to conduct a public auction of property of an estate without first obtaining the Court's specific prior approval of the auctioneer's employment, filing with the Court a bond in an amount fixed by the United States trustee, and furnishing the United States trustee with a copy of that bond. The bond shall be conditioned on the faithful performance of the auctioneer's duties and the auctioneer's accounting for all money and property of the estate that comes into his or her possession.

(B) To avoid the necessity of filing separate bonds for smaller auction sales, the auctioneer may file with the Court a blanket bond similarly conditioned in a base amount fixed from time to time by the United States trustee to cover various cases in which the auctioneer may act. The auctioneer shall also provide the United States trustee with a copy of the blanket bond. If at any time the value of goods of various estates in the auctioneer's custody exceeds the amount of the blanket bond, the auctioneer shall obtain a separate bond or bonds so that the full amount of all goods of various bankruptcy estates in the auctioneer's custody is covered.

(C) As a condition of the employment of an auctioneer in any bankruptcy estate, the auctioneer shall file a statement under the penalty of perjury that all goods of bankruptcy estates in the auctioneer's custody are fully covered at all times by separate bonds or blanket bonds or both. The auctioneer shall also state (i) his or her qualifications, (ii) where the auctioneer is licensed, (iii) whether the auctioneer is in good standing in all jurisdictions in which he or she is licensed, and (iv) whether the auctioneer is subject to any disciplinary proceedings or has been subject to any disciplinary proceedings in the five years preceding the filing of the application.

(4) *Attendance at Auction Sale.*

The estate representative or a representative of the trustee shall be present at an auction sale.

(5) *Auctioneer's Compensation and Expenses.*

(A) The auctioneer shall file and serve an application for compensation and reimbursement of expenses setting forth the amount requested, services rendered, time spent, and actual expenses incurred as required by Fed. R. Bankr. P. 2016(a).

(B) Auctions of Personal Property. Unless otherwise ordered by the Court, with respect to auctions of personal property, the auctioneer's compensation shall not exceed the following percentages of gross proceeds:

(i) 10% of the first ten thousand dollars ($10,000) or part thereof;

(ii) 7% of the next ten thousand dollars ($10,000) or part thereof;

(iii) 6% of the next thirty-five thousand dollars ($35,000) or part thereof; and

(iv) 5% of the balance.

(C) Real Estate Auctions. Unless otherwise ordered by the Court, with respect to sales of real property, the auctioneer's compensation shall not exceed the greater of:

(i) 10% of the first fifty thousand dollars ($50,000) realized in excess of the amount of encumbrances, plus 2½% of the balance of the equity; or

(ii) $500.00.

(D) Auction Expenses. The auctioneer shall be reimbursed for actual and necessary expenses incurred in connection with an auction, including advertising, if the auctioneer has obtained approval by the Court in advance of the auction for these expenses. Unless otherwise ordered by the Court, the auctioneer shall not be reimbursed for any overhead expense associated with the auction, including labor, cleaning, setting up, lotting, and tagging.

c) Internet Auction Mechanisms.

(1) With prior Court approval, after appropriate notice as required by Fed. R. Bankr. P. 2002 (a), the estate representative, or an auctioneer or other professional authorized by the Court to sell estate property, may sell any asset or assets of the estate by public auction through the use of an automated Internet auction, listing, or brokerage mechanism ("Internet Auction Mechanism").

(2) In any motion requesting such approval, the estate representative must state:

(A) The name and uniform resource locators (URL) of the proposed Internet Auction Mechanisms;

(B) Why the estate representative believes that use of the Internet Auction Mechanism is in the best interests of the estate;

(C) Whether the estate representative has or any party in interest is known to have any connections with the proposed Internet Auction Mechanism or any expected bidder;

(D) All fees associated with use of the Internet Auction Mechanism;

(E) Whether use of the Internet Auction Mechanism is subject to rules, policies, procedures or terms or conditions and, if so: (i) provide either a copy thereof or the URL at which they can be examined and (ii) summarize any such rules, policies, procedures or terms or conditions that are likely to result in any restrictions on bidding for the asset(s) proposed to be sold or limitations on the estate representative in offering asset(s) for sale with full or partial reserve or otherwise controlling the determination to sell each asset;

(F) The mechanism for payment to the estate; and

(G) That the Internet Auction Mechanism will not provide auction services or any other services beyond access to its automated on-line services and related customer support.

(3) Any such motion must request authority for the estate representative to (a) comply with any rules, policies, procedures, or terms or conditions of the Internet Auction Mechanism and enter into any required agreements, (b) consummate such sale, and (c) pay any and all fees associated with use of the Internet Auction Mechanism, each without further order of the Court.

(4) Nothing in this rule shall limit applicability of the requirements of Local Rule 6004–1(b) with respect to any auctioneer hired by an estate representative to provide services beyond access to an Internet Auction Mechanism.

(5) Unless the Court orders otherwise, a listing placed on an Internet Auction Mechanism shall state the bankruptcy case name and number and that the sale procedure has been approved by the United States Bankruptcy Court for the District of Massachusetts.

(d) For the purposes of this rule, the term estate representative shall include a chapter 7 trustee, chapter 11 trustee, chapter 11 debtor in possession, chapter 12 trustee, and chapter 13 debtor.

Effective August 1, 1997; amended effective January 1, 2005.

RULE 6005–1. APPRAISERS AND BROKERS

(a) An appraiser may be employed after allowance by the Court of a motion to employ and shall be paid at an hourly rate to be set from time to time by the Court or at a flat rate approved by the Court.

(b) A broker may be employed after allowance by the Court of a motion to employ and shall be paid a commission at a rate approved by the Court.

(c) No party or firm may act as an appraiser, and as a broker, and as an auctioneer, in any combination, in the same case.

Effective August 1, 1997.

RULE 6006–1. MOTION FOR ASSUMPTION OR REJECTION OF EXECUTORY CONTRACT OR UNEXPIRED LEASE

If a party files a motion seeking an extension of the deadline for filing a motion to assume or reject an executory contract or an unexpired lease within fifteen (15) days prior to the expiration of the sixty (60) day period found in 11 U.S.C. § 365(d), the movant must also file a motion for an emergency hearing. If the Court is unable to schedule a hearing before the expiration of the sixty (60) day period, the deadline shall be automatically extended to the date of the hearing on the motion for extension or until the Court has acted on the motion, but in no event shall the deadline be extended for more than thirty (30) days beyond the original deadline. Nothing in this rule shall be deemed to limit the Court's ability to grant additional extensions for cause shown.

Effective August 1, 1997.

RULE 6007–1. ABANDONMENT OF ESTATE PROPERTY

(a) **Requesting Notice.** The Clerk shall include in the initial notice of a meeting of creditors pursuant to 11 U.S.C. § 341 the following language:

Notice is hereby given that any creditor or other interested party who wishes to receive notice of the estate representative's intention to abandon property of the estate pursuant to 11 U.S.C. § 554(a) must file with the Court and serve upon the estate representative and the United States trustee a written request for such notice within ten (10) days from the date first scheduled for the meeting of creditors.

(b) **Estate Representative's Abandonment of Property.** After the expiration of the ten (10) day period referenced in section (a), the estate representative is authorized to limit notice of an abandonment of property to the debtor, debtor's counsel, any creditor claiming an interest in the property concerned, those creditors who have requested notice of such action in accordance with section (a), and those parties who have filed appearances and requested service of all notices and pleadings, provided that the value to the estate of the property concerned is less than $5,000.00. If the value to the estate of the property concerned is greater than $5,000.00, the estate representative shall provide notice of abandonment to all creditors and parties in interest in accordance with Fed.R.Bankr.P. 6007.

This rule is not intended to imply that estate representatives are required to abandon property with a value to the estate of less than $5,000.00, or that estate representatives are in any manner restricted from liquidating or administering such property in any other fashion.

(c) Estate Representative's Discretion to Utilize Full Notice. Nothing in this rule shall be deemed to prevent the estate representative from utilizing greater notice than that set forth for property with a value to the estate of less than $5,000.00 if the estate representative, in his or her discretion, determines that notice of a greater magnitude is warranted.

(d) Within three (3) court days of receipt of a written request by the debtor, estate representative, or other party in interest, the Clerk shall issue a certificate of no objections concerning the abandonment of property of the estate.

Effective August 1, 1997.

RULE 7003–1. INFORMATION TO ACCOMPANY COMPLAINT IN ADVERSARY PROCEEDINGS

The original complaint commencing an adversary proceeding filed with the Clerk shall be accompanied by a completed adversary proceeding cover sheet.

Effective August 1, 1997.

RULE 7016–1. PRETRIAL PROCEDURE

(a) Upon consent of all parties, the Court may enter an order referring a proceeding to mediation or arbitration or other procedure for alternative dispute resolution upon such terms and conditions as the parties may agree in writing. Such terms and conditions shall include the procedure for selection and compensation of the mediator or arbitrator, the power and authority of the mediator or arbitrator, the deadline for the mediator or arbitrator's report to the Court on whether the matter has been resolved, and the procedures for protecting the confidentiality of the information disclosed at mediation or arbitration, including the protection of proprietary information and preservation of privileges.

(b) Any request for an extension of any deadline or for modification of a party's obligations under Fed. R.Bankr.P. 7016 shall be made by written motion which shall state the basis for the relief requested. The Court will not consider any such motion unless consented to or accompanied by a certification made with particularity (time, date and circumstances) that the moving party has made a reasonable and good faith effort to reach agreement with the opposing party on the matter that is the subject of the motion.

(c) If relief is sought under Fed.R.Civ.P. 26(c) (as made applicable by Fed.R.Bankr.P. 7026) or Fed. R.Bankr.P. 7037, copies of the relevant portions of disputed documents shall be filed with the Court contemporaneously with any motion for order compelling disclosure or discovery. In addition, the Court will not consider any such motion unless accompanied by a certification made with particularity (time, date and circumstances) that the moving party has made a reasonable and good faith effort to reach agreement with the opposing party on the matter that is the subject of the motion.

Effective August 1, 1997. Amended effective January 1, 2002.

RULE 7024–2. NOTIFICATION OF CLAIM OF UNCONSTITUTIONALITY

(a) Whenever in any action, suit, or proceeding to which the United States or any agency, officer or employee thereof is not a party, the constitutionality of any Act of Congress affecting the public interest is drawn into question, the party raising such question shall file a notice to enable the Court to comply with 28 U.S.C. § 2403(a), and shall serve a copy of the notice upon the United States trustee, giving the title of the cause, a reference to the questioned statute sufficient for its identification, and the respects in which it is claimed to be unconstitutional.

(b) Whenever in any action, suit or proceeding to which a State of the Union or any agency, officer or employee thereof is not a party, the constitutionality of any statute of that State is drawn into question, the party raising such question shall file a notice to enable the Court to comply with 28 U.S.C. § 2403(b), and shall serve a copy of the notice upon the United States trustee, giving the title of the cause, a reference to the questioned statute sufficient for its identification, and the respects in which it is claimed to be unconstitutional.

Effective August 1, 1997.

RULE 7026–1. GENERAL PROVISIONS GOVERNING DISCOVERY

(a) Depositions upon oral examinations, transcripts, interrogatories, requests for documents, requests for admissions, and answers and responses thereto, shall not be filed unless so ordered by the Court or for use in the proceeding. The party taking a deposition or obtaining any material through discovery is responsible for its preservation and delivery to the Court if needed or so ordered. If, for any reason, any party believes that any of the above-named documents should be filed, a motion for authority to file such documents may be made together with the reasons for the request. If the moving party under Fed. R.Bankr.P. 7056 or the opponent relies on discovery documents, copies of the pertinent parts thereof shall be filed with the motion or opposition. The Court also may order the filing of documents sua sponte and, in addition, may order the parties to disclose any information and documentation that the Court determines are discoverable by the submission of sworn statements of any party.

(b) Any request for an extension of any deadline or for modification of a party's obligations under Fed. R.Bankr.P. 7026 shall be made by written motion which shall state the basis for the relief requested. The Court will not consider any such motion unless consented to or accompanied by a certification made with particularity (time, date and circumstances) that the moving party has made a reasonable and good faith effort to reach agreement with the opposing party on the matter that is the subject of the motion.

(c) If relief is sought under Fed.R.Civ.P. 26(c) (as made applicable by Fed.R.Bankr.P. 7026) or Fed. R.Bankr.P. 7037, copies of the relevant portions of disputed documents shall be filed with the Court contemporaneously with any motion for order compelling disclosure or discovery. In addition, the Court will not consider any such motion unless accompanied by a certification made with particularity (time, date and circumstances) that the moving party has made a reasonable and good faith effort to reach agreement with the opposing party on the matter that is the subject of the motion.

Effective August 1, 1997. Amended effective January 1, 2002.

RULE 7027–1. DEPOSITIONS

For purposes of Fed.R.Civ.P. 45(b)(2), made applicable to bankruptcy cases by Fed.R.Bankr.P. 9016, and without order of the Court:

(a) Boston shall be deemed a convenient place for the taking of a deposition of any person who resides, is employed, or transacts his or her business in person in any of the following counties: Suffolk, Bristol, Essex, Middlesex, Norfolk and Plymouth.

(b) Springfield shall be deemed a convenient place for the taking of a deposition of any person who resides, is employed, or transacts his or her business in person in any of the following counties: Berkshire, Franklin, Hampden and Hampshire.

(c) Depositions of parties residing within the counties of Worcester, Barnstable, Dukes or Nantucket shall be held within their respective counties.

Effective August 1, 1997.

RULE 7033–1. INTERROGATORIES

(a) Number of Interrogatories. A party may proffer no more than twenty-five (25) interrogatories to another party without leave of Court.

(b) Form of Response.

(1) Answers and objections in response to interrogatories served pursuant to Fed.R.Bankr.P. 7033 shall be made in the order of the interrogatories.

(2) Each answer, statement, or objection shall be preceded by the interrogatory to which it responds.

(3) Each objection and the grounds for the objection shall be stated separately.

(c) Provisions of MLBR 9013–1 Applicable to Objections. The provisions of MLBR 9013–1(e) shall be applicable to any motions relating to objections to interrogatories.

(d) Answers to Interrogatories Accompanying or Following Objection.

(1) When there is an objection to part of an interrogatory which is separable from the remainder, the part to which there is no objection shall be answered.

(2) Answers to interrogatories with respect to which objections were served and which are subsequently required to be answered shall be served within fifteen (15) days after entry of an order determining that they should be answered, unless the Court directs otherwise.

(e) Supplemental Answers to Certain Interrogatories. If a party has served an answer to an interrogatory which directly requests information concerning the identity and location of persons having knowledge of relevant facts, and the party later learns that the answer is substantially incomplete, that party shall file a supplemental answer or objection within seven (7) days after learning that the answer is substantially incomplete.

Effective August 1, 1997.

RULE 7036–1. REQUESTS FOR ADMISSION

(a) Form of Response.

(1) Answers and objections in response to requests for admission served pursuant to Fed.R.Bankr.P. 7036 shall be made in the order of the requests for admission.

(2) Each answer, statement, or objection shall be preceded by the request for admission to which it responds.

(3) Each objection and the grounds for the objection shall be stated separately.

(b) Provisions of MLBR 9013–1 Applicable to Objections. The provisions of MLBR 9013–1(e) shall be applicable to any motions relating to objections to requests for admission.

(c) Statements in Response to Requests for Admission After Objection. When there is an objection to a request for admission and it is subsequently determined that the request is proper, the matter for which admission is requested shall be deemed admitted unless within ten (10) days after entry of an order making such determination, or such other period as the Court directs, the party to whom the request was directed serves a statement denying the matter or setting forth the reasons why the matter cannot be admitted or denied, as provided in Fed.R.Bankr.P. 7036.

Effective August 1, 1997.

RULE 7037–1. FAILURE TO MAKE DISCOVERY; SANCTIONS

(a) Fed.R.Civ.P. 37 applies in adversary proceedings and contested matters, except that any reference to Fed.R.Civ.P. 26(a) shall be deleted and substituted with a reference to MLBR 7026–1(b).

(b) Prior to the filing of any motion relating to a discovery dispute, including a motion to compel discovery, a motion for a protective order, or a motion for sanctions, counsel for the parties or any pro se party shall confer by telephone or in person in a good faith effort to resolve the discovery dispute and to eliminate as many areas of the dispute as possible without the necessity of filing a motion. It shall be the responsibility of the party seeking the discovery order to arrange for the conference. Unless relieved by order of the Court, the conference shall take place within ten (10) days of the service of a letter requesting the conference. Failure of any party to respond to a request for a discovery conference within seven (7) days of a request for the conference shall be grounds for sanctions, which may include substantive and/or monetary sanctions. Any motion relating to discovery must be accompanied by a statement signed under the penalty of perjury that the movant has complied with the provisions of this section.

(c) If the parties are unable to resolve a discovery dispute and a discovery motion is filed, the parties shall file a joint stipulation specifying separately and with particularity (1) the date of the discovery conference and, if it was not held, the reason why; (2) the matters on which the parties reached agreement; (3) each contested discovery issue that remains to be determined by the Court; and (4) a statement of each party's position as to each contested issue, with supporting legal authority. The stipulation shall be filed within seven (7) days after the discovery motion. Notwithstanding the foregoing, if the only discovery dispute constitutes a failure of a party to serve any response, the discovery motion shall so state, and the joint stipulation need not be filed. The failure of any party or attorney to cooperate in resolving discovery disputes may result in the imposition of sanctions, including but not limited to, the sanctions provided in Fed.R.Civ.P. 37.

Effective August 1, 1997; Amended effective January 1, 2005.

RULE 7052–1. JUDGMENTS— PREPARATION AND ENTRY

Subject to the provisions of Fed.R.Bankr.P. 7054, upon a general verdict of a jury or upon a decision by the Court that a party shall recover only money or costs or that all relief shall be denied, the Clerk, unless the Court orders otherwise, shall forthwith prepare, sign and enter the judgment without further order of the Court; provided, however, that upon either a decision by the Court granting other relief or upon a special or general verdict accompanied by answers to interrogatories, the Court shall enter the judgment. The judgment shall be set forth on a separate document, in accordance with Fed.R.Civ.P. 58, and shall be effective only upon its entry on the docket, pursuant to Fed.R.Civ.P. 79(a). Entry of the judgment shall not be delayed for the taxing of costs.

Effective August 1, 1997.

RULE 7055–1. JUDGMENT BY DEFAULT

Judgment by default may be signed and entered by the Clerk in such circumstances as are specified in Fed.R.Civ.P. 55(b)(1) when accompanied by an affidavit that the person against whom judgment is sought is not an infant, an incompetent person, or serving in the armed forces within the meaning of the Soldiers and Sailors Civil Relief Act of 1940, 50 U.S.C. § 520(1). Upon application of any party, the Clerk shall make and file a certificate of default as to any party in default for the convenience of the Court or of the party applying for the default judgment. When application is made to the Court under Fed.R.Civ.P. 55(b)(2), made applicable through Fed.R.Bankr.P. 7055, for a default judgment, unless the Court orders otherwise, the Clerk shall schedule a hearing and notify counsel of the hearing date. If the party against whom judgment by default is sought has appeared in the action or proceeding, the party seeking the default judgment and the Clerk shall give notice of the hearing as required by Fed.R.Civ.P. 55(b)(2). With leave of Court, proof may be submitted by affidavit, and the Court may order such further hearing as it deems necessary.

Effective August 1, 1997.

RULE 7055–2. DISMISSAL FOR WANT OF PROSECUTION

(a) Dismissal of Proceedings Inactive for Six Months.

(1) The Clerk shall mail notice to all persons who have entered an appearance in any adversary proceeding in which no action was taken by any party during the preceding six months that, subject to the provisions of subsection (3) of this section, the adversary proceeding will be dismissed thirty (30) days after the date of the notice.

(2) After the thirtieth day following the sending of the notice, the Clerk shall, subject to the provisions of

subsection (3), enter an order of dismissal without prejudice and serve the order upon the parties.

(3) An adversary proceeding shall not be dismissed by the Clerk for want of prosecution if, within thirty (30) days of the sending of notice:

(A) there are further proceedings in the adversary proceeding; or

(B) a response is filed in opposition to the proposed dismissal.

(b) Effect of Dismissal. The dismissal of an adversary proceeding pursuant to this rule shall be without prejudice and without costs unless the Court on motion of a party directs otherwise.

Effective August 1, 1997.

RULE 7056-1. SUMMARY JUDGMENT

District Court Local Rule 56.1 is adopted and made applicable to proceedings in the Bankruptcy Court.

Effective August 1, 1997.

RULE 7067-1. REGISTRY FUNDS

The provisions of U.S. District Court Local Rules 67.2, 67.3, and 67.4 shall be applicable to proceedings in the United States Bankruptcy Court for the District of Massachusetts. References in specific United States District Court Local Rules to the "Clerk, United States District Court" or the "United States District Court" shall be replaced with "Clerk, United States Bankruptcy Court" or the "United States Bankruptcy Court," respectively.

Effective August 1, 1997.

RULE 9004-1. FONT SIZE

The font size of all original documents, other than the Petition, Schedules and Statement of Affairs, shall be not less than 12 point type. The font size of the Petition, Schedules and Statement of Affairs shall be not less than 10 point type.

Effective March 1, 2003.

RULE 9006-1. EXTENSIONS OF TIME FOR DISCHARGE COMPLAINTS AND OBJECTIONS TO EXEMPTIONS

If the Court is unable to act on any motion to extend any deadline for filing complaints relating to the debtor's discharge or for filing objections to the debtor's claim of exemptions, which motion to extend was filed before the expiration of the deadline, the deadline shall be automatically extended to the date that the Court acts on the motion.

Effective September 1, 1999.

RULE 9009-1. OFFICIAL LOCAL FORMS

The forms adopted by this Court as MLBR Official Local Forms and the official forms promulgated by the Judicial Conference of the United States shall be utilized in cases and proceedings filed in this Court under Title 11 of the United States Code. The MLBR Official Local Forms may be amended and supplemented from time to time.

Effective August 1, 1997.

RULE 9009-2. CASE MANAGEMENT

Upon motion of the estate representative or *sua sponte*, the Court may order that one or more case management procedures be employed in order to ease the administrative burden on the parties or the Court. Such procedures may relate to, *inter alia*, omnibus hearing dates, notices of agenda, and payment of interim compensation and reimbursement of expenses and other matters typical to Chapter 11 cases or cases under other Chapters with sufficient complexity. Sample case management procedures are contained in Appendix 6. A motion requesting case management orders shall highlight, in bold-faced type, those provisions which would vary from those set forth in Appendix 6.

Effective January 1, 2005.

RULE 9010-1. REPRESENTATION AND APPEARANCES

(a) A person who is a member in good standing of the bar of United States District Court for the District of Massachusetts may appear and practice before this Court.

(b) Except as provided in subsection (d) of this rule, an attorney who is not a member of the bar of the United States District Court for the District of Massachusetts, but is a member of the bar of any other United States District Court or the bar of the highest court of any state may appear and practice in this Court in a particular case or adversary proceeding only by leave granted in the discretion of the Court, provided such attorney files a certificate attesting that (1) the attorney is a member of the bar in good standing in every jurisdiction where the attorney has been admitted to practice; (2) there are no disciplinary proceedings pending against such attorney as a member of the bar in any jurisdiction; and (3) the attorney is familiar with the Local Rules of this Court. An attorney seeking admission under this subsection may not enter an appearance or sign any pleadings until admission is granted, except that the attorney may sign a complaint or any other pleading necessary to prevent entry of default or the passage of any deadline, provided such complaint or other pleading is accompanied by the attorney's application for admission under this subsection in proper form. An attorney seeking admission under this subsection more frequently than twice in any 12 month period shall additionally certify (1) the attorney's efforts to seek admission to the bar of the United States District Court for the District of Massachusetts; or (2) why such efforts have not been undertaken.

(c) A corporation, partnership or trust, by and through an officer or agent, or a person authorized by a power of attorney, may file a proof of claim or an application for payment of unclaimed monies due such entity, and may be heard on objections to claims or applications for payment. Otherwise, such entities shall appear only through counsel.

(d) An attorney need not obtain leave to appear and practice in a particular case merely to file a request for service or a proof of claim.

Effective August 1, 1997. Amended effective September 1, 1999.

RULE 9010-3. NOTICE OF APPEARANCE

(a) The filing of any pleading or other document by an attorney shall constitute an appearance in the case or proceeding in which the pleading or document is filed by the attorney who signs it, unless the pleading or document states otherwise.

(b) An appearance in a case or proceeding by a member of the bar of the United States District Court for the District of Massachusetts may be made by filing a notice of appearance which shall contain the name, address, telephone number and any registration number assigned by the Board of Bar Overseers of the Commonwealth of Massachusetts (the "BBO number") of the attorney entering the appearance. If the Court has authorized the attorney to appear pro hac vice with respect to a particular matter pursuant to MLBR 9010-1(b), the Clerk shall assign a Bankruptcy Court registration number (the "PHV number") to the attorney which number must be set forth by the attorney in any pleadings filed in this Court in connection with the matter.

(c) If an attorney wishes to receive copies of all notices and pleadings, the attorney must file an appearance with a specific request to be so served and must serve a copy of such request on the trustee and counsel for the trustee or debtor in possession and counsel for the debtor; otherwise, the attorney will receive only those notices, pleadings and orders that affect his or her client as required by the Federal Rules of Bankruptcy Procedure.

(d) An attorney representing a debtor in a bankruptcy case is required to represent the debtor in any adversary proceeding filed within the bankruptcy case in which the debtor is a named defendant unless the debtor expressly agrees otherwise in writing at the commencement of the representation.

(e) The Clerk shall maintain a general appearance list within each case and make it available to any attorney or party upon request. The Clerk shall also maintain a general appearance list on the PACER system.

Effective August 1, 1997. Amended effective September 1, 1999.

RULE 9011-1. SIGNING OF PAPERS

Any pleading filed with the Court shall set forth the name, address, telephone number, and BBO or PHV number, *see* MLBR 9010-3, of the attorney signing the pleading.

Effective September 1, 1999.

RULE 9013-1. MOTIONS

(a) A request for an order shall be made by motion. Unless it is made during the course of a hearing or trial, the motion must be in writing, setting forth each allegation in a numbered paragraph, and must be filed with the Clerk. Any request that is made by letter need not be considered by the Court.

(b) Before the filing of any motion, except a motion for an emergency hearing under MLBR 9013-1(h) or a routine motion unlikely to be opposed by any party in interest, the movant shall make a reasonable and good faith effort to determine whether or not the motion is unopposed.

(c) The movant may file together with the motion a separate supporting memorandum, including argument and citations to authorities. If the motion is based upon affidavits and documents evidencing facts on which the motion is based, the affidavits and documents must be filed with the motion, unless they are unavailable at the time that the motion is filed. Letters from counsel or parties will not be accepted as memoranda in support of a motion and may be disregarded by the Court.

(d) The Court, in its discretion, may schedule a motion for hearing or establish a deadline for filing objections or responses to a motion. Any party opposing entry of the order requested by a motion must file a response to the motion no later than the response date set in the hearing notice, or if no response date is set in the hearing notice, within ten (10) days of service of the motion, inclusive of the three (3) day mailing period set forth in Fed.R.Bankr.P. 9006(f). All hearing dates and response deadlines shall be set by the Clerk. The Clerk shall notify the movant of the hearing date and/or response deadline and the manner of service.

(e) The Court may act upon a motion without a hearing under appropriate circumstances, including the following:

(1) if no objection is filed to the motion (A) within ten (10) days of the date of service of the motion, or (B) after any specific objection deadline established by the Court, whichever is later, or

(2) prior to the expiration of any applicable objection period, if the motion is:

(A) a non-adversarial motion of a routine nature;

(B) a motion to which all affected parties in interest have consented;

(C) a motion that is without merit in light of the law and the established facts of the case; and

(D) a motion that is opposed only by objections which are, given the law and the established facts of the case, without merit.

(f) The Court, in its discretion, may remove from the hearing list any motion that has been scheduled for hearing if no timely written response or objection has been filed. The Court may consider and act upon such matters without a hearing and may enter the proposed order submitted with the motion, request from the movant a modified order indicating the lack of timely opposition and the fact that no hearing was held, or enter an appropriate order of its own.

(g) Expedited Hearings. If movant seeks to have a motion considered by the Court earlier than seven (7) court days after the motion is filed, the movant shall file a separate motion entitled "Motion for Expedited Hearing."

(1) *Motion for Expedited Hearing.* The motion for expedited hearing shall set forth in detail all facts and circumstances which justify expedited hearing and may include or be accompanied by documents, affidavits or a memorandum which includes citations to pertinent authority.

(2) *Limitation of Notice.* If the facts and circumstances leading to the request for an expedited hearing or the nature of the relief requested warrant limitation of notice, the motion for expedited hearing shall include a request that notice be limited to designated recipients and recommend a practical manner of notice reasonably calculated to inform affected parties that the motion is pending and that a hearing is requested on an expedited basis. It is the duty of the party seeking an expedited hearing and limitation of notice to make a reasonable and good faith effort to advise all affected parties of the pending motion and of the time and date of the hearing. Such reasonable and good faith efforts may include providing notice of the substance of the motion and request for expedited hearing by telephone or by facsimile transmission in appropriate circumstances.

(3) *Responses to Expedited Motions.* Written responses to expedited motions shall be filed within the time established by the Court. The content of responses to expedited motions, to the extent possible under the existing circumstances, shall include the information required for responses to non-expedited motions. If no response time is established by the Court, responses to expedited motions shall be filed no later than the business day preceding the day of the hearing.

(4) *Hearings on Expedited Motions.* The Court shall set such conditions for any hearing and shall schedule and conduct the hearing, telephonically or otherwise, as appropriate under the circumstances.

(h) Emergency Motions. If a movant seeks to have a motion considered by the Court earlier than two (2) court days after the motion is filed, it shall file a separate motion denominated "Motion for Emergency Hearing."

(1) *Contents of Motion for Emergency Hearing.* The motion for emergency hearing shall set forth in detail all facts and circumstances which necessitate an emergency hearing and may be accompanied by documents, affidavits or a memorandum which includes citations to pertinent authority.

(2) *Limitation of Notice.* If the necessity of an emergency hearing precludes the movant's ability to provide notice in a timely manner to the parties otherwise required by these rules or the Federal Rules of Bankruptcy Procedure, the motion for emergency hearing shall include a request that notice be limited to designated recipients and recommend a practical manner of notice reasonably calculated to inform affected parties that the motion is pending and that an emergency hearing may take place. It is the duty of the party seeking an emergency hearing to make a reasonable and good faith effort to advise all affected parties of the motion and of the time and date for hearing. Such reasonable and good faith efforts may include providing notice of the substance of the motion and of the date and time of hearings by telephone or by facsimile transmission. Such efforts may, and in appropriate circumstances should, include attempts to provide notice of the motion and a motion for an order limiting notice in advance of filing the motions.

(3) *Responses to Emergency Motions.* Notwithstanding any other provisions of these rules, written responses to emergency motions are not required. However, written responses are encouraged and may be filed up to the time that the hearing is convened.

(4) *Hearings on Emergency Motions.* The Court shall set such conditions for the emergency hearing and shall schedule and conduct the hearing, telephonically or otherwise, as appropriate in the circumstances.

(i) Ex Parte Motions. A motion seeking ex parte relief may be filed only in circumstances in which immediate action is required to maintain the status quo until an appropriate hearing on notice can be conducted. A motion for ex parte relief shall be verified or supported by affidavit and shall set forth specific facts and circumstances necessitating ex parte relief. The motion shall include a statement as to why proceeding under this rule's procedures for expedited or emergency hearing is not practical. All orders or proposed orders providing ex parte relief shall include the finding that the relief requested could not be delayed and that affected parties may request a hearing on the subject matter addressed by the ex parte motion by filing a motion for review of the ex parte action within ten (10) days of service of the order for ex parte relief. The Court shall schedule a hearing on such a post-order motion, if appropriate, as soon as is practicable.

(j) Oppositions. In any opposition to a motion, the opposing party shall admit or deny each allegation of the motion, state any affirmative defense to the motion, and state specifically why the relief requested in the motion should not be granted.

Effective August 1, 1997. Amended effective September 1, 1999.

RULE 9013–3. SERVICE OF PLEADINGS AND NOTICES

(a) Motions and Other Documents. Upon filing a motion requesting action by the Court, with the exception of an adversary complaint, counsel (or a pro se party) shall immediately serve the motion upon all interested parties and upon all parties who have filed their appearances and requested service of all pleadings filed in the case. A certificate of service shall be filed with the motion and served in the same manner and on the same parties as the motion, unless otherwise directed by the Court.

(b) Notice of Hearing. Upon receipt of a notice of hearing from the Court, counsel (or a pro se party) shall immediately serve the notice upon all interested parties and parties who have filed their appearances and requested service of all notices in the case. A certificate of service shall be filed with the Clerk at the same time as service of the notice of hearing and shall be served in the same manner and on the same parties as the notice of hearing, unless otherwise directed by the Court.

(c) Statement on Scope of Service. A certificate of service shall list the name and address of each person and attorney being served with the pleading and the name of the party or parties that an attorney represents. If service is required to be made upon all creditors pursuant to Fed.R.Bankr.P. 2002, the certificate of service shall specifically state whether all creditors have been served and shall list the names and addresses of the parties served.

(d) Sanctions. Failure to comply with the provisions of this rule may result in the imposition of monetary sanctions, non-monetary sanctions, or denial of the relief sought as the Court, in its discretion, deems proper.

Effective August 1, 1997. Amended effective September 1, 1999.

RULE 9015–1. JURY TRIALS

(a) In any bankruptcy case or proceeding, issues triable by jury shall be tried by a jury if a party timely demands a jury trial in accordance with the provisions of this rule. Nothing in this rule shall be deemed to (1) create or imply a right to jury trial where no such right exists under applicable law or (2) violate a party's right of trial by jury as set forth in the Seventh Amendment to the Constitution or in any statute of the United States. On motion or on its own initiative, the Court may determine whether there is a right to trial by jury in any adversary proceeding or contested matter or whether a jury demand should be granted or stricken.

(b) Any party may demand a jury trial of any issue triable by jury by filing with the Court and serving upon the other parties a written demand for jury trial no later than the deadline for filing the answer or the reply to a counterclaim or cross claim in an adversary proceeding, or in a contested matter no later than the deadline for filing the initial responsive pleading or opposition. A jury demand may be made in any pleading and need not be made in a separate pleading. The failure of a party to file and serve a demand constitutes a waiver of the right to trial by jury. A demand for a jury trial may not be withdrawn without the consent of all parties.

(c) The bankruptcy judge may conduct a jury trial pursuant to 28 U.S.C. § 157(e) if the right to a jury trial applies and a timely demand has been made, provided that the parties file a pleading entitled "Joint Statement of Consent to Jury Trial in the Bankruptcy Court" no later than the date established by the Court for the filing of the Joint Pretrial Memorandum pursuant to MLBR 7016–1 or such other time as the Court may fix. If the parties do not file the Joint Statement of Consent to Jury Trial in the Bankruptcy Court, the Bankruptcy Court shall conduct all pretrial proceedings and thereafter transfer the case or proceeding to the appropriate United States District Court for trial.

Effective August 1, 1997. Amended effective September 1, 1999.

RULE 9018–1. IMPOUNDMENT OF PAPERS

(a) For cause reflecting a genuine risk of substantial harm to any party in interest, the court may order that some or all of the papers in the case be impounded by the clerk. Such impounded papers shall be maintained under clerk custody separate and apart from files to which the public has access; no computer or other images thereof shall be made for public viewing.

(b) A request for impoundment shall be made by motion. The papers sought to be impounded shall be placed in a sealed envelope or container conspicuously marked "filed subject to pending impoundment motion," and shall be filed simultaneously with the motion. The motion shall contain (i) a statement under oath setting forth the grounds for impoundment, (ii) a statement of the earliest date on which the impounding order may be lifted, or a statement, supported by good cause, that the material should be impounded until further order of the court, and (iii) suggested custody arrangements for the post-impoundment period, if any.

(c) The court shall review the papers sought to be impounded in camera. If the motion for impoundment is denied, the papers shall be returned to the party requesting impoundment and, if refiled, shall be filed with other pleadings in the case to which public access is allowed. If the motion for impoundment is granted, the order of impoundment shall be filed with the pleadings in the case. The impounded papers shall be transferred to the custody of the clerk for special storage. The clerk shall attach a copy of the order of impoundment to the envelope or other container holding the impounded material. Thereafter, access to the impounded papers shall be limited to the court, the clerk, the party for whose benefit the impoundment order was granted, and any party who, upon motion, notice to the party for whose benefit the impoundment order was granted and an opportunity to be heard, receives relief from the impoundment order in whole or in part.

(d) If the impoundment order expires by its terms but provides no arrangements for post-impoundment custody of the impounded papers, or if the impoundment order provides for post-impoundment custody of the impounded papers, but the impounded papers are not timely retrieved, the clerk shall provide notice of no less than thirty (30) days to the party for whose benefit the impoundment order was granted, or his, her or its attorney, that the said papers shall, in the absence of timely objection made prior to the expiration of the notice period, be placed in the public file.

(e) For good cause shown by affidavit attesting to a risk of irreparable harm if advance notice is given to any other party, the motion for impoundment may be heard ex parte.

Effective January 1, 2002.

RULE 9019–1. STIPULATIONS; SETTLEMENTS

(a) All stipulations affecting a case or proceeding before the Court, except stipulations which are made in open court, shall be in writing, signed, and filed with the Court. No stipulation shall have the effect of relieving the parties from a prior order of the Court, including a scheduling order, unless such stipulation is approved by the Court in writing.

(b) When a proceeding or matter is settled, the parties shall, within seven (7) days or such other time

as the Court may direct, file a signed stipulation or agreement for judgment or such other document as the Court may direct.

(c) A settlement of any controversy that affects the estate, except the settlement of complaints pursuant to 11 U.S.C. § 523, shall be accompanied by a motion to approve the stipulation pursuant to Fed.R.Bankr.P. 9019 and, unless otherwise ordered by the Court, the stipulation and motion to approve the stipulation shall be served on all creditors and interested parties in accordance with Fed.R.Bankr.P. 2002. The settlement of a complaint under 11 U.S.C. § 523 may be documented by the filing of a stipulation of dismissal or an agreement for judgment in the adversary proceeding. A stipulation with respect to a motion for relief from stay shall be accompanied by a motion and shall be served in accordance with Fed.R.Bankr.P. 4001(d).

Effective August 1, 1997.

RULE 9022–1. NOTICE OF ENTRY OF ORDERS AND JUDGMENTS

The Clerk's mailing to either attorneys of record or pro se parties of copies of orders or judgments showing the date such orders or judgments were entered shall constitute notice of entry pursuant to the provisions of Fed.R.Civ.P. 77(d). The Clerk shall indicate the date of such mailing on the Court docket.

Effective August 1, 1997.

RULE 9027–1. REMOVAL

Upon motion, the Court, in its discretion, may permit the filing of a certified docket and photocopies of all records and proceedings in a state or federal court, upon the representation of counsel for the party removing the action that the pleadings are true and accurate copies of the pleadings on file with the state or federal court.

Effective August 1, 1997.

RULE 9029–1. APPLICATION

(a) These rules shall govern all cases and civil proceedings arising under Title 11 or related to cases under Title 11 that are referred to or otherwise being heard by the bankruptcy judges in this district. All prior local rules are hereby repealed.

(b) To the extent that a conflict appears or arises between these rules and the Federal Rules of Bankruptcy Procedure promulgated by the Supreme Court of the United States, the latter shall govern.

(c) The Appendices annexed hereto may be amended, from time to time, by joint order of the bankruptcy judges. Nothing in these rules shall prohibit the issuance by one or more individual bankruptcy judges of standing orders relative to the conduct of cases and proceedings before them. A copy of any standing order shall be annexed to these rules by the Clerk.

Effective August 1, 1997.

RULE 9029–3. APPLICABILITY OF U.S. DISTRICT COURT LOCAL RULES

The following U.S. District Court Local Rules shall be applicable in the United States Bankruptcy Court for the District of Massachusetts:

26.5 (Uniform Definitions in Discovery Requests)

56.1 (Motions for Summary Judgment)

67.2 (Registry Funds)

67.3 (Disbursement of Registry Funds)

67.4 (Payments and Deposits Made With the Clerk)

81.2 (Definition of Judicial Officer)

83.5.1(b) (Student Practice Rule) (insofar as applicable to civil proceedings)

83.6 (Rules of Disciplinary Enforcement)

201 (Reference to Bankruptcy Court)

202 (Bankruptcy Court Jury Trials)

203 (Bankruptcy Appeals)

204 (Bankruptcy Court Local Rules)

205 (Disciplinary Referrals by Bankruptcy *Judges*)

The other Local Rules of the United States District Court shall not govern cases or proceedings before the United States Bankruptcy Court.

Effective August 1, 1997. Amended effective September 1, 1999; January 1, 2005.

RULE 9036–1. ELECTRONIC FILING

All cases open as of the effective date of these rules or filed thereafter will be administered through the Electronic Case Filing System (the "ECF System"). The procedures for electronic filing set forth in Appendix 8 hereof, as amended from time to time, shall be known as the Electronic Filing Rules of the United States Bankruptcy Court for the District of Massachusetts, and shall be referred to in abbreviation as "MEFR." Except as expressly provided in MEFR 1,

parties in interest shall file all petitions, motions, applications, memoranda of law or other pleadings or documents only through the ECF System. To the extent that the MEFR conflict with any other provision of the Massachusetts Local Bankruptcy Rules or their appendices, the provisions of the MEFR shall govern.

Effective March 1, 2003; Amended effective January 1, 2005.

RULE 9070–1. EXHIBITS

After a trial, exhibits shall remain in the custody of the Court. If there is no appeal from the Court's decision after the time for filing a notice of appeal has elapsed, or after any appeal has been finally determined, the Clerk shall notify the parties that the exhibits should be removed from the Court within thirty (30) days and that if they are not removed within that time, the Clerk will dispose of them. If the exhibits are not removed or another arrangement made with the Clerk within thirty (30) days, the Clerk may, without further notice, destroy or otherwise dispose of them. If a notice of appeal is filed, the Clerk shall make the exhibits available to the parties for duplication for the record on appeal. After any appeal has been finally determined, the Clerk shall make any disposition of the exhibits required by the Clerk of the appellate court or as otherwise permitted under this rule.

Effective August 1, 1997.

RULE 9074–1. APPEARANCES BY TELE-PHONE OR VIDEOCONFERENCE

Request to Appear By Telephone or Videoconference. A person may appear at a pretrial conference or non–evidentiary hearing by telephone or by videoconference, for good cause shown. The request shall be in writing and timely filed with the Clerk and will be allowed only if appropriate under the circumstances, considering, without limitation, the nature of the hearing, proximity of the person requesting such an appearance and the resulting savings in travel time and reduction of expenses of that person and/or the court. The telephone numbers and facsimile numbers for the courtroom deputies are set forth in Appendix 5.

Effective January 1, 2005.

APPENDICES

APPENDIX 1. CHAPTER 13 RULES

13–1. APPLICABILITY

These chapter 13 rules relate to chapter 13 cases filed in all divisions of the Court, and supersede any

previous orders in conflict with these provisions. To the extent that these rules conflict with the provisions of the Massachusetts Local Bankruptcy Rules ("MLBR"), the provisions of these rules shall prevail. In all other respects, the MLBR shall apply in all chapter 13 cases.

13–2. COMMENCEMENT OF CASE

(a) The debtor[1] shall file each of the following documents:

1. the petition;

2. Schedules A through J and the Statement of Financial Affairs;

3. the chapter 13 plan;

4. the Statement required under Fed.R.Bankr.P. 2016(b) (if applicable);

5. an application and proposed order authorizing payment of the filing fee in installments (if applicable); and

6. the matrix (original only) in conformity with MLBR Official Local Form 1 listing the names, addresses and zip codes in alphabetical order of all creditors, parties in interest, debtor's counsel, the debtor, the chapter 13 trustee, and the United States trustee.

7. If the debtor is a debtor engaged in business, the debtor shall also file and serve on the chapter 13 trustee:

   A. the Statement of Financial Affairs for debtor engaged in business;

   B. a profit and loss statement for the calendar year or fiscal year, whichever is applicable, preceding the year in which the case is filed, and a profit and loss statement for the period from the end of the calendar or fiscal year to the date of the filing of the petition;

   C. a statement by the debtor as to whether the debtor's business incurs trade debt;

   D. a statement of quarterly income and expenses incurred, regardless of whether the debtor incurs trade debt, within thirty (30) days of the close of each quarter, with a copy served on the chapter 13 trustee; and

   E. within five (5) days after the commencement of the case:

      (i) evidence of appropriate business insurance; and

      (ii) evidence that appropriate debtor in possession checking accounts were opened at the time of the filing of the petition;

8. an executed copy of the engagement agreement by and between the debtor and any attorney retained by the debtor, in the form set forth in Official Local Form 8.

(b) Failure to timely submit the documents required by subsection (a) may result in dismissal of the case pursuant to 11 U.S.C. §§ 109(g)(1) or 1307. Upon the debtor's filing of a motion prior to the expiration of the deadlines established by this section, and upon a showing of good cause, the Court may excuse the debtor from filing some or all of the documents required in subsection (a).

(c) The matrix must be filed within three (3) court days of the commencement of the case, failing which the case shall be dismissed without further notice. If the documents specified in paragraphs 13–2(a)(2)–(7) and, if applicable, 13–2(b) are not filed with the petition, the Court shall issue an order notifying the debtor and debtor's counsel that, if the missing documents are not filed within fifteen (15) days from the date of commencement of the case and the Court has not allowed a motion filed within that time to extend the time for filing the missing documents, the case may be dismissed pursuant to 11 U.S.C. § 109(g) at the expiration of that period.

(d) A motion requesting an extension of time to file the documents required under this paragraph shall set forth the specific cause for the request, the amount of additional time requested, the date the petition was filed, and a proof of service evidencing that the motion was served on the chapter 13 trustee.

(e) Any motion to amend a voluntary petition or statement shall be served upon all parties affected by the amendment and the chapter 13 trustee. The motion and proposed amendment shall be accompanied by a certificate of service identifying those parties served. A motion to amend to add a creditor to the debtor's schedules shall be served upon that creditor and the chapter 13 trustee. An amendment adding a creditor or party in interest shall be accompanied by 1) the fee prescribed by the Administrative Office of the United States Courts, if applicable, and 2) an amended matrix including the names and addresses of the added parties.

Amended effective March 1, 2003; January 1, 2005.

13–3. DISCLOSURE OF RELATED CASES

The debtor shall disclose in the petition other previous or pending bankruptcy cases and adversary proceedings, whether filed in this or any other district, which are related to the bankruptcy case being filed. Related cases and adversary proceedings include all those involving:

1. a spouse or ex-spouse of the debtor; or

2. an affiliate, as defined in 11 U.S.C. § 101(2); or

3. an insider, as defined in 11 U.S.C. § 101(31); or

4. the same debtor using any aliases or fictitious names.

Failure to comply with these disclosure requirements may result in sanctions, including dismissal of the case pursuant to 11 U.S.C. § 109(g).

---

1. For the purposes of these chapter 13 rules, the use of the term debtor shall include both debtors in a joint case.

13–4. CHAPTER 13 PLAN

(a) Form of Plan. A chapter 13 plan shall conform to MLBR Official Local Form 3, with such alterations as may be appropriate to suit the circumstances.

(b) Service of Plan. Concurrently with the filing of the plan, the debtor or the debtor's attorney shall cause a copy of the plan to be served by first class mail upon the chapter 13 trustee, all creditors of the debtor, all attorneys who have filed appearances and requested service of all pleadings, and other parties in interest. The debtor or his attorney shall file with the plan a certificate of service.

(c) If a debtor proposes payments to creditors over a period that exceeds three (3) years, the debtor shall set forth in the plan the reasons for such longer payment period.

13–5. SERVICE OF MOTIONS

All motions and requests for orders must be served on the chapter 13 trustee, the debtor, the debtor's attorney, persons who have filed appearances and requested service of all pleadings, and all creditors with the following exceptions:

(1) a motion for relief from the automatic stay shall be served on debtor, debtor's attorney, and all persons with an interest in or lien on the subject collateral;

(2) a chapter 13 trustee's motion to dismiss shall be served on the debtor and the debtor's attorney;

(3) a debtor's motion to dismiss or notice of conversion to chapter 7 or 11 when there have been no prior conversions shall be served on the chapter 13 trustee;

(4) objections to claims shall be served on the chapter 13 trustee, the claimant, and the claimant's attorney;

(5) objections to confirmation shall be served in accordance with paragraph 13–8.

13–6. ATTORNEYS

(a) An attorney who represents a debtor at the time a chapter 13 case is commenced or when a case under another chapter of the Bankruptcy Code is converted to chapter 13 has a continuing duty to represent the debtor in all matters, including the section 341 meeting and court hearings, until the occurrence of the earliest of the following:

(1) dismissal of the case;

(2) closing of the case; or

(3) the entry of an order allowing the attorney to withdraw from further representation of the debtor.

(b) If an attorney for a debtor is unable to contact the debtor in connection with any matter, the attorney shall file a statement informing the Court of this fact, which statement shall include the efforts the attorney has made to contact the debtor. The attorney shall serve a copy of the statement on the debtor at his or her last known address.

(c) The chapter 13 trustee or a representative of the chapter 13 trustee shall be present at any hearing held in a chapter 13 case, unless excused for cause prior to the hearing.

13–7. PROFESSIONAL FEES; PREPETITION RETAINERS

(a) Prepetition Retainers. The amount of any retainer received by debtor's counsel shall be included in the Statement of Attorney Compensation filed pursuant to Fed.R.Bankr.P. 2016(b).

(b) Unless otherwise ordered by the Court, if debtor's counsel's total compensation prior to confirmation of a plan is $2,500 or less, the disclosure of the compensation in the Rule 2016(b) Statement shall be sufficient notwithstanding compensation for post confirmation services in amount not exceeding $500, and the filing of an itemized application for compensation shall be excused, unless the Court orders otherwise.

(c) Application for Additional Attorney's Fees. An attorney who proposes to charge a debtor more than $2,500 in the aggregate for legal services in a chapter 13 case prior to confirmation, or $500 in the aggregate for such services after confirmation, shall file an application for compensation in accordance with Fed.R.Bankr.P. 2016 and MLBR 2016–1. Unless otherwise ordered by the Court, debtor's Counsel shall serve a copy of the application on all creditors, parties requesting service of all pleadings, and the Chapter 13 trustee and shall file a certificate of Service to that effect with the application. If no objections are filed within twenty (20) days of service, the Court shall award fees in its discretion, with or without a hearing, in accordance with applicable law.

13–8. OBJECTIONS TO CONFIRMATION

(a) Deadline for Filing. Any objection to confirmation of a chapter 13 plan shall be filed no later than the later of (i) thirty (30) days after the first date set for the section 341 meeting or (ii) thirty (30) days after service of a modified plan, unless otherwise ordered by the Court.

(b) Service of Objection. An objection to confirmation shall be filed with the Court and served on the chapter 13 trustee, the debtor, the debtor's attorney, and any other party or attorney who has filed an appearance and requested service of pleadings. The objection shall be accompanied by a certificate of service evidencing compliance with this requirement.

13–9. SECTION 341 MEETING OF CREDITORS

(a) The Clerk shall serve on all creditors notice of the section 341(a) meeting of creditors and initial confirmation hearing date along with a proof of claim form in accordance with Fed.R.Bankr.P. 2002(a) and 2003(a).

(b) If the debtor fails to appear at the section 341 meeting, the case may be dismissed upon motion of a party in interest pursuant to 11 U.S.C. § 109(g).

(c) The debtor shall file any due but unfiled tax returns no later than the deadline for filing claims, unless the time to do so is extended by the Court. When the tax return is filed, the debtor shall file with the Clerk and serve on the chapter 13 trustee a notice of the filing of the return, which shall disclose the amount of the tax liability or the amount of the refund.

13–10. AMENDMENTS TO PLAN PRIOR TO CONFIRMATION

(a) Amendments to a plan which do not adversely affect creditors may be made at or prior to the section 341(a) meeting without leave of court by a separate pleading entitled "Modification of Plan," which shall be filed with the Court and served on the chapter 13 trustee and any party or attorney who has filed an appearance and requested service of pleadings in the case. The modification shall be accompanied by a certificate of service. If no objections to the modification are filed within ten (10) days after service, the Court shall consider confirmation of the plan as amended.

(b) Where an amendment to a plan adversely affects creditors, the debtor shall file with the Court an amended plan and a motion to approve the amended plan. The debtor shall serve a copy of the amended plan and motion to approve the amended plan on the chapter 13 trustee, all creditors, and all parties and attorneys who filed appearances and request for service of all pleadings in the case. The motion shall be accompanied by a certificate of service. If no objections to the motion to approve the amended plan or the amended plan are filed within thirty (30) days of the filing of the certificate of service, the Court may allow the motion without a hearing.

13–11. CONFIRMATION

(a) Where no objection to confirmation of a chapter 13 plan is filed within the time limits established by paragraph 13–8(a) of this order, the Court may enter an order confirming the plan without a hearing.

(b) Where a timely objection to a chapter 13 plan is filed, the Court shall hold a hearing on the objection. The Clerk shall schedule a confirmation hearing and advise the objecting party and/or its counsel of the hearing date. The objecting party shall provide notice of the confirmation hearing to the debtor, debtor's counsel, all creditors, interested parties, and all parties who filed appearances and requested service of all pleadings, and shall file a certificate of service regarding the notice of the hearing.

(c) The chapter 13 trustee shall submit a proposed order of confirmation to the Court in conformity with MLBR Official Local Form 4 within twenty (20) days after the later of 1) the Court's order overruling any objection to confirmation; 2) the withdrawal of an objection to confirmation; or 3) in the event that there are no objections to confirmation, the deadline for filing objections to confirmation. The chapter 13 trustee shall attach a copy of the plan to the proposed order of confirmation. The chapter 13 trustee shall serve a copy of the proposed order of confirmation on the debtor's attorney, the debtor, and all parties and attorneys who have filed appearances and requests for service of pleadings in the case.

13–12. AMENDMENTS TO PLAN AFTER CONFIRMATION

(a) A debtor who seeks to amend a chapter 13 plan after confirmation shall do so by filing a motion to amend the plan with a copy of the proposed amended plan attached. The motion to amend shall include a summary and statement of the reason for the amendment. In conjunction with the motion to amend, the debtor shall file updated schedules I and J if plan payments are changing under the terms of the amended plan. The chapter 13 trustee, in his or her discretion, may schedule a new section 341 meeting with respect to the amended plan.

(b) The debtor shall serve a copy of the motion, amended plan, updated schedules I and J, and the amended statement on the chapter 13 trustee, all creditors, and parties and attorneys who have filed appearances and requests for service of pleadings in the case. In the event that the debtor proposes more than one amended plan, each amended plan shall be titled "First Amended Plan," "Second Amended Plan," and so on as may be appropriate.

(c) The Court shall not consider any amendments to a plan unless they are set forth in an amended plan that conforms to MLBR Official Local Form 3.

(d) Approval of an amended plan after confirmation of a prior plan may be granted without a hearing if no objections are timely filed. Objections to an Amended Plan shall be filed no later than thirty (30) days from the date of service of the motion to amend. In the event that no objections to the motion are timely filed, the Court may, in its discretion, allow the motion to amend without a hearing. If a party in interest files a timely objection to the motion, the Court shall set the motion and objection for hearing. The objecting party shall serve a notice of hearing on the debtor, debtor's counsel, all creditors, the chapter 13 trustee, and all parties who filed appearances and requested service of pleadings at least seven (7) days before the hearing date, and shall file a certificate of service.

(e) The trustee shall submit a proposed order confirming an amended plan in conformity with MLBR Official Form 4 within twenty (20) days after the Court allows the motion to amend the plan. The chapter 13 trustee shall attach a copy of the amended plan to the proposed order of confirmation. The chapter 13 trustee shall serve a copy of the proposed order confirming an amended plan on the debtor, debtor's attorney, and all parties and attorneys who have filed appearances and requests for service of pleadings in the case.

13-13. PROOFS OF CLAIM AND OBJECTIONS

(a) The provisions of MLBR 3007-1(a), (b) and (c) shall apply to chapter 13 cases. All creditors must timely file a proof of claim to participate in distributions under the plan.

(b) Objections to claims shall be served and filed with the Court within thirty (30) days after the deadline for filing proofs of claims or within such additional time as the Court may allow upon the filing of a motion to extend time and for good cause shown. Any claim to which a timely objection is not filed shall be deemed allowed and paid by the chapter 13 trustee in accordance with the provisions of the confirmed plan. The Court, in its discretion, may overrule an untimely objection to a proof of claim.

(c) If the Court has determined the allowed amount of a secured or unsecured claim in the context of a valuation hearing pursuant to 11 U.S.C. § 506, the debtor or trustee need not file an objection to a secured creditor's proof of claim that varies from the Court's determination, and the chapter 13 trustee shall make distribution in accordance with the Court's order.

13-14. SALE OF ESTATE PROPERTY

(a) Any sale of the property of the estate outside the ordinary course of business, including but not limited to, the debtor's principal residence, real property, or other property must be approved by the Court after notice and a hearing. A motion for such approval shall be made in accordance with 11 U.S.C. § 363, Fed.R.Bankr.P. 4001 or 6004, and MLBR 6004-1, as applicable, and the notice of sale shall conform to MLBR Official Local Form 2A. The motion to sell shall include a proposed distribution of the proceeds of the sale. All motions to sell shall be served on the chapter 13 trustee, all creditors, all parties who

have filed appearances and any other entity as the Court may direct.

(b) If an appraiser or real estate broker is involved in the sale, the debtor must obtain Court authority to employ the appraiser or broker by way of motion. The motion must be accompanied by an affidavit of disinterestedness signed by the broker and comply with the requirements of MLBR 2014(a)-1 and 6005-1.

13-15. BORROWINGS OR REFINANCING OF ESTATE PROPERTY

The provisions and requirements of MLBR 4001-2 shall apply in chapter 13 cases. Any motion for approval of a borrowing or refinancing shall include all the material terms of the proposed credit arrangement. A copy of any borrowing agreement shall be attached to the motion.

13-16. MOTIONS FOR RELIEF FROM STAY

(a) In addition to the requirements of MLBR 4001-1, a motion for relief from the automatic stay shall provide the following information:

1. the date of filing of the chapter 13 petition;

2. the total amount owed to the moving party;

3. the date of confirmation of the plan (if the plan has been confirmed);

4. the amount of the monthly payment at issue;

5. the total amount of the post-petition or post-confirmation payments (principal and interest) in default as of the date of the filing of the motion and due as of the anticipated date of hearing, and the total amount of any other post-petition charge due or anticipated as of each of these dates;

6. the total amount of the prepetition arrearage;

7. the identity and an estimation of the amounts due all lienholders, in order of their priority;

8. an opinion of the value of the property (by declaration), if such value is an issue to be determined; and

9. if the motion for relief from stay is based on defaults in payments to or through the chapter 13 trustee, the motion must show that the debtor has not made the payments to the chapter 13 trustee.

The Court, in its discretion, may deny a motion for relief from stay in the absence of an objection, if the above information is not set forth in the motion.

(b) Stipulations Relating to Motions for Relief from Stay. A motion for approval of a stipulation relating to a motion for relief from stay between the debtor and a party that has a lien on property of the estate shall be filed with the stipulation and served on the chapter 13 trustee, debtor's attorney, any other entity with an interest in the property, and any party requesting service of pleadings in the case. Unless otherwise ordered by the Court, the moving party shall serve the stipulation together with a notice that objections to the approval of the stipulation must be filed within fifteen (15) days of the mailing of the notice, unless the Court fixes a different time. If no objection is filed, the Court may approve the stipulation without a hearing. The Court, in its discretion, may approve a stipulation that is not accompanied by a motion for its approval.

(c) A stipulation resolving a motion for relief from stay shall be served on the chapter 13 trustee, any other entity with an interest in the property, including any lienholder or co-owner, and any attorney who has filed an appearance requesting service of pleadings in the case. The debtor's attorney (or the debtor, if appearing pro se) shall file a certificate of service reflecting compliance with this rule. Unless otherwise ordered by the Court, an objection to a stipulation resolving a motion for relief from stay shall be filed within fifteen (15) days from the date of service of the stipulation. Notwithstanding this requirement, the Court, in its discretion, may cancel a hearing scheduled on a motion for relief from stay which is the subject of a stipulation and may approve a stipulation resolving a motion for relief from stay without a hearing.

13–17. MOTIONS TO DISMISS AND CONVERT

(a) A party who files a motion to dismiss a chapter 13 case shall serve the motion on the debtor, debtor's attorney, all creditors, any party who filed an appearance in the case, and the chapter 13 trustee, and shall file a certificate of service. The motion shall state with particularity the cause for dismissal. A party who opposes a motion to dismiss shall file a response to the motion to dismiss within twenty (20) days of service of the motion.If no response to the motion to dismiss is filed, the Court, in its discretion, may allow the motion without a hearing.

(b) In a case not previously converted under 11 U.S.C. §§ 706, 1208, or 1112, a debtor electing to have the case dismissed may file a motion to voluntarily dismiss the case, pursuant to 11 U.S.C. § 1307, which motion shall be served on the chapter 13 trustee. The debtor's motion to dismiss shall contain a statement as to whether the case has been converted previously. If the Court enters an order dismissing the case, the Clerk shall provide timely notice of the dismissal to all creditors on the matrix and to the chapter 13 trustee.

(c) If the Court denies confirmation of the debtor's plan, the case shall be dismissed by the Court without further notice unless, within ten (10) days after denial of confirmation, or a different time fixed by the Court:

1. the debtor files an amended plan;

2. the debtor moves to convert the case to one under another chapter of the Bankruptcy Code;

3. the debtor files a Motion for Reconsideration or appeals the denial of confirmation, and obtains a stay of the dismissal order; or

4. the Court otherwise orders.

13–18. CONVERSION FROM CHAPTERS 11 OR 7 TO CHAPTER 13

Within fifteen (15) days after conversion of a case from chapter 11 or chapter 7 to chapter 13, the debtor shall file with the Court those documents required by paragraph 13–2 of this order and serve copies on the chapter 13 trustee.

13–19. COMMENCEMENT AND CONTINUANCE OF PAYMENTS TO THE CHAPTER 13 TRUSTEE; DISMISSAL FOR FAILURE TO MAKE REQUIRED PAYMENTS

(a) Payments to the chapter 13 trustee pursuant to either 11 U.S.C. § 1326(a) or the terms of a confirmed plan shall be made by certified check or money order. Each payment shall be legibly marked with the bankruptcy case number and the name of the debtor as it appears in the caption of the case.

(b) Payments to the chapter 13 trustee pursuant to either 11 U.S.C. § 1326(a) or the terms of a confirmed plan shall continue until the case has been dismissed, the debtor has completed all payments required by the plan, the debtor has moved for either a hardship discharge pursuant to 11 U.S.C. § 1328(b) or voluntary dismissal, or the debtor has requested that the case be converted to a case under another chapter of the Bankruptcy Code.

(c) The Court will not consider, allow or approve motions or stipulations for direct payment to the chapter 13 trustee from the debtor's employer or any other entity.

(d) In the event that a chapter 13 case is dismissed or converted prior to confirmation of the plan, the chapter 13 trustee shall be entitled to retain from any monies collected from the debtor the amount of $150.00, which shall constitute an administrative expense pursuant to 11 U.S.C. § 503(b).

13–20. DISTRIBUTION

Unless otherwise directed by the Court, the distribution of any proceeds pursuant to a confirmed plan shall be mailed to the address of the creditor as designated pursuant to Fed.R.Bankr.P. 2002(g).

13–21. CHAPTER 13 TRUSTEE'S FINAL ACCOUNT

When the chapter 13 trustee determines that the plan has been completed, the trustee shall file and serve a final report and account on all creditors with allowed claims, all attorneys who have filed appearances and requested service of pleadings in the case, the debtor, and debtor's counsel. The report shall state the allowed amount of each claim and the amount paid on each claim. The chapter 13 trustee shall give notice that any objection to the final report and account shall be filed within thirty (30) days after service. The chapter 13 trustee shall file a certificate of service reflecting service of the final report and account and objection deadline. In the absence of a timely filed objection, the Court may approve the final report and account without a hearing.

Amended effective January 1, 2002.

13–22. ORDER OF DISCHARGE

(a) The order of discharge shall include findings that

1. all allowed claims have been fully paid in accordance with the provisions of the confirmed plan; or

2. with respect to secured claims which continue beyond the term of the plan, any pre-petition or post-petition defaults have been cured and such claims are in all respects current, with no escrow balance, late charges, costs or attorneys' fees owing.

(b) The order of discharge shall direct that

1. creditors who held secured claims which were fully paid execute and deliver to the debtor a release or other discharge certificate suitable for recording; and

2. creditors who hold secured claims which continue beyond the term of the plan take no action inconsistent with the findings provided for in subsection (a).

Effective August 1, 1997. Amended effective September 1, 1999.

APPENDIX 2. EXPENSES

In lieu of calculating the actual cost of the following expenses, the applicant may request the rates of reimbursement set forth below:

(i)	copies	$0.15 per page
(ii)	incoming telecopier transmissions	$0.15 per page
(iii)	auto mileage	at the rate set forth from time to time pursuant to 41 CFR § 301–4.2

Effective August 1, 1997.

APPENDIX 3. FILING FEES

(a) New Case, Ancillary Proceeding and Case Reopening. The following fees apply to the filing or reopening of cases:

1.	Chapter 7 (Filing)	$ 209.00
2.	Chapter 7 (Reopening)	$ 155.00
3.	Chapter 9	$ 839.00
4.	Chapter 11 Non–Railroad	$ 839.00
5.	Chapter 11 Non-Railroad (Reopening)	$ 839.00
6.	Chapter 11 Railroad	$1,039.00
7.	Chapter 12 (when authorized)	$ 239.00
8.	Chapter 13	$ 194.00
9.	Chapter 13 (Reopening)	$ 155.00
10.	11 U.S.C. § 304 (Ancillary Proceeding)	$ 839.00
11.	The fee due upon conversion from a chapter 7 or chapter 13 case to a chapter 11 case is $645.00.	

(b) Motions.

1. The fee for the filing of a motion for relief from the automatic stay under 11 U.S.C. § 362(d) is $150.00.

2. The fee for the filing of a motion to withdraw the reference is $150.00.

3. The fee for the filing of a motion to compel abandonment of property of the estate is $150.00.

4. The fee for the filing of a motion to convert or a notice of conversion to a chapter 7 case is $15.00.

(c) Adversary Proceedings. The filing fee for a complaint is $150.00, except that no fee is required if the United States or the debtor in a chapter 7 or chapter 13 case is the plaintiff. The debtor in possession in a chapter 11 case must pay the filing fee. If a trustee in a case under Title 11 is the plaintiff, the fee shall be payable only from the estate to the extent of available funds. The Court may, upon motion of a trustee, defer payment of the filing fee.

(d) Miscellaneous Fees.

1. Notice of Appeal from Final Order $255.00

2. Cross Appeal $255.00

3. Notice of Appeal from Inter-locutory Order (If a motion for leave to appeal is allowed, an additional $250.00 will be due.) $ 5.00

4. Amendment to Schedules D, E and F or List of Creditors $ 26.00

5. Clerk's Certificate $ 18.00

6. Records Search $ 26.00

(If copies are requested, a copy charge also will be assessed.)

7. Retrieval of Closed File from Federal Records Center $ 45.00

8. Certification of Document $ 9.00

9. Copies per page $ .50

10. Registering a Judgment from Another District $ 39.00

11. Reproduction of a Tape Recording $ 26.00

12. Check Returned Due to Insufficient Funds $ 45.00

Effective August 1, 1997. Amended effective September 1, 1999; December 29, 1999; March 1, 2003; November 1, 2003; January 1, 2005.

APPENDIX 4. NOTICES TO THE UNITED STATES OF AMERICA AND THE COMMONWEALTH OF MASSACHUSETTS

(a) Whenever notice is required to be given to the Internal Revenue Service, it shall be mailed to:

Internal Revenue Service
Special Procedures Function STOP 20800
P.O. Box 9112
JFK Building
Boston, MA 02203

(b) Whenever notice is required to be given to the Securities and Exchange Commission, it shall be mailed to:

Securities and Exchange Commission
Boston District Office
73 Tremont Street, 6th Floor
Boston, MA 02108

Securities and Exchange Commission
450 Fifth Street, N.W.
Washington, DC 20549

(c) Whenever notice is required to be given to the United States Attorney, it shall be mailed to:

United States Attorney
United States Courthouse
John Joseph Moakley One Courthouse Way, Suite

9200
Boston, MA 02210

(d) Fed.R.Bankr.P. 7004(a)(4) governs service of process upon the United States in adversary proceedings.

(e) Whenever notice is required to be given to the Massachusetts Department of Revenue, it shall be mailed to:

Massachusetts Department of Revenue
Bankruptcy Unit
P.O. Box 55484
Boston, MA 02205

(f) Whenever notice is required to be given to the Massachusetts Division of Employment and Training, it shall be mailed to:

Commonwealth of Massachusetts
Division of Employment and Training
Attn: Chief Counsel
Hurley Bldg—Government Center
Boston, MA 02114

(g) Whenever notice is required to be given to the Massachusetts Attorney General, it shall be mailed to:

Office of the Attorney General
Commonwealth of Massachusetts
One Ashburton Place
Boston, MA 02108

Effective August 1, 1997. Amended effective September 1, 1999; March 1, 2003.

APPENDIX 5. COURT DIVISIONS AND CLERK'S OFFICE

(a) **Divisions.** The District of Massachusetts shall contain the following two (2) divisions:

(1) *Eastern Division*: The Eastern division shall consist of (A) the counties of Barnstable, Bristol, Dukes, Nantucket, Norfolk, Plymouth, and Suffolk, (B) the county of Essex, with the exception of the towns specifically assigned to the Western Division in section (2), and (C) the following towns in Middlesex County: Arlington, Ashland, Belmont, Burlington, Cambridge, Everett, Framingham, Holliston, Lexington, Lincoln, Malden, Medford, Melrose, Natick, Newton, North Reading, Reading, Sherborn, Somerville, Stoneham, Wakefield, Waltham, Watertown, Wayland, Weston, Wilmington, Winchester, and Woburn.

The address of the Eastern division is: Clerk, U.S. Bankruptcy Court, 1101 Thomas P. O'Neill Jr. Federal Building, 10 Causeway Street, Boston, MA 02222–1074.

(2) *Western Division*: The Western division shall consist of (A) the counties of Berkshire, Franklin, Hampden, Hampshire, and Worcester, (B) the county of Middlesex, with the exception of the towns specifically assigned to the Eastern Division in section (1), and the following towns in Essex County:

Essex: Andover, Boxford, Bradford, Haverhill, Lawrence, Methuen, and North Andover;

The address of the Western Division is: Clerk, U.S. Bankruptcy Court, Donohue Federal Building, 595 Main Street, Worcester, MA 01608–2076.

(b) **Emergency Filings.** Filings can be made before 8:30 AM or after 4:30 PM on court days or on weekends or holidays for cause and by prior arrangement or in emergency circumstances, as determined by the Clerk or his or her designee. With respect to Eastern Division cases, parties should contact the Clerk's office at (617) 565–8950 and press (0) or (617) 565–8956 during business hours. With respect to Western Division cases, parties should contact the Clerk's office in Worcester at (508) 770–8900 during business hours. At other times, parties should contact the Clerk or his or her designee by calling **beeper no. (800)759–8888 and enter PIN #1309280.**

(c) **Emergency Closings or Delayed Opening.** Information as to an emergency closing or delayed opening of the Court is available by calling 1-866-419-5695 (Toll Free).

(d) **Courtroom Deputies.** The telephone numbers, fax numbers and e-mail addresses (to be employed for forwarding proposed orders), for each of the following courtroom deputies are set forth below:

For Chief Judge Joan N. Feeney's Session

Telephone: (617) 565–6067
Fax: (617) 565–6651
E-mail: jnf@mab.uscourts.gov

For Judge William C. Hillman's Session

Telephone: (617) 565–6073
Fax: (617) 565–6652
E-mail: wch@mab.uscourts.gov

For Judge Henry J. Boroff's Session

Telephone: (508) 770–8936
Fax: (508) 770–8958
E-mail: hjb@mab.uscourts.gov

For Judge Joel B. Rosenthal's Session

Telephone: (508) 770–8927
Fax: (508) 793–0189
E-mail: jbr@mab.uscourts.gov

For Session of Judge (to be designated)

Telephone: (617) 565–5280
Fax: (617) 565–6650
E-mail: (to be designated)

Effective August 1, 1997; amended effective March 1, 1999; September 1, 1999; March 1, 2003; January 1, 2005.

APPENDIX 6. SAMPLE CASE MANAGEMENT PROCEDURES

(a) **Omnibus Hearing Dates and Notices of Agenda.**

(1) Unless the Court otherwise orders, the Court will conduct omnibus hearings in this case on a (weekly) (bimonthly) (monthly) basis ("Omnibus Hearing Dates").

(2) All matters requiring a hearing shall be set for and be heard on one of the Omnibus Hearing Dates unless alternative hearing dates are approved by the Court for good cause shown.

(3) In order for a pleading to be heard on an Omnibus Hearing Date, a party must first contact the Court's courtroom deputy and request the scheduling of the hearing. The courtroom deputy shall set the pleading for the first available Omnibus Hearing date, taking into account the time required for notice to other parties and the remaining time available on the Omnibus Hearing Date; and shall set an objection deadline, if any. No motion or application shall be set for hearing absent compliance with Fed. R. Bankr. P. 2002(a) nor shall the hearing be set for less than 7 days from service of that motion or application, unless the Court has allowed a request for expedited determination. The requesting party must file and serve the pleading no later than forty-eight (48) hours after the courtroom deputy has set the pleading for an Omnibus Hearing Date and must indicate on the first page of the pleading the time of the hearing and the deadline for objections, if any.

(4) The provisions of MLBR 9013–1 shall continue to govern, except insofar as they may specifically conflict with the procedures set forth above.

(5) Counsel to the estate representative shall maintain, file and serve a Notice of Agenda for each Omnibus Hearing Date as follows:

(A) A proposed Notice of Agenda shall be filed before 12:00 noon on the day that is two (2) court days before the Omnibus Hearing Date.

(B) Resolved or continued matters shall be listed ahead of unresolved matters.

(C) The Notice of Agenda shall be promptly amended as necessary and served on all parties in interest. All amended Notices of Agenda shall list matters as listed in the original Notice of Agenda with all edits and additional information being listed in boldface type.

(D) For each motion or application, the Notice of Agenda shall indicate:

(i) the name of the movant or the applicant, the nature of the motion or application, and the docket number (Supporting papers of the movant or applicant shall be similarly denoted);

(ii) the objection deadline, any objection filed and its docket number, if available; and

(iii) whether the matter is going forward, whether a continuance is requested (and any opposition to the continuance, if known), whether any or all of the objections have been resolved, and any other pertinent status information.

(E) When a matter in an adversary proceeding is scheduled to be heard, the Notice of Agenda shall indicate the adversary proceeding number and the corresponding docket number for pleadings filed in the adversary proceeding, together with the information contained in subparagraph (d) above, insofar as applicable.

(b) Procedures Governing Payment of Interim Compensation and Reimbursement of Expenses to Professionals Pursuant to 11 U.S.C. §§ 105(a) and 331.

(1) Scope of Applicability. All professionals retained in a Chapter 11 case pursuant to 11 U.S.C. §§ 327 and 1103 (each, a "Professional") may seek post-petition interim compensation pursuant to these procedures (the "Administrative Fee Order").

(2) Submission and Monthly Statements. On or before the twenty-fifth (25th) day of each month following the month for which compensation is sought, each Professional seeking compensation pursuant to the Administrative Fee Order shall serve a monthly fee and expense statement (the "Monthly Fee Statement") upon the following persons:

(A) the officer designated by the debtor to be responsible for such matters;

(B) counsel to the debtor;

(C) any Chapter 7 or 11 trustee;

(D) counsel to all official committees;

(E) the Office of the United States Trustee;

(F) counsel to all post-petition lenders or their agents; and

(G) any other party the Court may so designate.

(3) Content of Monthly Fee Statement. Each Monthly Fee Statement shall contain an itemization of time spent and the applicable hourly rate. All time-keepers must maintain contemporaneous time entries in increments of one-tenth (1/10th) of an hour.

(4) Review Period. Each person receiving a Monthly Fee Statement shall have twenty (20) days after service of the Monthly Fee Statement to review it and serve an objection (the "Objection Period").

(5) Payment. In the absence of a timely served objection, the estate representative will promptly pay each Professional an amount (the "Interim Payment") equal to the lesser of (i) ninety percent (90%) of the fees and 100 percent (100%) of the expenses requested in the Monthly Fee Statement, or (ii) ninety percent (90%) of the fees and 100 percent (100%) of the expenses not subject to any partial objection.

(6) Objections

(A) If any party objects to a Monthly Fee Statement, it must serve a written objection (the "Notice of Objection to Monthly Fee Statement") and serve it upon the Professional and each of the parties served with the Monthly Fee Statement as set forth above, so that the Notice of Objection to Monthly Fee Statement is received on or before the last day of the Objection Period.

(B) The Notice of Objection to Monthly Fee. Statement must set forth the nature of the objection and the amount of fees and/or expenses at issue.

(C) If an estate representative receives an objection to a particular Monthly Fee Statement, the estate representative shall withhold payment of that portion of the Monthly Fee Statement to which the objection is directed, and shall promptly pay the remainder of the fees and disbursements in the percentages set forth above.

(D) If the parties to an objection are able to resolve their respective dispute(s) following the service of a Notice of Objection to Monthly Fee Statement, and the Professional and the objecting party serve upon each of the parties served with the Monthly Fee Statement as set forth above a statement indicating that the objection is withdrawn, in whole or in part, describing in detail the terms of the resolution, then the estate representative shall promptly pay in accordance with the percentages listed above that portion of the Monthly Fee Statement which is no longer subject to an objection.

(E) If the parties are unable to reach a resolution to the objection within twenty (20) days after service of the objection, the affected Professional may either (a) move to compel the payment with the Court, together with a request for payment of the difference, if any, between the total amount of the Interim Payment sought and the portion of the Interim Payment as to which there is an objection (the "Incremental Amount"); or (b) forgo payment of the Incremental Amount until the next interim or final fee application, or any other date and time so directed by the Court, at which time it will consider and dispose of the objection, if so requested.

(F) Neither an objection to a Monthly Fee Statement nor the failure to object thereto shall prejudice a party's right to object to any fee application on any ground.

(G) Failure of a professional to timely serve a Monthly Fee Statement shall not prejudice such professional in seeking interim or final allowance of fees or expenses. Further, any Monthly Fee Statement served after the deadline for such Monthly Fee Statement shall be deemed served at the time that such professional serves a Monthly Fee Statement for the next subsequent period and shall be subject to the Objection Deadline for the Monthly Fee Statement for such subsequent period.

(7) Fee Applications

(A) Parties seeking compensation pursuant to an Administrative Fee Order shall file at four (4) month intervals or such other intervals directed by the Court ("Interim Period") an interim fee application. Each Professional seeking approval of its interim fee application shall file with the Court an interim application for allowance of compensation and reimbursement of expenses, pursuant to 11 U.S.C. § 331, of the amounts sought in the Monthly Fee Statements issued during such period (the "Interim Fee Application").

(B) The Interim Fee. Application shall comply with the mandates of the Bankruptcy Code, Rules 2014 and 2016 of the Federal Rules of Bankruptcy Procedure and the Local Rules for the United States Bankruptcy Court for the District of Massachusetts.

(C) The Interim Fee. Application must be filed within forty-five (45) days after the conclusion of the Interim Period.

(D) In the event any Professional fails to file an Interim Fee Application when due, such Professional will be ineligible to receive further interim payments or fees or expenses under the Administrative Fee Order until such time as the Interim Fee Application is submitted.

(E) The pendency of a fee application, or a Court order that payment of compensation or reimbursement of expenses was improper as to a particular Monthly Fee Statement, shall not disqualify a Professional from the further payment of compensation or reimbursement of expenses as set forth above, unless otherwise ordered by the Court. Additionally, the pendency of an objection to payment of compensation or reimbursement of expenses will not disqualify a Professional from future payment of compensation or reimbursement of expenses, unless the Court orders otherwise.

(F) Neither the payment of, nor the failure to pay, in whole or in part, monthly compensation and reimbursement as provided herein shall have any effect on the Court's interim or final allowance of compensation and reimbursement of expenses of any Professionals. All compensation is subject to final approval by the Court.

(G) Counsel for each official committee may, in accordance with the foregoing procedure for monthly compensation and reimbursement to professionals, collect and submit statements of actual expenses incurred, with supporting vouchers, from members of the committee such counsel represents, provided, however, that such committee counsel ensures that these reimbursement requests comply with the applicable rules and those guidelines.

8. Miscellaneous

(A) Any party may object to requests for payments made pursuant to the Administrative Fee Order for good cause, including, without limitation, that the estate representative has not timely filed monthly operating reports or remained current with its administrative expenses and 28 U.S.C. § 1930 fees.

(B) The estate representative shall include all payments to Professionals on its monthly operating reports, including details of the amount paid to each Professional.

(C) All fees and expenses paid to Professionals are subject to disgorgement until final allowance by the Court.

Effective August 1, 1997; amended effective January 1, 2005.

APPENDIX 7. APPLICATION FOR COMPENSATION SAMPLE NARRATIVE OF SERVICES RENDERED [DELETED]

Effective August 1, 1997; Deleted effective January 1, 2005.

APPENDIX 8. ELECTRONIC FILING RULES

RULE 1. SCOPE OF ELECTRONIC FILING

Electronic filing of petitions, motions, applications, memoranda of law or other pleadings or documents (hereafter "documents") shall be mandatory as set forth in MLBR 9036–1, excepting only documents:

(a) constituting proofs of claim;

(b) filed by parties in interest who are pro se;

(c) constituting a request for ex parte determination or a request for impoundment, pursuant to MLRB 9018–1.

(d) filed by attorneys who:

(1) personally, or by an agent, hand deliver the document(s) to the Clerk's Office and scan the document(s) electronically employing equipment supplied and procedures as directed by Clerk's Office personnel; or

(2) are unable to file electronically on account of temporary equipment or system breakdown in the attorney's office or the Clerk's Office; or

(e) accepted in paper form with prior permission of the Clerk, the Deputy Clerk or their designee, leave to be given only on a showing of temporary exigent circumstances other than equipment or system breakdown.

Effective March 1, 2003; amended effective January 1, 2005.

RULE 2. ELIGIBILITY, REGISTRATION, PASSWORDS

(a) **Registered User.** The term "Registered User" as employed in these rules shall be deemed to mean an individual who has registered to use this Court's ECF System, with full or limited access, pursuant to subsection (b) hereof. Limited access allows an attorney or non–attorney to become a Registered User for the sole purpose of filing proofs of claim, notice requests, transfers or assignments of claim, and withdrawals of claims.

(b) **Eligibility.** Attorneys admitted to the bar of the United States District Court for the District of Massachusetts (including those admitted pro hac vice, pursuant to Local Rule 9010–1(b)), attorneys representing the United States of America or any state, the United States trustee and his/her assistants, Chapter 7, 11, 12, or 13 trustees, limited access users, and others as the Court may allow in its discretion on prior motion and order, may register as Registered Users of the ECF System after completion of such electronic filing training as the Clerk of this Court may establish and require from time to time.

(c) **Registration.** Application for registration as a Registered User shall be made on a form prescribed by the Clerk as amended from time to time and posted on the Court's website, *www.mab.uscourts.gov.* All registration application forms shall be mailed or delivered to the Office of the Clerk, United States Bankruptcy Court, 10 Causeway Street, 11th Floor, Boston, Massachusetts 02222, ATTN: FINANCE, PERSONAL AND CONFIDENTIAL. Each approved registrant will receive a notice from the Clerk to retrieve from the Clerk's Office (in Boston or Worcester, as designated by the registrant) a sealed envelope containing a log-in name and assigned password. Only the applicant or an authorized representative may retrieve the envelope; except that, at the written request of an approved registrant, the Clerk may e–mail the log-in name and password to the registrant. The Clerk is authorized to employ such further precautions which in the Clerk's judgment will ensure security in the distribution of passwords. Each Registered User shall be entitled to only one password, except that additional passwords may be issued to a single user for good cause shown and in the discretion of the Clerk.

(d) **Withdrawal or Amendment of Registration.** A Registered User who wishes to withdraw or amend a registration shall e–mail a request for such change to the Clerk on a form prescribed by the Clerk as amended from time to time and posted on the Court's website, *www.mab.uscourts.gov.*

(e) **Security.** Registration constitutes a Registered User's agreement to protect the security of his or her assigned password and immediately notify the Clerk if the Registered User learns that the security of the password has been compromised. No Registered User shall knowingly permit the password to be utilized by anyone other than an authorized agent of the Registered User. Upon notice to the Clerk that a password has been compromised, the Clerk shall promptly provide a substitute password to the Registered User.

(f) **Waivers.** Registration constitutes the Registered User's: (1) agreement to receive documents electronically and waiver of the right to receive notice by any other means; and (2) consent to service of all documents electronically and waiver of the right to service by any other means, excepting only service of process in an adversary proceeding or with respect to an involuntary petition, or as otherwise ordered by the Court. The aforesaid waiver of service and notice by non-electronic means shall include waiver of notice by first class mail of the entry of an order or judgment under Fed. R. Bank. P. 9022.

(g) **Involuntary Termination of Registration; Sanctions.** On notice from the Clerk that a Registered User and/or his or her agents has/have repeatedly and/or egregiously failed to comply with the procedures established by the Court for use of the ECF System or failed to comply with reasonable password security precautions, the Court may, after notice and hearing, sanction a Registered User for such failure, including, without limitation, by suspending the Registered User from use of the ECF System.

Effective March 1, 2003; amended effective January 1, 2005.

RULE 3. CONSEQUENCES OF ELECTRONIC FILING

(a) **Filing and Entry.** Transmission of a document to the ECF System consistent with these rules, together with the transmission of a Notice of Electronic Filing from the Court, constitutes the filing of the document for all purposes of the Federal Rules of Bankruptcy Procedure and the local rules of this Court, and constitutes entry of the document on the docket kept by the Clerk pursuant to Fed. R. Bank. P. 5003.

(b) **Official Record.** When a document has been filed electronically, the official record is the electronic recording of the document as stored by the Court, and the filing party is bound by the document as filed. A document filed electronically is deemed filed on the date and the time stated on the Notice of Electronic Filing from the Court.

(c) **Filing Deadline.** A document may be filed at any time, except that:

(1) where the Court orders that filing must be completed by a specific date and time, filing a document electronically does not alter the filing deadline for that document; and

(2) where the Court orders that filing must be completed by a specific date but does not specify the time, entry of the document into the ECF System must be completed before 4:30 p.m. Eastern Standard (or Daylight, if applicable) Time in order to be deemed timely filed.

Effective March 1, 2003.

RULE 4. ENTRY OF COURT ORDERS

The Clerk shall enter all orders, judgments, and proceeding memos on the docket kept by the clerk under Fed. R. Bankr. P. 5003 and 9021 in electronic format. Any order entered electronically without the original signature of a judge shall have the same force and effect as if the judge had affixed his or her signature to a paper copy of the order.

Effective March 1, 2003; amended effective January 1, 2005.

RULE 5. ATTACHMENTS AND EXHIBITS

(a) If the exhibit(s) to any document constitutes) more than 50 pages in the aggregate, the exhibit(s) must be filed separately from the underlying document. In such event, the Registered User must file

with the underlying document (a) a list of all of the exhibits, identifying clearly the subject matter of each exhibit, and (b) a summary of the content of each exhibit of 50 or more pages in length. If any recipient is unable to open an exhibit for any reason, it is the responsibility of the recipient to notify the transmitting Registered User of the recipient's inability to open the exhibit and to request paper copies. The Registered User shall respond promptly to any such request.

(b) Exhibits may, but need not, be attached to Proofs of Claim when filed electronically. The claimant shall promptly provide any party in interest all exhibits upon request.

Effective March 1, 2003.

RULE 6. SEALED OR IMPOUNDED DOCUMENTS

Any motion to seal or impound a document, pursuant to MLBR 9018–1, and the subject document, shall not be filed electronically, unless specifically authorized by the Court. In the event that the motion to seal or impound is granted, the Court shall determine the extent to which the motion and/or the document(s) shall be electronically filed.

Effective March 1, 2003.

RULE 7. STATEMENTS UNDER OATH; RETENTION REQUIREMENTS

(a) Unless the Court orders otherwise, all electronically filed documents, (including, without limitation, affidavits or a debtor's petition, schedules, statement of affairs, or amendments thereof) requiring signatures under the penalties of perjury shall also be executed in paper form, together with a Declaration Re: Electronic Filing in the form of Official Form 7. The Declaration Re: Electronic Filing shall be filed with the Court as an imaged, and not electronically created, document, together with or in addition to the document electronically filed with the Court. Said Declaration shall be valid for the declarant for all subsequently filed documents requiring a signature in the case.

(b) Notwithstanding subsection (a) above, the paper forms of the electronically filed document(s) and the Declaration Re: Electronic Filing shall be retained by the Registered User until five (5) years after the closing of the case. Said paper documents shall be deemed property of the Court and not property of the declarant or the Registered User. The Registered User must produce all such original documents for review or filing at the request of a party in interest or upon order of the Court.

Effective March 1, 2003; amended effective January 1, 2005.

RULE 8. SIGNATURES

(a) The user log-in and password required to submit documents to the ECF System serve as the Registered User's signature on all electronic documents filed with the Court. They also serve as a signature for purposes of Fed. R. Bankr. P. 9011, the Federal Rules of Bankruptcy Procedure, the local rules of this Court, and any other purpose for which a signature is required. Electronically filed documents must set forth the name, address, telephone number, e–mail address of a Registered User and, if an attorney, his or her BBO or PHV number (see MBLR 9010–3(b)). In addition, the document must include a signature block where the name of the Registered User and/or affiant is typed, but preceded by an "/s/," or is set forth as an imaged or electronically created signature.

(b) Where an electronically filed document sets forth the consent of more than one party, the additional consents may be supplied by: (1) a scanned document containing all of the necessary signatures; or (2) a representation that the Registered User has authority to consent on behalf of the other parties who are purported signatories to the document; or (3) a notice of endorsement filed by the other signatories no later than three business days after filing of the document; or (4) any other manner approved by the Court.

(c) All electronic documents filed after the commencement of the case must contain the case caption and number.

(d) Notwithstanding Fed. R. Bankr. P. 9011(a), an attorney may electronically file an application for compensation for a professional who is not a registered user but whose employment in that case has been authorized previously by order of the court.

Effective March 1, 2003; amended effective January 1, 2005.

RULE 9. SERVICE OF DOCUMENT BY ELECTRONIC MEANS

(a) Transmission by the Court of the "Notice of Electronic Filing" constitutes service or notice of the filed document, except that persons not deemed to have consented to electronic notice or service are entitled to conventional notice or service of any electronically filed document according to the Federal Rules of Bankruptcy Procedure and the local rules.

(b) Service by electronic transmission shall be deemed equivalent to service by mail for the purposes of Fed. R. Bankr. P. 9006(f).

Effective March 1, 2003.

RULE 10. NOTICE OF COURT ORDERS AND JUDGMENTS

Upon the entry of an order or judgment in a case or an adversary proceeding, the Clerk will transmit notice to Registered Users in the case or adversary proceeding in electronic form. Transmission of a Notice of Electronic Filing constitutes the notice required by Fed.R.Bankr.P. 9022. The Clerk shall give conventional notice to a person who has not consented to electronic service in accordance with the Federal Rules of Bankruptcy Procedure.

Effective March 1, 2003.

RULE 11. TECHNICAL FAILURES

A Registered User whose filing is made untimely as a result of a technical failure may seek appropriate relief from the Court, including, without limitation, leave to file by facsimile and defer payment of any filing fee.

Effective March 1, 2003; amended effective January 1, 2005.

RULE 12. PUBLIC ACCESS

A person may view electronically filed documents that have not been impounded by the Court at the Clerk's Office. A person may also access the ECF System at the Court's Internet site, *www.mab.us-courts.gov*, by obtaining a PACER login and password. A person who has PACER access may retrieve dockets and documents. Only a Registered User may file documents electronically.

Effective March 1, 2003.

OFFICIAL LOCAL FORMS

OFFICIAL LOCAL FORM 1. MATRIX LIST OF CREDITORS

This form is a sample master mailing matrix creditor list required to be filed with a bankruptcy petition. **This form can be printed out or submitted on a 3½" floppy disk, following the same guidelines for both.** The following format must be observed:

1. Listing must be in a single column containing as many pages as are required to list all creditors. Page numbers or page headings must not be included in the list.

2. The margins at the top and bottom of the page must be at least one inch each.

3. The matrix shall be produced with a quality computer printer or typewriter. If a dot matrix printer is used, it should have near letter quality. Standard type size shall be used. The name and address of each creditor must not consist of more than five (5) lines.

At least one blank line shall be inserted between each creditor listing.

4. If not filed on disk, an original of the matrix or amended matrix must be filed with the Clerk's Office; because our optical character reader will not read a faxed document, a matrix cannot be filed by fax.

5. If submitting matrix on a floppy disk, please save the file as an ASCII (DOS) text file, and write the debtor's name and town on the disk.

EXAMPLE:

Donut and Coffee National Bank
Post Office Box 3391
Beaumont, TX 77703

Pyramid Investing Corp.
3001 Ghost Street
Reno, NV 86068

Hammer and Anvil Mediation, Inc.
10 Garrison Blvd.
Los Angeles, CA 90905

Spotted Owl Furniture
83 Timber St.
Lakewood, CA 98323

SPECIFICATIONS FOR FLOPPY DISK CREDITOR MATRIX

The following format for a floppy disk containing creditors' names and addresses must be observed:

1. Data must be in ASCII format.

2. Each creditor name and corresponding address ("record") must be on a single line.

3. Each record may consist of up to five (5) fields of data.

4. Each field cannot exceed forty (40) characters. The field may contain fewer characters or be nonexistent.

5. Each field must end with a "separator." The preferred separator is the pipe/vertical bar symbol (|). Do not use a letter, digit, or underscore as the separator.

EXAMPLE:

John Dee | 1846 Main Street | Boston, MA 02222 |

Hook, Line, and Sinker, P.C. | P.O. Box 49085432 |
Tampa, FL 15362 |

ABC Company | Granite Bldg. | Suite 101 | P.O.
Box 87 | Hartford, CT 06105 |

Effective August 1, 1997. Amended effective September 1, 1999; March 1, 2003.

OFFICIAL LOCAL FORM 2A. NOTICE OF INTENDED PRIVATE SALE

UNITED STATES BANKRUPTCY COURT
DISTRICT OF MASSACHUSETTS

_____

In re   )
)
) Chapter
) Case No.
)
   Debtor)
_____)

NOTICE OF INTENDED PRIVATE SALE OF ESTATE PROPERTY, DEADLINE FOR SUBMITTING OBJECTIONS AND HIGHER OFFERS AND HEARING DATE

To Creditors and Parties in Interest:

Notice is hereby given, pursuant to 11 U.S.C. Section 363, Fed.R.Bankr.P. 2002(a)(2) and 6004, and MLBR 2002–5 and 6004–1, that the Trustee (or, where applicable, the Debtor), _____, intends to sell at private sale the Debtor's right, title and interest in certain property of the estate consisting of: ___ (Property Description) ___.

The Trustee (or where applicable, the Debtor) has received an offer to purchase ___ (Property) ___ for the sum of ___ (Purchase Price) ___ in cash (or state other consideration) from ___ (Proposed Buyer) ___. The relationship of the proposed buyer to the Debtor (or Trustee, if applicable) is: _____.

The sale shall take place on or before _____. The proposed buyer has paid a deposit in the sum of $_____. The terms of the proposed sale are more particularly described in a Motion for Order Authorizing and Approving Private Sale of Property of the Estate (the "Motion to Approve Sale") filed with the Court on _____ and a written purchase and sale agreement dated _____. The Motion to Approve Sale and the purchase and sale agreement are available upon request from the undersigned.

The ___ (Property) ___ will be sold free and clear of all liens, claims and encumbrances. Any perfected, enforceable valid liens shall attach to the proceeds of the sale according to priorities established under applicable law.

Any objections to the sale and/or higher offers shall be filed in writing with the Clerk, United States Bankruptcy Court at _____ (either Boston or Worcester address as applicable) on or before _____ at 4:30 PM (the "Objection Deadline"). A copy of any objection or higher offer also shall be served upon the undersigned. Any objection to the sale must state with particularity the grounds for the objection and why the intended sale should not be authorized. Any objection to the sale shall be governed by Fed.R.Bankr.P. 9014.

Through this Notice, higher offers for the Property are hereby solicited. Any higher must be accompanied by a cash deposit of $_____ in the form of a certified or bank check made payable to the undersigned. Higher offers must be on the same terms and conditions provided in the Purchase and Sale Agreement, other than the purchase price.

A hearing on the Motion to Approve Sale, objections or higher offers is scheduled to take place on _____ at ____AM/PM before the Honorable _____, United States Bankruptcy Judge, Courtroom ____, _____, _____, Massachusetts. Any party who has filed an objection or higher offer is expected to be present at the hearing, failing which the objection will be overruled or the higher offer stricken. If no objection to the Motion to Approve Sale or higher offer is timely filed, the Bankruptcy Court, in its discretion, may cancel the scheduled hearing and approve the sale without hearing.

At the hearing on the sale the Court may 1) consider any requests to strike a higher offer, 2) determine further terms and conditions of the sale, 3) determine the requirements for further competitive bidding, and 4) require one or more rounds of sealed or open bids from the original offeror and any other qualifying offeror.

The deposit will be forfeited to the estate if the successful purchaser fails to complete the sale by the date ordered by the Court. If the sale is not completed by the buyer approved by the Court, the Court, without further hearing, may approve the sale of the Property to the next highest bidder.

Any questions concerning the intended sale shall be addressed to the undersigned.

Respectfully Submitted,

TRUSTEE (or Debtor)

By _____

Dated: _____

Effective August 1, 1997.

OFFICIAL LOCAL FORM 2B. NOTICE OF INTENDED PUBLIC SALE OF ESTATE PROPERTY

UNITED STATES BANKRUPTCY COURT
DISTRICT OF MASSACHUSETTS

```
_____ )
In re                      )  Chapter
                           )  Case No.
                           )
        Debtor             )
_____ )
```

NOTICE OF INTENDED PUBLIC SALE OF ESTATE PROPERTY

To Creditors and Parties in Interest:

Notice is hereby given, pursuant to 11 U.S.C. § 363, Fed.R.Bankr.P. 2002(a)(2) and 6004, and MLBR Rule 2002–5 and 6004–1, that the Trustee (or, where applicable, the Debtor), _____, intends to sell at public sale the Debtor's right, title and interest in certain property of the estate consisting of: ____(Property Description)____.

The sale will be conducted by ____(Auctioneer)____ at ____(Address)____ on ____(Date)____ at ____(Time)____. The proposed sale procedures are more particularly described in the Debtor's Motion for Order Authorizing and Approving Public Sale of Property of the Estate (the "Motion to Approve Sale").

The ____(Property)____ will be sold free and clear of all liens, claims and encumbrances, with such valid liens, claims and encumbrances, if any, attaching to the net proceeds of the sale to the same extent and in the same order of priority as such liens, claims and encumbrances attached to the ____(Property)____.

Objections, if any, to the Motion to Approve Sale and the intended public sale of the Debtor's interest in the ____(Property)____ must be filed with the Clerk of the United States Bankruptcy Court on or before _____ at 4:30 PM (the "Objection Deadline"). A copy of the objection must also be served upon the Trustee (or, where applicable, the Debtor or Debtor's Counsel).

A hearing is scheduled to take place on _____ at _____ AM/PM before the Honorable _____, United States Bankruptcy Judge, Courtroom ____, _____, _____, Massachusetts. If no objection to the sale is timely filed, the Bankruptcy Court, in its discretion, may cancel the scheduled hearing and grant the Motion.

Respectfully submitted,

_____

(Name, address, telephone number)

Dated: _____

Effective August 1, 1997.

OFFICIAL LOCAL FORM 3.   CHAPTER 13 PLAN AND COVER SHEET

UNITED STATES BANKRUPTCY COURT
DISTRICT OF MASSACHUSETTS

CHAPTER 13 PLAN COVER SHEET

Filing Date: _____	Docket #: _____
Debtor: _____	Co–Debtor: _____
SS#: _____	SS#: _____
Address: _____	Address: _____
_____	_____
_____	_____

Debtor's Counsel: _____
Address: _____
_____
_____

Telephone #: _____
Facsimile #: _____

ATTACHED TO THIS COVER SHEET IS THE CHAPTER 13 PLAN FILED BY THE DEBTOR(S) IN THIS CASE.   THIS PLAN SETS OUT THE PROPOSED TREATMENT OF THE CLAIMS OF CREDITORS.   THE CLAIMS ARE SET FORTH IN THE BANKRUPTCY SCHEDULES FILED BY DEBTOR(S) WITH THE BANKRUPTCY COURT.

YOU WILL RECEIVE A SEPARATE NOTICE FROM THE BANKRUPTCY COURT OF THE SCHEDULED CREDITORS' MEETING PURSUANT TO 11 U.S.C. § 341.   THAT NOTICE WILL ALSO ESTABLISH THE BAR DATE FOR FILING PROOFS OF CLAIMS.

PURSUANT TO THE MASSACHUSETTS LOCAL BANKRUPTCY RULES, YOU HAVE UNTIL THIRTY (30) DAYS AFTER THE SECTION 341 MEETING TO FILE AN OBJECTION TO CONFIRMATION OF THE CHAPTER 13 PLAN, WHICH OBJECTION MUST BE SERVED ON THE DEBTOR, DEBTOR'S COUNSEL AND THE CHAPTER 13 TRUSTEE.

UNITED STATES BANKRUPTCY COURT
DISTRICT OF MASSACHUSETTS

CHAPTER 13 PLAN

Docket # _____

DEBTORS: (H) _____   SS# _____
(W) _____   SS# _____

TERM OF THE PLAN _____ Months

(If the plan is longer than thirty-six (36) months, a statement of cause pursuant to 11 U.S.C. § 1322(d) must be attached hereto.)

PLAN PAYMENT: Debtor(s) to pay monthly: $ _____

I. SECURED CLAIMS
  A. CLAIMS TO BE PAID THROUGH THE PLAN (INCLUDING AR-REARS):

Creditor	Description of claim (pre-petition arrears, purchase money, etc.)	Amount of claim
_____	_____	$_____
_____	_____	$_____
_____	_____	$_____
		$_____

Total of secured claims to be paid through the Plan $_____

  B. CLAIMS TO BE PAID DIRECTLY TO CREDITORS (Not through Plan):

Creditor	Description of Claim
_____	_____
_____	_____
_____	_____
_____	_____

II. PRIORITY CLAIMS

Creditor	Description of claim	Amount of claim
_____	_____	_____
_____	_____	_____
_____	_____	_____

Total of priority claims to be paid through the plan $ _____

III. ADMINISTRATIVE CLAIMS

A. Attorneys fees (to be paid through the plan): $_____
(to be paid in first 12 months of plan)

B. Miscellaneous fees:

Creditor	Description of claim	Amount of claim
_____	_____	_____
_____	_____	_____

  C. The chapter 13 trustee's fee is determined by order of the United States Attorney General. The calculation of the Plan payment set forth below utilizes a 10% trustee's commission. In the event that the trustee's commission is less than 10%, the additional funds collected by the trustee shall be disbursed to unsecured creditors up to 100% of the allowed claims.

IV. UNSECURED CLAIMS
The general unsecured creditors shall receive a dividend of ___% of their claims.

A. General unsecured claims: $_____

B. Undersecured claims arising after lien avoidance/cramdown:

Creditor	Description of claim	Amount of claim
_____	_____	_____
_____	_____	_____

Total of A + B general unsecured claims: $_____

    C. Multiply total by percentage of dividend: $_____ (Example: Total of $38,500.00 × .22 dividend = $8,470.00)

    D. Separately classified unsecured claims (co-borrower/student loan, etc.):

Creditor	Description of claim	Amount of claim
_____	_____	_____
_____	_____	_____
_____	_____	$_____

Total amount of separately classified
claims payable at _____%: $_____

V. <u>OTHER PROVISIONS</u>

    A. Liquidation of assets to be used to fund plan: _____

    B. Modification of Secured Claims: Set forth details of modifications below or on attached sheets. This information should include name of creditor and detailed explanation of the modification. The total amount of the secured claim that is to be paid through the plan (inclusive of interest) should be set forth in Section I of this Plan.

        _____

        _____

        _____

        _____

    C. Miscellaneous provisions: _____

        _____

        _____

VI. <u>CALCULATION OF PLAN PAYMENT</u>

a. Secured claims (Section I–A Total): $_____

b. Priority claims (Section II Total):   + $_____

c. Administrative claims (Section III A + B Total):   + $_____

d. General unsecured claims (Section IV–C Total):   + $_____

e. Separately classified unsecured claims
      (Section IV–D Total):   + $_____

f. Total of (a) through (e) above: = $_____

g. Divide (f) by .90 for total including
Trustee's fee: Cost of Plan= $_____

(This represents the total amount to be paid into the chapter 13 plan)

h. Divide (g) Cost of Plan by Term of plan: _____ months

i. Round up to nearest dollar: Monthly Plan Payment: $____
                                      (Enter this amount on page 1)

Pursuant to 11 U.S.C. § 1326(a)(1), unless the Court orders otherwise, a debtor shall commence making the payments proposed by a plan within thirty (30) days after the plan is filed.

LIQUIDATION ANALYSIS

I.   Real Estate:

Address   Fair Market Value   Recorded Liens
                                                            (Schedule D)

_____ $_____ $_____
_____ $_____ $_____
_____ $_____ $_____

Total Net Equity for Real Property: $_____
Less Exemptions (Schedule C): $_____
Available Chapter 7: $_____

II.   Automobile (Describe year, make and model):

_____ Value $_____ Lien $_____ Exemption $_____
_____ Value $_____ Lien $_____ Exemption $_____
Net Value of Equity: $_____
Less Exemptions (Schedule C): $_____
Available Chapter 7: $_____
III.   All Other Assets (All remaining items on Schedule B):
(Itemize as necessary)

Value: $_____   Less Exemptions (Schedule C): $_____
                             Available Chapter 7: $_____
SUMMARY (Total amount available under Chapter 7):
Net Equity (I and II) Plus Other Assets (III) less all claimed
exemptions: $_____

Additional Comments regarding Liquidation Analysis:

_____
_____

Pursuant to the Chapter 13 rules, the debtor or his or her counsel is required to
serve a copy of the Amended Plan upon the Chapter 13 trustee, all creditors and
interested parties, and to file a certificate of service accordingly.

_____   _____
Debtor's counsel   Date

Address: _____

_____

_____
Telephone#:_____

I/WE DECLARE UNDER THE PENALTIES OF PERJURY THAT THE FORE-
GOING REPRESENTATIONS OF FACT ARE TRUE AND CORRECT TO THE
BEST OF OUR KNOWLEDGE AND BELIEF.

_____   _____
Debtor   Date

_____   _____
Debtor   Date

Effective August 1, 1997.

OFFICIAL LOCAL FORM 4. ORDER CONFIRMING CHAPTER 13 PLAN

UNITED STATES BANKRUPTCY COURT DISTRICT OF MASSACHUSETTS

```
                              )
In re                         )
                              ) Chapter 13
                              ) Case No.
                              )
                              )
          Debtor              )
                              )
```

ORDER CONFIRMING CHAPTER 13 PLAN

The debtor(s) filed a First Amended Chapter 13 Plan (the "Plan") on _____. The debtor(s) filed a Certificate of Service on _____, reflecting that the Plan was served on all creditors and parties in interest. No objections to the confirmation of the Plan were filed, or all objections were overruled by the Court or resolved by the parties. Upon consideration of the foregoing, the Court hereby orders the following:

1. The Plan is confirmed. The term of the Plan ____ months.

2. The debtor(s) shall pay to the chapter 13 trustee the sum of _____ per month commencing _____ which payments shall continue through completion of the Plan and shall be made on the first day of each month unless otherwise ordered by the Court. Payments shall be made by Money Order or Bank Treasurer's check (personal checks will not be accepted) and shall be made payable to and forwarded to; Chapter 13 Trustee, P.O. Box 8250, Boston, MA 02114 or, if applicable, Chapter 13 Trustee, P.O. Box 16607, Worcester, MA 01601.

3. The effective date of confirmation of the Plan is _____. The disbursements to be made by the chapter 13 trustee pursuant to the confirmed plan are set forth on the attached summary which is incorporated by reference. Interested parties should consult the detailed provisions of the Plan for treatment of their particular claims and other significant provisions of the Plan. Unless otherwise ordered by the court, all property of the estate as defined in 11 U.S.C. §§ 541 and 1306, including, but not limited to, any appreciation in the value of real property owned by the debtor as of the commencement of the case, shall remain property of the estate during the term of the plan and shall vest in the debtor(s) only upon discharge. All property of the estate shall remain within the exclusive jurisdiction of the bankruptcy court. The debtor(s) shall not transfer, sell or otherwise alienate property of the estate other than in accordance with the confirmed plan or other order of the bankruptcy court. The debtor shall be responsible for, preserving and protecting property of the estate.

Dated: _____, 200__

```
_____
United States Bankruptcy Judge
```

SUMMARY OF DISBURSEMENTS TO BE MADE UNDER THE PLAN

A. SECURED CLAIMS

1. Modified Secured Claims

The secured claim of (Creditor) is being modified as follows: (describe modified treatment). The secured creditor is retaining its lien on (describe property) to the following extent: _____. The balance of the claim will be treated as an unsecured claim in the sum of $_____ as set forth below.

2. Unmodified Secured Claims

(Creditor) is retaining its lien on (describe property). The debtor(s) shall continue to make regular monthly payments in accordance with the contract with (creditor). (Creditor) will be paid its prepetition arrearage in the sum of $_____ over _____ months in the sum of $_____ per month.

3. Administrative Claims

(Creditor) will be paid $_____ over _____ months.

4. Priority Claims

   a) Tax Claims

   b) Other

5. Unsecured Claims

6. Other Pertinent Provisions

Effective August 1, 1997. Amended effective September 1, 1999.

OFFICIAL LOCAL FORM 5. ORDER AND NOTICE FIXING DEADLINE FOR FILING PROOFS OF CLAIM IN CHAPTER 11 CASES

UNITED STATES BANKRUPTCY COURT DISTRICT OF MASSACHUSETTS

```
                              )
In re                         )
                              ) Chapter 11
                              ) Case No.
                              )
          Debtor              )
                              )
```

ORDER AND NOTICE FIXING DEADLINE FOR FILING PROOFS OF CLAIM IN CHAPTER 11 CASES

This matter having come before the Court on the Motion for an Order Fixing Deadline for Filing Proofs of Claim (the "Motion"), and good cause having been shown, it is hereby

ORDERED, ADJUDGED and DECREED:

1. Except as provided in paragraphs 2 or 3 below, any individual or entity asserting a claim against the estate of the Debtor must file a proof of claim with the Clerk's Office, United States Bankruptcy Court for the District of Massachusetts, _____ (address) _____, on or before 4:00 p.m. on _____, 200_ (the "Bar Date"). A proof of claim shall not be deemed filed until it is actually received and time stamped by the Clerk of the United States Bankruptcy Court at the above address.

2. No proof of claim shall be required with respect to any claim listed as liquidated, undisputed and not contingent in the Debtor's Schedules of Liabilities filed with this Court on _____, 200_, *provided, however*, that no such claim may be allowed in an amount exceeding the amount as listed unless a proof of claim for a higher amount is filed.

3. Any individual or entity asserting a claim of the type described in 11 U.S.C. § 502(g), (h) or (I) shall file a proof of claim with the Clerk's Office, United States Bankruptcy Court for the District of Massachusetts, at the address specified above by the Bar Date

or, if later, the 30th day after (a) in the case of the claim of the type described in 11 U.S.C. § 502(g), entry of an Order of this Court approving the rejection of the executory contract or unexpired lease giving rise to such claim; (b) in the case of a claim of a type described in 11 U.S.C. § 502(h), entry of an Order or Judgment avoiding such transfer; or (c) in the case of a claim of the type described in 11 U.S.C. § 502(I), the date such type of claim arises.

4. Any claim against the Debtor for which a proof of claim is required, but is not timely filed under the terms of this Order, shall be forever disallowed and barred as a claim against the Debtor whether for purposes of voting, sharing in any distribution, or in any other way participating as a party in interest in this proceeding.

5. The Debtor shall serve a copy of this Order upon all creditors listed in the Schedules, and all parties who filed or entered their appearance in this case, within ten (10) days after the entry of this Order. Service of this Order shall constitute effective notice of the Bar Date. The Debtor shall promptly file a certificate of service with this Court.

Entered at Boston, Massachusetts, this _____ day of _____, 200___.

_____
United States Bankruptcy Judge

Effective August 1, 1997.

OFFICIAL LOCAL FORM 6. REAFFIRMATION AGREEMENT

UNITED STATES BANKRUPTCY COURT
DISTRICT OF MASSACHUSETTS

Debtor's Name   Bankruptcy Case No.
                                          Chapter

Creditor's Name and Address

Instructions: 1) Attach a copy of all court judgments, security agreements and evidence of their perfection.
                     2) File all the documents by mailing them or delivering them to the Clerk of the Bankruptcy Court.

NOTICE TO DEBTOR

This agreement gives up the protection of your bankruptcy discharge for this debt.

As a result of this agreement, the creditor may be able to take your property or wages if you do not pay the agreed amounts. The creditor may also act to collect the debt in other ways.

You may rescind (cancel) this agreement at any time before the bankruptcy court enters a discharge order or within 60 days after this agreement is filed with the court, whichever is later, by notifying the creditor that the agreement is canceled.

<u>You are not required to enter into this agreement by any law.</u> It is not required by the Bankruptcy Code, by any other law, or by any contract (except another reaffirmation agreement made in accordance with Bankruptcy Code § 524(c)).

<u>You are allowed to pay this debt without signing this agreement.</u> However, if you do not sign this agreement and are later unwilling or unable to pay the full amount, the creditor will not be able to collect it from you. The creditor also will not be allowed to take your property to pay the debt unless the creditor has a lien on that property.

If the creditor has a lien on your personal property you may have a right to <u>redeem</u> the property and eliminate the lien by making a single payment to the creditor equal to the current value of the property, as agreed by the parties or determined by the court.

This agreement is not valid or binding unless it is filed with clerk of the bankruptcy court. If you were not represented by an attorney during the negotiation of this reaffirmation agreement, the agreement cannot be enforced by the creditor unless 1) you have attended a reaffirmation hearing in the bankruptcy court, and 2) the agreement has been approved by the bankruptcy court. (Court approval is not required if this is a consumer debt secured by a mortgage or other lien on your real estate.)

REAFFIRMATION AGREEMENT

The debtor and the creditor named above agree to reaffirm the debt described in this agreement as follows.

THE DEBT

Total Amount of Debt When Case Was Filed		$_____
Total Amount of Debt Reaffirmed	$_____	
Above total includes the following:		
Interest Accrued to Date of Agreement	$_____	
Attorney Fees	$_____	
Late Fees	$_____	
Other Expenses or Costs Relating to the Collection of		
this Debt	$_____	
(Describe)		
Annual Percentage Rate (APR)	_____%	
Amount of Monthly Payment	$_____	
Date Payments Start	_____	
Total Number of Payments to be made	_____	
Total of Payments if paid according to schedule	_____	
Date Any Lien Is to Be Released if paid according to		
schedule	_____	

The debtor agrees that any and all remedies available to the creditor under the security agreement remain available.

All additional Terms Agreed to by the Parties (if any):

_____

_____.

Payments on this debt [were] [were not] in default on the date on which this bankruptcy case was filed. This agreement differs from the original agreement with the creditor as follows:

_____

_____

_____.

CREDITOR'S STATEMENT CONCERNING AGREEMENT
AND SECURITY/COLLATERAL (IF ANY)

Description of Collateral. If applicable, list manufacturer, year and model. _____
_____.

Value $_____

Basis or Source for Valuation _____

Current Location and Use of Collateral _____

Expected Future Use of Collateral _____

Check Applicable Boxes:

☐ Any lien described herein is valid and perfected.

☐ This agreement is part of a settlement of a dispute regarding the dischargeability of this debt under section 523 of the Bankruptcy Code (11 U.S.C. § 523) or any other dispute. The nature of dispute is _____
_____.

DEBTOR'S STATEMENT OF EFFECT OF AGREEMENT
ON DEBTOR'S FINANCES

My monthly income (take home pay plus any other income received) is $_____.

My current monthly expenses total $_____, not including any payment due under this agreement or any debt to be discharged in this bankruptcy case.

I believe this agreement [will] [will not] impose an undue hardship on me or my dependents.

DEBTOR'S STATEMENT CONCERNING DECISION TO REAFFIRM

I agreed to reaffirm this debt because _____
_____
_____.

I believe this agreement is in my best interest because _____
_____
_____.

I [considered] [did not consider] redeeming the collateral under section 722 of the Bankruptcy Code (11 U.S.C. § 722). I chose not to redeem because _____
_____
_____.

I [was] [was not] represented by an attorney during negotiations on this agreement.

CERTIFICATION OF ATTACHMENTS

Any documents which created and perfected the security interest or lien [are] [are not] a attached. [*If documents are not attached*: The documents which created and perfected the security interest or lien are not attached because _____
_____.]

SIGNATURES

_____   _____
(Signature of Debtor)   (Name of Creditor)

Date _____
                                         _____
                                         (Signature of Creditor
                                         Representative)

Date _____
                                         _____
                                         (Signature of Joint Debtor)

Date _____

CERTIFICATION BY DEBTOR'S ATTORNEY (IF ANY)

I certify that 1) this agreement represents a fully informed and voluntary agreement by the debtor(s); 2) this agreement does not impose a hardship on the debtor or any dependent of the debtor; and 3) I have fully advised the debtor of the legal effect and consequences of this agreement and any default under this agreement.

Date _____
                                         _____
                                         (Signature of Debtor's Attorney, if any)

Effective September 1, 1999.

OFFICIAL LOCAL FORM 7.   DECLARATION RE: ELECTRONIC FILING

UNITED STATES BANKRUPTCY COURT
DISTRICT OF MASSACHUSETTS

In re   )
)   Chapter
)   Case No.
)
)
      Debtor(s)   )
)

DECLARATION RE: ELECTRONIC FILING

PART I—DECLARATION

I[We] _____ and _____, _hereby declare(s) under penalty of perjury_ that all of the information contained in my _____ (singly or jointly the "Document"), filed electronically, is true and correct. I understand that this _DECLARATION_ is to be filed with the Clerk of Court electronically concurrently with the electronic filing of the Document. I understand that failure to file this _DECLARATION_ may cause the Document to be struck and any request contained or relying thereon to be denied, without further notice.

I further understand that pursuant to the Massachusetts Electronic Filing Local Rule (MEFR) 7(b) all paper documents containing original signatures executed under the penalties of perjury and filed electronically with the Court are the property of the bankruptcy estate and shall be maintained by the authorized CM/ECF Registered User for a period of five (5) years after the closing of this case.

Dated:

Signed: _____
                (Affiant)

Signed: _____
                (Joint Affiant)

PART II—DECLARATION OF ATTORNEY (IF AFFIANT IS REPRESENTED BY COUNSEL)

I certify that the affiant(s) signed this form before I submitted the Document, I gave the affiant(s) a copy of the Document and this *DECLARATION*, and I have followed all other electronic filing requirements currently established by local rule and standing order. This *DECLARATION* is based on all information of which I have knowledge and my signature below constitutes my certification of the foregoing under Fed.R.Bankr.P. 9011. I have reviewed and will comply with the provisions of MEFR 7.

Dated:

Signed: _____
                Attorney for Affiant

Effective March 1, 2003; amended effective January 1, 2005.

OFFICIAL LOCAL FORM 8. CHAPTER 13 AGREEMENT BETWEEN DEBTOR AND COUNSEL—RIGHTS AND RESPONSIBILITIES OF CHAPTER 13 DEBTORS AND THEIR ATTORNEYS

UNITED STATES BANKRUPTCY COURT
FOR THE DISTRICT OF MASSACHUSETTS

In re   )   Chapter
)   Case No.
)
)
Debtor(s)   )
)

CHAPTER 13 AGREEMENT BETWEEN DEBTOR AND COUNSEL
RIGHTS AND RESPONSIBILITIES OF CHAPTER 13 DEBTORS
AND THEIR ATTORNEYS

It is important for debtors who file bankruptcy cases under Chapter 13 to understand their rights and responsibilities. It is also useful for debtors to know what their attorney's responsibilities are, and understand the importance of communicating with their attorney to make the case successful. Debtors should also know that they may expect certain services to be performed by their attorney. To encourage that debtors and their attorneys understand their rights and responsibilities in the bankruptcy process, the following terms are agreed to by the debtors and their attorneys.

BEFORE THE CASE IS FILED:

The DEBTOR agrees to:

1. Provide the attorney with accurate financial information; and

2. Discuss with the attorney the debtor's objectives in filing the case.

The ATTORNEY agrees to:

1. Meet with the debtor to review the debtor's debts, assets, income and expenses;

2. Counsel the debtor regarding the advisability of filing either a Chapter 7 or Chapter 13 case, discuss both procedures with the debtor, and answer the debtor's questions;

3. Explain what payments will be make through the plan, and what payments will be made directly by the debtor for mortgage and vehicle loan payments, as well as which claims accrue interest;

4. Explain to the debtor how, when, and where to make the Chapter 13 plan payments, as well as the debtor's obligation to continue making mortgage payments, without interruption, and the likely consequences for failure to do so;

5. Explain to the debtor how the attorney's fees and trustee's fees are paid, and provide an executed copy of this document to the debtor;

6. Explain to the debtor that the first plan payment must be made to the Trustee within 30 days of the date the plan is filed;

7. Advise the debtor of the requirement to attend the 341 Meeting of Creditors, and instruct debtor as to the date, time and place of the meeting;

8. Advise the debtor of the necessity of maintaining appropriate insurance on all real estate, motor vehicle and business assets; and

9. Timely prepare and file the debtor's petition, plan and schedules.

AFTER THE CASE IS FILED:

The DEBTOR agrees to:

1. Keep the Trustee and attorney informed for the debtor's address and telephone number;

2. Inform the attorney of any wage garnishments or attachments of assets which occur or continue after the filing of the case;

3. Contact the attorney if the debtor loses his/her job or has other financial problems (the attorney may be able to have the Chapter 13 plan payments reduced or suspended in those circumstances), or alternatively obtains a material increase in income or assets;

4. Advise counsel if the debtor is sued during the case;

5. Inform the attorney if tax refunds to which the debtor is entitled are seized or not received;

6. Advise counsel and the Trustee before buying or selling property or before entering into any long-term loan agreements, to determine what approvals are required;

7. Provide the Trustee and the attorney, prior to the Section 341 meeting of creditors, with documentary evidence as the debtor's income from all sources and the value of any asset in which the debtor has an interest, together with a copy of any declaration of homestead covering the debtor's real estate, proof of insurance on any real property or automobiles in which the debtor has an interest, and any other documents which the Trustee might reasonably request in order to assess whether the debtor's proposed plan should be confirmed.

The ATTORNEY agrees to provide the following legal services in consideration of the compensation further described below:

1. Appear at the 341 Meeting of Creditors with the debtor;

2. Respond to objections to plan confirmation, and where necessary, prepare an amended plan;

3. Prepare, file and serve one necessary modification to the plan which may include suspending, lowering, or increasing plan payments;

4. Prepare, file and serve necessary amended schedules in accordance with information provided by the debtor;

5. Prepare, file and serve necessary motions to buy, sell or refinance real property;

6. Object to improper or invalid claims, if necessary, based upon documentation provided by the debtor;

7. Represent the debtor in motions for relief from stay;

8. Where appropriate, prepare, file and serve necessary motions to avoid liens on real or personal property; and

9. Provide such other legal services as necessary for the administration of the case.

The initial fees charged in this case are $_____. Any and all additional terms of compensation and additional services agreed to be rendered, if any, are set for the in writing and annexed hereto. If the initial fees are not sufficient to compensate the attorney for the legal services rendered in this case, the attorney further agrees to apply to the court for additional fees. If the debtor disputes the legal services provided or the fees charged by the attorney, an objection may be filed with the court and the matter set for hearing.

Debtor signature: _____ Dated:_____

Co–debtor signature: _____ Dated:_____

Attorney for the debt-   _____ Dated:_____
or(s) signature:

Effective March 1, 2003.

RULES OF PROCEDURE OF THE JUDICIAL PANEL ON MULTIDISTRICT LITIGATION

Effective July 1, 1993

Renumbered and Amended Effective November 2, 1998

Including Amendments Effective April 2, 2001

Research Note

Use WESTLAW ® *to find cases citing a rule. In addition, use* WESTLAW *to search for specific terms or to update a rule; see the US–RULES and US–ORDERS Scope Screens for further information.*

Amendments to Rules of Procedure of the Judicial Panel on Multidistrict Litigation are published, as received, in Federal Reporter 3d, Federal Supplement 2d *and* Federal Rules Decisions *advance sheets.*

Table of Rules

I. GENERAL RULES/RULES FOR MULTIDISTRICT LITIGATION UNDER 28 U.S.C. § 1407

RULE 1.1 DEFINITIONS

As used in these Rules "Panel" means the members of the Judicial Panel on Multidistrict Litigation appointed by the Chief Justice of the United States pursuant to Section 1407, Title 28, United States Code.

"Clerk of the Panel" means the official appointed by the Panel to act as Clerk of the Panel and shall include those deputized by the Clerk of the Panel to perform or assist in the performance of the duties of the Clerk of the Panel.

"Chairman" means the Chairman of the Judicial Panel on Multidistrict Litigation appointed by the Chief Justice of the United States pursuant to Section 1407, or the member of the Panel designated by the Panel to act as Chairman in the absence or inability of the appointed Chairman.

A "tag-along action" refers to a civil action pending in a district court and involving common questions of fact with actions previously transferred under Section 1407.

Former Rule 1 adopted May 3, 1993, effective July 1, 1993; renumbered Rule 1.1 September 1, 1998, effective November 2, 1998.

RULE 1.2 PRACTICE

Where not fixed by statute or rule, the practice shall be that heretofore customarily followed by the Panel.

Former Rule 5 adopted May 3, 1993, effective July 1, 1993; renumbered Rule 1.2 September 1, 1998, effective November 2, 1998.

RULE 1.3 FAILURE TO COMPLY WITH RULES

The Clerk of the Panel may, when a paper submitted for filing is not in compliance with the provisions of these Rules, advise counsel of the deficiencies and a date for full compliance. If full compliance is not accomplished within the established time, the non-complying paper shall nonetheless be filed by the Clerk of the Panel but it may be stricken by order of the Chairman of the Panel.

Former Rule 4 adopted May 3, 1993, effective July 1, 1993; renumbered Rule 1.3 and amended September 1, 1998, effective November 2, 1998.

RULE 1.4 ADMISSION TO PRACTICE BEFORE THE PANEL AND REPRESENTATION IN TRANSFERRED ACTIONS

Every member in good standing of the Bar of any district court of the United States is entitled without condition to practice before the Judicial Panel on Multidistrict Litigation. Any attorney of record in any action transferred under Section 1407 may continue to represent his or her client in any district court of the United States to which such action is transferred. Parties to any action transferred under Section 1407 are not required to obtain local counsel in the district to which such action is transferred.

Former Rule 6 adopted May 3, 1993, effective July 1, 1993; renumbered Rule 1.4 September 1, 1998, effective November 2, 1998.

RULE 1.5 EFFECT OF THE PENDENCY OF AN ACTION BEFORE THE PANEL

The pendency of a motion, order to show cause, conditional transfer order or conditional remand order before the Panel concerning transfer or remand of an action pursuant to 28 U.S.C. § 1407 does not affect or suspend orders and pretrial proceedings in the district court in which the action is pending and does not in any way limit the pretrial jurisdiction of that court. A transfer or remand pursuant to 28 U.S.C. § 1407 shall be effective when the transfer or remand order is filed in the office of the clerk of the district court of the transferee district.

Former Rule 18 adopted May 3, 1993, effective July 1, 1993; renumbered Rule 1.5 September 1, 1998, effective November 2, 1998.

RULE 1.6 TRANSFER OF FILES

(a) Upon receipt of a certified copy of a transfer order from the clerk of the transferee district court, the clerk of the transferor district court shall forward to the clerk of the transferee district court the complete original file and a certified copy of the docket sheet for each transferred action.

(b) If an appeal is pending, or a notice of appeal has been filed, or leave to appeal has been sought under 28 U.S.C. § 1292(b) or a petition for an extraordinary writ is pending, in any action included in an order of transfer under 28 U.S.C. § 1407, and the original file or parts thereof have been forwarded to the court of appeals, the clerk of the transferor district court shall notify the clerk of the court of appeals of the order of transfer and secure the original file long enough to prepare and transmit to the clerk of the transferee district court a certified copy of all papers contained in the original file and a certified copy of the docket sheet.

(c) If the transfer order provides for the separation and simultaneous remand of any claim, cross-claim, counterclaim, or third-party claim, the clerk of the transferor district court shall retain the original file and shall prepare and transmit to the clerk of the transferee district court a certified copy of the docket sheet and copies of all papers except those relating exclusively to separated and remanded claims.

(d) Upon receipt of an order to remand from the Clerk of the Panel, the transferee district court shall prepare and send to the clerk of the transferor district court the following:

(i) a certified copy of the individual docket sheet for each action being remanded;

(ii) a certified copy of the master docket sheet, if applicable;

(iii) the entire file for each action being remanded, as originally received from the transferor district court and augmented as set out in this rule;

(iv) a certified copy of the final pretrial order, if applicable; and

(v) a "record on remand" to be composed of those parts of the files and records produced during coordinated or consolidated pretrial proceedings which have been stipulated to or designated by counsel as being necessary for any or all proceedings to be conducted following remand. It shall be the responsibility of counsel originally preparing or filing any document to be included in the "record on remand" to furnish on request sufficient copies to the clerk of the transferee district court.

(e) The Clerk of the Panel shall be notified when any files have been transmitted pursuant to this Rule.

Former Rule 19 adopted May 3, 1993, effective July 1, 1993; renumbered Rule 1.6 and amended September 1, 1998, effective November 2, 1998.

RULE 5.1   KEEPING RECORDS AND FILES

(a) The records and files of the Panel shall be kept by the Clerk of the Panel at the offices of the Panel. Records and files may be temporarily or permanently removed to such places at such times as the Panel or the Chairman of the Panel shall direct. The Clerk of the Panel may charge fees, as prescribed by the Judicial Conference of the United States, for duplicating records and files. Records and files may be transferred whenever appropriate to the Federal Records Center.

(b) In order to assist the Panel in carrying out its functions, the Clerk of the Panel shall obtain the complaints and docket sheets in all actions under consideration for transfer under 28 U.S.C. § 1407 from the clerk of each district court wherein such actions are pending. The Clerk of the Panel shall similarly obtain any other pleadings and orders that could affect the Panel's decision under 28 U.S.C. § 1407.

Former Rule 2 adopted May 3, 1993, effective July 1, 1993; renumbered Rule 5.1 and amended September 1, 1998, effective November 2, 1998.

RULE 5.11   PLACE OF FILING OF PAPERS

All papers for consideration by the Panel shall be submitted for filing to the Clerk of the Panel by mailing or delivering to:

Clerk of the Panel
Judicial Panel on Multidistrict Litigation
Thurgood Marshall Federal Judiciary Building
One Columbus Circle, N.E., Room G–255, North Lobby
Washington, D.C. 20002–8004

No papers shall be left with or mailed to a Judge of the panel.

Former Rule 3 adopted May 3, 1993, effective July 1, 1993; renumbered Rule 5.11 and amended September 1, 1998, effective November 2, 1998.

RULE 5.12   MANNER OF FILING OF PAPERS

(a) An original of the following papers shall be submitted for filing to the Clerk of the Panel: a proof of service pursuant to Rule 5.2(a) and (b) of these Rules, a notice of appearance pursuant to Rule 5.2(c) and (d) of these Rules, a corporate disclosure statement pursuant to Rule 5.3 of these Rules, a status notice pursuant to Rules 7.2(f), 7.3(e) and 7.4(b) of these Rules, a notice of opposition pursuant to Rules 7.4(c) and 7.6(f)(ii) of these Rules, a notice of related action pursuant to Rules 7.2(i), 7.3(a) and 7.5(e) of these Rules, an application for extension of time pursuant to Rule 6.2 of these Rules, or a notice of presentation or waiver of oral argument pursuant to Rule 16.1(d) of these Rules. An original and eleven copies of all other papers shall be submitted for filing to the Clerk of the Panel. The Clerk of the Panel may require that additional copies also be submitted for filing.

(b) When papers are submitted for filing, the Clerk of the Panel shall endorse thereon the date for filing.

(c) Copies of motions for transfer of an action or actions pursuant to 28 U.S.C. § 1407 shall be filed in each district court in which an action is pending that will be affected by the motion. Copies of a motion for remand pursuant to 28 U.S.C. § 1407 shall be filed in the Section 1407 transferee district court in which any action affected by the motion is pending.

(d) Papers requiring only an original may be faxed to the Panel office with prior approval of the Clerk of the Panel. No papers requiring multiple copies shall be accepted via fax.

Former Rule 7 adopted May 3, 1993, effective July 1, 1993; renumbered Rule 5.12 and amended September 1, 1998, effective November 2, 1998; amended effective April 2, 2001.

RULE 5.13 FILING OF PAPERS: COMPUTER GENERATED DISK REQUIRED

(a) Whenever an original paper and eleven copies is required to be submitted for filing to the Clerk of the Panel pursuant to Rule 5.12(a) of these Rules, and where a party is represented by counsel, one copy of that paper must also be submitted on a computer readable disk and shall be filed at the time the party's paper is filed. The disk shall contain the entire paper exclusive of computer non-generated exhibits. The label of the disk shall include i) "MDL #___," ii) an abbreviated version of the MDL descriptive title, or other appropriate descriptive title, if not yet designated by the Panel, iii) the identity of the type of paper being filed (i.e. motion, response, reply, etc.), iv) the name of the counsel who signed the paper, and v) the first named represented party on the paper.

(b) The paper must be on a 3½ inch disk in Word-Perfect for Windows format.

(c) One copy of the disk may be served on each party separately represented by counsel. If a party chooses to serve a copy of the disk, the proof of service, as required by Rule 5.2 of these Rules, must indicate service of the paper in both paper and electronic format.

(d) A party may be relieved from the requirements of this Rule by submitting a written application for a waiver, in a timely manner in advance of submission of the paper, certifying that compliance with the Rule would impose undue hardship, that the text of the paper is not available on disk, or that other unusual circumstances preclude compliance with this Rule. The requirements of this Rule shall not apply to parties appearing pro se. Papers embraced by this Rule and submitted by counsel after June 1, 2000 without a computer disk copy or Panel-approved waiver of the requirements of this Rule shall be governed by Rule 1.3 of these Rules.

Effective June 1, 2000.

RULE 5.2 SERVICE OF PAPERS FILED

(a) All papers filed with the Clerk of the Panel shall be accompanied by proof of previous or simultaneous service on all other parties in all actions involved in the litigation. Service and proof of service shall be made as provided in Rules 5 and 6 of the Federal Rules of Civil Procedure. The proof of service shall indicate the name and complete address of each person served and shall indicate the party represented by each. If a party is not represented by counsel, the proof of service shall indicate the name of the party and the party's last known address. The proof of service shall indicate why any person named as a party in a constituent complaint was not served with the Section 1407 pleading. The original proof of service shall be filed with the Clerk of the Panel and copies thereof shall be sent to each person included within the proof of service. After the "Panel Service List" described in subsection (d) of this Rule has been received from the Clerk of the Panel, the "Panel Service List" shall be utilized for service of responses to motions and all other filings. In such instances, the "Panel Service List" shall be attached to the proof of service and shall be supplemented in the proof of service in the event of the presence of additional parties or subsequent corrections relating to any party, counsel or address already on the "Panel Service List."

(b) The proof of service pertaining to motions for transfer of actions pursuant to 28 U.S.C. § 1407 shall certify that copies of the motions have been mailed or otherwise delivered for filing to the clerk of each district court in which an action is pending that will be affected by the motion. The proof of service pertaining to a motion for remand pursuant to 28 U.S.C. § 1407 shall certify that a copy of the motion has been mailed or otherwise delivered for filing to the clerk of the Section 1407 transferee district court in which any action affected by the motion is pending.

(c) Within eleven days of filing of a motion to transfer, an order to show cause or a conditional transfer order, each party or designated attorney shall notify the Clerk of the Panel, in writing, of the name and address of the attorney designated to receive service of all pleadings, notices, orders and other papers relating to practice before the Judicial Panel on Multidistrict Litigation. Only one attorney shall be designated for each party. Any party not represented by counsel shall be served by mailing such pleadings to the party's last known address. Requests for an extension of time to file the designation of attorney shall not be granted except in extraordinary circumstances.

(d) In order to facilitate compliance with subsection (a) of this Rule, the Clerk of the Panel shall prepare and serve on all counsel and parties not represented by counsel, a "Panel Service List" containing the names and addresses of the designated attorneys and the party or parties they represent in the actions under consideration by the Panel and the names and addresses of the parties not represented by counsel in the actions under consideration by the Panel. After the "Panel Service List" has been received from the Clerk of the Panel, notice of subsequent corrections relating to any party, counsel or address on the "Panel Service List" shall be served on all other parties in all actions involved in the litigation.

(e) If following transfer of any group of multidistrict litigation, the transferee district court appoints liaison counsel, this Rule shall be satisfied by serving each party in each affected action and all liaison counsel. Liaison counsel designated by the transferee district court shall receive copies of all Panel orders concerning their particular litigation and shall be responsible for distribution to the parties for whom he or she serves as liaison counsel.

Former Rule 8 adopted May 3, 1993, effective July 1, 1993; renumbered Rule 5.2 and amended September 1, 1998, effective November 2, 1998.

RULE 5.3   CORPORATE DISCLOSURE STATEMENT

(a) Any nongovernmental corporate party to a matter before the Panel shall file a statement identifying all its parent corporations and listing any publicly held company that owns 10% or more of the party's stock.

(b) A party shall file the corporate disclosure statement within eleven days of the filing of a motion to transfer or remand, an order to show cause, or a motion to vacate a conditional transfer order or a conditional remand order.

(c) Once a corporate disclosure statement by a party has been filed in an MDL docket pursuant to subsection (b) of this Rule, such a party is required to update the statement to reflect any change in the information therein i) until the matter before the Panel is decided, and ii) within eleven days of the filing of any subsequent motion to transfer or remand, order to show cause, or motion to vacate a conditional transfer order or a conditional remand order in that docket.

Effective April 2, 2001.

RULE 6.2   APPLICATIONS FOR EXTENSIONS OF TIME

Any application for an extension of time to file a pleading or perform an act required by these Rules must be in writing, must request a specific number of additional days and may be acted upon by the Clerk of the Panel. Such an application will be evaluated in relation to the impact on the Panel's calendar as well as on the basis of the reasons set forth in support of the application. Any party aggrieved by the Clerk of the Panel's action on such application may submit its objections to the Panel for consideration. Absent exceptional circumstances, no extensions of time shall be granted to file a notice of opposition to either a conditional transfer order or a conditional remand order. All applications for extensions of time shall be filed and served in conformity with Rules 5.12, 5.2 and 7.1 of these Rules.

Former Rule 15 adopted May 3, 1993, effective July 1, 1993; renumbered Rule 6.2 and amended September 1, 1998, effective November 2, 1998.

RULE 7.1   FORM OF PAPERS FILED

(a) Averments in any motion seeking action by the Panel shall be made in numbered paragraphs, each of which shall be limited, as far as practicable, to a statement of a single factual averment.

(b) Responses to averments in motions shall be made in numbered paragraphs, each of which shall correspond to the number of the paragraph of the motion to which the responsive paragraph is directed. Each responsive paragraph shall admit or deny wholly or in part the averment of the motion, and shall contain the respondent's version of the subject matter when the averment or the motion is not wholly admitted.

(c) Each pleading filed shall be:

(i) flat and unfolded;

(ii) plainly written, typed in double space, printed or prepared by means of a duplicating process, without erasures or interlineations which materially deface it;

(iii) on opaque, unglazed, white paper (not onionskin);

(iv) approximately 8–1/2 x 11 inches in size; and

(v) fastened at the top-left corner without side binding or front or back covers.

(d) The heading on the first page of each pleading shall commence not less than three inches from the top of the page. Each pleading shall bear the heading "Before the Judicial Panel on Multidistrict Litigation," the identification "MDL Docket No.___" and the descriptive title designated by the Panel for the litigation involved. If the Panel has not yet designated a title, an appropriate descriptive title shall be used.

(e) The final page of each pleading shall contain the name, address and telephone number of the attorney or party in active charge of the case. Each attorney shall also include the name of each party represented.

(f) Except with the approval of the Panel, each brief submitted for filing with the Panel shall be limited to twenty pages, exclusive of exhibits. Absent exceptional circumstances, motions to exceed page limits shall not be granted.

(g) Exhibits exceeding a cumulative total of 50 pages shall be fastened separately from the accompanying pleading.

(h) Proposed Panel orders shall not be submitted with papers for filing.

Former Rule 9 adopted May 3, 1993, effective July 1, 1993; renumbered Rule 7.1 and amended September 1, 1998, effective November 2, 1998; amended effective April 2, 2001.

RULE 7.2 MOTION PRACTICE

(a) All requests for action by the Panel under 28 U.S.C. § 1407 shall be made by written motion. Every motion shall be accompanied by:

(i) a brief in support thereof in which the background of the litigation and factual and legal contentions of the movant shall be concisely stated in separate portions of the brief with citation of applicable authorities; and

(ii) a schedule giving

(A) the complete name of each action involved, listing the full name of each party included as such on the district court's docket sheet, not shortened by the use of references such as "et al." or "etc.";

(B) the district court and division in which each action is pending;

(C) the civil action number of each action; and

(D) the name of the judge assigned each action, if known.

(b) The Clerk of the Panel shall notify recipients of a motion of the filing date, caption, MDL docket number, briefing schedule and pertinent Panel policies.

(c) Within twenty days after filing of a motion, all other parties shall file a response thereto. Failure of a party to respond to a motion shall be treated as that party's acquiescence to the action requested in the motion.

(d) The movant may, within five days after the lapse of the time period for filing responsive briefs, file a single brief in reply to any opposition.

(e) Motions, their accompaniments, responses, and replies shall also be governed by Rules 5.12, 5.2 and 7.1 of these Rules.

(f) With respect to any action that is the subject of Panel consideration, counsel shall promptly notify the Clerk of the Panel of any development that would partially or completely moot the matter before the Panel.

(g) A joinder in a motion shall not add any action to the previous motion.

(h) Once a motion is filed, any other pleading that purports to be a "motion" in the docket shall be filed by the Clerk of the Panel as a response unless the "motion" adds an action. The Clerk of the Panel, upon designating such a pleading as a motion, shall acknowledge that designation by the distribution of a briefing schedule to all parties in the docket. Response time resulting from an additional motion shall ordinarily be extended only to those parties directly affected by the additional motion. An accelerated briefing schedule for the additional motion may be set by the Clerk of the Panel to conform with the hearing session schedule established by the Chairman.

(i) Any party or counsel in a new group of actions under consideration by the Panel for transfer under Section 1407 shall promptly notify the Clerk of the Panel of any potential tag-along action in which that party is also named or in which that counsel appears.

Former Rule 10 adopted May 3, 1993, effective July 1, 1993; renumbered Rule 7.2 and amended September 1, 1998, effective November 2, 1998; amended effective April 2, 2001.

RULE 7.3 SHOW CAUSE ORDERS

(a) When transfer of multidistrict litigation is being considered on the initiative of the Panel pursuant to 28 U.S.C. § 1407(c)(i), an order shall be filed by the Clerk of the Panel directing the parties to show cause why the action or actions should not be transferred for coordinated or consolidated pretrial proceedings. Any party or counsel in such actions shall promptly notify the Clerk of the Panel of any other federal district court actions related to the litigation encompassed by the show cause order. Such notification shall be made for additional actions pending at the time of the issuance of the show cause order and whenever new actions are filed.

(b) Any party may file a response to the show cause order within twenty days of the filing of said order unless otherwise provided for in the order. Failure of a party to respond to a show cause order shall be treated as that party's acquiescence to the Panel action contemplated in the order.

(c) Within five days after the lapse of the time period for filing a response, any party may file a reply limited to new matters.

(d) Responses and replies shall be filed and served in conformity with Rules 5.12, 5.2 and 7.1 of these Rules.

(e) With respect to any action that is the subject of Panel consideration, counsel shall promptly notify the Clerk of the Panel of any development that would partially or completely moot the matter before the Panel.

Former Rule 11 adopted May 3, 1993, effective July 1, 1993; renumbered Rule 7.3 and amended September 1, 1998, effective November 2, 1998.

RULE 7.4 CONDITIONAL TRANSFER ORDERS FOR "TAG–ALONG ACTIONS"

(a) Upon learning of the pendency of a potential "tag-along action," as defined in Rule 1.1 of these Rules, an order may be entered by the Clerk of the Panel transferring that action to the previously designated transferee district court on the basis of the prior hearing session(s) and for the reasons expressed in previous opinions and orders of the Panel in the litigation. The Clerk of the Panel shall serve this order on each party to the litigation but, in order to afford all parties the opportunity to oppose transfer, shall not send the order to the clerk of the transferee district court for fifteen days from the entry thereof.

(b) Parties to an action subject to a conditional transfer order shall notify the Clerk of the Panel within the fifteen-day period if that action is no longer pending in its transferor district court.

(c) Any party opposing the transfer shall file a notice of opposition with the Clerk of the Panel within the fifteen-day period. If a notice of opposition is received by the Clerk of the Panel within this fifteen-day period, the Clerk of the Panel shall not transmit said order to the clerk of the transferee district court until further order of the Panel. The Clerk of the Panel shall notify the parties of the briefing schedule.

(d) Within fifteen days of the filing of its notice of opposition, the party opposing transfer shall file a motion to vacate the conditional transfer order and brief in support thereof. The Chairman of the Panel shall set the motion for the next appropriate hearing session of the Panel. Failure to file and serve a motion and brief shall be treated as withdrawal of the opposition and the Clerk of the Panel shall forthwith transmit the order to the clerk of the transferee district court.

(e) Conditional transfer orders do not become effective unless and until they are filed with the clerk of the transferee district court.

(f) Notices of opposition and motions to vacate such orders of the Panel and responses thereto shall be governed by Rules 5.12, 5.2, 7.1 and 7.2 of these Rules.

Former Rule 12 adopted May 3, 1993, effective July 1, 1993; renumbered Rule 7.4 and amended September 1, 1998, effective November 2, 1998; amended effective April 2, 2001.

RULE 7.5   MISCELLANEOUS PROVISIONS CONCERNING "TAG–ALONG ACTIONS"

(a) Potential "tag-along actions" filed in the transferee district require no action on the part of the Panel and requests for assignment of such actions to the Section 1407 transferee judge should be made in accordance with local rules for the assignment of related actions.

(b) Upon learning of the pendency of a potential "tag-along action" and having reasonable anticipation of opposition to transfer of that action, the Panel may direct the Clerk of the Panel to file a show cause order, in accordance with Rule 7.3 of these Rules, instead of a conditional transfer order.

(c) Failure to serve one or more of the defendants in a potential "tag-along action" with the complaint and summons as required by Rule 4 of the Federal Rules of Civil Procedure does not preclude transfer of such action under Section 1407. Such failure, however, may be submitted by such a defendant as a basis for

opposing the proposed transfer if prejudice can be shown. The inability of the Clerk of the Panel to serve a conditional transfer order on all plaintiffs or defendants or their counsel shall not render the transfer of the action void but can be submitted by such a party as a basis for moving to remand as to such party if prejudice can be shown.

(d) A civil action apparently involving common questions of fact with actions under consideration by the Panel for transfer under Section 1407, which was either not included in a motion under Rule 7.2 of these Rules, or was included in such a motion that was filed too late to be included in the initial hearing session, will ordinarily be treated by the Panel as a potential "tag-along action."

(e) Any party or counsel in actions previously transferred under Section 1407 or under consideration by the Panel for transfer under Section 1407 shall promptly notify the Clerk of the Panel of any potential "tag-along actions" in which that party is also named or in which that counsel appears.

Former Rule 13 adopted May 3, 1993, effective July 1, 1993; renumbered Rule 7.5 and amended September 1, 1998, effective November 2, 1998; amended effective April 2, 2001.

RULE 7.6   TERMINATION AND REMAND

In the absence of unusual circumstances—

(a) Actions terminated in the transferee district court by valid judgment, including but not limited to summary judgment, judgment of dismissal and judgment upon stipulation, shall not be remanded by the Panel and shall be dismissed by the transferee district court. The clerk of the transferee district court shall send a copy of the order terminating the action to the Clerk of the Panel but shall retain the original files and records unless otherwise directed by the transferee judge or by the Panel.

(b) Each action transferred only for coordinated or consolidated pretrial proceedings that has not been terminated in the transferor district court shall be remanded by the Panel to the transferor district for trial. Actions that were originally filed in the transferee district require no action by the Panel to be reassigned to another judge in the transferee district at the conclusion of the coordinated or consolidated pretrial proceedings affecting those actions.

(c) The Panel shall consider remand of each transferred action or any separable claim, cross-claim, counterclaim or third-party claim at or before the conclusion of coordinated or consolidated pretrial proceedings on

(i) motion of any party,

(ii) suggestion of the transferee district court, or

(iii) the Panel's own initiative, by entry of an order to show cause, a conditional remand order or other appropriate order.

(d) The Panel is reluctant to order remand absent a suggestion of remand from the transferee district court. If remand is sought by motion of a party, the motion shall be accompanied by:

(i) an affidavit reciting

(A) whether the movant has requested a suggestion of remand from the transferee district court, how the court responded to any request, and, if no such request was made, why;

(B) whether all common discovery and other pretrial proceedings have been completed in the action sought to be remanded, and if not, what remains to be done; and

(C) whether all orders of the transferee district court have been satisfactorily complied with, and if not, what remains to be done; and

(ii) a copy of the transferee district court's final pretrial order, where such order has been entered.

Motions to remand and responses thereto shall be governed by Rules 5.12, 5.2, 7.1 and 7.2 of these Rules.

(e) When an order to show cause why an action or actions should not be remanded is entered pursuant to subsection (c), paragraph (iii) of this Rule, any party may file a response within twenty days of the filing of said order unless otherwise provided for in the order. Within five days of filing of a party's response, any party may file a reply brief limited to new matters. Failure of a party to respond to a show cause order regarding remand shall be treated as that party's acquiescence to the remand. Responses and replies shall be filed and served in conformity with Rules 5.12, 5.2 and 7.1 of these Rules.

(f) Conditional Remand Orders.

(i) When the Panel has been advised by the transferee district judge, or otherwise has reason to believe, that pretrial proceedings in the litigation assigned to the transferee district judge are concluded or that remand of an action or actions is otherwise appropriate, an order may be entered by the Clerk of the Panel remanding the action or actions to the transferor district court. The Clerk of the Panel shall serve this order on each party to the litigation but, in order to afford all parties the opportunity to oppose remand, shall not send the order to the clerk of the transferee district court for fifteen days from the entry thereof.

(ii) Any party opposing the remand shall file a notice of opposition with the Clerk of the Panel within the fifteen-day period. If a notice of opposition is received by the Clerk of the Panel within this fifteen-day period, the Clerk of the Panel shall not transmit said order to the clerk of the transferee district court until further order of the Panel. The Clerk of the Panel shall notify the parties of the briefing schedule.

(iii) Within fifteen days of the filing of its notice of opposition, the party opposing remand shall file a

motion to vacate the conditional remand order and brief in support thereof. The Chairman of the Panel shall set the motion for the next appropriate hearing session of the Panel. Failure to file and serve a motion and brief shall be treated as a withdrawal of the opposition and the Clerk of the Panel shall forthwith transmit the order to the clerk of the transferee district court.

(iv) Conditional remand orders do not become effective unless and until they are filed with the clerk of the transferee district court.

(v) Notices of opposition and motions to vacate such orders of the Panel and responses thereto shall be governed by Rules 5.12, 5.2, 7.1 and 7.2 of these Rules.

(g) Upon receipt of an order to remand from the Clerk of the Panel, the parties shall furnish forthwith to the transferee district clerk a stipulation or designation of the contents of the record or part thereof to be remanded and furnish the transferee district clerk all necessary copies of any pleading or other matter filed so as to enable the transferee district clerk to comply with the order of remand.

Former Rule 14 adopted May 3, 1993, effective July 1, 1993; renumbered Rule 7.6 and amended September 1, 1998, effective November 2, 1998; amended effective April 2, 2001.

RULE 16.1   HEARING SESSIONS AND ORAL ARGUMENT

(a) Hearing sessions of the Panel for the presentation of oral argument and consideration of matters taken under submission without oral argument shall be held as ordered by the Panel. The Panel shall convene whenever and wherever desirable or necessary in the judgment of the Chairman. The Chairman shall determine which matters shall be considered at each hearing session and the Clerk of the Panel shall give notice to counsel for all parties involved in the litigation to be so considered of the time, place and subject matter of such hearing session.

(b) Each party filing a motion or a response to a motion or order of the Panel under Rules 7.2, 7.3, 7.4 or 7.6 of these Rules may file simultaneously therewith a separate statement limited to one page setting forth reasons why oral argument should, or need not, be heard. Such statements shall be captioned "Reasons Why Oral Argument Should [Need Not] Be Heard," and shall be filed and served in conformity with Rules 5.12 and 5.2 of these Rules.

(c) No transfer or remand determination regarding any action pending in the district court shall be made by the Panel when any party timely opposes such transfer or remand unless a hearing session has been held for the presentation of oral argument except that the Panel may dispense with oral argument if it determines that:

(i) the dispositive issue(s) have been authoritatively decided; or

(ii) the facts and legal arguments are adequately presented in the briefs and record, and the decisional process would not be significantly aided by oral argument.

Unless otherwise ordered by the Panel, all other matters before the Panel, such as a motion for reconsideration, shall be considered and determined upon the basis of the papers filed.

(**d**) In those matters in which oral argument is not scheduled by the Panel, counsel shall be promptly advised. If oral argument is scheduled in a matter the Clerk of the Panel may require counsel for all parties who wish to make or to waive oral argument to file and serve notice to that effect within a stated time in conformity with Rules 5.12 and 5.2 of these Rules. Failure to do so shall be deemed a waiver of oral argument by that party. If oral argument is scheduled but not attended by a party, the matter shall not be rescheduled and that party's position shall be treated as submitted for decision by the Panel on the basis of the papers filed.

(**e**) Except for leave of the Panel on a showing of good cause, only those parties to actions scheduled for oral argument who have filed a motion or written response to a motion or order shall be permitted to appear before the Panel and present oral argument.

(**f**) Counsel for those supporting transfer or remand under Section 1407 and counsel for those opposing such transfer or remand are to confer separately

prior to the oral argument for the purpose of organizing their arguments and selecting representatives to present all views without duplication.

(**g**) Unless otherwise ordered by the Panel, a maximum of twenty minutes shall be allotted for oral argument in each matter. The time shall be divided equally among those with varying viewpoints. Counsel for the moving party or parties shall generally be heard first.

(**h**) So far as practicable and consistent with the purposes of Section 1407, the offering of oral testimony before the Panel shall be avoided. Accordingly, oral testimony shall not be received except upon notice, motion and order of the Panel expressly providing for it.

(**i**) After an action or group of actions has been set for a hearing session, consideration of such action(s) may be continued only by order of the Panel on good cause shown.

Former Rule 16 adopted May 3, 1993, effective July 1, 1993; renumbered Rule 16.1 and amended September 1, 1998, effective November 2, 1998; amended effective April 2, 2001.

RULE 16.2 NOTICE OF PRESENTATION OR WAIVER OF ORAL ARGUMENT, AND MATTERS SUBMITTED ON THE BRIEFS [REPEALED]

Former Rule 17 adopted May 3, 1993, effective July 1, 1993; renumbered Rule 16.2 and amended September 1, 1998, effective November 2, 1998; repealed effective April 2, 2001.

II. RULES FOR MULTICIRCUIT PETITIONS FOR REVIEW UNDER 28 U.S.C. § 2112(a)(3)

RULE 17.1 RANDOM SELECTION

(**a**) Upon filing a notice of multicircuit petitions for review, the Clerk of the Panel or designated deputy shall randomly select a circuit court of appeals from a drum containing an entry for each circuit wherein a constituent petition for review is pending. Multiple petitions for review pending in a single circuit shall be allotted only a single entry in the drum. This random selection shall be witnessed by the Clerk of the Panel or a designated deputy other than the random selector. Thereafter, an order on behalf of the Panel shall be issued, signed by the random selector and the witness,

(i) consolidating the petitions for review in the court of appeals for the circuit that was randomly selected; and

(ii) designating that circuit as the one in which the record is to be filed pursuant to Rules 16 and 17 of the Federal Rules of Appellate Procedure.

(**b**) A consolidation of petitions for review shall be effective when the Panel's consolidation order is filed at the offices of the Panel by the Clerk of the Panel.

Former Rule 24 adopted May 3, 1993, effective July 1, 1993; renumbered Rule 17.1 September 1, 1998, effective November 2, 1998.

RULE 25.1 FILING OF NOTICES

(**a**) An original of a notice of multicircuit petitions for review pursuant to 28 U.S.C. § 2112(a)(3) shall be submitted for filing to the Clerk of the Panel by the affected agency, board, commission or officer. The term "agency" as used in Section II of these Rules shall include agency, board, commission or officer.

(**b**) All notices of multicircuit petitions for review submitted by the affected agency for filing with the Clerk of the Panel shall embrace exclusively petitions for review filed in the courts of appeals within ten days after issuance of an agency order and received by the affected agency from the petitioners within that ten-day period.

(c) When a notice of multicircuit petitions for review is submitted for filing to the Clerk of the Panel, the Clerk of the Panel shall file the notice and endorse thereon the date of filing.

(d) Copies of notices of multicircuit petitions for review shall be filed by the affected agency with the clerk of each circuit court of appeals in which a petition for review is pending that is included in the notice.

Former Rule 20 adopted May 3, 1993, effective July 1, 1993; renumbered Rule 25.1 and amended September 1, 1998, effective November 2, 1998.

RULE 25.2 ACCOMPANIMENTS TO NOTICES

(a) All notices of multicircuit petitions for review shall be accompanied by:

(i) a copy of each involved petition for review as the petition for review is defined in 28 U.S.C. § 2112(a)(2); and

(ii) a schedule giving

(A) the date of the relevant agency order;

(B) the case name of each petition for review involved;

(C) the circuit court of appeals in which each petition for review is pending;

(D) the appellate docket number of each petition for review;

(E) the date of filing by the court of appeals of each petition for review; and

(F) the date of receipt by the agency of each petition for review.

(b) The schedule in Subsection (a)(ii) of this Rule shall also be governed by Rules 25.1, 25.3 and 25.4(a) of these Rules.

Former Rule 21 adopted May 3, 1993, effective July 1, 1993; renumbered Rule 25.2 and amended September 1, 1998, effective November 2, 1998.

RULE 25.3 SERVICE OF NOTICES

(a) All notices of multicircuit petitions for review shall be accompanied by proof of service by the affected agency on all other parties in all petitions for review included in the notice. Service and proof of service shall be made as provided in Rule 25 of the Federal Rules of Appellate Procedure. The proof of service shall state the name and address of each person served and shall indicate the party represented by each. If a party is not represented by counsel, the proof of service shall indicate the name of the party and his or her last known address. The original proof of service shall be submitted by the affected agency for filing with the Clerk of the Panel and copies thereof shall be sent by the affected agency to each person included within the proof of service.

(b) The proof of service pertaining to notices of multicircuit petitions for review shall certify that copies of the notices have been mailed or otherwise delivered by the affected agency for filing to the clerk of each circuit court of appeals in which a petition for review is pending that is included in the notice.

Former Rule 22 adopted May 3, 1993, effective July 1, 1993; renumbered Rule 25.3 September 1, 1998, effective November 2, 1998.

RULE 25.4 FORM OF NOTICES

(a) Each notice of multicircuit petitions for review shall be

(i) flat and unfolded;

(ii) plainly written, typed in double space, printed or prepared by means of a duplicating process, without erasures or interlineations which materially deface it;

(iii) on opaque, unglazed white paper (not onionskin);

(iv) approximately 8–1/2 x 11 inches in size; and

(v) fastened at the top-left corner without side binding or front or back covers.

(b) The heading on the first page of each notice of multicircuit petitions for review shall commence not less that three inches from the top of the page. Each notice shall bear the heading "Notice to the Judicial Panel on Multidistrict Litigation of Multicircuit Petitions for Review," followed by a brief caption identifying the involved agency, the relevant agency order, and the date of the order.

(c) The final page of each notice of multicircuit petitions for review shall contain the name, address and telephone number of the individual or individuals who submitted the notice on behalf of the agency.

Former Rule 23 adopted May 3, 1993, effective July 1, 1993; renumbered Rule 25.4and amended September 1, 1998, effective November 2, 1998.

RULE 25.5 SERVICE OF PANEL CONSOLIDATION ORDER

(a) The Clerk of the Panel shall serve the Panel's consolidation order on the affected agency through the individual or individuals, as identified in Rule 25.4(c) of these Rules, who submitted the notice of multicircuit petitions for review on behalf of the agency.

(b) That individual or individuals, or anyone else designated by the agency, shall promptly serve the Panel's consolidation order on all other parties in all petitions for review included in the Panel's consolidation order, and shall promptly submit a proof of that service to the Clerk of the Panel. Service and proof of that service shall also be governed by Rule 25.3 of these Rules.

(c) The Clerk of the Panel shall serve the Panel's consolidation order on the clerks of all circuit courts of appeals that were among the candidates for the Panel's random selection.

Former Rule 25 adopted May 3, 1993, effective July 1, 1993; renumbered Rule 25.5 and amended September 1, 1998, effective November 2, 1998.

CONVERSION TABLE

Renumbered Rule	Previous Rule
1.1	1
1.2	5
1.3	4
1.4	6
1.5	18
1.6	19
5.1	2
5.11	3
5.12	7
5.13	—
5.2	8
5.3	—
6.2	15
7.1	9
7.2	10
7.3	11
7.4	12
7.5	13
7.6	14
16.1	16, 16.2 & 17
17.1	24
25.1	20
25.2	21
25.3	22
25.4	23
25.5	25

*

FEDERAL COURTS MISCELLANEOUS FEE SCHEDULES

COURT OF APPEALS FEE SCHEDULE

Issued in Accordance With 28 U.S.C. § 1913
Effective October 1, 1979

Including Amendments Effective January 1, 2005

Following are fees to be charged for services provided by the courts of appeals. No fees are to be charged for services rendered on behalf of the United States, with the exception of those specifically prescribed in items 2, 4 and 5. No fees under this schedule shall be charged to federal agencies or programs which are funded from judiciary appropriations, including, but not limited to, agencies, organizations, and individuals providing services authorized by the Criminal Justice Act, 18 U.S.C. § 3006A, and Bankruptcy Administrator programs.

(1) For docketing a case on appeal or review, or docketing any other proceeding, $250. A separate fee shall be paid by each party filing a notice of appeal in the district court, but parties filing a joint notice of appeal in the district court are required to pay only one fee. A docketing fee shall not be charged for the docketing of an application for the allowance of an interlocutory appeal under 28 U.S.C. § 1292(b), unless the appeal is allowed.

(2) For every search of the records of the court and certifying the results thereof, $26. This fee shall apply to services rendered on behalf of the United States if the information requested is available through electronic access.

(3) For certifying any document or paper, whether the certification is made directly on the document, or by separate instrument, $9.

(4) For reproducing any record or paper, 50 cents per page. This fee shall apply to paper copies made from either: (1) original documents; or (2) microfiche or microfilm reproductions of the original records. This fee shall apply to services rendered on behalf of the United States if the record or paper requested is available through electronic access.

(5) For reproduction of recordings of proceedings, regardless of the medium, $26, including the cost of materials. This fee shall apply to services rendered on behalf of the United States if the reproduction of the recording is available electronically.

(6) For reproduction of the record in any appeal in which the requirement of an appendix is dispensed with by any court of appeals pursuant to Rule 30(f), F.R.A.P., a flat fee of $71.

(7) For each microfiche or microfilm copy of any court record, where available, $5.

(8) For retrieval of a record from a Federal Records Center, National Archives, or other storage location removed from the place of business of the court, $45.

(9) For a check paid into the court which is returned for lack of funds, $45.

(10) Fees to be charged and collected for copies of opinions shall be fixed, from time to time, by each court, commensurate with the cost of printing.

(11) The court may charge and collect fees commensurate with the cost of providing copies of the local rules of court. The court may also distribute copies of the local rules without charge.

(12) The clerk shall assess a charge for the handling of registry funds deposited with the court, to be assessed from interest earnings and in accordance with the detailed fee schedule issued by the Director of the Administrative Office of the United States Courts.

Publisher's Note Regarding Registry Fees

Effective June 12, 1989, the Administrative Office issued regulations assessing a fee equal to the first 45 days' income earned on registry fund accounts, for the handling of funds deposited with the court in noncriminal proceedings and held in interest bearing accounts or instruments. See 54 F.R. 20407 (May 11, 1989) for further information.

Effective December 1, 1990, registry fee assessment provisions were converted to a charge of ten percent of all income earned on funds while held in the court registry, and the fee was extended to any funds placed into the court's registry and invested regardless of the nature of the action underlying the deposit. The new method of computing the fee applied to new investments of funds placed into court beginning on the effective date, but was not applicable to investments in cases from which a fee had been exacted under 54 F.R. 20407. See 55 F.R. 42867 (October 24, 1990) for further information.

Effective February 3, 1992, the registry fee is based on a variable rate, dependent on the amounts deposited and, in certain cases, the length of time funds are held in the courts' registry. For investments of less than $100,000,000, the revised fee is ten percent of the total income received during each income period. For investments of $100,000,000 or more, the ten percent fee is reduced by one percent for each increment of $50,000,000 over the initial $100,000,000. For deposits placed in the registry by court order for a time certain, the fee is further reduced 2.5 percent for each five-year interval or part thereof. The total minimum fee is no less than two percent of the income on investments. The new fee schedule applies to investments on and after the effective date, but does not apply to earnings on investments in cases administered under 54 F.R. 20407. See 56 F.R. 56356 (November 4, 1991) for further information.

These registry fees do not apply in the District Court of Guam, the Northern Mariana Islands, the Virgin Islands, the United States Court of Federal Claims, or any other federal court whose fees are not set under the governing statutes.

(13) Upon the filing of any separate or joint notice of appeal or application for appeal from the Bankruptcy Appellate Panel, or notice of the allowance of an appeal from the Bankruptcy Appellate Panel, or of a writ of certiorari, $5 shall be paid by the appellant or petitioner.

(14) The court may charge and collect a fee of $200 per remote location for counsel's requested use of videoconferencing equipment in connection with each oral argument.

(15) For original admission of attorneys to practice, $150 each, including a certificate of admission. For a duplicate certificate of admission or certificate of good standing, $15.

Instructions for Processing the New Attorney Admission Fee for the Courts of Appeals

- The payment of the attorney admission fee–including both the new fee under 28 U.S.C. § 1913(15) and the fee set by local rule–should be made with one check, made payable to: Clerk, United States Court.

- The receipt of these funds must be recorded in FAS4T.

- The receipt of funds will be split so that funds are deposited into the appropriate accounts.

- The new fee of $150 should be credited to account 510000 (the judiciary's fee account).

- The additional local fee should be credited to a new deposit fund 6855AP.

- On a monthly basis, the court of appeals clerk's office should create and enter in FAS4T a pay-

ment authorization for the amount of funds deposited into 6855AP during the prior month.

- The payment authorization will be disbursed by the district clerk's office to the custodian of the locally held library or bar fund.

- The AO's Accounting and Financial Systems Division will prepare its CAS and FAS4T databases, and develop or modify policies and procedures for the addition of the new fund (6855AP) to ensure that the fund is available for use on January 1, 2005.

- **The AO Accounting and Financial Systems Division will provide additional information to you regarding any changes that need to be made to local court systems, along with applicable policies and procedures.**

DISTRICT COURT FEE SCHEDULE

Issued in Accordance With 28 U.S.C. § 1914(b)
Effective October 1, 1979

Including Amendments Effective June 1, 2004

Following are fees to be charged for services provided by the district courts. No fees are to be charged for services rendered on behalf of the United States, with the exception of those specifically prescribed in items 2, 4 and 5. No fees under this schedule shall be charged to federal agencies or programs which are funded from judiciary appropriations, including, but not limited to, agencies, organizations, and individuals providing services authorized by the Criminal Justice Act, 18 U.S.C. § 3006A, and Bankruptcy Administrator programs.

(1) For filing or indexing any document not in a case or proceeding for which a filing fee has been paid, $39.

(2) For every search of the records of the district court conducted by the clerk of the district court or a deputy clerk, $26 per name or item searched. This fee shall apply to services rendered on behalf of the United States if the information requested is available through electronic access.

(3) For certification of any document or paper, whether the certification is made directly on the document or by separate instrument, $9. For exemplification of any document or paper, twice the amount of the fee for certification.

(4) For reproducing any record or paper, $.50 per page. This fee shall apply to paper copies made from either: (1) original documents; or (2) microfiche or

microfilm reproductions of the original records. This fee shall apply to services rendered on behalf of the United States if the record or paper requested is available through electronic access.

(5) For reproduction of recordings of proceedings, regardless of the medium, $26, including the cost of materials. This fee shall apply to services rendered on behalf of the United States, if the reproduction of the recording is available electronically.

(6) For each microfiche sheet of film or microfilm jacket copy of any court record, where available, $5.

(7) For retrieval of a record from a Federal Records Center, National Archives, or other storage location removed from the place of business of the court, $45.

(8) For a check paid into the court which is returned for lack of funds, $45.

(9) For an appeal to a district judge from a judgment of conviction by a magistrate in a misdemeanor case, $32.

(10) For original admission of attorneys to practice, $50 each, including a certificate of admission. For a duplicate certificate of admission or certificate of good standing, $15.

(11) The court may charge and collect fees commensurate with the cost of providing copies of the local rules of court. The court may also distribute copies of the local rules without charge.

(12) The clerk shall assess a charge for the handling of registry funds deposited with the court, to be assessed from interest earnings and in accordance with the detailed fee schedule issued by the Director of the Administrative Office of the United States Courts.

(13) For filing an action brought under Title III of the Cuban Liberty and Democratic Solidarity (LIBERTAD) Act of 1996, P.L. 104–114, 110 Stat. 785 (1996), $5,431. (This fee is in addition to the filing fee prescribed in 28 U.S.C. § 1914(a) for instituting any civil action other than a writ of habeas corpus.)

BANKRUPTCY COURT FEE SCHEDULE

Issued in Accordance With 28 U.S.C. § 1930(b)
Effective October 1, 1979

Including Amendments Effective June 1, 2004

Following are fees to be charged for services provided by the bankruptcy courts. No fees are to be charged for services rendered on behalf of the United States, with the exception of those specifically prescribed in items 1, 3, and 5, or to bankruptcy administrators appointed under Public Law No. 99–554, § 302(d)(3)(I). No fees under this schedule shall be charged to federal agencies or programs which are funded from judiciary appropriations, including, but not limited to, agencies, organizations, and individuals providing services authorized by the Criminal Justice Act, 18 U.S.C. § 3006A.

(1) For reproducing any record or paper, $.50 per page. This fee shall apply to paper copies made from either: (1) original documents; or (2) microfiche or microfilm reproductions of the original records. This fee shall apply to services rendered on behalf of the United States if the record or paper requested is available through electronic access.

(2) For certification of any document or paper, whether the certification is made directly on the document or by separate instrument, $9. For exemplification of any document or paper, twice the amount of the charge for certification.

(3) For reproduction of recordings of proceedings, regardless of the medium, $26, including the cost of materials. This fee shall apply to services rendered on

behalf of the United States, if the reproduction of the recording is available electronically.

(4) For amendments to a debtor's schedules of creditors, lists of creditors, matrix, or mailing lists, $26 for each amendment, provided the bankruptcy judge may, for good cause, waive the charge in any case. **No fee is required when the nature of the amendment is to change the address of a creditor or an attorney for a creditor listed on the schedules or to add the name and address of an attorney for a listed creditor.**

(5) **For every search of the records of the bankruptcy court conducted by the clerk of the bankruptcy court or a deputy clerk, $26 per name or item searched. This fee shall apply to services rendered on behalf of the United States if the information requested is available through electronic access.**

(6) **For filing a complaint, a fee shall be collected in the same amount as the filing fee prescribed in 28 U.S.C. § 1914(a) for instituting any civil action other than a writ of habeas corpus. If the United States, other than a United States trustee acting as a trustee in a case under title 11, or a debtor is the plaintiff, no fee is required. If a trustee or debtor in possession is the plaintiff, the fee should be payable only from the estate and to**

the extent there is any estate realized. If a child support creditor or its representative is the plaintiff, and if such plaintiff files the form required by § 304(g) of the Bankruptcy Reform Act of 1994, no fee is required.

(7) For filing or indexing any document not in a case or proceeding for which a filing fee has been paid, $39.

(8) In all cases filed under title 11, the clerk shall collect from the debtor or the petitioner a miscellaneous administrative fee of $39. This fee may be paid in installments in the same manner that the filing fee may be paid in installments, consistent with the procedure set forth in Federal Rule of Bankruptcy Procedure 1006.

(9) Upon the filing of a petition under chapter 7 of the Bankruptcy Code, the petitioner shall pay $15 to the clerk of the court for payment to trustees serving in cases as provided in 11 U.S.C. § 330(b)(2). An application to pay the fee in installments may be filed in the manner set forth in Federal Rule of Bankruptcy Procedure 1006(b).

(10) Upon the filing of a motion to convert a case to chapter 7 of the Bankruptcy Code, the movant shall pay $15 to the clerk of court for payment to trustees serving in cases as provided in 11 U.S.C. § 330(b)(2). Upon the filing of a notice of conversion pursuant to section 1208(a) or section 1307(a) of the Code, $15 shall be paid to the clerk of the court for payment to trustees serving in cases as provided in 11 U.S.C. § 330(b)(2). If the trustee serving in the case before the conversion is the movant, the fee shall be payable only from the estate that exists prior to conversion.

(11) For filing a motion to reopen a Bankruptcy Code case, a fee shall be collected in the same amount as the filing fee prescribed by 28 U.S.C. § 1930(a) for commencing a new case on the date of reopening, unless the reopening is to correct an administrative error or for actions related to the debtor's discharge. The court may waive this fee under appropriate circumstances or may defer payment of the fee from trustees pending discovery of additional assets. If payment is deferred, the fee shall be waived if no additional assets are discovered.

(12) For each microfiche sheet of film or microfilm jacket copy of any court record, where available, $5.

(13) For retrieval of a record from a Federal Records Center, National Archives, or other storage location removed from the place of business of the court, $45.

(14) For a check paid into the court which is returned for lack of funds, $45.

(15) For docketing a proceeding on appeal or review from a final judgment of a bankruptcy judge pursuant to 28 U.S.C. § 158(a) and (b), the fee shall be the same amount as the fee for docketing a case on appeal or review to the appellate court as required by Item 1 of the Courts of Appeals Miscellaneous Fee Schedule. A separate fee shall be paid by each party filing a notice of appeal in the bankruptcy court, but parties filing a joint notice of appeal in the bankruptcy court are required to pay only one fee. If a trustee or debtor in possession is the appellant, the fee should be payable only from the estate and to the extent there is any estate realized.

(16) For filing a petition ancillary to a foreign proceeding under 11 U.S.C. § 304, the fee shall be the same amount as the fee for a case commenced under chapter 11 of title 11 as required by 28 U.S.C. § 1930(a)(3).

(17) The court may charge and collect fees commensurate with the cost of providing copies of the local rules of court. The court may also distribute copies of the local rules without charge.

(18) The clerk shall assess a charge for the handling of registry funds deposited with the court, to be assessed from interest earnings and in accordance with the detailed fee schedule issued by the Director of the Administrative Office of the United States Courts.

Publisher's Note Regarding Registry Fees

Effective June 12, 1989, the Administrative Office issued regulations assessing a fee equal to the first 45 days' income earned on registry fund accounts, for the handling of funds deposited with the court in noncriminal proceedings and held in interest bearing accounts or instruments. See 54 F.R. 20407 (May 11, 1989) for further information.

Effective December 1, 1990, registry fee assessment provisions were converted to a charge of ten percent of all income earned on funds while held in the court registry, and the fee was extended to any funds placed into the court's registry and invested regardless of the nature of the action underlying the deposit. The new method of computing the fee applied to new investments of funds placed into court beginning on the effective date, but was not applicable to investments in cases from which a fee had been exacted under 54 F.R. 20407. See 55 F.R. 42867 (October 24, 1990) for further information.

Effective February 3, 1992, the registry fee is based on a variable rate, dependent on the amounts deposited and, in certain cases, the length of time funds are held in the courts' registry. For investments of less than $100,000,000, the revised fee is ten percent of the total income received during each income period. For investments of $100,000,000 or more, the ten percent fee is reduced by one percent for each increment of $50,000,000 over the initial $100,000,000. For deposits placed in the registry by court order for a time certain, the fee is further reduced 2.5 percent for each five-year interval or part thereof. The total minimum fee is no less than two percent of the income on investments. The new fee schedule applies to investments on and after the effective date, but does not apply to earnings on investments in cases administered under 54 F.R. 20407. See 56 F.R. 56356 (November 4, 1991) for further information.

These registry fees do not apply in the District Court of Guam, the Northern Mariana Islands, the Virgin Islands, the United States Court of Federal Claims, or any other federal court whose fees are not set under the governing statutes.

(19) When a joint case filed under § 302 of title 11 is divided into two separate cases at the request of the debtor(s), a fee shall be charged equal to the current filing fee for the chapter under which the joint case was commenced.

(20) For filing a motion to terminate, annul, modify, or condition the automatic stay provided under § 362(a) of title 11, a motion to compel abandonment of property of the estate pursuant to Rule 6007(b) of the Federal Rules of Bankruptcy Procedure, or a motion to withdraw the reference of a case or proceeding under 28 U.S.C. § 157(d), a fee shall be collected in the amount of the filing fee prescribed in

28 U.S.C. § 1914(a) for instituting any civil action other than a writ of habeas corpus. No fee is required for a motion for relief from the co-debtor stay or for a stipulation for court approval of an agreement for relief from a stay. If a child support creditor or its representative is the movant, and if such movant files the form required by § 304(g) of the Bankruptcy Reform Act of 1994, no fee is required.

(21) For docketing a cross appeal from a bankruptcy court determination, the fee shall be the same amount as the fee for docketing a case on appeal or review to the appellate court as required by Item 1 of the Courts of Appeals Miscellaneous Fee Schedule. If a trustee or debtor in possession is the appellant, the fee should be payable only from the estate and to the extent there is any estate realized.

JUDICIAL PANEL ON MULTIDISTRICT LITIGATION FEE SCHEDULE

Issued in Accordance With 28 U.S.C. § 1913
Effective October 1, 1979

Including Amendments Effective June 1, 2004

Following are fees to be charged for services provided by the Judicial Panel on Multidistrict Litigation. No fees are to be charged for services rendered on behalf of the United States, with the exception of those specifically prescribed in items 1 and 3. No fees under this schedule shall be charged to federal agencies or programs which are funded from judiciary appropriations, including, but not limited to, agencies, organizations, and individuals providing services authorized by the Criminal Justice Act, 18 U.S.C. § 3006A.

(1) For every search of the records of the court conducted by the clerk of the court or a deputy clerk, $26 per name or item searched. This fee shall apply to services rendered on behalf of the United States if the information requested is available through electronic access.

(2) For certification of any document or paper, whether the certification is made directly on the document or by separate instrument, $9.

(3) For reproducing any record or paper, $.50 per page. This fee shall apply to paper copies made from either: (1) original documents; or (2) microfiche or microfilm reproductions of the original records. This fee shall apply to services rendered on behalf of the United States if the record or paper requested is available through electronic access.

(4) For retrieval of a record from a Federal Records Center, National Archives, or other storage location removed from the place of business of the court, $45.

(5) For a check paid into the Panel which is returned for lack of funds, $45.

ELECTRONIC PUBLIC ACCESS FEE SCHEDULE

Including Amendments Effective January 1, 2005

As directed by Congress, the Judicial Conference has determined that the following fees are necessary to reimburse expenses incurred by the judiciary in providing electronic public access to court records. These fees shall apply to the United States unless otherwise stated. No fees under this schedule shall be charged to federal agencies or programs which are funded from judiciary appropriations, including, but

not limited to, agencies, organizations, and individuals providing services authorized by the Criminal Justice Act, 18 U.S.C. § 3006A, and bankruptcy administrator programs.

I. For electronic access to court data via dial up service: sixty cents per minute. For electronic access to court data via a federal judiciary Internet site:

eight cents per page, with the total for any document, docket sheet, or case-specific report not to exceed the fee for thirty pages–provided however that transcripts of federal court proceedings shall not be subject to the thirty-page fee limit. Attorneys of record and parties in a case (including pro se litigants) receive one free electronic copy of all documents filed electronically, if receipt is required by law or directed by the filer. No fee is owed under this provision until an account holder accrues charges of more than $10 in a calendar year. Consistent with Judicial Conference policy, courts may, upon a showing of cause, exempt indigents, bankruptcy case trustees, individual researchers associated with educational institutions, courts, section 501(c)(3) not-for-profit organizations and pro bono ADR neutrals from payment of these fees. Courts must find that parties from the classes of persons or entities listed above seeking exemption have demonstrated that an exemption is necessary in order to avoid unreasonable burdens and to promote public access to information. Any user granted an exemption agrees not to sell for profit the data obtained as a result. Exemptions may be granted for a definite period of time and may be revoked at the discretion of the court granting the exemption.

II. For printing copies of any record or document accessed electronically at a public terminal in the courthouse: ten cents per page. This fee shall apply to services rendered on behalf of the United States if the record requested is remotely available through electronic access.

III. For every search of court records conducted by the PACER Service Center, $20.

JUDICIAL CONFERENCE POLICY NOTES

Courts should not exempt local, state or federal government agencies, members of the media, attorneys or others not members of one of the groups listed above. Exemptions should be granted as the exception, not the rule. A court may not use this exemption language to exempt all users. An exemption applies only to access related to the case or purpose for which it was given. The electronic public access fee applies to electronic court data viewed remotely from the public records of individual cases in the court, including filed documents and the docket sheet. Electronic court data may be viewed free at public terminals at the courthouse and courts may provide other local court information at no cost. Examples of information that can be provided at no cost include: local rules, court forms, news items, court calendars, opinions, and other information–such as court hours, court location, telephone listings–determined locally to benefit the public and the court.

†